Immigration, Asylum and Human Rights

Nicholas Blake QC

and

Raza Husain

Series Editor: John Wadham

OXFORD
UNIVERSITY PRESS

OXFORD

UNIVERSITY PRESS

Great Clarendon Street, Oxford OX2 6DP

Oxford University Press is a department of the University of Oxford.
It furthers the University's objective of excellence in research, scholarship,
and education by publishing worldwide in

Oxford New York

Auckland Bangkok Buenos Aires Cape Town Chennai
Dar es Salaam Delhi Hong Kong Istanbul Karachi Kolkata
Kuala Lumpur Madrid Melbourne Mexico City Mumbai Nairobi
São Paulo Shanghai Taipei Tokyo Toronto

Oxford is a registered trade mark of Oxford University Press
in the UK and in certain other countries

Published in the United States
by Oxford University Press Inc., New York

© Blake and Husain 2003

The moral rights of the author have been asserted

Database right Oxford University Press (maker)

First published 2003

British Library Cataloguing in Publication Data

Data available

Library of Congress Cataloging in Publication Data

Data available

ISBN 1–84174–140–X

1 3 5 7 9 10 8 6 4 2

Typeset in Times
by Cambrian Typesetters, Frimley, Surrey
Printed in Great Britain
on acid-free paper by
Antony Rowe Ltd., Chippenham

Contents

Preface

We are conscious that this book has been overlong in its gestation and delivery. The first chapters were originally drafted in the summer of 2000 when the brave new world of the commencement of the Human Rights Act 1998 was imminent. Completing the text proved problematic and needed constant revision in the light of subsequent developments whilst the typescript was under preparation. We hope that the disadvantage of delay has been compensated for by the ability to report and comment on the emerging case law after the coming into force of the Human Rights Act 1998 as it impacts on immigration law. The text was ready for printing in September 2001, when the events of September 11 proved likely to have a profound effect on immigration and asylum. We accordingly added a post-script on the effect of the Anti-Terrorism Crime and Security Act 2001 that came into force in December 2001. We had hoped to make 1 August 2002 our terminus point for reflecting on new cases, and even then were conscious that with the volume of new decisions from the IAT, the Administrative Court, and elsewhere, there almost certainly would be omissions. Once again, developments in this fast-moving field of law overtook us, while the final proofs were being corrected.

Some of the case law of the courts in the period from September to December 2002 has been noted in final revision of the proofs. We have only added cases that overturned or qualified previous passages of the text.

More significantly a new Nationality Immigration and Asylum Bill was rushed through Parliament. The Nationality Immigration and Asylum Act 2002 received Royal Assent on 7 November 2002, when certain provisions came into force. The Act was not, however, published until 28 November 2002.

The Act essentially represents a further shift towards greater discretionary powers of the Home Secretary, although there are welcome changes in the removal of the offensive and discriminatory nature of some of our nationality laws. We note two principal areas of concern. First, provision is made for the issue of 'clearly unfounded' certificates, the effect of which is to deprive individuals of rights of suspensive appeal against the rejection of their human rights and asylum claims. Such certificates were issued after 7 November 2002 but before 28 November 2002, when the relevant provisions were in force but not publicly available. Second, section 55 and Schedule 3 restrict access to social support by asylum seekers as from 8 January 2003, save where human rights obligations otherwise require. The meaning of these provisions is being tested in the Courts as this book goes finally to the printers.

At the same time, some politicians seem to be squaring up for yet another round of asylum legislation focusing on the UK's international obligations. At least it cannot be said that the subject of this book is some arid recondite area of the law. We hope that this book, in focusing upon the principles of the Convention, will prove of assistance to all those engaged in the difficult task of determining how far Convention obligations will assist in the arrival of fair, just and reasonable decisions in immigration cases.

We are grateful to our long-suffering publishers for their forbearance. We owe a debt of thanks to our professional colleagues, particularly those at our former home at 2 Garden Court and our current colleagues at Matrix Chambers, and to the wider immigration and human rights community with whom so many ideas have been debated and refined.

We owe particular thanks to our families, for whom too many a weekend and holiday has seen us disappear to our respective word processors for further articulation of the meaning of respect for family life; to Anna Edmundson for assistance with research, and to Satnam Singh for assistance with the footnotes.

Nicholas Blake would like to dedicate this book to his wife, Clio; Raza Husain dedicates this book to his parents. However, this book is most of all for our respective children Lydia, Sophia, Sebastian and Zakaria, loved beyond the stars. We wish them a fairer and safer world, free of cruelty, discrimination, intolerance, prejudice, and racial hatred, and a state and civil society that understands, respects and adheres to human rights norms.

Nicholas Blake
Raza Husain
1 January 2003

Table of Cases

Table of Primary Legislation

Primary Legislation (EC)

Primary Legislation (Antigua and Barbuda)

Primary Legislation (Austria)

Primary Legislation (Canada)

Primary Legislation (Costa Rica)

Primary Legislation (Grenada)

Table of Secondary Legislation

Table of International Instruments

Introduction

This book appears two years after the coming into force of the Human Rights Act 1998. The higher courts have now been grappling with the meaning of the European Convention on Human Rights (ECHR) and its domestic application in a regular flow of cases, and each passing week adds to a developing body of knowledge. Some of the decisions have not been consistent. There has been no ordered linear development, indeed we might adopt Sir Isaiah Berlin's celebrated borrowing from Kant and refer to the 'Crooked Timber of Human Rights'.[1]

Thus on the vexed issue of s. 22(4) of the Human Rights Act (HRA) 1998 and the applicability of the ECHR to decisions taken before 2 October 2001 there is a 'present conflict of judicial opinion at the highest level'[2] with inconsistent majority reasoning in three House of Lords judgments. Much of the discussion that follows in chapter one was based on the reasoning in the decision of the House of Lords in *R v DPP, ex parte Kebilene* [2000] 2 AC 326 where the issues were fully and fairly argued. This led the Court of Appeal quite sensibly to conclude that where the meaning of statutes falls to be decided after 2 October 2000 (i.e. the date by which the HRA 1998 was fully in force), the principles of interpretation governed by s. 3 of the HRA 1998 should apply.[3] In the case of *R v Lambert* [2001] 3 WLR 206 (Lord Steyn dissenting on retrospectivity) the House of Lords threw doubt on the accepted wisdom that both s. 3 (the duty of interpretation) and s. 6 (the duty to act compatibly) apply to appeals from decisions that pre-dated the coming into force of the HRA 1998. Out of fidelity to the doctrine of precedent *Lambert* was followed in *R v Kansal No. 2* [2001] UKHL 62[4] although a majority thought *Lambert* to be wrongly decided. Lord Steyn (at para. 27) considered that since the issue did not concern the entire future of the HRA 1998 but rather a transitional provision on which the House had recently

---

[1] *The Crooked Timber of Humanity* (John Murray, 1990): 'Out of timber so crooked as that from which man is made nothing entirely straight can be carved.'

[2] *R v Kansal* [2001] UKHL 62, Lord Lloyd at paragraph 19. See also *R v DPP ex parte Kebilene* [2000] 2 AC 326; [1999] 3 WLR 969; *R v Lambert* [2001] 3 WLR 206; *Preiss v General Medical Council* [2001] 1 WLR 1926. In light of such conflict the Court of Appeal has accepted that *Lambert* 'should not be applied beyond its strict ratio': *R v Saunders and others* [2001] EWCA Civ 2860, 21 December 2001, para. 46.

[3] *Wilson v First County Trust No. 2* [2001] 3 WLR 422 CA; *Pye v Graham* [2000] Ch 676; leave to appeal to the House of Lords granted in both cases.

[4] Lords Slynn, Lloyd, Steyn, Hutton; Lord Hope dissenting.

ruled, it would be wrong to depart from the majority in *Lambert*. Lord Lloyd went as far as to say that *Lambert* was 'plainly erroneous' (at para. 17) but considered that the only satisfactory way of resolving the conflict of opinion was by a rehearing before a panel of seven law lords, absent which *Lambert* should be followed (at para. 19). It was perhaps unfortunate, in the circumstances, that the justification for following *Lambert* was itself a speech of Lord Hoffman in *Lewis* v *Attorney-General of Jamaica* [2001] 2 AC 50 in which he was in the minority on the issue (see *R* v *Kansal* at para. 20). Lord Hope considered that the majority judgment in *Lambert* was not even 'eminently possible' (at para. 51) but was alone in considering that *Lambert* should be departed from.

The implications of the suggestion that the whole of the HRA 1998 is a hermetically sealed, separate scheme which commenced only on 2 October 2000 are at the least highly surprising and would produce results incompatible with both legal certainty and the most obvious dictates of common sense. Taken to its logical extreme, the Court of Appeal criminal division may have to rule that a statute means something different in two cases decided on the same day depending on whether the prosecution commenced before or after 2 October 2000. In the case of *Porter* v *Magill* [2001] UKHL 67, para. 82 Lord Hope, with whom all the law lords agreed, has left open the possibility that the position may be different in civil appeals, and went on to determine the appeal on the basis that the HRA 1998 and the ECHR applied to a decision of a district auditor taken long before incorporation was even thought about. Matters may become clearer as time passes, but in the meantime, some of the reasoning in chapter 1 may be more tentative and subject to correction than we had first imagined.

The decision in *Lambert* had little immediate impact in immigration cases however, where immigration decisions remained to be executed after 2 October 2000. The case law from the Immigration and Asylum Act (IAA) 1999 has emerged slowly, essentially as a result of the terms of the Immigration and Asylum Act 1999 (Commencement No. 6, Transitional and Consequential Provisions) Order 2000 (SI 2000/2444), arts. 3, 4(1)(a), 4(2), Sch 2, para. 1(7) for the human rights appeal under s. 65 of the IAA 1999 and the decision in *Pardeepan* v *Secretary of State for the Home Department* [2000] INLR 447 on 12 October 2000 that only decisions made by the Secretary of State after commencement were subject to such an appeal, although the corollary was that fresh decisions might need to be taken in human rights cases after the disposal of asylum claims. The result of this was that no expulsion decision could be implemented after 2 October 2000 without consideration being given to underlying human rights issues and either an appeal or a certificate capable of challenge by judicial review. This was consistent with the prospective nature of the issues thrown up in immigration cases, issues somewhat removed from the problem of the impact of historic convictions on a contemporary appeal court.

The position has been altered by the judgment in *R (Kariharan and others)* v

Secretary of State for the Home Department [2001] EWHC Admin 1004, 5 December 2001. Here the High Court held that a decision by the Secretary of State to refuse an application to remain on human rights grounds after 2 October 2000[5] and thereafter to set removal directions was not a decision 'in relation to that person's entitlement to enter or remain in the United Kingdom' and thus did not attract appeal rights under s. 65, in circumstances where an earlier asylum application, which traversed the same factual territory as the human rights claim, had been determined and previous appeal rights exhausted before 2 October 2000. The High Court held that a decision to issue removal directions was predicated on the absence of entitlement to enter or to remain in the United Kingdom, but nevertheless was not a decision relating to such entitlement. The High Court considered that s. 65 distinguished between decisions declaring, creating or terminating a right to enter or remain, or affecting the terms of such a right, and administrative decisions, such as a decision to require a person who had no right to enter or to remain in the United Kingdom to leave, and a decision to enforce that requirement. The High Court further held that the Home Office's policy announced on 19 July 2001 not to furnish a s. 65 appeal right in these circumstances unless there was an appeal available or pending on 2 October 2000 was rational and consistent with the *Pardeepan* undertaking, which it considered related solely to pending appeals.

What *Kariharan* however did not consider,[6] was that the courts have held that leave is not a unitary concept in immigration law,[7] such that an application for leave to remain on a different ground from that made earlier requires a fresh formal notice of decision and it is not sufficient simply to rely upon an earlier formal decision. In the terms of the dichotomy erected in *Kariharan* the later decision is declaratory of rights, rather than a mere enforcement of a decision already taken denying such rights or requiring a person to leave. It remains to be seen what impact the decision in *Kariharan* will have, especially since the Home Office retains a discretion to issue further notices of decision in order to generate appeal rights.[8]

In our opinion, an application for leave to enter or remain on human rights grounds may certainly generate a decision that relates to a right of entry, and the failure of *Kariharan* to consider the case law on successive applications may render it unreliable as a binding authority. Doubtless, the courts will not be astute

---

[5] The commencement date for IAA 1999, s. 65.

[6] It appears that argument was not advanced on the point. The case has been reversed by the Court of Appeal whilst the proofs of this book were being prepared: [2002] INLR 383.

[7] *R v IAT, ex parte Secretary of State* (the Sri Lankan Tamils) [1990] 1 WLR 1126; *R v Secretary of State, ex parte Kazmi* [1995] Imm AR 73, 76–80; *Saad, Diriye and Osorio v Secretary of State* [2001] EWCA Civ 2008, 19 December 2001, Court of Appeal, para. 44.

[8] *R v Secretary of State, ex parte Kazmi* [1995] Imm AR 73, *R v Secretary of State, ex parte Onibiyo* [1996] Imm AR 370. The Secretary of State's policy however was itself the subject of unsuccessful challenge in *Kariharan*.

to preserve purely empty appeal rights where all material issues of fact and law have been authoritatively disposed of previously. Further, even outside the context of IAA 1999, s. 65 appeal rights, we adhere to the opinion expressed elsewhere that the HRA 1998, s. 3 duty of interpretation of statutes will be relevant to the construction of IAA 1999 and rules whenever the executive decision was taken, and even where there is no IAA 1999, s. 65 appeal the Secretary of State will have to act compatibly with s. 6 of the HRA 1998.

The European Court meanwhile continues to produce a large number of admissibility and merits decisions in the field of immigration, from an ever-widening list of countries who are members of the Council of Europe. To cope with its case load many such decisions are being taken under the Protocol 11 procedures without oral hearings and solely on the written pleadings and observations. It is somewhat surprising that a case of such importance as *Bensaid* v *United Kingdom* (2001) 33 EHRR 10 (where the applicant lost) and *Keenan* v *United Kingdom* (2001) 33 EHRR 38 (where he succeeded) should be decided on the paper submissions alone, and without the benefit of final oral submissions on the issues. The European Court has shown no great enthusiasm for referring chamber decisions to the Grand Chamber although this course has been adopted in the environmental noise case of *Hatton* v *UK* (2002) 34 EHRR 1.

We hope that one advantage in delaying the publication of this work has been to take on board in the text itself at least some of these developments, and so some provisional conclusions can be drawn on the central question: will the Human Rights Act 1998 make a difference to the common law in the field of immigration and asylum? This introduction was saved to the last so that we could reflect on any overall themes emerging in the application of human rights to immigration and asylum and partly so there would be one last chance to review developments that might reflect on what we had written to date. However, we considered that the events of 11 September 2001 and the legislative response of the United Kingdom deserved special consideration in a postscript.

It is apparent that despite the government's low key approach on commencement, 'you'll probably never need it, but it's nice to know it's there', the domestic incorporation of parts of the Convention is a significant event that has already changed the intensity of judicial scrutiny of executive decisions. These conclusions have most notably been felt in the field of mental health detention, criminal law, inquest law, prison law and in respect of the law relating to children. On 31 July 2001, Turner J announced his decision (although not his reasons) in the case of *R* v *Secretary of State for the Home Department, ex parte Farrakhan* (31 July 2001)[9] indicating that he would quash a decision to maintain a 15-year exclusion

---

[9] Reasons were given on 2 October 2001; the Court of Appeal granted the Secretary of State permission to appeal and the decision was reversed on the merits in April 2002: [2002] 3 WLR 481.

order on the controversial black religious and political leader. The editorials the following day responded with a range of views (mostly perforce taken in ignorance of the material facts, issues, and reasoning process) as to the merits of such a decision, but perhaps united in the belief that it had only been made possible by the Human Rights Act 1998. This is surely right.

The claimant in that case invited the court to judge the legality of the continued exclusion by reference to the proportionality of its interference with the claimant's right to express, and the black community's right to receive controversial ideas that many might find offensive. Here for the first time was a set of values and a developed jurisprudence on the application of those values against which the discretion of the Secretary of State could be judged. This took the place of the previous personal decision to exclude taken, without governing immigration rules or right of appeal, and in practice only capable of judicial review in theory, if the decision-taker was kind enough to supply a manifest error of approach on the face of the record. The light of reason enlightened the dark recondite recesses of the prerogative but, contrary to some tabloid reaction, this was not judicial usurpation of political functions. Apart from the obvious fact that it was Parliament that passed the law in question, the principle of legality requires more than a passing nod to ensure that the executive has proper authority to make the decision in hand.

Human rights abuses do not just occur when the state assumes powers of interference which it does not have in domestic law, but also embrace the occasion of the use of powers granted in domestic law in a manner that intrudes excessively on the rights of those whose political power is insufficient to ensure respect for their minority rights of expression, association, residence and the like. The techniques of *Wednesbury*[10] review, designed to keep courts from usurping the statutory function of local authorities in licensing Sunday afternoon cinemas in post Second World War Birmingham, are really beyond their sell-by date and no longer represent a useful model of uniform application, and are also apparently devoid of ethical content where the rights of minorities are concerned (see below at 5.145 et seq). It is not sufficient to trust the executive as the conscientious repository of the nation's political and social consensus, particularly where the evidence suggests that political accountability to Parliament is at an all-time low, while public enthusiasm for the electoral process itself reveals record levels of cynicism and indifference. If the law itself does not articulate the precise values and relevant considerations to be taken into account by the executive in certain finely tuned judgments, and if the judiciary must resist the temptation to restate its moral values and opinions as the only sensible arbiter of justice, where are sound values to be found? There is always public opinion, but which public and whose opinion? Even where an impartially administered plebiscitary democracy

---

[10] *Associated Provincial Picture Houses Ltd* v *Wednesbury Corp* [1948] KB 223.

exists (which is a very tall order in any event), mere expression of opinion misses the point of debate, reasoning, identifying relevant evidence and the like. The free press has a valuable role in informing, educating, disseminating and reflecting the opinion of its readerships but public opinion cannot be equated with the thundering of the editorials, particularly where they descend into somewhat hysterical attacks on judge rule. In the case of *Velino* v *Chief Constable of Manchester* [2001] EWCA Civ 1249, 31 July 2001 Sedley LJ noted:

> The House of Lords in *Tinsley* v *Milligan* [1996] 1 AC 340 rejected the 'public conscience' test articulated by Hutchison J in *Thackwell* v *Barclays Bank Ltd* [1986] 1 All ER 676 as a filter on claims with a criminal dimension. We are not now required, in other words, to look over our shoulders at what we fear the press will make of our decisions in this already difficult field. The public conscience, an elusive thing, as often as not turns out to be an echo chamber inhabited by journalists and public moralists. To allow judicial policy to be dictated by it would be as inappropriate as to let judges dictate editorial policy. It is not difficult, for example, to visualise how some sections of the media would choose to report a decision along the lines which I have proposed. The Law Commission's scholarly and constructive working paper has so far been reported under the headline 'Law paves way for thugs to sue victims' (*Daily Express*, 30 June 2001) and has earned the Law Commission the sobriquet 'Enemy of the people' (*Sunday Times*, 1 July 2001). In a free society such comment is perfectly permissible and its influence on public opinion no doubt considerably greater than that of a judgment or a Law Commission paper. The public may one day have to decide through the democratic process whether it wants the law to legitimise the use of firearms against intruders in a society which at present has a gun homicide rate 150 times lower than the United States. But to expect a judiciary to modify its decisions as to what the law and justice require because of what it fears the media would make of them is to ask for the surrender of judicial independence. The 'fair, just and reasonable' test is now the established judicial control on ground-breaking in tort. If the law were ever to revert to an exogenous test, it should be one which gauges the response of people who actually know what the court's reasoning is; and no court which has confidence in its own reasoning should be worried about that.

As Lord Steyn said in the Privy Council decision of *Bennett and John* v *Grenada* (Appeal No. 74 of 2000, 17 July 2001) as to the role of public opinion on the desirability of a retrial for murder (at para. 49):

> In this context the majority refer to the *dicta* of Lord Diplock in *Reid* v *R* [1980] AC 343 about the state of public opinion in Jamaica. Certainly I accept that public opinion in Grenada would favour a retrial in a serious case where it is just and appropriate to order one. On the other hand, I would not for a moment entertain the idea that public opinion in Grenada would demand a retrial even if it cannot take place without injustice to an accused. If I am wrong on this point, I would say that the baying of a lynch mob is no more acceptable in Grenada than elsewhere. The Constitution of Grenada is the silent sentinel guarding against such pressures. And the Privy Council is the ulti-

mate guarantor of the enforcement of the Constitution of Grenada and the integrity of its criminal justice system.

Public opinion is not to be equated with mob rule, lynch law, or hysterical and unreasoned condemnation. Democracy is thus electoral accountability plus due process and the rule of law. The latter embraces not just rule by law, but laws that are just. Human rights norms under the ECHR and related evidence of international practice and standards therefore help to provide an objective standard and method of approach when judges are confronted with issues of political controversy.

Faced with new responsibility and a new array of legal tools with which to examine and adjudicate on legislative and executive rule and decision-making, it is perhaps not surprising that the judges have moved cautiously in the opening months of the HRA 1998 and there has been much reference to the margin of discretion even in cases where judicial expertise was particularly conversant with the subject matter in hand, such as fair trial. The longest chapter in this book is chapter 5, which seeks to chart domestic and European Court case law on the judicial function in human rights cases through use of the margin of appreciation, discretionary area of judgment, proportionality and the like, where differing approaches had come forcefully to light in a sequence of immigration cases. It is apparent that human rights claims will not speedily trump carefully formulated and reasoned immigration policies concerned with family reunion, entry clearance, and deportation of serious criminal wrongdoers. Further, practitioners will know by now that bare recitation of the text of the ECHR and a long, hopeful punt that this will lead to the desired result is unhelpful and inadequate. The scrutiny may be more intense after 2 October 2000, but a proper constitutional distance must be maintained between executive and judiciary. So much is clear, but what is 'proper' and how far is 'distant'?

The European Court itself was not persuaded to refine its margin of appreciation jurisprudence in the context of planning policies for gypsies and Article 8 of the ECHR. In *Smith v UK* (2001) 33 EHRR 30 paras. 97–101, the invitation to revisit *Buckley v UK* (1997) 23 EHRR 101 paras. 74 and 75 was not taken up. The Court of Appeal has nevertheless concluded that Article 8 questions have to be specifically considered and addressed in the enforcement of planning decisions against travellers.[11] One can see that an international judge may need to be even more sensitive to national moral religious and social sensibilities than a domestic one. Applying human rights within the domestic arena should in principle lead to substantially trimmed margins for reasons we note in chapter 1 as well as chapter 6, yet even in the field of the right of silence and the articulation

---

[11] *South Buckinghamshire DC and others* v *Porter and others* [2001] EWCA Civ 1549, 12 October 2001.

of the express and implied rights to a fair criminal trial, the discretionary area of judgment made a controversial debut after 2 October 2000 in *Brown* v *Stott* [2001] 2 WLR 817. For many commentators what was troubling was not the result in that case but rather some of the reasoning, apparently deferring to executive choice, without an indication of where those limits were. In particular there was concern at the failure of their lordships to note that implied restrictions or interferences cannot be permitted to destroy the essence of the right. More recently, the limits of deference have been identified. First in *R* v *A (No. 2)* [2001] 2 WLR 1546 (the rape shield case), a notable example of the principles of purposive interpretation we discuss in chapter 1, and then a few weeks later in the judgment in *Daly* v *Secretary of State for the Home Department* [2001] 2 AC 532. In both cases, the limits to deference were discovered not so much in the case law of the European Court or the pithy restatement of the principles of proportionality in the European Union Charter of Human Rights, but in the dictum of Lord Clyde in the Privy Council decision of *De Freitas* v *Permanent Secretary of Agriculture, Fisheries, Land and Housing* [1999] 1 AC 69 that proportionality requires that the means used to impair the right or freedom are no more than is necessary to accomplish the objective. We discuss *De Freitas* in greater detail below at 5.186 et seq.

Daly is of particular importance to immigration lawyers on account of the references to the immigration cases of *Secretary of State* v *Isiko* [2001] INLR 175 175 and *R (Mahmood)* v *Secretary of State for the Home Department* [2001] 1 WLR 840, its consideration in *Samaroo* v *Secretary of State* [2002] INLR 55, and the conclusion (per Lord Steyn at paras. 25–8) that Lord Phillips MR's formulation of the test to be asked, i.e. could a reasonable Secretary of State have concluded that the interference was necessary in a democratic society, was an insufficient advance on the common law position to reflect the court's new responsibilities to decide rather than defer. *Daly* identifies that the judge in examining an executive decision for compatibility may need to go further than traditional grounds of review have afforded and direct attention to the relative weight of interests and considerations It may require:

> the reviewing court to assess the balance which the decision-maker has struck, not merely whether it is within the range of rational or reasonable decisions . . . even the heightened scrutiny test is not necessarily appropriate to the protection of human rights.

This does not mean that the judicial review court is a substitute decision-taker, or has complete control of all aspects of the merits. Laws LJ's search for a proper constitutional distance was endorsed specifically. Further, despite *Daly*, it would appear that a single test as to the requirements of proportionality in all cases where the ECHR permits a balance, is as inappropriate in ECHR law as it has been in European Community law. The key message is that context is all, and here context includes the different human right at stake, the subject matter of the issues, and the extent to which it involves the formulation of policy that is the peculiar province of the executive. On some occasions the question is asked, is the interference no more than is necessary (or even strictly necessary) to give effect to the legitimate policy that narrows the ambit of the right? Excluding all cross-examination of a rape complainant on material that the court considered relevant and probative was excessive on this test, just as insisting on the right to open legal correspondence in the absence of a prisoner may be. But can a deportation of a drug trafficker with strong family ties to the UK be examined in such a light?

On 17 July 2001, the Court of Appeal gave judgment in the case of *Samaroo v Secretary of State* [2002] INLR 55 and had the benefit of having heard argument on *Daly v Secretary of State for the Home Department* [2001] 2 AC 532. Here the Court of Appeal accepted the respondent's submission that there was a difference between proportionality of means and proportionality of ends. Whereas the former is appropriate to adjudicate on interferences with substantive rights granted in domestic or international law, a more general approach of whether deportation was a fair balance between the interests of the individual and that of the community was the appropriate question to be decided in Article 8 deportation cases. Whilst it is the court that decides whether the balance is fair, rather than the posited reasonable Secretary of State, it should take account of the essential legitimacy under the ECHR of the policy of deterring others and discouraging future traffickers by deporting convicted ones, despite the great hardship to the family and the absence of any propensity to reoffend. We examine the right to respect for family life and the legitimacy of interferences with it in chapter 4.

Three days after *Samaroo* the Court of Appeal gave judgment in *R (P and Q and QB) v Secretary of State* [2001] EWCA Civ 1151, 20 July 2001, a challenge to the Prison Service's policy of separating babies from their mothers at 18 months. The Court of Appeal noted that it itself had to determine the proportionality of the interference with Article 8(1) while paying appropriate deference to the conclusions of the Prison Service, and held, overturning the decision of the Divisional Court, that the Prison Service was not entitled to operate its policy in a rigid fashion irrespective of the merits of the individual case given the aims of the policy itself, and because there might be cases where under the rubric of Article 8 the combined interests of mother and baby outweighed other considerations arising from the mother's imprisonment and relating to the implications for the prison and the Prison Service generally.

The 'fair balance' test in the context of criminal wrongdoing of a very serious nature may not in the end seem a very significant advance on the test under the domestic case law of whether the compassionate circumstances of the case outweigh the public interest in deporting, despite the requirement that the

Secretary of State is to establish the justification of the interference by reference to the necessity of the decision in question. Clearly the human rights of serious class A drug traffickers and even those of innocent members of their family are unlikely to prove the testing ground for the limits of deference to a policy of deterrence. Immigration law is however, full of policies of greater or lesser importance, procedural or substantive, whose rigid application will cause injustice. Not all those who make late applications and overstay are in the same moral position; some overstay cases are near misses under strict rules and some have no element of expectation of success. While the content of the duty of respect for human rights remains obscure, and whilst the European Court refuses to acknowledge immigration as a civil right, and restates that respect for family life does not mean a right to live in a country of one's choice, the impact of the HRA 1998 at higher court level will remain unclear. It is to be hoped that adjudicators whose knowledge of immigration patterns is very much greater than the Administrative Court will be able to detect an ECHR 'deserving' case as a disproportionate interference without fear of intrusion on the margin of deference.

Certainly in the field of Article 3 the Tribunal, in an important preliminary ruling in the case of *Kacaj* v *Secretary of State* [2001] INLR 354 (Starred), has rejected the Home Office contention of a supposed higher standard of proof in Article 3 than in Refugee Convention (ie the UN Convention relating to the Status of Refugees 1951) cases, and an even more extravagant submission that Articles 2 and 4 have no 'extra territorial' effect. See, however, *Ullah* v *Special Adjudicator* [2002] EWCA Civ 1856 where the Court of Appeal held that no Article other than Article 3 of the ECHR was engaged by an act of exclusion or expulsion. Leave to appeal to the House of Lords was granted.

The appellate authorities remain substantially concerned with the problems of harm to Roma and others from Eastern Europe, and the elucidation and application of the difficult concept of sufficiency of protection adumbrated by the House of Lords in *Horvath* v *Secretary of State* [2001] 1 AC 489. It seems unlikely that their lordships intended that asylum seekers should be returned to persecution because although the risk was real, the state's aspirations for protection were sufficient. The Court of Appeal was not prepared to grant permission to review the application of the *Horvath* test in *Cikos and others* v *Secretary of State* [2001] EWCA Civ 1716, 1 November 2001 and practitioners will have to live with the concept of sufficiency of protection if the draft EU Directive on Asylum is adopted into EC law. It is peculiar that the Divisional Court required higher standards of safety for former soldiers giving evidence in Londonderry than appears to have been afforded to Roma asylum seekers. In *R (Widgery soldiers and others)* v *Lord Saville and others* [2001] EWHC Admin 888, 16 November 2001 the Divisional Court concluded that the common law affords greater protection to the right to life than that demanded by ECHR principles. The case concerned the risks to soldier witnesses arising out of their giving evidence to the 'Bloody Sunday' enquiry in Northern Ireland. The court held that:

> 32. . . . in proceeding to apply the *Osman* [29 EHRR 245] test the Tribunal in our judgment fell into error. The *Osman* and *ex parte A* [*R* v *Lord Saville, ex parte A* [2001] 1 WLR 1855] tests are, as it seems to us, conspicuously different in purpose and effect. In *Osman* the European Court of Human Rights limited the obligation of the state to intervene to protect against the activities of third parties to those circumstances in which there is a real and immediate risk to life. In *ex parte Fernandez* [[1971] 1 WLR 987] the House of Lords and in *ex parte A* the Court of Appeal defined the obligation of a public authority more broadly as being not to make a decision exposing anyone to the real possibility of a risk to life in the future. This misdirection fundamentally flaws the Tribunal's decision.

It remains to be seen whether the heightened common law test for the protection of life has repercussions for domestic law application of ECHR concepts, particularly given the reliance in *Horvath* itself on the judgment of the European Court in *Osman*. The ECHR test is simpler and broader: are there substantial grounds for fearing a real risk of ill treatment? While in *Kacaj* [2001] INLR 354 the Tribunal held that even under the analysis required by the ECHR, the test of 'sufficiency of protection' should be applied to risks emanating from non-state actors, it made it clear that a best endeavours test was not coterminous with sufficiency of protection, and in the Tribunal's view the requisite protection would be lacking if the state's best endeavours are shown to be 'ineffective'. The question has recently been considered by the Court of Appeal in the case of *Macpherson* v *Secretary of State* [2001] EWCA Civ 1955, 19 December 2001 where an overstayer and drug offender faced a real risk of domestic violence from her former partner. The question was whether new legislation in Jamaica provided an effective level of deterrence to prevent such conduct. Arden LJ concluded at paragraph 38:

> Accordingly to be effective, measures for the purposes of Article 3 must be those which attain an adequate degree of efficacy in practice as well as exist in theory. If the appellant were able to show to the requisite degree of proof that the remedies provided under the law of Jamaica against domestic violence are unlikely to be an effective deterrent, in my judgment she would have shown that her removal from the United Kingdom to Jamaica would violate her rights under Article 3.

Sedley LJ at paragraph 22 restated Jamaica's obligation in terms of the *Osman* test and the requirement of reasonable measures to make the necessary protection available. In *Dhuma* [2002] INLR 243 the Divisional Court has brought welcome harmony between the real risk of persecution and the test for Article 3, by concluding that the latter is made out where the former exists. The point of

Article 3 is to preclude expulsions from the UK where future ill-treatment is fore-seeable to the requisite degree. Where the source of the risk is a private person, and the state has practical and effective measures for deterring such conduct, the risk is unlikely to be considered real, but it is the likelihood of the occurrence that is the focus of the human rights obligation.

In assessing this likelihood it is at any rate clear that the personal experiences of the claimants are of great importance. In the case of *Conka* v *Belgium* (App. No. 51564/99, 13 March 2001) the European Court declared inadmissible complaints of violation of Article 3 pursuant to expulsion of Roma to Slovakia. It indicated that whilst the documents and reports furnished to the European Court by the applicants contained information about the violence and discrimination to which the Gypsy community in Slovakia were subjected, they did not however establish that the applicants were personally under threat. In that connection, substantial weight had to be attached to the lack of any evidence that the applicants had suffered any violence or ill-treatment since their return to Slovakia and to the fact that their son had chosen to rejoin them of his own free will in April 2000. The European Court subsequently found other violations of Article 5 and Protocol 4 in connection with these expulsions (5 February 2002). By contrast, therefore, where the claimants had fled from personal threat that still continued, it would seem difficult to dispute that the fear is substantial, simply because the state does not encourage such discrimination and is taking certain measures to combat it. What matters therefore is the reality of the risk rather than the reasons for it, as we have commented below at 2.84 et seq.

No occasion has yet arisen to examine what deference is owed in Article 3 cases to the decision-taker's assessment of risk on the basis of primary findings of fact. We discuss the judgment in *Turgut* v *Secretary of State* [2001] 1 All ER 719 and its implications at some length below at 5.214 et seq. The comments of Lord Hoffman in *Rehman* v *Secretary of State* [2001] 3 WLR 877, para. 54 and see para. 57, support the proposition that no deference will be due: 'Whether a sufficient risk exists (of torture) is a question of evaluation and prediction based on evidence. In answering such a question, the executive enjoys no constitutional prerogative.'[12]

Again, the assertion of judicial responsibility for human rights decisions in *Daly* is helpful in deflecting the courts away from an approach that is content with asking questions merely as to whether the decision-maker's approach was reasonable. In the context of removal of asylum seekers to third countries in the EU, however, the Administrative Court has pronounced on the new regime after

---

[12] In *X* v *Secretary of State* [2001] INLR 205, para. 10 the Court of Appeal (on appeal from a dismissed application for judicial review) was prepared to assume that it itself was required to come to a conclusion whether removal would breach Article 3. See also Michael Beloff QC in 'Judicial Review' [2001] 6(3) JR 154–60, para. 24.

the coming into force of s. 11 of the IAA 1999 and certificates of without foundation under s. 72. On 7 June 2001[13] Collins J decided that a certificate excluding a human rights appeal in the case of a Sri Lankan Tamil threatened with return to Colombo should be upheld. The argument was that Germany's refusal to extend its internal application of Article 3 to non-state agents made it an unsafe place for return given the difficulties in securing temporary protection there. His Lordship noted (at para. 26):

> The question therefore is whether the indication of concerns in Germany about whether section 53(6) will provide the necessary protection, together with the further evidence about the high standard required to obtain protection under section 53(6) mean that the Secretary of State could not properly regard this claim as manifestly unfounded. In my judgment, the material does not cast any doubt upon the propriety of the Secretary of State's decision. He has clearly, as appears from the evidence put before me through Mr Sainsbury, considered the position in Germany. He is satisfied that the German authorities will conscientiously apply the European Convention and will not return anyone and will not return this applicant if he establishes that there is a real risk that he will suffer treatment contrary to Article 3. That is what the European Court of Human Rights found was the position in *TI* [[2000] INLR 211]. The fact that there may be some questions raised in Germany itself as to whether section 53(6) should be amended is nothing to the point, provided always that the Secretary of State was justified in concluding that there was no real risk that this applicant would be returned in contravention of the Convention. As I have said, it seems to me that he was entirely justified in that conclusion.

Where there is an effective and conscientious application of a system of temporary protection, therefore, a return to an EU or other designated country as a safe third country will not raise human rights concerns. The court will scrutinize the evidence to see whether the decision is justified. Collins J continued (at para. 27):

> This is not to say that automatically a decision to return to a European Member State in accordance with section 11 means that there cannot possibly be a well-founded claim under section 65. For example, as one of the applications before me indicated, there may be arguments that the mere act of return itself, for whatever reason, can create a breach of one of the Articles, for example Article 8, even possibly Article 3 in exceptional cases, because there is a potential breach of human rights other than that created by the possibility of return to the country where persecution or ill-treatment is feared. Equally, it may be possible that, in a given case, the evidence establishes that there is a real risk of return, for whatever reason, to the possible persecution. That is not, as I

---

[13] *R (Thangarasa)* v *Secretary of State* [2001] EWHC Admin 420, affirmed on appeal to the Court of Appeal in *R (Yogathas and Thangarasa)* v *Secretary of State* [2001] EWCA Civ 1611, 21 September 2001; dismissed by House of Lords in *Yogathas and Thangarasa* v *Secretary of State* [2002] UKHL 41.

say, the position here. But it must not be thought that the mere fact that section 11 can be used precludes the possibility of a claim under the Human Rights Act. I am sure the Secretary of State would not approach it on that basis and I am not prepared to assume that he does. I simply indicate that each case has to be given, and I am quite satisfied this case has been given, the separate consideration that is needed in all these cases.

One paradox of the advent of the HRA 1998 has been temporarily to draw human rights points away from the incremental development of the common law, and for courts to ask a harder-edged question: has there been a violation of the ECHR? There is no warrant for this. To give just one recent example, in the mother and baby prison case[14] Lord Phillips MR acknowledged (at para. 67) that English common law had been 'enriched' by European Court jurisprudence long before the Human Rights Act 1998 came into force. Incorporation and incremental development of the common law go hand in hand. Given the age of the ECHR itself, it is not surprising if more developed standards are not to be found in other instruments, whether treaties, Conventions, or political accords. As Lord Cooke has remarked in his concurring judgment in *Daly*, the decision in that case was reached by both the common law and the ECHR route, but reliance on the ECHR was not necessary for the result:

> The truth is, I think, that some rights are inherent and fundamental to democratic civilised society. Conventions, constitutions, bills of rights and the like respond by recognising rather than creating them.

The task of a human rights sensitive common law must be to continue to search for and recognize rights, whether as evidence of international consensus in the subject matter or by the more precarious route of legitimate expectation. The European Court has already demonstrated how such standards can be brought to bear on ECHR problems. Thus in *T and V v UK* (1999) 30 EHRR 121 it had regard to the Convention on the Rights of the Child and the political declarations of international community in determining whether maintaining the age of criminal majority at 10 was a violation of Article 3:

> 71. In this connection, the Court observes that, at the present time there is not yet a commonly accepted minimum age for the imposition of criminal responsibility in Europe. While most of the Contracting States have adopted an age-limit which is higher than that in force in England and Wales, other States, such as Cyprus, Ireland, Liechtenstein and Switzerland, attribute criminal responsibility from a younger age. Moreover, no clear tendency can be ascertained from examination of the relevant international texts and instruments (see paragraphs 43–44 above). Rule 4 of the Beijing Rules which, although not legally binding, might provide some indication of the exist-

---

[14] *R (P and Q and QB) v Secretary of State* [2001] EWCA Civ 1151, 20 July 2001.

ence of an international consensus, does not specify the age at which criminal responsibility should be fixed but merely invites States not to fix it too low, and Article 40(3)(a) of the UN Convention requires States Parties to establish a minimum age below which children shall be presumed not to have the capacity to infringe the criminal law, but contains no provision as to what that age should be.

72. The Court does not consider that there is at this stage any clear common standard amongst the member States of the Council of Europe as to the minimum age of criminal responsibility. Even if England and Wales is among the few European jurisdictions to retain a low age of criminal responsibility, the age of ten cannot be said to be so young as to differ disproportionately from the age-limit followed by other European States.

The implications are significant. Regard was had to a non-binding declaration in order to determine consensus on a specific content of a right. A search for a European consensus was held to be of importance. The implications of this for the non-binding but legally precise EU Charter of Rights are significant. Here member states have agreed precise statements of values that they recognize, including the right to conscientious objection. It is likely that such a Charter will provide a useful background to common European values when articulating the issues under the ECHR and common law respect for human rights. The rejection of the Charter's recognition of a right to conscientious objection by the majority in the case of *Sepet and Bulbul* v *Secretary of State for the Home Department* [2001] INLR 376 is antithetical to the logic of the common law and the ECHR in this respect. Rights that are recognized politically by the democratically elected representatives of states enter the currency of rights that may have legal significance in disputes between the executive and the individual. Although regional agreements cannot be used to read down the universal standards of protection under the Refugee Convention adhered to by the United Kingdom and others, there is no reason why such agreements cannot result in state practices of benefit to the individual applicable within Europe (Article 53 ECHR); for 'reading down' as a technique of statutory construction to give effect to human rights obligations see *R* v *A* [2001] UKHL 25 para. 44. The Court of Appeal in *Sepet and Bulbul* posed the question: did the UN instrument require the Secretary of State to recognize a right of conscientious objection as opposed to merely permitting him to do so? But as the minority judgment found, if the UK was permitted to apply asylum law recognizing such rights the evidence strongly suggests that it has already done so, and its adherence to the Charter would be strong confirmation of that proposition. A more progressive use has been made of the Charter in *R (Robertson)* v *ERO Wakefield* [2001] EWHC Admin 915.

Human rights and the detention of aliens and asylum seekers remain difficult and controversial. We have examined these issues below at 3.36 et seq where we discuss the decision of the Court of Appeal in the Oakington judgment on Article

5.[15] The Court granted leave to appeal to the House of Lords its judgment that the presumption of detention on arrival for certain classes of nationals operated in the Oakington reception centre regime was compatible with Article 5. The appeal was dismissed: [2002] 1 WLR 3131. The message from the European Court since the case of *Amuur* v *France* (1996) 33 EHRR 533 has been unclear. In the case of *Doughoz* v *Greece* (2001) 10 BHRC 306, the detention of a Syrian asylum seeker with repeat convictions for drug offending was held to be incompatible with Article 5 where the criminal court and the Minister of the Interior made conflicting assessments of dangerousness. It is unclear whether the decision turned on the absence of sufficiently effective procedural rights in Greece, or whether the European Court's decision can also be read as requiring an element of necessity of detention when such cases come before the courts. In the United Kingdom a potentially important judgment on the compatibility of the apparent presumption in favour of detention under Sch. 3 of the Immigration Act 1971 and the terms of the Human Rights Act 1998 was avoided by a consent order.[16] Asylum seekers and others who have served a criminal sentence and have been recommended for deportation in custody can only be released when the Secretary of State so agrees. There is at present no right for them to seek bail and so the only means of ensuring compatibility with Article 5(4) is the pursuit of judicial review or a writ of habeas corpus. The Home Office agreed that there could be no presumption in favour of detention, and an individualized assessment of risk and of the need for such detention was called for in the particular case. Speedy decisions should be made to ensure that detainees do not languish in immigration detention long after their sentence has been served, particularly if they have claims to remain that require determination and adjudication. All this suggests that Article 5 is not simply concerned with procedures, but also imports judicial protection against arbitrariness.

In summary the Human Rights Act 1998 is no quick fix for immigration and asylum problems, which still need to be addressed in terms of the substantive law and procedures, but in interpreting that law, in identifying minimum standards for the content of immigration rights, in precluding certain expulsions, and ensuring that judicial review may in appropriate cases penetrate deeper into the merits of competing considerations than had previously been the case, it makes a significant contribution to the culture of respect for human rights and judicial enforcement of those rights through litigation. We hope that the following pages will prove of some assistance to the general reader and practitioner alike in seeing to what extent the Human Rights Act 1998 may assist, and in warning of the circumstances when it will not.

---

[15] *R (Saadi and others)* v *Secretary of State* [2001] EWCA Civ 1512, 19 October 2001, [2002] 1 WLR 356

[16] *R (Sedrati, Buitrago-Lopez, Anaghatu)* v *Secretary of State for the Home Department* [2001] EWHC Admin 418, 17 May 2001.

Finally, in reviewing recent events we could hardly fail to mention the response of the United Kingdom to the terrorist attacks in America, and the risk of violence directed against the United Kingdom. Rather than rewrite the book and indeed this introduction in the light of these events and the Anti-Terrorism Crime and Security Act 2001, we have collected our thoughts in a postscript when the final text of the 2001 Act became available. What is clear to an even greater extent than in October 2000 is that judicial scrutiny of human rights claims and a willingness to vindicate them in favour of aliens who are otherwise without political friends or legal recourse is as vital today as ever before.

Chapter One

The Human Rights Act 1998 and the Immigration and Asylum Act 1999

INTRODUCTION

1.1   For most areas of public law the Human Rights Act (HRA) 1998 will apply on top of the existing framework of the statutory scheme. Thus the law of education, public housing, social security, criminal investigation will remain substantially as before but with public officials required to perform their tasks compatibly with the rights laid down in the European Convention on Human Rights (ECHR). In the field of immigration and asylum, the coming into force of the HRA 1998 coincided with the last phase of implementation of the Immigration and Asylum Act (IAA) 1999, which has significantly overhauled the system of immigration control. Immigration practitioners have thus had to get used to two new statutory schemes at the same time.

1.2   The purpose of this chapter is to introduce the new schemes and examine how they interrelate. We first examine how the HRA 1998 works and make some general observations about interpreting and applying the ECHR. We then look at the new scheme of immigration appeals and how human rights points may there be taken. Most HRA 1998 questions will be decided by adjudicators in the course of statutory appeals under the IAA 1999. One of the most significant rights of appeal under the old system was appeal on the merits against a decision to deport on the grounds of breach of conditions (Immigration Act 1971, s. 15).[1]

1.3   Henceforth those who breach conditions of admission or obtain a leave to remain by deception (IAA 1999, s. 10) can be removed without a prior right of appeal, either on the issue as to whether there was power in law to remove or on the general merits of the balance of the public interest and compassionate factors

---

[1]   See *R* v *Secretary of State, ex parte Bakhtaur Singh* [1986] 1 WLR 910. This right was significantly restricted in 1988 to those who had been resident in the UK for seven years prior to the decision to deport: see Immigration Act 1988, s. 5; *R* v *Secretary of State, ex parte Oladahinde* [1991] 1 AC 254.

as under a s. 3(5)(b) of the Immigration Act 1971 deportation appeal.[2] In place of the old merits appeal, a specific right of appeal on human rights grounds is provided. This necessarily means that submissions that might previously have been made on compassionate grounds will now be made on human rights grounds. Finally we examine the other courts where human rights issues will arise in the immigration and asylum context.

THE SCHEME OF IMMIGRATION CONTROL

1.4   Immigration law involves a wide variety of public officials. A journey to the United Kingdom may start with an application for entry clearance[3] for a purpose provided for by the Immigration Rules[4] or a recognized statutory concession.[5] If the person is seeking employment his proposed employer will have already sought a work permit from the Department for Education and Employment.[6] Others may be seeking admission as a visitor, student or other temporary capacity; or to run a business or enter in a self-employed capacity or as an investor or as a family member of a person already settled here or resident with an entitlement to settlement. The visa form is completed and the fee paid. In due course there may be an interview and the visa either granted or refused. If the visa is refused there is likely to be an appeal.[7] The appeal will be heard by an adjudicator in the United Kingdom unless national security grounds are involved and the ordinary right of appeal excluded. In this case the right of appeal is to the Special Immigration Appeals Commission (Special Immigration Appeals Commission Act 1997, s. 2). In ordinary immigration cases there may be a right to appeal with leave to the Immigration Appeal Tribunal (IAA 1999, Sch. 4, para. 22) and thereafter an appeal on a point of law to the Court of Appeal (para. 23).

---

[2]   *R* v *IAT, ex parte Patel* [1989] AC 910 as to the power to remove; judicial review on a precedent fact basis is however available in relation to reliance on the s. 10 removal power: see further below at 3.97.

[3]   Visas are required for visa nationals, entry clearances are required for others. Certificates of entitlement are issued for those with claims to exemption from immigration control on the grounds of British nationality. See Immigration Rules, HC 395, para. 6, Appendix 1. The generic term 'entry clearance' is used here.

[4]   The Immigration Rules are rules of policy in the administration of the Immigration Act 1971 laid under s. 3(2) of that Act. The current rules date from 1994 and have been subsequently amended many times. The rules can be found at the Home Office IND website at *http://www.ind.homeoffice.gov.uk*.

[5]   A number of well-established concessions in immigration law exist outside the Immigration Rules. The principal concessions are published on the Home Office IND website (see above at footnote 4).

[6]   Details of the work permit scheme can be obtained from the DfEE website at *www.dfee.gov.uk/ols*. The issue of work permits is not a matter for the Home Office although possession of a work permit is a mandatory requirement for those who come to the UK to be engaged in most kinds of employment.

[7]   The rights of appeal are provided for in ss. 59(2) and 60 of the IAA 1999.

Where there is no decision, or no right of appeal the process of entry clearance may give rise to an application for judicial review in the High Court.

1.5   If these appellate procedures result in the issue of the requisite visa, the journey will continue with the purchase of a travel ticket and the boarding of an aeroplane. If the traveller comes from a region where it is suspected that a significant number of passengers are asylum seekers, the scrutiny of the documentation by the airline may also involve reference to an immigration liaison officer posted abroad by the Home Office. Any advice which the liaison officer gives to the airline may result in the contract of carriage being annulled and the would-be migrant is back to square one (see *Farah* v *Home Office* (6 December 1999 CA)). All carriers will be concerned to ensure that those who require visas are in possession of them, or else they may face carriers sanctions in the United Kingdom (IAA 1999, s. 40). If the ship or aircraft is successfully boarded, the carrier may be required to give advance information to the British immigration authorities as to the identity of its passengers (IAA 1999, ss. 18–21). If the traveller enters via the Channel Tunnel he or she may encounter immigration officers operating in France under bilateral arrangements made between the UK and France.

1.6   Eventually the traveller arrives at a designated port of entry in the United Kingdom and then has to submit to an examination by an immigration officer on arrival (Immigration Act 1971, Sch. 2). If he or she is in possession of a valid visa the examination should be fairly short to determine whether the document was properly obtained or there has been a change of circumstances. A valid travel document or laissez-passer may then be stamped with a notice in writing giving leave to enter for a limited or unlimited period, and if the former there will be other conditions attached to the leave. Those whose cases excite suspicion, or who have no visa because they do not need one may have to submit to a longer examination. This will certainly be the case for asylum seekers who will be unable to obtain a prior visa to claim refugee status and may have arrived at the frontiers without any valid travel documents at all.

1.7   If the immigration officer remains unsatisfied as to identity or the purpose of entry, the examination may be adjourned and the person either admitted on temporary admission, in which case they are deemed not to have entered the United Kingdom, or detained in a detention centre run by a contracted out authority or in a prison. Prolonged detention of up to eight days will require the person to be brought before a judicial authority to review the necessity of detention (IAA 1999, s. 44). This may be an immigration adjudicator or a magistrate.

1.8   Asylum seekers who are not detained may well be destitute and have to apply for assistance under the new asylum support scheme set up by the IAA 1999, Part IV. This will involve more forms being filled, claims being processed, and rights of appeal from negative decisions to an asylum support adjudicator.

Support may be provided by the local authority, private landlords, voluntary organizations and others. Subsistence vouchers may have to be cashed at designated stores (IAA 1999, s. 96).

1.9 Eventually the examination process is brought to an end after one or more interviews. Leave to enter may be given or refused. Those who came to attention after passing through immigration control by deceit or clandestinely or evading immigration control altogether will be served with notices stating that they are illegal entrants and liable to be removed as such. Those who were in possession of a valid visa at the time of the intended entry will have an in country right of appeal. So will most asylum seekers if they are not being removed to a designated safe third country (IAA 1999, ss. 69, 71). Others would normally only be able to appeal from abroad. Everybody will have an opportunity to appeal before removal on human rights grounds, unless the factual basis of the human rights claim was considered in an earlier appeal, the underlying immigration decision pre-dates 2 October 2000 (IAA 1999, s. 65)[8] and any claim is not certified as being without foundation: see *R (Razgor)* v *Secretary of State for the Home Department* [2002] EWHC Admin 2554.

1.10 If an entrant has been given leave to enter the United Kingdom, it may be for either a limited or an indefinite period. If limited leave is granted it will be subject to conditions that must be adhered to unless varied. The most important of these is the time limits on the stay. People with a limited leave must either leave the country or seek an extension of stay from the Home Office using one of the approved forms issued for the purpose. Such extensions of stay should be sought within the time period of the initial one. People who overstay their time period or breach one of the conditions imposed on entry will face summary removal by immigration officers (IAA 1999, s. 10). People who are admitted under the Immigration Rules may be restricted from having access to public funds and may be charged for medical treatment (see Immigration Rules, HC 395, para. 6). Only those who are infirm and destitute may now pray in aid the residual powers of social support under the National Assistance Act 1948.

1.11 A migrant may wish to marry in the United Kingdom, in which case the registrar of marriages may take an interest in the application for a licence and be under a duty to report any suspicions to the Home Office (IAA 1999, s. 23). Aliens staying longer than six months may well be required to register their address with the police. The police will have functions to investigate crime, arrest and detain under the IAA 1999. If the person seeks advice from an immigration

---

[8] See *R (Kariharan)* v *Secretary of State* [2001] EWHC Admin 1004, 5 December 2001; now reversed by the Court of Appeal [2002] INLR 383.

consultant or others not exempt from registration, the adviser will have to apply to a commissioner for authority to practice (IAA 1999, s. 84), there may be rights of appeal against refusals (IAA 1999, s. 88).

1.12   At the end of the immigration process, a traveller may eventually be granted leave to remain indefinitely and in due course apply to the Home Office for naturalization as a British citizen. Alternatively he or she may be removed as an irregular migrant or face deportation on the grounds of conducive to the public good. Detention may once again follow and then placement, by force if necessary, on a flight back to the country of origin or any other country to which he or she is admissible.

1.13   This short survey is intended to introduce the range of officials concerned in some way with immigration and asylum: work permit officer, entry clearance officer, immigration liaison officer, immigration officer, housing officer, asylum support officer, benefit officer, registrar, Home Office official, police officer, adjudicator, special adjudicator, Tribunal member, judge. These are all public officials within the meaning of the HRA 1999. So too are prison and custody officers and those who move the detained person around from one place to another. Even those who are employed by international carriers and who have functions thrust on them by regulations may for certain purposes be public officials (*Poplar Housing and Regeneration Community Association Ltd* v *Donoghue* [2001] 3 WLR 183). All these have new enforceable duties thrust upon them to act compatibly with the ECHR. What does the HRA 1998 mean for them and those affected by their actions?

THE DUTY TO ACT COMPATIBLY

Convention rights

1.14   Section 6(1) is the centrepiece of the HRA 1998 making it unlawful for a public authority to act in a way which is incompatible with an ECHR right. The ECHR rights referred to are those set out in Schedule 1 to the HRA 1998 and consist of Articles 2 to 12 and 14 of the ECHR, Articles 1 to 3 of the First Protocol and Article 1 of the Sixth Protocol. This reflects the substantive ECHR obligations that the United Kingdom has ratified, save that the right to an effective remedy under Article 13 has been omitted. We consider the implications of this factor in greater detail below at 5.126 et seq.

1.15   We will see that the ECHR rights protected by the HRA 1998 apply to all those within the jurisdiction of a contracting state or those abroad affected by acts of its officials. Nationality of the contracting state is thus not a requirement of eligibility for human rights. Nevertheless those who are not British citizens and do not have the right of abode or a right of free movement, entry and residence under EC law, cannot normally found a complaint of a violation of ECHR rights in respect of decisions relating to immigration and asylum. The ECHR gives no foreign national a right to enter or remain in the territory of the United Kingdom. There is not even a right to enter to seek asylum from persecution (*Vilvarajah* v *UK* (1991) 14 EHRR 248). Although the right to seek asylum is listed as one of the rights in the Universal Declaration on Human Rights which inspired the drafting of the ECHR, the ECHR makes no reference to it.

1.16   The only reference to aliens in the original rights afforded under Articles 1 to 13 of the ECHR, indeed, is in the context of Article 5(1)(f) identifying detention for immigration purposes as a potential justification to detention without trial. Subsequently in 1963 the contracting states agreed Protocol 4, Articles 2 to 4 of which gave certain rights in the context of immigration. In 1984 Protocol 7 was adopted, Article 1 of which gave certain procedural rights to aliens. The UK has not ratified these additional Protocols nor incorporated them into domestic law. The European Court has recently pointed to the existence of the procedural rights under Protocol 7, Article 1 to suggest that 'States were aware that Article 6.1 of the Convention did not apply to procedures for the expulsion of aliens and wished to take special measures in that sphere.' (*Maaoui* v *France* (2001) 33 EHRR 42). In the following chapters we will explain how foreigners came to have human rights connected with their immigration asylum and nationality status.

Territorial effect

1.17   The HRA 1998 also failed to incorporate Article 1 of the ECHR that requires the states parties to the ECHR to 'secure to everyone within their jurisdiction the rights and freedoms'. Immigration law raises immediately the question of territorial effect of the s. 6 of the HRA 1998 duty. One narrow reading of the duties owed to immigrants by public authorities under domestic law suggests that a duty is only owed to those who have entered and are lawfully resident in the territory of a member state. Such an approach is inapplicable to the ECHR and the HRA 1998 which applies it to the United Kingdom. Three general propositions can be advanced which are derived from the case law on the ECHR.

1.18   First, the rights safeguarded are not restricted to those who are lawfully in the United Kingdom (*D* v *UK* (1997) 24 EHRR 423). Of course, the immigration status of a person affected by a decision of a public official may be highly relevant in deciding whether the action violates an ECHR right or not (*Berrehab* v *Netherlands* (1988) 11 EHRR 322). However, everyone in the jurisdiction is entitled to their rights irrespective of their status. The duty to secure the rights and freedoms to everyone within the jurisdiction includes everyone who is physically present in the territory of a state whether they are deemed to have entered the United Kingdom or not (*D* v *UK* (1997) 24 EHRR 423, para. 48).[9] This is to be contrasted with certain provisions of the Refugee Convention that are applicable only to those who are lawfully within the territory and can exclude those who are awaiting a decision on leave to enter or who have been refused leave to enter (*Bugdacay* v *Secretary of State for the Home Department* [1987] AC 514, 526).[10] The reason the government has given that Article 1 has not been enacted is that the United Kingdom fulfils the duty of securing rights to all within the jurisdiction by enacting the HRA 1998. The case law on Article 1 will still need to be visited however to understand the scope of the obligations that now form part of domestic law.

1.19   Secondly, the duties under s. 6 of the HRA 1998 apply to all public authorities, wherever they are located. There is no restrictive territorial limitation to the HRA 1998 in the text itself. The ECHR case law suggests that whenever a state exercises its authority abroad its officials will be accountable under the ECHR (*Loizidou* v *Turkey* (1995) 20 EHRR 90). The *Loizidou* case involved the Turkish army's occupation of Northern Cyprus and the exercise of governmental control over its inhabitants. A similar approach was applied when Turkey seized a suspected criminal abroad (*Issa and others* v *Turkey* (App. No. 31821/96, 30 May 2000) and *Öcalan* v *Turkey* (App. No. 46221/99, 14 December 2000)) and when the Italian navy intercepted a ship carrying refugees (*Xhavara and others* v *Italy and Albania* (App. No. 39473/98, 11 January 2001).[11] Subsequently the European Court concluded that Turkey could be liable for the acts of the civilian administration it installed in Northern Cyprus and not just for the acts of its own troops (*Cyprus* v *Turkey* (10 May 2001)).

1.20   The meaning of jurisdiction in cases of military activity abroad has been recently examined in great detail in the case of *Bankovic and others* v *Belgium and other NATO states* (12 December 2001), that concerned the bombing of the Belgrade TV station by NATO forces during the Kosovo conflict. The European Court concluded that the Yugoslav victims were not within the jurisdiction of the NATO states signatory to the ECHR. Jurisdiction was essentially territorial in scope but could extend to extraterritorial acts where the state sought to exercise extraterritorial control over others[12] or by reason of some special link with

---

9   See also *R* v *Secretary of State, ex parte Yiadom* (Case C-357/98) [2001] INLR 300.

10   See also *Kaya* v *London Borough of Haringay* [2001] EWCA Civ 677.

11   This involved the alleged deliberate striking of an Albanian ship by an Italian naval vessel 35 nautical miles off the coast of Italy.

12   At para. 70 the European Court concluded 'Moreover, in that first Loizidou judgment (*preliminary objections*), the Court found that, bearing in mind the object and purpose of the Convention, the responsibility of a Contracting Party was capable of being engaged when as a consequence of military action (lawful or unlawful) it exercised effective control of an area outside its national territory.

persons concerned. Cases where states were liable for acts of public officials outside their territory were exceptional therefore. The European Court concluded at paragraphs 71 to 73:

> In sum, the case-law of the Court demonstrates that its recognition of the exercise of extra-territorial jurisdiction by a Contracting State is exceptional: it has done so when the respondent State, through the effective control of the relevant territory and its inhabitants abroad as a consequence of military occupation or through the consent, invitation or acquiescence of the Government of that territory, exercises all or some of the public powers normally to be exercised by that Government. In line with this approach, the Court has recently found that the participation of a State in the defence of proceedings against it in another State does not, without more, amount to an exercise of extra-territorial jurisdiction (*McElhinney v Ireland and the United Kingdom* (dec.), no. 31253/96, p. 7, 9 February 2000, unpublished). Additionally, the Court notes that other recognised instances of the extra-territorial exercise of jurisdiction by a State include cases involving the activities of its diplomatic or consular agents abroad and on board craft and vessels registered in, or flying the flag of, that State. In these specific situations, customary international law and treaty provisions have recognised the extra-territorial exercise of jurisdiction by the relevant State.

It is clear that nationality of a contracting state, grant of travel documents or even prior residence or domicile there may be a sufficient link to bring consular acts within the jurisdiction of the contracting state for the purposes of Article 1.[13]

1.21 The European Court in *Bankovic* accepted the government argument that a different formula is used in international instruments concerned with the laws of war when intended to apply to acts done overseas, and that a high degree of control is needed before jurisdiction is being exercised. This decision is a realistic recognition of some boundaries in the application of the ECHR where the issue is aerial warfare, land forces are not engaged and indeed the principal participant in the bombing is not subject to the ECHR at all. In our opinion, however, the case law cited in this decision should make it plain that where British armed forces operate under their own initiative abroad, the treatment of

---

The obligation to secure, in such an area, the Convention rights and freedoms was found to derive from the fact of such control whether it was exercised directly, through the respondent State's armed forces, or through a subordinate local administration' (our emphasis). The European Court concluded that the acts of which the applicant complained were capable of falling within Turkish jurisdiction within the meaning of Article 1 of the ECHR.

[13] See *X v FRG* (App. No. 1611/62, 25 September 1965) where the Commission concluded 'in certain respects the nationals of a Contracting state are within its jurisdiction even when domiciled or resident abroad; whereas in particular the diplomatic and consular representatives of their country of origin perform certain duties with regard to them which may in certain circumstances, make that country liable in respect of the Convention'. See also *East African Asians* case (1973) 3 EHRR 76, but see *R (on the application of Suresh) v Secretary of State for the Home Department* [2001] EWHC Admin 1028, 16 November 2001 and *R (Abbasi) v Secretary of State for the Home Department* [2002] EWCA Civ 1598.

suspects and detainees must accord with the fundamental requirements of Articles 2 and 3.[14]

1.22   Outside the field of warfare, the question is whether the public authority is purporting to exercise jurisdiction over an individual in accordance with its domestic law or the principles of international law. This will include cases of arrest with a view to extradition, refusal of visas, or other exercise of official authority carried out with the acquiescence or consent of the sovereign state. This raises potentially difficult issues if the public authority amenable to the UK court is acting abroad and acts incompatibly as a result of local foreign laws that it has to obey. However entry clearance officers, for example, are consular officials subject to diplomatic immunity and their discretionary decisions relating to the grant of visas will attract the section 6, HRA 1998 duty to act compatibly. The performance of their functions may require particular care to ensure confidentiality when dealing with information that may place a person at risk by the local laws and local traditions, such as where applications are made by same-sex partners, unmarried couples or others whose personal status might well be disapproved of locally. The mere fact that an alien applies for an entry clearance abroad does not of itself engage the responsibility of the contracting state for all the consequences of a refusal of a visa.[15] Nevertheless there is a difference between the question whether the ECHR applies in principle and what the particular obligations are under the ECHR in the context of international relations.

1.23   The third observation about jurisdiction is that acts done by public authorities in the United Kingdom may have consequences elsewhere outside the United Kingdom (*Soering* v *UK* (1989) 11 EHRR 439). Indeed they may produce

---

[14]   See *Loizidou* v *Turkey* (1995) 20 EHRR 90; *Ilascu* v *Moldova* (App. No. 48787/99, 4 July 2001). In its report in the *Coard* case (Report No. 109/99, case No. 10.951, *Coard et al.* v *United States*, 29 September 1999, §§ 37, 39, 41 and 43), the Inter-American Commission of Human Rights examined complaints about the applicants' detention and treatment by United States' forces in the first days of the military operation in Grenada and commented: 'While the extraterritorial application of the American Declaration has not been placed at issue by the parties, the Commission finds it pertinent to note that, under certain circumstances, the exercise of its jurisdiction over acts with an extraterritorial locus will not only be consistent with, but required by, the norms which pertain. The fundamental rights of the individual are proclaimed in the Americas on the basis of the principles of equality and non-discrimination – "without distinction as to race, nationality, creed or sex". . . Given that individual rights inhere simply by virtue of a person's humanity, each American State is obliged to uphold the protected rights of any person subject to its jurisdiction. While this most commonly refers to persons within a state's territory, it may, under given circumstances, refer to conduct with an extraterritorial locus where the person concerned is present in the territory of one state, but subject to the control of another state—usually through the acts of the latter's agents abroad. In principle, the inquiry turns not on the presumed victim's nationality or presence within a particular geographic area, but on whether, under the specific circumstances, the State observed the rights of a person subject to its authority and control.'

[15]   See *R* v *Secretary of State, ex parte Sritharan* [1993] Imm AR 184 concerned with the Refugee Convention, and see also *R (on the application of Suresh)* v *Secretary of State for the Home Department* [2001] EWHC Admin 1028, 16 November 2001.

effects in states that are outside the Council of Europe altogether. This does not matter. If a public authority within the jurisdiction of the contracting state acts in a way that causes a violation of an ECHR right, the public authority may be liable for that act (*Chahal* v *Secretary of State for the Home Department* (1996) 23 EHRR 413). In the context of immigration this means that if there are substantial grounds for concluding that the consequence of an expulsion to country X is the pronouncement of the death penalty,[16] execution, torture or exposure to inhuman or degrading treatment (Article 3), slavery (Article 4(1)) or other consequence prohibited by the core values of the ECHR, the act of expulsion is unlawful.[17] The ECHR is not being applied to prohibit acts governed by laws of states that are outside its competence. The relevant treatment is the 'act' of expulsion: *Pretty* v *UK* (2002) 35 EHRR 1, para. 53. It prohibits acts done by officials subject to its jurisdiction that cause harm to the individual wherever the end result of the harm is occasioned. This follows whether the consequence is direct by expelling a person to a state where ill-treatment is feared, or indirect by sending the person to another state from where he may be expelled, even if the other state is itself a party to the ECHR (*TI* v *UK* [2000] INLR 211).

1.24   The European Court reviewed the reasoning behind these decisions in the *Bankovic* case. It noted at paragraphs 67 to 68:

> In keeping with the essentially territorial notion of jurisdiction, the Court has accepted only in exceptional cases that acts of the Contracting States performed, or producing effects, outside their territories can constitute an exercise of jurisdiction by them within the meaning of Article 1 of the Convention. Reference has been made in the Court's case-law, as an example of jurisdiction 'not restricted to the national territory' of the respondent State (the *Loizidou* judgment (*preliminary objections*), at para. 62), to situations where the extradition or expulsion of a person by a Contracting State may give rise to an issue under Articles 2 and/or 3 (or, exceptionally, under Articles 5 and/or 6) and hence engage the responsibility of that State under the Convention (the above-cited *Soering* case, at para. 91, *Cruz Varas and Others* v *Sweden* judgment of 20 March 1991, Series A no. 201, paras. 69 and 70, and the *Vilvarajah and Others* v *the United Kingdom* judgment of 30 October 1991, Series A no. 215, para. 103). However, the Court notes that liability is incurred in such cases by an action of the respondent State concerning a person while he or she is on its territory, clearly within its jurisdiction, and that such cases do not concern the actual exercise of a State's competence or jurisdiction abroad (see also, the above-cited *Al-Adsani judgment,* at para. 39).

> In addition, a further example noted at paragraph 62 of the *Loizidou judgment* (*preliminary objections*) was the *Drozd and Janousek* case where, citing a number of admissibility decisions by the Commission, the Court accepted that the responsibility of Contracting Parties (France and Spain) could, in principle, be engaged because of

---

[16] But see Protocol 6 which changes the *Soering* debate: see 2.49 et seq.
[17] See the starred IAT determination in *Kacaj* v *Secretary of State* [2001] INLR 354. See, however, *Ullah* v *Special Adjudicator* EWCA Civ 1856 (leave to appeal to House of Lords granted).

acts of their authorities (judges) which produced effects or were performed outside their own territory (the above-cited *Drozd and Janousek* judgment, at para. 91).

1.25   As this summary illustrates, the principle has not hitherto extended to expulsions that cause a person some restriction of human rights which he or she enjoyed in the United Kingdom, thus diminished rights to practise a religion, to marry, freedom of expression and association do not of itself make an expulsion unlawful.[18] The public authority in the United Kingdom is not responsible for all conduct by others anywhere in the world that falls short of ECHR standards. However, all the foreseeable consequences of an expulsion are factors to be considered. Thus a refusal of admission or expulsion to a family member may result in an unjustifiable interference with family or private life and be taken into account when deciding whether the expulsion is lawful (*Abdulaziz* v *UK* (1985) 7 EHRR 471; *Gul* v *Switzerland* (1996) 22 EHRR 93; *Bensaid* v *UK* [2001] INLR 325). We will consider the practical elaboration of these principles when considering particular ECHR rights in the following chapters.

Acting in accordance with primary legislation

1.26   The duty to act compatibly with a right in the ECHR does not apply if the public authority was required to act in the particular way by an act of primary legislation (HRA 1998, s. 6(2)). This introduces the principle stressed throughout the HRA 1998 that Parliament is supreme and can choose to legislate otherwise than in conformity with the ECHR if it so desires. If a piece of legislation cannot be interpreted in a way that is compatible with the ECHR and leaves the public authority no choice in how to go about its task so that 'the authority could not have acted differently' it will not be acting unlawfully. There is a slightly broader exception to the duty in the case where a public authority was acting so as to give effect to or enforce provisions of, or made under, primary legislation (HRA 1998, s. 6(2)(b)). However, this exception must be closely linked to the enforcement concerned, it could be no defence that a public authority acted incompatibly with an ECHR right to give effect to primary legislation if it did not have to give effect to such legislation or could have given effect in a different way that was not incompatible.

1.27   It is sufficient for present purposes to summarize a number of points about the special status of Parliament. First, neither House of Parliament nor those exercising functions connected with Parliamentary proceedings are a public authority (HRA 1998, s. 6(3)). This exemption does not include the Judicial Committee of

---

18 See for example *Drozd and Janousek* v *France and Spain* (1992) 14 EHRR 745 at para. 110. See also *Holub* v *Secretary of State for the Home Department* [2001] INLR 219. The issue was considered by the Court of Appeal in *Z, AM* v *Secretary of State for the Home Department* [2002] EWCA Civ 952. In *Ullah* v *Secretary of State for the Home Department* [2002] EWCA Civ 1856 the Court of Appeal held that no Art other than Art 3 was engaged in the context of an exclusion or expulsion decision. Leave to appeal to the House of Lords has been granted.

the House of Lords or the Privy Council when sitting as a court in the United Kingdom (HRA 1998, s. 6(4)). Secondly, a failure to introduce a proposal for legislation or a failure to make any primary legislation or a remedial order under the HRA 1998 is not an act capable of being unlawful under HRA 1998, s. 6 (s. 6(6)). Thus it would seem that a failure to bring into force a statute already passed by Parliament cannot be attacked on human rights grounds. Thirdly, incompatible subordinate legislation must be followed if primary legislation prevents the subordinate legislation from being compatible (HRA 1998, s. 4(4)). It will be apparent that where there is a general power to make rules or orders under a section of primary legislation both the failure to make rules or the making of incompatible rules could be an unlawful act if the decision-maker could have acted differently, although an order or other instrument made under primary legislation that brings into effect or amends a provision of primary legislation is itself treated as primary legislation (HRA 1998, s. 21(1)). Fourthly, where the legislation cannot be interpreted compatibly with an ECHR right, the lower courts can offer no relief to the victim of the violation. The higher courts can however make a declaration of incompatibility if proper notice is given to the appropriate member of the executive (HRA 1998, s. 4(5)). Fifthly, where either a declaration of incompatibility is made by the domestic courts or a finding of a violation is made by the European Court, the appropriate member of the executive can remedy the incompatibility by a remedial order to be laid before Parliament (HRA 1998, s. 10, Sch. 2). Finally, when enacting new legislation a Minister of the Crown in charge of a Bill in either House of Parliament must, before second reading, make a statement in writing of his view that the provisions of the Bill are compatible with the ECHR or that the government wishes to proceed with the legislation despite being unable to make such a declaration (HRA 1998, s. 19).

1.28   The general position is thus that primary legislation cannot be struck down for incompatibility and cannot be disapplied in the same way that it could if incompatible with EC law. The government of the day will have the right to introduce future incompatible legislation, but where legislation is declared incompatible, it will have the right to take speedy remedial action if it thinks fit. The HRA 1998 also obliges the government to review periodically the existing derogations from and reservations to ECHR rights (HRA 1998, s. 17). Primary legislation means any Act of Parliament, a Measure of the Church Assembly or General Synod of the Church of England, an Order in Council made in exercise of the royal prerogative, the Northern Ireland constitutional legislation or under an amending provision of legislation (HRA 1998, s. 21(1)).

1.29   The rules of the European Union are thus not primary legislation and their vires is a matter for the European Court of Justice (*R* v *Secretary of State for Health, ex parte Imperial Tobacco Ltd* [2001] 1 WLR 127). However measures given effect by national law may be. Subordinate legislation includes all other rule-making measures including other kinds of Orders in Council and the Acts of the Scottish Parliament and the Northern Ireland Assembly and Parliament. This means that immigration rules, immigration appeal procedure rules and statutory instruments governing fees for applications, and every other aspect of immigration and nationality regulation will in general not be primary legislation; obedience to them will not protect a public authority from s. 6, HRA 1998 illegality by acting incompatibly. We shall examine the consequence of this for immigration adjudicators below.

Public authorities

1.30 We must now examine the question of who are the public authorities that are subject to the s. 6, HRA 1998 duty. Apart from excluding the Houses of Parliament in order to preserve Parliamentary sovereignty, the HRA 1998 offers a broad and inclusive approach that will have to be determined on a case by case basis (HRA 1998, s. 6(2)).[19] It includes a court or tribunal at any level throughout the jurisdiction. This has particular implications for immigration proceedings. It also includes any person 'certain of whose functions are of a public nature' but not if the nature of the particular act complained of is private.

1.31 With these few indications, the question of what is a function of a public nature will be left to interpretation. This is a topic dealt with in greater detail in other textbooks and learned journals[20] where there are unresolved debates as to the status of or the scope of public functions of the BBC, sporting organizations, self-regulatory bodies of the media and industry, health authorities and others. In the context of immigration and asylum, with the possible exception of airlines and other carriers, the nature of public functions is fairly easy to identify and would constitute the 'obvious' public authorities to which the Minister referred in the passage of the legislation.

1.32 We would suggest that, although the ultimate test is to have regard to the function, the first approach is whether the person exercising the function is regarded as a public body. This includes all those whose acts are presently subject to judicial review. Judicial review of course reaches certain bodies exercising regulatory functions that would have been exercised by a public authority but for self-regulation. Ministers of the Crown, civil servants, local government officers, bodies whose functions are created by statute, statutory regulatory bodies are all obvious examples. Secondly, there are bodies that are not apparently public but which may be so having regard to their powers and activities. Thus case law on

---

[19] See the detailed discussion in *Poplar Housing and Regeneration Community Association Ltd v Donoghue* [2001] 3 WLR 183, para. 58.

[20] See Dawn Oliver, 'The Frontiers of the State' [2000] PL 476.

which commercial entities are emanations of the state for the purpose of European Community law may be relevant to the classification of the act.[21] Private commercial bodies part-owned by the state that have statutory powers to carry out their business by way of entry to premises and occupy public space are likely to be public authorities (*Foster v British Gas* [1991] 1 QB 405). Private bodies such as security firms and prison companies to which the state has contracted out functions that were formerly performed by state institutions would be performing public functions.[22] Finally there are private bodies which are regulated by the state in respect of the activity in question and which are required to act in conformity with that regulation. Could a private landowner providing accommodation to an asylum seeker be exercising a public function when formulating rules for the occupation of premises and terminating occupation?[23] Where an airline refuses a passenger admission to a flight because of a perceived duty not to bring those without visas to the United Kingdom, is this an act done to give effect to a public obligation and thus the exercise of a public function?[24]

THE ENFORCEMENT OF THE DUTY

1.33   The HRA 1998 provides that where a public authority has acted or proposes to act in contravention of s. 6(1) a person can either bring proceedings or defend proceedings brought against him or her if he or she is or would be the victim of the act. The term victim is used in the sense of the case law of the ECHR. This tends to mean a person directly affected by a relevant act or omission. Where close family members have been affected by the decision and the direct victim is dead or otherwise unable to bring a case, the family member is considered to be a victim (*McCann v UK* (1995) 21 EHRR 97; *Abdulaziz and others v UK* (1985) 7 EHRR 471). A company or other organization can be the victim of a violation of an ECHR right. A local authority is unlikely to be a victim of an ECHR right, save perhaps in respect of its ownership of property. A public interest body concerned with the application of the law in particular areas is unlikely to be a victim. The test in the HRA 1998 was deliberately kept different from those who presently have standing in judicial review. This can add confusion when a decision is being attacked on general public and human rights grounds in the same claim.

1.34   In most cases the victim test is narrower than in judicial review but in

---

[21] See for example *NUT v Governing Body of St Mary's Church* [1997] ICR 334.

[22] See the comments of Wright J in *Quaquah v Home Office* (23 May 2001).

[23] The answer is likely to be 'Yes' in the light of *Poplar Housing v Donoghue* (2001) (see above at footnote 19).

[24] A claim in negligence has been held to be arguable against both the airline and the Home Office in such circumstances: *Farah v Home Office* (6 December 1999).

some respects it is broader. The ECHR concept of victim includes those who are threatened by the very existence of the law even though no direct action has been taken against the person (*Dudgeon* v *UK* (1981) 4 EHRR 149). Once the person has become a victim the status continues until the authority recognizes the incompatibility of its action.[25] Thus a mere desistance from enforcement action without an acknowledgement from the state that the immigration action was incompatible with the ECHR will not destroy the status of victim (*Ahmed* v *Austria* 24 EHRR 278).[26] Although in judicial review, claims may proceed with the consent of the court after the decision in question has been revoked (*Salem* v *Secretary of State for the Home Department* [1999] 1 AC 450), there are often difficulties in persuading the funding authority such as the Community Legal Service that continued provision of legal aid is appropriate. Where the person remains a victim of a violation of an ECHR right, proceedings for appropriate declaratory or other relief should continue and the Community Legal Service may itself act incompatibly with ECHR rights if it withdraws funding.

Remedies

1.35   Whether a victim is bringing or resisting proceedings the court may grant such relief or remedy or make such order within its powers as it considers just and appropriate (HRA 1998, s. 8(1)). It is an important principle of the HRA 1998 that there is no procedural exclusivity in taking ECHR points. They can be taken in any tribunal where the subject matter of the dispute naturally falls. However, the HRA 1998 does not give ordinary courts and tribunals additional powers by way of remedies. They must apply the ECHR within the limits of their existing jurisdiction. Courts that already have power to make an award of damages will be able to award statutory compensation for violation of ECHR rights (HRA 1998, s. 8(2)).

1.36   The judicial bodies before which HRA 1998 points are likely to be taken are:

(a)   adjudicators, special adjudicators, the Tribunal, the Special Immigration Appeals Commission (SIAC) and other appellate bodies established under the IAA 1999;

(b)   magistrates' courts and the Crown Court in connection with certain bail applications, or criminal prosecutions;

---

[25] *De Jong* v *Netherlands* (1984) 8 EHRR 201; *Inze* v *Austria* (1987) 10 EHRR 394. In *Hay* v *UK* (App. No. 41894/98), the European Court found the family of the deceased were no longer victims having accepted an offer of compensation because 'there is no indication that the Government have attempted to avoid compliance with their obligations under the Convention by means of the mere payment of money'.

[26] See also the views of the United Nations Committee Against Torture (UNCAT) in Article 3 cases; see 2.54.

(c)   the Administrative Court of the High Court in connection with claims for judicial review or habeas corpus;

(d)   the Court of Appeal on appeal from the IAT, SIAC or on appeal on renewed application from the High Court and thereafter the House of Lords;

(e)   the county court and possibly the High Court with respect to claims for damages for torts, breaches of contract and the like.

1.37   We will examine the statutory jurisdiction of the immigration appellate authorities in more detail below. Essentially they are limited to dismissing or allowing an appeal and giving consequential directions. In some cases they may remit the case to the Secretary of State. They have no power to award damages, strike down rules, or make declarations of the law one way or the other. Where detention is concerned the authorities can grant bail with or without sureties but do not issue the writ of habeas corpus. In most immigration cases where an appellant is arguing that he or his family members should be admitted to the UK, granted leave to remain or not be deported or removed from the UK, allowing of the appeal can be accompanied by directions either that the person be granted the requisite leave, or that the Home Office might re-examine the case in the light of the judicial findings.

1.38   In cases where there is no immigration right of appeal, or other relief is sought the proceedings will normally be issued in the High Court where orders quashing decisions, requiring decisions to be taken, declarations as to a person's rights and declarations of incompatibility can be made. A claim for compensation can be made in addition to these remedies. Where the only issue is a claim for damages or compensation for a clear breach of duty, the ordinary civil courts may be the appropriate venue

Compensation

1.39   At present there is no general right to damages for wrongful administrative acts causing loss to an individual unless the claim can be brought within the scope of one of the nominate torts: negligence, false imprisonment, malicious prosecution, misfeasance in public office and the like (*W v Home Office* [1997] Imm AR 302). Where an authority has acted in contravention of an ECHR right then courts that have the power to award damages may award compensation if satisfied that an award is necessary to afford just satisfaction to the person in whose favour the award is made. Such compensation cannot be awarded for loss caused by a judicial act save where it is required under Article 5(5) of the ECHR in respect of damages for detention in contravention of the ECHR.

1.40   The HRA 1998 requires the court awarding the compensation to take into account the principles applied by the European Court in relation to its awards of compensation under Article 41 of the ECHR. We now summarize the European Court case law as to speak of principles in this area may be overstating the case.[27] Sometimes, the European Court considers that its decision on violation is a sufficient remedy when accompanied by orders for costs. At other times it will award any pecuniary damage occasioned by the breach of the ECHR in question. This is most clearly identified in cases where loss or diminution in the value of property has resulted from the breach. The most controversial award is of moral damages or general damages for a violation. This may be awarded where the state has behaved particularly outrageously, where the victim has suffered indignity or humiliation or where the breach of the ECHR has caused detention or a prolongation of detention.[28] There is a specific duty for a contracting state to ensure that anyone who had been the victim of a violation of any of the limbs of Article 5 shall have an enforceable right to compensation (Article 5(5)). In cases where the whole detention was illegal in national law or incapable of justification under any of the provisions of Article 5(1) it is fairly plain that compensation must follow for the detention. There is no reason to believe that it should be at any lesser rate than that awarded by the domestic courts for wrongful imprisonment (see *R (Bernard)* v *Enfield LBC* (25 October 2002). The loss is the same; the route to proving the loss is different.

1.41 The problem arises where the detention is unlawful because there was no access to a court that was capable of reviewing the detention and granting bail or release, or where the detention followed an unfair trial. In these cases awards are not made per se but follow the court's assessment of what would have happened had the relevant procedure been in place. In *Caballero* v *UK* (2000) *The Times*, 28 February it was common ground that the mandatory denial of bail was a violation of the ECHR in a case for murder. The parties were agreed that if the applicant had been able to apply for bail he would probably have obtained it in the light of the particular facts of his case. The court was therefore able to award compensation for the loss of liberty. In the case of *Chahal* v *United Kingdom* (1996) 23 EHRR 413, the court found that Mr Chahal's six-year detention was unlawful as there was no appellate body capable of reviewing his case and ordering his release where the detention was on national security grounds. The European Court however made no order for compensation. Mr Chahal pursued the matter by application to the Secretary of State for ex gratia payment, it being clear that the detention was lawful in national law. The application was refused and in the case of *R* v *Secretary of State, ex parte Chahal (No 2)* [2000] UKHRR 215

---

[27] A point made by many of the commentators: Harris, O'Boyle and Warwick, *Law of the European Convention on Human Rights*, Butterworths, 1995; Simor and Emmerson, *Human Rights Practice*, Sweet & Maxwell, 2001; Clayton and Tomlinson, *The Law of Human Rights*, OUP, 2001.
[28] See the award in *Keenan* v *UK* (2001) 33 EHRR 38; and in *Z* v *UK* (2002) 34 EHRR 3.

reviewed on appeal in the Court of Appeal. The Court of Appeal sought to assess the prospects of Mr Chahal being released earlier than he was, and was content to adopt the domestic approach of loss of a real chance to obtain liberty. Nevertheless the European Court's case law is quite strict as to proof of loss of real chance and even when damages are awarded they have not been at a noticeably generous level. This topic is discussed further in chapter 4 where we deal with Article 5 in greater detail.

Time limits for instituting and defending proceedings

1.42   A victim of an immigration decision that contravenes s. 6(1) of the HRA 1998 will normally bring proceedings by way of appeal to the immigration appellate authorities or by way of judicial review. The appropriate time limits will be those provided for in rules made under statute or the rules governing the procedure. In other cases the time limits will be a year beginning with the date of the act complained of or such longer period as the court considers equitable having regard to all the circumstances (HRA 1998, s. 7(5)).

1.43   In immigration cases, the immediate question arises of whether the HRA 1998 applies to refusals or expulsion decisions taken before 2 October 2000 when the appeal comes on after that date. The HRA 1998 itself indicates, in s. 22(4), that where legal proceedings brought by a public authority before 2 October 2000 are continued after that date, the individual may rely on ECHR rights *whenever* the act in question took place. Thus a criminal prosecution for illegal entry will have to be human rights compliant whenever the charge was laid, if some part of the proceedings is outstanding after 2 October 2000. Although 'legal proceedings' are defined non-exhaustively to include proceedings brought by or at the instigation of a public authority or an appeal against the decision of a court or tribunal (HRA 1998, s. 7(6)), on the present state of the case law, appeals (at least in the criminal sphere) are excluded from the definition of proceedings for the purposes of s. 22(4).[29]

1.44   Does the Home Office bring legal proceedings against a person when it decides to make a decision to deport? On the one hand it can be said that the whole process of deportation is a formal proceeding with legal consequences. It begins with a decision to deport on statutory grounds and ends with the signing of an order that requires a person to leave the United Kingdom. The order has an immediate effect on status and cancels any existing leave to remain. Removal directions against illegal entrants or overstayers, however, seem more likely to be

---

[29] The case law will need to be carefully re-examined in the light of the conflict in judicial opinion in the House of Lords in *R v Lambert* [2001] 3 WLR 206, *R v Kansal* [2001] UKHL 62, and *Porter v Magill* [2001] UKHL 67. See above at Introduction.

acts of administrative discretion available against those vulnerable to the exercise of the power.[30] On the other hand it may be that the legislator intended legal proceedings to mean proceedings brought by the public authority before a court or tribunal as suggested in the second limb of HRA 1998, s. 7(6). If an appeal against an administrative decision of the Home Office was intended to be included in proceedings for the purpose of the defence, one would have expected to have seen this spelt out, although Lord Hope had no difficulty in concluding that a challenge to a district auditor's assessment were proceedings brought by a public authority in *Porter* v *Magill* [2001] UKHL 67.

1.45   An alternative approach is to regard the decision to remove that has not been implemented as of 2 October 2000 as provisional only. We know from the case law of the European Court that the relevant date to examine whether an expulsion contravenes the ECHR is the date of the proposed actual expulsion rather than the original decision to expel. The decision to remove may thus be seen to be a continuing act that may be defended on the basis of a violation of s. 6(1) of the HRA 1998 if it has not been executed before commencement.[31] Moreover, if there is an appeal outstanding after 2 October 2000 from a decision made before that date, and it is apparent that an expulsion or a continued refusal to admit would contravene an ECHR right, then the immigration adjudicator as a public authority would appear to be under an independent duty to ensure that removal is not effected in violation of the ECHR. The confusion created by *Lambert* does not help resolution of this issue. However, in *Lambert* and *Kansal* the House of Lords were examining purely historic convictions that were regular under the binding statute law applicable at the time of the trial. In immigration cases, the court is examining whether a decision yet to be implemented is compatible with an ECHR right.

1.46   This is the significant feature of the HRA 1998. It is not merely a confined set of statutory duties imposed on a body of officials and enforced by a court. It is a duty to act compatibly imposed on the courts and tribunals themselves within the limits of their jurisdiction.

1.47   The IAT decided in the case of *Pardeepan* v *Secretary of State* [2000] INLR 447 (starred) that where an asylum appeal was refused before 2 October 2000, there was no need to consider human rights grounds along with the asylum claim. This was for two reasons. First, because Article 3(1)(a) of the IAA 1999 (Commencement No. 6 etc) Order 2000 (SI 2000/2444) applied to events which

---

[30] This was the view in *R (Kariharan)* v *Secretary of State* (5 December 2001) concerning a different question under s. 65 of the IAA 1999, but see *Porter* v *Magill* above at footnote 29.

[31] The decision of the Administrative Court in *R (Kariharan)* v *Secretary of State* (5 December 2001) is necessarily silent on this issue, concerned as it is only with the s. 65 appellate regime. See also, on appeal, at [2002] INLR 383.

took place after 2 October 2000. Secondly, the IAT was assured by the Secretary of State that 'those whose appeals are refused, for example, on asylum grounds will be given the opportunity to raise, if they think fit human rights objections to removal.' Thus it appeared that anyone facing removal after 2 October 2000 could raise an allegation that their removal would violate the ECHR. This would require the Home Office to respond by making a decision and serving a requisite removal notice that would trigger an IAA 1999 s. 65 right of appeal or certificate under s. 71 or s. 72. Although this process may have prolonged claims that could be considered in one go, it at least ensured that human rights points were not taken by ambush. Manifestly findings of fact by adjudicators were relevant to both refugee status and Article 3 issues.

1.48   The *Pardeepan* undertaking was subsequently modified on 19 July 2001 so as to exclude appellate rights from those whose claims to refugee status and asylum appeals had been dismissed prior to 2 October 2000 and covered the same ground as the human rights claim sought to be relied upon after that date. In these cases there would be no further decision issued attracting a s. 65 appeal right. The exception was where there was an appeal pending or available as at 2 October 2000. The legality of this modification was upheld by the Administrative Court in *R (Kariharan)* v *Secretary of State* (5 December 2001) as a lawful and rational formulation of policy consistent with the *Pardeepan* undertaking, which related solely to pending appeals. The Court of Appeal has now reversed this decision ([2002] INLR 383). It is hoped that the confusions surrounding retrospective effect will shortly disappear from practical importance. Presumably any challenge to such a removal as incompatible with human rights would have to be by way of judicial review.

1.49   What *Kariharan* did not expressly consider (and it appears that argument was not advanced on the point), was that the courts have held that leave is not a unitary concept in immigration law,[32] such that an application for leave to remain on a different ground to that made earlier requires a fresh formal notice of decision and it is not sufficient simply to rely upon an earlier formal decision. In the terms of the dichotomy erected in *Kariharan* the later decision is declaratory of rights, rather than a mere enforcement of a decision already taken denying such rights or requiring a person to leave. It remains to be seen what impact the decision in *Kariharan* will have, especially since the Home Office retains a discretion to issue further notices of decision in order to generate appeal rights.[33] In our view, whilst the transitional provisions are still being played out, advisers should

---

[32] See *R* v *IAT, ex parte Secretary of State* (the Sri Lankan Tamils) [1990] 1 WLR 1126; *R* v *Secretary of State, ex parte Kazmi* [1995] Imm AR 73, 76–80; *Saad, Diriye and Osorio* v *Secretary of State* (19 December 2001 CA), para. 44.

[33] *R* v *Secretary of State, ex parte Kazmi* [1995] Imm AR 73; *R* v *Secretary of State, ex parte Onibiyo* [1996] Imm AR 370. The Secretary of State's policy however was itself the subject of unsuccessful challenge in *Kariharan*.

be proactive in formulating claims to remain on human rights grounds after dismissals of earlier, pre 2 October 2000 appeals not raising the human rights claim, rather than waiting for enforcement action in the expectation that an appeal will be offered on a plate. Any refusal of such a claim may lead to a right to an IAA 1999, s. 65 appeal notwithstanding *Kahiharan*, as these arguments were not canvassed in that case and the authority is therefore not binding.[34]

1.50   Secondly, the decision in *Pardeepan* restricted the duty placed upon the IAT by s. 6 of the HRA 1998 to act in an ECHR-compatible manner by considering that its act in dismissing an appeal did not touch upon the human rights of an appellant because the Home Office had undertaken to afford a subsequent appellate remedy in a pending case. While the Court of Appeal has rejected the submission that it was obliged as a court to enforce ECHR rights (*Ramirez* v *Secretary of State* [2001] EWCA Civ 1365 at para. 33 per Sedley LJ), this was because it possessed appellate rather than original jurisdiction. However unlike the Court of Appeal, the Adjudicator and IAT possess original jurisdiction to review the facts upon which the decision is based and have been considered in the asylum context at least to be part of the decision-making process.[35] We would suggest that where there is an appeal other than under s. 65 of the IAA 1999 being heard before the Adjudicator after 2 October 2000, the proceedings are in the nature of the trial of the human rights point (whether the proposed expulsion is in accordance with the law[36]) and the Adjudicator has full authority to examine this question. In those circumstances we would suggest that the *Lambert* and *Kansal* decisions do not bite, concerned as they were with pre-HRA 1998 trials conducted in full accordance with the law as it stood at the time. Section 6 of the HRA 1998 would thus operate not so much to impugn the legality of the historic decision, but to preclude a course of action whose natural result would be violative of ECHR rights. Were this not the position, it is difficult to see the legal relevance of the Home Office's undertaking to the IAT's functions in *Pardeepan* itself.

1.51   A pragmatic approach has been taken in judicial review proceedings. In most other cases the court makes the assumption that the Human Rights Act 1998 was already in force at the material time, and gives a decision on the requirements of the ECHR. This is clearly the case where the immigration decision has been reviewed for human rights compliance after the grant of permission and 2 October 2000. In the case of *R* v *Secretary of State ex parte Mahmood* [2001]

---

[34] See *R (Kadhim)* v *LB Brent Housing Benefit Review Board* [2001] QB 955; *R* v *Secretary of State, ex part Ku* [1995] QB 364.

[35] See IAA 1999, Sch. 4, paras. 21(3), 22(2); *Ravichandran* v *Secretary of State* [1996] Imm AR 97.

[36] Even in a refugee appeal under s. 8 of the Asylum and Immigration Appeals Act (AIAA) 1993 (and analogously s. 69 of the IAA 1999) the Court of Appeal has held in *Saad, Diriye and Osorio* v *Secretary of State* [2002] INLR 34 that the Adjudicator still exercises the 'not in accordance with the law' jurisdiction originally provided under s. 19 of the IA 1971 and now by IAA 1999, Sch. 4, para. 21.

1 WLR 840 judicial review proceedings were initiated before 2 October 2000, but proceeded on appeal after that date. Laws LJ held (at para. 27) that s. 22(4) of the HRA 1998 was plainly not applicable. He also concluded (at paras. 28–30) that despite acceptance of the contrary proposition by the Crown, the court was not reviewing the future decision to remove but only a past decision that may not be implemented. It was not called upon to speculate as to the consequences of that decision. In the argument for leave to appeal following the handing down of the judgment, it was apparent that the court was influenced in this approach by the *Pardeepan* decision and the Secretary of State's undertaking therein. It concluded that removal in that case would require a further decision that might be capable of human rights challenge. This intervening decision apart, it is respectfully submitted that after 2 October 2000, the court on judicial review of removal decisions is precisely concerned with the consequences of a decision if implemented. This is manifestly true in Article 3 cases and also in Article 8 cases, where the impact would be separation of families.[37]

1.52   The scheme for which the Home Office has opted in implementing s. 65 of the IAA 1999 is problematic, however, in that only those who expressly raise the allegation that removal would infringe human rights will be informed that they have a right of appeal. The IAT in *Pardeepan* found this most unsatisfactory as it plainly contemplates that asylum seekers whose claims to refugee status are dismissed might be removed without their being aware that they would have a second appeal on Article 3 grounds. For this reason, until the matter is clarified by sensible Home Office practices, advocates should expressly raise human rights points before pending appeals, and adjudicators whose findings of fact raise Article 3 issues should perhaps be encouraged to say so when dismissing asylum appeals. This should at least put the appellant and the Home Office on notice that further considerations may be required.

1.53   Further s. 3 of the HRA 1998 comes into play immediately, whether there is a special human rights appeal or not. Although the right of appeal under s. 65 of the IAA 1999 may only apply to post 2 October 2000 decisions, other aspects of the HRA 1998 will be applicable immediately. In the case of *Pye* v *Graham* [2001] 2 WLR 1293[38] Keene LJ held that the meaning of a statute to be interpreted in accordance with s. 3, HRA 1998 after 2 October 2000 is the same whenever the underlying decision to which the statute applies took effect. This decision is now under appeal following the *Lambert* decision. For reasons we

---

[37] See *Samaroo* v *Secretary of State* [2001] EWCA Civ 1139; see further Lord Phillips MR at paragraph 36 in *R* v *Mahmood* [2001] 1 WLR 840. For the proposition that the trial court in judicial review is entitled to have regard to fresh, post-decision evidence because of the inherently updating nature of the decision see *R* v *Secretary of State for the Home Department, ex parte Turgut* [2001] 1 All ER 719.

[38] See also *Wilson* v *First County Trust Ltd (No. 2)* [2001] 3 WLR 42, para. 22. But see *R* v *Lambert* [2001] 3 WLR 206.

refer to in the Introduction, we believe the decision in *Pye* v *Graham* is plainly right and the consequences would be absurd if it were not. (See, however, *Wainwright* v *Secretary of State for the Home Department* [2002] 3 WLR 405). It follows that in interpreting the Immigration Rules or any immigration statute, the s. 3 principle of construction that we discuss below will be paramount.

THE APPLICATION AND INTERPRETATION OF THE CONVENTION

1.54   When examining the meaning of legislation or subordinate legislation a wholly new principle of statutory interpretation is brought into play. All legislation whenever passed must be read and given effect to in a way which is compatible with the ECHR rights under the HRA 1998 'so far as it is possible to do so'. This is a general duty of interpretation and applies whenever legislation engages an ECHR question. It makes the restriction on bringing proceedings to victims a little pointless. If a public interest group is challenging legislation in the High Court, that court will have to apply an interpretation of the law that is compatible with the ECHR whether the interest group is a victim or not. Laws do not change their meaning depending on who the party is to the proceedings.

1.55   The new duty of compatible interpretation means that previous decisions of even the highest courts in the land may no longer be binding on the most inferior tribunal, at least until they have considered the ECHR compatible meaning of the legislation and there has been no subsequent clarification from the European Court. Where an ECHR right is concerned old decisions on a topic must be revisited and the process of reasoning subjected to ECHR scrutiny.[39]

1.56   What does the term 'so far as is possible' mean? This is borrowed directly from EC law, and we therefore suggest that a similar intensity of presumption applies to questions of interpretation. In *Marleasing SA* v *La Comercial Internacional de Alimentacion SA* (Case C-106/89) [1990] ECR 1-4135 the European Court of Justice stated that where there are EC law rules national legislation must be interpreted as being in conformity with these rules wherever it is possible to do so without distorting the legislation in question. This EC law principle has nothing to do with discovering the intent of the legislator as it applies to laws whenever passed even before the relevant EC rules came into being. It is nothing to do with the clarification of ambiguities by resort to supplementary means of interpreting. It is even stronger than the purposive approach to legislation where the meaning of an international instrument is to be ascertained. Rather it is a process of subjecting the legislation to the international requirement where a compatible result can be achieved without distortion. For this purpose it is

---

[39] But see *Kaya* v *London Borough of Haringey*, *The Times*, 14 June 2001.

permissible to read in words necessary to give effect to the requirement or even to read out subordinate phrases that detract from compatibility. The House of Lords applied this approach in *Litster* v *Forth Dry Dock Engineering Co Ltd* [1990] I AC 546.

1.57 A similar process of interpretation will now apply to ECHR rights and it will be for courts to decide whether it is possible to find a compatible meaning or whether reading in a compatible meaning would fundamentally distort the true nature of the text to be interpreted.[40] The distortion concerned may not necessarily be in the particular phrase under scrutiny but has to be set against the terms of the statute as a whole (*Poplar Housing* v *Donoghue* [2001] 3 WLR 183). There was some initial timidity by the courts to make legislation yield an ECHR compatible meaning. In one decision the court preferred to give a declaration of incompatibility rather than read down a statutory scheme for the detention of mental patients (*R (on the application of H)* v *Mental Health Review Tribunal for NE London* [2001] EWCA Admin 414, 28 March 2001). The decision of the House of Lords in *R* v *A (No. 2)* [2001] 2 WLR 1546 demonstrates what is both possible and necessary by way of interpretation where the literal words of the statute have exceeded the requirements of the ECHR. In that case the interference with the right of fair trial of an alleged rapist was greater than was needed to protect the private life of rape victims. Apparently mandatory words limiting cross-examination were read down to give a judicial discretion to act compatibly with Article 6.

1.58 Although the principle of interpretation is derived from EC law the application of the principle will work a little differently in the context of the ECHR. This is because EC legislation is usually very specific about the result to be achieved whereas the ECHR is much more general in its terms and approach. So the first task of the interpreting court will be to find out what the requirements of the ECHR are. In the task of determining any ECHR question that has arisen, the court or tribunal must take into account any relevant judgment, decision, declaration or opinion of the European Court, the former European Commission of Human Rights or the Committee of Ministers (HRA 1998, s.2).[41] It is to be noted that the requirement is 'to take into account' and not 'be bound by' such decisions. Even amongst themselves these various sources of learning are of different authority.

1.59 This principle of interpretation does not exist in a vacuum but alongside a

---

[40] For the clearest approach to a s. 3, HRA 1998 interpretation that results in reading down a section of a statute see *R* v *A (No. 2)* [2001] 2 WLR 1546. For the need to make the Children Act 1989 compatible with the ECHR see *Re W and B* [2001] EWCA Civ 757, 23 May 2001.

[41] See also *R (Alconbury Ltd)* v *Secretary of State for the Environment* [2001] 2 WLR 1389, per Lord Slynn.

strong common law tradition that has moved some way to giving effect to a presumption that Parliament intends to legislate compatibly with fundamental human rights. In his speech in *R* v *Secretary of State ex parte Simms* [2000] 2 AC 115 Lord Hoffman explained that the principle of legality means that:

> Parliament must squarely confront what it is doing and accept the political cost. Fundamental rights cannot be overridden by general or ambiguous words. This is because there is too great a risk that the full implications of their unqualified meaning may have passed unnoticed into the democratic process. In the absence of express language or necessary implication, the courts therefore presume that even the most general words were intended to be subject to the basic rights of the individual.

1.60   There are therefore three approaches to interpretation under the common law and the HRA 1998. The first approach does not refer to an international instrument unless there is positive ambiguity or lack of clarity. This was the formula controversially stated in *Brind* [1991] 1 AC 696. The second assumes that Parliament intends to respect fundamental human rights recognized by the common law, unless it has addressed its mind specifically to the task in hand and unambiguously legislated in a contrary manner (the *Simms* [2000] 2 AC 115 approach). The third is an even more positive approach to finding a compatible meaning, and involves reading into the particular statute whenever passed a compatible meaning, including by reading in and reading out collateral phrases, unless this would distort the statute and it is not possible to reach the compatible result. This is the *R* v *A* [2001] 2 WLR 1546 approach and it is this that applies under the HRA 1998.

Finding the ECHR meaning

1.61   Clearly the greatest weight is attached to a judgment of the European Court. By its nature this is a fully reasoned judicial opinion determining the impact of the ECHR on the question in point. Decisions of the former European Commission on the merits may also be helpful where there is no court jurisprudence on the question. Decisions of the former European Commission on admissibility will also indicate lines of reasoning on the question, but such decisions are largely written by the secretariat rather than the judicial officers themselves, have not been exposed to as full an argument as court decisions, and are less fully reasoned. Decisions of the Committee of Ministers may be helpful in determining what additional measures beyond the formal order of the European Court the Committee of Ministers considered sufficient measures taken by the contracting state in response to a European Court judgment. These decisions may give glimpses of the afterlife of the case where an immigrant facing deportation has had the order revoked, and leave to remain given, for example.

1.62   The UK court must have regard to the decisions of the ECHR institutions whenever the decision was given. However, as the ECHR is a living instrument to be given an updating interpretation in the light of social developments (*Rees v UK* (1986) 9 EHRR 56; *Cossey v UK* (1991) 13 EHRR 622) and other comparable measures of international law,[42] the meaning of an ECHR right may change with time. Earlier decisions may now be a poor guide to what the ECHR presently requires. One can see this process clearly at work in the development of Article 3. In the case of *Tyrer v UK* (1970) 2 EHRR 1 the court held that the notion of degrading treatment had developed from 1950 so that corporal punishment in state schools would now be considered degrading. In *Selmouni v France* (2000) 29 EHRR 403 the European Court said that what is now considered torture has developed in recent years and plainly includes serious assaults in custody. It has to be doubted whether the European Court would adhere today to its judgment in *Ireland v UK* (1970) 2 EHRR 25 where certain practices of inhuman and degrading treatment of suspects were not considered to reach the severity of torture. Equally the application of Article 3 to extraterritorial expulsion was influenced by the terms of Article 3 of the UN Convention Against Torture 1984 that itself was based on earlier indications in the case law of the former European Commission. There is a general sense that international standards develop and, absent sudden emergencies in the life of a nation justifying restrictions or derogations, the application of the core principles of the ECHR is meant to be progressive.

Margin of appreciation

1.63   We have noted that the ECHR develops principles, an ordered hierarchy of values and questions to be resolved rather than a series of binding norms. Clearly the UK must apply the values and principles and reasoning as to the scope of the ECHR otherwise it will not be acting compatibly. Particular decisions of the European Court may not be binding as to the results, however. The evidence or the arguments may have changed, and greater weight may be attached to one of the competing values by a national court.

1.64   Further, where there are competing interests and the rights concerned are balanced rather than absolute ones, the European Court applies the doctrine of the margin of appreciation. This is an international doctrine based on the premise of subsidiarity that it is for contracting states and their courts to find the facts, to identify the moral values of particular significance to that society, and to balance the competing interests for themselves.[43] The margin of appreciation afforded to

---

[42] Article 53 provides that nothing in the [ECHR] shall be construed as limiting or derogating from any of the human rights and fundamental freedoms which may be ensured under the laws of any High Contracting party or under any other agreement to which it is a party. See the spectacular reversal of the trans-sexual jurisprudence in *Goodwin v UK* (2002) 35 EHRR 18.

[43] e.g. *James v UK* (1986) 8 EHRR 123, para. 46.

contracting states may be wide or narrow depending upon the subject matter of the litigation and the nature of the rights at stake. States may enjoy a wide margin of appreciation in the solution to certain ECHR questions particularly in the field of planning, child care, and moral and ethical issues.[44] Where it comes to matters close to more absolute rights such as detention, fair trial, reasonable measures to preserve life and respect for dignity and intimate aspects of private life, a narrow margin may be called for (*Lustig-Preane* v *UK* (2000) 29 EHRR 493 at para. 82). In any event this means that in the application of the principles of the ECHR to the facts, the European Court builds in an element of additional deference to the national authorities in reaching its conclusions on violations of the ECHR. It does so principally because it is an international body, but there is also some element of court deference to legitimate democratic choice on matters peculiarly within the legislative province.

1.65   But the doctrine of the margin of appreciation is an international doctrine. It is not one that will be applied by domestic courts, who are closer to the fact-finding function and the assessment of social and moral values than the international courts. The national court compared to the international court will call for a more intense scrutiny of executive decisions. The IAT, unlike the European Court, is not having to deal with the range of moral, religious and ethical opinions from Ireland to Russia, or Iceland to Turkey. The margin of appreciation is thus inapplicable in domestic law.[45] In the field of immigration this may mean that a European Court decision that an interference with family life was justifiable will not always be followed in the United Kingdom. Take away the additional element afforded to the margin of appreciation in a closely balanced case and the result could well be different. The converse is not always true: where an interference has been held to be a violation even allowing for the margin of appreciation then the national court is bound to conclude that the same follows if identical facts were to re-emerge in a future case.

1.66   In the decision of the Privy Council on appeal from a devolution issue in Scotland in *Brown* v *Stott* [2001] 2 WLR 817 Lord Steyn concluded (at p. 842):

> Under the Convention system the primary duty is placed on the domestic courts to secure and protect Convention rights. The function of the European Court of Human Rights is essential but supervisory. In that capacity it accords to domestic courts a margin of appreciation, which recognises that national institutions are in principle better placed than an international court to evaluate local needs and conditions. That principle is logically not applicable to domestic courts. On the other hand, national

---

[44]   See e.g. *Buckley* v *UK* (1996) 23 EHRR 101; *XYZ* v *UK* (1997) 24 EHRR 143.

[45]   For the commentators see Lester and Pannick, *Human Rights Law and Practice*, Butterworths, 1999, para. 3.20–3.21; Singh, Hunt and Demetriou, 'Is there a Role for the "Margin of Appreciation" in National Law after the Human Rights Act?' [1999] EHRLR 15.

courts may accord to the decisions of national legislatures some deference *where the context justifies it.*

Discretionary area of judgment

1.67 The courts will in turn give the executive a range of permissible options. The European Court has recognized that 'inherent in . . . the Convention is a search for a fair balance between the demands of the general interest of the community and the requirements of the protection of the individual's fundamental rights' (*Soering* v *UK* (1989) EHRR Series A No. 161, 35 at para. 89). The House of Lords first considered the question in the case of *R* v *DPP, ex parte Kebilene* [1999] 3 WLR 972. Lord Hope concluded (at p. 994) that the margin of appreciation was not applicable but that:

> Difficult choices may have to be made by the executive or the legislature between the rights of the individual and the needs of society . . . there is an area of judgment within which the judiciary will defer, on democratic grounds, to the considered opinion of the elected body or person whose act . . . is said to be incompatible with the Convention.

1.68 The implication of these remarks is being worked out in the developing jurisprudence of the courts.[46] We discuss at greater length in chapter 6 what effect, if any, the HRA 1998 has had on the intensity of scrutiny on judicial review, particularly in the immigration context. Debate has focused on four cases. The first, *B* v *Secretary of State* [2000] INLR 361 was an appeal on a point of law from the IAT to the Court of Appeal in an EC law deportation case. The IAT misdirected itself by concluding that Article 8 of the ECHR added little to the question whether the deportation of an Italian national for a sexual offence was proportionate and justified. The Court of Appeal concluded that because:

(a)   it was common ground that proportionality was a matter of law, and
(b)   a wrong approach had been adopted below, and
(c)   the necessary facts had been found by the IAT

it could examine for itself the question of competing considerations and reach a conclusion on proportionality. The Court of Appeal acknowledged Lord Hope's endorsement of the discretionary area of judgment but concluded that the length of residence in the UK meant that deportation was tantamount to exile in disproportionate contravention of private life.

1.69 The next case that came before the Court of Appeal was very different. In delivering the leading judgment in *R* v *Secretary of State, ex parte Mahmood* [2001] 1 WLR 840, Laws LJ observed that:

---

[46] See Introduction and *R (Daly)* v *Secretary of State* [2001] 2 WLR 1622.

much of the challenge presented by the enactment of the 1998 Act consists in the search for a principled measure of scrutiny which will be loyal to Convention rights, but loyal also to the legitimate claims of power.

1.70   In this case an illegal entrant had married late in the day after notice of dismissal of his asylum claim had been served. Under the applicable policy he had to apply to make an application for entry clearance from abroad, and there were no insuperable obstacles to his doing so. Applying the common law approach, the Court of Appeal concluded that in reviewing the Secretary of State's decision it was appropriate to give weight to his lawful policy of considering marriage claims from abroad, and constitutional propriety required a principled distance between the court and the decision-taker. Laws LJ recognized (at para. 33) that a more muscular approach to review was called for where the ECHR was engaged but the starting point at least was the search for a reasonable justification by the decision-taker to any interference with human rights:

> For present purposes that principled distance is to be found in the approach I have taken to the scope of judicial review in this case, built on what the common law has already done in *Smith*, *Launder*, and *Lord Saville*. For the future, when the court is indeed applying the Convention as municipal law, we shall no doubt develop a jurisprudence in which a margin of discretion (as I would call it) is allowed to the statutory decision-maker; but in the case of those rights where the Convention permits interference with the right where that is justified by reference to strict criteria (Arts. 8–11, paragraph 2 in each case) its length will no doubt be confined by the rigour of those criteria in light of the relevant Strasbourg case-law, and the gravity of the proposed interference as it is perceived here.

1.71   On the facts, there was no positive duty of respect for family life, and therefore proportionality was not involved. The Master of the Rolls assumed (at para. 40) that a version of the test in *R* v *MOD ex parte Smith* would normally suffice: 'applying an objective test, whether the decision-maker could reasonably have concluded that the interference was necessary to achieve one or more of the legitimate aims recognised by the Convention'.

1.72   The Court of Appeal was not referred to *B* v *Secretary of State* [2000] INLR 361 and so did not have to determine the scope of the Court of Appeal's own function in ensuring that a proportionate answer was arrived at. This was the subject of the decision in the third case, *Secretary of State* v *Isiko* [2001] INLR 175. This was another case of a migrant who had unlawfully entered the UK and had moreover committed a criminal offence. He challenged the application of the Secretary of State's policy dealing with removals on the grounds that the effect upon him was disproportionate. The Court of Appeal endorsed the deferential approach to matters of policy outlined in *Mahmood*, and would have preferred that case if it was in conflict with the *B* v *Secretary of State* approach. It concluded that the Court of Appeal does not substitute its decision for that of the decision-taker in judicial review proceedings. It reviews the decision having regard to the need for the executive to demonstrate that there was no interference or a proportionate and justified interference with human rights. The graver the impact of the decision, the more substantial the justification will be required. It concluded that 'this more intrusive mode of supervision will in broad terms and in most instances suffice as the beginning of a proper touchstone for review when the Convention is in play'.

1.73   The need to go further has now been confirmed by the House of Lords in the fourth case, *R (Daly)* v *Secretary of State* [2001] 3 WLR 1622 where it concluded that the ultimate question is whether the decision is proportionate and compatible with human rights and not whether a reasonable decision-maker could think it so. The question of compatibility is a matter for the decision-maker and not for the court. We discuss some of the recent developments and the application of *Daly* and *Samaroo* [2002] INLR 55 in the Introduction above.

The principles of the ECHR

1.74   There is a further good reason why the duty is to have *regard* to rather than being bound by the case law. The common law may itself have developed standards as good as or better than the requirements of the ECHR (see Article 53 above in the Introduction to this book). The ECHR cannot be used in those circumstances to reduce the law and restrict rights (see ECHR Articles 15 and 18). In the United Kingdom there is also the experience of the constitutional jurisprudence of other common law jurisdictions, some of which still retain the Judicial Committee of the Privy Council as the court of last appeal. Where the rights concerned are similar to those provided for in the constitutions and human rights law of these countries assistance may be derived from the decisions of the Privy Council or the higher courts of Canada, Australia, and New Zealand. Decisions of the UN Human Rights bodies and other regional human rights courts may also be persuasive as to the result to be followed. In Scotland where the courts have had a head start in applying the ECHR, the leading decisions are notable for their broad citation of comparable international material.[47]

1.75   The case law of the European Court is the repository of the articulated values and principles of the ECHR that are to be applied by the national courts in the light of the applicable social and political conditions and the decisions of democratically elected governments. What then are the European Court principles?

---

[47] See e.g. *Starrs* v *Ruxton* [2000] UKHRR 78. See also *Anderson* (2000) *The Times*, 22 June.

1.76   First, there is a clear commitment to the rule of law and accountability of the executive to the judiciary.[48] In *Klass* v *Germany* (1970) 2 EHRR 144 at para. 55 it was said:

> The rule of law implies *inter alia* that an interference by the executive authorities with an individual's rights should be subject to an effective control which should normally be controlled by the judiciary, at least in the last resort, judicial control offering the best guarantees of independence, impartiality and a proper procedure.

1.77   The discretionary area of judgment afforded to the executive must be examined with the appropriate degree of scrutiny by the judges to pass muster. Lord Steyn observed that 'it is a basic premise of the ECHR system that only an entirely neutral, impartial, and independent judiciary can carry out the primary task of securing and enforcing ECHR rights' (*Brown* v *Stott* [2001] 2 WLR 817 at p. 840). This is an important observation in the context of immigration where respect for rights is not adequately protected by the interests of the electorate. Heightened vigilance and judicial activism is called for where the subject of the decision may be particularly vulnerable or politically unpopular.[49] It will be particularly important in cases where liberty is interfered with by the executive (*Brogan* v *UK* (1998) 11 EHRR 117 at para. 58).

1.78   Secondly, pluralism, tolerance and broadmindedness are core values, requiring respect for the different ways individuals lead their private lives (*Dudgeon* v *UK* (1981) 4 EHRR 149 at para. 53) and the kinds of things they may want to say, disseminate or believe in. The notion of respect however is not clear-cut, and much will depend upon whether mere interference is called for by the executive, or whether positive measures of legislative change need to be under-taken to make society more tolerant and accommodating. The limits of the posit-ive obligation of the notion of respect were explored in the transsexual case of *Rees* v *United Kingdom* (1986) 9 EHRR 56 (see now *Goodwin* v *UK* (2002) 35 EHRR 18). Here the UK as a long-established multicultural society perhaps has greater experience of understanding respect for diversity than a number of other European societies. The necessity of immigration measures restricting admission and authorizing expulsion should respect these aspects of our society. Retention of indigenous traditions and use of the language of origin is unlikely to be seen as a factor against integration of migrants in the host state as has been suggested in some decisions on Article 8 (*R (Samaroo)* v *Secretary of State* Case No. CO/4973/1999, 20 December 2000, per Thomas J). Integration is not the same as cultural assimilation.

---

[48]   The rule of law is referred to as part of the common heritage of European traditions. In 1950 this might be considered more pious aspiration than historical truth.

[49]   See Singh, Hunt and Demetriou, 'Is there a Role for the "Margin of Appreciation" in National Law after the Human Rights Act?' [1999] EHRLR 15, 22 point 6; cited with approval by Lord Steyn in *Brown* v *Stott* [2001] 2 WLR 817 at p. 842.

1.79   Thirdly, the ECHR is to be interpreted in a way that makes it practical and effective (*Loizidou* v *Turkey* (1995) 20 EHRR 99). Rights must not be interpreted in a way that makes them theoretical and illusory. In certain cases the duty of securing that rights become available extends from mere non-interference to a positive duty to promote legislative and other measures to give effect to them. Thus it may be necessary to read in a right of access to a court to give effect to a right of fair trial in civil and criminal proceedings. This requires no interference with correspondence between a prisoner and his lawyer, and in certain cases provision of a system of legal aid in order to give effect to a right of access to court (*Johnstone* v *Ireland* (1986) 9 EHRR 203). Elsewhere a practical and effective application of the concept of respect may require the state to abolish laws interfering with personal conduct or stigmatizing illegitimacy, or to regulate intrusive surveillance activities (*Malone* v *UK* (1985) 7 EHRR 14; *Halford* v *UK* (1997) 24 EHRR 523).

1.80   This principle draws inspiration from Article 13 of the ECHR which requires an effective remedy in cases of arguable violations of ECHR rights. Although this Article has not been incorporated into the HRA 1998 on the grounds that the Act is itself an effective remedy, the case law of the European Court drawing on Article 13 and setting the standards of judicial scrutiny in respect of the different ECHR rights will all be matters to which the national courts and tribunals must have regard. As we have noted the ECHR is not static in its field of application but a living instrument, responding to developing social needs and new problems that require judicial resolution in a principled way that may not have been foreseen in 1950. An updating approach is thus part of the requirement of practicality and effectiveness.

1.81   Fourthly, the ECHR concepts are autonomous and do not depend on national law characterization of a measure. Thus 'law' in Article 5(1) means both a measure having the force of law in the contracting state and also the ECHR principle of legality. A law must be sufficiently precise and accessible to have the status of law in the ECHR however it is regarded domestically. Similarly lawfulness in Article 5(4) refers to ECHR concepts and is not just restricted to authority in national law. It is more controversial whether in this particular context the lawfulness includes ECHR concepts of proportionality and necessity.[50] Whether a law is criminal in character will not be exclusively determined by national characterization but can take account of other factors such as the penalty that follows, the characterization elsewhere in Europe, whether the measure regulates a specific class of people or is general in impact (*Benham* v *UK* (1996) 22 EHRR 293 at para. 56).

---

[50] See the Court of Appeal's judgment in *R (Saadi)* v *Secretary of State* [2001] EWCA Civ 1512 (19 October 2001); House of Lords [2002] UKHL 41, and see the Introduction to this book.

1.82   Fifthly, where a balance has to be maintained between rights and interests, the principle of proportionality applies. There must be a reasonable relationship between the means employed and the legitimate objectives (*Fayed* v *UK* (1994) 18 EHRR 393 at para. 71). This is much more than a requirement of good faith. Article 18 expressly precludes restrictions being applied for any purpose other than those for which they have been prescribed. An interference is only necessary in a democratic society if it is for a legitimate purpose recognized by the ECHR, addresses a pressing social need and is proportionate in the sense that the restriction is no more intrusive than necessary to meet the legitimate purpose contemplated by the ECHR.[51] This was applied in the case of *Brown* v *Stott* [2001] 3 WLR 817 where Lord Bingham concluded (and Lord Steyn approached the problem in similar terms):

> limited qualification of these rights is acceptable if reasonably directed by the national authorities towards a clear and proper public objective and if representing no greater qualification than the situation calls for.

1.83   In *B* v *Secretary of State* [2000] INLR 361 the Court of Appeal approved those commentators suggesting that the concept of proportionality in EC law and under the ECHR was essentially the same, although the rights that are subject to examination may be of greater or lesser weight. It concluded:

> In essence it amounts to this: a measure which interferes with a Community or human right must not only be authorised by law but must correspond to a pressing social need and go no further than is strictly necessary in a pluralistic society to achieve its permitted purpose.

1.84   The strictness of the necessity is, however, dependent on the nature of the right and the context of the decision, and in Article 8 cases subsequent decisions have confirmed that deportation may be necessary where a fair balance has been achieved between the competing interests. See in particular *Samaroo* v *Secretary of State for the Home Department* [2002] INLR 55. We have noted these developments above in the Introduction and below in chapters 4 and 6.

1.85   To summarize, where the national court is engaged in interpreting the ECHR and considering whether legislation is compatible with it:

(a)   it must first consider the text of the ECHR and the nature of the right at stake, whether absolute, procedural or presumptive subject to justified interference;

---

[51] See *R (Daly)* v *Secretary of State* [2001] 2 AC 532 citing *De Freitas* v *Permanent Secretary of Agriculture, Fisheries, Land and Housing* [1999] 1 AC 69; *R* v *A (No. 2)* [2001] 2 WLR 1546; see also *Samaroo* v *Secretary of State for the Home Department* [2002] INLR 55.

(b)   it should identify the ECHR principles applying to the interpretation of the right and give effect to them;

(c)   it will find the principles most clearly exposed in the case law of the European Court and the reasoned decisions of the former European Commission;

(d)   it may also consider other international instruments to which the UK is a party and any provisions of domestic law giving as good or greater protection and must achieve a result that incorporates all these standards;

(e)   it may have regard to other constitutional, common law or international jurisprudence;

(f)   it applies an updating and living instrument interpretation that may require it to take a more advanced position than one articulated in an old judgment of the European Court;

(g)   it is looking for a purposive construction of the right and a decision that gives practical effect to the right. It is not looking at a purely linguistic construction of the Article devoid from its policy and purposes;

(h)   it must determine whether interference with rights is justified and decide whether it considers that the proportionality requirement is met. It does not afford the same international deference to the contracting state as the European Court does through the margin of appreciation, whilst nevertheless recognizing that in difficult matters of policy, respect for the decisions of the legislature and the executive is appropriate;

(i)   it is looking for the autonomous ECHR approach to particular terms rather than being bound by purely domestic classification;

(j)   it will be astute to detect discrimination in the application of ECHR rights.

1.86   Once the requirements of the ECHR have been identified by these principles the national court looks at the text of the domestic legislation in question bearing the following precepts in mind:

(a)   it will strive to find an interpretation that is compatible with the ECHR if this is at all possible, reading in and reading down words in the legislative provision to do so;

(b)   where a subordinate instrument is incompatible it may be disapplied to the extent that it is necessary to do so to achieve compatibility save when the incompatibility is mandated by a provision of primary legislation;

(c)   where the incompatibility is driven by or found in primary legislation and the court can find no unlawfulness, then courts of the level of High Court and above can make a declaration of incompatibility;

(d)   laws remain valid and in force notwithstanding a declaration of incompatibility, until any remedial measure is taken to amend them;

(e)   where the court has a discretion under a statute it should act to give effect to the ECHR right unless mandated to the contrary by other provisions of primary legislation.

IMMIGRATION APPEALS

1.87   We have seen that the HRA 1998 will apply in immigration appeals as well as in the High Court. It is beyond the scope of this introductory chapter to give a detailed assessment of the scheme of immigration appeals as amended by the IAA 1999. A brief description of the kinds of decisions that are subject to an appeal will suffice. Immigration appeals have been a feature of modern immigration law since the Commonwealth Immigration Act 1968 which was shortly thereafter absorbed into Part 2 of the Immigration Act 1971. The rights of appeal were restricted and amended on a number of occasions between 1981 and 1996. In addition there are appeal rights for European Economic Area (EEA) nationals and members of their family under the Immigration (European Economic Area) Regulations 2000 (SI 2000/2326) and for those who are to be excluded on national security or political grounds by the Special Immigration Appeals Commission Act 1997. Part 2 of the Immigration Act 1971 is now repealed and replaced by Part 4 of the IAA 1999.

1.88   The new system of appeals is largely restrictive and highly circumscribed by procedural requirements that significantly cut down the breadth of the right of appeal being offered. There is one very significant loss, namely the absence of a full right of appeal on the merits of a decision to remove a person who has remained in breach of conditions. Further, those who are alleged to have obtained leave to remain by deception are added to this class. Such people will be in the same position as illegal entrants in the future. Under the statute they are able to challenge the jurisdiction to remove by a post removal appeal. Of course nobody with serious grounds to challenge will proceed by this ridiculous route, and as at present will rely on judicial review before removal to challenge the jurisdiction to interfere with their liberty.

1.89   Although they will not be able to appeal to an adjudicator on the grounds that discretion should have been exercised differently on the basis that the compassionate circumstances of the case outweigh the public interest in removal, there may be judicial review challenges to the precedent fact necessary for triggering removal if that is disputed, or to the rationality of the decision to treat a person under the summary removal powers.

1.90   It is difficult to see how consistency and fairness in the exercise of discretion between one case and another is to be achieved, and how sensible exercise of humanitarian discretion will be exercised without appellate review. The consequences will almost certainly be the opposite of what the government intended: either an increase in applications for judicial review of removal decisions, or a shift from compassionate factors to asylum and human rights grounds.

1.91   There are four positive developments enlarging on the scheme in existence before October 2000. First, a person who is a family visitor has the right of appeal against a refusal of entry clearance restored to them (IAA 1999, s. 60(5)(a)). However such an applicant may be required to pay a fee for the costs of the appeal, in addition to the costs of the entry clearance application, and if successful the sponsor of the visitor may be required to lodge a bond ensuring compliance with the immigration rules. Secondly, people who have been granted exceptional leave to remain on an application being made for asylum are now clearly granted a right of appeal to upgrade to refugee status. This clarifies the confusing position under s. 8 of the AIAA 1993.[52] Thirdly, and most significantly there is a new right of appeal on human rights grounds under s. 65 of the IAA 1999. Fourthly, there is now an appeal on race discrimination grounds.

1.92   We shall now look at the appeal structure in a little more detail and examine the measures taken to reduce multiple and repeat appeals or abuse of the human rights appeal.

1.93   The IAA 1999 has replaced and re-enacted the scheme of statutory appeals under the previous laws. It provides for rights of appeal against the following immigration decisions:

(a)   refusals of entry clearance or certificates of entitlement (s. 59(2));

(b)   decisions that a person requires leave to enter (s. 59(1)(a));

(c)   decisions refusing a person leave to enter (s. 59(1)(b));

(d)   refusals of variation of leave if as a result of the refusal a person may be required to leave the UK within 28 days of the decision (s. 61);

(e)   a decision to deport a person or a dependent family member on grounds conducive to the public good or a refusal to revoke a deportation decision (s. 63);

(f)   against removal directions as an illegal entrant or overstayer, and if in possession of a work permit or current entry clearance, against a refusal of leave to enter on the grounds that a person ought to be removed to a different country from that identified by the Secretary of State (s. 67(1)).

---

[52] In the case of *Saad, Diriye and Osorio* v *Secretary of State* [2002] INLR 34, the Court of Appeal removed much of the confusion by making it clear that the asylum appellate regime conferred an appeal on the question of status under Article 1, as well as the issue of *refoulement* under Article 33. It confined *Massaquoui* v *Secretary of State* [2001] Imm AR 309, a case which appeared to yield the contrary results, to its own facts.

1.94   These rights of appeal are restricted by significant procedural require-ments about possession of relevant documents at the time of the decision, and one stop procedures preventing unnecessary duplication. We discuss the extent to which the ECHR requires an opportunity to appeal or fairness in the determina-tion of any appeal provided, in chapter 5 and aspects of the appeal system as it affects family rights, in chapter 4.

SECTION 65 OF THE IAA 1999

1.95   As we have examined above, s. 6 of the HRA 1998 requires all public authorities throughout the United Kingdom to act compatibly with the ECHR within the confines of their particular jurisdiction. The HRA 1998 did not of itself grant a right of appeal where none existed previously and does not enable an adjudicator to grant a remedy beyond his or her statutory jurisdiction. Even before the coming into force of the IAA 1999 it was apparent that there were certain kinds of immigration decisions relating to expulsion or exclusion where human rights might well be violated but where an adjudicator did not have or may not have had jurisdiction.

1.96   The wholesale removal of deportation of overstayers and a right of appeal against those who have overstayed created an even greater jurisdictional hiatus. For example, it is unlikely that a person who objected to removal under s. 67(2) of the IAA 1999 without naming a different country for the proposed removal could have used the occasion to challenge independently the decision to remove at all on human rights grounds. The original response of the government to concerns voiced by immigration practitioners was to implement what is now s. 7(11) of the HRA 1998 whereby the Minister who has power to make procedure rules (in the case of immigration the Lord Chancellor) could promote rules to ensure that any tribunal can provide an appropriate remedy in relation to an act of a public author-ity that would be unlawful as a result of s. 6(1) of the HRA 1998.

1.97   In the event, however, immigration law was overhauled before the HRA 1998 came into effect and we now have s. 65(1) of the IAA 1999 that is designed to provide an independent right of appeal on human rights grounds. It is never-theless important to note that s. 65 is not a general replacement for the HRA 1998 in the field of immigration and asylum, but a supplementary measure designed to ensure compatibility in these spheres. Adjudicators hearing visitor and entry clearance appeals will have to apply the HRA 1998 in the construction of the immigration rules and in deciding the legality of immigration decisions, whether a s. 65 appeal is formally raised or not. The draftsman has acted perhaps out of an abundance of caution in providing in s. 65(3) and s. 65(4) that wherever a question arises of compatibility of an immigration decision with the human rights of the appellant the appellate authority has jurisdiction to act.

1.98   Irrespective of s. 65 the authority has a plain duty to act compatibly with ECHR rights, because any failure by the Home Office to act compatibly with human rights will mean that its decision is not in accordance with the law. The jurisdiction of adjudicators and the tribunal hearing appeals is generally governed by Sch. 4, para. 21 of the IAA 1999 whereby an appeal must be allowed if 'the decision or action against which the appeal is brought was not in accordance with the law . . .'. The question is now put beyond doubt. Thus in the course of an asylum appeal under s. 69 of the IAA 1999, in respect of a decision taken after 2 October 2000, the adjudicator must consider not merely whether the appellant is a refugee under the 1951 Refugee Convention but also whether the consequences of the decision would violate rights under the HRA 1998. Clearly grounds of appeal and the procedure rules should seek to focus argument in advance of the hearing so all parties are prepared to argue the relevant issues fully.

1.99   Section 65(5) makes plain that in addition to the general grounds for allowing an appeal provided for elsewhere in the statute, the adjudicator can also allow an appeal on the grounds that it contravenes the appellant's human rights. Again, such a power was strictly unnecessary in the case of appeals where para. 21 of Sch. 4 of the IAA 1999 applied, but may clarify any doubts as to the availability of those powers in asylum appeals (see observations of Laws J in *R v Secretary of State, ex parte Mehari* [1994] QB 474; see now *Saad, Diriye and Osorio v Secretary of State* [2002] INLR 34).

1.100   Section 65(1) grants a right of appeal where a person alleges that an authority has, in taking any decision under the Immigration Acts relating to that person's entitlement to enter or remain in the United Kingdom, acted in breach of that person's human rights. Further, as a result of the Race Relations Act 2000, it also enables a person to complain of racial discrimination in connection with entry or remaining in the UK. There are a number of observations about the scope of this appeal.

1.101   First, it is restricted to decisions taken under the Immigration Acts. On the face of it decisions about naturalization or other matters taken under the British Nationality Act 1981 would be outwith the scope of the appeal right. However, decisions taken in respect of certificates of entitlement would be decisions taken under the Immigration Acts as they relate to the grant of documents provided for in those Acts. The Immigration Acts are defined in s. 167(1) of the IAA 1999.

1.102   Secondly, the decision must be related to entitlement to enter or remain. Entitlement to enter or remain must be read broadly as any claim to enter or remain as, strictly speaking, all those who do not have the right of abode or entitlement to exemption from immigration control, enter by permission as opposed to of right. The subject matter of the decision must relate to entering or remaining in the

United Kingdom. There is no reason why a decision refusing temporary admission or release or any other adjectival decision consequent upon a claim to admission or remaining could not come within the section,[53] although other appeal rights may exist in such circumstances. We deal with the question of using s. 65 to ventilate detention issues in chapter 4.

1.103   However, authority is given a narrower meaning than under s. 6 of the HRA 1998 and for the purposes of s. 65(1) of the IAA 1999 is confined by s. 65(7) to the Secretary of State, immigration officer, or person responsible for the grant or refusal of entry clearance. This would therefore preclude a direct challenge under this section to a decision of the Department for Education and Skills relating to work permits.

1.104   Thirdly, the person concerned must allege that the authority has acted in breach of his or her human rights. This appears to be a little narrower than the s. 6, HRA 1998 question as to whether an authority has acted incompatibly 'with a Convention right'. The language of s. 65(2) and s. 65(5) is to similar effect. Arguable breaches of the ECHR that have no impact on the merits of the decision relating to entry or remaining are thereby excluded. In the context of family life, however, there is little scope for an argument that an immigration decision may infringe the child's right to family life under Article 8 but not the overstaying father's. The appellant's ECHR rights are inextricably bound up with the impact of his deportation on others: a child, partner or other family member. The weighing of the proportionality of the decision and the necessity for any interference with family life requires consideration of all of the relevant circumstances and to hear any material evidence as to the consequences for others.

1.105   Moreover, the ECHR itself would conclude that an assessment of the justification for an interference with the right to family life that proceeded by breaching the provisions of national law would result in a violation of the applicant's human rights. If we were to assume for the purposes of this argument that a decision to remove a father of a young child violated the child's human rights of respect for family life, and the question was whether it also violated the father's rights, the father could argue that the decision was not in accordance with the law as required by Article 8(2) because the immigration authorities had breached s. 6(1) of the HRA 1998 in acting incompatibly with the child's rights. If that is so then the case never proceeds to the next stage of justification on the grounds of necessity in a democratic society, a decision that is contrary to the domestic law is incapable of justification.[54]

---

[53] See however *R (Kariharan and others)* v *Secretary of State for the Home Department* [2001] EWHC Admin 1004, 5 December 2001 and see the Introduction.

[54] See for example *Khan* v *UK* 8 BHRC 310; see also the similar reasoning in *R* v *Governor of Brockhill Prison ex parte Evans* (No. 2) [2000] 3 WLR 843 per Lord Hope at 857–9.

1.106 Such an approach precludes the need to consider the difficult issue of the impact of para. 21 of Sch. 4 in s. 65 appeals. It would be peculiar indeed if the adjudicator were required to dismiss an appeal against a decision to expel where he or she concluded that the decision was not in accordance with the law because an authority had not acted compatibly with s. 6 HRA 1998. There is nothing in the permissive language of s. 65(5) of the IAA 1999 to suggest that Parliament had intended such an absurd consequence to follow. It would certainly be inconsistent with the aim of economy and efficiency of appellate proceedings to require an aggrieved spouse or child to take judicial review proceedings to quash an intended removal of an aberrant partner or parent on the grounds of illegality vis à vis them, following any failed appeal determined on a narrow basis against the appellant under s. 65.

1.107 Fourthly, the s. 65 appeal is not available if the decision is capable of appeal to the Special Immigration Appeals Commission which is, of course, a public authority itself bound by s. 6(1) of the HRA 1998 and appellants will be able to argue ECHR points before it. The IAA 1999 in s. 65(6) contemplates that a s. 65 appeal could be brought in respect of a decision made after the conclusion of the SIAC proceedings presumably on fresh circumstances arising since then.

1.108 Prima facie, therefore whenever a person is faced with an adverse immigration decision he may appeal under s. 65 irrespective of the previous immigration history and prior appeals or absence of them. Any refusal to revoke an unexecuted removal direction may therefore raise a human rights issue.[55]

PREVENTION OF ABUSE

1.109 This state of affairs could result in the abuse of endless repeated applications and appeals on the same grounds, and so the legislator has provided methods to ensure that the human rights appeal is not abused. First there is the one stop procedure. Where an appealable decision is taken under the Immigration Rules to refuse leave to enter or remain, to vary or refuse to vary a limited leave to enter or remain that may require a person to leave the United Kingdom within 28 days of the decision, or a decision is taken to deport a person, the decision-taker is required to serve on the person affected a notice requiring the recipient to state any additional grounds he or she may have for wishing to enter or remain in the United Kingdom (IAA 1999, s. 74(1)–(4)). The recipient must then within the prescribed period serve on the Secretary of State details of any additional claim to be made. These additional grounds must include any claim for asylum or any allegation that an act breaches his human rights (s. 74(7)). A complementary duty

---

[55] But see *Kariharan* (above at footnote 53) discussed in the Introduction.

arises where there is no right of appeal against a refusal of leave to enter or a person is being removed as an illegal entrant, or under s. 10 and a person has claimed either asylum or made a human rights allegation (s. 75(1)–(3)).

1.110   The form of the notice and the definition of family members on whom it should be served are prescribed by orders made under the principal sections. The Immigration and Asylum Appeals (One-Stop Procedure) Regulations 2000, SI 2000/2244 set out the details of the scheme. Notices can be served on the applicant or his or her representative by hand or post or fax. The notice contains a form of statement of additional grounds that must be completed in English and returned within ten days in ordinary appeals or five days in SIAC appeals. Notices must be served on the principal applicant and dependent family members as defined in the regulations.

1.111   Failure to include the additional claim, including the human rights claim, means that in the subsequent appeal the person will not be able to rely on that ground for entry or remaining in the UK if they were aware of the ground at the material time (IAA 1999, s. 76(2)(b)). The material time must mean the prescribed period for giving the notice in response.

1.112   Then there are powers in the Secretary of State to certify that a human rights allegation is manifestly unfounded. This can be done under s. 72(2)(a) where a person challenges removal under s. 11, IAA 1999 to another member state for the purpose of asylum determination. Alternatively a certificate can be issued under s. 73(2)(a) if it is alleged that the human rights or discrimination claim could have been raised earlier and was not, one purpose of the claim was to delay removal and there was no other legitimate purpose for making the claim. People who fail to comply with the s. 74 procedure for giving details of related or further claims when faced with immigration action, may find themselves vulnerable to the exercise of such power.

1.113   Where the person concerned is subject to a decision that can only be appealed to the SIAC then the SIAC will have jurisdiction to determine the human rights points. Cases can proceed on final determinations of appeals from the SIAC or the IAT on a question of law with permission to the Court of Appeal. Where there is no further right of appeal, cases may proceed by judicial review if the decisions of adjudicators or non-final decisions of the IAT show legal errors of approach. We consider the adequacy of the compliance of this appellate structure with the requirements of Articles 6 and 13 in chapter 5. We examine the procedures for review of detention in chapter 3.

1.114   However, this automatic exclusion from arguing the supplementary grounds does not apply if the additional ground is a claim for asylum or a claim that the act breached the applicant's human rights, or in any case where the

Secretary of State considers that the applicant had a reasonable excuse for the omission.

1.115   Late human rights or asylum claims are intended to be curtailed by a certification procedure. In the case of a late claim for asylum where the person has failed to include the claim in the notice required under s. 74, the Secretary of State may certify under s. 76(5) that one purpose of making the claim for asylum was to delay the removal from the United Kingdom of the applicant or of any member of his family and the applicant had no other legitimate purpose for making the application. We shall call these two conditions the abusive delay requirements. The certificate has the effect of precluding an asylum appeal proceeding under s. 69.

1.116   In human rights cases, the certification power only precludes a fresh appeal arising on human rights grounds after the final determination or another appeal (s. 73(1)). If a notice of appeal is served making a claim that the authorities have acted in breach of the claimant's human rights, the Secretary of State may certify (s. 73(2)) that the human rights claim could either have been raised in the original appeal or a s. 74 notice and was not and in addition the abusive delay conditions apply. Alternatively the Secretary of State may certify that the human rights complaint was in fact considered in the previous appeal (s. 73(5)). The words used suggest that actual consideration is necessary rather than the deeming provisions of s. 77(2) that we consider below. In either case, the effect of the certificate is to deem that there are no appeals outstanding and that the claimed appeal has been finally determined thus precluding any bar to removal of the claimant and the family members concerned. A certificate barring a human rights appeal can also be issued where an asylum claimant is being sent to a safe third country designated under statutory instrument (Asylum (Designated Safe Third Countries) Order 2000 (SI 2000/2245)). Where the appellant responds by making a s. 65 appeal, the Secretary of State can respond by certifying that the allegation is manifestly unfounded (IAA 1999, s. 72(2)(a)). Further, the Secretary of State or the immigration officer may certify that the abusive delay conditions are met in the case of any fresh application made to them (s. 73(7), (8)) and no appeal can be brought against such a certified decision (s. 73(9)).

1.117   Clearly certificates that are inappropriately issued may be challenged by judicial review and it may be doubted whether a complex exclusionary regime is preferable to relying on the good sense of the appellate authorities to determine and dismiss abusive claims without merit summarily. The criteria for certification are stringent. Given the tight timetable for service of a counternotice, it is unlikely that the conditions could be met where a late notice was served before the appeal through difficulty in seeking or obtaining or responding to competent legal advice. Late claims will require explanation, as indeed is the case at present if they are to have any credibility, but where the application reveals serious arguable grounds for a claim to remain it is difficult to conclude that a certificate could state that the only reason for making the claim was to delay removal. A claim made to prevent removal at all is not an abusive attempt to delay the inevitable. Thus the merits of the claim would have to be considered before any conclusion could be reached on why it was made. Equally, it cannot be considered that the fact that the Secretary of State proposes to send an asylum seeker to another EU country, Switzerland or North America, precludes any arguable violation of ECHR rights. The case of *TI v UK* [2000] INLR 211 demonstrates that in principle the UK can be responsible for the onward return of an asylum seeker from the third country to a place where treatment contrary to Article 3 is encountered, but that no substantial grounds for such a fear will arise where the third country adopts de facto policies and practices that would preclude such a consequence. In other words it will all depend on a detailed examination of the law and policies of those third countries whether in fact someone is at risk of expulsion to face torture, or inhuman or degrading treatment.[56]

1.118   If these stringent conditions for certification are applied in practice, it is unlikely that the regime as a whole will be declared incompatible with the ECHR. See also the decision of the House of Lords in *R (Thangarasa) v Secretary of State for the Home Department* [2002] UKHL 36 considered in *R (Razgor) v Secretary of State for the Home Department* [2002] EWHC Admin 2554. The European Court has held that time limits can be applied even to claims of Article 3 ill-treatment, making a failure to ventilate the complaint promptly a failure to exhaust domestic remedies (*Bahaddur v Netherlands* (1998) 26 EHRR 278). However, each case depends on its facts, and the overall purpose of the law and the ECHR is to prevent the UK acting inconsistently with its international obligations rather than refusing to consider arguable claims because of the inconvenience it would cause to government.

1.119   When the appellate authority hears an appeal, s. 77(2) provides that the appellant is to be treated as also appealing on any additional grounds which he may have for appealing the decision and that he is not prevented by s. 76 or s. 72(2) from relying on. With the exception of the safe third country issue addressed by s. 72(2), this means that even where a counternotice alleging a human rights complaint has not been served, the appellant is to be treated as appealing on these grounds. In asylum and human rights appeals post decision evidence of relevant events and circumstances is admissible, whereas in ordinary immigration appeals the admissible evidence is confined to what was known by

---

[56] In *TI v UK* [2000] INLR 211 the European Court concluded that German practices precluded such a risk. See also *Suresh v Minister for Immigration* [2002] SC, Supreme Court of Canada.

the Secretary of State or which relates to the relevant facts at the date of the decision.

1.120 Thus as far as human rights allegations are concerned the statutory scheme is that these matters should be raised in counternotices when any other immigration appeal is pending, but that a failure to serve such a notice will not prevent the appellate authority considering the human rights ground and any post decision evidence in support of it when the appeal is heard. It is only if the claim was considered in the original appeal, or subsequent to this appeal the applicant makes a human rights claim that should have been considered earlier and to which the abusive delay conditions apply, that he or she will be cut out, subject to the certificate being lawfully issued. In other cases, the failure to ventilate the claim in the notice may be of evidential but not jurisdictional significance.

1.121 If one has the case of a person who enters with leave, overstays without applying for an extension and remains for some time when he or she establishes family life in the United Kingdom, then whether on an application for regularization or a response to removal directions, the applicant will be able to allege that the decision infringes his human rights. The allegation, if not accepted by the Secretary of State, will then result in the service of notice of an appealable decision under reg. 4 of the Immigration and Asylum Appeals (Notices) Regulations 2000, SI 2000/2333. The applicant is then brought within the timetable for service of notice of appeal under the Immigration and Asylum Appeals (Procedure) Rules 2000. No question of a s. 74 notice or certification arises. If the same applicant had made an unsuccessful application for variation of leave before overstaying, the critical question is whether he or she appealed against such a decision. A s. 74 notice can be served on the rejection of the initial application, but will have no effect unless the applicant enters an appeal, and the criteria for s. 73 certification arise if the human rights claim is raised subsequently. No such certification can be made if there is no first appeal entered. Thus appealing merely to extend time may have significant consequences for a subsequent human rights claim. If an appeal is made but not pursued by the applicant, and no human rights claim actually raised, it is our opinion that the Secretary of State could not subsequently certify the case as having been considered in the earlier appeal, even when there was an opportunity to have raised it. In those circumstances the abusive delay criteria have to be met. Where a previous appeal has raised a human rights point, or a certificate is issued that it could reasonably have done, then no subsequent application is likely to give rise to an opportunity to serve notice of a s. 65 appeal unless the certificate is challenged on judicial review. A certificate could not be issued if there has been a material change of circumstances since the first appeal, there was a reasonable excuse for not raising the claim earlier, or the merits of the claim suggest that there was another reason for making it other than merely to delay an inevitable removal.

1.122   Where there is a right of appeal and the appeal has been dismissed by the adjudicator and there is a right of appeal to the IAT, there is a final measure to prevent abuse contained in the IAA 1999 that deserves mention. By s. 79, the IAT may inform an applicant at any time before it determines an appeal that it considers it has no merit. In those circumstances pursuit of an unsuccessful appeal after receipt of the notice may render the appellant or his or her representative liable to a specified penalty under regulations to be made by the Lord Chancellor. This is a provision that may create considerable problems for representatives unless exercised in a highly restrained way. Frequently appeals that appear hopeless on a cursory examination reveal a more complex issue on fuller debate, and whether the applicant is ultimately successful or not, an appellant or his representative cannot be penalized for persisting with an arguable point, notwithstanding indications of judicial disapproval. In the civil courts punitive wasted costs orders are not made merely because an advocate has taken what a judge concludes is a bad point. Given that an applicant who alleges that his human rights have been violated must exhaust all domestic remedies before ventilating his complaint elsewhere, it would be harsh and arguably inconsistent with Article 13 of the ECHR itself for an applicant to be penalized for taking a point unsuccessfully in domestic proceedings. In our opinion, the IAT should give a very strict construction to the term 'no merit'. It should not embrace any appeal where there is a legitimate purpose in proceeding despite some overall weakness in the case: the redetermination of a matter of central fact, the clarification of the meaning of a particular rule, the existence of a previously undetermined argument of ECHR or human rights law. Where a genuinely unmeritorious appeal has been pursued after an adverse indication, then any penalty should be proportionate to the means of the claimant, who will be the principal person on whom it is imposed unless he or she waives legal professional privilege and attributes responsibility for pursuing the point to the representative.

SPECIAL IMMIGRATION APPEALS COMMISSION

1.123   Hitherto our discussion has focused on immigration appeals that raise no question of national security considerations which would take the case out of the ordinary appeal system and into the jurisdiction of the Special Immigration Appeals Commission. SIAC was set up by the SIAC Act 1997 following the decision in the case of *Chahal* v *United Kingdom* (1996) 23 EHRR 413. It is not surprising that the passage of the statute was marked with government assurances that SIAC would be able to allow an appeal if it concluded that the exclusion or the removal in question conflicted with the human rights of the applicant. It is pertinent to observe that the jurisdiction of SIAC to allow appeals reflects that of Sch. 4, para. 21 of the IAA 1999. Thus by s. 4(1) of SIAC Act 1997 the Commission must allow an appeal if it considers that 'the decision . . . was not in accordance with the law or with any immigration rules applicable to the case or where it involved the exercise of discretion, that the discretion should have been exercised differently'.

1.124   In its decision in *Mukhtiar Singh and Paramjit Singh* v *Secretary of State for the Home Department* (31 July 2000), SIAC allowed an appeal from two applicants accused of association with international terrorism, on the basis that 'substantial grounds were shown for believing that each of the appellants if expelled would face a real risk of torture if returned to India'. This was notwithstanding that each applicant represented a danger to the national security of the UK by reason of association with terrorism and for the same reason each was excluded from the protection of the Refugee Convention by Article 1F of that Convention. Since the Home Office conceded that the appeal should be allowed if the risk subsisted, it was not necessary for SIAC to determine the precise jurisdictional basis for allowing the appeal. Where the HRA 1998 is in force, the decision would not have been in accordance with the law; before then the discretion to deport should have been exercised differently in the light of the present policy not to act in violation of the ECHR. In any event SIAC jurisdiction is ample confirmation of the fact that it is not always necessary to have a specific s. 65 human rights appeal to succeed on a human rights question. The powers and function of SIAC have been reviewed by the Court of Appeal and the House of Lords in the case of *Rehman* v *Secretary of State for the Home Department* [2001] 3 WLR 877 and have been amended by the anti-terrorism legislation that we discuss in the postscript to this book. It is plain, however, that the SIAC approach to human rights and the contravention of Article 3 has been endorsed in *Rehman* by Lord Hoffman. For further decisions of SIAC in the field of human rights see chapter 7 below, discussing the Anti-Terrorism, Crime and Security Act 2001.

Chapter Two

The Protection of Life, Bodily Integrity and Human Dignity

INTRODUCTION

2.1 We have seen at 1.15 and 1.16 that the ECHR rights protected by the HRA 1998 apply to all those within the jurisdiction of a contracting state or those abroad affected by acts of its officials.

2.2 The only reference to aliens in the original rights afforded under Articles 1 to 13 of the ECHR is in the context of Article 5(1)(f) identifying detention for immigration purposes as a potential justification to detention without trial.

2.3 The European Court has frequently emphasized that a state has the right under both national and international law to control its own frontiers and to decide whom it wishes to admit or not (*Vilvarajah* v *UK* (1991); *Abdulaziz* v *UK* (1985) 7 EHRR 471). There is no right to a choice of the country of residence. Nevertheless, within these parameters, notwithstanding the absence of any promising material in the text itself, case law has developed whereby the state's exercise of its rights to control its own frontiers is subject to the requirements of the ECHR.

2.4 The most significant development in this respect has been the progressive interpretation of Article 3 to prevent expulsion of a foreign national from a contracting state in certain circumstances. Once it was recognized that respect for human rights might prevent expulsions then, despite the absence of immigration rights in the ECHR, it was clear that in principle immigration decisions might infringe human rights. The great development in the application of the ECHR to the field of immigration came with the recognition that a person can be subjected to torture by means of an expulsion to another state where there is a risk of harm.[1] A text that at

---

[1] See *Soering* v *UK* (1989) 11 EHRR 439; *Cruz Varas* v *Sweden* (1991) 14 EHRR 1; *Vilvarajah* v *UK* (1991) 14 EHRR 248; *Chahal* v *UK* (1996) 23 EHRR 413; *Ahmed* v *Austria* (1997) 24 EHRR 278; *HLR* v *France* (1997) 26 EHRR 29; *Hilal* v *UK* (2001) 33 EHRR 2; *Bensaid* v *UK* (2001) 33

first blush failed to afford any rights to those seeking protection from persecution, has thus now extended protection in some areas beyond that provided by the Refugee Convention itself (see 2.84 et seq for comparisons). The case law of the European Court both anticipated and was itself the inspiration for Article 3(1) of the UN Convention Against Torture 1984 (*Chahal* v *UK* (1996) 23 EHRR 413).

2.5   In this chapter we are primarily considering the circumstances where a foreign national faces possible harm and suffering by reason of expulsion from the UK. For this purpose we shall principally be concerned with the case law on Article 2 and Article 1. We will also touch upon issues arising under Article 8 as we seek to discuss here all forms of protection against threats to life, mental and physical integrity and other forms of distressing and humiliating harm (see, however, *Ullah* v *Special Adjudicator* [2002] EWCA Civ 1856 (leave to appeal to House of Lords granted)). We will examine the scope of Article 8 more fully again in chapter 4 where we consider the right to respect for private and family life in its different aspects.

2.6   This book is principally concerned with immigration decisions and its relevance to human rights, rather than the human rights of immigrants in other spheres of civil society. Everyone is entitled to the equal protection of the criminal law in the UK whatever their immigration status. Thus torture, inhuman treatment, assaults of sufficient severity at the hands of public authorities or others, are violations of Article 3. Where there is a credible complaint of such actions taken against migrants or members of a racial minority, the ECHR requires the state to investigate actively and to prosecute where there is available evidence.[2] Asylum seekers and immigrants facing removal are a group liable to detention and the ECHR imposes core minimum obligations as to their treatment in custody that will be discussed here. Threats to bodily integrity or dignity inconsistent with the ECHR could arise in the way that an asylum seeker is treated by the authorities in the United Kingdom pending resolution of his or her status or in the manner of removal. This may embrace such questions as access to urgent medical treatment,[3] social support and shelter.[4] Once indefinite leave to remain has been

---

EHRR 10. Note that the judgment in *Soering*, which gave rise to this jurisprudence, was itself informed by the earlier decision of the European Court in *Abdulaziz* v *UK* (1985) 7 EHRR 471, paras. 59 and 60, on Article 8: see para. 85 of the judgment in *Soering*.

[2]   See *R* v *DPP ex parte Manning* [2000] 3 WLR 663 citing *Assenov* v *Bulgaria* (1998) 28 EHRR 652; *Aydin* v *Turkey* (1997) 25 EHRR 251; *Kaya* v *Turkey* (1998) 28 EHRR 1. See recently *Jordan* v *UK* (4 May 2001); *R (Wright and Bennet)* v *Secretary of State* [2001] EWHC Admin 520; *R (Amin)* v *Secretary of State* (5 October 2001).

[3]   In *Pretty* v *DPP* UKHL 61 (29 November 2001) the House of Lords considered the application of Article 3 to cases of deprivation of medical treatment.

[4]   In *R (Husain)* v *Asylum Support Adjudicator* [2001] EWHC Admin 832, (2001) *The Times*, 15 November Stanley Burnton J considered obiter that a total deprivation of social support to an asylum seeker would be a contravention of Article 3.

granted, a foreign national will generally be entitled to equal treatment with British nationals in terms of their social and economic rights. A difference in treatment between people who are essentially in the same position as lawful residents of a territory is likely to constitute discrimination contrary to Article 14 of the ECHR (*Gaygusuz* v *Austria* 23 EHRR 364). In exceptional circumstances treatment that is racially discriminatory could itself be said to be inhuman or degrading (*East African Asians* v *UK* (1981) 3 EHRR 76).

SCOPE OF APPLICATION: DELIBERATE HARM

2.7   Article 2 of the ECHR provides that:

1. Everyone's right to life shall be protected by law. No one shall be deprived of his life intentionally save in the execution of a sentence of a court following his conviction for a crime for which this penalty is provided by law.

2. Deprivation of life shall not be regarded as inflicted in contravention of this Article when it results from the use of force which is no more than is absolutely necessary:

   (a)   in defence of any person from unlawful violence;
   (b)   in order to effect a lawful arrest or prevent the escape of a person lawfully detained;
   (c)   in action lawfully taken for the purpose of quelling a riot or insurrection.

2.8   Article 3 of the ECHR states that

No one shall be subjected to torture or inhuman or degrading treatment or punishment.

2.9   These Articles thus prohibit the following:

   (a)   intentional killing;
   (b)   torture;
   (c)   inhuman treatment;
   (d)   inhuman punishment;
   (e)   degrading treatment;
   (f)   degrading punishment.

Many of these issues can sensibly be considered together. The European Court frequently does not see the necessity to distinguish between inhuman or degrading treatment. Killing does raise particular issues and so we shall first examine the scope of Article 2 and then turn to Article 3. We will then consider some examples of how these Articles might apply to immigration decisions in the United Kingdom.

Deprivation of life

2.10   There are two essential requirements set out in Article 2. First, the intentional killing of an independent living being is prohibited save for the lawful application of the death penalty following due process of law, and where lethal force is absolutely necessary to prevent specific serious crimes and escape from arrest and lawful custody. This is essentially a negative obligation. We shall consider the special position of the application of Article 2 to death penalty cases below at 2.49 et seq.

2.11 Secondly, there is also a positive obligation. The principal aspect of this positive obligation is that states must promote laws and a system of justice that effectively respect the right to life and deter those who might kill (*McCann v UK* (1996) 21 EHRR 97). This is the primary obligation. The positive obligation may go beyond this and in certain cases require the state to provide individual measures of protection against a threat to life. It does not require the contracting state to ensure that no one is unlawfully killed. It is necessary to take all reasonable measures to guard against a foreseeable threat to life however (*McCann v UK* (1996)). The European Court reviewed these aspects of Article 2 in the case of *Osman v UK* (2000) 29 EHRR 245 and concluded at paragraphs 115 and 116:

> 115. The Court notes that the first sentence of Article 2 § 1 enjoins the State not only to refrain from the intentional and unlawful taking of life, but also to take appropriate steps to safeguard the lives of those within its jurisdiction. . . . It is common ground that the State's obligation in this respect extends beyond its primary duty to secure the right to life by putting in place effective criminal-law provisions to deter the commission of offences against the person backed up by law-enforcement machinery for the prevention, suppression and sanctioning of breaches of such provisions. . . .

> 116. For the Court, and bearing in mind the difficulties involved in policing modern societies, the unpredictability of human conduct and the operational choices which must be made in terms of priorities and resources, such an obligation must be interpreted in a way which does not impose an impossible or disproportionate burden on the authorities. Accordingly, not every claimed risk to life can entail for the authorities a Convention requirement to take operational measures to prevent that risk from materialising. . . . In the opinion of the Court where there is an allegation that the authorities have violated their positive obligation to protect the right to life in the context of their above-mentioned duty to prevent and suppress offences against the person . . . it must be established to its satisfaction that the authorities knew or ought to have known at the time of the existence of a real and immediate risk to the life of an identified individual or individuals from the criminal acts of a third party and that they failed to take measures within the scope of their powers which, judged reasonably, might have been expected to avoid that risk.[5]

---

[5] See also *R (Widgery Soldiers and others) v Lord Saville* [2001] 1 EWHC Admin 888, 16 November 2001 (on appeal [2002] 1 WLR 1249) for the proposition that the common law affords greater protection than Article 2 to the right to life; discussed above in the Introduction.

2.12   The debate in *Osman* concerned what is reasonable where there was positive evidence of a threat to a child and his family from a deranged school teacher. The European Court did not

> accept the Government's view that the failure to perceive the risk to life in the circumstances known at the time or to take preventive measures to avoid that risk must be tantamount to gross negligence or wilful disregard of the duty to protect life. . . . Such a rigid standard must be considered to be incompatible with the requirements of Article 1 of the Convention and the obligations of Contracting States under that Article to secure the practical and effective protection of the rights and freedoms laid down therein, including Article 2 [citing *McCann* v *UK* (1996) 21 EHRR 97 at para. 146]. For the Court, and having regard to the nature of the right protected by Article 2, a right fundamental in the scheme of the Convention, it is sufficient for an applicant to show that the authorities did not do all that could be reasonably expected of them to avoid a real and immediate risk to life of which they have or ought to have knowledge.

2.13   In *Mastromatteo* v *Italy* (App. No. 37703/97, 14 September 2000 the Court declared a claim admissible under Article 2 where a child was killed by dangerous bank robbers, whose release on home leave whilst serving a prison sentence for violent crime, had been authorized without adequate inquiry. The claim subsequently failed on its merits (European Court of Human Rights, 24 October 2002). The state's positive duties may here have been violated even though there was no evidence that the child was at particular risk. A complaint was held inadmissible in *Bromiley* v *UK* (App. No. 33747/96, 23 November 1999) where there was no evidence that a prisoner was dangerous or that a particular victim was at risk.

2.14   Many cases have arisen from Turkey where the authorities have failed to protect persons at risk. One such recent case is *Kilic* v *Turkey* (App. No. 22492/93, 28 March 2000). The European Court found a violation of Article 3 where the state permitted or fostered a lack of accountability of members of the security forces which was not compatible with the rule of law in a democratic society. In addition, there was an absence of operational measures of protection. A wide range of measures was available which would have assisted in minimizing the risk to Kilic's life and which would not have involved an impractical diversion of resources, but there was no evidence that any steps were taken in response to his request. The authorities failed to take reasonable measures available to them to prevent a real and immediate risk to Kilic's life.

2.15   Where someone has been killed, the positive obligation requires the state to conduct a proper inquiry by the public authorities. There must be a vindication of the right to life by appropriate prosecution where there is evidence of a crime. In the case of *Kaya* v *Turkey* (1999) 28 EHRR 1 the court found a violation of Article 2 in this respect. During the investigation, the file changed hands several times, the autopsies were incomplete, and there was no forensic examination of the scene or investigation concerning how the victims were transported. The prosecutors took steps in response to information provided by the victims' relatives, but these steps were often limited and superficial. The investigation was also dilatory and there were periods during which no apparent activity took place. In view of the serious allegations of misconduct implicating the security forces, it was incumbent on the authorities to respond actively and with reasonable expedition. The European Court was not satisfied that the investigation was adequate or effective.

2.16 A particularly strong obligation arises where a person dies at the hands of the state, when in police custody following arrest or whilst detained in prison.[6] There must be an investigation by the competent authorities of the state into all the circumstances of the killing and the family must have access to the investigation.[7] Where the investigation reveals that the person died at the hands of a state official, then the state must establish that the killing was strictly necessary for a purpose recognized by the ECHR (*McCann* v *UK* (1996) 21 EHRR 97).

2.17 When the European Court itself investigates whether the state has intentionally deprived someone within its jurisdiction of life, it applies a high standard of proof beyond reasonable doubt.[8] This is because it is essentially finding the state guilty of the most serious criminal offence in the canon, and a violation of the first and most obvious norm of national and international law. This is *not* the test to be applied when considering prevention of future killing or whether state action would place the person in danger of loss of life.[9] No crime has yet been committed, and it is not the criminal culpability of a contracting state that is engaged, but its positive obligation to take reasonable steps to protect life. Thus

---

[6] See *Velikova* v *Bulgaria* (27 April 2000, paragraph 80); and see *Salman* v *Turkey* (27 June 2000, paragraph 99).

[7] See *Assenov* v *Bulgaria* (1998) 28 EHRR 652 at paragraph 117; *Aydin* v *Turkey* (1997) 25 EHRR 251 at paragraph 103; *Jordan* v *UK* (4 May 2001); *R (Wright and Bennett)* v *Secretary of State* [2001] EWHC Admin 520; *R (Amin)* v *Secretary of State* (5 October 2001). For the limitations and potential of a coroner's jurisdiction see Friedmann, 'The Human Rights Act and the Inquest Process' (2001) *Legal Action*, November at p. 31 and December at p. 16. See now *R (Amin)* v *Secretary of State, R (Middleton)* v *Secretary of State* [2002] EWCA Civ 390, and see *Edwards* v *UK* (14 March 2002).

[8] See *Ireland* v *UK* 2 EHRR 25 at paragraph 161. Where certain primary facts are proved, a failure by the State to rebut them or provide a sufficient explanation supported by evidence, may enable the European Court to draw the inferences necessary to establish the violation: *Salman* v *Turkey* (27 June 2000, paragraph 100).

[9] Especially in domestic law in light of *R (Widgery Soldiers)* v *Lord Saville* [2001] 1 EWHC Admin 888. See also *Gonzalez* v *Spain* (App. No. 43544/98), 29 June 1999), where the applicant complained that extradition to the USA exposed him to serious risk to his life from drug-cartels, since he had co-operated with the federal government. The European Court drew no distinction between the standard of proof needed to show that extradition would amount to a violation of Article 2, and the standard of proof that would give rise to a violation of Article 3.

in the Turkish cases the European Court has sometimes found that it is not satisfied on the evidence that the state killed the victim in violation of Article 2 but may nevertheless find that there were inadequate measures of protection or an inadequate investigation.[10]

2.18   One obviously does not protect life by handing over a person to another whom it is known or suspected will kill the individual in question. In one of the early decisions, the former European Commission declared admissible a case against the United Kingdom where a Moroccan military officer fled to Gibraltar after an unsuccessful coup against the King (*Amekrane v UK* (1973) 16 YB 356).[11] He was summarily returned to Morocco despite the obvious risk of reprisals that followed immediately on return. His widow instituted proceedings against the UK and sought damages for the death caused by the expulsion. The case was subsequently settled. This case was an early demonstration that the ECHR could have effect in respect of events outside the frontiers of states that were parties to the ECHR or territories for which they were responsible.

2.19   Although this has sometimes been referred to as extraterritorial application of the ECHR, the better view is that the ECHR prohibits acts done within the territory of states parties to it: namely the expulsion or indeed exclusion (*East African Asians v UK* (1981) 3 EHRR 76) of an individual, where the consequences of the acts are reasonably foreseeable. The relevant act is the act of expulson (*Pretty v UK* ((2002) 35 EHRR 1, para. 53)). Responsibility is thus a direct one for the foreseeable consequences of the action rather than an indirect or vicarious responsibility for the acts of states not party to the ECHR. Under both Article 2 and Article 3 the question is not whether the applicant can prove what would happen, but whether there is a sufficiently real risk of personal jeopardy.

2.20   There is a continuum of risk. At one end of the spectrum there is the extradition case where a person is wanted by the authorities in another state, which threatens to deprive that person of his life for reasons of some alleged wrongdoing. At the other end is the risk that a person may become the innocent victim of a deadly crime perpetrated in the country of origin. Each case will require careful examination of the facts at the moment of expulsion to ascertain what the likely or foreseeable consequences are. A mere possibility of harm is generally insufficient to engage the responsibility of a contracting state.[12] There is no obligation on any state to guarantee absolute safety either within its territory or beyond.

---

[10] See for example the case of *Kilic v Turkey* (App. No. 22492/93, 28 March 2000) and *Kaya v Turkey* (1999) 28 EHRR 1.

[11] See Harris, O'Boyle and Warwick, *Law of the European Convention on Human Rights*, Butterworths, 1995, at 74 for details of the friendly settlement.

[12] See *Vilvarajah v UK* (1991) 14 EHRR 248; *HLR v France* (1997) 26 EHRR 29; *Slepeik v Netherlands* 86-A DR 176 (persecution of Roma if returned to Czech Republic).

Evidence of harm by state agents such as special forces, brutal police or prison officers and the like, will more obviously raise the question of real risk than the unpredictable acts of criminals. We will consider the appropriate standard of proof in these circumstances at 2.85 et seq when discussing Article 3 and its applications to expulsions, because the case law is more developed in this context.

Torture

2.21 In the early case of *Ireland* v *UK* (1978) 2 EHRR 25 at para. 167 torture was defined by the European Court as 'deliberate inhuman treatment causing very serious and cruel suffering'. The contrast with inhuman treatment is that the latter does not have to be deliberate and the intensity of the physical and mental suffering it causes is less than the threshold for torture. As the European Court has recapitulated in *Selmouni* v *France* (1999) 29 EHRR 403 at para. 96:

> In order to determine whether a particular form of ill-treatment should be qualified as torture, the Court must have regard to the distinction, embodied in Article 3, between this notion and that of inhuman or degrading treatment. . . . it appears that it was the intention that the Convention should, by means of this distinction, attach a special stigma to deliberate inhuman treatment causing very serious and cruel suffering.[13]

2.22 In the *Greek* case (1969) 12 YB 1 the former European Commission determined that 'deliberate' meant not merely the deliberate infliction of the physical or mental acts causing the suffering, but also the intention to provoke or cause such suffering. Torture cannot, therefore, arise by mere oversight, or be the unintended by-product of another act. Acts or omissions that simply cause intense physical or mental suffering will however be inhuman treatment. Torture often takes the form of an aggravated assault and battery.[14]

2.23 Violence that is inflicted in self-defence, or to effect a lawful arrest or prevent a crime will not have been inflicted with the intention of causing suffering, but such violence must be strictly necessary in all the circumstances and is prohibited once a person is taken into custody.[15] There is no scope for a defence

---

[13] See *Ireland* v *United Kingdom* (1978) 2 EHRR 25 at para. 167. There, reference was made to Article 1, Resolution 3452 adopted by the General Assembly of the UN on 9 December 1975 (the precursor to the United Nations Convention Against Torture 1984): 'Torture constitutes an *aggravated* and deliberate form of cruel, inhuman or degrading treatment or punishment.'

[14] See e.g. *Aksoy* v *Turkey* (1997) 23 EHRR 553 ('Palestinian hanging'); *Aydin* v *Turkey* (1997) 25 EHRR 51 (rape).

[15] See *Ribbitsch* v *Austria* (1995) 21 EHRR 573 at para. 38; concurring opinion of Judge de Meyer in *Tomasi* v *France* (1992) 15 EHRR 1; *Sur* v *Turkey* (Commission Report 3.9.96) (paragraph 43). However compare *Raninen* v *Finland* (1997) 26 EHRR 563 paras. 56 and 57, where the government conceded that handcuffing had not been strictly necessary but the European Court considered the effects were not sufficiently serious to give rise to a violation of Article 3; see also *Selmouni* v *France* (1999) 29 EHRR 403.

that inhuman treatment can be legitimately applied to obtain information to prevent a future outrage or relieve the sufferings of others.[16] Once a person has been taken into custody in apparent good health, there is a burden on the authorities to investigate diligently with a view to prosecution and compensation for the victims and their families, any death or injury caused in detention (*Aksoy* v *Turkey* (1997) 23 EHRR 553). A similar duty arises with respect to the use of lethal force in anti-terrorist operations (*McCann* v *UK* (1996) 21 EHRR 97; *Jordan* v *UK* (4 May 2001)). Where injuries have been found on a person who was unharmed on detention there is a duty on the state to explain the injuries consistent with there having been no violation (*Aksoy* v *Turkey* (1997)). This means that where force has been used it must be no more than was absolutely necessary in all the circumstances (*Ribbitsch* v *Austria* (1995)). A failure to provide an explanation or produce relevant documentary material to prove or disprove the claim will lead the European Court to conclude that the claim has not been rebutted (*Timurtas* v *Turkey* (13 June 2000)).

2.24 We have seen that intent to cause suffering is an important component part of the definition of torture. It is not *necessary* to demonstrate a particular motive however. Thus in *Aydin* v *Turkey* (1997) 25 EHRR 251, paras. 85 and 86 a finding of torture where a woman was raped whilst in custody by a state official was not precluded simply because there was no evidence that the suffering was inflicted with the direct objective of acquiring information. The severity of the harm and intention to cause it were the essential touchstones. By contrast in *Ireland* v *UK* (1978) 2 EHRR 25, para. 167 there was no dispute that the five techniques of interrogation (wall standing, hooding, subjection to noise, sleep deprivation and deprivation of food and drink) were systematically used to extract information, but they did not amount to torture because the level of suffering caused was not sufficiently cruel or intense. The European Court held that those five techniques amounted only to inhuman and degrading treatment. We consider that in the light of developing standards and the decision in *Selmouni* v *France* (2000) 29 EHRR 403, it is unlikely that the same conclusion on torture would be reached today.[17]

2.25 Frequently as part of the scrutiny of the facts the European Court will carefully examine any evidence as to why such actions are undertaken, and motive may be relevant. Thus in one British case, the Court of Appeal agreed that a mere

---

[16] This is clear from the European Court's reference to the absolute character of the obligation.

[17] See below at 2.40. At paragraph 167 of its judgment the European Court in *Ireland* v *UK* (1978) 2 EHRR 25 described the five techniques in the following terms: 'The five techniques were applied in combination, with premeditation and for hours at a stretch; they caused, if not actual bodily injury, at least intense physical and mental suffering to the persons subjected thereto and also led to acute psychiatric disturbances during interrogation. . . . They were such as to arouse in their victims feelings of fear, anguish and inferiority capable of humiliating and debasing them and possibly breaking their physical and moral resistance.'

assault would not ordinarily be torture by itself, but even comparatively minor physical force could be said to be torture if used for the purpose of extracting information in circumstances likely to put the person in fear *R v Secretary of State for the Home Department, ex parte Singh* (3 March 2000) per Roch LJ.[18] The deliberate use of violence by security agencies in order to obtain information is thus a material factor in the classification of the treatment, but it is not part of the definition.[19] In *Selmouni v France* (2000) 29 EHRR 403 at para. 98 the European Court noted:

> The course of the events also shows that pain and suffering were inflicted on the applicant intentionally for the purpose of, *inter alia*, making him confess to the offence which he was suspected of having committed.

By contrast where the injuries are not of the greatest severity and there is some doubt as to the surrounding circumstances the absence of a motive to extract a confession is relevant in the treatment falling short of torture.[20]

2.26 There is no requirement in the ECHR (a) that torture or inhuman or degrading treatment has to be inflicted by or with the acquiescence of a state official or (b) that the treatment be inflicted for a particular purpose. We suggest that evidence of deliberate sadistic treatment without any apparent ulterior motive would not preclude a finding of torture. This state of affairs contrasts with the definition of torture under the United Nations Convention Against Torture that we examine below at 2.54 et seq.[21] Doubtless, torture is usually an abuse of official authority in some form; whilst this is a sufficient or relevant consideration, it is not a mandatory one. The European Court has expressly determined that inhuman treatment does not have to emanate from the state (*HLR v France* (1997) 26 EHRR 29), and similar reasoning should apply to torture.

Inhuman treatment

2.27 Inhuman treatment is conduct that causes substantial mental or physical suffering but is not intended to have that effect or otherwise does not reach the standards of severity of torture. In practice, the European Court tends to examine

---

[18] See also *R v Special Adjudicator ex parte Singh* [1999] INLR 632, 637.

[19] See *Ireland v UK* (1978) 2 EHRR 25, para. 167; *Greek* case (1969) 12 YB 1. See the different emphasis in *Ireland v UK* (1978). See *Ireland v UK* (1978) 2 EHRR 25 for Sir Gerald Fitzmaurice's conclusion that a specific purpose was not necessary for torture. See further *Denizi v Cyprus* (23 May 2002), where the European Court held that ill-treatment and beating of detainees did not amount to torture since it had not been shown to be for the purposes of extracting confessions. See also *Egmez v Turkey* (21 December 2000) and *Peers v Greece* (2001) 33 EHRR 51 (poor prison conditions not torture).

[20] Note however *Denizi v Cyprus* (23 May 2001, above at footnote 19).

[21] Contrast also Criminal Justice Act 1988, s. 134(1).

first whether the conduct in question is inhuman, before considering whether the particular level of severity and cruelty has been reached to constitute torture.[22] Assaults that do not reach the severity of torture such as a threat of torture (*Campbell and Cosans* v *UK* (1982) 4 EHRR 293), psychological interrogation techniques (*Ireland* v *UK* (1978) 2 EHRR 25), and the deprivation of food and water to detainees (*Cyprus* v *Turkey* 4 EHRR 482 at 541) have all been considered inhuman treatment.

2.28 Such treatment may take subtler forms such as the deliberate causing of mental suffering to relatives of dead or missing persons or detainees, by insulting and threatening them or by failing to investigate the loss of their close relatives. In the case of *Kurt* v *Turkey* (1998) 27 EHRR 373[23] the European Court cited with approval the submissions of Amnesty International that the phenomenon of 'disappearances' was a form of harm that the international community had recognized as torture or inhuman treatment that continued as long as the grievances were unacknowledged. Suppression of a right to protest about these disappearances also perpetuated this ill-treatment. This approach was repeated in the case of *Timurtas* v *Turkey* (13 June 2000) where the callous disregard of the authorities for the concerns of relatives, and the prolongation of the anguish by denial of the truth, all led to a finding of a violation of Article 3.

Degrading treatment

2.29 Degrading treatment is treatment that humiliates or debases (*Tyrer* v *UK* (1970) 2 EHRR 1, para. 30). While one of the factors the European Court considers is whether the object of the treatment was to humiliate and debase, the absence of any such purpose does not rule out a finding of a violation.[24] Again there must be a minimum level of severity. Conduct that arouses in the victim a feeling of fear, anguish and inferiority is capable of humiliating and debasing the victim and possibly breaking his physical or moral resistance. The question is whether a person of the applicant's sex, age and sensibilities would be humiliated. The test is thus dependent on the victim rather than a universal standard.

2.30 The 'shuttlecocking' of asylum seekers, where the individual is repeatedly removed to a state which rejects responsibility for the claim and refuses admission, may amount to degrading treatment.[25] Equally issues may arise under

---

[22] See *Selmouni* v *France* (2000) 29 EHRR 403 and see below at 2.44.

[23] See also the decision of the Inter-American Court of Human Rights in *Velasquez Rodriguez* (1988) Series C, No. 49 HRLJ 212. See also *Cakici* v *Turkey* (App. No. 23657/94, 8 July 1999); *Akdeniz* v *Turkey* (App. No. 23954/94, 31 July 2001); *Tas* v *Turkey* (App. No. 24396/94, 14 November 2000).

[24] See *Peers* v *Greece* (2001) 33 EHRR 51, paras. 67 and 68 and *Price* v *UK* (2001) *The Times*, 13 August.

[25] See *Giama* v *Belgium* 21 DR 73; *Z* v *Netherlands* 38 DR 145; *Harabi* v *Netherlands* 46 DR 112.

Article 3 where the refusal of admission in the receiving state occurs because the identity of the deportee cannot be established (*Giama* v *Belgium* 21 DR 73; *Harabi* v *Netherlands* 46 DR 112). Where the ambiguity as to identity arises solely because of lack of co-operation by the individual, such as where different nationalities are advanced to the authorities, responsibility for the consequences of repeated deportation to different countries cannot be ascribed to the expelling state (*Z* v *Netherlands* 38 DR 145).[26]

2.31   The illegitimate infringement of human dignity is important. Aggravating features will include humiliation linked to a person's racial origin. In *East African Asians* v *UK* (1981) 3 EHRR 76 (followed by the European Court in *Cyprus* v *Turkey* (10 May 2001) paras. 304–309) the European Commission observed:

> special importance should be attached to discrimination based on race; publicly to single out a group of persons for differential treatment based on race might, in certain circumstances, constitute a special form of affront to human dignity, and that differential treatment of a group of persons on the basis of race might therefore be capable of constituting degrading treatment when differential treatment on some other ground would raise no such question.

2.32   The statement has to be seen in the context of legislation that denied British nationals a right to enter their country of nationality at a time when they were being expelled from the country of residence. The European Commission found that the consequent insecurity and denial of responsibility combined with the implicitly racist basis of distinguishing between citizens of the United Kingdom and colonies cumulatively exceeded the minimum level of severity that must exist for the conduct in question to violate the standards of Article 3.

2.33   This does not mean that every occasion of racial discrimination is ipso facto degrading treatment. Most such issues naturally fall to be considered under Article 14 and the new UK legislation outlawing discrimination in the field of immigration. In *Abdulaziz* v *UK* (1985) 7 EHRR 471[27] the European Court did not find a violation of Article 3 where immigration rules for the admission of spouses made distinctions on the grounds of gender or ancestral connection with the UK. It concluded that:

> the difference of treatment complained of did not denote any contempt or lack of respect for the personality of the applicants and that it was not designed to, and did not, humiliate or debase, but was intended solely to achieve the aims of [maintaining a firm immigration control].

---

[26] See also *R* v *Secretary of State, ex parte Andries* (10 December 1999) (immigration limbo caused by contradictions in applicant's account not unlawful).

[27] See also paras 84 to 86; see also below at 6.7.

Inhuman or degrading punishment

2.34   Where the infliction of a punishment lawful under domestic law is concerned, the European Court's task of characterization itself involves a balance between the interests of the community and those of the victim of the treatment (*Soering* v *UK* (1989) 11 EHRR 439). It will consider the method of punishment: severe punishments such as flogging will be considered disproportionate and unacceptable in a modern society (*Tyrer* v *UK* (1970) 2 EHRR 1; *Jabari* v *Turkey* [2001] INLR 136). The effect on the victim is important, since not all victims can be assumed to be of equal stamina and endurance. The duration of the punishment, and the possibility of release from prison when the offender has served a penal part of the sentence and is no longer considered a threat to society are relevant to whether the punishment is inhuman and degrading.[28] The European Court reviewed the principles in *T and V* v *UK* (2000) 30 EHRR 121 where it concluded that prosecuting 10-year-olds was not contrary to Article 3, but detaining them indefinitely without a fair procedure to secure their release on rehabilitation would be.[29] At the other end of the scale, the European Court has had to deal with elderly war criminals in cases against the UK and France, and concluded that the enormity of the crimes justified the detention even at such an advanced age (*Sawoniuk* v *UK* (29 May 2001); *Papon* v *France* (7 June 2001).

2.35   For there to be a violation the consequence of the punishment must be over and above that inherent in the legitimate purpose of the punishment itself.[30] Disciplinary measures relating to detention and solitary confinement, and the system for review, will be considered in the context of the proportionality of these measures to the legitimate aims, on the one hand and the conduct of the particular individual on the other.

2.36   In certain circumstances, the state has a positive duty to ensure that private persons do not use inhuman or degrading treatment. Thus a state may be required to outlaw corporal punishment in school (*Costello-Roberts* v *UK* (1995) 19 EHRR 112), or legislate to restrict the scope of the reasonable chastisement defence relied on by a parent as a defence to assault (*A* v *UK* (1999) 27 EHRR

---

[28]   But see *B, H and L* v *Austria* 64 DR 264 at 271 (Article 3 cannot be interpreted to require a procedure for remission, but the applicant had not established that there was no hope of release following extradition and conviction in USA).

[29]   See also *Weeks* v *UK* (1988) 10 EHRR 293; *Hussain and Singh* v *UK* (1996) 22 EHRR 1.

[30]   See *Altun* v *Germany* 36 DR 209 para. 8 (Article 3 may apply where extradition request under colour of ordinary law used to prosecute in breach of the specialty rule for political offences or because of individual's political opinion. European Commission required to assess risk of unjustified or disproportionate sentence being passed); *A* v *Switzerland* 46 DR 257 (extradition to Turkey for political offences); *C* v *FRG* 46 DR 176 (expulsion of an applicant facing a 10-year sentence for refusing to undertake military service in Yugoslavia was held by the European Commission not to raise any issue under Article 3).

611). The nature of these positive obligations should not be confused with the negative obligation not to expose the claimant to harm of a sufficient severity to contravene Article 3 whoever is the agent inflicting the harm.

ABSOLUTE NATURE OF THE OBLIGATION

2.37 Article 3 encompasses one of the core values of the ECHR: an absolute duty not to subject someone to torture or inhuman or degrading treatment.[31] The abysmal history of human rights violations in Europe and elsewhere in the twentieth century has demonstrated that disrespect for human dignity and discriminatory denial of human rights is a process whereby unequal treatment can move through a spectrum of gravity until perpetrators of torture believe they are justified in using terrible methods of causing pain and mutilation on their victims. Torture is the activity at the extreme end of this spectrum.

2.38 In many ways torture is a more serious matter than death, which may be unintended, not premeditated, and undiscriminating in its general impact.[32] Torture may be prolonged, repeated and extremely painful and debilitating, whereas death may be comparatively speedy and painless. There is the paradox that on the existing case law it is not a violation of Article 2 to execute someone, but it may be a violation of Article 3 to expose them to physical and mental suffering whilst awaiting execution. As we have seen, Article 2 is not in terms absolute in scope; apart from preserving the death penalty as a permissible punishment, it contemplates other circumstances in which loss of life might be justified, including the saving of the lives of others.[33] The prohibition on Article 3 is subject to no exception or exclusion.

2.39 Neither Article 2 nor Article 3, nor indeed Article 4 (prohibition on slavery) nor Article 7 (prohibition on retrospective criminal penalties) is one from which a derogation can ever be made, even in wartime or at other moments of national emergency (Article 15(2), ECHR). There can be no justifiable torture or inhuman or degrading treatment. In *Soering* v *UK* (1989) 11 EHRR 439 the European Court did refer to a balance between the interests of society and those of the individual, but that was in the context of determining whether the lawful punishment in question led to consequences that were inhuman or degrading. Once the frontiers of its applicability have been mapped, Article 3 permits no

---

[31] See *Chahal* v *UK* (1996) 23 EHRR 413.

[32] On 14 December 2000 the case of *Ocalan* v *Turkey* (App. No. 46221/99, 14 December 2000) was declared admissible where the European Court will have to consider whether the death penalty per se is a violation of Article 3 when employed in a contracting state, as well as issues relating to Articles 2, 6 and 8.

[33] See the reference to Article 2 in the Siamese twins case: *In re A (Children) (Conjoined Twins)* [2001] 2 WLR 480, at 537, 544, 571, 589.

balance of competing interests and no considerations of proportionality or margin of appreciation. In *Ravichandran* v *Secretary of State for the Home Department* [1996] Imm AR 97, when considering the meaning of refugee status, Staughton LJ suggested that persecution involved persistent and unjustified ill-treatment. It is highly unlikely that the Court of Appeal was considering that there could be such a thing as justified ill-treatment, and certainly there can be no such concept in the field of Article 3. It thus lends itself to a norm of universal application, prohibited irrespective of the particular circumstances in which a person may be subject to its provisions.[34] The European Court repeated its jurisprudence in *Selmouni* v *France* (1999) 29 EHRR 403 at paragraph 95 in the following terms:

> The Court reiterates that Article 3 enshrines one of the most fundamental values of democratic societies. Even in the most difficult circumstances, such as the fight against terrorism and organised crime, the Convention prohibits in absolute terms torture or inhuman or degrading treatment or punishment. Unlike most of the substantive clauses of the Convention and of Protocols Nos. 1 and 4, Article 3 makes no provision for exceptions and no derogation from it is permissible under Article 15(2) even in the event of a public emergency threatening the life of the nation.

2.40   The absolute nature of the prohibition was most clearly established in *Chahal* v *UK* (1996) 23 EHRR 413. The Secretary of State sought to deport a suspected Sikh militant on the grounds that he represented a danger to the national security of the United Kingdom. The UK argued that whereas a contracting state could not seek to justify the infliction of torture or inhuman or degrading treatment within its own state on grounds of national security, the position was different if it had compelling reasons to expel a foreign national and the assessment of the risk of ill-treatment as a consequence of the expulsion was difficult and uncertain. The European Court rejected this reasoning. Where the threshold test for preventing an expulsion was met, the reasons prompting the expulsion were irrelevant. The prohibition on the expulsion was absolute and the protection extended significantly further than the non-*refoulement* provision of the UN Refugee Convention.

2.41   The UK government did not seek to argue Article 17 of the ECHR in this context, despite the gravity of the unproven allegations made against the victim. Article 17 precludes the ECHR being interpreted so as to imply a right by a person to engage in any activity or perform any act aimed at the destruction of any rights and freedoms set forth herein. It is possible that, in proven cases, Article 17 may have some impact in limiting the rights of racists and terrorists to operate with impunity in threatening the lives and freedoms of others (*Lehideur*

---

[34] See *R* v *Bow Street Magistrate ex parte Pinochet Ugarte* [2000] 1 AC 61, 147.

and Isorni v *France* (1998) 5 BHRC 540 (holocaust denial)). The European Court's absolute rejection of any diminution of the protection of Article 3, however, would preclude it from applying Article 17 to justify exposure to torture or inhuman treatment or punishment. There are other ways of protecting the safety of the realm than by exposing alleged terrorists to torture abroad.

2.42 The prohibition on torture has almost certainly now reached the status of *jus cogens*, a binding obligation in international customary law, irrespective of treaty obligations voluntarily adhered to. Treaties such as the 1984 UN Convention Against Torture are to be read as imposing special obligations on states to prevent torture and secure the effective apprehension and punishment of those who perpetuate it. In *R* v *Secretary of State for the Home Department, ex parte Pinochet Ugarte (No. 3)* [1999] 2 WLR 827 AT 841 Lord Browne-Wilkinson referred to torture as a peremptory norm of international law which may be punished by any state. The Treaty is thus a reflection of developing international norms rather than the source of a novel obligation to desist from the activity of torture in the first place.

2.43 Torture is moreover essentially recognizable in whatever society it takes place. In the paradigm case, the severe ill-treatment of suspects in state custody is torture, whatever the sophistication of the technique or lack of it. There is no room for debate about cultural relativity when dealing with electrocution, attempts to suffocate, Palestinian hanging, the administering of *falaka* or other forms of beating, sexual assaults on suspects and the like. It is pertinent to note that by 1949, the Geneva Conventions relating to the treatment of prisoners of war and civilians at the time of international armed conflict, prohibited the infliction of 'violence to life and person, murder of all kinds, mutilation, cruel treatment and torture . . . outrages upon personal dignity, inhuman and degrading treatment'.[35] These were the standards expected from a belligerent power towards enemy nationals in time of war. It was a reasonable step to demand that a civilized state did not cause foreign nationals to be exposed to similar treatment by others.

INCREMENTAL AND UPDATING APPROACH

2.44 Findings that torture has been used by the state were rare, and until the 1990s the only such conclusion was by the former European Commission in the *Greek* case (1969) 12 YB 1. Controversially, the European Court overturned a powerful decision of the former European Commission in the case of *Ireland* v *UK* (1978) 2 EHRR 25 (and see above at 2.24 and footnote 17) where five techniques of interrogation of internees short of actual battery were used. It is unlikely

---

[35] Geneva Convention Relative to Prisoners of War 1949 III and also Geneva Convention IV (Civilians) Article 3(1).

that a court reviewing similar facts today would have been content with the conclusion that the techniques were inhuman treatment but not torture. First, there is greater awareness of the adverse psychological effects of interrogation. Secondly, standards advance and expectations of civilized behaviour by states are raised.

2.45   In *Tommasi* v *France* (1993) 15 EHRR 1 an assault on a suspect in a police station by punching slapping and kicking was held to be contrary to Article 3 as inhuman treatment. In *Selmouni* v *France* (1999) 29 EHRR 403 a few years later, the European Court revisited this question and held that serious violence in a police station was sufficiently severe to constitute torture. It established first that the degree of violence administered was clearly sufficient to constitute inhuman treatment and continued:

> 100. . . . it remains to establish in the instant case whether the 'pain or suffering' inflicted on Mr Selmouni can be defined as 'severe' within the meaning of Article 1 of the United Nations Convention. The Court considers that this 'severity' is, like the 'minimum severity' required for the application of Article 3, in the nature of things, relative; it depends on all the circumstances of the case, such as the duration of the treatment, its physical or mental effects and, in some cases, the sex, age and state of health of the victim, etc.

> 101. . . . having regard to the fact that the Convention is a 'living instrument which must be interpreted in the light of present-day conditions' . . . the Court considers that certain acts which were classified in the past as 'inhuman and degrading treatment' as opposed to 'torture' could be classified differently in future. It takes the view that the increasingly high standard being required in the area of the protection of human rights and fundamental liberties correspondingly and inevitably requires greater firmness in assessing breaches of the fundamental values of democratic societies . . .

2.46   Applying an updating and living instrument approach, the European Court concluded that the evidence of persistent assaults throughout a prolonged period in police custody

> committed against the applicant's person caused 'severe' pain and suffering and was particularly serious and cruel. Such conduct must be regarded as acts of torture for the purposes of Article 3 of the Convention.

2.47   The same principles apply to what is inhuman treatment. Classification of treatment as inhuman will depend on social developments and the elaboration of particular standards by the international community. Corporal punishment in schools would doubtless not have been considered inhuman or degrading in 1950, but in the case of *Tyrer* v *UK* (1978) 2 EHRR 1 was considered objectionable as a form of punishment irrespective of parental consent to the application of such treatment in state schools. Social developments are reflected in the elaboration of Human Rights Conventions such as the International Covenant on Civil and Political Rights 1966, the UN International Convention on the Elimination of All Forms of Racial Discrimination 1966, the UN Convention on the Elimination of All Forms of Discrimination against Women 1979, the UN Convention Against Torture 1984, and the UN Convention on the Rights of the Child 1989. The European Court has regard to internationally accepted standards when developing the ECHR incrementally. It will also pay particular attention to social and political developments in the Council of Europe. Potentially inter-state agreements such as the European Social Charter and the decisions of the Parliamentary Assembly of the Council of Europe can influence the direction of the jurisprudence, although they are not directly enforceable by the European Court or the British courts under the HRA 1998.[36]

2.48 The question of whether the conduct is torture or inhuman treatment or punishment is thus resolved on a case by case basis in the light of all the circumstances. The principal questions relevant to the classification will be the seriousness of the injury caused, the period of time over which the treatment was inflicted, the degree of control exercised over the victim, the degree of pre-planning and pre-meditated harm, the use of instruments or particularly cruel forms of injury, accompanying threats and abuse, the targeting of racial or religious minorities, the deliberate exploitation of vulnerability, the use of sexual abuse particularly on women, the age and state of health of the victim and its effect on him or her. We have already noted that the intense suffering required may be mental and psychological rather than physical. Deliberate creation of anguish caused by threats to family members or announcement of pending execution may well be torture. A deliberate failure to investigate a claim of death of a relative or put the family out of the agony of suspense may also amount to torture (see above at 2.21).

EXPULSION CASES AND THE DEATH PENALTY

2.49 In the landmark case of *Soering v UK* (1989) 11 EHRR 439, the European Court had to consider whether a German national held in the United Kingdom on an extradition warrant to the US state of Virginia for the murder of his girlfriend's parents faced inhuman treatment or punishment. The Virginia prosecutor intended to charge Soering with capital murder and seek the death penalty. The

---

[36] See for example the approach of the European Court in the transsexual cases of *Rees v UK* (1986) 9 EHRR 56; *Cossey v UK* (1991) 13 EHRR 622; *B v France* (1993) 16 EHRR 1; *XYZ v UK* (1997) 24 EHRR 143; and *Sheffield and Horsham v UK* (1999) 27 EHRR 163. International policy of the treatment of the AIDS epidemic was cited to the Commission and the Court in the case of *D v UK* (1997) 24 EHRR 423. *Sepet and Bulbul v Secretary of State* [2001] INLR 376 Court of Appeal.

state of Virginia was not directly bound by the terms of the extradition treaty between the UK and the USA that permitted the UK to withhold extradition in the absence of assurances from the US State Department that the death penalty would not be implemented.[37] The direct route of declaring the death penalty unlawful as a violation to the right of life was not permissible given the express exemption in Article 2. For similar reasons, the European Court was unable to conclude that the death penalty per se was inhuman punishment, as there would be a conflict between Articles 2 and 3. Instead the European Court went on to consider whether the death row phenomenon was inhuman treatment by way of prolonging the agony of suspense, and occasioning acute mental suffering over a prolonged period of time. The evidence was that a person sentenced to death would languish for many years in death row pending appeals before finally learning whether he was to be executed or have the sentence commuted. The European Court also noted the age and mental state of the applicant and referred to the International Covenant on Civil and Political Rights and the American Convention on Human Rights, both of which prohibit the visitation of the death penalty on persons aged less than 18 at the time of the offence. The European Court concluded that such treatment was contrary to Article 3, overruling the earlier decision of the Commission in *Kirkwood* v *UK* 37 DR 158.

2.50   Three observations should be made about this case. First, it was decided at a time before the United Kingdom had acceded to the Sixth Protocol to the ECHR. The answer to any future case where a person may be returned to face judicial execution is now much simpler to resolve. During the passage of the HRA 1998, Parliament included the Sixth Protocol to the ECHR as part of the corpus of ECHR rights to be respected by a public authority in the United Kingdom, even though at the time the UK had not ratified this Protocol of the ECHR. Article 1 of the Sixth Protocol provides 'The death penalty shall be abolished.' By itself this would only be directed to the law of the contracting state or any overseas territories for which a contracting state is responsible. However, the Article continues 'No one *shall be condemned* to such penalty or executed' (our emphasis). This is much wider. By analogy with the case law on Article 3, it must mean that the contracting state must not cause anyone to be executed by surrendering them to a territory or state where there are substantial grounds to conclude that there is a real risk that such a consequence could follow. Further, it is not sufficient that the sentence of a condemned man may be commuted, even pursuant to a long standing convention on the exercise of the prerogative of mercy. The Protocol provides that no one is to be sentenced to death. In the case

---

[37] The European Court considered that the assurances given by the US federal government and accepted by the state authorities that in practice the death penalty would not be carried out, were insufficient to remove the real risk that the applicant would be subject to the death row phenomenon.

of *Jin* v *Hungary* (App. No. 58073/00, 6 November 2000)[38] a Chinese national faced capital charges in China, and the European Court declared the application admissible notwithstanding the fact that the Hungarian authorities had obtained an assurance from the Chinese government that the death sentence would not be imposed or, if imposed, would not be carried out.

2.51 In the future it is suggested that extradition is only possible to states that retain the death penalty, if a binding and effective assurance is given that the death penalty will not be sought at all.[39] The European Court will no longer have to engage in the intellectual gymnastics of whether a suspension of execution is inhuman treatment. This proposition will apply with equal strength to a case of deportation or expulsion where there is a risk of capital punishment being pronounced or carried out. It may therefore be argued that a state that has ratified the Sixth Protocol has removed the exemption to the right to life contained in Article 2(1).

2.52 Secondly, even without the intervention of the Sixth Protocol, the application of the death sentence may be outside the proviso to Article 2(1) if the law permitting it is arbitrary, uncertain, disproportionate, or applied following a trial that does not meet internationally acceptable standards of fairness. The case law in Europe remains undeveloped because the Western European states have been de facto or de jure abolitionists for many years. The concept of 'law' in Article 2(1) is an autonomous concept that is defined by the European Court and not every domestic pronouncement will have the character of law. It is highly unlikely that the European Court would permit lesser standards than those developed by the Human Rights Committee under Article 6 and 14 of the International Covenant on Civil and Political Rights 1966. We would also suggest that the treatment or punishment may be a violation of Article 2(1) if the sentence was not reserved for the most serious offences, if there was no fair trial in the presence of the defendant with effective representation,[40] a right of appeal or to seek commutation of the sentence in the light of any mitigating circumstances.

2.53 Thirdly, the punishment of death may be inhuman treatment despite the terms of Article 2, depending on the form of capital punishment used and the method of its implementation. Thus in the case of *Jabari* v *Turkey* [2001] INLR 136 the European Court concluded that the proposed expulsion of an Iranian woman from Turkey would involve a violation of Article 3 where the applicant feared the infliction of the Islamic punishments of flogging or stoning to death for

---

[38] See also *Dehwari* v *Netherlands* (2000) 29 EHRR CD 74 and the criticism of this Commission decision in *Kacaj* v *Secretary of State for the Health Department* [2001] INLR 354.

[39] See e.g. *Aylor Davis* v *France* 76-B DR 164 (assurances from USA authorities accepted).

[40] See e.g. DR v France 76-A DR 174 (death sentence imposed in absentia by Algerian authorities; French authorities agreed not to expel applicant).

adultery. In the case of *Ocalan* v *Turkey* (App. No. 46221/99, 14 December 2000) the European Court declared the case admissible and may well have to decide whether the death penalty is itself inhuman or degrading. This would require the *Soering* case to be revisited in the light of subsequent international developments and in particular the landmark decision of the South African Constitutional Court in *Makwanyane* v *the State* [1995] LRC 269, where the South African court concluded that the death penalty was in itself unconstitutional as amounting to torture and inhuman and degrading treatment. The Inter-American Commission on Human Rights has concluded that the death penalty can amount to an arbitrary violation of the right to life in a sequence of cases starting with *Baptiste* v *Grenada*.[41]

THE UN CONVENTION AGAINST TORTURE 1984

2.54   The United Nations Convention Against Torture and Other Cruel, Inhuman or Degrading Treatment or Punishment 1984 came into force on 26 June 1987. Communications about non-compliance are addressed to the United Nations Committee Against Torture (UNCAT). This Convention is specifically concerned with state acts. Article 1 states:

> 1. For the purposes of this Convention, the term 'torture' means any act by which severe pain or suffering, whether physical or mental, is intentionally inflicted on a person for such purposes as obtaining from him or a third person information or a confession, punishing him for an act he or a third person has committed or is suspected of having committed, or intimidating or coercing him or a third person, or for any reason based on discrimination of any kind, when such pain or suffering is inflicted by or at the instigation of or with the consent or acquiescence of a public official or other person acting in an official capacity . . .

Article 16, paragraph 1 states:

> Each State Party shall undertake to prevent in any territory under its jurisdiction other acts of cruel, inhuman or degrading treatment or punishment which do not amount to torture as defined in Article 1, when such acts are committed by or at the instigation of or with the consent or acquiescence of a public official or other person acting in an official capacity . . .

2.55   The UN Convention Against Torture provides a narrower definition of torture than the ECHR in respect of both state acquiescence and motivation. The

---

[41] The Inter-American Court of Human Rights will consider this question in the cases of *Hilaire, Constantine and Benjamin* v *State of Trinidad and Tobago*. (Admissibility Decision 15 September 2001; Commission decision confirmed by the court, July 2002).

decisions of UNCAT should be applied with some care to Article 3 of the ECHR therefore. Nevertheless the approach of UNCAT to the assessment of risk within the field of application of the UN Convention Against Torture provides some helpful guidance to the resolution of ECHR problems. The European Court takes particular account of this jurisprudence and attempts to develop its case law in line with comparable international developments.[42]

2.56 The UN Committee Against Torture has indicated that in deciding whether there are substantial grounds for believing that someone would be in danger of being subjected to torture upon return to another country, a general pattern of human rights abuse and violations is relevant but not determinative. The aim of the decision is to establish whether a person would be personally at risk. One can have a general pattern of abuse and no personal risk and vice versa.[43] This is an approach reflected in the European Court decisions of *Vilvarajah* v *UK* (1991) 14 EHRR 248 and *Vijaynathan* v *France* (1993) 15 EHRR 62 where the risks were considered general and not specific to an individual.

2.57 However, doubts about credibility and unexplained inconsistencies do not diminish the existence of substantial grounds for fearing a personal risk where the objective medical evidence shows past torture and there is a continuing present pattern of abuse (*Matumbo* v *Switzerland* (1994) 15 HRLJ 164). A similar approach was adopted by the European Commission in the case of *Hatami* v *Sweden* 27 EHRR CD 8.[44] In contrast to refugee decisions where the case law has tended to emphasize the need for a genuinely held fear and credibility has been the principal focus of decision makers,[45] expulsion to torture or inhuman or degrading treatment is based more on an objective consideration of risk.

2.58 This approach has been adopted in *Hilal* v *UK* (2001) 33 EHRR 2. This was a case where a claim for asylum from Tanzania was rejected on credibility grounds, and both leave to appeal to the IAT and a fresh hearing were refused when fresh evidence was obtained to address the defects in credibility. The UK government then switched tack to allege that in any event there was a safe haven

---

[42] See *Al Adsani* v *UK* (App. No. 35763/97, 21 November 2001) where, by a majority of one, the UK rules against suing a foreign sovereign for torture committed abroad were upheld as being consistent with the ECHR.

[43] See Communication No. 96/1997 against the Netherlands CAT/c/23/d/96/1977, 24 January 2000, para. 7.2. CAT decisions can be found on its website at www.unhchr.ch/tbs.

[44] Here the former European Commission held that the domestic authorities had not established the facts correctly and that the applicant's deportation to Iran would violate Article 3.

[45] See for example *Mbanza* v *Secretary of State* [1996] 1 WLR 507 but note *Gashi* v *Secretary of State* [1997] INLR 96 at 110 and *Ramirez* v *Secretary of State* [2001] EWCA Civ 1365 at para. 11, quoting the IAT decision to the effect that the requirement of 'fear' in the refugee definition did not connote a condition of foreboding, but rather of apprehension, otherwise it was difficult to see how child claimants, or for that matter those mentally impaired by ill-treatment, could ever satisfy the definition.

in the country, despite the fact that human rights observers and the IAT had concluded that political activists from Zanzibar were not safe in mainland Tanzania. The European Court found that removal would violate Article 3 and based its decision on the objective evidence that the government had not rebutted or shown to be false. Despite the successive catalogue of denial of judicial remedies, it however found that judicial review was an effective remedy for the purposes of Article 13 (see further below at 5.126 et seq, 5.144).

2.59   The Human Rights Committee under the ICCPR has decided that the risk of expulsion is not obviated by the mere grant of a temporary permit with no expectation that it will be renewed as long as the risk exists.[46] This develops the European Court's concept of the continuing nature of victim status.[47]

2.60   Articles 1 and 16 of the UN Convention Against Torture confine torture or other forms of inhuman or degrading treatment to cases 'when such pain or suffering is inflicted by or at the instigation of or with the consent or acquiescence of a public official or other person acting in an official capacity'. This has given rise to debates over whether a particular group in society is acting as a state functionary in circumstances where no effective state may exist. The situation in Somalia has given rise to particular problems where it is universally recognized that there is no government in operation at all and therefore no official state functionaries who could commit violations of human rights.[48] In the case of *Elmi v Australia* [1999] INLR 341,[49] the state argued that no expulsion to Somalia could violate Article 3(1) of the UN Convention Against Torture as there was no state to whom torture within the meaning of Article 1 could be attributed. The UN Committee disagreed and stated at paragraph 6.5 ([1999] INLR 341 at 353):

> The Committee notes that for a number of years Somalia has been without a central government, that the international community negotiates with the warring factions and that some of the factions operating in Mogadishu have set up quasi-governmental institutions and are negotiating for the establishment of a common administration. It follows then that de facto those factions exercise certain prerogatives that are comparable to those normally exercised by legitimate governments. Accordingly the members of the factions can fall, for the purposes of the application of the Convention within the phrase 'public officials or other persons acting in an official capacity' contained in Article 1.

---

[46] See Communication No. 96/1997 para. 7.3 (above at footnote 43).

[47] In *Ahmed v Austria* (1997) 24 EHRR 278, Ahmed remained a victim, despite a temporary suspension of removal, without the grant of a residence permit.

[48] See e.g. *Republic of Somalia v Woodhouse Drake and Carey* [1993] QB 54.

[49] Note that the reports of UNCAT are available on its web site at http://www.unhchr.ch/tbsdoc. nsf/.

HARM BY NON-STATE AGENTS

2.61 By contrast to the UN Convention Against Torture, Article 3 of the ECHR requires no such state complicity. The European Court has avoided an over precise prescriptive definition which enables the instrument to be developed to give effective protection from serious harm, without the need for such forms of supplementary reasoning. The flexible approach of the European Court system allows incremental development on a case by case basis in the light of evolving standards without the need to resort to fictions such as 'de facto' authorities in cases where the state as such has collapsed and is no longer in existence. Similarly there is no need to define the limits of 'acquiescence' if the evidence established that the state is unable to prevent the harm in question for whatever reason.

2.62 The issue was directly raised in the case of *HLR* v *France* (1997) 26 EHRR 29,[50] where the applicant feared murder at the hands of the members of drug cartels after he had given information to the French police about drug trafficking. The European Court observed at para. 40:

Owing to the absolute character of the rights guaranteed, the Court does not rule out the possibility that Article 3 of the Convention may also apply where danger emanates from persons or groups of persons who are not public officials. However it must be shown that the risk is real and that the authorities of the receiving state are not able to obviate the risk by providing appropriate protection.

2.63 Five months earlier, the European Court had concluded in the case of *Ahmed* v *Austria* (1997) 24 EHRR 278 that the expulsion of a Somali national who had been recognized as a refugee in Austria but had lost that status following a conviction for a serious criminal offence would be contrary to Article 3, without having to consider the 'non-state agent point'. Some countries like Germany refused to follow the decision in *Ahmed* and the observations in *HLR*, and persisted in determining that both persecution under the Geneva Convention and risk of ill-treatment contrary to Article 3 required official acquiescence or participation.

2.64 In the case of *TI* v *UK* [2000] INLR 211 the European Court had to consider the case of a failed Tamil asylum seeker whom the United Kingdom proposed to return to Germany despite the fact that he feared ill-treatment at the hands of non-state agents. In its decision on admissibility the European Court heard argument from the German government in support of its views on non-state agents, but concluded (at p. 228):

---

[50] See also *YH* v *Germany* 51 DR 258; *Altun* v *Germany* 36 DR 209.

The Court's case law further indicates that the existence of [the obligation not to return in violation of Article 3] is not dependent on whether the source of the risk of the treatment stems from factors which involve the responsibility, direct or indirect, of the authorities of the receiving country. Having regard to the absolute character of the right guaranteed, Article 3 may extend to situations where the danger emanates from persons or group of persons who are not public officials, or from the consequences to health from the effect of serious illness. In any such case contexts, the Court must subject all the circumstances surrounding the case to a rigorous scrutiny.

2.65   The case law on Article 2, noted above, may be relevant to ascertain the level of protection a state should provide against ill-treatment by third parties. In the case of *Kaya v Turkey* (1999) 28 EHRR 1, the European Court had found that there was a violation of Article 2 in respect of a doctor who had been threatened for providing medical assistance to Kurds. The authorities knew or ought to have known that the doctor was at risk of being targeted and the failure to protect his life placed him in danger not only of extra-judicial execution but also of ill-treatment from persons who were unaccountable for their actions. The government was therefore responsible for the ill-treatment he suffered after his disappearance.

APPLICATION TO EXPULSIONS

Sufficiency of protection

2.66   The principal use of Article 3 in immigration and asylum cases will be to prevent expulsions not otherwise prohibited by the Refugee Convention to countries where the immigrant faces treatment contrary to the provisions of Article 3. The case law of the European Court has also been cited in the interpretation of the Refugee Convention itself and in particular whether there is a sufficiency of protection in the country of return.[51] Doubtless there is some value in considering whether a person will be ill treated by private persons if returned abroad in considering what the obligations of a state are in domestic and international law and how those obligations are discharged in practice.

2.67   It is, however, misleading for the scope of Article 3 in expulsion cases to be judged by whether another foreign state is in breach of its positive obligations to provide a practical level of protection (see, in particular, *R (A and others) v Lord Saville and others* [2002] 1 WLR 1249). This is not why Article 3 applies to expulsion cases. The courts have been at pains to point out that there is no extra territorial attribution of responsibility at all in such cases. As we have pointed out above at 1.17 et seq this is not strictly an extra territorial application of the ECHR, but an application of it to those plainly within the jurisdiction of the contracting

---

[51] Notably in the case of *Horvath v Secretary of State for the Home Department* [2001] 1 AC 489.

state who may well be harmed by its decision to remove. We are thus in the realm of assessment of future risks and not civil responsibility for historic wrongs, as was the case in *Osman*. It is thus necessary to examine why contracting states may be responsible for the harm caused by an intended or actual expulsion and see what kind of harm is embraced within the prohibition on Article 3.

2.68   It was not until the case of *Soering* v *UK* (1989) 11 EHRR 439 that the European Court endorsed the previous case law of the Commission and held that a decision to remove to another country could be contrary to Article 3 of the ECHR. This statement of principle was applied to failed refugee cases in *Cruz Varas* v *Sweden* (1992) 14 EHRR 1 and *Vilvarajah* v *United Kingdom* (1992) 14 EHRR 248. It led to the conclusion that return would be prohibited in the case of *Chahal* v *UK* (1996) 23 EHRR 413 and a sequence of following cases.[52]

2.69   The European Court in these cases refined the approach it has subsequently adopted. First, it examines the facts at the date of the expulsion or proposed expulsion and not just as of the initial decision to expel. This may require a review of changed circumstances and excludes an approach that limits protection claims to one occasion or a prescribed period of time.[53] The analysis may extend to after the expulsion has taken place. In *Mansi* v *Sweden* (App. No. 15658/89, 9 March 1990) a Jordanian Palestinian was removed to Jordan, in the face of a request by the former European Commission that the Swedish authorities postpone the expulsion. The applicant was subsequently tortured in Jordan and sought refuge in Denmark. By way of a friendly settlement, the Swedish authorities agreed to readmit the applicant.

2.70   Secondly, the European Court is not concerned with state responsibility for killing or deliberately administering torture but with the protection principle. Given the irreversible nature of the harm, the issue is not whether the state will cause the applicant to be ill treated, but whether there is a risk of such ill-treatment. The absolute and solemn nature of the obligation means it is not sufficient if there is a mere possibility of such a risk occurring; there have to be substantial grounds. The European Court thus asks the question 'are there substantial grounds for fearing a real risk of exposure to ill-treatment contrary to Article 3?'

2.71   Thirdly, the responsibility of the contracting state is engaged because of the foreseeable consequences of its own expulsion decision and not because of any extraterritorial application or vicarious liability for the acts (*TI* v *UK* [2000]

---

[52] *Ahmed* v *Austria* (1997) 24 EHRR 278; *HLR* v *France* (1997) 26 EHRR 29; *Hilal* v *UK* (2001) 33 EHRR 2; *Bensaid* v *UK* (2001) 33 EHRR 10; *MAR* v *UK* (App. No. 28038/95, 19 September 1997).
[53] The European Court is presently considering the case of *Amrollahi* v *Denmark* (App. No. 56811/00) where the applicant's subsequent appeal against expulsion to Iran following his drugs conviction was dismissed on the basis that he was only entitled to one appellate decision on the merits.

INLR 211 at 228) of others. In principle this responsibility remains the same even if the place of expulsion is a state that has responsibilities of its own under human rights conventions.

2.72 However, expulsion may be contrary to Article 3 even if the circumstances of the individual would not violate the receiving state's obligations. A significant development in the case law came with the case of *D v UK* where the European Court concluded that it may be inhuman to send someone to a country where urgently needed medical and social treatment is not available. This is not because there is necessarily any obligation on a state to provide such treatment, but because to remove someone who is receiving such treatment to a place where they cannot continue to receive it, may be contrary to the providing state's obligations to respect human dignity.[54] Even where the consequences of such deprivation of medical treatment may be life threatening, cases of expulsion to third countries have generally been reviewed by the European Court under Article 3, rather than Article 2 (*D v UK* 24 EHRR 423).[55]

2.73 Questions about the level of health care in a third country doubtless raise a complex number of considerations. The European Court does not want to develop the positive obligations to such an extent as to encourage migration to contracting states for the purpose of receiving health care superior to that which is available in the home state. Save in the most exceptional cases, it will be generally be more appropriate to examine health care cases in a broader spectrum ranging from respect for mental and physical integrity through to degrading treatment, rather than posing the extreme question of measures to preserve life under the provisions of Article 2.

Expulsions and denial of health care

2.74 In *D v UK* 24 EHRR 423 the applicant was a national of a small Caribbean island and had been diagnosed as suffering from an advanced state of AIDS after he had been sentenced to a substantial term of imprisonment for importing drugs. This infection pre-dated his arrival in the UK. He was deemed not to have entered the United Kingdom, though the European Court and the European Commission regarded this as a fiction in the light of his substantial physical presence here. The case was an unusual one in that it combined:

(a) a substantial period of time when the applicant was receiving treatment to suppress the deterioration of the immune system and substantial

---

[54] This is of course a fact-sensitive question: *X v Secretary of State* [2001] INLR 205, para. 14.

[55] A similar approach was adopted in *SCC v Sweden* (App. No. 46553/99, 15 February 2000), where the European Court examined the application of Articles 2 and 3 together.

prophylactic treatment to prevent his succumbing to secondary infection;

(b)   a threatened summary withdrawal of this treatment on which he had become dependent at the end of his sentence;

(c)   a complete absence of comparable medical facilities in his own country;

(d)   an absence of any effective social or family support enabling him to die with some dignity.

The European Court held that his expulsion would contravene Article 3. Although the European Court was mindful of the need to deter drug trafficking it repeated its conclusions that once Article 3 is engaged it cannot be diminished or balanced against sound reasons of social policy for the expulsion.

2.75   This decision has had a substantial effect on state practice in Europe and has led to policies being developed and implemented to prevent expulsion in similar cases. In the United Kingdom the instructions to the asylum directorate establish that exceptional leave to remain may be granted:

> where there is credible medical evidence that return due to the medical facilities in the country concerned would reduce the applicant's life expectancy and subject him to acute mental and physical suffering in circumstances where the UK can be regarded as having assumed responsibility for his care.[56]

2.76   *Tatete* v *Switzerland* (App. No. 41874/98, 6 July 2000) is an example of a more familiar kind of immigration case, without the complicating factor of serious crimes having been committed. The applicant, from the Democratic Republic of Congo, entered Switzerland illegally and was refused asylum. Shortly before her case was finally rejected, she was admitted to hospital and found to have AIDS and, in particular, to be suffering from pneumonia. In the hospital's view this meant that her return to her country of origin would have to be postponed. After being admitted to hospital for a second time, the applicant, relying on her state of health, requested the Swiss authorities responsible for asylum matters to reconsider her situation. In support of her request, she produced a medical certificate which stated, inter alia, that her HIV infection was at the C3 stage and that she had tuberculosis and pneumonia. At that stage, a monthly medical examination was necessary and, once the tuberculosis had been treated, a tritherapy against AIDS could be undertaken in order to reduce the risk of developing fresh diseases and to improve her long-term life expectancy. The document concluded

---

[56] Asylum Directorate Instructions July 1998. The March 1998 instructions were cited in *Bensaid* v *UK* (2001) 33 EHRR 10. These instructions have been amended recently and the Home Office website should be consulted for the latest version. See also 2.130 below.

that if the applicant's treatment should cease abruptly as a result of her being returned to her country of origin her short-term health would deteriorate. This request for a reconsideration of her situation was rejected, on the grounds that tuberculosis and hepatitis could be treated in Kinshasa and that although the care given in Switzerland might postpone the development of AIDS, that disease was fatal sooner or later. The Swiss authorities also pointed out that the applicant's family circle in her country of origin would be beneficial to her and, last, that she could be given medicines and instructions for her future doctors when she left Switzerland. Following the declaration that the case was admissible the parties reached a friendly settlement when the applicant was granted temporary leave to remain and paid 6,000 Swiss francs by way of lump-sum compensation for all the harm sustained. The European Commission had found that there would be a violation in similar circumstances in the case of *BB* v *France* (28 September 1998). In that case, the French government avoided a finding of a violation of Articles 2 and 3 by undertaking not to expel the applicant, who was suffering from AIDS, to a country where no medical treatment was available.

2.77   In the case of *SCC* v *Sweden* (App. No. 46553/99, 15 February 2000), a different approach was taken by the European Court. The applicant was from Zambia and had originally lived in Sweden as the wife of a diplomat before returning home. Whilst in Zambia in 1995 she was diagnosed as being HIV positive. In 1996 she returned to Sweden and sought permission to reside there unsuccessfully. On appeal she raised her HIV condition. The Swedish health authorities concluded that her HIV status by itself did not preclude expulsion. There was some treatment available in Zambia and she had family and friends there to help care for her. The case was found not to be admissible by the European Court.[57]

2.78   The key point in *SCC* v *Sweden* was that the applicant appeared to be conscious of her medical condition when seeking to return to Sweden and in the circumstances the responsibility of the state to provide her with medical treatment was not engaged. We suggest that responsibility is engaged where the knowledge of the symptoms develops after arrival during a period of lawful residence in the state, during a period of an examination of an asylum claim, or during a period of detention in the contracting state. Further, where treatment has been provided and there is a lack of available treatment in the state of origin, the state's responsibil-

---

[57] See also *MM* v *Switzerland* (1999) 27 EHRR 356 CD where the applicant was infected with HIV and faced return to the Democratic Republic of Congo. Declaring the application inadmissible, the former European Commission distinguished *D* v *UK:* the applicant did not suffer from any HIV-related illness; the Swiss authorities had agreed to pay for a year's treatment on return, and the applicant could obtain supplementary treatment by way of blood tests in South Africa without having to leave his country, after which his immune system could be expected to recover.

ity will be engaged if it terminates the treatment without an effective alternative. We discuss the impact of *D* v *UK* on Home Office policy and the approach of the courts below 2.124 et seq.

2.79   In *R* v *Secretary of State ex parte Njai* (1 December 2000) a decision ordering the expulsion of a schizophrenic was quashed where the evidence suggested that there was no comparable treatment available at an accessible cost in Gambia. In the case of *Bensaid* v *UK* (2001) 33 EHRR 10, a person suffering from long-term schizophrenia was to be returned to a part of Algeria where the necessary treatment was only available to inpatients at a hospital some distance away. The European Court accepted (at paras. 36 and 37) that deterioration in mental condition causing the risk of self-harm resulting from difficulties in obtaining medication, as well as restrictions in social functioning, were in principle within the scope of Article 3.[58] On the facts however, it held (at para. 40) that those consequences were speculative and the case was not made out evidentially.

2.80   An expulsion may be contrary to Article 8(1) in its private life aspects if the consequences do not meet the minimum level of severity required to engage Article 3. In *Bensaid* v *UK* the European Court also found that there was no violation of Article 8 in the light of its finding that the risk of damage to health was hypothetical. Where the evidence established a real as opposed to a speculative risk, it recognized that Article 8 would be engaged (para. 47):

> Private life is a broad term not susceptible to exhaustive definition. The Court has already held that elements such as gender identification, name and sexual orientation are important elements of the personal sphere protected by Article 8 . . . Mental health must also be regarded as a crucial part of private life associated with the aspect of moral integrity. Article 8 protects the right to identity and personal development, and the right to establish and develop relationships with other human beings and the outside world . . . The preservation of mental stability is in that context an indispensable precondition to effective enjoyment of the right to private life.

See also *Pretty* v *UK* (2002) 35 EHRR 1 and *R (Ahmadi)* v *Secretary of State for the Home Department* [2002] EWHC Admin 1897.

GENERALIZED FAILURE OF PROTECTION

2.81   The European Court has focused on whether there are substantial grounds

---

[58]   See also *Harron and Alayo* v *Sweden* 87-A DR 126 (Swedish authorities granted right to remain, on basis of medical reports indicating serious risk that the applicants would commit suicide or sustain serious physical or mental injuries if removed to Uganda). But see also *R* v *Chief Immigration Officer, ex parte R* (24 October 2001).

for the risk rather than the reasons for the risk or whether the risk is personal to the applicant as an individual rather than as a member of a group. Nevertheless the case law establishes that the grounds will not be considered substantial unless there is some specific evidence that the applicant will be of interest to the authorities in his or her country or to others whom the authorities are powerless to control. Such interest may arise because of past conduct, or membership of an ethnic group or even the fact that the individual has fled abroad and been expelled.

2.82   In cases where the state has broken down altogether and there is generalized violence, it may be that a broader approach should be taken. The evidence may establish a level of break down of law and order such as has prevailed in Somalia and Sierra Leone. One approach in such cases is to conclude that there must be substantial grounds for anyone returned to such places to be at risk. Another is that in addition to considering whether a person is at particular risk by reason of ethnic identity or past individual experience, it will be necessary to examine whether a person is being deprived of the protection of a system of law to protect life. We have noted the primary obligation under Article 2 as set out in the sense described in the *Osman* judgment above and the apparently broader protection afforded to the right to life by the common law (*R (Widgery Soldiers) v Lord Saville* [2001] EWHC Admin 888, see the Introduction and see now *R (A and others) v Lord Saville and others* [2002] 1 WLR 1249).

2.83   These societies are also ones where the maintenance of the basic facilities of life, such as employment, housing, education, and social support will be lacking. Taking Articles 2 and 3 together, at the very least it could be said that an expulsion to such a state of affairs is likely to be inhuman and degrading, because of the denial of respect to human dignity a return to such conditions represent.

APPLICATION IN THE UNITED KINGDOM

Distinctions with persecution under the Refugee Convention

2.84   The primary instrument for the protection of those seeking asylum in the United Kingdom will remain the UN Convention Relating to the Status of Refugees. The status of refugee and its concomitant specific rights of residence, new documentation, and access to the host society, should be accorded those who have a well-founded fear of persecution for a Refugee Convention reason.[59]

---

[59] See most recently *Saad, Diriye and Osorio* v *Secretary of State* (19 December 2001) Court of Appeal.

Human rights norms inform both the meaning of the term persecution,[60] and other central elements of the refugee definition.[61]

2.85 In its domestic application there should be no material difference between the approaches to the standard of proof under the two instruments (*Kacaj v Secretary of State* [2001] INLR 354; and see the Introduction). In both cases the focus is on the risk of future ill-treatment occurring, but there has to be real risk or substantial likelihood rather than a speculative possibility. The European Court has been rigorous in its application of the concept and has required objective evidence of risk to the individual by reason of his personal history or distinguishing characteristic before reversing assessments made at national level.[62] Even so there may be room for differences. 'Substantial grounds' in the ECHR jurisprudence may reflect a marginally higher test than 'reasonable degree of likelihood'.[63] 'Persecution' includes a persistent course of harassment without the need to characterize the effect on the individual as 'inhuman or degrading'. It is important that the domestic application of the ECHR does not diminish the existing scope of protection of the Refugee Convention. The rights afforded under one instrument cannot be used to restrict the rights under another (Article 53 of the ECHR; s. 11 of the HRA 1998).

2.86 Nevertheless there may be cases where asylum claims have been dismissed or could never have been made with any degree of success, where the protection of the ECHR is broader and complementary. We here summarize the essential differences.

2.87 First, the ECHR applies even to those who fall outside the protection of the Convention by reason of their conduct before or after arrival in the host state. There is no exclusion clause in Article 3 of the ECHR and no derogation from the protection of non-*refoulement* by reason of the commission of a criminal offence or because the claimant is a threat to the national security of the host state. Article 3 of the ECHR provides a broader protection than Article 33 of the Refugee Convention (*Chahal v UK* (1996) 23 EHRR 413).

2.88 Secondly, the ECHR focuses on the objective nature of the treatment and is not independently concerned with the credibility of the applicant's fears or the motives for ill-treatment. There is no need to characterize the ill-treatment as

---

[60] See e.g. submissions of the UNHCR and the IAT's conclusion in *Gashi v Secretary of State* [1997] INLR 205.

[61] See *R v Secretary of State ex parte Shah and Islam* [1999] 2 AC 629; *Danian v Secretary of State* [2000] Imm AR 96.

[62] See e.g. *Hatami v Sweden* 27 EHRR CD 8 for an example of where the Strasbourg Commission reversed findings of fact made by the national authority.

[63] See *Karanakaram v Secretary of State for the Home Department* [2000] INLR 122 for the approach of the Refugee Convention.

being for a specific ECHR reason.[64] Of course, where a credible account of a past history has been given that explains why an individual is at particular risk, that will be highly significant to the assessment of whether substantial grounds for a real risk exist. But clear evidence of past torture in a country where continued torture is still prevalent, may speak louder as to the objective nature of risk than the usual distracting minutiae of asylum decisions as to why a person should have so suffered, why he did not claim protection elsewhere, and why there was delay or inconsistency in setting out his or her account.

2.89   Thirdly Article 3 focuses on the expulsion itself and its foreseeable consequences rather than an administrative decision as to the existence of a status. Change of circumstances, or fresh material that throws substantial light on the risks must be considered and evaluated. Time limits or other restrictions on Article 3 claims would thus appear to be inconsistent with the ECHR.[65] In *Jabari* v *Turkey* [2000] INLR 136 the European Court was not persuaded that the Turkish authorities had conducted any meaningful assessment of the applicant's claim, including whether it was arguable. The applicant's failure to comply with a national five-day time limit denied her any scrutiny of the factual basis of her fears. The automatic and mechanical application of such a short time limit for an asylum application was considered at variance with the protection of the fundamental value embodied in Article 3.

2.90   Fourthly, whereas the Refugee Convention does not expressly prescribe a standard of review and a system of appeals (*Saad, Diriye and Osorio* v *Secretary of State* [2002] INLR 34), the ECHR by Article 13 requires that there must be effective remedies available to prevent expulsions in violation of Article 3. In *Jabari* v *Turkey* [2001] INLR 136 there was no assessment by the domestic authorities of the risk claimed by the applicant and there was no appeal against the refusal to consider her asylum request. Although she could challenge the lawfulness of the deportation order, this did not entitle her to either a suspension of its implementation or an examination of the merits of her claim. The European Court repeated its jurisprudence first spelt out in the case of *Chahal* v *UK* (1996) 23 EHRR 413. Given the irreversible nature of the harm that might occur, the notion of an effective remedy in such circumstances required independent and rigorous scrutiny of such a claim and the possibility of having the measure suspended. Since the Administrative Court failed to provide any of these safeguards, the judicial review proceedings relied on by the government did not

---

[64] On the nature of the requisite causal nexus in the refugee definition, see *Sivakumar* v *Secretary of State* [2001] EWCA Civ 1196.

[65] In *Bahadur* v *Netherlands* (1998) 26 EHRR 278 the European Court stressed there was a requirement to exhaust domestic remedies even in Article 3 cases, and a failure to take the opportunity of national procedures could be held against the person. On the facts the Dutch authorities were now reconsidering the claim, however.

satisfy the requirements of Article 13. We consider the efficacy of judicial review as an effective remedy below at 5.126 et seq. However in the context of Article 3 and in light of the recognition in *Turgut* v *Secretary of State* [2001] 1 All ER 716 that the Administrative Court has a special responsibility to examine the facts and is as well (if not better) placed as the Secretary of State to make an evaluation of risk if all the relevant material is placed before it, judicial review may finally move from being a theoretically available remedy to prevent incompatible results and might for the first time perform the function that the Strasbourg judges indicate that it ought to.[66] In any event, in the case of human rights decisions made after 2 October 2000, the independent scrutiny will be performed by adjudicators who have the necessary powers to make fresh findings of fact without any deference to the approach of the decision-maker if it is not supported by evidence.

2.91   Fifthly, whereas persecution for the purposes of the Refugee Convention always requires some deliberate act by human agents, whether state or non-state according to national jurisprudence, Article 3 of the ECHR extends to degrading consequences from the point of view of the individual. In the refugee context, see *Katrinak* v *Secretary of State for the Home Department* [2001] INLR 499, para. 21. In particular circumstances these may include severe measures of social and health deprivation that are different from persecution because of the lack of the element of intentionality. The focus is not on why this may happen to the individual concerned, but whether the foreseeable consequences are of sufficient severity.

Conditions of detention

2.92   Special considerations arise where a person is in custody (*Hurtado* v *Switzerland* (1994) Series No. A 280). The UN Minimum Rules and the recommendations of the Committee for the Prevention of Torture, make plain that a state assumes particular obligations to those whom it incarcerates and detains.

2.93   These principles were reviewed in the case of *Kudla* v *Poland* (App. No. 30210/96, 26 October 2000), where the European Court was concerned with the detention of a suicidal prisoner held on remand in custody for criminal offences despite suffering from a recognized psychiatric condition. The European Court observed that for Article 3 to be applicable the humiliating factors had to go beyond those necessarily inherent in any lawful sentence or detention.

---

[66] See further *Rehman* v *Secretary of State* [2001] 3 WLR 877, paras. 54 and 57 per Lord Hoffman; *X* v *Secretary of State* [2001] INLR 205, para. 10; Michael Beloff QC at [2001] 6(3) JR 154–60 at para. 24; and see the Introduction.

93. Measures depriving a person of his liberty may often involve such an element. Yet it cannot be said that the execution of detention on remand in itself raises an issue under Article 3 of the Convention. Nor can that Article be interpreted as laying down a general obligation to release a detainee on health grounds or to place him in a civil hospital to enable him to obtain a particular kind of medical treatment.

94. Nevertheless, under this provision the State must ensure that a person is detained in conditions which are compatible with respect for his human dignity, that the manner and method of the execution of the measure do not subject him to distress or hardship of an intensity exceeding the unavoidable level of suffering inherent in detention and that, given the practical demands of imprisonment, his health and well-being are adequately secured by, among other things, providing him with the requisite medical assistance.

2.94 Thus special obligations to protect the health and well-being of prisoners is assumed because of the element of control inherent in a sentence of custody. These obligations may then survive beyond the period of detention. In the case of *D* v *UK* (1997) 24 EHRR 423 it was the withdrawal of life-supporting medical treatment afforded to a prisoner in custody when the sentence had come to an end that amounted to the ill-treatment.

2.95 Findings of actual violations of Article 3 in this context are rare, but the case law indicates the kinds of considerations to be taken into account. In the case of *Price* v *United Kingdom* (2001) *The Times*, 13 August the applicant was a four-limb deficient thalidomide victim and suffered from kidney problems. She was ordered to be detained in custody for a week in respect of civil proceedings to recover a debt. The European Court unanimously held that her detention violated Article 3. The European Court found no evidence of any positive intention to humiliate or debase the applicant. However it considered that the failure to provide her with suitably adapted facilities to accommodate her severe disabilities constituted degrading treatment, even though her detention was of the order of a few hours overnight in a police station and a few days in prison before being transferred to a civilian hospital. This suggests that incarceration of those with acute medical needs will only be possible where suitable arrangements have been made in advance. In the case of *Keenan* v *United Kingdom* (2001) 33 EHRR 38, the European Court concluded that there had been a violation of Article 3 where the prison service had failed to take adequate measures to treat a suicidally depressed prisoner, but had instead punished him by placing him in solitary confinement.

2.96 In the case of *Zhu* v *United Kingdom* (App. No. 36790/97) a Chinese national was detained in prison following his illegal entry of a forged passport. His complaint was of social isolation with the absence of other Mandarin speakers and denial of access to an interpreter in prison for six months, inadequate exercise, and violence and abuse from other inmates. The government disputed various aspects of the applicant's contention. It agreed that the applicant had no interpreter for six months, but maintained that thereafter he had access to one on a weekly basis; it added that the ligature-free 'suicide watch' cell where he was placed after his suicide attempt was provided with a sleeping bag. A report of the authorities concerning, inter alia, the detention of persons awaiting deportation established that they were subjected to verbal abuse and intimidation in overcrowded prisons where they were detained together with convicted detainees. The European Court concluded that it was undesirable that immigration detainees be held in the same location as convicted prisoners but declared the complaint of a violation of Article 3 as unfounded and inadmissible because the prison authorities made efforts to alleviate the applicant's situation. He was provided with an interpreter and special measures were taken after his suicide attempt to prevent any other attempt, thus taking due account of his suicidal tendencies. The applicant did not complain about the authorities as such and it was not substantiated that the aggressive behaviour of the other inmates towards the applicant was sufficiently grave to render the conditions of his detention contrary to Article 3.

Lack of health care and social support

2.97 We have seen that treatment that offends the concept of human dignity is an important aspect of what is degrading for the purpose of Article 3.[67] A minimum level of severity has to be met, but in our view degrading treatment can in principle apply to the provision or denial of basic services needed to provide a dignified existence such as access to health, housing, social security, or the education and protection of children.

2.98 In *Tanko* v *Finland* 77-A DR 133 the former European Commission recognized the possibility that 'a lack of proper medical care in a case where someone is suffering from a serious illness could in certain circumstances amount to a treatment contrary to Article 3'.

2.99 Even though the ECHR affords no express right to medical treatment or housing we have seen in the detention cases that certain minimum standards are imposed. We would suggest that the rationale is because the prisoner is dependent on the state for his or her welfare. The same degree of reliance may be present when considering the position of others who cannot support themselves. The position of children who require protection and particular measures to promote their social welfare may also engage Article 3.

---

[67] See also Professor Feldman's two articles in *Public Law* [1999] PL 682, and [2000] PL 61; and see *Pretty* v *UK* (2002) 35 EHRR 1.

2.100   In the case of *Fadele* v *UK* 70 DR 159 the Commission found a complaint admissible that the return to Nigeria of children of a deported Nigerian national, after the death of the children's mother, raised questions under Article 3. The children were ill, isolated, uneducated and suffering the loss of the facilities they enjoyed in the United Kingdom.[68]

2.101   In *Nsona* v *Netherlands* (28 November 1996), the applicants complained that the method of removal of a minor infringed Article 3. On its facts, the case was not made out and the authorities had arranged for an adult apparently acquainted with the child to accompany her from the Netherlands to Zaire via Zurich. She was unaccompanied on the last leg of the journey because her lawyer had requested a stay when she was in Switzerland. The European Court accepted that such expulsions could raise Article 3 issues but concluded on the facts that the authorities had made adequate arrangements for the care and reception of the child.

2.102   If prisoners and children are special cases, then it is equally arguable that so are asylum seekers, who are precluded from independently supporting themselves by employment or access to the general welfare regime and are accordingly dependent on the state's regime of benefits for support. These matters are also properly to be considered as a part of the individual's right to respect for bodily and physical integrity as an aspect of private life protected under Article 8 (see above at 2.80). Such an approach has the advantage for the contracting state that in less extreme cases there is a balance between a right to respect and other social and economic obligations to others. In his judgment in *Pretty* v *DPP* [2001] UKHL 61 Lord Bingham observed at paragraph 13:

> Article 3 enshrines one of the fundamental values of democratic societies and its prohibition of the proscribed treatment is absolute: *D* v *United Kingdom* (1997) 24 EHRR 423 at p 447, para 47. Article 3 is, as I think, complementary to Article 2. As Article 2 requires states to respect and safeguard the lives of individuals within their jurisdiction, so Article 3 obliges them to respect the physical and human integrity of such individuals.

See also *Pretty* v *UK* (2002) 35 EHRR 1.

2.103   In the case of *HLR* v *France* (1997) 26 EHRR 29 Cabral Barreto was a concurring member of the Commission who concluded that where a proposed expulsion of a drug dealer was contrary to Article 3, more than mere abstinence from expulsion was required to respect the ECHR. He noted that the consequence of deportation was to render the applicant illegal in domestic law and unable to obtain a residence permit or to work. He noted:

---

[68] See also *Taspinar* v *Netherlands* 44 DR 262 (Dutch authorities grant child right to remain following admissibility decision under Article 3).

In my opinion, an alien who lives in a particular country but who has no access to the employment market and cannot benefit from the social security scheme is in a situation which fails to meet the requirements of Article 8 of the Convention.[69]

2.104   The point has particular relevance in the light of the sad history of *Ahmed v Austria* (1997) 24 EHRR 278. In that case the European Court concluded that it would be a violation of Article 3 for Austria to have expelled Ahmed, but subsequently no residence permit or authority to remain was granted. Following several months of precarious assistance, without stability or ability to support himself, Ahmed committed suicide. Where social deprivation may have such consequences, there could be little doubt that the minimum level of severity for Article 3 purposes has been reached. Suffering can be caused by deprivation of facilities as well as deliberate harm.

2.105   In the absence of further guidance from the European Court attention should be focused on the resolutions of the Council of Ministers noting measures adopted by contracting states where friendly settlements have been agreed. In our opinion there can be no legal ambiguity of a foreign national in the UK. If the law precludes his or her removal, then a status permitting residence and the ability to acquire some semblance of a normal life is required.[70] This is not to say that state's do not enjoy a wide margin when it comes to setting up their social security schemes.

2.106   This problem has been examined independently of the ECHR by the UK courts on a number of occasions. In the case of *R* v *Secretary of State for Social Security ex parte JCWI and B* [1997] 1 WLR 295 social security regulations that would deny emergency income support to asylum seekers pending appeal were struck down on the grounds that their consequences were unduly harsh. In *R* v *Kensington and Chelsea LBC ex parte Kihara* 29 HRL 147 the same Court decided that a penniless asylum seeker was in priority need for the purpose of duties towards the homeless. In *R* v *Westminster CC ex parte M* [1997] 1 CCLR 85 the Court of Appeal concluded that asylum seekers were entitled to qualify for assistance under the National Assistance Act 1948 as a result of their predicament after they arrived in the UK because:

---

[69] Whether Article 8 is breached by Home Office delay in failing to grant recognition of refugee status following a successful appeal is to be considered in *R (Mambakasa)* v *Secretary of State* (CO/3140/01) and *R (Boladale Allie)* v *Secretary of State* CO/4388/01).

[70] See *R* v *Secretary of State ex parte Quaquah (No.1)* [2000] INLR 196 (failure to take into account Article 6 in expulsion meant decision was flawed); *R* v *Secretary of State ex parte Quaquah (No. 2)* (1 September 2000) (bare denial of status flawed for want of reasons). The third set of proceedings (CO 729 2001) in respect of the Home Office's continuing failure to grant status was compromised through the grant of limited leave following the grant of permission by Collins J on (22 June 2001). Note however *R* v *Secretary of State ex parte Andries* (10 December 1999) (immigration limbo caused by fundamental contradictions in applicant's account as to his nationality and origins not unlawful).

of the effect on them of the problems under which they are labouring. In addition to the lack of food and accommodation is to be added their inability to speak the language, their ignorance of this country and the fact that they have been subject to the stress of coming to this country in circumstances which at least involve contending to be refugees. . . . The authorities can anticipate the deterioration which would otherwise take place . . . they do not need to wait until the health of the asylum seeker has been damaged.

2.107   The Court of Appeal subsequently had to consider the problem created by the restriction of these duties (IAA 1999, s. 116) before the full implementation of a new statutory scheme for the social support of asylum seekers under the IAA 1999. In the case of *R v Wandsworth LBC ex parte O* [2000] 1 WLR 2539 asylum seekers were losing any form of social assistance between the rejection of their claim and the subsequent acceptance that they should be given exceptional leave to remain on health grounds. Local authorities were only providing such assistance where the applicants were already unfit to travel. See also *R (Westminster City Council) v NASS* [2002] 1 WLR 2956.

2.108   The Court of Appeal concluded that the facts of *D v UK* (1997) 24 EHRR 423 were highly exceptional. They described the principle established in the case that Article 3 can be violated even though:

   (a)   the applicant is fit to travel now;

   (b)   removal to another country would not result in a breach of that other country's human rights obligations.

The Court of Appeal concluded that it would not apply in the majority of cases where expulsion would substantially damage the health of the subject. It may be right that mere damage to health will not automatically lead to a violation of Article 3, but the Court of Appeal may have imagined that *D v UK* is somewhat more restrictive than it is. Severe suffering caused by an expulsion is absolutely prohibited, even if the suffering is a substantial aggravation of an existing disease.

2.109   The Court of Appeal in *R v Wandsworth LBC ex parte O* [2000] 1 WLR 2539 overruled a High Court decision *R v Brent LBC, ex parte D* [1997] CCLR 234 to the effect that illegal entrants other than asylum seekers could not benefit from the residual duties under the National Assistance Act 1948 as they could always voluntarily return to their home countries. There may be other obstacles to returning home other than a well-founded fear of persecution. The Court of Appeal's decision is consistent with the requirements of the ECHR. In the decision of *R (Husain) v Asylum Support Adjudicator* (5 October 2001), *The Times Law Reports* 15 November 2001 Stanley Burnton J concluded that a total deprivation of social support for asylum seekers would violate Article 3.

2.110   In *R v North West Lancashire Health Authority ex parte A, D and G*

[2001] 1 WLR 977 at 995, 996 another division of the Court of Appeal was dismissive of the proposition that the standards of Article 3 of the ECHR could assist in the determination of the legality of a policy by a health authority not to fund gender reassignment surgery for transsexuals without any consideration of the ECHR case law. It considered that the issue of human rights arose under Article 8, if at all, where questions of the balance of competing claims for resources could be taken into account. Expenditure on social and health provision has hitherto been considered a matter supremely for central government and its delegates, and an area in which the courts would not intervene once the decision-maker had correctly addressed himself to the nature of the medical problem in hand. In *Pretty* v *DPP* [2001] UKHL 61, however, the House of Lords concluded by analogy that a deliberate denial of palliative treatment might contravene Article 3. Having considered *D* v *UK* (1997) 24 EHRR 423, Lord Bingham observed (at para. 14):

> An analogy might be found in the present case if a public official had forbidden the provision to Mrs Pretty of pain-killing or palliative drugs. But here the proscribed treatment is said to be the Director's refusal of proleptic immunity from prosecution to Mr Pretty if he commits a crime. By no legitimate process of interpretation can that refusal be held to fall within the negative prohibition of Article 3.

2.111   The right to physical and bodily integrity may require the expenditure of social resources. The European Court recently communicated the case of *Van Kuck* v *Germany* (App. No. 35968/97) as raising issues under Articles 6, 8, and 14. The applicant was a male to female transsexual. She brought an action against the health insurance company to which she was affiliated and claimed reimbursement of the pharmaceutical expenses of her hormone treatment. She also requested a declaratory judgment to the effect that the defendant company would be liable to reimburse 50 per cent of the expenses of the gender reassignment operations and further hormone treatment. In the light of medical evidence, the Regional Court dismissed the applicant's claims, considering notably that hormone treatment and gender reassignment could not be deemed a necessary medical treatment in her case. She unsuccessfully appealed against this decision to the Court of Appeal which found that she had caused her disease deliberately.

Torture in certified cases

2.112   In the context of immigration and asylum, it is usually immaterial to have to distinguish between treatment or punishment that constitutes torture or that which is merely inhuman or degrading. The question is normally a global one: would a proposed removal or expulsion infringe Article 3? However, evidence that a person *has been* tortured precludes certification of an asylum appeal (Asylum and Immigration Act 1996, Sch. 2, para. 5; IAA 1999, Sch. 4, para. 9).

2.113 In *R (Roszkowski)* v *A Special Adjudicator* (31 October 2000) Keene J noted at para. 26 of his judgment that the Home Office instructions provided that there was no need for the torture to have been inflicted by a public official or a person acting in an official capacity. We suggest that this is an accurate reflection of torture in international law. More controversially the judge suggested (at paras. 40–8) obiter that in the context of an asylum claim torture required an absence of sufficiency of protection in the home state.[71] In our view, this is an inappropriate gloss on the standard and universal definition of torture in the UN Convention Against Torture (see 2.54 above). It should be noted that Turner J had no difficulty applying this definition in the context of certification (*R (Javed and Ali)* v *Secretary of State for the Home Department* [2001] EWHC Admin 7; this part of the reasoning was not challenged in the Court of Appeal).

2.114 In general, however, the courts have been reluctant to provide a comprehensive definition of torture which may narrow its scope of application and have preferred instead to leave the issue to the good sense of adjudicators for application on a case by case basis.[72]

2.115 In a decision granting permission to apply for judicial review the Administrative Court held in *R (Prabaharen)* v *Special Adjudicator* [2001] EWHC Admin 754[73] that where the Secretary of State erroneously asserts in support of his certificate that the applicant had 'adduced no evidence relating to torture', it was not open to a Special Adjudicator to agree with the certificate on the basis that the evidence which *had* been produced before the Secretary of State was not credible.[74]

2.116 The new scheme for certification in IAA 1999, Sch. 4, para. 9 covers both asylum and human rights appeals. Its provisions were considered in *Zenovics* v *Secretary of State* (01/TH/0631 starred) where the IAT held that once the

---

[71] See also comments of Scott Baker J in *R* v *IAT ex parte Brylewicz* (26 March 1999). The question whether a person has been tortured for the purpose of a certificate is a wholly different consideration from whether a person would be persecuted in the future. Official acquiescence is relevant to the degree of severity and likelihood of repetition of the ill-treatment but it is not an essential requirement of the definition in asylum or human rights law. Moreover, it does not, we suggest, follow that because, as Keene J in *Rozkowski* held at para. 47, the torture must be 'related' to the substantive claim for asylum, the ill-treatment suffered cannot be torture unless there is an absence of sufficient protection from the state.

[72] See *R* v *Special Adjudicator ex parte Singh* [1999] INLR 632; *R* v *Special Adjudicator ex parte Okonkwo* [1998] Imm AR 502.

[73] Collins J considered that exceptionally the decision should be reported notwithstanding that he was merely granting permission to apply for judicial review.

[74] This approach is consistent with the increasing recognition that immigration proceedings are in essence adversarial whose primary focus is to determine the issues between the parties: see *MNM* v *Secretary of State* [2000] INLR 576; see further the comments of the Court of Appeal in *Saad, Diriye and Osario* v *Secretary of State* [2002] INLR 34 on *Ravichandran* v *Secretary of State* [1996] Imm AR 97. See also *Nanthakumar* v *Secretary of State* (22 May 2000).

Secretary of State had certified only one part of a mixed human rights and asylum claim, an Adjudicator was constrained to agree or disagree with only that part of the claim which had been certified, even though the consequence was that there would be no right of appeal to the IAT on any ground, including the non-certified ground.

2.117 The IAT recognized that proper thought had not been given to the provisions of IAA 1999, Sch. 4, para. 9 by Parliament and that the injustice and unfairness of denying an appeal to the IAT on a non-certified part of the claim had not been expressly contemplated:

13. In the circumstances we would expect that each claim is in some way regarded as defective before an appeal right which otherwise exists could be removed. That is not the effect of paragraph 9(4) and 9(5). [Counsel for the Secretary of State] argued that Parliament did deliberately so provide because otherwise there would be problems if, as was likely, the IAT needed to revisit findings of fact which resulted in the upholding of the certification on, say, the asylum claim. This argument assumes that Parliament would have countenanced that justice and fairness should be subordinated to convenience. We find that unlikely; at least, we would be surprised if it were done consciously with no dissenting voices. But in reality the argument contains the seeds of its own destruction. If the claims under the two Conventions are based on the same facts or the findings on one should determine the other both ought to be certified if certification under sub-paragraph (4) or (5) is considered appropriate.

14. In our view, the explanation for the difficulties created by paragraph 9 lies in the draftsman's incorporation of the new right of appeal created by s. 65 of the 1999 Act (the human rights appeal) with the existing paragraph dealing with certification. We strongly suspect that those responsible at the Home Office did not initially realise that to certify sub-paragraph (4) would, if the Adjudicator agreed, remove the right of appeal in respect of the human rights claim as well. . . . It is our clear view that, if a certificate is considered appropriate, and if there are claims under both Conventions based on the same facts, both claims or neither should be certified. Otherwise unfairness will result. Since paragraph 9(2) requires, if the right of appeal is to be denied, that the Adjudicator agrees with the opinion expressed in the certificate, he can only so agree if both claims were properly certified. He must agree with the whole and not only part of the opinion.

2.118 We consider that the conclusion reluctantly reached by the IAT, which it acknowledged created injustice and unfairness through denial of the second tier of appellate remedy in respect of a perfectly cogent (non-certified) claim, is open to doubt.[75] The right of access to the immigration appellate authority is recognized

---

[75] There is a present challenge pending in *R (Romario)* v *Secretary of State* (CO 4033 2001), where certification of the refugee claim proceeded for the technical reason that the claimant could not show an ECHR reason for persecution. That had and could have had nothing whatsoever to do with the

by the common law as a fundamental or constitutional right akin to the right of access to the courts (*R* v *Secretary of State, ex parte Saleem* [2001] 1 WLR 443). The IAT found that Parliament had not explicitly considered the ouster of the non-certified part of the appeal. A robust construction of the relevant statutory provisions, informed by the principle that Parliament cannot be taken to intrude on fundamental rights unless it does so in the clearest terms,[76] would permit the retention of appeal to the IAT on the non-certified part of the claim. The IAT's decision in *Zenovics* has been overturned by the Court of Appeal: [2002] INLR 219.

Third country removals

2.119   Where the Secretary of State proposes to remove an asylum claimant to another member state of the European Union under the Dublin Convention 1990, IAA 1999, s. 11 provides that such a removal is not unlawful. This is despite the judgment of the House of Lords in *Adan and Aitsegeur* [2001] 2 WLR 143 that removal to certain member states could violate the UK's obligations under the Refugee Convention, because a more restrictive interpretation is given to its scope in the field of non-state agents of persecution. A suspensive human rights appeal will remain, although this will be ousted in the case of a manifestly ill-founded allegation: IAA 1999, s. 72(2)(a).[77] It is clear from the decision in *TI* v *UK* [2000] INLR 211 that the responsibility of one contracting state is still engaged in principle despite the fact that it proposes to send the claimant to another contracting state. International agreements such as the Dublin Convention cannot remove the liability of states for the causal consequences of their expulsion decisions. The primary consideration will be on the evidence of actual practice in the other member state.[78] If there is evidence that border guards or others send claimants on to unsafe countries without proper consideration of their claims, then the Dublin Convention and IAA 1999, s. 11 cannot prevail.

---

merits of the claimant's claim to be in need of international protection under the ECHR. The only issue on the Article 3 ground was whether a real risk, of treatment accepted to be sufficiently severe at the hands of non-state agents in Colombo, was made out.

[76]   The principle of legality: *R* v *Secretary of State ex parte Simms* [2000] 2 AC 115.

[77]   See Introduction and the comments of Collins J in *R (Thangarasa)* v *Secretary of State* [2001] EWHC Admin 420, para. 27: 'This is not to say that automatically a decision to return to a European Member State in accordance with section 11 means that there cannot possibly be a well-founded claim under section 65 . . . It must not be thought that the mere fact that section 11 can be used precludes the possibility of a claim under the Human Rights Act'. See also *R (Ibrahim)* v *Secretary of State* [2001] EWCA Civ 519 (Secretary of State's discretion to certify under s. 11 cannot be impugned on a refugee law challenge). See further *R (Mohammad and others)* v *Secretary of State for the Home Department* [2002] EWHC Admin 57.

[78]   See *R (Yogathas and Thangarasa)* v *Secretary of State* [2001] EWCA Civ 1611; followed in the House of Lords: [2002] 3 WLR 1276.

2.120 Undoubtedly there is a humanitarian discretion in the Secretary of State to consider the claim on broad human rights grounds notwithstanding the statutory presumption of safety, or to desist from certification where a human rights appeal is lodged (see above at 1.109 et seq). We would suggest that discretion might be engaged where:

(a) there has been a full hearing of a previous claim and there has been a perverse rejection of it;[79]

(b) there is substantial fresh evidence and no adequate procedure in the other state for reopening decisions;

(c) the procedures in the other state are so poor or effectively inaccessible as to amount to a violation of the right to an effective remedy under Article 13, and guidance can be obtained from the Council of Europe recommendations on minimum procedural standards;

(d) there is cogent evidence that removal would create mental or physical suffering by reason of the interruption or deprivation of essential medical or psychiatric care, or family and social support.[80]

2.121 Clearly, discretion is only likely to be exercised in clear cases where respect for human dignity and safety requires it. In the absence of common EU minimum standards binding on member states and consistent with the provisions of the ECHR, and the recommendations in the field of asylum procedures, problems of harmonization and individual injustice are bound to occur. Criteria for temporary protection, standards of social assistance during the reception process, and a guarantee of status after a decision that the claimant is entitled to protection are all called for. Shuffling the problem ad hoc between states without a commitment to effective standards will not do.

2.122 The European Court was perhaps exceptionally generous to Germany in assuming that de facto protection to prevent a violation of Article 3 would be available to a Tamil claimant returned from the UK in the case of *TI v UK* [2000] INLR 211. There was no evidence that such cases had been successfully reopened and status given under the particular provisions of the relevant Code. Theoretical possibilities of protection are not enough, although undoubtedly it is preferable that the problem is addressed in all member states and not just the UK.

---

[79] See *R v Secretary of State ex parte Dahmas* (17 November 1999) CA, unreported, reversing HC at [2000] Imm AR 151; *R v Secretary of State ex parte Stefan Chiper and Ionel* [1995] Imm AR 410. But see *R (Ibrahim) v Secretary of State* [2001] EWCA Civ 519 (Secretary of State's discretion to certify under s. 11 cannot be impugned on basis that France was unsafe in light of *Adan* (see below and footnote 81) and *Aitsegeur* [2001] 2 AC 477).

[80] See family links policy published 21 March 1991, cited and considered in *R v Secretary of State ex parte Arif* CO 628 99 (1 February 2000). See also *R (Ahmadi) v Secretary of State for the Home Department* [2002] EWHC Admin 1897, and *R (Nadarajah) v Secretary of State for the Home Department* [2002] EWHC Admin 2595 (appeal pending before Court of Appeal).

2.123   A recent admissibility decision before the European Court demonstrates the problems that still remain in some member states. In the case of *Kalantari* v *Germany* (App. No. 51342/99) the applicant, an Iranian national, fled Iran and entered Germany where he applied for the status of political refugee. The Federal Office for Refugees rejected his application. That rejection was upheld by the courts. A new application made by the applicant was also rejected by the Federal Office for Refugees and the Administrative Court dismissed his application to have the expulsion order stayed. The Federal Constitutional Court dismissed the appeal. The trial on the merits was still pending in the Administrative Court, but since it had no suspensive effect, the applicant could have been expelled to Iran at any moment. He fled to France, where he was probably still hiding. In January 2000 the Fourth Section asked the parties for more information (applying Rule 39 of the Rules of the European Court) relating in particular to the persecution suffered by the applicant's family. The government informed the European Court that it was not in a position to furnish the information requested. The applicant's sister, however, produced documents relating to the persecution suffered by her family. The Special Rapporteur on Torture at the UN Human Rights Commission sent the European Court an extract from a public report which mentioned an appeal by the Special Rapporteur against the applicant's expulsion in August 1999 owing to the risk of the applicant being tortured in Iran. When dismissing the application for refugee status the German authorities had not mentioned the fate of the members of the applicant's family in Iran or the dangers he would run if he was sent back there, despite the fact that the applicant had from the very first hearing before the Federal Office of Refugees emphasized the persecution to which his sisters in Iran had been subjected. In addition, the German authorities had received evidence during the proceedings of the persecution suffered by the applicant's sisters and must have been aware of the appeals against his expulsion made by certain international organizations and associations, such as the UN Human Rights Commissioner. The evidence regarding the situation of the applicant's family in Iran coupled with his political activities during his exile should have enabled the authorities to assess the risks of torture which the applicant would run if he was expelled to Iran. It was for the authorities to seek further information if they considered it necessary. Furthermore, the applicant had already made a further application for political asylum, which was still pending on its merits, and a number of unsuccessful applications for a stay of execution of the expulsion order. Lastly, under the domestic legislation in force on aliens, a fresh application for political asylum had to be made in principle within three months of the applicant becoming aware of the existence of new evidence. In the case before the European Court, that period had long since expired. In conclusion, the applicant could not be required to bring new proceedings concerning his application for asylum. Thus, the government's objection that domestic remedies had not been exhausted was unfounded.

Health policies

2.124   The Home Office's criteria when considering applications from those who are subject to immigration control but suffer from AIDS or other serious illnesses are contained in rules, instructions and policies, and are the subject of consideration by the courts.

2.125   The starting point is the provisions of the medical visitor rules, which in essence provide for the grant of limited leave to enter in cases where the treatment is of finite duration, and the applicant can fund the treatment and intends to leave the UK (Immigration Rules, HC 395, paras. 51–6).

2.126   In August 1995 an instruction, BDI 3/95 was issued to give guidance on AIDS or HIV positive cases. The fact that a person was suffering from AIDS/HIV was neither sufficient for nor determinative against the grant of leave (paras. 2.1 and 2.2 of BDI 3/95). The policy for port cases was to adhere to the provisions of the rules, otherwise on-entry permission was to be refused (para. 4.1 of BDI 3/95). This fettered the discretion of the Immigration Officer since the policy governed the realm of extra-rule discretion under s. 4 of the Immigration Act 1971.[81] In a case heard by Dyson J, leave to move for judicial review was granted on this basis and the case settled after evidence was submitted by the Secretary of State indicating that each case was considered on its merits even in on-entry cases.[82] However, it is unfortunate that a policy framed in misleadingly harsh and unlawful terms remained unaltered for almost six years until its replacement in June 2001.

2.127   The provisions for after-entry cases in BDI 3/95 were more generous. Although the starting point for consideration was again the Immigration Rules, provision was made for the compassionate exercise of discretion outside the Rules (BDI 3/95, para. 5.2). The core test for in-country cases was that a grant of leave to remain would 'normally be appropriate' where there are 'no facilities for treatment available' in the home country and such absence of treatment would significantly shorten life expectancy (BDI 3195, para. 5.4). This core test was interpreted by the Secretary of State in an absolutist manner: there had to be a

---

[81]   See *Adan* v *Secretary of State* [1999] AC 293, 301 (submissions of Counsel for Secretary of State).

[82]   *R* v *Secretary of State, ex parte K* (1999). Affidavit of Lauren Shukru, 7 January 1999, para. 14: 'Thus while the AIDS and HIV guidelines draw a distinction between applications for leave to enter and applications for leave to remain, the Secretary of State looks at each case individually to see whether, even though the requirements of the Rules are not met and the guidelines do not avail an applicant, the circumstances are so exceptional that it is appropriate to grant leave to enter.' The justification for the different regimes in BDI 3/95 was given at para. 12: '*generally* persons seeking leave to remain have closer links with the UK than persons seeking leave to enter' (emphasis supplied).

complete absence of treatment, rather than no available treatment.[83] The difficulty with the Secretary of State's interpretation, at its logical extreme, was that if a rich individual were able to import treatment into the country, the claim would be defeated since there would be *some* treatment notionally available.

2.128 A parallel policy, the asylum/exceptional leave to enter/remain policy, did not differentiate between on-entry and in-country cases. The single test as of 20 March 1998[84] for the grant of leave was the existence of '*credible* evidence that return would result in substantial damage to the physical or psychological health of the applicant or his dependants' (para. 2.1 of the exceptional leave policy, 20 March 1998). This generously framed policy was short-lived. The policy changed and the test hardened in June 1998 in terms reflective of the judgment in *D* v *UK* (1997) 24 EHRR 423 (above at 2.72–2.74)[85] so that leave would only be granted if additionally it could be shown that removal would 'subject (the applicant) to acute mental and physical suffering, in circumstances where the UK can be regarded as having assumed responsibility for his care'.

2.129 But even this policy did not stipulate any requirement of a complete absence of treatment causative of ill-treatment.[86] However, the application of the exceptional leave to enter/remain policy to AIDS/HIV cases was thrown into substantial doubt by the decision of the Court of Appeal in *R* v *Secretary of State ex parte Kasasa* (16 February 2000). Here the Court of Appeal held, accepting a submission that 'was rather far down in the bucket' from Treasury Counsel, that the exceptional leave to enter/remain policy only applied to those seeking asylum during the pendancy of the asylum process. Once that was finished, the applicable policy was the AIDS/HIV policy, interpreted so as to require a complete absence of relevant treatment in the home country. There was accordingly no solace from the 'complete absence test' for AIDS/HIV sufferers in the excep-

---

[83] Some support for this interpretation perhaps could be derived from the decision in *I* v *Secretary of State* [1997] Imm AR 172. Here the Court of Appeal refused leave to move for judicial review on a renewed application where the claimant and her infant daughter, both HIV sufferers, faced return to Uganda to inferior treatment 80 miles away from their home in Kampala. However, this was a case regarding superable difficulties of *access* rather than insuperable difficulties of *cost*: the Court of Appeal noted (at p. 176): 'There is no evidence to show that there are no facilities available which she could take advantage of, such as they are, albeit that she may do so with difficulty.'; see comments of Staughton LJ in *R* v *Secretary of State ex parte Kasasa* (16 February 2000). It is to be noted that *I* v *Secretary of State* was decided before *D* v *UK* 24 EHRR 423 and a leave application is not binding: *Clarke* v *University of Lincolnshire and Humberside* [2000] 1 WLR 1988, para 43; *R* v *Secretary of State ex parte Robinson* [1998] QB 929.

[84] Cited in *Bensaid* v *UK* (2001) 33 EHRR 10.

[85] See comments of Sullivan J in *R* v *Secretary of State ex parte M* CO 4975 98 (23 July 1999).

[86] Thus the applicant in *R* v *Secretary of State ex parte M* CO 4975 98 (23 July 1999) was successful merely by showing life-shortening, acute mental and physical suffering under the exceptional leave policy. Assumption of responsibility appears not to have been a point taken by the Secretary of State.

tional leave to enter/remain policy. *Kasasa* is, in our view, a difficult decision to comprehend. A number of points arise. First, it meant that those suffering less severe diseases than HIV/AIDS who happened to be asylum-seekers had greater protection under the law. Secondly, it encouraged repeat abusive asylum claims to gain access to the exceptional leave to enter/remain policy. Thirdly, there was no temporal limitation in the exceptional leave policy and no evidence appears to have been submitted to the Court to that effect. The decision was expressly contrary to the evidence submitted by the Secretary of State in *R* v *Secretary of State, ex parte K* (1999).[87]

2.130 A new policy was published on the Home Office website in June 2001 in Immigration Directorate Instructions, Chapter 1, Section 8. The core test is as follows:

i. the UK can be regarded as having assumed responsibility for a person's care; and
ii. there is credible medical evidence that return, due to a complete absence of medical treatment in the country concerned, would significantly reduce the applicant's life expectancy; and
iii. subject them to acute physical and mental suffering.

2.131 We discuss the notion of engagement of responsibility above at 2.78. In *D* v *UK* (1997) EHRR 423 the European Court stated (at para. 53) that:

The Court also notes in this respect that the respondent State has assumed responsibility for treating the applicant's condition since August 1994. He has become reliant on the medical and palliative care which he is at present receiving and is no doubt psychologically prepared for death in an environment which is both familiar and compassionate. Although it cannot be said that the conditions which would confront him in the receiving country are themselves a breach of the standards of Article 3, his removal would expose him to a real risk of dying under most distressing circumstances and would thus amount to inhuman treatment.

2.132 August 1994 was the date on which the applicant (whilst serving a prison sentence) suffered an attack of PCP (a form of pneumonia which is a complication of AIDS) and started receiving treatment. The infection pre-dated entry. While in *D* v *UK* (1997) the concept of assumption of responsibility appeared to

---

[87] Affidavit of Lauren Shukru, 7 January 1999, para. 14: 'AIDS and HIV guidelines are just that. They give guidance . . . They are not a rigid code. *They also need to be read in conjunction with the ELE* [exceptional leave to enter] *policy.*' (emphasis supplied). *Kasasa*, as a decision refusing permission to apply for judicial review, is not binding: *Clarke* and *Robinson* (see above at footnote 83). On 16 May 2000 Jowitt J in *R* v *Secretary of State ex parte Kiwanuka (No. 2)* CO 881 2000 granted permission to apply for judicial review, where the claimant sought to argue that *Kasasa* was wrongly decided on this and other points. The claimant's application was dismissed by Jackson J on the basis that an alternative remedy had become available in the form of a s. 65 appeal: [2002] EWHC Admin 2013.

be of incidental rather than focal importance, it appears to be the basis upon which later cases have been decided. The key distinction appears to be awareness of the condition on arrival.[88] We have suggested above at 2.78 that responsibility is engaged where the knowledge of the symptoms develops after arrival during a period of lawful residence in the state, during a period of an examination of an asylum claim, or during a period of detention in the contracting state. Further, where treatment has been provided and there is a lack of available treatment in the state of origin, the state's responsibility will be engaged if it terminates the treatment without an effective alternative. Thus the statement in the new policy that:

> The Strasbourg Court has found in *SCC v Sweden* that a person who is subject to removal cannot in principle claim any entitlement to remain in the territory of a Contracting State in order to continue to benefit from medical, social or other forms of assistance provided by the removing State.

as a blanket statement oversimplifies the position.

2.133   Once assumption of responsibility is established, we suggest that all that then may be required is the last condition, namely subjection of the individual to acute mental and physical suffering through removal. If this reaches the threshold minimum level of severity, then there may be no need to go further for Article 3 purposes, albeit that HIV/AIDS cases will concern life shortening as well. But that may be an incidental or relevant consideration rather than essential feature of the analysis.[89]

2.134   The policy requires there to be a causal connection between the absence of available treatment and life shortening. An important issue is whether the absence of treatment must be total.[90] In *Kasasa* the Court of Appeal appeared to give the Secretary of State some latitude in construing the absence of treatment test, allowing for a 'complete absence' construction at least on the facts of that case. We suggest that even allowing for the traditional *Wednesbury* approach to questions of policy construction,[91] there can be no room for an interpretation which renders Article 3 protection illusory and theoretical rather than practical and effective (see *R (Kiwanuka) v Secretary of State for the Home Department*

---

[88] See *Tatete v Switzerland* (App. No. 41874/98); *BB v France* (App. No. 30930/96) rejection of admissibility by the European Court in *SCC v Sweden* (App. No. 46553/99) (note however the decision in *Karara v Finland* (App. No. 40900/98) which is difficult to reconcile with the other cases).

[89] See e.g. *Bensaid v UK* (2001) 33 EHRR 10.

[90] This issue will be considered in *R v Secretary of State ex parte Kiwanuka (2)* (above at footnote 87).

[91] *R v Secretary of State ex parte Urmaza* [1996] COD 479 and *R v Secretary of State ex parte Gangadeen* [1998] COD 216; see Craig, P., *Administrative Law* (4th edn) 1999, (Sweet & Maxwell, 629–30).

c/2002/2180, 19 December 2002, CA; refusal of permission to appeal). In the critical passage in *Kasasa*, the Court of Appeal appears with respect to have misunderstood *D* v *UK* in stating that:

> Would it be inhuman or degrading treatment to send Mr K back to Uganda on the grounds that he may or may not be able to afford all the treatment that he requires? It does seem to me that, if we were to accede to that argument, we would be in effect adopting a rule that any country which did not have a health service which was available free to all people within its bounds, would be a place to which it would be inhuman and degrading to send someone. I do not consider that the ECtHR would reach that conclusion.

But *D* v *UK* concerned withdrawal of treatment already being enjoyed in the host state rather than the issue of access from abroad. The Court in *D* v *UK* indeed did not contemplate the latter issue since it held that removal to conditions which *in themselves* would not breach Article 3 may do so in other circumstances.

Chapter Three

Protection from Arbitrary Detention

INTRODUCTION

3.1   The detention of immigrants and asylum seekers is a politically charged issue. It is noteworthy that, despite the fact that the numbers of asylum seekers entering Western Europe have stabilized, the numbers being detained have increased.[1] Yet despite this increase, the case law on Article 5(1)(f) of the ECHR, the provision allowing for a deprivation of liberty for immigration-related reasons, is underdeveloped in comparison to the other sub-Articles of Article 5. In this chapter we examine the requirements of Article 5 of the ECHR in the context of immigration detention. We consider the judgment of the Court of Appeal in *R (Saadi)* v *Secretary of State* [2001] EWCA Civ 1512, 19 October 2001 (which was upheld by the House of Lords: [2002] UKHL 41) on the compatibility with Article 5 of the Secretary of State's detention regime at Oakington reception centre, described (at para. 1) as a 'cornerstone of the government's current procedure for processing applications for asylum'. We also consider the compatibility with the ECHR scheme of the provisions of the Anti-Terrorism Crime and Security Act 2001 permitting internment for suspected international terrorists whose expulsion is prevented by international obligations (essentially Article 3 of the ECHR) or other practical obstacles, together with the UK's proposed derogation from Article 5(1) under Article 15(3) of the ECHR. We return to this issue in chapter 7, the postscript to this book.

3.2   We then consider the powers of administrative detention available to the Secretary of State under the Immigration Act (IA) 1971, the available modes of challenge and the likely impact of Article 5 of the ECHR in its field of application. The issue of whether conditions in detention breach ECHR rights is considered above at 2.34 et seq.

---

[1] UNHCR, Recommendations as Regards Harmonisation of Reception Standards for Asylum Seekers in the EU, Part A: Summary of State Practice (Geneva, UNHCR July 2000) 31.

THE REQUIREMENTS OF ARTICLE 5: THE RIGHT TO LIBERTY AND SECURITY OF THE PERSON

3.3 The right to liberty is a prized and fundamental right not only of English common law.[2] The ECHR devotes Article 5 to its protection, and the European Court has repeatedly emphasized that it is one of the fundamental principles of a democratic society that a state must strictly observe the rule of law when interfering with the right of personal liberty (*Brogan* v *UK* (1988) 11 EHRR 117, para. 58). Article 5 may in essence be treated as providing two safeguards for detainees: (1) a test for the legality of detention; (2) a set of procedural rights for detainees. The right protected is liberty in the narrow or classic sense, namely the physical liberty of the person (*Engel* v *Netherlands* (1976) EHRR 647, para. 58). The underlying aim of Article 5 is 'to ensure that no one should be dispossessed of his liberty in an arbitrary fashion'.[3] The reference to 'security of the person' serves to emphasize the requirement that detention should not be arbitrary (*Bozano* v *France* (1986) 9 EHRR 292, paras. 54 and 60), is to be read in the context of physical liberty rather than physical safety (*East African Asians* v *UK* (1973) EHRR 76, para. 220), and thus does not impose positive obligations on the state to provide physical protection from private actors *X* v *Ireland* (1973) 16 YB 388,[4] and does not extend to a right to social security (*X* v *FRG* (1972) 1 Digest 288).[5]

3.4 The importance of the right is demonstrated by the provision in Article 5(5), which uniquely imposes a substantive and procedural duty directly upon the state to provide compensation for its breach. While Article 6 has been held not to apply to the field of immigration in general (*Maaoiua* v *France* (2001) 33 EHRR 42; see chapter 5), challenges to immigration detention may. The essential scheme is that no one can be deprived of their liberty save in accordance with a procedure established by law and for a purpose recognized by the ECHR. Any person deprived of their liberty has the right under Article 5(4) to apply to a court for a speedy review of the legality of the detention and to be released from detention if the detention is not lawful. The wider rights afforded to criminal suspects to apply to a court to review the expediency of detention pending trial under Article 5(3) do not apply to immigration detainees not charged with criminal conduct.

---

[2] See e.g. *R (Saadi)* v *Secretary of State* [2001] EWCA Civ 1512, 19 October 2001, para. 69; *In Re Wasfi Suleiman Mahmood* [1995] Imm AR 311; *R (Abbasi)* v *Secretary of State for the Home Department* [2002] EWCA Civ 1598.

[3] See e.g. *Engel* v *Netherlands* (1976) 1 EHRR 647, para. 58; *Guzzardi* v *Italy* (1980) 3 EHRR 333, para. 92; *Bozano* v *France* (1986) 9 EHRR 292, para. 54.

[4] In the context of positive obligations to protect security and safety see 2.11–2.16 and 2.92–2.111 (positive obligations to protect against a violation of the right to life, and from inhuman and degrading treatment, and from violations of physical and moral integrity).

[5] In *Theory and Practice of the ECHR* (3rd edn), Kluwer Law, 1997 345, Van Dijk and Van Hoof question whether this restrictive approach does justice to the right to security of the person.

Civil detention of immigrants is thus likely to be concerned with the following questions: is the detention in accordance with the law; is the detention for a purpose permitted by Article 5(1)(f), and what are the factors that go to the legality of the detention during a review under Article 5(4)?

Article 5(1): Scope

Voluntary confinement

3.5 Article 5 will not apply where the individual clearly and unequivocally consents to the restraint. However, the decision of the European Court in *Amuur* v *France* (1996) 22 EHRR 533 firmly establishes that the state cannot argue that asylum seekers held in a transit zone of an airport are free to leave the territory and are thereby not deprived of their liberty. In a decision paying due regard to the reality of the situation as opposed to the notional freedom relied upon by the French government, the European Court rejected the proposition that the confinement in those circumstances was voluntary, and concluded (at para. 48) that Article 5 was capable of application to such a situation, especially where the only destination for the asylum seeker would be to another state providing inferior protection. Van Dijk and Van Hoof find the contrary view, adopted by the European Commission both in the *Amuur* case and in an earlier case[6] to be 'rather remarkable'[7] and overly 'formalistic'. Thus the European Court stated in *Amuur* (at para. 48) that:

> The mere fact that it is possible for asylum seekers to leave voluntarily the country where they wish to take refuge cannot exclude a restriction on liberty, the right to leave any country, including one's own, being guaranteed, moreover, by Protocol No. 4 to the Convention. Furthermore, this possibility becomes theoretical if no other country offering protection comparable to the protection they expect to find in the country where they are seeking asylum is inclined or prepared to take them in.

Restriction and deprivation of liberty

3.6 In domestic law, any confinement of an individual amounts to a deprivation of liberty and is actionable as such.[8] However, Article 5 is not concerned with mere restrictions on liberty of movement (*Engel* v *Netherlands* (1976) EHRR 647 at para. 58). The distinction between a restriction on and a deprivation of liberty is sometimes elusive since the difference is 'merely one of degree and intensity, and not one of nature or substance'.[9] The starting point for determining whether

---

[6] 19066/91 SSCBA 1992, *AM and YSM* v *Austria*, *SM and MT* v *Austria* (1993) 74 DR 179.

[7] Van Dijk and Van Hoof, *Theory and Practice of the ECHR* (above at footnote 5) 347.

[8] *Clerk and Lindsell on Torts* (17th edn) (Sweet & Maxwell) paras. 12–17 and 12–18.

[9] See *Amuur* v *France* (1996) 22 EHRR 533 at para. 43; *Guzzardi* v *Italy* (1981) 3 EHRR 333 at para. 92.

there is a deprivation is the individual situation of the person concerned.[10] Other relevant factors include the character of the interference with liberty, its duration, effects, and the manner of implementation of the restraining measure.[11] Once the threshold of deprivation is crossed, the burden of providing justification for the detention falls on the state.

3.7 The case law of the European Court recognizes that the process of examining those who are seeking entry to another country involves incidental and necessary interference with liberty at port. It is thus legitimate to impose restrictions on liberty for the purposes of examination of a claim. Such interferences do not engage Article 5 but are instead governed by Article 2 of the Fourth Protocol to the Convention, to which the UK is not a party. The intention of the authorities to question rather than detain is relevant, but where the conditions of confinement are of sufficient severity or the confinement is unduly prolonged and disproportionate to the process of examination, the European Court will consider that there has been a deprivation of liberty and Article 5 will then be engaged (*Amuur* v *France* (1996) 22 EHRR 533 at para. 42). The controversial issue posed by the Court of Appeal judgment in the Oakington case (above at 3.1; and upheld by the House of Lords: [2002] UKHL 41), is whether Article 5 permits a deprivation of (as opposed merely to a restriction on) liberty for the purposes of an examination of a claim, even if the deprivation of liberty 'falls at the bottom end of the scale of interference with the right' as was the case in *Saadi* owing to the relatively liberal quality of the Oakington regime (see *R (Saadi)* v *Secretary of State* [2001] EWCA Civ 1512 at para. 69 and see below at 3.53).

3.8 Thus in *Amuur* v *France* (1996) 22 EHRR 533 the European Court held that holding asylum seekers in the international zone of an airport for 20 days amounted to a deprivation of liberty in circumstances where they were placed under constant police surveillance, provided with no legal or social assistance, in particular as to the progressing of their claims, and there was no review by a court of the length of or necessity for their confinement.

3.9 In *Guzzardi* v *Italy* (1981) 3 EHRR 333 at para. 56 the European Court held that a compulsory residence order requiring the applicant, a suspected Mafia member, to live on a small island subject to strict police supervision amounted to a deprivation of liberty. This was to be contrasted with another phase of his detention, when he was held on the Italian mainland subject to a less strict regime. In *NC* v *Italy* (App. No. 24952/94) at para. 33 the European Court accepted that house arrest constituted a deprivation of liberty.

---

[10] Van Dijk and Van Hoof, *Theory and Practice of the ECHR* (above at footnote 5) 346.
[11] See *Guzzardi* v *Italy* (1981) 3 EHRR 333 at para. 92; *Engel* v *Netherlands* (1976) EHRR 647 at paras. 58 and 59.

3.10   Whether a restraint amounts to a deprivation of liberty may also depend upon the level of 'residual liberty' otherwise enjoyed by the individual. Thus a disciplinary order confining a prisoner to his cell may not lead to an additional deprivation of liberty (*X v Switzerland* (1978) 11 DR 216 at para. 2), whilst an order for the forfeiture of remission will be regarded as imposing an additional period of detention (see *Campbell and Fell* v *UK* (1984) 7 EHRR 165 at para. 72).[12]

Extraterritorial effect

3.11   Article 5 has consequences outside the territorial jurisdiction in two senses. First, it applies to an arrest or detention by agents of the contracting state, even if this is effected outside the jurisdiction. Contracting states are bound to secure ECHR rights 'to all persons under their actual authority and responsibility, whether that authority is exercised within their own territory or abroad'.[13] Thus as we have seen above at 3.5–3.8, the protection of Article 5 cannot be denied on the basis that an applicant for entry into a country is in an international zone at a port and thus not on the territory of the contracting state (*Amuur* v *France* (1996) 22 EHRR 533 at para. 48). The extraterritorial consequences of the UK's ECHR obligations in general are discussed above at 1.17–1.25.

3.12   Secondly, an expulsion of an individual to a country where he will be detained following a conviction that was a 'flagrant denial of justice' will breach Article 5.[14] Article 5 (and Article 6) may exceptionally be engaged in those circumstances, so that responsibility for the breach remains with the expelling state.[15] Thus, in *MAR* v *UK* (App. No. 28038/95, 19 September 1997) it was argued by analogy with Article 3 case law that detention and trial in flagrant breach of Article 5 (and Article 6) would be attributable to the UK. The case was settled before an opinion on the merits was adopted by the European Commission. Similarly, where a contracting state receives custody of a person detained by a non-contracting state, responsibility for the fairness of the trial leading to the detention is not normally attributed to the receiving state unless there are exceptional circumstances and a serious violation of the ECHR (*Drozd and Janousek* v *France and Spain* 14 EHRR 745). However, the Court of Appeal in *Ullah* v *Special Adjudicator* [2002] EWCA Civ 1856 have decided that no Article, save for Article 3, is engaged in the expulsion context. Leave to appeal to the House of Lords has been granted.

---

[12]   See however *R* v *Secretary of State ex parte Greenfield* [2001] 2 WLR 865; effectively reversed by *Ezeh and Connors* v *UK* (2002) 35 EHRR 28. The case has been referred to the Grand Chamber.

[13]   See *Cyprus* v *Turkey* (1975) 2 DR 125 at 136; *Freda* v *Italy* (1980) 21 DR 250.

[14]   See *Drozd and Janousek* v *France and Spain* (1992) 14 EHRR 745 para. 118; *Soering* v *UK* (1989) 11 EHRR 439.

[15]   See also *Bankovic* v *Belgium and Other NATO States* (12 December 2001) at paras. 67 and 68 discussed above at 1.20.

Article 5(1): no one shall be deprived of his liberty save in the following cases and in accordance with a procedure prescribed by law

3.13 The permissible grounds for detention set out in Article 5(1) are exhaustive (*Ireland* v *UK* (1978) 2 EHRR 25 para. 194), and are to be given a narrow interpretation[16] (*McVeigh, O'Neill and Evans* v *UK* (1981) 25 DR 15) but are not mutually exclusive. Thus a requirement for an immigrant to submit to further examination can be an obligation under Article 5(1)(b) and a permissible ground for deprivation of liberty (*McVeigh et al* v *UK* (1981)). The Article 5 requirement that every deprivation of liberty be 'prescribed by law' which imports a requirement of procedural legality is closely related to the requirement that detention must be 'lawful' under the permitted grounds under paragraphs (a) to (f) since the notion of 'lawful' covers both substantive and procedural matters. In practice, the European Court sometimes merges consideration of these two requirements by asking if the deprivation of liberty was 'lawful'.[17] Legality has two elements: domestic legality, and ECHR legality. It follows that an ECHR review of detention will necessarily provide greater protection than a pure domestic law assessment.

3.14 In *R* v *Governor of HMP Brockhill ex parte Evans (No. 2)* [2000] 3 WLR 843 Lord Hope summarized the approach of the European Court as follows:

The jurisprudence of the European Court of Human Rights indicates that there are various aspects to Article 5(1) which must be satisfied in order to show that the detention is lawful for the purposes of that Article. The first question is whether the detention is lawful under domestic law. Any detention which is unlawful in domestic law will automatically be unlawful under Article 5(1). It will thus give rise to an enforceable right to compensation under Article 5(5), the provisions of which are not discretionary but mandatory. The second question is whether, assuming that the detention is lawful under domestic law, it nevertheless complies with the general requirements of the Convention.

These are based upon the principles that any restriction on human rights and fundamental freedoms must be prescribed by law: see Articles 8 to 11 of the Convention. They include the requirements that the domestic law must be sufficiently accessible to the individual and that it must be sufficiently precise to enable the individual to foresee the consequences of the restriction: *Sunday Times* v *United Kingdom* (1979–80) 2 EHTT 245; *Zamir* v *United Kingdom* (1985) 40 DR 42, paras 90–91. The third question is whether, again assuming that the detention is lawful under domestic law, it is nevertheless open to criticism on the ground that it is arbitrary because, for example, it was resorted to in bad faith or was not proportionate: *Engel* v *Netherlands* [1976] 1 EHRR 647, para. 58; *Tsirlis and Kouloumpas* v *Greece* [1997] 25 EHRR 198, para. 56.

---

[16] See *Guzzardi* v *Italy* (1981) 3 EHRR 333 paras. 98 and 100; *Winterwerp* v *Netherlands* (1979) 2 EHRR 387 para. 37; *Quinn* v *France* (1995) 21 EHRR 529 para. 42.
[17] Harris, O'Boyle and Warwick, *Law of the European Convention on Human Rights* (Butterworths, 1995) 105.

Domestic legality

3.15 Domestic legality includes directly applicable provisions of Community law (*Caprino v UK* (1978) 12 DR 14). It is the primary function of the national authorities, and especially in this context, the courts, to interpret and apply domestic law (*Bozano v France* (1986) 9 EHRR 297 para. 58), but the European Court retains the ultimate or long-stop function of determining whether detention is in accordance with national law (*Bozano* para. 58). A certain margin of appreciation will be afforded to the domestic courts owing to 'the limits inherent in the logic of the European system of protection'.[18] We have seen in chapter 1 that such limits are neither inherent nor necessarily appropriate under the Human Rights Act 1998, where a national court is examining detention. The Court of Appeal has stated that deference will be paid to the Secretary of State's assessment of the need for immigration detention, notwithstanding the Court's experience and function of adjudicating upon the propriety of detention (*R (Sezek) v Secretary of State* [2001] INLR 675). The critical question is whether the court is reviewing expediency akin to a bail review under Article 5(3) or legality under Article 5(4). We return to the issue of deference in the context of challenges to detention below at 3.114.

3.16 In *E v Norway* (1990) 17 EHRR 30 para. 49 the European Court held that an 'arrested or detained person is entitled to a review of the "lawfulness" of his detention in the light not only of the requirements of domestic law, but also of the text of the Convention, the general principles embodied therein, and the aim of the restrictions permitted by Article 5(1)'. In *Zamir v UK* (1983) 40 DR 42 the European Commission had earlier stated (at para. 87) that:

> While Article 5(1)(e) requires that the substantive conditions justifying detention are met,[19] Article 5(1)(f) does not require the Commission to provide its own interpretation on questions of national law concerning the legality of the detention or deportation. The scope of the Commission's review is limited to examining whether there is a legal basis for the detention and whether the decision of the courts on the question of lawfulness could be described as arbitrary in light of the facts of the case.

ECHR legality

3.17 The general principles of ECHR law include the 'rule of law'[20] and the requirement that the domestic law upon which a detention is based must have

---

[18] See *Bozano v France* (1986) 9 EHRR 297 para. 58; *Weeks v UK* (1987) 10 EHRR 293 para. 50; *Winterwerp v Netherlands* (1979) 2 EHRR 387 para. 40.

[19] i.e. the existence of a mental disorder warranting compulsory confinement.

[20] See *Brogan v UK* (1988) 11 EHRR 117 para. 58; *Engel v Netherlands* (1976) EHRR 647 para. 69.

sufficient qualities of accessibility and precision so as to avoid arbitrariness.[21] This is particularly important with regard to asylum seekers. The issue was raised by the Council of Europe Parliamentary Assembly in 1997, when it recommended that member states develop and promote clear criteria for detention.[22] In *Amuur* v *France* (1996) 22 EHRR 533 the European Court stated (at para. 50) that:

> It remains to be determined whether the deprivation of liberty found to be established in the present case was compatible with Article 5(1). Where the 'lawfulness' of detention is in issue, including the question whether 'a procedure prescribed by law' has been followed, the Convention refers essentially to national law and lays down the obligation to conform to the substantive and procedural rules of national law, but it requires in addition that any deprivation of liberty should be in keeping with the purpose of Article 5, namely to protect the individual from arbitrariness. . . .
>
> In laying down that any deprivation of liberty must be effected 'in accordance with a procedure prescribed by law', Article 5(1) primarily requires any arrest or detention to have a legal basis in domestic law. However, these words do not merely refer back to domestic law; like the expressions 'in accordance with the law' and 'prescribed by law' in the second paragraphs of Articles 8 to 11, they also relate to the quality of the law, requiring it to be compatible with the rule of law, a concept inherent in all the Articles of the Convention.
>
> In order to ascertain whether a deprivation of liberty has complied with the principle of compatibility with domestic law, it therefore falls to the Court to assess not only the legislation in force in the field under consideration, but also the quality of the other legal rules applicable to the persons concerned. Quality in this sense implies that where a national law authorises deprivation of liberty—especially in respect of a foreign asylum seeker—it must be sufficiently accessible and precise, in order to avoid all risk of arbitrariness. These characteristics are of fundamental importance with regard to asylum seekers at airports, particularly in view of the need to reconcile the protection of fundamental rights with the requirements of states' immigration policies.

3.18 In *Dougoz* v *Greece* (2001) 10 BHRC 306 a complaint under Article 5(1)(f) succeeded because the law under which the applicant was detained was of insufficient quality to ensure that detention was necessary. The European Court noted (at paras. 56 to 58) that Greek law:

> provides for the detention of an alien on condition that the execution of an administrative order for expulsion taken by the Minister of Public Order is pending, and that the alien is considered to be a danger to public order or might abscond.
>
> In the present case the expulsion of the applicant was ordered by a court and not by

---

[21] See *Zamir* v *UK* (1983) 40 DR 42 paras. 90 and 91; *Steel* v *UK* [1999] EHRLR 109; *Amuur* v *France* (1996) 22 EHRR 533 para. 50.

[22] Council of Europe Parliamentary Assembly, Recommendation 1327 on the Protection and Reinforcement of the Human Rights of Refugees and Asylum Seekers in Europe, 1997, http://stars.coe.fr/ta/ta97/ERREC1327.htm

an administrative decision. Moreover, the applicant was not considered a danger to public order. The indictments chamber, which ordered his release from prison in July 1997, held that it transpired from the applicant's conduct during detention that he was not going to commit any further offences when released and that it was not necessary to prolong his detention.

57. The Court further notes that on 1 April 1993 the Deputy Public Prosecutor of the Court of Cassation opined that decision No. 4803/13/7A/18–26.6.92 applied by analogy in cases of expulsion ordered by courts. The Court does not consider that the opinion of a senior public prosecutor—concerning the applicability by analogy of a ministerial decision on the detention of persons facing administrative expulsion—constituted a 'law' of sufficient 'quality' within the meaning of the Court.

58. In these circumstances, the Court finds that there has been a breach of Article 5(1) of the Convention in the present case.

Thus where national law permits detention pending deportation only where the deportee is a risk to public order or an absconding risk, and a court has ruled that the deportee does not present such risks, continued detention will breach Article 5(1)(f). In the UK, however, there are provisions of the law permitting detention pending removal.

Arbitrariness

3.19 Convention legality also importantly includes a requirement for an absence of arbitrariness either in motivation or effect.[23] The requirement that detention must not be arbitrary encompasses cases of bad faith where the detention is not in keeping with the purposes of the restrictions set out in Article 5. In *Bozano* v *France* (1987) 9 EHRR 297 an Italian national who had been convicted in his absence of murder by an Italian court was forcibly taken by French police to the Swiss border and handed into Swiss police custody pursuant to what transpired to be an unlawful deportation order in order to circumvent a French court's ruling. The European Court held the deprivation of liberty to be arbitrary in motivation and unlawful: the detention was ostensibly for the purpose of deportation but in reality was a disguised illegal extradition.

---

[23] See *Amuur* v *France* (1996) 22 EHRR 533; *Winterwerp* v *Netherlands* (1979) 2 EHRR 387 at paras. 37–9; note that the concern to prevent arbitrary detention is expressly stated in Article 9 of the UN International Covenant on Civil and Political Rights. In *R* v *Governor of HMP Brockhill ex parte Evans No. 2* [2000] 3 WLR 843, Lord Hope held that detention by a prison governor in accordance with an erroneous construction of legislation as to release dates was not arbitrary under Article 5, where the construction was based on Divisional Court authority subsequently overruled by the Court of Appeal. In *R* v *Offen* [2001] 1 WLR 514 the Court of Appeal considered that the imposition of an automatic life sentence under s. 2 of the Crime (Sentences) Act 1997 could be arbitrary unless the exceptional circumstances proviso was interpreted widely to allow the Court to consider risk and dangerousness on an individuated basis.

Proportionality

3.20 However, even if properly motivated and otherwise lawful, a deprivation of liberty may be arbitrary in effect by being disproportionate to the aim pursued. In *Litwa v Poland* (4 April 2000) a case concerning Article 5(1)(e), the European Court held (at para. 78) that:

> The notion of 'lawfulness' runs through Article 5. As a result it is not enough simply to establish that one of the grounds for detention under Article 5(1)(a) to (f) is made out, detention must also be necessary. And detention will not be necessary unless the authorities can show that other measures short of detention were considered.

3.21 In *A v Australia* (1997) 4 BHRC 210 the UN Human Rights Committee considered Article 9 of the UN International Covenant on Civil and Political Rights[24] which provides as follows:

> 9.1 Everyone has the right to liberty and security of the person. No one shall be subjected to arbitrary arrest or detention. No one shall be deprived of his liberty except on such grounds and in accordance with such procedures as are established by law.

3.22 The concern of Article 5 of the ECHR to protect against arbitrary detention is thus made explicit in Article 9 of the ICCPR. *A v Australia* concerned a four-year detention of a Cambodian asylum seeker. The UN Human Rights Committee noted that arbitrariness embraced questions of necessity, and held (Communication No. 560/1993, Butterworths Immigration Law Service):

> the notion of 'arbitrariness' must not be equated with 'against the law' but be interpreted more broadly to include such elements as inappropriateness and injustice. Furthermore, remand in custody could be considered arbitrary if it is not necessary in all the circumstances of the case, for example to prevent flight or interference with evidence: the element of proportionality becomes relevant in this context. . . .
>
> The Committee observes however, that every decision to keep a person in detention should be open to review periodically so that the grounds justifying detention can be assessed. In any event, detention should not continue beyond the period for which the State can provide appropriate justification. For example, the fact of illegal entry may indicate a need for investigation and there may be other factors particular to the individual, such as the likelihood of absconding and lack of co-operation, which may justify detention for a period. Without such factors detention may be considered arbitrary, even if entry was illegal.

---

[24] The UK is a signatory to the ICCPR 1966 although does not presently recognize the right of individual petition. Further Articles 17 and 53 of the ECHR require interpretation of ECHR obligations in a manner consistent with other international obligations of the contracting state, and the jurisprudence relating to the two instruments has been developed in parallel; see also s. 11 of the HRA 1998.

3.23   This approach is also reflected in Detention Guidelines published by the UNHCR,[25] which specify that legality requires that the law authorizing detention must be in conformity with general principles of international human rights law, and that the review of detention must embrace the question of whether the detention is and continues to be necessary in the particular circumstances of the case. The UNHCR has also commented that the detention of asylum seekers is 'inherently undesirable',[26] and is only acceptable if it is brief, absolutely necessary and is instituted after other options have been implemented.[27]

3.24   We return to the question of proportionality below at 3.36 et seq when we consider the 'Oakington case'.

Reasons

3.25   Reasons for detention may be relevant to a consideration of whether the detention is arbitrary. The UN Body of Principles for the Protection of All Persons Under Any Form of Detention or Imprisonment provide at Principle 32 that the detainee should be able to challenge not only whether the detention is lawful but also the reasons for the detention. In *Chahal* (1997) 23 EHRR 413, the European Court noted that the Secretary of State's view that the applicant's detention was required by national security considerations was open to a limited form of review by the advisory panel procedure,[28] the gist of the reasons for detention were given to the applicant, and therefore held that the combination was a sufficient guarantee against the detention being arbitrary and a violation of Article 5(1). That procedure however was insufficient for the purposes of Article 5(4), because the advisory panel was not a court, could not direct release and the procedures before it were not sufficiently court-like. The European Court made plain that Article 5(4) did not require a complete review of the expediency of the detention, and the underlying reasons for the expulsion, but a sufficient control of legality for Article 5(1) purposes.

Article 5(1)(f)

3.26   Article 5(1)(f) is the only provision in the ECHR which explicitly refers to immigration control in recognizing that the detention of persons to prevent unauthorized entry into a country or in order to remove those liable to expulsion is a permissible exception to the right of individual liberty. Its importance lies in the

---

[25] UNHCR, Guidelines on applicable Criteria and Standards relating to the Detention of Asylum seekers (Geneva, 1999, www.unhcr.hr).

[26] *ibid*, para. 1.

[27] UNHCR EXCOM Conclusion 44 ('Detention of Refugees and Asylum seekers') UN Doc A/AC.96/688.

[28] Replaced by the Special Immigration Appeals Commission set up by the Special Immigration Appeals Commission Act 1997.

fact that although the ECHR does not grant to aliens a right of admission or residence in contracting states, the minimum guarantees against arbitrary detention are provided by Article 5(1)(f) where the authorities arrest or detain an alien pending a decision on his admission, deportation or extradition.

3.27　The critical question in immigration law is: what do those minimum guarantees comprise? Detention is only justified 'to prevent (a person's) unauthorised entry into the country' or where 'action is being taken with a view to deportation or extradition'. On its face, the Article appears to speak to two discrete classes of persons: (1) those at the frontier seeking entry and (2) those detained pending deportation.

Prevention of unauthorized entry
3.28　In *Amuur* v *France* (1996) 22 EHRR 533 the European Court held, in respect of the first category under Article 5(1)(f), that:

> 43. Holding aliens in the international zone does indeed involve a restriction upon liberty, but one which is not in every respect comparable to that which obtains in centres for the detention of aliens pending deportation. Such confinement, accompanied by suitable safeguards for the persons concerned, is acceptable only in order to enable States to prevent unlawful immigration while complying with their international obligations, particularly under the 1951 Geneva Convention Relating to the Status of Refugees and the European Convention on Human Rights. States' legitimate concern to foil the increasingly frequent attempts to circumvent immigration restrictions must not deprive asylum seekers of the protection afforded by these Conventions.

3.29　Whilst this passage might have been expressed in clearer terms, we suggest that the natural reading is that the justification for detention of the first class of immigrant is narrow: it is acceptable only to *prevent* unlawful immigration. The use of the term 'prevent' in both Article 5(1)(f) and *Amuur* also suggests that there must be a causal connection between the detention and the unlawful immigration. And an immigrant claiming asylum is not thereby without more seeking unlawful or unauthorized entry. In *R* v *Naillie* [1993] AC 674, the House of Lords held that where asylum seekers arrived, but did not seek entry, by means including deception, they could not be treated as illegal entrants. UNHCR Detention Guidelines[29] make the related point that asylum seekers who arrive without documentation because they are unable to obtain any in their country of origin should not be detained solely for that reason: detention is only permissible where asylum seekers who travel on no, or fraudulent, documentation intend to mislead the authorities or refuse to co-operate. Commentators have noted that asylum seekers can be said to enjoy presumptive refugee status until it is established that they are not

---

[29] See footnote 25 above.

refugees.[30] As the European Court stated in *Amuur* at para. 43, asylum seekers cannot be treated as criminals, and Article 31 of the Convention relating to the Status of Refugees 1951 forbids the imposition of penalties upon asylum seekers who illegally enter or are illegally present in the host territory.[31] Asylum seekers, without more, should not be treated in the same manner as illegal immigrants. However, a different approach to causation was taken by the Court of Appeal in *R (Saadi) v Secretary of State* [2001] EWCA Civ 1512 (upheld by the House of Lords: [2002] UKHL 41). There the Court of Appeal held that a short-term detention of the order of a week in the relatively liberal regime of Oakington Reception Centre, for the purposes of examination of a claim even where there was no risk of absconding, was compatible with Article 5(1)(f). The only issue was whether the detention was overlong and whether the conditions of detention were suitable. We discuss *Saadi* below at 3.36–3.54. As to length of detention, see below at 3.31.

Action with a view to deportation or extradition

3.30   The terms permitting detention of the second class of immigrants are more widely drawn: all that is necessary is that 'action is being taken with a view to deportation . . .'. There is no causal condition: the Article does not require, for example, detention in order to facilitate deportation. According to the European Court's case law, it is clear that at least in this class of case detention is not confined to the situation where the deportee is an absconding risk or may otherwise misbehave. In *Chahal v UK* (1997) 23 EHRR 413 the European Court held (at para. 112):

> The Court recalls that it is not in dispute that Mr Chahal has been detained 'with a view to deportation' within the meaning of Article 5(1)(f).
>
> Article 5(1)(f) does not demand that the detention of a person against whom action is being taken with a view to deportation be reasonably considered necessary, for example to prevent his committing an offence or fleeing; in this respect Article 5(1)(f) provides a different level of protection from Article 5(1)(c).[32]
>
> Indeed, all that is required under this provision is that 'action is being taken with a view to deportation'. It is therefore immaterial, for the purposes of Article 5(1)(f) whether the underlying decision to expel can be justified under national or Convention law.

Due diligence as an aspect of 'lawfulness'

3.31   The European Court in *Chahal* did however limit the power of detention

---

[30] See J. Vedsted-Hansen in F. Nicholson and P. Twomey (eds), *Refugee Rights and Realities: Evolving International Concepts and Regimes* (Cambridge University Press, 1999) at 275.

[31] See *R v Uxbridge MC ex parte Adimi* [2001] QB 667.

[32] See also *Bozano v France* (1986) 9 EHRR 297 para. 60; *Al-Nashif v Bulgaria* (App. No. 50963/99).

under this limb of Article 5(1)(f) by stipulating that detention was only lawful so long as the underlying deportation proceedings were being pursued with due diligence, and that even where the proceedings were diligently pursued, if they continued for an exceptional length of time, some explanation had to be provided otherwise the detention would be arbitrary.[33]

3.32 The Commission had earlier noted in 1976 in *Lynas v Switzerland* (1976) 6 DR 141 that while Article 5(1)(f) sets no 'reasonable time' limit on the length of detention, proceedings had to be pursued with due diligence.[34] In practice, extended periods of detention of immigrants have been permitted with the European Court considering the actions of the individual as well as those of the state. Thus in *Kolompar v Belgium* (1992) 16 EHRR 197, where the applicant was detained for almost three years, there was no breach of Article 5(1)(f) because he had delayed proceedings and impliedly consented to the prolongation of his detention. In *Chahal* itself, a three and a half year detention was not excessive, having regard to the complexity of the proceedings and the gravity of the issues at state.[35]

3.33 The protection offered by the ECHR as regards the permissible length of detention is less than that promoted by other international organs. The Parliamentary Assembly has recommended in a number of resolutions that member states be encouraged to introduce a maximum period of detention into law.[36] Both the UNHCR and the European Council for Refugees and Exiles have also stated that an absolute maximum period of detention should be specified in national law,[37] and principles relating to detention of asylum seekers published by the UN Working Group on Arbitrary Detention also state that in no case should detention be unlimited or of excessive length.[38]

Expulsion as an aspect of lawfulness
3.34 In *Ali v Switzerland* (1998) 28 EHRR 304 the European Commission concluded that where deportation is impossible, Article 5(1)(f) will not permit

---

[33] *Chahal* v *UK* (1997) 23 EHRR 413 para. 113; *Quinn* v *France* (1969) 21 EHRR 529 para. 48; note that the duration of detention is only mentioned in Article 5(3), referring to criminal cases under Article 5(1)(c).

[34] See also *X* v *UK* 12 DR 207 at 209; *Farmakopoulos* v *Belgium* 64 DR 52.

[35] *Chahal* v *UK* (1997) 23 EHRR 413 para. 117.

[36] See Council of Europe Parliamentary Assembly, Recommendation 1327 on the Protection and Reinforcement of Human Rights of Refugees and Asylum Seekers in Europe, 1997; Council of Europe Parliamentary Assembly, Arrival of Asylum Seekers and European Airports (Doc 8761, June 2000).

[37] UNHCR, Guidelines on applicable Criteria and Standards relating to the Detention of Asylum Seekers, Geneva, 1999 (www.unhcr.hr).

[38] UN Commission on Human Rights Working Group on Arbitary Detention, Body of Principles for the Protection of All Persons under Any Form of Detention or Imprisonment Regarding the Situation of Immigrants and Asylum Seekers, UN Doc E/CN. 4/2000/4/Annex 2 (1999) Principle 7.

detention. The European Commission noted that the Swiss authorities wanted to extradite the applicant to Somalia but were unable to do so because he had no travel documents. Since the execution of the extradition was impossible, the detention could no longer be considered 'with a view to extradition' within Article 5(1)(f). These requirements appear to mirror the duty of expedition on the Secretary of State for the Home Department and the further implied limits to the statutory power of detention held to exist by Woolf J in *Hardial Singh* [1984] 1 WLR 704 at 706.

3.35 Thus the practical impossibility of removal will be one of the essential ingredients of the legality of the detention, required to be speedily reviewed by a court under Article 5(4). Equally where removal is prohibited owing to the nature of the treatment which would prevail in the receiving state following expulsion, a deprivation of liberty pending such expulsion would be unlawful. In this situation, the court on an Article 5(4) review would not be examining the merits or expediency of the decision to detain, but rather one of the essential ingredients of its legality.

The Oakington case
3.36 In *R (Saadi)* v *Secretary of State* [2001] EWCA Civ 1512, 19 October 2001 the Court of Appeal controversially allowed the Secretary of State's appeal against the judgment of Collins J [2001] EWHC Admin 670, 7 September 2001 in which the regime of detention at Oakington Reception Centre was declared to be in violation of Article 5. The House of Lords upheld the Court of Appeal's decision [2002] UKHL 41).

3.37 The case is important because the Oakington regime was described 'a cornerstone of the government's current procedure for processing applications for asylum'. The claimants were four Iraqi asylum seekers who had entered the UK legally and illegally and were detained at Oakington Reception Centre. They were detained for not more than 10 days. Their detention was designed to facilitate a speedy decision on their claims for asylum by ensuring that they were available at all times for interview. None of the claimants were considered to be at risk of absconding or committing offences; indeed lack of such a risk was a condition for detention at Oakington. Collins J considered (at paras. 43 to 45) that detention was not justified under the first limb of Article 5(1)(f) since ensuring that the claimants attended interviews was a matter of administrative convenience, no alternatives had been tried, and detention was disproportionate to the prevention of unauthorized entry and a clear breach of Article 5(1)(f).

Detention in accordance with domestic law
3.38 The Court of Appeal considered that at domestic law there was a power to detain pending a decision on leave to enter, with an implicit limitation only on the

)ersisted for so long as was reasonably neces-
ınd reach the decision.[39] It was clear that the
simply because the individual did not present
t situation there would equally be no power to
the power to grant temporary admission only
ed ([2001] EWCA Civ 1512, 19 October 2001,
her the use made of the national law power to
s.

iidered that under the Home Office policy on
hite Paper, *Firmer Faster Fairer—A Modern
:ylum* the applicants would have had an unan-
ed for initial detention no longer than necessary
the nature of the claim, with a subsequent grant
ıy reason to believe that they would not comply
ıdmission (para. 16). But the policy changed on
:ional criterion for detention was announced.
tained at Oakington for about a period of seven
ıat a speedy decision could be reached. If that
lmission would be granted, or a period of further
detention would be imposed in accordance with existing criteria (para. 17). The
Secretary of State submitted that even temporary absences could impair the expeditious consideration of cases, and have domino effects on systemic efficiency
(para. 24). The Court of Appeal noted that if it was not necessary to detain to
process claims speedily (the stated purpose of the detention) then detention would
be irrational. While the Court of Appeal entertained doubts about the necessity of
detention, those doubts were speculative. While detention in circumstances where
the individuals did not present an absconding risk was 'extreme', it was not irrational to ensure efficient working of the system, and was a measure of last resort
given the influx of asylum seekers to the UK (paras. 26 and 27).

3.40   Importantly, the Court of Appeal were at pains to emphasize the quality of
the regime. It was not 'markedly different' from temporary admission with residence conditions, and the additional element of confinement could be imposed
under domestic law (para. 28).

The position under the Convention
3.41   The Court of Appeal noted that at the heart of the issue under Article

---

[39] [2001] EWCA Civ 1512, 19 October 2001, para. 14; applying by analogy *R v Secretary of State
ex parte Hardial Singh* [1984] 1 WLR 704, 706; *Tan Te Lam v Superintendent of Tai A Chau
Detention Centre* [1997] AC 97, 111.

5(1)(f) of the ECHR was the question of what was meant by the term 'unauthorized entry'. The Secretary of State's submission was that unauthorized entry was simply entry which had not been authorized. When an alien set foot in the territory of a state, that state could authorize entry or refuse it. 'Unless and until it authorises entry, the alien will, if he or she moves within the territory, be effecting unauthorised entry. Article 5(1)(f) recognises the right of a state to prevent this by detaining the person seeking to enter.' (para. 32).

3.42   Collins J had rejected this submission (at para. 33), essentially because the causal element in Article 5(1)(f) was not satisfied:

> Once it is accepted that an applicant has made a proper application for asylum and there is no risk that he will abscond or otherwise misbehave, it is impossible to see how it could reasonably be said that he needs to be detained to prevent his effecting an unauthorised entry. He is doing all that he should to ensure that he can make an authorised entry.

Thus, where a person exercised the international human right to seek asylum in compliance with national law procedures, they were not seeking an unauthorized entry, and detention could not prevent that which in law was not being sought.

3.43   The Court of Appeal considered (at para. 40) that at least in 1950 Article 5(1)(f) bore the meaning for which the Secretary of State contended, noting that the right of a state to determine whether aliens should enter its territory was a firmly entrenched principle of public international law (citing the decision in *A v Australia* (1997) 4 BHRC 210 quoted above at 3.21). The Court concluded that the judgment in *Chahal v UK* (1997) 23 EHRR 413 gave rise to three propositions (see para. 54):

(a)   *Chahal* was inconsistent with the contention that the justification for detaining a person with a view to deportation was that this was necessary to prevent absconding or other misbehaviour;

(b)   detention could only be justified if the deportation proceedings were pursued with due diligence;

(c)   even where the proceedings were diligently pursued, if they continued for an exceptional length of time, some explanation had to be provided otherwise the detention would be arbitrary.

The applicants argued that a different approach applied to the first limb of Article 5(1)(f) where an individual, against whom there was no deportation order, had applied for asylum, and relied on *Amuur v France* (1996) 22 EHRR 533.

3.44   The Court of Appeal (at para. 61) considered that the reasoning in *Amuur* was unclear, but critically drew the following conclusions:

64. The [European] Court is expressly comparing 'mere restriction on liberty', which does not infringe Article 5, with 'deprivation of liberty', which does. Yet the examples of what constitutes 'mere restriction of liberty' look very like 'lawful detention to prevent unauthorised entry, or while action is being taken with a view to deportation', which is permitted by Article 5(1)(f). It seems to us that the [European] Court contemplates that it will be lawful to confine aliens in a centre of detention pending deportation or in an international zone for the time that is inevitably needed to organise the practical details of the alien's repatriation or while his application for leave to enter the territory in order to be afforded asylum is considered, provided always (1) that confinement is accompanied by suitable safeguards and (2) that it is not prolonged excessively.

65. It is significant that the [European] Court treats together both detention of the person seeking to enter and detention of the person awaiting deportation. *Amuur* must be read with the later decision in *Chahal*. It seems to us that the Court is considering as lawful detention pending the consideration of an application for leave to enter or the making of arrangements for deportation and not applying a test of whether the detention is necessary in order to carry out those processes. The inroad that we believe that the European Court has made into the right of immigration authorities to detain aliens pending consideration of the applications for leave to enter, or their deportation, is that these processes must not be unduly prolonged. It is in relation to the duration of detention that the question of proportionality arises.

3.45 In the instant case the Court of Appeal concluded that a detention in the order of a week was not too long, and that the Secretary of State's detention policy was more generous than that required by the Convention (para. 67). This was unsurprising because the common law recognized as part of our heritage the fundamental importance of liberty, and the 'deprivation of liberty with which this appeal is concerned falls at the bottom end of the scale of interference with that right' (para. 69).

Analysis

3.46 There are a number of difficult questions raised by the Court of Appeal's judgment in *Saadi* (which judgment was upheld by the House of Lords: [2002] UKHL 41). In our opinion, the Court of Appeal's analysis of the ECHR principles with respect to detention of immigrants is flawed and could lead to widespread schemes of indefinite detention of the variety favoured by Australia but inconsistent with human rights standards.

3.47 First, there is, with respect, an important difference between those who are being deported and those whose unauthorised entry is being prevented. Deportees have violated the criminal or immigration laws of the country and are facing removal because of their infringements of the law. Asylum seekers are not violating domestic law when they apply for entry at the port (see above at 3.29). They require no documents or visas to enter for the purposes of asylum.

3.48   Secondly, the Court of Appeal has focused on a broad construction of 'unauthorized entry'. Once an asylum application is going to take weeks to consider rather than days, the situation does not correspond to the normal immigration scenario of a brief interview on arrival and administrative restriction of liberty for a few hours or possibly days as checks are made. Neither the international community in 1950 nor the drafters of the Immigration Act 1971 foresaw the problem of determining large numbers of asylum claims at the frontier. Once large numbers of asylum claims meant significant delays in decision-making at the port, national practice in the UK has always been to grant temporary admission where possible in the absence of countervailing factors. It is obvious that such a policy promotes the principle of minimal interference with liberty and does not penalize those who are exercising an international right to seek protection abroad. Temporary admission is not unauthorized entry; manifestly the state is authorizing physical admission in those circumstances. Neither does liability to temporary admission expose without more the individual to a deprivation of liberty, simply because the state has in international law the right to control conditions of admission and a grant of temporary admission does not preclude a subsequent detention.

3.49   Thirdly, as a result of this elision between temporary admission and a deprivation of liberty, the Court of Appeal did not explain that deprivation of liberty had to be necessary to prevent unauthorized entry. Temporary admission, which as we have explained is a restriction rather than a deprivation of liberty, will in most cases be sufficient where there is no reason to suspect a future breach of its terms. International principles of construction require the exception to the right of liberty to be strictly and narrowly construed. What should have been the subject of the Court of Appeal's analysis was whether deprivation of liberty was a proportionate means of preventing unlawful entry where a restriction of liberty was available.

3.50   Fourthly, the Court of Appeal has not identified any factor going to arbitrariness other than the duration of the detention, and the conditions of the detention regime. It cited but did not address nor follow the opinion of the UN Human Rights Committee in the case of *A v Australia*. We would argue that the logic of the European Court's decision in *Amuur* and that of the UN Human Rights Committee in *A v Australia* is consistent with the approach we suggest and requires the court to ask: is the interference necessary and proportionate?

3.51   The *Chahal* judgment did not revise *Amuur*. The European Court in *Chahal* was dealing with a very different issue. Chahal was clearly detained with a view to being deported and the European Court concluded that in the light of the complexities of the case the deportation was not unlawful by reason of excessive detention. If that was all that the national court needed to do by way of Article 5(4) then judicial review and habeas corpus would have provided sufficient remedies under the ECHR but they did not. They did not, we suggest, because a reviewing court had to go beyond the outlines for legal detention and give some examination to whether there were national security reasons to deny bail. The High Court could not do this and the advisory panel is not a court so there was a violation. This could only be because legality required some consideration of the necessity or propriety of detention, but not a complete review of the merits or expediency of deportation in the first place. Applying this logic to the different case of preventing unlawful entry, it is plain that the prevention of arbitrariness requires the reviewing court to consider whether the deprivation is necessary or proportionate, and in this function while the length of the detention period is important it is not the only consideration.

3.52 It is perhaps somewhat ironic that Iraqi asylum seekers as a class were chosen for detention at Oakington, on the basis that speedy decisions could be made in their cases, even though the resolution of their claims is proving notoriously difficult, with complex questions arising in the context of the refugee definition as to the status of the Kurdish autonomous region, the operation of the internal protection alternative and, moreover, removals cannot be effected to Iraq.[40] A lack of a proper objective basis for the selection of such claims which prove difficult to resolve within the seven-day detention period contemplated by the policy and the Court of Appeal may raise issues under Article 14 in conjunction with Article 5.

3.53 The relatively liberal nature of the regime must be emphasized. The quality of detention featured at three junctures of the Court of Appeal's judgment: first, in providing support for the conclusion that detention was lawful and necessary at common law in that detention at Oakington was not markedly different from a grant of temporary admission with residence conditions (para. 28); and secondly and critically in the Court of Appeal's pivotal consideration of the *Amuur* case to the effect that *Amuur* was contemplating a confinement similar to that which obtains at Oakington; and thirdly in its concluding remarks that *Saadi* concerned an interference with the right to liberty that was at the bottom end of the scale. We would suggest that even on the Court of Appeal's analysis of the ECHR a generalized confinement in a harsher regime, with difficulty of access to legal representation, and with detention routinely prolonged beyond seven days would violate Article 5(1)(f) as being disproportionate in length and therefore arbitrary. The inference would arise that detention was being used as a deterrent[41]

---

[40] See *Gardi* v *Secretary of State* [2002] 1 WLR 2755 (declared a nullity on jurisdictional grounds: [2002] EWCA Civ 1560); and *R (Hwez and Khadit)* CO/2405/2001, CO/5118/2001.

[41] This would also arguably violate other international obligations in Article 31 of the Refugee Convention: *R* v *Uxbridge Magistrates' Court ex parte Adimi and others* [2001] QB 667.

rather than as a means of facilitating the expeditious examination of claims,[42] and mixed purposes extraneous to Article 5(1) are not permitted.

3.54 There is no support either in the text of the ECHR itself or in the case law of the European Court for the view that a deprivation of liberty is permitted for administrative convenience in the expeditious processing of a claim. If indeed the restrictions were so minimal and necessary for effective examination at the frontier then, applying *Amuur*, Article 5(1) would not be engaged at all, but this was never the government's case. The terminology of Article 5(1)(f)—at least the starting point for discerning its true meaning[43]—is careful to isolate the purpose of preventing unauthorized entry for the detention of those in respect of whom there is no pending deportation process. The mere fact that deportation may follow a rejected claim for entry is not to the point since detention with a view to deportation is only permitted for the pendency of that process.

Article 5(2): right to be informed of the grounds of detention

3.55 Article 5(2) requires that anyone arrested or detained be 'informed promptly, in a language which he understands, of the reasons for his arrest and of any charge against him'. The Article is not restricted to criminal cases and extends to detention on any ground in Article 5(1) (*Van der Leer* v *Netherlands* (1990) 12 EHRR 567, paras. 27–9). The purpose of the requirement is to enable a detainee to formulate a challenge under Article 5(4), and accordingly he or she must be told in simple, non-technical language the essential legal and factual basis for his detention (*Fox, Campbell and Hartley* v *UK* (1990) 13 EHRR 157, para. 40). The extent of the information required depends on the circumstances, but mere recitation of the source detention power is unlikely to be sufficient (para. 41).

Article 5(4)

3.56 Article 5(4) provides a *lex specialis* remedy for detention as compared with the more general protection of an effective remedy embodied in Article 13.

---

[42] Van Dijk and Van Hoof, *Theory and Practice of the ECHR* (above at footnote 5) 364, contemplate at least such a role for proportionality in Article 5(1)(f): 'Article 5(1)(f) implies the guarantee that the detention must have no purpose other than that of preventing the admission of the alien in question to the country or of making it possible to decide on his deportation or extradition. Article 18. . . . which prohibits restrictions of the rights and freedoms for any purpose other than that for which they have been permitted, applies here as well. In the first place this means . . . that the deprivation of liberty is unlawful if the deportation order, and the way in which it is enforced, constitute a misuse of power. In the second place it follows that the detention must not be attended with more restrictions for the person concerned and must not last longer than is required for a normal conduct of the proceedings.' Harris, D. J., Warwick, C. and O'Boyle, M., *Law of the European Convention on Human Rights* (Butterworths, 1995) 127, appear to agree with Van Dijk and Van Hoof in stating that 'the principle of proportionality provides a convincing basis for insistence upon "reasonable diligence".'

[43] See Article 31 of the Vienna Convention, *Fothergill* v *Monarch Airlines* [1981] AC 251.

Its engagement does not depend on the detention being unlawful under Article 5(1): it is a discrete free-standing right (*Kolompar* v *Belgium* (1992) 16 EHRR 197, para. 45). What is required is speedy access to a court competent to review the legality of detention, both in ECHR and domestic senses of the term, with a view to directing release. Since the purpose is to secure release, a person lawfully at liberty cannot invoke it to challenge his detention retrospectively (*X* v *Sweden* (1983) 32 DR 303 at 305), although complaint may be made about the speediness of any review which took place (*X* v *UK* (1982) 28 DR 235 at 239). Where the grounds for detention may change over time, *periodic* review is required (*Bezichen* v *Italy* (1989) 12 EHRR 210).

3.57 On any Article 5(4) review, the burden of justifying the detention falls on the state (*Zamir* v *UK* (1983) 5 EHRR 242, para. 58). The extent of the remedy required varies according to the nature of the detention challenged but restriction to the narrow question of whether there is jurisdiction to detain according to national law will be insufficient.[44] Thus in *Chahal* v *UK* (1997) 23 EHRR 413 the European Court stated:

127. The Court further recalls that the notion of 'lawfulness' under Article 5(4) has the same meaning as in Article 5(1), so that the detained person is entitled to a review of his detention in the light not only of the requirements of domestic law but also of the text of the Convention, the general principles embodied therein and the aim of the restrictions permitted by Article 5(1).

The scope of the obligations under Article 5(4) is not identical for every kind of deprivation of liberty . . . this applied notably to the extent of the judicial review afforded. Nonetheless, it is clear that Article 5(4) does not guarantee a right to judicial review of such breadth as to empower the court, on all aspects of the case including questions of pure expediency, to substitute its own discretion for that of the decision-making authority. The review should, however, be wide enough to bear on those conditions which are essential for the 'lawful' detention of a person according to Article 5(1).

128. The Court refers again to the requirements of Article 5(1) in cases of detention with a view to deportation. . . . It follows from these requirements that Article 5(4) does not demand that the domestic courts should have the power to review whether the underlying decision to expel could be justified under national or Convention law.

129. The notion of 'lawfulness' in Article 5(1)(f) does not refer solely to the obligation to conform to the substantive and procedural rules of national law; it requires in addition that any deprivation of liberty should be in keeping with the purpose of Article 5. The question therefore arises whether the available proceedings to challenge the lawfulness of Mr Chahal's detention and to seek bail provided an adequate control by the domestic courts.

---

[44] See *Amuur* v *France* (1996) 22 EHRR 533 at paras, 50 and 53; *A* v *Australia* (1997) 4 BHRC 210, para. 9.5.

3.58   Thus the Article 5(4) court reviews the legality of the detention rather than the expediency or merits,[45] so that it is more a habeas corpus court than a bail court (examination of the merits is required by Article 5(3) which applies only to criminal cases (*Aquilina* v *Malta* (App. No. 25642/94, 29 April 1999) para. 47)). But the extent of the remedy required will depend upon the nature of the detention at issue.[46] The court must be able to consider as part of its function of reviewing the essential conditions for the legality of detention: (1) domestic legality; (2) ECHR legality including the question of whether detention is proportionate which will involve consideration, at minimum, of duration and the conditions of detention, and arguably, at least in non-expulsion cases, the necessity of detention in all the circumstances (see above at 3.48). The court will need to review any necessary facts to ensure that detention is not arbitrary and is restricted to the purpose claimed.[47] Thus it may need to review the question of whether there are impediments to removal, whether practical (*Ali* v *Switzerland* (1998) 28 EHRR 304; see above at 3.34) or legal, where the power of detention is linked to that question.

3.59   The procedure followed must be judicial in character and commensurate with the kind of deprivation of liberty in question.[48] In *Chahal* v *UK* while the advisory panel procedure provided sufficient guarantees against arbitrariness under Article 5(1)(f), it was not a court for Article 5(4) purposes for a combination of reasons: the applicant did not have the right of legal representation before it, he was given only an outline of the grounds for the notice of intention to deport; the panel had no power to give a binding decision, and its advice was not disclosed to him.[49] The European Court also found that Article 5(4) had been

---

[45]   In *Zamir* v *UK* (1983) 5 EHRR 242 para. 100 states in the context of deportation: 'It is not a requirement of this provision . . . that judicial control of detention under Art 5(1)(f) extend to a complete review on all questions of fact of the exercise of the power to detain.'

[46]   See *X* v *UK* (1981) 4 EHRR 188 (habeas corpus insufficient to challenge medical grounds for detention); *Weeks* v *UK* (1987) 10 EHRR 293 (judicial review insufficient to challenge recall of a post-tariff discretionary lifer).

[47]   See *Amuur* v *France* (1996) 22 EHRR 533, paras. 50 and 52; *Litwa* v *Poland* (4 April 2000), para. 78.

[48]   *X* v *UK* (1981) 4 EHRR 188 at para. 53; *Winterwerp* v *Netherlands* (1979) 2 EHRR 387, para. 60 (procedural guarantees under Article 5(4) are not always those required by Article 6(1)); cf *Lamy* v *Belgium* (1989) 11 EHRR 529, para. 29 (appraisal of need for remand in custody in a criminal case and subsequent determination of guilt too closely linked to allow different rules on prosecution disclosure); *De Wilde Ooms and Versyp* v *Belgium* (1970) 1 EHRR 373 at 407, 408 paras. 78 and 79 (procedural guarantees appropriate to a criminal prosecution required in proceedings relating to detention of vagrants).

[49]   *Chahal* v *UK* (1997) 23 EHRR 413 at para. 130. Following the *Chahal* judgment Parliament enacted the Special Immigration Appeals Commission Act 1997 establishing the SIAC; see also *Dougoz* v *Greece* (2001) 10 BHRC 306, paras. 60 to 63 (applicant suffers violation of Article 5(4) where he can only challenge his detention pending deportation by appealing to the discretionary leniency of the Ministers of Justice and Public Order).

violated because national security considerations prevented the courts on judicial review or habeas corpus from reviewing the merits of the decision to detain the applicant with a view to deportation on national security grounds (*Chahal* v *UK* at para. 130). Where there was no national security element to the detention of an illegal entrant, judicial review was found to be sufficient to establish the lawfulness of detention under Article 5(1)(f) (*Zamir* v *UK* (1983) 40 DR 42, para. 100).

3.60 A further requirement of Article 5(4) is that the application for release must be determined speedily. The European Court has emphasized that 'speedily' cannot be defined in the abstract and is context-sensitive. Relevant considerations are the diligence of the authorities, whether delay was caused by the detainee and factors outside the state's responsibility. But neither an excessive workload (*Bezicheri* v *Italy* (1989) 12 EHRR 210, para. 25) nor a holiday period (*E* v *Norway* (1990) 17 EHRR 30) can justify inactivity on the part of the judicial authorities. Time runs from the moment that proceedings are instituted and ends with the final determination of the legality of the detention.[50] Delays of even six and eleven days have been held to be unlawful.[51] In *Amuur* v *France* (1996) 22 EHRR 533, para. 42 the European Court observed 'although by force of circumstances the decision to order holding must necessarily be taken by the administrative or police authorities, the prolongation requires speedy review by the Courts, the traditional guardians of personal liberties'.[52]

3.61 Procedurally, the principles derived from, or at least more commonly associated with, Article 6 have informed the protection afforded to the right to secure liberty before a court under Article 5(4). The Court of Appeal in *A, X and Y and others* v *Secretary of State for the Home Department* [2002] EWCA Civ 1502 considered, at para. 57, that the detention, under immigration powers, of a suspected international terrorist pursuant to the Anti-Terrorism, Crime and Security Act 2001 engaged the civil limb of Article 6. Indeed the right to liberty has been recognized by the European Court as a civil right in *Aerts* v *Belgium* (2000) 29 EHRR 50, para. 59 for the purposes of Article 6. The requirements are as follows:

(a) the 'court' must be independent of the executive and the parties, impartial, and have power to give a legally binding judgment as to release from detention;

---

[50] See *Van der Leer* v *Netherlands* (1990) 12 EHRR 567, para. 35; *Luberti* v *Italy* (1984) 6 EHRR 440.

[51] See *De Jong, Baljet and Van den Brink* v *Netherlands* (22 May 1984) Series A No.77; see also *GB and MB* v *Switzerland* (30 November 2000) (21 days unlawful).

[52] See also principle 4 of the UN Body of Principles on All Forms of Detention (1988).

(b)   the 'equality of arms' principle applies to an Article 5(4) review;[53]

(c)   the detainee must be told the reasons for his detention (*X* v *UK* (1982) 28 DR 235, para. 66),[54] a broad outline is insufficient (*Chahal* v *UK* (1996) 23 EHRR 413, para. 130), and must be given disclosure of all relevant evidence in the possession of the authorities (*Lamy* v *Belgium* (1989) 11 EHRR 529, para. 29);

(d)   he must have adequate time to prepare an application for his release (*Farmakopoulos* v *Belgium* (1992) 16 EHRR 187);

(e)   where detention may be for prolonged periods, the procedure should not be markedly inferior to those in criminal courts (*De Wilde, Ooms and Versyp* v *Belgium* (1971) 1 EHRR 373, paras. 78 and 79);

(f)   there is a proactive duty on the state to provide legal assistance, both during and prior to an Article 5(4) hearing, whenever this is necessary to enable the detainee to make an effective application for release.[55] In *Amuur* v *France* (1996) 22 EHRR 533, para. 53 the European Court held the detention to be incompatible with Article 5(1) because the administrative circulars 'did not provide for legal, humanitarian and social assistance, nor did they lay down procedures and time limits for access to such assistance so that asylum seekers . . . could take the necessary steps'.

(g)   the detainee or his legal representative should generally be permitted to participate in an oral hearing (*Keus* v *Netherlands* (1991) 13 EHRR 700, para. 27), albeit in the extradition context a written procedure was held to be sufficient (*Sanchez-Reisse* v *Switzerland* (1986) 9 EHRR 71, para. 51), but a violation was found because the principle of equality of arms was breached owing to an inability to comment on a late report from the authorities that was before the European Court.

3.62   The position is well-illustrated in *Garcia* v *Germany* (App. No. 23541/94, 13 February 2001):

39 . . . A court examining an appeal against detention must provide guarantees of a judicial procedure. The proceedings must be adversarial and must always ensure 'equality of arms' between the parties, the prosecutor and the detained person. Equality of arms is not ensured if counsel is denied access to those documents in the investigation file

---

[53] The suggestion that the equality of arms principle does not apply to Article 5(4) in *Neumeister* v *Austria* (1968) 1 EHRR 91 at paras. 22–5 and in *Matznetter* v *Austria* (1969) 1 EHRR 198 at para. 13 has not been followed, and the following later authorities are to be preferred: *Toth* v *Austria* (1991) 14 EHRR 551, para. 84; *Lamy* v *Belgium* (1989) 11 EHRR 529, para. 29 and *Sanchez-Reisse* v *Switzerland* (1986) 9 EHRR 71, para. 52.

[54] See also principle 11(3) of the UN Body of Principles on All Forms of Detention (1988).

[55] See *Megveri* v *Germany* (1992) 15 EHRR 584, para. 27; *Woukan Noudefo* v *France* (1988) 13 EHRR 549; *Winterwerp* v *Netherlands* (1979) 2 EHRR 387, para. 60; *A* v *Australia* (1997) 4 BHRC 210 para. 9.5; UN Body of Principles on All Forms of Detention (1988), principle 17(1).

which are essential in order effectively to challenge the lawfulness of his client's detention. . . .

These requirements are derived from the right to an adversarial trial as laid down in
Article 6 of the Convention, which means, in a criminal case, that both the prosecution
and the defence must be given the opportunity to have knowledge of and comment on
the observations filed and the evidence adduced by the other party. According to the
Court's case law, it follows from the wording of Article 6—and particularly from the
autonomous meaning to be given to the notion of 'criminal charge'—that this provision has some application to pre-trial proceedings. . . . It thus follows that, in view of
the dramatic impact of deprivation of liberty on the fundamental rights of the person
concerned, proceedings conducted under Article 5(4) of the Convention should in principle also meet, to the largest extent possible under the circumstances of an on-going
investigation, the basic requirements of a fair trial, such as the right to an adversarial
procedure. While national law may satisfy this requirement in various ways, whatever
method is chosen should ensure that the other party will be aware that observations
have been filed and will have a real opportunity to comment thereon. . . .

Article 5(5)

3.63 The importance in the ECHR of the right to liberty and of effective judicial
supervision of its deprivation is emphasized by Article 5(5) which is unique in the
ECHR[56] in requiring the *national* authority to implement domestic measures to
compensate for detention, as opposed to providing for general measures of redress
to vindicate rights guaranteed under the ECHR. An *ex gratia* scheme is unlikely to
comply with the right to an *enforceable* right to compensation.[57]

3.64 The detainee must have suffered damage, which can include pecuniary and
non-pecuniary loss, to claim compensation (*Wassink* v *Netherlands* (1990) Series
A/185-A, para. 38). Breaches which attract compensation are not limited to those
under Article 5(1) (*Brogan* v *UK* (1988) 11 EHRR 117). The principles to be
employed are those used by the European Court in assessing just satisfaction for
the purposes of Article 41 (formerly Article 50), although as we note above at
1.40 it may be overstating the case to refer to 'principles' in this context. Where
procedural breaches are alleged[58] so that damage is contingent on the hypothetical actions of the Secretary of State, it may be legitimate to award a measure of
damages commensurate with the chance that the Article 5(4) court would have
acted in the detainee's favour.[59]

---

[56] Article 3 of the Seventh Protocol has similar provision for miscarriages of justice which may
involve a breach of Article 6; the UK has yet to ratify the Seventh Protocol.
[57] Harris, O'Boyle and Warwick, *Law of the European Convention on Human Rights*
(Butterworths, 1995) 159.
[58] For example a failure to provide an Article 5(4) court: *R* v *Secretary of State for the Home
Department, ex parte Chahal No. 2* [2000] UKHRR 215.
[59] See *Allied Maples* v *Simmons and Simmons* [1995] 1 WLR 1602, 1604–11; *Benham* v *UK*
(1996) 22 EHRR 293.

3.65   Article 5(5) does not require proof of bad faith on the part of the authorities (*Santa Cruz Ruiz* v *UK* [1998] EHRLR 208). This principle is reflected in s. 9(3) of the HRA 1998 which provides for an exception from the general rule that damages for breaches of s. 6 of the HRA 1998 are not to be awarded against the court or appellate authority for judicial acts done in good faith. Where a judicial act has led to a violation of Article 5, the Lord Chancellor may be required to compensate the claimant.

3.66   Article 5(5) does not give rise to any entitlement to exemplary damages since the right is exclusively compensatory. The right arises where the detention decision was reached without jurisdiction, but not where the decision is merely reversed on appeal.[60] Thus a decision to detain that is subsequently declared unlawful by the court does not necessarily render the whole detention unlawful for its duration: *Benham* v *UK* (1996) 22 EHRR 293. The question remains whether there was sufficient authority in a court or other body of competent jurisdiction to detain in the first place or whether there was a mere flaw in the way that the discretion to detain was executed. It would only be in the former class of 'jurisdiction' case that a quashing of the deportation order is likely to have implications for any interim detention in pursuance of the order. Thus the European Court appears to draw a distinction between cases of a power exercised from the outset in bad faith and a *bona fide* decision subsequently found to be unlawful. In the former case, the detention is likely to be retrospectively unlawful.[61]

3.67   In *Cumber* v *UK* [1997] EHRLR 191 the European Commission held that if the level of compensation awarded was so low as no longer to be 'enforceable' Article 5(5) would be breached. The applicant had been awarded £350 for five hours' false imprisonment. The European Commission considered this was low but not negligible and declared the application manifestly ill-founded. In *Thompson and Hsu* v *Commissioner of Police of the Metropolis* [1998] QB 498 the Court of Appeal gave guidelines for the assessment of damages in false imprisonment cases. It expressly disapproved of the award in *Cumber* and held that in a basic case, basic damages should start at £500 per hour, on a decreasing hourly rate, up to a maximum of about £3000 for the first 24 hours.[62]

3.68   Article 5(5) informed the approach of the House of Lords to the tort of false imprisonment in *R* v *Governor of HMP Brockhill ex parte Evans No. 2*

---

[60] See *Van der Leer* v *Netherlands* (1990) 12 EHRR 567; *Benham* v *UK* (1996) 22 EHRR 293.

[61] See *Bozano* v *France* (1986) 9 EHRR 297, para. 55, contrast *Caprino* v *UK* (1980) 22 DR 5. See *McGrath* v *Chief Constable of Royal Ulster Constabulary* [2001] UKHL 39 (wrong warrant).

[62] The Court of Appeal also gave guidance on aggravated damages. The guidance does not apply where there is unlawful detention at the end of an otherwise lawful sentence of imprisonment: *R* v *Governor of Brockhill Prison, ex part Evans No. 2* [1999] QB 1043 (£5000 awarded for 59 days' loss of liberty, subsequently approved by the House of Lords).

[1999] QB 1043. Lord Hope refused to extend the defence of justification to the acts of a prison governor performed in obedience to erroneous construction of legislation by binding judicial authority. If, as was the case, the detention fell to be regarded as unlawful in domestic law, it would be incompatible with Article 5(5) to refuse compensation.

Derogation

3.69 Article 15 permits contracting states to derogate from Article 5 in times of war or other public emergency threatening the life of the nation. The derogation must be limited to the extent strictly required by the exigencies of the situation, and must not be inconsistent with states' other obligations under international law.

3.70 The UK entered a limited derogation from Article 5(3) following the judgment of the European Court in *Brogan* v *UK* (1988) 11 EHRR 117 where the provisions of the Prevention of Terrorism (Temporary Provision) Act 1984 which permitted detention for four days and six hours, were held to be incompatible with the requirement that the detainee be brought promptly before a judge. The derogation permitted detention up to seven days, and was expressly retained by the HRA 1998, s. 14, Sch. 3 for five years subject to renewal by order of the Secretary of State (HRA 1998, s. 16). The derogation was however withdrawn with effect from 26 February 2001.[63] Many people in the UK would have concluded that with improving prospects of peace in Northern Ireland there would be no need to consider future derogations, however this was not to be. The Human Rights Act 1998 (Designated Derogation) Order 2001 (SI 2001 No. 3644, in force 13 November 2001) was made in anticipation of the UK's proposed derogation from Article 5(1), subsequently communicated to the Council of Europe.

3.71 Presently, other than the UK, only Turkey of the 43 Council of Europe contracting states has a derogation in force, and no contracting state has yet sought to derogate from Article 5 in the light of the events of 11 September 2001 other than the UK. The United Kingdom concluded that derogation was necessary because Article 5(1)(f) does not permit detention where there is no prospect of removal (*Ali* v *Switzerland* (1998) 28 EHRR 304), while section 23 of the Anti-Terrorism Crime and Security Act 2001 permits the indefinite detention of those subject to immigration control (s. 23(2)), who are suspected international terrorists posing a threat to national security, and whose expulsion is prevented by international obligations or other practical obstacles (s. 23(1)).

---

[63] HRA (Amendment) Order 2001 (SI 2001 No. 1216, in force 1 April 2001) amended the HRA 1998 to reflect the withdrawal of the derogation, which followed the implementation of Sch. 8 to the Terrorism Act 2000.

3.72   The European Court held in *Lawless* v *Ireland* (1961) 1 EHRR 15, 31[64] that the words 'other public emergency threatening the life of the nation' refer to:

> an exceptional situation of crisis or emergency which affects the whole population and constitutes a threat to the organised life of the community of which the State is part.

3.73   The European Court requires the asserted emergency to be supported by evidence. A wide margin of appreciation is however left to the national authorities, on the familiar international principle that they are 'in principle better placed than the international judge . . . to decide on the presence of such an emergency'.[65] The decision in *Rehman* v *Secretary of State for the Home Department* [2001] 3 WLR 877 would suggest that substantial deference would be paid by a domestic court to the Secretary of State's assertion in recognition of its status as court and the Secretary of State's status as an accountable Minister.

3.74   While the European Court resists the temptation to judge the efficacy of measures with the benefit of hindsight (*Ireland* v *UK* (1978) 2 HRR 205, paras. 214, 220), the standard of strict necessity demands a high intensity of review of the proposed derogating measure. Thus in *Aksoy* v *Turkey* (1997) 23 EHRR 553) the European Court ruled that the public emergency in south-east Turkey could not justify a detention on suspicion of terrorist involvement lasting 14 days, and without judicial supervision or access to lawyers, doctors, relatives or friends (paras. 78, 83–4).

3.75   We examine the Anti-Terrorism, Crime and Security Act (ATCSA) 2001 and the proposed derogation in more detail in chapter 7, the postscript to this book.

THE DOMESTIC LEGAL FRAMEWORK

3.76   In the UK, the power of administrative detention for immigrants is provided by Schedules 2 and 3 to the Immigration Act (IA) 1971.[66] Such detention may be challenged by an application for bail under the IA 1971 or the Special Immigration Appeals Commission Act 1997, by application for habeas corpus, by invoking the inherent jurisdiction of the High Court to grant bail as ancillary

---

[64] See also *Aksoy* v *Turkey* (1997) 23 EHRR 533, para. 70.

[65] *Ireland* v *UK* (1978) 2 EHRR 25, para. 207; *Brannigan and McBride* v *UK* (1993) 17 EHRR 539, para. 43; *Aksoy* v *Turkey* (1997) 23 EHRR 553, para. 68.

[66] The use of administrative detention has been the subject of criticism: see most recently, Weber, L. and Gelsthorpe, L., *Deciding to Detain* (thesis, Cambridge University, June 2000). The long-standing previous arrangements had led to criticism by the UN Human Rights Committee (see Concluding Observations/Comments on the 4th Periodic Report of the UK (CCPR/C/95/Add.3) July 1995). See earlier Ashford, *Detained Without Trial* (JCWI, 1993); Amnesty International, *Prisoners Without a Voice: Asylum seekers detained in the UK* (1994).

relief on judicial review, or by application for judicial review of the detention itself on grounds of, for example, a failure to follow policy or an otherwise unlawful exercise of discretion. In cases certified under the ATCSA 2001, the sole means of challenge is before SIAC, and thence the Court of Appeal. The jurisdiction of the High Court is ousted. We discuss these provisions in detail in chapter 7.

The source of detention power

3.77 Immigration detention is authorized by the IA 1971 in the following circumstances:

(a) during examination by an immigration officer to ascertain whether an individual needs or should be granted leave to enter;[67]

(b) pending the giving of removal directions and removal for those refused leave to enter, for those considered to be illegal entrants and for those subject to administrative removal under s. 10 of the IAA 1999;[68]

(c) pending removal of those served with notice of intention to deport (under s. 3(5) IA 1971), those subject to a signed deportation order and those recommended for deportation (Sch. 3, para. 2);

(d) members of the crew of a ship or aircraft who stay longer than permitted or who are reasonably expected of intending to do so pending the giving of removal directions and pending removal (Sch. 2, paras. 12, 13 and 16(2)).

3.78 It is noteworthy that there is no freestanding detention power in ATCSA 2001. The indeterminate detention without trial contemplated by ATCSA 2001 is under paragraph 16, Schedule 2 and Schedule 3 to the IA 1971. It is thus only immigrants who are within the scope of ATCSA 2001 (and see chapter 7).

3.79 The grant of temporary admission to a specific address (with an option of requiring sureties) is an alternative to detention. There is no statutory time limit set to the length of the period of examination pending a decision on leave to enter (*R* v *Secretary of State for the Home Department, ex parte Thirakumar* [1989]

---

[67] IA 1971, Sch. 2, para. 16(1) and para. 16(1A) inserted by IAA 1999, Sch. 14, para. 60 to cater for the detention of persons being examined who were granted leave to enter the UK prior to their arrival here (a new concept introduced by the IAA 1999).

[68] IA 1971, Sch. 2, paras, 8, 9 and 16(2) as amended by IAA 1999, s. 140(1). The amendment to para. 16(2) fortifies the decision in *Secretary of State for the Home Department* v *Khan* [1995] Imm AR 348 that the prohibition on removal pending the pursuit of an asylum claim does not preclude exercise of the detention power, and also prevents a false imprisonment claim by a person who establishes that they did not fall within s. 10 of the IAA 1999 because they did not, say, breach their conditions of entry. It does not alter the precedent fact approach to illegal entry or indeed to a s. 10 removal; see below at 3.100, 3.101.

Imm AR 402), nor indeed to the period of detention. The power is impliedly limited by the need to conduct the examination with reasonable diligence (*R (Saadi)* v *Secretary of State* [2001] EWCA Civ 1512, 19 October 2001).

3.80 Section 4 of the IAA 1999 gives the Secretary of State power to admit persons to temporary admission at appointed accommodation. The IAA 1999 amends paragraph 21, Schedule 2 to the IA 1971 by allowing for conditions attached to temporary admission which restrict residence to be made by regulation, by allowing for such regulations to prohibit residence in particular areas and to prohibit absence from appointed accommodation.[69]

Exercise of the detention power

3.81 The Immigration Rules stipulate that powers of detention must be exercised without regard to race, colour or religion (Immigration Rules, HC 395, paragraph 2).

The policy
3.82 The present Home Office policy on detention is contained in Chapter 38, Operational Enforcement Manual, 21 December 2000.[70] This is a detailed document which begins by providing as follows:

(a)   detention is only to be used as a last resort (38.1);

(b)   detention will usually only be appropriate to effect removal, establish identity or the true basis of the claim, or prevent absconding (38.1);

(c)   asylum seekers will be detained at Oakington[71] where it appears the claim can be decided quickly (38.1);

(d)   it is not an effective use of detention space to detain people for lengthy periods if it would be practical to effect detention later in the process once any rights of appeal have been exhausted (38.1);

(e)   while the government is committed to a strategy of detaining in ded-

---

[69] IA 1971, Sch. 2, paras. 2A and 2B inserted by IAA 1999, Sch. 14, para. 62. There is however a power to make 'different provisions for different cases' (IA 1971, Sch. 2, para. 2D).

[70] The previous long-standing departmental instructions were first issued in 1991, and subsequently revised in 1994. They were disclosed to Amnesty International and became known to practitioners in 1996: *R* v *Secretary of State for the Home Department, ex parte Brezinski and Elowacka* (19 July 1996, CO 4251/95), cited in *R* v *Special Adjudicator and Secretary of State for the Home Department, ex parte AKB* [1998] INLR 315 at 317–18. The Court of Appeal in *R* v *Secretary of State ex parte Lamin Minteh* (8 March 1996) considered that the policy embodied a presumption in favour of bail. In *R (Sedrati and others)* v *Secretary of State* [2001] EWHC Admin 418 Moses J declared that there was no presumption in favour of detention even in cases concerning detention under Sch. 3 pursuant to a criminal court's recommendation to deport the individual.

[71] A reception centre with a relaxed regime, unsuitable for absconding risks.

icated detention and holding centres, even in the long term, it is likely that a number of detainees will need to be held in prisons (38.1);

(f)   detention where removal is not *necessary* for the purposes of removal of the individual is not compatible with Article 5: detention for deterrence purposes is not permitted (38.1.1.1);

(g)   where detention interferes with rights to respect for family life, it must go 'no further than was strictly necessary' to achieve the Article 8(2) (see chapter 4) aims.

3.83   The criteria for detention are set out below at 3.146.

3.84   Reviews of detention are to be conducted after 24 hours, and thereafter weekly or as advised, subject to a minimum of a further review after 28 days: 'It must always be considered whether continued detention is essential when detention is being reviewed.' (38.6).

3.85   Criminal detainees subject to deportation, if sentenced to 12 months or more, are not to be transferred into Immigration Service accommodation but retained within the Prison Service estate until deportation can be effected unless granted bail or temporary admission (38.8).[72]

3.86   The location of detention is determined in accordance with the Immigration (Places of Detention) Direction 1999, which includes as permissible places of detention police cells, detention accommodation, local prisons or discrete accommodation provided by the Prison Service. Home leave for prisoners subject to removal action is a matter for the discretion of the governor, in liaison with the Chief Immigration Officer (38.18). But where the prisoner is the subject of a deportation order, home leave should only be granted in the most exceptional circumstances (38.18).

Challenges to detention

Bail applications in the Immigration Appellate Authority
3.87   The impact of the Asylum and Immigration Act 1996 was to provide for a statutory right to apply for bail to an adjudicator in almost all circumstances in which detention could be authorized (IA 1971, Sch. 2, para. 22 (IA)). The exception where there was still no right to bail was where detention was authorized pursuant to the deportation process and there was no pending appeal. This lacuna is to be filled by section 54(4) of the IAA 1999, which when in force will extend the right to apply for bail to an adjudicator in all deportation cases, even in the

---

[72] These provisions are to be revised following *R (Sedrati and others)* v *Secretary of State* [2001] EWHC Admin 418.

situation where the individual is in immigration detention following a recommendation for deportation by the sentencing court which failed to direct his release on the expiry of the criminal sentence (IA 1971, Sch. 2, para. 2(1) amended by IAA 1999). However in this last class of case there is no statutory presumption in favour of bail. On the fact of it the position is therefore neutral with the relevant considerations to be weighed by the court on a case by case basis. The burden of justification still lies with the Secretary of State. It appears that the s. 54 regime will not now be brought into force.

3.88 Prior to the coming into force of s. 54(4) of the IAA 1999, there is a right to apply for bail to the appellate authority in all cases save for deportation. In deportation cases, bail is only available where certain appeals are pending (IA 1971, Sch. 3, para. 3). Those appeals are appeals against administrative removal (IAA 1999, s. 66), appeals objecting to destination where an alternative destination must be specified (IAA 1999, s. 67), appeals against 'conducive to the public good' deportations (IAA 1999, s. 63(1)(a)), and asylum appeals (IAA 1999, s. 69(4)(a)). Significantly there is no right to apply for bail in the appellate authority in a deportation case where the only appeal being pursued is that on human rights grounds under s. 65 of the IAA 1999.

3.89 Under the current and long-standing 'elective' bail regime there is no presumption in favour of release and no detailed criteria for the granting of bail in either primary or subordinate legislation (IA 1971, Sch. 2, paras. 22–34).

3.90 However, the IAA 1999 makes further significant changes to the statutory right to apply for bail:

(a) section 45 provides for a system of routine bail hearings at different fora (the appellate authority, SIAC, or magistrates' court depending on context) for all those detained under IA 1971 powers save for those recommended for deportation by a criminal court. The hearings must take place before the 10th and 38th days of detention;

(b) section 46 enacts a general presumption in favour of bail whose impact is limited by the number of exceptions thereafter set out.

Despite the government's intentions in 1999, this provision has still not been brought into force and there has been no commencement date set.[73]

3.91 It is significant that the contemplated regime does not affect the position of those who are newly arrived in the UK and are awaiting a decision as to leave

---

[73] It now appears that these provisions in the IAA 1999 will not be brought into force.

to enter. They remain unable to apply for bail until seven days after arrival (IA 1971, Sch. 2, paras. 22(1), 22(1B) and 22(1)(aa); IAA 1999, s. 44(4)).

3.92 Where detention is certified as being in the interests of national security under s. 3 of the Special Immigration Appeals Commission Act 1997 (enacted following the judgment in *Chahal* v *UK* (1996) 23 EHRR 412 on Article 5(4)), the application for bail is made to the SIAC, which reviews sensitive material in 'closed session' from which the detainee is barred but at which a 'special advocate' is present to represent the detainee's interests. It is of interest that the Special Immigration Appeals Commission Act 1997 does not provide for another ground of detention but refers to the powers contained in IA 1971 (Special Immigration Appeals Commission Act 1997, s. 3, Sch. 3). Thus there is no power in domestic immigration law to detain a person simply on national security grounds where no 'immigration objective' (removal or examination) can be identified,[74] save where the individual is a suspected international terrorist. National security concerns[75] would however be relevant to the propriety of continued detention on a bail application (*R* v *Secretary of State for the Home Department, ex parte Ben Taher* (24 September 1999); Home Office Operation Enforcement Manual 2000, 38.5.2).

3.93 Similarly where there is certification permitting indeterminate detention without trial under the ATCSA 2001 in respect of a suspected international terrorist immigrant who is a threat to national security, the application for bail is made to the SIAC. It is difficult to see the circumstances, short of near fatal illness, which would justify the grant of bail given the nature of the ground for detention. As we note above at 3.76, the power to detain is derived from IA 1971, s. 23.

Bail guidelines
3.94 Both the Home Office and the Adjudicators have issued bail guidelines. The Home Office policy is contained in Chapter 39, Operational Enforcement Manual. Two points are worthy of note. First, one of the conditions contemplated is the surrendering of a passport (introduction to 39), presumably to prevent departure from the UK. This appears difficult to justify at least in most circumstances and appears to be at odds with the following comments of the Court of Appeal in *Doku* v *Secretary of State* (30 November 2000, para. 6), where the applicant sought permission to appeal the refusal of bail by Keene J:

---

[74] See the release from detention and subsequent grant of exceptional leave to enter to Egyptian nationals detained under national security certificates: *R* v *Secretary of State for the Home Department, ex parte Hany Youssef* (CO 706/99; CO 1649/99) and the immediate release of Chahal following the judgment of the European Court finding a prospective breach of Article 3 were he to be deported to India: *Chahal* v *UK* (1996) 23 EHRR 413. It was essentially for this class of case that the detention provisions of ACSA 2001 were enacted.

[75] Defined broadly, see *Rehman* v *Secretary of State for the Home Department* [2001] 3 WLR 877, 894 per Lord Slynn.

(the Applicant) advances three grounds which he submits might in another case be no more than arguments on the facts, but in this case, he submits, are elevated to issues of law by their starkness. He says, first, that there was simply no evidence upon which a risk of the nature spelt out in Schedule 1 of the Bail Act could be held to exist. Secondly, and it is perhaps another way of putting the same point, he says that Keene J engaged in a speculation about the risk, which in its nature was impermissible. Thirdly, he submits that, entering into the argument although it does not enter into the judgment, was the submission that if he was given bail Mr Doku might leave the United Kingdom. As to the last of these it is certainly right that counsel for the Home Secretary in an unguarded moment did so submit. Keene J however was not seduced by that argument. It is as well he was not.

3.95 Secondly, the policy appears to contemplate the taking of sureties as a norm in a fact-insensitive manner (39.5) which may raise issues as to its compatibility with Article 5(1) or at least, in light of the Court of Appeal's decision in *R (Saadi)* v *Secretary of State* [2001] EWCA Civ 1512, 19 October 2001, with the case by case justification of any confinement of liberty required by the common law.

3.96 The guidance issued by the Chief Adjudicator, His Honour Judge Hodge,[76] provides that there is a common law presumption in favour of bail applicable to immigration applications (1.4). The burden is on the Secretary of State to prove that detention is necessary, on a balance of probabilities (2.6.1). If the burden is not discharged the applicant will normally be entitled to bail (2.6.1). Attendance of the applicant will be necessary if there is a dispute over issues of fact (2.1.2)). Conditions must only be imposed so far as *necessary* to ensure that the applicant answers to bail (2.4.2).

3.97 The guidance considers that, for the purposes of Article 5 'Not all asylum seekers are attempting to gain unauthorised entry' (7.3). While this is a realistic approach to 'unauthorised entry', and entirely valid in the context of a bail hearing, it is probably inconsistent with the reasoning in *R (Saadi)* v *Secretary of State for the Home Department* [2001] EWCA Civ 1512, [2002] UKHL 41.

Bail applications in the High Court
3.98 Bail applications can also be made pursuant to the inherent jurisdiction of the High Court as ancillary relief in a judicial review action. Where there is a statutory right to bail, the High Court, and Court of Appeal on appeal (Supreme Court Act 1981, s. 15(3)), will exercise original jurisdiction: *R (on the application of Sezek)* v *Secretary of State* [2001] INLR 675, *R* v *SSHD ex parte Doku* (30

---

[76] Namely, 'BAIL: Guidance Notes for Adjudicators from the Chief Adjudicator, His Honour Judge Hodge, revised January 2002 (available at http://www.iasuk.org/document_store/Doc115.doc).

November 2000) per Sedley LJ, *R* v *SSHD ex parte Kelso* [1998] INLR 603, distinguishing *Vilvarajah* v *SSHD* [1990] Imm AR 457. Whilst, following basic principles, the statutory right to apply for bail should be exhausted before relief is sought from the High Court on judicial review, the High Court has shown a marked preparedness to entertain bail applications where a refusal of bail by an adjudicator would itself lead to further proceedings, or where the issue can be expeditiously dealt with.[77] The jurisdiction of the High Court is however ousted in respect of suspected international terrorists detained under section 21(9) of the ATCSA 2001. The Court of Appeal however has all the powers of the High Court on statutory appeal from the SIAC.

Habeas corpus
3.99 An application for habeas corpus is available where a condition precedent to the power of detention is challenged (*R* v *Secretary of State for the Home Department, ex parte Muboyayi* [1992] QB 244), save where the detention is certified under ATCSA 2001, where the jurisdiction of the High Court is ousted. The Court of Appeal however has all the powers of the High Court on statutory appeal from the SIAC. In the celebrated case of *R* v *Governor of Durham Prison ex parte Hardial Singh* [1984] 1 WLR 704[78] Woolf J held that the power of detention was limited to the express purpose provided by statute and was further limited to a fact-sensitive period that was reasonably necessary to enable the machinery of deportation (or removal) to be carried out, there being a duty of all reasonable expedition on the Secretary of State for the Home Department. Thus the power to detain will cease to exist where removal is not a practical possibility for whatever reason (lack of transport connections, lack of travel documents, refusal of admission, no prospect of return consistent with obligations under Article 3 of the ECHR) (*R* v *Secretary of State for the Home Department, ex parte Hany Youssef* (CO 706/99; CO 1649/99)). Where the grounds for making out the claim are established the remedy is not discretionary, although it may be an abuse of process to proceed by habeas corpus where the identical issue has been previously adversely determined in judicial review proceedings. The answer is that if any judicial review application shows signs of being refused on discretionary grounds it should be converted into a habeas corpus application at the time, rather than run the risk of sequential failures.[79] Habeas corpus remains available where

---

[77] See *R* v *Secretary of State for the Home Department, ex parte Kelso* [1998] INLR 603; *R* v *Secretary of State for the Home Department, ex parte Ben Taher* (24 September 1999).

[78] Approved in *Tan Te Lam* v *Superintendent of Tai A Chau Detention Centre* [1997] AC 97 and followed in *Re Wasfi Suleiman Mahmood* [1995] Imm AR 311. See also *I* v *Secretary of State for the Home Department* (C/2002/0743) CA.

[79] In *R* v *Secretary of State ex parte Sheikh* [2001] INLR 98 the Court of Appeal held that an application for habeas corpus was an abuse of process in circumstances where a judicial review application challenging the detention had been refused for want of promptness. In the 1999 lecture to the

a person is liable to summary detention but has in the meantime been given bail or temporary admission.[80]

Judicial review

3.100 Judicial review is available to challenge an unlawful exercise of discretion to detain where a clear public law error can be shown, e.g. a failure to follow departmental instructions.[81] In the illegal entry context, the court will regard the question of the immigrant's status as a question of precedent jurisdictional fact to be proven by the Secretary of State for the Home Department, since it is that fact which is the precondition to the power of removal (IA 1971, Sch. 2, para. 9).

3.101 The amendment to IA 1971, Sch. 2, para. 16 which permits detention of a person in respect of whom there are reasonable grounds for suspecting that removal directions may be given, does not alter the precedent fact analysis to the question of illegal entry established in *Khawaja* v *SSHD* [1984] AC 74 (see IA 1971, Sch. 2, para. 16(2)) where there is a challenge to the giving of removal directions. The statute makes plain that liability to the summary removal power still arises because the person *is* an illegal entrant, not because the Secretary of State thinks that the person is (IA 1971, Sch. 2, para. 9), and 'illegal entrant' is still defined in objective terms (IA 1971, s. 33). Similarly the power of administrative removal under s. 10 of the IAA 1999 arises only where objective conditions are met.[82] What has changed is that the statute authorizes detention where there are reasonable grounds for concluding that someone can be removed.

THE IMPACT OF ARTICLE 5

3.102 The effect of incorporation into domestic law of Article 5 is perhaps at present unclear, given that the meaning of Article 5(1)(f) is yet to be authoritatively determined by the House of Lords (although see now [2002] UKHL 41). However practices and procedures relating to immigration detention appear to have, to some extent, been informed by considerations deriving from Article 5

Administrative Law Bar Association, 'Habeas Corpus—A New Chapter', Simon Brown LJ had urged that the procedure for applying for judicial review and habeas corpus become unified, and that it was inconceivable that a judicial review application in respect of an unlawful detention would be refused on discretionary grounds. While the procedure is now unified, CPR Part 54 makes it clear that habeas corpus lies as of right.

[80] See *R* v *Secretary of State, ex parte Sheikh* [2001] INLR 98; see also Sharpe, *The Law of Habeas Corpus*, 2nd edn (Clarendon Press, 1989).

[81] See *R* v *A Special Adjudicator and SSHD ex parte AKB* [1998] INLR 315, where a declaration was granted to the effect that an immigrant's detention became unlawful as against the weight of all available evidence.

[82] e.g. the person may be removed if 'having only a limited leave to enter or remain, he does not observe a condition attached to the leave . . .': s. 10(1)(a) of the IAA 1999.

which in turn have informed the common law.[83] The Home Office policy on detention, if not that relating to bail, provides a considerable level of Article 5 compliant protection: (1) detention as a last resort; (2) limited use of detention; (3) exclusive use of detention for the permitted purposes and only when necessary to promote those purposes; (4) the provisions of reasons;[84] and (5) regular reviews, are all important aspects of the exercise of the detention power which serve to promote rights guaranteed by Article 5. The concerns which remain in the policy are (1) detention being contemplated to establish identity or the 'true' basis of the claim (but see *R (Saadi)* v *Secretary of State* [2001] EWCA Civ 1512, [2002] UKHL 41); (2) the reference to 'space-oriented' detention considerations, noted by Leanne Weber and Loraine Gelsthorpe (see above at footnote 66) as leading to an arbitrariness of practice on the ground; (3) the contemplation of Oakington type detention based on speed considerations rather than the express permitted purposes under Article 5(1)(f); (4) the contemplation of immigration detainees being kept with convicted criminals; and (5) the reason for detention that 'You have used or attempted to use deception in a way that leads us to consider that you may continue to deceive' which may allow an inappropriate focus on asylum seekers who use no deception to *enter* the UK, but travel on forged passports to *arrive* here (*R* v *Naillie* [1993] AC 674), and which may ignore the protection conferred on clandestine entrants by Article 31 of the Refugee Convention (*R* v *Uxbridge Magistrates' Court, ex parte Adimi and others* [2000] 3 WLR 434).

3.103   The Chief Adjudicator's bail guidance also achieves higher standards of protection than before in recognizing (1) the application of a common law presumption in favour of bail; (2) the importance of oral testimony on disputed questions of fact; (3) that conditions must be imposed only so far as necessary to ensure that the applicant answers to bail; and (4) the purposes stipulated by Article 5(1)(f) (but note *Saadi*). The concern in the guidance remains that if the Home Office fails to make out an exception permitting detention, the applicant is 'normally' entitled to bail. We suggest that it would be the very exceptional case where the (evidential) onus on the Secretary of State was not discharged but continued detention was permitted: the common law and the European Court presumption of liberty would require release in cases of doubt.

3.104   These provisions, together with Part III of the IAA 1999, address most of the concerns of the report of the UN EcoSoc Working Group on Arbitrary

---

[83] The 'background' relevance of Article 5 in the detention context was recognized in: *Birdi* v *Secretary of State* [1975] 119 SJ 322 and *R* v *Secretary of State ex parte Bhajan Singh* [1976] QB 198; but see *R* v *IAT ex parte Minta* (1991) *The Times*, 24 June 1991; *R* v *Secretary of State ex parte Brezinski* (19 July 1996).

[84] See also the declaration granted by Moses J in *R (on the application of Sedrati and others)* v *Secretary of State* [2001] EWHC Admin 418.

Detention in the UK.[85] The issues which remain unaddressed are (1) the location of detention (para. 30); (2) the failure to set out criteria for detention in primary or secondary legislation (para. 32); and (3) the failure to set an absolute maximum duration for the detention of asylum seekers. These omissions in the detention scheme are part of a wider failure to specify *in legislation* measures relating to the detention of immigrants that would promote ECHR compliance and clarity in domestic law.

3.105   We now turn to examine specific issues raised by the application of Article 5 to immigration detention.

Jurisdiction

3.106   The first issue is jurisdiction. It appears that some adjudicators are declining to consider Article 5 issues on bail hearings. We suggest that there are two routes to the conclusion that adjudicators have Article 5 jurisdiction.

3.107   The first route is through the human rights appeal under s. 65 of the IAA 1999. This as we have seen provides for a right of appeal where a person alleges that an authority has 'in taking *any* decision under the Immigration Acts *relating* to that person's entitlement to enter or remain in the UK . . . acted in breach of his human rights' (s. 65(1)). Section 65(4) grants jurisdiction to the appellate authority to consider the question.

3.108   The first point to note is that the right of appeal under s. 65 is framed in wide terms: *any* decision . . . *relating* . . . to an entitlement to enter or remain in the UK. The draftsman could easily have specified the decisions appealable on human rights grounds as being 'removal-centric' refusals of leave to enter or remain, or the setting of removal decisions etc. on analogy with s. 69 of the IAA 1999 (asylum appeals).

3.109   Secondly, a detention pending removal or pending appeal is a decision under the Immigration Acts which *relates* to an entitlement to enter or remain. The detention power is parasitic on the removal/deportation power; at least once the substantive issue of removal is put in issue (either on an appeal or by representations) the detention decision *relates* to the entitlement to enter or remain: it is a negation of it, or an enforcement of the denial of that entitlement. This analysis is however not supported by the dichotomy set up in *R (Kariharan)* v *Secretary of State* [2001] EWHC Admin 1004, 5 December 2001 (see above at Introduction and at 1.48, 1.49), which views the setting of removal directions as outwith the scope of the section (now reversed by the Court of Appeal: [2002]

---

[85]   E/CN.4/1999/63/Add.3, 18.12.98.

INLR 383). However, the position is strongest when an appeal is lodged on some other non-detention ground, the resolution of which would determine the removal question and hence the detention issue.

3.110 The interpretative obligation in s. 3 of the HRA 1998 would assist the argument, since it is compatible with ECHR rights to secure a speedy and ECHR-compliant remedy in respect of detention. There would be no retrospectivity problem given the continuing nature of the decision to detain (see above at Introduction).

3.111 The question of jurisdiction on appeal in general is a matter for the appellate authority and cannot be unilaterally determined by the Secretary of State through a refusal to forward appeal forms to the appellate authority (*Lokko* v *Secretary of State* [1990] Imm AR 111, affirmed [1990] Imm AR 539).

3.112 Alternatively, in this context the adjudicator's bail jurisdiction can be considered both a means of adjudicating on whether the detainee will abscond and a means of giving effect to Article 5 obligations. There is no legislative stricture preventing adjudicators from acting in an ECHR compliant manner as they are mandated to do by s. 6 of the HRA 1998. While on this approach the historic decision to detain would be outside the reach of the appellate authority owing to jurisdictional limitations, the continuing decision to detain would attract the appellate authority's obligations under the HRA 1998. Thus the appellate authority could direct release if satisfied there was a breach of Article 5, but not rule retrospectively to quash the historic decision.

3.113 The jurisdiction would then extend to consideration of the underlying legality of the detention. As well as the usual question of whether the applicant is good for bail, the appellate authority would be mandated to review the essential conditions for the detention: domestic legal authority, duration of the detention, and arbitrariness. Proportionality would enter by a number of routes: the Home Office criteria themselves require strict proportionality to be applied, and a review based on domestic legal criteria would oblige the same standard to be applied by the reviewing court. We have discussed the *Saadi* judgment above at 3.46, 3.47 and the resolution by the House of Lords as to the extent of the proportionality review required under Article 5(4) in respect of immigration detention under Article 5(1)(f). We suggest that the focus on arbitrariness, as explained most clearly by *A* v *Australia* (1997) 4 BHRC 210, *Amuur* v *France* (1996) 22 EHRR 533, para. 43 and in *Litwa* v *Poland* (4 April 2000) raises issues of proportionality and necessity in detention under the first limb of Article 5(1)(f). This analysis does not, however, survive *Saadi* v *Secretary of State for the Home Department* [2002] UKHL 41.

3.114 We consider that no deference to the Secretary of State's view would be due: the appellate authority is well used to assessing the detention decisions and is vested with the final decision by the legislative scheme. The European Court recognizes that the courts are 'the traditional guardians of personal liberties' (*Amuur* v *France* (1996) 22 EHRR 533, para. 43). This however appears not to have been the view taken in *R (on the application of Sezek)* v *Secretary of State* [2001] INLR 675 where the Court of Appeal held that weight had to be given to the Secretary of State's view that detention was necessary and to his reasons for objecting to release. We suggest it would be difficult to justify such a deferential approach at least in the appellate authority given its independence, extensive fact-centric jurisdiction and great experience in adjudicating on bail issues.

Procedural breaches

3.115 The question of procedural or technical breaches of Article 5, such as the failure to provide reasons, or make disclosure, or delays in listing, raises the issue as to the relief the appellate authority should award. Whilst release would not be required merely by virtue of such a breach, the appellate authority would fail in its duty under s. 6 of the HRA 1998 if it did not require the breach to be corrected, for example, through requiring the provision of reasons and proper disclosure. If on a subsequent occasion, release was ordered, and it could be established with hindsight that there was some causal connection between the procedural breach and prolongation of detention (*W* v *Home Office* [1997] Imm AR 302), then compensation would be available under Article 5(5) and s. 9(3) of the HRA 1998.

Detention following entry and Oakington

3.116 We have seen above from cases such as *Amuur* that at the very least restrictions on the liberty of immigrants at the frontier are permitted for the purposes of establishing identity and examining the basis of the claim to enter. However once this margin is exceeded by detention of more than a few hours, or where the detention regime is sufficiently severe, there is likely to be a finding of a deprivation of liberty for the purposes of Article 5(1). Following the appeal to the House of Lords in *Saadi*, at that point, there may be an issue as to whether detention will then require justification under Article 5(1)(f) by the need to detain for the *purpose* of preventing illegal entry through absconding or breaching conditions of temporary admission (*Akhtar* v *Governor of Pentonville Prison* [1993] Imm AR 424), rather than for the broad purpose of examination to determine admissibility. See now the House of Lords decision in *Saadi* [2002] UKHL 41.

3.117 The problem is exacerbated by inflexible procedures available to challenge detention for persons newly arrived, where bail is not available for seven days. In context this may breach the ECHR requirement of sufficient guarantees against arbitrariness and the right of speedy access to a detention reviewing court under Article 5(4). The present seven day bar on bail applications appears to equate arriving immigrants with suspects held under the prevention of Terrorism Act 1989,[86] and where conditions of detention are suitably onerous this absence of judicial supervision is likely to amount to a deprivation rather than a mere restriction of liberty (*Amuur* v *France* (1996) 22 EHRR 533; *R (Saadi)* v *Secretary of State* [2001] EWCA Civ 1512.

3.118 Asylum seekers arriving without lawful documents may be vulnerable under present Home Office practice and policy. The focus on use or attempted use of deception 'in a way that leads us to consider that you may continue to deceive' as a basis for detention may facilitate a propensity to detain asylum seekers who use no deception to enter the UK, but travel on forged passports to arrive here (*R* v *Naillie* [1993] AC 694), and who may be protected as clandestine entrants by Article 31 of the Refugee Convention (*R* v *Uxbridge Magistrates' Court, ex parte Adimi and others* [2001] QB 667, and see IAA 1999, s. 31).

3.119 The contemplation of Oakington type detention based on speed considerations may also raise issues under Article 5(1)(f). Whilst sometimes referred to as a 'reception' or 'holding' centre, the Operation Enforcement Manual plainly refers to it as a 'detention centre',[87] and in individual cases, especially where family members of vulnerable applicants are present in the UK, the interference with liberty may assume sufficient gravity so as to amount to a deprivation within Article 5. If that threshold is crossed, the speed oriented concerns which lead to confinement of new arrivals in Oakington together with the impossibility of seeking bail for seven days, are likely to breach Article 5(1)(f) and Article 5(4). If there is evidence of specific nationalities being singled out for detention, issues may also arise under Article 14.

3.120 Policies of mandatory detention of all asylum seekers, or of wholesale classes of asylum seekers have been mooted as a means of addressing the failure to deliver a fast and firm system of immigration control. Unless the regime is relaxed and does not differ markedly from temporary admission with residence, and unless expedition can routinely be achieved, we consider that any such policy of mandatory detention may well place the UK in breach of the Article 5 prohibition on arbitrary detention. The decision in *Saadi* would not protect such a scheme for reasons we suggest above at 3.53.

---

[86] See the derogation entered by the UK under Article 15 of the ECHR in respect of Article 5(3) and retained by s. 14 of the HRA 1998 permitting detention of terrorist suspects in Northern Ireland for up to seven days. The derogation was a response to the judgment in *Brogan* v *UK* (1988) 11 EHRR 117.

[87] See also 2 November 1999, Hansard, vol. 606, no. 147, col. 733.

3.121   The power contained in s. 4 of the IAA 1999 and para. 21, Sch, 2 to the IA 1971 (as amended by IAA 1999, Sch. 14, para. 62) to restrict residence to and prohibit absence from appointed accommodation chosen in an area where the individual is isolated from his community may also cross the threshold so as to attract Article 5 safeguards.[88] The power to prevent a person being absent from appointed accommodation has been described as 'amounting to a power to impose house arrest'.[89] If the Rubicon is crossed and Article 5 applies, the fact-insensitive imposition of such residence conditions *by regulation* is likely to breach the guarantee against arbitrariness. The new basis for attaching residence conditions to grants of temporary admission contrasts with the previous provisions which required imposition on an individual and thus more ECHR compatible basis (IA 1971, Sch. 2, para. 21(2), Sch. 3, para. 2(5)).

Section 10 cases

3.122   Section 10 of the IAA 1999 widens the class of persons at risk of detention. By allowing for overstayers and those who breach conditions (perhaps innocently) to be administratively removed without an in-country right of appeal save on human rights grounds, the ability to justify detention, which is adjectival on the prospect of a quick removal, is increased.

3.123   We take the following classes of case: a student who inadvertently breaches an employment condition; an inadvertent overstayer who submits his application for leave to remain a day late; an immigrant who disputes that he obtained leave by deception historically; an immigrant who accepts he used deception 12 years ago but has strong compassionate factors and roots in the community. There is a cogent case that all these persons, who are subject to summary administrative removal under s. 10 and accordingly at risk of summary detention, would be able to mount a strong argument that detention was disproportionate if only at present as a matter of common law and Home Office policy. In relation to the last category, the UN EcoSoc Working Group on Arbitrary Detention in the UK has raised significant concerns.[90]

Deportees

3.124   Deportees have no rights to apply for bail, save where certain appeals are pending (IA 1971, Sch. 3, para. 3). Those appeals are appeals against adminis-

---

[88] See by analogy *Guzzardi* v *Italy* (1981) 3 EHRR 333 and *Cyprus* v *Turkey* (Comm Report 10 July 1976).

[89] See the House of Lords Select Committee on Delegated Powers and Deregulation, 27th Report, 27 October 1999, para. 42. In *NC* v *Italy* (App. No. 24952/94) the European Court accepted at para. 33 that house arrest constituted a deprivation of liberty.

[90] UN EcoSoc Working Group on Arbitrary Detention in the UK, E/CN.4/1999/63/Add.3, para. 22.

trative removal (IAA 1999, s. 66), appeals objecting to destination where an alternative destination must be specified (s. 67), appeals against 'conducive to the public good' deportations (s.63(1)(a)), and asylum appeals (s. 69(4)(a)). Significantly there is no right to apply for bail in the appellate authority in a deportation case where the only appeal being pursued is that on human rights grounds under s. 65 IAA 1999.

3.125 The position for persons detained pursuant to the recommendation for deportation of a criminal court under s. 3(6) of the IA 1971 (see Sch. 3, para. 2(1)) is stark. Paragraph 2(1), Sch. 3 of the IA 1971, which governs the position for this group of detainees, if read literally, embodies a presumption in favour of detention:

> Where a recommendation for deportation made by a court is in force in respect of any person, and that person is detained neither in pursuance of the sentence or order of any court nor for the time being released on bail by any court having power so to release him, he shall, unless the court by which the recommendation is made otherwise directs, be detained pending the making of a deportation order in pursuance of the recommendation, unless the Secretary of State directs him to be released pending further consideration of his case.

3.126 This is contrary to Article 5(1). Moreover, quite apart from the difficulty of a sentencing court directing the release on bail of a defendant months and possibly years before the event, the Home Office has long recognized that conducting a review as to whether to follow the recommendation for deportation is a time-consuming process during which time the detainee is required to submit to administrative detention.[91]

3.127 The position has been clarified by a series of declarations consented to by the Secretary of State following the three joined judicial review claims in *R (Sedrati)* v *Secretary of State* [2001] EWHC Admin 418). The Secretary of State accepted that he had applied the wrong test in erecting a presumption in favour of detention in 'recommendation' cases, that there was no such presumption in favour of detention, that a scheme would be devised whereby the Secretary of State would consider the release of a detainee before the expiry of the criminal sentence, that reasons would be given if detention was maintained, that criteria governing the exercise of the detention power would be published, and that representations could be made as to the location of detention on the expiry of the criminal sentence.

---

[91] See Home Office circular: *Immigration Act 1971: detention pending deportation* (Home Office circular No. 113/1978).

Location of detention

3.128 The location of detention is determined in accordance with the Immigration (Places of Detention) Direction 2001, which includes as permissible places of detention police cells, detention accommodation, local prisons or discrete accommodation provided by the Prison Service. The Home Office is committed to reducing the numbers of detainees held in prisons, but envisages even in the long term that immigration detainees may still need to be held in prison detention. This violates soft law provisions, such as those of the European Prison Rules, which stipulate that convicted and non-convicted prisoners should not be held together.

3.129 The right to challenge the location of detention primarily arises under Article 5(1)(e) which provides for 'the lawful detention of persons for the prevention of the spreading of infectious diseases, of persons of unsound mind, alcoholics or drug addicts or vagrants'. In *Aerts* v *Belgium* (2000) 29 EHRR 50 the European Court held (at para. 46) that:

> there must be some relationship between the ground of permitted deprivation of liberty relied upon and on the place and conditions of detention. In principle the 'detention' of a person as a mental health patient will only be 'lawful' for the purposes of Article 5(1)(e) if effected in a hospital, clinic or other appropriate institution.

In finding a breach in *Amuur* v *France* (1996) 22 EHRR 533 the European Court held inter alia that none of the texts under which the applicants were detained 'allowed the ordinary courts to review the conditions under which aliens were held . . .' (at para. 53). We have seen above at 3.53 that the conditions of detention may inform the proportionality of detention even if the proportionality question is limited to duration.

3.130 In *R (on the application of Sedrati)* v *Secretary of State* [2001] EWHC Admin 418 as we have seen, Moses J granted a declaration whereby the Secretary of State would consider representations on the propriety of administrative detention at immigration detention centres rather than prisons. Plainly an immigration detainee who suffers pre-existing trauma or a deterioration of mental health would be able to argue on analogy with Article 5(1)(e) that detention with convicted prisoners in the Prison estate was inappropriate and arbitrary. The position is exacerbated by what appear to be harsh regimes as to escorted absences and transfer to open conditions operated by the Prison Service.

Prison detainees

3.131 There are no statutory criteria governing the interface between criminal detention pursuant to a court order and administrative detention under the IA

1971. The position appears to be regulated by unclear and apparently inconsistent policies. These are unlikely to be Article 5 compliant.

3.132   The Operation Enforcement Manual provides (at para. 38.8) that criminal detainees subject to deportation, if sentenced to 12 months or more, are not to be transferred into Immigration Service accommodation but retained within the Prison estate until deportation can be effected unless granted bail or temporary admission. This provision will be revised in light of the declaration in *Sedrati and others* [2001] EWHC Admin 418.

3.133   Home leave for prisoners subject to removal action is a matter for the discretion of the Governor, in liaison with the Chief Immigration Officer (para. 38.18). But where the prisoner is the subject of a deportation order, home leave should only be granted in the most exceptional circumstances (para. 38.18). This appeared to conflict with policies operated by the Prison Service. Apparently on a Home Office mandate, Prison Service policy was to exclude, as a class, decategorization to open conditions in the cases of those subject to removal, and to prohibit to those subject to deportation orders the granting of escorted absences from prison as preparation for open conditions. The policy was changed following the grant of permission in *R v Secretary of State for the Home Department, ex parte Madezia* (CO/1260/2001).

Children

3.134   The detention of unaccompanied minors may breach Article 5 as a disproportionate deprivation of liberty, even if measured only in terms of the conditions and duration of detention. A ground for detention includes the category of case of an unaccompanied minor who needs alternative arrangements for his or her care.[92] This may breach the provisions of the UN Convention on the Rights of the Child 1989, including those relating to refugee children under Article 22 which require state parties to take measures to ensure that a child seeking refugee status whether unaccompanied or not, receives appropriate protection and humanitarian assistance.

Damages[93]

3.135   Where detention is unlawful in either domestic law or under the Convention, there will be a breach of Article 5 giving rise to a damages claim under Article 5(5) and s. 9(3) of the HRA 1998.

---

[92] See below at 3.150.
[93] See also above at 3.63–3.68.

3.136   Article 5(5) does not require proof of bad faith on the part of the authorities (*Santa Cruz Ruiz* v *UK* [1998] EHRLR 208). This principle is reflected in s. 9(3) of the HRA 1998 which provides for the general rule that damages for breaches of s. 6 of the HRA 1998 are not to be awarded against the court or appellate authority for judicial acts done in good faith, but stipulates an exception where the award is for compensation for breaches of Articles 5(1)–(4) and thus required by Article 5(5).

3.137   What is required is demonstration of some causal connection between the breach and damage (*R* v *Secretary of State, ex parte Chahal (No. 2)* [2000] UKHRR 215, which may include non-pecuniary loss. An analysis of comparative law indicates that exemplary damages are generally not awarded for breaches of constitutional instruments,[94] and Article 5(5) is no different.

3.138   In judicial review claims, damages must be expressly pleaded. Otherwise damages are recoverable from any court with the power to make the award. The appellate authority is accordingly excluded as an appropriate court.

3.139   The measure of damages are the principles under Article 41 (old Article 50). Since it is perhaps unrealistic to speak of 'principles' it may be more appropriate to bring an action in tort.

False imprisonment
3.140   Detention without authority, in the sense that there was no power to detain, will found an action for false imprisonment. Equally, however, an unlawful exercise of a power to detain will be actionable: see on analogy with the 'wrongful arrest' cases *Holgate-Mohammed* v *Duke* [1984] 1 AC 437[95] where Lord Diplock stated, in a passage with which the remainder of the Law Lords agreed, that:

> The *Wednesbury* principles . . . are applicable to determining the lawfulness of the exercise of the statutory discretion of a constable under s. 2(4) . . . not only in proceedings for judicial review but also for the purpose of founding a cause of action at common law for damages for that species of trespass to the person known as false imprisonment . . .

In *R* v *(1) Special Adjudicator (2) Secretary of State, ex parte AKB* [1998] INLR 315 the claimant successfully obtained a declaration that his detention prior to eventual release was unlawful following which an award of £18,000 damages for two months' detention was made. Exemplary damages are available.

---

[94] See *Nilabati Behera* v *State of Orissa* [1994] LRC 99 for a notable exception.
[95] See also *Castorina* v *Chief Constable of Surrey* (10 June 1988); *Lyons* v *Chief Constable of West Yorkshire* (16 April 1997).

3.141   As we have seen above at 3.68, Article 5(5) has already had an impact on the development of the common law: in *R* v *Governor of Brockhurst Prison ex parte Evans (No 2)* [2000] 3 WLR 843 Lord Hope held that the result dictated by Article 5(5) was consistent with rejecting the defence of justification to the tort of false imprisonment in circumstances where the detainor was reliant at the material time on a judgment of a court subsequently declared to have been wrong.

Misfeasance in public office

3.142   The constituent elements of this tort are (1) a malicious exercise of power by a public official, or (2) a knowingly unlawful or objectively reckless exercise with probable consequential damage. The tort was authoritatively considered by the House of Lords in *Three Rivers District Council* v *Bank of England (No. 3)* [2000] 2 WLR 1220. Malice, wilful illegality or objective recklessness will be difficult to prove. The tort attracts exemplary damages, but there is a question mark in cases of vicarious liability (*Kuddus* v *Chief Constable of Leicestershire* [2001] 2 WLR 1789).

Negligence

3.143   The present state of the law is that an Immigration Officer in general and absent an assumption of responsibility owes no duty of care to an immigrant in deciding whether or not to exercise the statutory discretion to detain: *W* v *Home Office* [1997] Imm AR 302. Accordingly no action for negligent detention will in general lie.[96] This may be revisited in light of the incremental developments in the law of negligence following the judgment of the European Court in *Osman* v *UK* (2000) 29 EHRR 245 and notwithstanding the subsequent clarification in *Z* v *UK* [2000] 2 FCR 245 (the European Court 'limb' of *X* v *Bedfordshire*).

Miscarriages of justice

3.144   A scheme exists under s. 133 of the Criminal Justice Act 1988 to provide compensation in accordance with this requirement, and where those criteria are not satisfied an *ex gratia* scheme also exists. This scheme is based on the following principles set out in answer to a Commons Question by the Home Secretary, Douglas Hurd on 29 November 85:[97]

---

[96] The Home Office may be liable for careless advice causing detention where it assumes a responsibility not otherwise thrust on it (see *Farah* v *(1) British Airways (2) Home Office* (CA, 6 December 1999).

[97] HC Official Report (6th Series), 29 November 1985, cols. 691–2; see also *R* v *Secretary of State ex parte Chahal No. 2* [2000] UKHRR 215; *R* v *Secretary of State ex parte Garner* (1999) 11 Admin LR 595 and cases referred to therein.

For many years . . . it has been the practice of the Home Secretary, in exceptional circumstances, to authorise on application ex gratia payments from public funds to persons who have been detained in custody as a result of a wrongful conviction . . . (resulting) from serious default on the part of a member of the police force or of some other public authority. There may be exceptional circumstances that justify compensation in cases outside these categories.

3.145 Substantial awards have been made under the *ex gratia* scheme for persons convicted and detained following prosecutions in breach of Article 31 of the Refugee Convention (*R v Uxbridge Magistrates' Court, ex parte Adimi and others* [2001] QB 667).

HOME OFFICE, OPERATIONAL ENFORCEMENT MANUAL, 21 DECEMBER 2000, CHAPTER 38

3.146 Paragrah 38.3 states as follows:

38.3 Factors influencing a decision to detain

There is a presumption in favour of temporary admission or temporary release. There must be strong grounds for believing that a person will not comply with conditions of temporary admission or temporary release for detention to be justified. All reasonable alternatives to detention must be considered before detention is authorised. Once detention has been authorised, it must be kept under close review to ensure that it continues to be justified. There are no statutory criteria for detention, and each case must be considered on its individual merits. The following factors must be taken into account when considering the need for initial or continued detention. The list is not exhaustive neither is it in any order of priority.

- what is the likelihood of the person being removed and, if so, after what timescale?
- is there any evidence of previous absconding?
- is there any evidence of a previous failure to comply with conditions of temporary release or bail?
- has the subject taken part in a determined attempt to breach the immigration laws? (e.g. entry in breach of a deportation order, attempted or actual clandestine entry);
- is there a previous history of complying with the requirements of immigration control? (e.g. by applying for a visa, further leave, etc);
- what are the person's ties with the United Kingdom? Are there close relatives (including dependants) here? Does anyone rely on the person for support? Does the person have a settled address/employment?
- what are the individual's expectations about the outcome of the case? Are there factors such as an outstanding appeal, an application for judicial review or representations which afford incentive to keep in touch?
- is the subject under 18?
- has the subject a history of torture?
- has the subject a history of physical or mental ill health?

3.147   Criteria for detention at Oakington are:

The purpose of Oakington Reception Centre is to enable the Immigration and Nationality Directorate to deal quickly with asylum applications, many of which prove to be unfounded. People are detained at Oakington for around a week while their asylum application is considered. They are then given temporary admission/release or moved to a longer-term detention centre. In addition to the criteria set out at Chapter 38.1,[98] Oakington detainees must belong to one of the nationalities listed in regular instructions to staff. The following are unsuitable for Oakington:

- any case which does not appear to be one in which a quick decision can be reached;
- any case which has complicating factors, or issues, which are unlikely to be resolved within the constraints of the Oakington process model;
- unaccompanied minors;
- age dispute cases, other than those where there is clear and irrefutable documentary evidence that the applicant is aged over 18 years;
- disabled applicants, save for the most easily manageable;
- any person with special medical needs, unless they can be managed within a GP surgery environment;
- any person who gives reason to believe that they might not be suitable for the relaxed Oakington regime, including those who are considered likely to abscond.

3.148   The policy goes on to provide for:

(a)   service of a form in all cases at the time of detention detailing the source power of detention, the reasons for detention, and the basis upon which the decision to detain was made. Thereafter reasons are to be given at appropriate intervals (38.5.2);

(b)   an explanation to the detainee of his bail rights (38.5.2);

(c)   interpretation of the contents of the form where the detainee does not read English, otherwise Article 5(2) may be breached (38.5.2).

3.149   Five possible reasons for detention are given (38.5.2):

- you are likely to abscond if given temporary admission or release;

---

[98] Ministers made it clear that in addition to existing detention criteria, asylum applicants will be detained at Oakington where it appears that their application can be decided quickly, including those applications which may be certified as manifestly unfounded.

- there is insufficient reliable information to decide on whether to grant you temporary admission or release;
- your removal from the United Kingdom is imminent;
- you need to be detained whilst alternative arrangements are made for your care;
- your release is not considered conducive to the public good.

3.150   Then, twelve factors are listed, which are apt to form the *basis* of the reasons for the decision to detain (38.5.2):

- you do not have enough close ties (e.g. family or friends) to make it likely that you will stay in one place;
- you have previously failed to comply with conditions of your stay, temporary admission or release;
- you have previously absconded or escaped;
- you have used or attempted to use deception in a way that leads us to consider that you may continue to deceive;
- you have failed to give satisfactory or reliable answers to an Immigration Officer's enquiries;
- you have not produced satisfactory evidence of your identity, nationality or lawful basis to be in the United Kingdom;
- you have previously failed, or refused to leave the United Kingdom when required to do so;
- you are a young person without the care of a parent or guardian and alternative arrangements need to be made for your care;
- your health gives serious cause for concern on grounds of your own well-being and/or public health or safety;
- you are excluded from the United Kingdom at the personal direction of the Secretary of State;
- you are detained for reasons of national security, the reasons are/will be set out in another letter;
- your unacceptable character, conduct or associations.

Chapter Four

The Protection of Family and Private Life

INTRODUCTION

4.1 Family and private life are broad concepts which engage a number of ECHR rights. Respect for family and private life is expressly required by Article 8(1), the central Article of relevance in immigration cases, which overlaps with the right to marry and found a family under Article 12. Discrimination in the enjoyment of these rights will violate Article 14 and in extreme cases the absolute prohibition against inhuman or degrading treatment under Article 3 may be engaged.

4.2 Article 8 guarantees the right to respect to four discrete personal interests: family and private life, home and correspondence. The concept of respect is essentially negative in character in the sense that the state is required not to interfere with the rights in question. However, in certain circumstances 'respect' imposes positive obligations and requires positive measures to be taken by the state authorities. In common with three other Articles where a balance is expressly involved (namely Articles 9, 10, and 11), Article 8 goes on to permit an interference with the right to respect for these personal interests in specified circumstances. Any interference that is permitted under the ECHR must be in accordance with law, which includes both domestic law and the autonomous ECHR concept of law. If an interference is not in accordance with the law, it is not permissible. Beyond that, an interference must be for a legitimate motive within the meaning of the ECHR, and must be necessary rather than merely desirable in the circumstances of the case. This last requirement brings in the concept of proportionality.

4.3 Article 12 provides for the right to marry and found a family, subject only to the requirement that the individuals seeking to marry are of marriageable age and they comply with marriage rules in domestic law.

4.4 In this chapter we look at the scheme of ECHR protection afforded to family and private life, and the right to marry and found a family. The basic questions which arise are:

(a)   Is there family life or private life being enjoyed?
(b)   Do the circumstances in which family life or private life is enjoyed require respect from the immigration authorities?
(c)   If so, is the interference constituted by the immigration decision justified, i.e. is it

   (i)   in accordance with law;
   (ii)   in pursuit of a legitimate aim;
   (iii) necessary, i.e. in pursuit of a pressing social need and proportionate to that need?

4.5   We then examine the impact on domestic immigration law of the incorporation of Article 8 by the Human Rights Act 1998.

4.6   We highlight one point at the outset: the jurisprudence of the European Court on cases involving Article 8 has been criticized as arbitrary[1] and incoherent[2] by none other than judges of the European Court itself. The helpful distillation of principles governing the application of family life cases under Article 8 in *R (Mahmood)* v *Secretary of State* [2001] 1 WLR 840, the first domestic case to consider the issue, is accordingly likely to prove a useful guide to the approach required to be taken as the domestic courts develop their own municipal human rights jurisprudence.[3] Similarly the judgment of the European Court in *Boultif* v *Switzerland* (2001) 33 EHRR 50 should provide a helpful set of principles to be applied in expulsion cases involving Article 8.

IS THERE FAMILY AND PRIVATE LIFE ENJOYED?

Scope: the meaning of family life

4.7   The primary significance of Article 8 in the context of immigration is the protection it affords to respect for family life. The question of whether family life exists is a question of fact, and turns on issues of substance rather than form. In *K* v *UK* (1986) 50 DR 199 at 207 the European Commission stated that the existence of family life depends upon 'the real existence in practice of close personal ties'. In *Marckx* v *Belgium* (1979) 2 EHRR 330 the Court held (at para. 31) that:

---

[1] *Boughanemi* v *France* (1996) 22 EHRR 228; Judge Martens, dissenting opinion, para. 3.
[2] *Sternja* v *Finland* (1997) 24 EHRR 195; Judge Wildhaber, concurring opinion.
[3] *R (M and La Rose)* v *Commissioner of Police for the Metropolis* [2001] EWHC Admin 553 para. 11; *R (Pro Life Alliance)* v *BBC* [2002] EWCA Civ 297 paras. 33–34.

By guaranteeing the right to respect for family life, Article 8 presupposes the existence of a family . . . Article 8 makes no distinction between the 'legitimate' and the 'illegitimate' family. Such a distinction would not be consonant with the word 'everyone' [in ECHR Article 1], and this is confirmed by Article 14 with its prohibition, in the enjoyment of the rights and freedoms enshrined in the Convention, of discrimination grounded on 'birth'.[4]

4.8   The two most important family relationships are those between husband and wife and parent and child. A lawful and genuine marriage will suffice to constitute family life between the couple even in the absence of cohabitation: *Abdulaziz, Cabales and Balkandali* v *UK* (1985) 7 EHRR 471 para. 62.[5] Relationships between parties to a formally invalid polygamous marriage fall within the scope,[6] albeit that it may be legitimate to preclude admission under Article 8(2) where the consequence would be the establishment of two wives residing together with their husband in a country which does not permit polygamy.[7] Prospective relationships may be within Article 8(1), such as those between fiancés.[8] A relationship of form only, such as a 'sham' marriage, is likely to fall outside the scope of Article 8, although in *Benes* v *Austria* 72 DR 271 the European Commission treated an annulment of such a marriage as requiring justification under Article 8(2). Informal relationships of sufficient substance and stability may fall within the ambit of family life, and so heterosexual relationships of this nature are recognized as amounting to family life.[10]

4.9   From the moment of the child's birth and by the fact of it, there exists between child and parents a bond amounting to 'family life' which subsequent events cannot break save in 'exceptional circumstances' (*Gul* v *Switzerland* (1996) 22 EHRR 93 para. 32). A child born of a subsisting marital union forms

---

[4] In J. Simor and B. Emmerson, *Human Rights Practice* (Sweet & Maxwell, 2000) the authors note, at para. 8.025, that in *B, R and J* v *Germany* 36 DR 130 the European Commission expressed its opinion that by virtue of Art. 12, the family based on marriage nevertheless enjoyed greater protection than the 'illegitimate' family, so that special legislation concerning children born out of wedlock could be justified. These statements have not been reiterated or relied upon since that decision.

[5] And see *Wakefield* v *UK* (1990) 66 DR 251; *Kroon* v *Netherlands* (1994) 19 EHRR 263 para. 30.

[6] See *A and A* v *Netherlands* (1992) 72 DR 118 at 121–3; *R* v *Secretary of State ex parte Glowacka* (26 June 1997), where the Secretary of State agreed to treat the parties to an invalid Roma marriage as if they were formally married for refugee family reunion purposes.

[7] See *Bibi* v *UK* (1992) (Application 19628/92); and see the Immigration Rules, HC 395, paras. 278–9.

[8] See *Abdulaziz et al* (1985) 7 EHRR 471 paras. 61–3; *Wakefield* v *UK* (1990) 66 DR 251 at 255; and see below at 4.9.

[9] See *Moustaquim* v *Belgium* (1991) 13 EHRR 802; *K* v *UK* 50 DR 199 at 207.

[10] See *Johnston* v *Ireland* (1986) 9 EHRR 203; *Keegan* v *Ireland* (1994) 18 EHRR 342 para. 44; *Marckx* v *Belgium* above at 4.7.

part of the family relationship.[11] Whether the marriage is monogamous or polygamous will be irrelevant,[12] as will whether the child is born in or out of wedlock. There is a general presumption in favour of family life between a natural father and child even where the relationship between the parents had ended at the time of birth (*Keegan* v *Ireland* (1994) 18 EHRR 342), but where the father retains no contact with or interest in the child or mother, the presumption may be defeated. Family life continues to exist between child and parents after divorce (*Berrehab* v *Netherlands* (1988) 11 EHRR 322), and the parent deprived of custody has the right to have contact with the child.[13] The natural family relationship is not terminated when a child is taken into care (*W* v *UK* (1997) 10 EHRR 29 para. 59).

4.10   The adoption of a child gives rise to family life between adoptive parents and child.[14] The European Court has held that there existed family life between a female to male transsexual and the child of his female partner, conceived by IVF treatment, to whom the applicant had always acted as 'father' (*X, Y and Z* v *UK* (1997) 24 EHRR 143 and see below at 6.30). But in the absence of close personal ties, family life will not exist between an anonymous donor of sperm for IVF treatment and the recipient mother or child, even where the donor enjoyed some contact with the child in the months after birth (*G* v *Netherlands* (1993) 16 EHRR CD 38). Family life was not established where one of two women, living as a lesbian couple in a long-term relationship, produced a child by IVF treatment (*Kerkhoven* v *Netherlands* (App. No. 15666/89). It is doubtful whether the UK courts would accept this: see *Mendoza* v *Ghaidan* [2002] EWCA Civ 1533 following *Fitzpatrick* v *Sterling Housing* [1999] UKHL 42.

4.11   Depending on the strength of emotional ties, relationships between siblings, grandparents and grandchildren,[15] and even between uncle and nephew are potentially within the scope of family life.[16] Thus in *Nhundu and Chiwera* v

---

[11]   See *Berrehab* v *Netherlands* (1988) 11 EHRR 322 para. 21; *Ciliz* v *Netherlands* [2000] 2 FLR 469 paras. 33, 44.

[12]   See *A and A* v *Netherlands* 72 DR 118 (see *Khan* v *UK* (1995) 21 EHRR CD 67 on bigamous marriages).

[13]   See *W* v *Germany* 50 DR 219; *M* v *Germany* 51 DR 245; *Irlen* v *Germany* 53 DR 225.

[14]   See *X* v *France* (1992) 31 DR 241. The provisions of the Immigration Rules concerning adoption (HC 395 paras. 310, 311 and 314, 315) which require adoption to be based on the inability of the natural parents to care for the child, and the cessation of all links with those parents, may not be compatible with Article 8. See 4.115 below.

[15]   See *Marckx* v *Belgium* (1979) 2 EHRR 330 at para. 45; *GBH* v *UK* [2000] EHRLR 545; *Hokkanen* v *Finland* (1995) 19 EHRR 139.

[16]   See *Moustaquim* v *Belgium* (1991) 13 EHRR 802; *X* v *Germany* (1968) 9 YB 449; *Marckx* (above footnote 15); *Boyle* v *UK* (1995) 19 EHRR 179. Of course, a relationship between an uncle or aunt with nephew or neice does not *necessarily* amount to family life: *R* v *Secretary of State for Health ex parte L* [2001] 1 FLR 406.

Secretary of State (01/TH/613, 1 June 2001), the IAT found (at para. 34) that there existed family life between an aunt and her nephew whom she had raised, and who was still a minor when she left him to come to the UK.[17]

4.12   The Strasbourg organs favour 'vertical' family relationships (minor children, parents, grandparents) over 'horizontal' ones (siblings, nieces and nephews). Thus relationships between adult siblings or adult children and their parents will not usually fall within the ambit of family life (*Advic v UK* (1995) 20 EHRR CD 125). In *A and Family v Sweden* (1994) 18 EHRR CD 209[18] the European Commission held that where an adult woman and her children formed an independent family unit, her deportation and separation from her parents and sisters did not engage Article 8(1). In *Uppal v UK* (1979) 3 EHRR 391 the European Commission declared admissible a complaint where removal would interfere with the family life between children, parents, grandparents and married sisters forming a close family unit.[19] A claim based (indirectly) on a sibling relationship succeeded in *Olsson v Sweden* (1989) 11 EHRR 259. In the context of immigration from South Asia or Somalia, where extended family units are recognized to be the norm,[20] we suggest that a broad and purposive approach is appropriate to the question of whether there exists family life for the purposes of Article 8.

4.13   Although the focus is on substance, form also has a role in the establishment of family life: we have noted above that parties to a genuine and lawful marriage may enjoy family life even in the absence of cohabitation, that there is a presumption in favour of family life between child and natural parents that may only be broken in exceptional circumstances, and that family life may be established through adoption.

4.14   Despite the general emphasis on substantive ties, same-sex relationships have consistently been held to be outside the ambit of 'family life' in Article 8.[21] Rather they are considered to be an aspect of private life, where the positive obligations required of respect are less developed. In the context of admission and expulsion the consequence has been that greater leeway is given to the national

---

[17] The IAT also found, perhaps rather harshly, that the time which the aunt had spent apart from the nephew's elder brother, whom she had also raised but who was an adult when the aunt left for the UK, meant that family life between the aunt and the brother was destroyed: para. 34.

[18]   And see *Papayianni v UK* [1974] Imm AR 7.

[19]   The case was the subject of a friendly settlement.

[20]   Paragraph 8.1, Somali Family Reunion Policy.

[21]   *S v UK* (1986) 47 DR 274 para. 2; *X v UK* (1983) 32 DR 220; *Kerkhoven v Netherlands* (above at 4.10); *Norris v Ireland* (1988) 13 EHRR 186; *Dudgeon v United Kingdom* (1981) 4 EHRR 149; *Grant v SW Trains* [1998] ECR I-621. In *X, Y and Z v UK* (1997) 24 EHRR 143, the relationship between a transsexual, her same-sex partner and their child was de facto family life.

authority.[22] The extent to which it would be appropriate for the UK courts to exclude stable same-sex relationships from the ambit of family life is discussed below at 4.125.

4.15 It has also been held by the European Commission that national provisions which, in order to protect the family, treat married couples and couples of opposite sex living together more favourably than same-sex couples, are not contrary to the anti-discriminatory provisions of Article 14.[23] This issue is considered below at 6.31.

Date of assessment

4.16 The approach of the European Court to the date on which family or private life is assessed has not been consistent. In the earlier cases, the European Court took into account developments which post-dated the making of the potential interfering measure in assessing that there was a breach of Article 8 (*Nasri* v *France* (1995) 21 EHRR 458, where the position was considered in 1995 after an exclusion order had been made in 1991), and also considered matters which post-dated its execution to support its conclusion that there was no interference under Article 8(1) (*Ahmut* v *Netherlands* (1996) 24 EHRR 62 para. 72). In *Boughanemi* v *France* (1996) 22 EHRR 228 para. 35, the European Court took into consideration family life which was only established after the execution of the challenged removal and in a subsequent period of illegal stay following re-entry in the contracting state.

4.17 Subsequent cases adopted a more restrictive approach, but again the jurisprudence was not entirely clear. In *Bouchelkia* v *France* (1997) 25 EHRR 686 para. 41, the European Court held that the material date for assessment was the execution of a deportation order (in 1990), and family life established in a period of illegal re-entry in 1992 could not be relied upon, even though a second application had been made in 1995 to rescind the order following re-entry. In *El Boujaidi* v *France* (2000) 30 EHRR 223 para. 33, the European Court held that the relevant date was when the measure became final following exhaustion of appeals (in 1989), and not the date when it was enforced (in 1993). Thus the applicant could not plead his relationship with a French woman, nor the fact that they had a child together. In *Boujlifa* v *France* (2000) 30 EHRR 419 para. 36, the European Court repeated its view that the critical date was when the impugned measure was adopted (in 1991), but also excluded matters which post-dated the time when the applicant was informed of the fact that deportation proceedings

---

[22] See *X and U* v *UK* (1983) 5 EHRR 601; *X* v *UK* (1989) 11 EHRR 49; *Secretary of State for the Home Department* v *Z* [2002] EWCA Civ 952.

[23] See *S* v *UK* (1986) 47 DR 274 para. 7; *B* v *UK* 64 DR 278 para. 2.

had commenced (in 1990). Accordingly the applicant could not rely on his relationship with a French woman.

4.18 The European Court appeared to relax its approach in *Dalia* v *France* (2001) 33 EHRR 26 para. 45, where it held, distinguishing the situation in *El Boujaidi*, that because the measure challenged was the refusal of the Court of Appeal to lift an exclusion order (in 1994) rather than the order itself (which became final in 1985), the relevant time was the former rather than the latter date. This was despite the fact that the applicant's application to lift the exclusion order had been made following re-entry in 1987 on a temporary visa and during a period of unlawful stay. This enabled the applicant to rely upon the birth of her son, a French national. This approach harked back to *Boughanemi* (where family life in illegal re-entry was taken into consideration), and the facts appear not to be markedly different from those in *Bouchelkia* (where such family life was excluded). In *Farah* v *Sweden* (App. No. 43218/98, 24 August 1999) in declaring the complaint inadmissible, the European Court took into account the fact that after the execution of the ten-year expulsion order (in 1997; the order had become final in 1994), the applicant's family had accompanied him to Tunisia. In *Ezzoudhi* v *France* (App. No. 47160/99, 13 February 2001) para. 25 the European Court followed the *Bouchelkia* and *El Boujaidi* line, albeit with little material consequence to the case before it. In *Bensaid* v *UK* (2001) 33 EHRR 10, in the context of a private life claim, the European Court borrowed from the analysis in Article 3, where the Court's well-established practice is to assess the position at the time of its own consideration of the case, and considered medical reports and country conditions in 1999 which post-dated both the refusal of leave to enter (in 1998) and setting of removal directions (in 1998).

4.19 We would suggest that where possible, it is the approach in *Dalia* v *France* that should be followed by domestic courts. That approach appears to reverse the position in *El Boujaidi* and *Boujlifa*, and indeed *Bouchelkia*, so that even family life which is only established in a period of illegal stay can be taken into account, as occurred in *Boughanemi*. This accords with the principle that ECHR obligations are engaged by physical presence in the territory, and lawful stay is not a condition precedent to locus as a victim, albeit it may be highly material to the final result: *D* v *UK* (1997) 24 EHRR 423. It also accords with the principle that emphasis should be placed on matters of substance rather than form. While it is clear that family life which is engaged in when the immigration position of one of the parties is precarious will only exceptionally found an Article 8 breach, there seems little reason to exclude such family life from analysis altogether (as occurred in *Boujlifa*), and so elevate form over substance. The important judgment of the Court of Appeal in *R (Mahmood)* v *Secretary of State* [2001] 1 WLR 840 acknowledges that such family life is unlikely to found an Article 8 breach, but should not be *a priori* excluded from analysis.[24] The general guidance contained in *Boultif* v *Switzerland* (2001) 33 EHRR 50 para. 48, while not explicitly addressing the issue, also supports this approach (see below at 4.63). What is highly unsatisfactory is an inconsistency of approach which permits reliance on the up-to-date situation which avails the Government to support a finding that there has been no violation (*Ahmut* and, far less compellingly, *Farah*), while excluding current matters which support the applicant.

4.20   In the appellate context, s. 77(4) of the IAA 1999 prevents adjudicators and tribunals from considering post-decision facts in non-Article 3 cases, save where the evidence was available to the Secretary of State at the time of his decision, or relates to relevant facts at that date. The latter saving enables evidence as to post-decision developments (such as living together or the birth of a child) to be admitted to prove issues that were in dispute at the time of the decision (e.g. the strength of the relationship). The tribunal in *Nhundu and Chiwera* v *Secretary of State for the Home Department* (01/TH/00613, 1 June 2001) at para. 69 considered that 'if the purport of s. 77(4) was to wholly exclude reliance upon post-decision facts insofar as they relate to a non-Article 3 claim, then the section is impossible to reconcile with Strasbourg jurisprudence on Article 8'. The section has now been 'read down' to be compatible: see *S and K* v *Secretary of State for the Home Department* [2002] UKIAT starred 05613, paras. 19–21.

Actual and prospective enjoyment
4.21   Article 8(1) only protects the rights of existing, established families and not the right of a person to enter a country in order to found a new family (*Abdulaziz et al* v *UK* (1985) 7 EHRR 471 para. 67). However, an engagement to marry, accompanied by sufficient evidence of the strength of future intention or establishment of past relations, may in certain circumstances give rise to family life.[25]

4.22   An application for entry clearance by a wife to join her husband in the UK would raise issues of family life, even though the couple are not presently living together.[26] The bond of marriage and the fact of any past cohabitation is sufficient to found actual family life as is the mere birth of a child to parents.

---

[24] See below. Laws LJ rejected, on classic judicial review principles, the proposition that the High Court on judicial review should examine the position at the date of hearing, supported by citation of *Nasri* v *France* (see above at 4.16). The recognition in *Turgut* v *Secretary of State* [2000] INLR 292 Court of Appeal, that some decisions are inherently updating and permit receipt of updating material at least at first instance, appears not to have been considered in *Mahmood*.

[25] See *Wakefield* v *UK* (1990) 66 DR 251 para. 255; *Abdulaziz etc* v *UK* at para. 62. Although the European Commission has held that an intention to marry cannot found a claim to family life under Article 8, the European Court held that 'this does not mean that all intended family life falls entirely outside its ambit'.

[26] See *Abdulaziz* (above at 4.21) para. 21; but a marriage of convenience will not be so regarded: *Benes* v *Austria* 72 DR 721.

Cohabitation at any one moment is not necessary provided there are sufficient continuing links.[27] A separation does not necessarily break family life (*Beljoudi v France* (1992) 14 EHRR 801 para. 76 (imprisonment did not terminate family life). The degree of respect to be afforded to the relationship would turn on the strength of relationship (*Soderback v Sweden* (1998) 29 EHRR 95).

Scope: the meaning of private life

4.23   Article 8 is also significant in the context of immigration in the protection afforded to respect for private life. Private life under Article 8 is a broad concept that cannot be exhaustively defined. In the leading case of *Niemietz v Germany* (1992) 16 EHRR 97 the European Court held (at para. 29) that:

> it would be too restrictive to limit the notion (of private life) to an 'inner circle' in which the individual may live his own personal life as he chooses and to exclude therefrom entirely the outside world not encompassed within that circle. Respect for private life must also comprise to a certain degree the right to establish and develop relationships with other human beings.

4.24   In the immigration context, questions of private life may be engaged where the individual facing expulsion has been integrated into or has resided in the expelling state.[28] In *Beljoudi v France* (1992) 14 EHRR 801, although the applicant won on the basis of an unjustified interference with his family life (para. 67), Judges Martens and De Meyer in concurring opinions considered that the severance of the 'social ties' through expulsion should be considered under the private life rubric. In *Nasri v France* (1995) 21 EHRR 458, the applicant was again successful in showing an interference with his family life which the French Government failed to justify. In the opinions of Judges Morenilla and Wildhaber, the approach under private life was to be preferred since it facilitated the consideration of the broad sum of the ties, or the 'whole social fabric', rather than the narrower question of the family ties established. However, in both these cases (as indeed in *Berrehab v Netherlands* (1988) 11 EHRR 322 and in *Moustaquim v Belgium* (1991) 13 EHRR 802) it was implicit in the approach of the European Court that broader questions of private life arising from historical connections with the contracting state were considered. In later cases, the European Court has been more explicit in its acknowledgement of private life as a factor to be considered in such cases: *C v Belgium* (App. No. 21794/93, 7 August 1996) para. 25; *Bouchelkia v France* at para. 41; *El Boujaidi v France* at para. 33; *Mehemi v*

---

[27]   For the principle in the case of children see *Kroon v Netherlands* (1994) 19 EHRR 263; *Keegan v Ireland* (1994) 18 EHRR 342; *Berrehab v Netherlands* (1988) 11 EHRR 322 para. 21; *Boughanemi v France* (1996) 22 EHRR 228.

[28]   See van Dijk, 'The Protection of Integrated Aliens Against Expulsion under the ECHR' [1999] 1 EJML 293; *Lamguindaz v UK* (1993) 17 EHRR 213, concurring opinion of Judge Schermers.

France (2000) 30 EHRR 739 para. 27; *Boujlifa* v *France* at para. 36; *Dalia* v *France* at para. 45. Thus, in *Nhundu and Chiwera* v *Secretary of State* (01/TH/00613, 1 June 2001) the IAT summarized the position at para. 26:

> In the context of immigration and asylum cases, the [European] Court has come to view the right to respect for private and family life as a composite right. This approach requires the decision-maker to avoid restricting himself to looking at the circumstances of 'family life' and to take into account also significant elements of the much wider sphere of 'private life'.

4.25 Private life also covers the right to be 'left alone' as well as the right to develop one's personality and inter-relate socially with others.[29] Thus sexual orientation and identity have been held to be most intimate aspects of private life (*Dudgeon* v *UK* (1981) 4 EHRR 149), where the margin of appreciation afforded to the state is narrow (see below at 6.31), and homosexual relations attract the protection of Article 8 under this head.[30]

4.26 The right to protection of a person's physical and moral integrity are important aspects of private life, and may come into play where the minimum level of severity necessary for the engagement of Article 3 cannot be shown (*Raninen* v *Finland* (1997) 26 EHRR 563). Individuals have the right not to be subjected to compulsory physical interventions and treatments, such as blood (*X* v *Austria* (1979) 18 DR 154) or urine tests (*Peters* v *Netherlands* (1994) 77-A DR 75) or corporal punishment. There is emergent jurisprudence that 'limbo' immigration status where removal is not contemplated violates the right to respect to moral and physical integrity as an aspect of private life. As European Commission member Cabral Barreto stated in *HLR* v *France* (1997) 26 EHRR 29, 'an alien who lives in a particular country but who has no access to the employment market and cannot benefit from the social security scheme is in a situation which fails to meet the requirements of Article 8 of the Convention'.

4.27 In *Bensaid* v *UK* (2001) 33 EHRR 10, a person suffering from long-term schizophrenia was to be returned to a part of Algeria where the necessary treatment was only available to in-patients at a hospital some distance away. The European Court accepted that deterioration in mental condition causing the risk of self-harm resulting from difficulties in obtaining medication, as well as restrictions in social functioning, were in principle within the scope of Articles 3 and 8 (paras. 36 and 37).[31] On the facts however, it held that those consequences were

---

[29] See *X* v *Iceland* (1976) 5 DR 86; *McFeeley* v *UK* (1980) 20 DR 44.

[30] See *Dudgeon* v *UK* (1981); *Norris* v *Ireland* (1988) 13 EHRR 186; *Modinos* v *Cyprus* (1993) 16 EHRR 485.

[31] See also *Harron and Alayo* v *Sweden* (App. No. 28783/95) 87-A DR 126 (Swedish authorities granted right to remain, on basis of medical reports indicating serious risk that the applicants would commit suicide or sustain serious physical or mental injuries if removed to Uganda).

speculative and the case was not made out evidentially (para. 40). As to the scope of private life the European Court stated (at para. 47):

> Private life is a broad term not susceptible to exhaustive definition. The Court has already held that elements such as gender identification, name and sexual orientation are important elements of the personal sphere protected by Article 8 . . . Mental health must also be regarded as a crucial part of private life associated with the aspect of moral integrity. Article 8 protects the right to identity and personal development, and the right to establish and develop relationships with other human beings and the outside world . . . The preservation of mental stability is in that context an indispensable precondition to effective enjoyment of the right to private life.

4.28   We have examined some of these aspects of Article 8 at 2.102 et seq above dealing with bodily and physical integrity.

INTERFERENCE WITH THE RIGHT TO RESPECT FOR FAMILY AND PRIVATE LIFE

4.29   Not every decision which impacts adversely on interests protected by Article 8 amounts to an interference with the right to respect for that interest. What is required by the notion of 'respect' cannot be precisely defined in the abstract and will depend on the circumstances in the particular case. In general, however, it is possible to say that different considerations may apply as to what is demanded by 'respect' in the immigration context to decisions to exclude from the frontier those subject to immigration control, as opposed to decisions to remove those who entered or remained unlawfully whose spouses knew the precarious nature of the immigration position at the time of marriage, and further contrasted again with decisions to remove those who have been residing lawfully in the UK. The European Court appears to have drawn a distinction along these lines (*Ahmut* v *Netherlands* (1996) 24 EHRR 62 para. 63). Admission is seen as raising issues concerning the state's positive obligations under Article 8,[32] whereas where a couple live together in an ECHR state, the removal of either of them is seen as a failure to respect their rights whatever the prospect of the one following the other,[33] unless the national spouse was aware of the fragility of the other's immigration position at the time of marriage. Thus, in the 'normal' removal case,[34] the

---

[32] *Gul* v *Switzerland* (1996) 22 EHRR 93; *Sen* v *Netherlands* (App. No. 31465/96, 21 December 2001) paras. 31–2; *Nhundu and Chiwera* v *Secretary of State for the Home Department* (01/TH/00613, 1 June 2001) para. 38.

[33] See *Berrehab* v *Netherlands* (1988) 11 EHRR 322; *Boughanemi* v *France* (1996) 22 EHRR 228; C. Warbrick, 'The Structure of Article 8' [1998] EHRLR 32, 39.

[34] Namely where there was no precariousness in the immigration position, or where the family life is not tenuous: *Nhundu and Chiwera* v *Secretary of State for the Home Department* (01/TH/00613, 1 June 2001) para. 42.

focus then shifts to see whether the interference, with the 'negative obligation to refrain from measures which cause family ties to rupture'[35] inherent in respect, is justified. The guidance given by Lord Phillips MR in *R (Mahmood)* v *Secretary of State* [2001] 1 WLR 840, although not conceptually framed in terms of positive and negative obligations, accords with this basic dichotomy of approach.

4.30   Whether in the expulsion or admission context, once it is established that the circumstances in which family life or private life is being enjoyed require respect by the immigration authorities, the exercise of immigration control will constitute an interference in all but the most unusual cases.[36] The question will then become whether the interference is justified, which we consider below at 4.66. Justification only arises once an interference is established.[37]

4.31   What respect requires is important because the task for the state to establish that no questions of respect arise under Article 8(1) is less onerous than the task of justifying an interference with a (now established) right under Article 8(2). Thus in an admission case where it is established that 'respect' for family life requires the grant of entry, and the threshold of 'respect' is set sufficiently high, it may be difficult if not conceptually impossible for the state to argue justification.[38] The elimination of any role for justification under Article 8(2) points towards the imposition of a lower threshold for respect under Article 8(1). By contrast in removal cases concerning lawfully present individuals, the debate centres on justification because the European Court effectively approximates the right to respect for family life with a right of residence.

4.32   A key consideration in both contexts, however, is the ability with which family life could be enjoyed elsewhere. It has been suggested by Judge Martens and the European Commission that the approach to Article 8 should be the same in both admission and removal cases.[39] This suggestion has been taken up, at least to some extent, by the European Court in its recognition that 'the boundaries between the state's positive and negative obligations under Article 8 do not lend themselves to precise definition' and the 'applicable principles are . . .

---

[35] *Ciliz* v *Netherlands* (App. No. 29192/95, 11 July 2000) para. 62. See also *Pretty* v *UK* (2002) 35 EHRR 1, para. 53; *Nhundu and Chiwera* v *Secretary of State for the Home Department* (01/TH/00613, 1 June 2001) para. 38.

[36] Exceptions include cases where it is not apparent that the measure will materially affect or has materially affected the individual in question, e.g. where a wealthy, long-settled immigrant was able to travel easily to the country of his non-national spouse.

[37] Harris, O'Boyle & Warbrick, *Law of the European Convention on Human Rights* (1995, Butterworths) 328.

[38] See e.g. *Sen* v *Netherlands* (2003) 36 EHRR 7, para. 42.

[39] See Judge Martens's concurring opinion in *Beljoudi* v *France* (1992) 14 EHRR 801, and his dissents in *Gul* v *Switzerland* (1996) 22 EHRR 93 paras. 7–9 and in *Boughanemi* v *France* (1996) 22 EHRR 228; see also European Commission decision in *Ahmut* v *Netherlands* (1996) 24 EHRR 62 paras. 44–5.

similar'[40] (especially given that even in entry cases there will be a family member resident in the contracting state). The important recent decision of the European Court in *Sen* v *Netherlands* (2003) 36 EHRR 7 concerning the admission of a child also reveals a greater similarity in overall approach across admission and expulsion cases (para. 31), with emphasis given to the quality of the resident parent's stay in the contracting state and the obstacles to relocation (para. 40), in determining whether the right to respect for family life was interfered with. Even in *Sen*, however, the finding that there was a breach of a positive obligation in Article 8(1) disposed of the entire case, with no consideration being given to whether the state could justify the breach of the positive obligation constituted by the denial of admission to the child. This approach still points to the threshold of 'respect' being set too high by the European Court in admission cases. Logically the next stage in the development of the jurisprudence would be an acknowledgement that what is required by 'respect', in admission as well as expulsion cases, should be set at a more realistic level, and that what are properly questions of justification should be assigned to their proper place in Article 8(2). Hitherto, while professing a similarity of approach to positive and negative obligations inherent in respect in Article 8, it is difficult to see how the European Court in practice has applied it.

Respect for family life

Abdulaziz
4.33 The leading case concerning the interrelation between the rights of the individual to respect for family life and those of the community in the context of immigration is *Abdulaziz, Cabales and Balkandali* v *UK* (1985) 7 EHRR 471, where the European Court held (at para 494) as follows:

> 59. The Government's principal submission was that neither Article 8 nor any other Article of the Convention applied to immigration control, for which Protocol No. 4 was the only appropriate text. In their opinion, the fact that that Protocol was, as stated in its preamble, designed to afford rights additional to those protected by Section I of the Convention conclusively demonstrated that rights in the field of immigration were not already accorded by the Convention itself, and in particular by Article 8 thereof. Furthermore, the applicants were claiming a right which was not secured to aliens, even by the Protocol, an instrument that in any event had not been ratified by the United Kingdom. The Commission rejected this argument at the admissibility stage. In doing so, it confirmed—and the applicants now relied on—its established case-law: the right of a foreigner to enter or remain in a country was not as such guaranteed by the

---

[40] *Sternja* v *Finland* Series A No. 299-B (1994) para. 38; *Keegan* v *Ireland* (1994) 18 EHRR 342 para. 49; *Gul* v *Switzerland* (1996) 22 EHRR 93 para. 38; *Ahmut* v *Netherlands* (1996) 24 EHRR 62 para. 63; *Ciliz* v *Netherlands* (App. No. 29192/95, 11 July 2000) para. 61.

Convention, but immigration controls had to be exercised consistently with Convention obligations, and the exclusion of a person from a State where members of his family were living might raise an issue under Article 8.

60. The Court is unable to accept the Government's submission. The applicants are not the husbands but the wives, and they are complaining not of being refused leave to enter or remain in the United Kingdom but, as persons lawfully settled in that country, of being deprived (Mrs. Cabales), or threatened with deprivation (Mrs. Abdulaziz and Mrs. Balkandali), of the society of their spouses there. Above all, the Court recalls that the Convention and its Protocols must be read as a whole; consequently a matter dealt with mainly by one of their provisions may also, in some of its aspects, be subject to other provisions thereof . . . Thus, although some aspects of the right to enter a country are governed by Protocol No. 4 as regards States bound by that instrument, it is not to be excluded that measures taken in the field of immigration may affect the right to respect for family life under Article 8. The Court accordingly agrees on this point with the Commission.

. . .

67. The Court recalls that, although the essential object of Article 8 is to protect the individual against arbitrary interference by the public authorities, there may in addition be positive obligations inherent in an effective 'respect' for family life. However, especially as far as those positive obligations are concerned, the notion of 'respect' is not clear-cut: having regard to the diversity of practices followed and the situations obtaining in the Contracting States, the notion's requirements will vary considerably from case to case. Accordingly, this is an area in which the Contracting Parties enjoy a wide margin of appreciation in determining steps to be taken to ensure compliance with the Convention with due regard to the needs and resources of the community and of individuals. In particular, in the area now under consideration, the extent of a State's obligation to admit to its territory relatives of settled immigrants will vary according to the particular circumstances of the persons involved. Moreover, the Court cannot ignore that the present case is concerned not only with family life but also with immigration and that, as a matter of well-established international law and subject to its treaty obligations, a State has the right to control entry of non-nationals into its territory.

68. The Court observes that the present proceedings do not relate to immigrants who already had a family which they left behind in another country until they had achieved settled status in the United Kingdom. It was only after becoming settled in the United Kingdom as single persons, that the applicants contracted marriage. The duty imposed by Article 8 cannot be considered as extending to a general obligation on the part of a Contracting State to respect the choice by married couples of a country of their matrimonial residence and to accept the non-national spouses for settlement in that country.

4.34 Thus, *Abdulaziz, Cabales and Balkandali* v *UK* authoritatively established, first, that while there are no rights to immigration as such in the ECHR, the state's well-established right in international law to control its own frontiers had to be exercised subject to obligations contained in the ECHR[41] and the exclusion of a person from a state where members of his family were living could give rise to an issue under Article 8.

4.35   Secondly, given the right of a state to control its frontiers, Article 8 does not impose on the state an obligation to respect, without more, the choice of matrimonial residence of a couple and accept the non-national spouse for settlement. It follows that immigration control of itself is not inconsistent with obligations under Article 8, but neither in all cases will the exercise of immigration control be compatible with Article 8. Everything will depend on the particular circumstances of the case. We discuss Judge Martens's analysis of para. 68 of the *Abdulaziz* judgment at 4.49 below.

Respect: the fair balance
4.36   *Abdulaziz* also established that the notion of 'respect' is not precise and abstract but case-sensitive. It is well settled that the question of what is required in any particular context to maintain 'respect' for a particular interest will be determined by weighing the needs and resources of the individual against the interests of the community (*Cossey* v *UK* (1990) 13 EHRR 622). The circumstances as a whole must be considered, and the following are relevant factors: the past residence of the parties;[42] the duration of any separations; their legal and practical ability to establish themselves abroad; the ability of the parties and especially of any children to adapt to conditions there;[43] the links between the family members and the proposed country of destination; the availability of adequate educational (*Fadele* v *UK*) resources, language difficulties; cultural, religious and social practices; and compelling health (*Fadele* v *UK*), employment or family imperatives;[44] the economic consequences of removal[45] and the risk of ill-treatment on return.[46]

---

[41] It is curiously noteworthy that when the European Court was considering for the first time the application of Article 6 to the immigration context, the French Government was successful in advancing the formally similar argument to that which had failed in *Abdulaziz, Cabales and Balkandali* v *UK*, namely that since Protocol 7, Article 1 expressly dealt with immigration matters, Article 6 did not apply: *Maaouia* v *France* (2001) 33 EHRR 42.

[42] See *Abdulaziz*: there the applicants were *not* immigrants who had already had a family which they left behind in another country until they had achieved settled status, implying that different norms might be applied to 'paradigm' family reunion cases; see *Gul* v *Switzerland* (1996) 22 EHRR 93, dissent of Judge Martens at para. 13; see below at 4.42.

[43] *Fadele* v *UK* (1990) 70 DR 159; (poor living conditions and lack of educational opportunities); *Sorabjee* v *UK* (App. No. 239938/93); *PP* v *UK* (1996) 21 EHRR CD 81; *Jaramillo* v *UK* (App. No. 24865/94.

[44] See *Adegbie* v *Austria* (9 April 1996, unreported) subsequently settled (1997) 90-A DR 31, where neither spouse had prior or familial connections in Nigeria.

[45] See *X and Y* v *UK* (App. Nos. 5445, 5446/72) and *Adegbie* v *Austria* (above footnote 44) where the Austrian spouse would have had to give up a career.

[46] See *Dreshaj* v *Finland* 77 DR 126 (Kosovan Albanians returning to post-war Kosovo).

4.37   The 'constructive deportation' of children with residence rights through the expulsion of a parent will be relevant but not decisive,[47] with age and adaptabilty and the degree of hardship to be encountered also being considered.

4.38   Knowledge of the precariousness of the immigration position of one of the parties to the marriage will also be very relevant to the question of what respect demands. This was a further reason for the failure of the applicants in *Abdulaziz, Cabales and Balkandali* v *UK*, which additionally concerned the entry of husbands abroad (para. 68).[48]

4.39   The duty of respect may impose a positive obligation to maintain a just and effective law capable of vindicating rights to family life,[49] and to protect the family from attacks by others (*Osman* v *UK* (2000) 29 EHRR 455). Thus, in *Ciliz* v *Netherlands* (App. No. 29192/95, 11 August 2000) the European Court held that the notion of 'respect' extended to the imposition of positive procedural duty on the Netherlands to facilitate the prosecution of domestic procedures in the family law courts so as to enable family life to be established in the immigration context (*Olson* v *Sweden (No. 2)* (1994) 17 EHRR 134). The Dutch authorities' refusal to extend a father's permit so that he could have trial visits with his child pre-judged the family court's decision on access, and Article 8 was breached by his subsequent expulsion where there was no immediate need for his removal. While the expulsion engaged the 'negative obligation to refrain from measures which cause family ties to rupture' (*Ciliz* v *Netherlands* (App. No. 29192/95 para. 62)), in the final analysis the European Court focused on the Dutch authorities' failure to co-ordinate proceedings to promote the positive obligation of enabling family ties to be developed.

4.40   The dispersal of asylum seekers to accommodation in isolated and hostile places may raise issues under Article 8 as well as Article 3. We have also considered these broader aspects above at 2.102.

Respect and admission cases

4.41   In admission cases, the European Court has considered that what is being claimed is a positive obligation to admit the individual.[50] Here the traditional view is that a wide margin of appreciation is afforded to the state in determining what is required to ensure respect (*Abdulaziz* para. 67).[51]

---

[47] See Nuala Mole, *Constructive Deportation* (1995) EHRLR 63.

[48] See also *Poku* v *UK* (1996) 22 EHRR CD 94; *Ajayi* v *UK* (App. No. 27663 95, 20 June 1999, unreported).

[49] See *Marckx* v *Belgium* (1979) 2 EHRR 330; *Kroon* v *Netherlands* (1994) 19 EHRR 263; *Hokkanen* v *Finland* (1996) 19 EHRR 139.

[50] See *Ahmut* v *Netherlands* (1996) 24 EHRR 62 para. 63; *Sen* v *Netherlands* (2003) 36 EHRR 7, paras. 31–2.

[51] See, however, the discussion at 4.29–4.32 above, and the recognition of the need for a greater harmonization of approach across cases raising positive and negative obligations.

4.42   A couple's mere preference to live in the contracting state will not suffice to show an interference with the right to respect for their family life, at least where the family life only arises subsequent to the non-national spouse's admission into the contracting state. The main consideration as to whether an exclusion constitutes a denial of respect is the question of whether there are real obstacles to the constitution of family life elsewhere or special reasons why the persons concerned ought not to be expected to do so. This was the primary basis upon which the applicants in *Abdulaziz, Cabales and Balkandali* v *UK* failed to show a lack of respect for family life (see para. 68).

4.43   There are, however, recent indications that the European Court has taken a more expansive approach to questions of family reunion, where parents achieve a settled or stable status and seek reunion with the children they left behind. We discuss the cases of *Gul* v *Switzerland* (1996) 22 EHRR 93, *Ahmut* v *Netherlands* (1996) 22 EHRR 62 and *Sen* v *Netherlands* (2003) 36 EHRR 7 below at 4.48 to 4.58.

4.44   Where it can be shown that the parties would suffer significant detriment by having to leave the UK and live elsewhere in order to continue to enjoy family life an interference should be established. Whilst mere economic hardship (*X* v *UK* (28 February 1996)) and illness (*Akhtar* v *UK* (12 February 1992)) have been held to be insufficient by themselves, we suggest that loss of property rights and cessation of access to health should be considered in the context as a whole. Social and economic reality cannot be ignored and people on low incomes cannot be expected to pay expensive air fares to fly around the world for access visits to maintain family life (*Berrehab* v *Netherlands* (1988) 11 EHRR 322 paras. 22–3).

4.45   Family life may be established through ties of dependency with the applicant living abroad, even in the absence of present cohabitation.[52] Thus where family life is being enjoyed through the nexus of financial provision being sent from earnings in the UK by the UK settled sponsor, which the sponsor would not earn in the home country, a refusal to admit the family may amount to an interference with respect for family life (*R* v *Secretary of State ex parte Arman Ali* [2000] Imm AR 134).

4.46   Regard to reality may also work the other way. A spouse with exceptional leave to remain status, who has travelled back to the country in which they fear ill-treatment, may not be able to establish a breach of Article 8 with the spouse or child living there, where those visits show that the fears of ill-treatment have dissipated.[53] Whether such fears have ceased to be well-founded is plainly a

---

[52] See *Rees* v *UK* (1986) 9 EHRR 56; *Berrehab* v *Netherlands* (1988) 11 EHRR 322 paras. 20–1; *R* v *Secretary of State ex parte Arman Ali* [2000] Imm AR 134 at 145.
[53] *Gul* v *Switzerland* (1996) 22 EHRR 93 para. 41; note that Counsel for the applicant expressly disavowed any present fear of return to Turkey.

question of fact: it would be difficult to argue that they did not continue to persist where, for example, there were compelling reasons as to the motive and duration of the visit.[54] Equally it would be difficult for the state to argue that family life could be established in another country where conditions there do not afford a safe or durable place for its enjoyment.

4.47 A trio of admission cases demonstrates the application of these principles.

Gul, Ahmut and Sen

4.48 In *Gul v Switzerland* (1996) 22 EHRR 93 the applicant was a Turkish national married to a Turkish wife. Both were lawfully resident in Switzerland but had no settlement rights. The applicant had originally claimed to be a refugee, but had withdrawn his claim as a condition of obtaining humanitarian residence rights. The applicant had worked for many years in Switzerland before he was incapacitated by an accident. His wife had suffered serious injuries in an epileptic fit and had joined him in Switzerland because she could not receive adequate medical care where she was living in Turkey. The couple were receiving social assistance in Switzerland. A daughter was born to them in Switzerland whom they could not look after and she was placed in public care. The applicant sought permission to bring into Switzerland his son whom he had left behind in Turkey, and who was at the time of the request eight years old. The Swiss authorities refused on grounds that the applicant had insufficient resources to maintain his son. The European Court considered the case under Article 8(1) and concluded that there were no insuperable obstacles to the enjoyment of family life in Turkey (at para. 42). The applicant had returned there from time to time, which tended to show (as confirmed by the applicant's Counsel) that his initial asylum reasons for leaving Turkey were no longer valid (para. 41), and the European Court was not satisfied that his wife would not be able to receive adequate medical treatment there (at para. 41). The son had always lived in Turkey and therefore had grown up in the cultural and linguistic environment of the country (at para. 42). In a controversially harsh decision, in which the European Court entirely failed to address the relationship of the parents with their daughter, the European Court concluded that respect for family life did not require the issue of residence permit enabling the son to enter Switzerland.

4.49 In a memorable dissent (approved by Judge Russo), Judge Martens (paras. 7 to 15) considered that the approach of the European Court should be the same in exclusion as in expulsion cases, that the European Court in *Abdulaziz* had

---

[54] See analogously Article 1C(1) of the Geneva Convention on the Status of Refugees and para. 125 UN Handbook.

impliedly concluded that where an immigrant *did* leave behind an established family, and achieved settled status (something which the Guls did not enjoy) in the contracting state, that state had to respect the couple's choice of residence on the basis that 'it is *per se* unreasonable, if not inhumane to give them the choice between giving up the position which they have acquired in the country of settlement or to renounce the mutual enjoyment by parent and child of each other's company which constitutes a fundamental element of family life'.[55] The daughter's position was not lost on Judge Martens: since it was in her interests to remain in Switzerland where she was being educated in a home, the Guls were faced with a choice of renouncing her or their son.

4.50   The impact of the *Gul* judgment was felt in *Ahmut* v *Netherlands* (1996) 24 EHRR 62 where a 5:4 majority of the European Court concluded that no issue of respect under Article 8(1) arose. The applicant, a dual Dutch and Moroccan national, sought to bring his son aged nine at the time of the request, to the Netherlands. The son had been brought up by his mother until she died, and then by other members of his family. The applicant sent funds for his son's upkeep. The son joined the applicant in the Netherlands but was refused permission to stay, and was sent back to Morocco where he started attending boarding school. The European Commission considered that the refusal of permission to stay interfered with the right of the applicant to respect for his family life (paras. 44 and 45). The majority of the European Court analysed the application as an allegation that the Netherlands had failed to comply with a positive obligation inherent in the concept of respect (para. 63), and concluded that the Netherlands had discharged such an obligation. The European Court noted that the son had strong links with the cultural and linguistic environment of Morocco (para. 69), and that there was nothing to stop the applicant returning to Morocco to live with his son or maintaining the level of family life he had voluntarily opted for himself when he left Morocco (para. 70). The applicant's preference for remaining in the Netherlands to maintain his family life there was not enough to show that the Dutch had failed to respect his rights under Article 8 (para. 71). The European Court also considered that by sending his son to boarding school, the applicant had arranged for his care in Morocco (para. 72).

4.51   The dissenting judges analysed the refusal of the residence permit as an

---

[55] Judge Martens also considered 'the Government's attempt to embellish the harsh, political objectives of their decision by pleading that in the first place it was designed to serve (the son's) interests as rather hypocritical' (para. 9) and that the European Court 'has to ensure, in particular, that State interests do not crush those of an individual, especially in a situation where political pressure—such as the growing dislike of immigrants in Member States—may inspire State authorities to harsh decisions.' (para. 15).

interference with the applicant's right to respect for family life, which could not be justified under Article 8(2).[56]

4.52 The important recent judgment in *Sen* v *Netherlands* (2003) 36 EHRR 7 marks a welcome retreat from the harsh reasoning in *Gul* and *Ahmut*. In *Sen* the European Court held that Article 8 demanded the grant of entry to a 13-year-old girl who had been left in the custody of her uncle in Turkey at the age of three when her parents moved to the Netherlands, and had spent her whole life in Turkey where she still had relatives.

4.53 The European Court considered that the admission of the daughter to the Netherlands raised issues as to the positive obligations inherent in the concept of 'respect' (paras. 31 and 32), albeit that the applicable principles were similar to the situation where negative obligations were engaged (para. 31). In a passage echoing the dissent of Judge Martens in *Gul* (see above at 4.49), the European Court observed that this was not a situation where family ties had only been established subsequent to entry in the contracting state, but rather pre-dated the parents' admission to the Netherlands (para. 37). The European Court considered that the case contained a number of similarities with the *Ahmut* decision, in particular the fact that the daughter's separation from her parents was the result of a voluntary decision of the parents, and that she had been cared for by her uncle in Turkey, where she enjoyed linguistic and cultural links (paras. 38 and 39).

4.54 However, contrary to the *Ahmut* and *Gul* decisions, there were major obstacles to the rest of the family's return to Turkey: the parents had settled in the Netherlands where they had been legally resident for many years, and they had two children who were born there, had always lived there, and went to school there. *Gul* was first distinguished on the basis that one of the parents had settlement in the Netherlands. Secondly, and more significantly, the European Court distinguished both *Gul* and *Ahmut* on the basis that the two younger children of the couple would themselves face significant obstacles if required to uproot to Turkey: they were born in, had grown up in, and attended school in the Netherlands. In those circumstances, the most appropriate place for family life to be constituted was the Netherlands, having regard to the daughter's age and the importance of her integration into the 'natural' family of her parents. While the separation of the daughter from her parents was a result of the parents' deliberate

---

[56] Judge Valticos was not far short of accusing the Dutch authorities of racism: 'The father had acquired Netherlands nationality, and in any country, a national is entitled to have his son join him, even if the son does not have the same nationality. How does it come about that in the present case this right was refused him? I cannot think that it is because the Dutch father was called 'Ahmut'. However, the suspicion of discrimination must inevitably lurk in people's minds. It is to be hoped that the Netherlands Government will swiftly remedy this blunder.'

decision, to cement that decision now by refusing admission would entail the definitive abandonment of any prospect of reunification of the family (para. 40). In those premises, it was not necessary to consider whether relatives in Turkey were able or willing to support the daughter (para. 41). In consequence a violation of Article 8 was found (para. 43).

4.55 In a concurring opinion, Judge Turmen endorsed the dissent of Judge Martens in both *Ahmut* and *Gul*, holding that where a father or mother obtain permanent residence in a country and seek reunion with their children, it was per se unreasonable if not inhumane to give them the choice of abandoning their residence or renouncing their reunion with their children. We would strongly agree with this concurring opinion, whose essence is reflected in the judgment of the European Court, and would hope that the domestic courts when faced with a similar problem would follow this line of reasoning in developing a municipal human rights jurisprudence.[57]

4.56 It is noteworthy that the basic facts in the *Sen* case were, if anything, less compelling than those in *Gul*, and not markedly different from those in *Ahmut*. The European Court in *Sen* first laid emphasis on the settled status of the applicant parents (para. 40), something which the parents in *Gul* lacked, despite having enjoyed considerable periods of lawful residence in Switzerland.[58] However, *Ahmut* was not distinguishable on this basis, for there the applicant father had achieved 'the best possible settled status: he ha[d] acquired Dutch nationality'.[59] The second distinguishing factor in *Sen*, namely the obstacles to relocation faced by the two younger children who had been brought up in the Netherlands, was not available to differentiate *Gul* (as noted above in 4.48 and 4.49), since there the daughter had not only been brought up in Switzerland but was in care there, and could hardly be expected to uproot to Turkey. Yet her position was simply not addressed by the European Court. While in *Ahmut* there was no child resident in the Netherlands whose family life could be invoked, Ahmut's son in Morocco was not only younger than the daughter in *Sen* but had lost his mother, had lived with his father in the Netherlands, and had been maintained by him even when he was in Morocco.

4.57 The judgment in *Sen* is perhaps best explained by the European Court's recognition that Article 8 presumptively embraces the reunion of the natural family, where parents leave their country of origin and achieve a settled or stable

---

[57] *R (M and La Rose)* v *Commissioner of Police for the Metropolis* [2001] EWHC Admin 553 para. 11; *R (Pro Life Alliance)* v *BBC* [2002] EWCA Civ 297 paras. 33–4.
[58] In *Gul* the father, although not settled, had lived for 13 years in Switerland, and had held a residence permit for seven years.
[59] *Ahmut* v *Netherlands* (1996) 24 EHRR 62, dissenting opinion of Judge Martens, para. 6

status in the contracting state;[60] hence the reference by the European Court in *Sen* at para. 40 to the importance of the daughter's reintegration into her 'natural' family. Such an approach of course also reflects increasing standards of humanity in the application of the ECHR, one of whose purposes as Judge Martens in *Gul* noted is to protect unpopular minorities from political pressure and the harsh decisions that may generate.

4.58   However, even the judgment in *Sen* leaves the problem that the threshold of respect in admission cases is set so high as to deprive Article 8(2) of any space in which to apply. Warbrick's reluctant analysis of *Gul* was that it appeared that nothing less than the demonstration of Article 3 risks would prevent the state arguing that denial of admission was consistent with respect for family life. This meant that there was no room for justification of the failure to comply with the duty of respect.[61] While the first part of this analysis cannot in our view survive *Sen*, the second part—the otiosity of Article 8(2)—remains an analytical problem even following the *Sen* judgment. The next step in the jurisprudence, we tentatively suggest, requires a modest adjustment of *Sen*, through an acknowledgement of a more appropriate conception of the standard of respect. We suggest that the European Court should recognize that the refusal to allow a lawfully resident and established parent to be reunited with their child of itself interferes with the duty to respect family life owed by the state to that parent. This allows questions which in essence relate to justification to be given their proper place in Article 8(2). Hitherto these questions have been subsumed into determining the content of the duty of respect under Article 8(1), with the conceptually unattractive result that Article 8(2) then becomes redundant.

Respect: expulsion cases

4.59   Expulsions of persons lawfully present in the UK raise different questions from questions concerning removals of those illegally here or denial of admission to those at the frontier, even though social and economic policy may be relevant in both cases. In removal cases, where there is no issue as to the precariousness of the situation when the relationship was formed, where the relationship is not otherwise wholly tenuous,[62] or where there is no question of attempted deceit to secure entry,[63] the right to respect for family life is seen as embracing a right to respect the choice of residence such that an expulsion decision will be seen to interfere with the negative obligation inherent in that right 'to refrain from

---

[60] *Sen* v *Netherlands* para. 37; *Abdulaziz* para. 68.
[61] C. Warbrick, 'The Structure of Article 8', [1998] EHRLR 32, 42.
[62] See *Nhundu and Chiwera* v *Secretary of State for the Home Department* (01/TH/00613, 1 June 2001) para. 42.
[63] See *Nsona* v *Netherlands* (App. No. 23366/94, 28 November 1996) para. 113.

measures that cause family ties to rupture',[64] and will also engage issues of respect for private life where the 'whole social fabric' (see above at 4.24) can be considered. The debate then centres on whether the state can justify the interference under Article 8(2). By contrast, as we have seen, the authorization of entry to the territory is seen as an aspect of the state's positive obligations to promote laws and practices that permit family union, and what 'respect' requires is a manifestation of a positive obligation where the state may have a greater margin of appreciation (albeit we note above at 4.32 that the approach of the European Court to both positive and negative obligations inherent in Article 8(1) is now professed to be 'similar').

4.60 In particular, it is to be noted that settled immigrants will historically have fulfilled criteria enabling them lawfully to stay, will have thereafter lived in the UK and typically will have become integrated into society. They enjoy established rights in the UK, and 'respect' in the Article 8 context engages the negative obligation not to interfere with historically established ties and rights attendant on legal status.

4.61 The case law on Article 8 and its application to removals is considered below at 4.77 when we consider 'justification' under Article 8(2). It suffices to state for present purposes that the European Court has recognized that in expulsion cases, the right of respect for family life includes the right of residence, interference with which must be justified, even where the family life claimed is rather tenuous (*C* v *Belgium* (App. No. 21794/93, 7 August 1996)) or where the applicant is an adult at the material time claiming family life with adult siblings and parents (*Boujlifa* v *France* (2000) 30 EHRR 419; *Mehemi* v *France* (2000) 30 EHRR 739). At this juncture, we simply consider the conception accorded to 'respect' in the landmark case of *Berrehab* v *Netherlands* (1988) 11 EHRR 322 and in the recent guideline case of *Boultif* v *Switzerland* (2001) 33 EHRR 50.

4.62 In *Berrehab* v *Netherlands* (1988) 11 EHRR 322 the applicant, a Moroccan national, challenged an order expelling him from the Netherlands which would prevent him from continuing to exercise his rights of access to his four-year old daughter from whose mother he was separated.[65] The European Court considered (at para. 23) that since the possibility of family life with his daughter being maintained by the applicant from Morocco was 'somewhat theoretical'—not least owing to financial difficulties and the fact that the applicant had been initially refused a temporary visa to travel to the Netherlands for access—the refusal to grant the applicant a new residence permit after his divorce and his

---

[64] See *Ciliz* v *Netherlands* (App. No. 29192/95, 11 July 2000) para. 62.

[65] Subsequently, the couple remarried and the applicant was granted permission to reside in the Netherlands: (1988) 11 EHRR 322 para. 13.

resulting expulsion amounted to interferences with his right to respect for family life under Article 8(1).

4.63 In *Boultif* v *Switzerland* (2001) 33 EHRR 50, the applicant, an Algerian national, entered Switzerland in 1992 at the age of 25. The following year he married a Swiss citizen, and committed a robbery in 1994 for which he was sentenced to two years' imprisonment in 1997. In May 1998, the Swiss authorities refused to renew his residence permit. Before proceeding to 'establish guiding principles' (para. 48) as to whether an interfering measure is necessary in a democratic society, the European Court was required to consider the issue of whether the refusal to renew the permit amounted to an interference with the right to respect for family life. It took the issue shortly, stating at para. 39 that 'the removal of a person from a country where close members of his family are living may amount to an infringement of the right to respect for family life' and at para. 40 that 'In the present case, the Applicant, an Algerian citizen, is married to a Swiss citizen. Thus, the refusal (of the permit) interfered with the Applicant's right to respect for his family life . . .'.

Respect for private life: regularization of status
4.64 The right to respect for private life may include the imposition of a positive duty on a state to regularize an immigrant's status with no prospect of removal within a reasonable timescale, where the result of limbo status is destitution through an inability to access the labour market together with a denial of access to the mainstream benefits regime.

Respect for private life: expulsions
4.65 Respect for private life may also require the immigration authorities in a contracting state to refrain from the expulsion of an immigrant, where the conditions in the country to which he is to be sent will unjustifiably interfere with his right to respect for private life. In *Bensaid* v *UK* (2001) 33 EHRR 10 the European Court appeared to recognize that an expulsion in such a context could engage the responsibility of the sending state. Thus a removal to a regime which criminalizes and prosecutes for consensual, non-violent, homosexual sex between adults in private, a prosecution which 'is not regarded by the international community at large as acceptable',[66] may interfere with the dignity of the immigrant and the duty of respect for the essence of the right owed by the expelling state.[67]

---

[66] *Jain* v *Secretary of State* [2000] INLR 71; see also the decision of the South African Constitutional Court in *National Association of Gays and Lesbians* v *Minister of Justice* (1999) (1) SA 6.

[67] See *Secretary of State* v *Z and Others* [2002] Imm AR 560, but see also *Ullah* v *Secretary of State* [2002] EWCA Civ 1856.

JUSTIFICATION: THE LAW

4.66 An interference with the right to respect for family or private life will become a violation of Article 8 unless the state demonstrates it to be in 'accordance with the law'. Any substantive breach of domestic law will therefore necessarily amount to a breach of Article 8.

4.67 This has important consequences for the jurisdictional limits of the appeal under s. 65 of the Immigration and Asylum Act 1999, where the right and ground of appeal appears to be limited to consideration as to whether the immigrant's human rights will be breached. But where the domestic law enjoins that an act is unlawful if it is a breach of a person's (victim's) human rights (ss. 6 and 7 of the Human Rights Act 1998) and the victim is not the subject of immigration action, the appellate review would have to include a consideration of that question owing to the requirement that an interference with the immigrant's human rights be in accordance with domestic law. See, however, the IAT's ruling in *Citajci* (22 August 2002, under review at present), *Kehinde* (01/TH/2668) and *Metsola* [2002] UKIAT 00295.

4.68 Domestic law is not law for the purposes of the ECHR if it is not adequately accessible and precise so that its consequences are foreseeable, and a law conferring a discretion must indicate the width of that discretion (*Silver v UK* (1983) 5 EHRR 347). However, the mere fact that an individual has to consult a lawyer for effective access to the law is not a breach of the accessibility rule (*Sunday Times v UK* (1979–80) 2 EHRR 245).

4.69 This means that leaked internal instructions such as DP/2/93 would not have complied with this requirement, especially in relation to its application to illegal entrants, whose position is not otherwise governed by the Immigration Rules. An illegal entrant whose right to respect for family life was interfered with through an expulsion decision based on secret guidelines may have been able to argue that the interference was not in accordance with the law: especially if they could show that had the guidelines been available, they would have regulated their conduct differently.

4.70 The present policy of transparent government, with published instructions, is likely to comply with this aspect of the ECHR concept of law. We suggest that all published instructions should be incorporated within the Immigration Rules, to avoid any possibility of misunderstanding and confusion as to the requirements of an opaque, extra-rule, regulatory framework, and in light of the status of the Immigration Rules. Immigration Rules simply represent the practice to be followed in the administration of immigration control and are not strictly delegated legislation in the conventional sense[68] albeit they have the force of law in the appellate system (IAA 1999, Sch. 4, para. 21). Indeed the impact of the ECHR can be discerned in the increasing formal status given to guidelines regulating the position of those historically not covered by the rules over time, e.g. the position of same-sex partners was initially governed by general extra-rule discretion, was then regulated by policy, and has now been incorporated into the Immigration Rules.

JUSTIFICATION: LEGITIMATE MOTIVES

4.71   An interference under Article 8(1) will found a violation unless the state demonstrates that the interference has the aim of protecting one of the interests listed in Article 8(2). These interests are:

> national security, public safety or the economic well-being of the country, for the prevention of disorder or crime, for the protection of health or morals, or for the protection of the rights and freedoms of others.

Article 18 provides that no additional qualification can be grafted onto the right in Article 8(1).

4.72   Immigration control has consistently been held by the European Court to relate to the the preservation of the economic well-being of the country, the prevention of disorder or crime, the protection of health and morals, and the protection of rights and freedoms of others. Exclusions or expulsions of illegal entrants are therefore likely to fall easily within a permissible competing interest under Article 8(2). It is important to note that immigration control is not of itself a valid end capable of justifying an interfering measure; it is rather the medium through which other legitimate aims are promoted.

4.73   The question of whether a deportation of a settled immigrant with no propensity to reoffend could fit within the permissible objects in Article 8(2) on the basis of past criminality alone, was considered by the Court of Appeal in *B* v *Secretary of State* [2000] INLR 361. The court held, leaving the issue open, that the interests listed in Article 8(2) were 'likely to engage questions of propensity rather than of past conduct'.[69] In *Samaroo* [2002] INLR 55, however, even though the individual appellant had no propensity to reoffend, the Secretary of State's policy

---

[68] *Hosenball* [1977] 1 WLR 766—they probably are delegated legislation for Human Rights Act 1998 purposes.

[69] It is plain that under domestic law, a sufficiently serious historic offence can found reasons conducive to the public good (s. 3(5)(b), Immigration Act 1971) for deportation. Even in the EU context, past conduct alone can constitute a present threat to the requirements of public policy (*R* v *Bouchereau* [1978] QB 732, 759; *Al Sabah* v *IAT* [1992] Imm AR 223; *Marchon* v *IAT* [1993] Imm AR 384; *Goremsandu* v *Home Secretary* [1996] Imm AR 250).

of deterring other international drug traffickers, which was promoted by the deportation of the appellant, fell within Article 8(2) as preventing crime and protecting others.

4.74 In EC law the European Court of Justice (ECJ) has held that 'Community law precludes the expulsion of a national of a Member State on general preventative grounds, that is to say an expulsion ordered for the purpose of deterring other aliens',[70] and that 'a measure expelling an alien as a matter of principle ordered on general preventative grounds following a criminal conviction for a specific offence must be considered to be incompatible' with the provisions regulating derogation from rights of establishment conferred under the Turkish–EEA Association Agreement.[71]

4.75 Given that as long ago as 1974 in *Rutili* v *Ministre de l'Intérieur* [1975] ECR 1219 the ECJ considered that its approach to derogation from rights of free movement under Directive 64/221 had to be inspired by ECHR jurisprudence, there is, however, some scope for the suggestion that general deterrence alone is not a legitimate aim under Article 8(2), at least where the issue is exclusively domestic without any international element and connection to immigration. Whatever the merits of such a position (and Thomas J in *Samaroo* appeared to consider that different considerations may arise under Community law, it is clear that the absence of propensity and the presence only of general deterrence as a justifying measure will be highly relevant to the necessity of the interfering measure.

4.76 Further issues arise in the case of an interference with private life through the failure to regularize status, and especially where the consequence of limbo status is an inability to access the courts effectively. The current asylum support regime excludes from support those seeking judicial review of asylum decisions. Ministers expressly excluded such persons so as to deter abusive applications. There is a parachute system of 'Hard Cases' support[72] designed to provide support for those who are destitute. Exposure to a sub-normal benefits system, or a denial of support altogether, may raise issues as to whether the measures pursued and the consequent interference with respect for private life pursues a legitimate aim. The aims listed in Article 8(2) are intended to be exhaustive; there is no scope for states inferentially to extend grounds that are not explicitly stated,[73] and moreover, those aims are construed strictly and in a way which does not permit interference with rights beyond their natural meaning. A desire to

---

[70] *Bonsignore* v *Stadt Köln* [1975] ECR 297, para. 7.
[71] *Nazli* v *Germany* [2000] ECR I-957, a case concering the importation of class A drugs.
[72] Currently administered by the Home Office under s. 4, Immigration and Asylum Act 1999.
[73] See *De Wilde, Ooms and Versyp* v *Belgium* (1979–80) 1 EHRR 373; *Golder* v *UK* (1979–80) 1 EHRR 524.

expel putative refugees generally may not qualify as a legitimate aim especially given the current debate as to the needs of the domestic labour market.[74]

JUSTIFICATION: PROPORTIONALITY AND NECESSITY

4.77   An interference with family life or private life will be a violation of Article 8 unless the state demonstrates that the interference was 'necessary in a democratic society'. The adjective 'necessary' is left undefined in the ECHR, and the European Court has held that it implies the existence of 'a pressing social need' and that the interfering measure is proportionate to the aim of responding to that need.

ECHR case law

4.78   In *Moustaquim* v *Belgium* (1991) 13 EHRR 802, the applicant was a Moroccan national and a petty criminal who had committed numerous offences, and had lived in Belgium since he was one year old. The European Court considered (at para. 36) that his deportation resulted in his being separated from his parents and seven siblings, and that accordingly there was an interference with his right to respect for family life under Article 8(1). Similarly in *Beljoudi* v *France* (1992) 14 EHRR 801, the applicant was an Algerian national, and a professional criminal who was married to a Frenchwoman. He had been brought to France by his family as an infant. The European Court shortly noted (at para. 67) that the enforcement of the challenged deportation order would constitute an interference with the right to respect for family life. In *Nasri* v *France* (1995) 21 EHRR 458, the European Court (at para. 34) was even more pithy in considering that the deportation of the applicant would amount to an interference under Article 8(1). The applicant was an Algerian national and deaf-mute, who had been convicted of numerous petty offences, but had also been convicted of one offence of gang rape. In *Mehemi* v *France* (2000) 30 EHRR 739, the applicant was an Algerian national born in France, who was made subject to a permanent exclusion order following a conviction for the illegal importation of drugs. It was suspected that he was a member of a drug trafficking network. He had lived his whole life, more than thirty years, in France, where his entire family resided, including his Italian wife, and he was the father of three minor children of French nationality. The French Government argued that the applicant's ties with his parents and siblings should not be considered because he had attained majority by the time that his

---

[74] The existence of such a desire can perhaps be the more readily inferred since the decision of the Divisional Court in *R* v *Home Secretary ex parte Adimi* [1999] Imm AR 560 where the court acknowledged that the system of prosecuting refugee claimants for use of false documentation in securing entry was intended to discourage refugees from coming to the UK and was in contravention of Article 31 CSR.

exclusion was ordered. The European Court took into account the applicant's history and ties with France, including his links with his parents and siblings, and was 'in no doubt' that the exclusion order amounted to interference with the right to respect for private and family life.

4.79 In none of the cases considered above at 4.78 were the respondent Governments able to demonstrate that the interference with the right to respect for family life was justified under Article 8(2).

4.80 In *Boughameni* v *France* (1996) 22 EHRR 228, the applicant, a Tunisian who had lived in France since the age of eight, was deported following his conviction for a number of offences. He returned to France illegally and formed a relationship with a woman, whose child he subsequently recognized. His parents and siblings were legally resident in France, but the applicant did not live with them. The European Court considered (at para. 35) that the deportation order would have the effect of separating the applicant from his child and his parents and siblings, and that it could accordingly be regarded as an interference under Article 8(1). In *C* v *Belgium* (App. No. 21794/93, 7 August 1996), the applicant was a Moroccan citizen who had lived in Belgium since the age of eleven, and who had married a Moroccan woman with whom he had a child. The couple divorced and the applicant was granted custody of his son. He was served with a deportation order on the ground of his criminal convictions for criminal damage and unlawful possession of drugs. The European Court considered (at para. 25) that the appellant had a family life and social ties in Belgium and that 'It follows that the Applicant's deportation amounted to interference with his right to respect for his family and private life.' In *Bouchelkia* v *France* (1998) 25 EHRR 686, the European Court held (at para. 41) that the deportation of the applicant, an Algerian national who had lived in France since the age of two, who at the material time was still living with his original family, and who had been convicted of rape, amounted to an interference with the right to respect for private and family life. In *El-Boujaidi* v *France* (2000) 30 EHRR 223 the applicant was a Moroccan national resident in France since the age of seven, who was subject to an exclusion order following his conviction for supplying heroin. The material date was the date when the order became final, and accordingly the applicant could not plead his relationship with a French woman, nor the fact that they had a child together (para. 33). Nevertheless, at the material time, the applicant had lived the majority of his life in France and his parents and siblings lived there. Accordingly (at para. 33), the European Court was 'in no doubt' that the expulsion order amounted to an interference under Article 8(1). In *Boujlifa* v *France* (2000) 30 EHRR 419 the applicant, a Moroccan national who had resided in France since the age of five, was the subject of a deportation order following a number of convictions including two for armed robbery and robbery. The Government argued that the applicant's ties with his parents and siblings could not be considered since he had attained the age of majority. Nor could his relationship and cohabitation with a French national since January 1991 be considered since that post-dated the time when the applicant was subject to a deportation order. At para. 36 the European Court considered that the material time was when the impugned measure was adopted in April 1991, but, accepting the French Government's argument, that he could not rely on his relationship since he had been informed in December 1990 that deportation proceedings had commenced. The European Court was, however, 'in no doubt' that the deportation amounted to an interference with private and family life, having regard to his history and schooling in France, and the presence of his parents and siblings. In *Dalia v France* (App. No. 26102/95, 19 February 1998) the applicant was an Algerian national who entered France aged 17 or 18 to join her family. She was subject to an exclusion order in 1985 following a conviction for drugs-related offences for which she received a twelve-month prison sentence. She was deported in 1987 but returned subsequently in 1989. Her mother and siblings were resident in France. In 1990 she gave birth to a child who had French nationality. The Government argued that the applicant had led a marginal existence in France before 1985, and since her trial had lived there in hiding. She had an independent social life in Algeria having spent her formative and adolescent years there, which she reactivated from 1987–89. Since her return to France her ties with her mother and siblings had been 'loose' and the material date was 1985, some five years before the birth of her son. The European Court considered (at para 45) that the applicant's complaint was not to the exclusion order which became final in 1985, but rather to the failure of the Court of Appeal to lift it in 1994. By teleological reasoning the European Court considered that 1994 was the material date, distinguishing *El-Boujaidi*, and held that the applicant could indeed rely on the birth of her son in 1990. Given her history and the birth of her son, for whom she had parental responsibility, the European Court concluded that there was 'no doubt' that the Court of Appeal's decision amounted to an interference with respect for private and family life.

4.81   The Strasbourg case law indicates a general disinclination to authorize deportation where the effect would be to separate the family, especially where family life is temporally well established in the respondent state.[75] In *Berrehab* (1989) 11 EHRR 322 the fact that the applicant, who was divorced and therefore no longer entitled to remain in the Netherlands, had close ties with his daughter which would probably be severed by his deportation, entailed a duty on the state not to deport him. Where deportation is based on criminal activity, it must go beyond repeat petty crime and have a more serious dimension. This approach was followed in *Moustaquim v Belgium* (1991) 13 EHRR 802 and *Beljoudi v France*

---

[75] See in particular the recent decision in *Sen v Netherlands* (above at 4.52–4.57) appearing to reverse the decisions in *Ahmut v Netherlands* and *Gul v Switzerland*.

(1992) 14 EHRR 801, where the appellants were accomplished petty criminals with substantial family ties to parents/siblings and to a wife respectively. By contrast in *Boughanemi* v *France* (1996) 22 EHRR 228 paras. 42–5 deportation was not disproportionate because of the serious crimes committed by the applicant and the maintenance of substantial links with Tunisia. In *Bouchelkia* v *France* (1997) 25 EHRR 686 Article 8 was not violated where a convicted rapist founded his family after the deportation order was signed. Propensity to reoffend will be relevant to proportionality (*B* v *Secretary of State*; see para. 4.73 above).

4.82 By contrast in finding that the expulsion of the immigrant-husband who had enjoyed substantial family life in France 'might imperil the unity or even the very existence of the marriage' the European Court in *Beljoudi* v *France* (1992) 14 EHRR 801 suggested the right to respect for such family life itself included a right of residence, such that any expulsion measures will amount to an interference and require justification.

4.83 The case law demonstrates that an important consideration is the extent to which there is already established family life in the state in which residence is sought,[76] and the related issue of the prospect of joint residence in the respondent state at the time the family was founded. Indeed Judge Martens in dissenting opinions has gone so far as to say that the position of an 'integrated alien' should be assimilated to that of a national who cannot be expelled from his or her own state.[77] This does not however reflect the approach of the European Court as a whole.

4.84 The judgment of the European Court of Human Rights in *Boultif* v *Switzerland* (2001) 33 EHRR 50 provides a helpful set of principles to be applied in expulsion cases involving Article 8. The Court stated:

> In assessing the relevant criteria in such a case, the Court will consider the nature and seriousness of the offence committed by the applicant; the length of the applicant's stay in the country from which he is going to be expelled; the time elapsed since the offence was committed as well as the applicant's conduct in that period; the nationalities of the various persons concerned; the applicant's family situation, such as the length of the marriage; and other factors expressing the effectiveness of a couple's family life; whether the spouse knew about the offence at the time when he or she entered into a family relationship; and whether there are children in the marriage, and if so, their age. Not least, the Court will also consider the seriousness of the difficulties which the spouse is likely to encounter in the country of origin, though the mere fact that a person might face certain difficulties in accompanying her or his spouse cannot in itself exclude an expulsion.

---

[76] *Berrehab* v *Netherlands* (1989) 11 EHRR 322; *Moustaquim* v *Belgium* (1991) 13 EHRR 802; *Beljoudi* v *France* (1992) 14 EHRR 801; *Boughanemi* v *France* (1996) 22 EHRR 228; *Bouchelkia* v *France* (1997) 25 EHRR 686; *Nasri* v *France* (1995) 21 EHRR 458.

[77] *Beljoudi* v *France* (1992) 14 EHRR 801.

The impact of the *Boultif* guidelines were felt in two liberal decisions where Article 8 considerations prevented expulsion: *Amrollahi v Denmark* (ECtHR, 11 July 2002) and *R v Secretary of State for the Home Department, ex parte Carpenter* (ECJ, 11 July 2002).

Proportionality

4.85 The principle of proportionality reflects the inherent concern of the ECHR to find a fair balance between the protection of individual rights and the interests of the community (*Soering v UK* (1989) 11 EHRR 439, para. 89). In early cases the UK courts reflected the views of the commentators that this fair balance could only be achieved if restrictions on individual's rights did not go beyond what is strictly necessary to achieving the legitimate aim they pursue.[78]

4.86 In *Samaroo v Secretary of State* (see above at 4.73), the Court of Appeal held that where there is no less intrusive means of achieving the desired objective than deportation, the only question is whether an overall fair balance has been struck by the Secretary of State. Here the policy of the Secretary of State was to deport international drug traffickers to deter others contemplating migration to the UK for that purpose. Nothing less than deportation would do, and it was accordingly inappropriate to apply a proportionality as to means test (namely, is there a less intrusive alternative?), and the only issue was whether there was proportionality as to ends (namely, had a fair balance been struck?).

4.87 In other contexts such as the application of the public funds test before allowing entry of family members, however, there may be a less restrictive measure that can be adopted and, absent some exceptional circumstance, this would be powerful evidence that the state has failed the test.[79] (See below at 4.58; and see further 6.29). In this context, once a violation of the right to respect for personal interests in Article 8(1) is shown, the burden will be on the Home Office to show by 'relevant and sufficient' reasons that there is no less restrictive alternative to the measure deployed.

4.88 This suggests that something more than a neutral balance is involved. Accordingly the suggestion of the Court of Appeal in *R v Secretary of State ex parte Gangadeen and Khan* [1998] Imm AR 106 and 117–19, a case which pre-dated the HRA 1998, that Article 8 is no different from the domestic scheme in that both domestic law and Article 8 enjoin a balance with the scales equal as between family life and the interets of immigration control, does not, we submit with respect, reflect these principles.[80] The Court of Appeal was of course look-

---

[78] See *B v Secretary of State* [2000] INLR 361 and commentators cited therein.
[79] See *Barthold v Germany* (1985) 7 EHRR 383; *Arman Ali* [2000] Imm AR 134.
[80] The suggestion that the interests of the child are relevant rather than primary or determinative in the immigration context of Article 8 is however, we submit, correct.

ing at the ECHR merely as an aspect of the Minister's own policy guidance rather than a matter of independent legal duty.

4.89   In *Isiko* [2001] INLR 175 and *Mahmood* [2001] 1 WLR 840 the Court of Appeal held that the mere fact that the presence of an individual and his family in the UK will not in itself constitute a threat to one of the interests enumerated in Article 8(2), did 'not prevent a decision to enforce a lawful immigration policy which applies in the individual's case from being lawful' given the effect on the rights and freedoms of others, including other putative immigrants where the relevant consideration is whether an individual ought to be permitted to jump the queue by having entry clearance requirements waived and being absolved from returning to his country. In *Samaroo* (see above at 4.73) the Court of Appeal held that the Secretary of State could not be required to prove that refraining from deporting the appellant would undermine his policy of deterring immigration for the purposes of drug trafficking. This was not a matter susceptible of proof.

4.90   Considerations relevant to proportionality will be: the reason for the interference; the applicant's ties with the UK; the extent of disruption to family life; the extent of obstacles to establishing family life elsewhere; and in criminal cases, the gravity of the offence and the applicant's past criminal record.

The Mahmood approach

4.91   Notwithstanding Judge Martens's observations that the European Court's approach to Article 8 in immigration cases has led to arbitrariness and has the appearance of a lottery, the following principles were distilled by the Court of Appeal in *Mahmood*:

(a)   A state has the right under international law to control the entry of non-nationals into its territory, subject always to treaty obligations.

(b)   Article 8 does not impose on a state any general obligation to respect the choice of residence of a married couple.

(c)   Removal or exclusion of one family member from a state where other members of the family are lawfully resident will not necessarily infringe Article 8 provided that there are no insurmountable obstacles to the family living together in the country of origin of the family member excluded, even when this involves a degree of hardship for some or all members of the family.

(d)   Article 8 is likely to be violated by the expulsion of a member of the family that has been long established in a state if the circumstances are such that it is not reasonable to expect the other members of the family to follow that member expelled.

(e)   Knowledge on the part of one spouse at the time of marriage that rights of residence of the other were precarious militates against a finding that an order excluding the latter violates Article 8.

(f)   Whether interference with family rights is justified in the interests of immigration will depend on:

(i)   the facts of the particular case and

(ii) the circumstances prevailing in the State whose action is impugned.

We respectfully agree with this helpful distillation of working propositions. In non-criminal cases, this guidance suggests that where there are insurmountable obstacles, separation of the family will breach Article 8. Where the family is settled or long established, it is enough for a violation that it would not be reasonable to relocate elsewhere and a degree of hardship may be relied upon, save that where the immigration position was known to be precarious, that would militate against a finding of a violation.

Deference

4.92   We suggest that within the field of immigration the extent of deference to be given to a decision which concerns family life should vary depending upon whether it regulates entry for those at the frontier, whether it concerns removal of persons who never lawfully entered or having so entered did not lawfully remain, or whether the decision intrudes upon family life being enjoyed by persons lawfully established in the UK.

APPLICATION

4.93   We have seen that the maintenance of immigration policies and controls does not of itself violate Article 8. In the UK, respect for family life is primarily sought to be achieved by the Immigration Rules, which increasingly incorporate policies formerly outside the rules. We have noted above that the ECHR has influenced the status of provisions regulating the position of persons such as same-sex partners, or separated parents seeking access to children, by elevating those provisions from the realms of general discretion, to published policies, and now to the Immigration Rules. The ECHR has also impacted on the content of the policies or rules.[81]

4.94   Since it is the Immigration Rules and policies that primarily provide

---

[81] For example, the provisions in the Immigration Rules allowing for leave to enter, remain and settlement as a parent seeking access reflect the reality that access visits from abroad were no general answer to an interference with family life.

respect for family life, it is plain that they should wherever possible be construed in an ECHR compliant manner so as to promote respect. As Collins J stated in *Arman Ali* [2000] Imm AR 134 at 146, 'Since it is clear that [the implementation of the Immigration Rules] can, given circumstances which are not likely to be particularly unusual, produce a breach of Article 8, they should, if possible, be given a construction which will avoid a breach.' *Ali* was decided without the aid of s. 3 of the Human Rights Act 1998; its injunction assumes greater force with the coming into force of that section. Where Immigration Rules and policies are so rigid in application that they interfere with family life disproportionately in individual cases, they will need to be read down, or circumnavigated given the primary obligation to respect ECHR rights (s. 6 of the Human Rights Act 1998).

The maintenance and accommodation requirements of the Immigration Rules

4.95 Family members seeking entry or stay in the UK have to show that they can be adequately maintained and accommodated without recourse to public funds.[82] The application of the condition is in general compliant with the Article 8(2) purpose of preserving the economic well-being of the UK (*Arman Ali* [2000] Imm AR 134 at 146).

4.96 The new Immigration Rules make it clear that it is only *additional* recourse to public funds that is prohibited: 'For the purposes of these Rules, a person is not to be regarded as having (or potentially having) recourse to public funds merely because he is (or will be) reliant in whole or in part on public funds provided to his sponsor, unless, as a result of his presence in the UK, the sponsor is (or would be) entitled to increased or additional public funds.' (para. 6A). The genesis of this incorporation demonstrates the impact of the ECHR both substantively on the content of the rule, and formally on its status. The impact of the ECHR is not, we suggest, extinguished by rule 6A: the position as to indirect reliance from third parties, and as to accommodation is not expressly covered and is accordingly also dealt with below at 4.98.

4.97 The requirement that there be no recourse to public funds was construed to prohibit *indirect reliance* on public funds[83] where the applicant is maintained by savings accrued in part by public funds or where the sponsor is already in receipt of public funds, and further to prevent support from a third party complying with the requirement of the rule. The former prohibition is addressed by paragraph 6A of the new Immigration Rules. The latter scenario is unlikely to be compatible with the s. 3, HRA 1998 duty to interpret legislation compatibly with

---

[82] See the Immigration Rules para. 281(vi) (spouse); para. 297(iv) (children).
[83] See *ex p Islam Bibi*, [1995] Imm AR 157.

ECHR rights where that is possible. Moreover, an over-rigid application of the requirement may produce results that are incompatible with Article 8.

Third party support

4.98   The rationale for the exclusion of third party support was typically that the Immigration Rules envisage the admission of self-sufficient family units.[84] In *Arman Ali* [2000] Imm AR 134 at 146, using Article 8 for the classic pre-incorporation device of resolving ambiguity in the rules[85] providing for the admission of spouses and children,[86] Collins J held this reasoning and the resulting interpretation was incompatible with Article 8, since it amounted to an interference with the right of respect for family life which was disproportionate to the legitimate aim pursued: 'the barrier (to admission) must not be greater than necessary'. The case could equally have been decided on the more fundamental basis that there was no legitimate aim being pursued since admission would not adversely affect the economic well-being of the country, in particular since the stated aim behind the Secretary of State's public funds requirements was not to increase the burden falling on the state in the form of additional recourse to benefits. This suggestion also demonstrates that immigration control is not a valid end in itself justifying interference, but rather can only be the medium to the enumerated aims in Article 8(2).

4.99   Thus where evidentially it could be shown that third party support in the long-term will indeed be forthcoming, or where children seeking admission could maintain themselves by their own earnings, the requirements even of the old rules would, on an ECHR compliant construction, have been met.

4.100   Further, the suggestion in the Immigration Rules (HC 395, para. 297) that the family must be accommodated in the same premises, excluding a situation where, for example, the children lived with settled grandparents whilst the spouses lived together, would be disproportionate to the aim of the legislation and in Collins J's view 'must be reconsidered before 2 October 2000' (*Arman Ali* at page 148). This as we have seen has occurred in respect of recourse to public funds arising from reliance on funds provided to the sponsor.

4.101   So the duty on the adjudicator hearing an appeal against a refusal of entry clearance where this issue of accommodation arises, would be either to construe the rule compatibly with Article 8, even where that meant a departure from the ordinary meaning of the rule provided the Article 8 compliant reading was 'poss-

---

[84] See e.g. *Ishaque Ahmed* (1992, IAT, unreported).
[85] *Garland* v *British Rail* [1983] 2 AC 751; *Arman Ali* [2000] Imm AR 134 at 142.
[86] See the Immigration Rules, HC 251, paras. 50, 52; and see the Immigration Rules, HC 395, paras. 281(v), (vi) and 297(iv).

ible',[87] or to allow the appeal on the basis of the 'not in accordance with the law' jurisdiction (Immigration and Asylum Act 1999, Sch. 4, para. 21).

Indirect reliance

4.102   By analogous reasoning, an interpretation of the Rules which excludes an applicant where admission would cause no *additional recourse* to public funds, would not be compliant with Article 8 since no legitimate purpose for the inter-ference with family life could be shown. Indirect present reliance, where the sponsor presently is in receipt of public funds is, we suggest, no different in prin-ciple from indirect historic reliance, through recourse to savings accrued with the aid of public funds in the past, and both are permissible on an ECHR compliant construction. The Divisional Court authorities which held to the contrary would no longer be binding.[88] It is perhaps unlikely that the Home Office will contest this point, since Home Office policy, drawn slightly wider than paragraph 6A of the Immigration Rules, is that:

> With regard to public funds there is no objection to other residents in the same house-hold receiving public funds to which they are entitled in their own right. The question is whether additional recourse to public funds would be necessary on the Applicant's arrival here.[89]

4.103   The present situation, where accommodation and reliance on third party support is concerned, that admission may be permitted by policy but is excluded by rules which cover identical subject-matter, is hardly satisfactory.[90]

Over-rigid application of requirements in applications for family reunion

Public funds

4.104   The very application of an otherwise ECHR compliant construction of the public funds requirements, prohibiting admission only where additional recourse to public funds is shown, may produce results incompatible with Article 8.

4.105   The issue arose in the case of *R* v *Secretary of State ex parte Belhocine* (1999). The applicant, an Algerian man granted exceptional leave to remain in the UK, applied for family reunion with his wife and son, from whom he had been separated for six years. The Entry Clearance Officer refused entry clearance to his wife because the couple would not be able to maintain themselves without recourse to public funds, as required by the Home Office policy on granting

---

[87] See *R* v *A (No. 2)* [2002] 1 AC 45.
[88] *Islam Bibi* [1995] Imm AR 157.
[89] See the responsible Minister's letter to (unnamed) MP, 5 October 1994.
[90] See observations of Mr Kinnell in *Cleavon Marcus Scott* v *Entry Clearance Officer Kingston* (13389, IAT) and *Kausar* v *Entry Clearance Officer Islamabad* [1998] INLR 141.

family reunion to sponsors with exceptional leave to remain status in the UK. The applicant had been tortured in Algeria. There was evidence that the continued separation of the applicant exacerbated his post-traumatic stress disorder, and that both the applicant's wife and son were suffering from depression in Algeria. The applicant argued that the imposition of a blanket and fact-insensitive requirement that there be no additional recourse to public funds as a condition precedent of granting family reunion to family members of UK sponsors granted protection from Article 3 risks in the form of exceptional leave, amounted to an unlawful fetter of the Secretary of State's discretion, which was apt to and did in fact lead to an interference with rights to respect for family life that was disproportionate to the legitimate aim of economic well-being pursued. Kay J granted permission to apply for judicial review (27 July 1999) following which the Secretary of State compromised proceedings by granting entry clearance, but also (in view of the claim for declaratory relief) by examining the need to revise the family reunion policy, and indicating that the policy would be operated as follows:[91]

> The family reunion concession applies to the pre-existing spouse and minor dependent children of someone who has been recognised as a refugee in the UK. People with exceptional leave to remain in the UK may also apply for their pre-existing spouse and minor children to join them under the terms of the family reunion concession after they have spent four years in the UK with exceptional leave to remain (ELR). The normal maintenance and accommodation requirements of the Immigration Rules, which are waived for those joining refugees, are expected to be met by those sponsors with ELR.
>
> Exceptionally, where there are compelling compassionate circumstances, family reunion for people with ELR can be considered before the four year point. *When considering whether it is appropriate to exercise discretion in this way, the Secretary of State will have due regard to the UK's international obligations. In such cases it might also be appropriate to exercise discretion with regard to the maintenance and accommodation requirements* . . . However the Secretary of State, while retaining his discretion to waive these requirements of the Rules if clearly warranted, considers it reasonable to expect ELR sponsors with four years leave to remain in the UK to be able to satisfy these requirements in the vast majority of cases. (emphasis supplied)

4.106 The question of whether this is sufficient publication to enable reliance by immigrants on legitimate expectation principles[92] is unlikely to arise after incorporation. The Secretary of State's response in *Belhocine* (see above at 4.105) indicates that any application of the public funds rule which is authorized by policy to be fact-insensitive will be vulnerable to challenge under sections 3 and 6 of the Human Rights Act 1998 for non-compliance with the principle of proportionality under Article 8(2).

---

[91] Letter from Peter Ring, IND to Treasury Solicitor, 20 January 2000.

[92] See Hobhouse LJ's comments as to the juridical nature of legitimate expectations in *Ahmed and Patel* [1998] INLR 570.

4.107   In cases where it is claimed that admission of relatives will only lead to a short-term reliance on public funds (because a child will soon be able to find employment, or a spouse will relieve the settled-parent of child-care duties), consideration will need to be given to the less restrictive alternative of, for example, granting entry clearance for *limited* leave to remain so as to enable the sponsor and applicants to enjoy family life, and permit the Home Office to review at the end of the period of leave the efforts made to relieve reliance on public funds.

4.108   Whilst the *Belhocine* case (see above at 4.105) concerned an extra-rule application of the public funds requirements, the same principles apply to the applications for family reunion made within the rules, where the sponsor enjoys settled status in the UK, but cannot meet the public funds requirements in the rules.

Qualifying relatives and age limits
4.109   The same observations apply to the restriction of qualifying relatives to spouse and minor children in the policy: if family life is established between, for example, a Somali adult son with exceptional leave to remain status in the UK and his elderly mother stranded in a refugee camp, the *a priori* exclusion of the mother as a qualifying relative in the policy is unlikely to be compliant with Article 8, not least because the Secretary of State has recognized the extended and unusual nature of the Somali family unit.[93]

4.110   The very restrictive provisions of the Immigration Rules for reunion with parents below 65, adult children, siblings or aunts and uncles are further unlikely to be compliant with Article 8 where family life with those relatives is established. Necessary conditions for qualifying under the Rules for such a relative include that they are 'living alone outside the UK in the most compassionate circumstances and [are] mainly dependent financially on relatives settled in the UK' (Immigration Rules, HC 395, para. 317(i)(f)) and they have 'no close relatives in [their] own country to whom [they] could turn for financial support'.

4.111   Age limits in the case of adult children or parents below 65 in the Rules are vulnerable to challenge as representing a case-insensitive and disproportionate obstacle where in fact family ties are established. The applicant in *Moustaquim* v *Belgium* (1991) 13 EHRR 802, where the European Court found an unjustifiable interference with the applicant's private and family life in circumstances where he had lived with his family since he was one year old, was 21 years old at the time of the deportation proceedings.

---

[93] Letter to Tower Hamlets Law Centre, para. 8.1.

Time

4.112 Similarly where the sponsor has not accrued four years' exceptional leave status, an over-rigid focus on 'compelling compassionate' circumstances as a necessary condition for the very entertaining of an application for family reunion is unlikely to comply with Article 8. Again in the Somali context, if an adult daughter with one year's exceptional leave can establish historical ties with her mother and children resident in a refugee camp in dire circumstances, it is difficult to conclude that a four-year separation absent compelling compassionate circumstances is consistent with her right to respect for her family life, or is a justified interference with that right.

4.113 Since the primary focus under Article 8 is not on the formal status of the sponsor, but rather on the quality and duration of family life established, and the ability to constitute such family life elsewhere, the requirement that an individual have settled status will self-evidently also not be an absolute bar to an application being successful. Enjoyment of settled status will however have the advantage under the Immigration Rules for qualifying relatives that, for example, real obstacles to enjoyment of family life elsewhere will not need to be shown. The preferential regime for those with settled status in the Rules is unlikely to be discriminatory under Article 14, there being a reasonable relationship of proportionality between the differential treatment and the permanent stay enjoyed.

Entry clearance

4.114 Where admission is sought by family members seeking reunion with a UK sponsor, the grant of a valid entry clearance is a necessary condition for admission.[94] While in general this is a permitted purpose under Article 8(2) (prevention of disorder), in cases where an elderly or infirm applicant for admission is required to return home, or to dire conditions in a refugee camp, the application of the condition may amount to a disproportionate interference with respect for family life. Absent such differentiating compassionate factors, waiver of entry clearance is unlikely to be dictated by considerations of proportionality having regard to the impact of others in the queue: while the Entry Clearance Officer is a separate entity from the Home Office, the effect on others waiting decisions at the Home Office cannot be ignored (*Amjad Mahmood* v *Secretary of State* [2001] 1 WLR 840 (per Laws LJ)).

Adoptions

4.115 The adoption of a child gives rise to family life between the adoptive parents and the child (*X* v *France* [1992] 31 DR 241). The Immigration Rules

---

[94] See Immigration Rules, HC 395, para. 317(i), (vi) (parents, grandparents, dependent relatives); 310 (xi), 314 (xii) (adoptive children); 297 (v) (children); 290 (viii) (fiancé(e)); 281 (vii) (spouses).

provide for an adoptive parent to be treated as a parent where 'a child was adopted in accordance with a decision taken by the competent administrative authority or court in a country whose adoption orders are recognised [Adoptions (Designation of Overseas Adoptions) Order 1973, SI 1973/19] by the UK (except where an application for leave to enter or remain is made under paragraphs 310–316)' (Immigration Rules, HC 395, para. 6). It is arguable that in these cases the governing regime is the straightforward regime for admission of children under paragraph 297.

4.116 The stricter regime under paragraphs 310 to 316 applies to adoptions made 'in accordance with a decision taken by the competent administrative authority or court in (the child's) country of origin or the country in which he is resident' (HC 395, para. 310(v)), but where the adoption order is not recognized by the UK. Beyond the condition that there has been a genuine transfer of parental responsibility (HC 395, para. 310(viii)), this regime includes the requirements that:

(a) the adoption took place at a time when both parents were resident together abroad, or either or both were settled in the UK (HC 395, para. 310(vi));

(b) the child was adopted 'due to the inability of the original parent(s) or current carer(s) to care for him' (HC 395, para. 310(viii));

(c) the child 'has lost or broken ties with his family of origin' (HC 395, para. 310(ix));

(d) 'the adoption was not one of convenience arranged to facilitate . . . admission to or remaining in the UK' (HC 395, para. 310(x)).

4.117 It is strongly arguable that these conditions are incompatible with Article 8. The existence of genuine ties between parent and adoptive child constitute family life and require respect under Article 8(1). An exclusion or expulsion based on an inability to show the conditions listed above would, we suggest, have no legitimate aim under Article 8(2), or would otherwise be a disproportionate interference with respect for family life between child and parent.

4.118 For example, a conscious decision may be taken by a woman to have her son adopted by her childless sister, who fails to meet the residence conditions at the time of adoption. The existence of stable and genuine ties between adoptive son and adoptive mother is quite consistent with:

(a) an absence of an inability to care for the child by the natural mother who on the contrary assists her sister in the care of the child;

(b) an absence of a breakdown in ties between child and natural mother who on the contrary retains a large degree of contact; and

(c) (more contentiously) the fact that one of the reasons or even the main reason for the adoption was the possibility of admission to the UK.[95]

---

[95] But see *Re H (A Minor) (Adoption: Non-Patrial)* [1996] 4 All ER 600.

Reliance on these conditions as absolute bars to admission where respect for the established and genuine ties between adoptive mother and adoptive child requires, in light of the factual matrix, a right of residence would, we suggest, either fail to pursue a legitimate aim under Article 8(2) or fail the test of proportionality.

4.119   *De facto* adoptions (the norm in Islamic jurisdictions) are not provided for by the rules. The framework is provided by policy outside the rules.[96] The additional conditions noted above at 4.116 apply and in appropriate cases of a genuine transfer of parental responsibility and genuine established ties (which would probably require cogent evidence given the absence of a formal authorizing procedure) could not, we submit, lawfully ground a refusal of admission or extension of stay.

4.120   Where a child is cared for by a relative in the UK and there is evidence that the natural parents have rejected the child, removal will almost certainly breach Article 8.[97]

Marital relationships; same-sex relationships; children

Marital relationships
4.121   An application for stay on the basis of marriage between a non-national and a person settled in the UK must be made at a time when 'the Applicant has limited leave to remain in the UK' (HC 395, para. 284(i)). Marriages entered into after the expiration of leave or indeed after the commencement of enforcement action call for discretionary treatment. Enforcement action, as we have seen, may well interfere with respect for family life where there has been a relationship of some duration and stability and there are obstacles to establishing family life elsewhere.

4.122   Where enforcement is by way of deportation for reasons conducive to the public good, the immigration rules will provide the framework (HC 395, paras. 364–7, 374–5). Extra-rule policies will be relevant to both deportations and other removals. An over-rigid application of the requirement that the relationship commenced prior to enforcement action, or that it had not existed for a particular prescribed qualifying period[98] may violate Article 8 where there is no reasonable prospect of enjoying family life elsewhere. However knowledge of vulnerable

---

[96] Immigration Direction Instructions, ch 8, Annexe R, December 2000.

[97] In *R v Secretary of State ex parte Sujon Miah* (6 December 1994) Ewbank J quashed as irrational removal directions in respect of an 11-year-old Bangladeshi child refused leave to enter whose parents had rejected him and were unwilling to receive him back.

[98] Para. 2, DP/2/93; para. 5(b) DP 3/96—the latter imposing an additional requirement that a marital and cohabitational relationship has existed for at least two years prior to enforcement action. See *R v Secretary of State for the Home Department, ex parte Carpenter* (ECJ, 11 July 2002).

immigration status militates against a breach of Article 8 (*Mahmood* v *Secretary of State* [2001] 1 WLR 840). A violation may also be shown where exclusion is pursued on the basis that a marriage post-dated an *earlier* unrelated enforcement decision, subsequent to which the applicant lawfully returned to the UK and, for the first time, establishes family ties.[99]

4.123 Relationships between men and women that are not legitimated by marriage are not provided for by the Immigration Rules. This means given the hermetic sealing of the Immigration Rules that an application for such a purpose would be bound to be refused under the Rules (HC 395, paras. 320(8) and 322(1)). Moreover such relationships appear not to be catered for in the realm of extra-rule discretion either, save where there is a legal impediment to marriage other than for reasons of consanguinity or age: the present policy requires satisfaction of the condition that it is *not possible* to form a marriage relationship.[100]

4.124 Whether such relationships involve issues of family life will depend on the length and stability of the relationship, the intentions of the parties, their commitment to one another and dependency between them.[101] Cohabitation is relevant but not essential (*Kroon* v *Netherlands* (1994) A-297 para. 30). Where family life is shown (without legal impediment to marriage) and there are real obstacles to its constitution elsewhere, the present domestic law position would fail to meet the autonomous ECHR concept of 'law' owing to a failure to delineate discretion or to pronounce accessible and precise criteria in respect of such cases.

Same sex relationships
4.125 We have seen above at 4.14 that same-sex relationships are not considered to fall within the scope of family life by the Strasbourg organs. Domestically, for the reasons listed below, the position ought to be different.

(a) In the UK there is increasing awareness and acceptance of same-sex relationships. The Secretary of State's extra-rule policies and Immigration Rules which are the route through which respect for family life and private life is promoted in the field of immigration, evidence changing mores. In 1993, the Home Office policy was to reject applications on the basis of same-sex relationships unless 'the circumstances

---

[99] The Secretary of State's construction of his policy adopting this approach has been upheld as rational in *Zellouf* [1997] Imm AR 120; *R* v *Secretary of State ex parte Resham Singh* (1 August 1996, unreported); and *Adebiyi* v *Secretary of State* [1997] Imm AR 57.
[100] 'Common-law and same sex (unmarried partners)' Immigration Direction Instructions, ch 8, section 7.
[101] See *Keegan* v *Ireland* (1994) 18 EHRR 342 paras. 44–5; *X, Y, Z* v *UK* (1995) 20 EHRR CD 6 paras. 50–1.

were wholly exceptional such as the grave illness of the British partner'.[102] In contrast, unmarried heterosexual couples were treated as
marriage cases and where the relationship had subsisted for two years or
more and appeared genuine, in general leave to remain would be
granted.[103] However on 13 October 1997 the Home Office published a
concession outside the rules for unmarried partners, drawing no distinction between same-sex and heterosexual couples. The requirement in the
concession that 'the parties have been living together in a relationship
akin to marriage which has subsisted for four years or more' was relaxed
to a two-year requirement. The concession outside the rules has now
been incorporated into the rules, with the imprimatur of Parliament (HC
395, para 295A-O).

(b)   Given the living tree approach to the ECHR and increasing levels of
tolerance expected as democracies develop, the increasing recognition
given in the UK to same-sex relationships as a valid social unit means
that a UK court, free of the constraints faced by the supra-national court,
should find that homosexual relationships constitute family life, or alternatively that similar considerations which justify an interference with
respect for family life should be invoked to warrant interfering with
respect for private life if same-sex relationships continue to fall under
the private life limb of Article 8.

(c)   We have noted that ECHR jurisprudence is not binding but must simply
be taken into account under the Human Rights Act 1998, section 2, and
that the ECHR was intended to provide a minimum bedrock of rights
leaving national legal systems to operate a more beneficial regime.

(d)   The question of family life is inherently contextual and so the difficult
question of supra-national applicability, raising sensitive cultural-reli-
gious issues as to the ambit of family life in different societies, will not
have to be considered by the UK courts when determining the issue.

(e)   Social mores are developing, indeed in the case concerning homosexual
members of the armed forces (*Smith* v *United Kingdom*; *Grady* v *United
Kingdom*; *Beckett* v *United Kingdom*; *Lustig-Prean* v *United Kingdom*
(2000) 29 EHRR 493) the European Court had regard to the 'widespread
and consistently developing views [and] the legal changes in the domestic laws of Contracting States in favour of the admission of homosexuals into the armed forces of those States'.

(f)   An example of this approach to the determination of family in the
context of the Rent Act 1977 is the decision of the House of Lords in
Fitzpatrick v *Sterling Housing Association* [2001] 1 AC 27 holding that

---

[102] See Home Office letter of 8 March 1993 addressed to Wilson & Co.
[103] *Smith et al* v *UK* (2000) 29 EHRR 493..

same-sex partners in a relationship of sufficient stability and duration were capable of being members of a family. See also *Mendoza* v *Ghaidan* [2002] EWCA Civ 1533 where the Court of Appeal confirmed that gay partners enjoy family life.

4.126 In the immigration context, serious obstacles may exist to the enjoyment of same-sex relationships in the non-national partner's country by, for example, the maintenance on the statute book of a law criminalizing private consensual homosexual conduct between adults.[104]

4.127 An over-rigid and case-insensitive application of the (now) two-year qualifying requirement in the rules would give rise to issues of proportionate interference with established family (or private) life.

Children

4.128 The vulnerability and dependency of children renders the child–parent relationship central to the meaning of family life in Article 8. The establishment of family life in children cases is often assumed.

4.129 In *Boughanemi* v *France* (1996) 22 EHRR 228, the European Court accepted that the existence of family life as between father and child was not broken even though the father was separated from his common-law spouse prior to the birth of the child and had not formally recognized the child until ten months after his birth, had not provided for the child, contributed to the child's education or demonstrated that he enjoyed parental rights.

4.130 In cases of divorced and separated parents, it may be difficult for the Secretary of State to maintain that family life has 'broken down' as between the separated partner and the child by reason of their ceasing to live together. Paragraph 6 DP 4/96, which states that 'in this type of case there is unlikely to be a breach of Article 8 of the ECHR as "family life" has already broken down', appears to be dissonant with the Court's case law.[105]

4.131 Moreover, the new Immigration Rules appear to recognize the importance to the child's well-being of maintaining contact with the separated parent in providing for leave to be granted for persons exercising rights of access to a child resident in the UK.[106] An over-rigid application of the requirement that the individual has extant leave to remain or has not stayed in breach of the immigration laws may violate proportionality. These new rules make more general provision for access by contemplating indefinite leave to remain in this capacity and replace

---

[104] *Dudgeon* v *United Kingdom* (1981) 4 EHRR 149; *Norris* v *Ireland* (1988) 13 EHRR 186.
[105] eg. *Berrehab* v *Netherlands* (1988) 11 EHRR 322.
[106] See new paras. 246–8 Immigration Rules HC 395 (changed in September 2000).

the rules allowing for access visits in the old paragraphs 246 to 248, HC 395. They can be seen as the immigration equivalent of the positive duty on states, as part of 'respect' for family life, to ensure that proper procedures are in place to facilitate access (*Ciliz* v *Netherlands* (App. No. 29192/95, 11 July 2000).

4.132   While the paramountcy principle probably does not apply in the immigration context[107] an interference with family life is more readily established where children are involved, and the burden will lie with the Secretary of State to show why interference is proportionate. The answer that the child's interests flow from a marriage which of itself is insufficient to show removal to be disproportionate appears unduly technical and ignores the practical reality of the situation facing the child.[108] Where however contact with a settled parent is minimal (for example by telephone only) removal of the child will have a minimal consequential effect (*Poku* v *UK* (1996) 22 EHRR CD 94).

4.133   A child's rights of residence/citizenship which cannot be enjoyed as a matter of practical reality in the state from which the parents are being expelled are not decisive.[109]

Application to private life

4.134   An asylum seeker taking judicial review proceedings against a decision of the IAT refusing leave to appeal, who is thereby excluded from Home Office administered asylum support and cannot access local authority care and assistance owing to the restrictive provisions of the Immigration and Asylum Act 1999, is likely to be able to invoke Article 3 and Article 8 considerations to fortify his domestic law challenge that the benefits regime interferes with his constitutional right of access to the courts.[110] Article 3 would be engaged in the extreme case where there was a denial of access to *any* benefits in conjunction with a legal bar on taking employment,[111] whereas Article 8 would speak to the lesser predicament of an individual with a discrete and proper reason to stay who is subjected to a sub-normal benefits regime (vouchers) and cannot work by reason of non-regularisation.[112]

---

[107] *Gangadeen and Khan* [1998] Imm AR 106, but note the observations as to other aspects of this judgment above at 4.88.

[108] This was the approach in *Mahmood* v *Secretary of State* [2001] 1 WLR 840.

[109] *Sorabjee* v *UK* 23938/93 (1995, unreported); *PP* v *UK* (1996) 21 EHRR CD 81; *Jaramillo* v *UK* 24865/94 (1995, unreported).

[110] *R* v *Lord Chancellor ex parte Witham* [1998] QB 575.

[111] *R (Husain)* v *Asylum Support Adjudicator* The Times, 15 November 2001.

[112] Note however that such an argument was tentatively rejected by Elias J in *Quaquah 2* CO/1028/98, although the decision in the result appears to recognize the force of the general point.

Chapter Five

Procedural Rights

INTRODUCTION

5.1   In this chapter we consider the protection of procedural rights in immigration both domestically and under the ECHR. Our discussion of the requirements of Articles 6 and 13 leads to the basic thesis that procedural protection is afforded to immigrants domestically by procedure rules and, where they are deficient, by the common law's approach to the protection of fundamental rights.

5.2   While the European Court decided in *Maaouia v France* (2001) 33 EHRR 42 that Article 6 does not apply in the immigration field (even though consequential on the determination of the immigration decision, pecuniary rights and family life rights will typically be engaged), and while the IAT in the 'starred' decision of *MNM v Secretary of State* [2000] INLR 576 has come to the same conclusion domestically, we suggest that this is likely to have limited practical significance, as the Tribunal itself noted, given the pre-existing position under the procedure rules and the common law. (Starred determinations are binding on adjudicators and should only be departed from by another IAT if clearly wrong: *Sepet and Bulbul v Secretary of State for the Home Department* [2001] INLR 376, 414 para. 99.)

5.3   This is not to say that it would not be appropriate for the national court to reach a different result as to the applicability of Article 6 to the immigration sphere, especially having regard to the mode of patriation of ECHR rights, and the availability of damages for a breach. At the very least, we consider that the decision of the Court of Appeal in *R v Secretary of State, ex parte Saleem* [2001] 1 WLR 443 indicates that where an appellate system is established, its workings attract Article 6 considerations at least by analogy within the common law.

5.4   In any event, as noted above, we consider that the applicability of Article 6 would in the main have normative rather than practical significance: we suggest it would consolidate juridically the qualitative protection already afforded by the common law inspired by ECHR principles rather than provide a quantitatively different level of protection. The exception would probably be the effect on the entitlement to a hearing within a reasonable time, and on the level of factual scrutiny afforded by the High Court to 'raw' challenges to discretionary decisions of the Secretary of State where appeal rights are excluded to classes of immigrants (rather than not effectively exercised), especially where those classes are unable to identify a right recognized as fundamental at common law, such as businessmen or students.

5.5   The remainder of the chapter then goes on to consider the intensity of review to be afforded on judicial review in immigration cases raising human rights issues. We note that the 'raw' Article 8 judicial review challenges to the Secretary of State's decisions raised in the sequence of transitional cases before the courts have become rarer following the coming into force of the IAA 1999, s. 65 right of appeal.[1] However human rights issues will obviously continue to be litigated in the higher courts even with the full force of s. 65, either by way of statutory appeal from the IAT on a material question of law to the Court of Appeal (IAA 1999, Sch. 4, para. 23(1)) or by judicial review of decisions taken where there is no available right of appeal. Accordingly the question of the proper approach of the higher courts in human rights cases will remain of fundamental importance.

5.6   The question has been resolved to a large degree by the decision of the House of Lords in *R (Daly) v Secretary of State* [2001] 2 WLR 1622 where it concluded that the ultimate question was whether the decision is proportionate and compatible with human rights, and not whether a reasonable decision-maker could come to that conclusion. The implications of *Daly* were considered by the Court of Appeal in *Samaroo v Secretary of State* [2001] EWCA Civ 1139, where the Court of Appeal concluded that the 'no more than necessary' limb of the proportionality test (proportionality as to means) did not apply to a deportation decision where the end of the measure was deterrence of international drug traffickers: that end could not be achieved by anything less than deportation, so the only question was proportionality as to ends, which required the Secretary of State to conduct a fair balance between the needs of the community and those of the individual. The Court of Appeal's role was to ask for itself whether the measure was proportionate in this sense, meanwhile allowing the Secretary of State significant deference where a matter of policy such as the efficacy of deterring drug traffickers through deportation was concerned. The debate has thus moved on from the trio of early cases, *B v Secretary of State* [2000] 2 CMLR

---

[1] Immigration and Asylum Act (Commencement No. 6 Transitional and Consequential Provisions) Order 2000, SI 2000/2444 dictated that s. 65 rights of appeal were not available to decisions taken prior to 2 October 2000; *Pardeepan v Secretary of State* [2000] INLR 447; *R (Kariharan) v Secretary of State* 5 December 2001; *R (Kumarakuraparan) v Secretary of State* [2002] EWHC 112, on appeal: [2002] INLR 383; see Introduction and see above at 1.47–1.52.

1086, *R* v *Secretary of State, ex parte Mahmood* [2001] 1 WLR 840, and *R* v *Secretary of State, ex parte Isiko* [2001] INLR 175.

THE REQUIREMENTS OF ARTICLE 6 AND THE POSITION AT COMMON LAW

5.7   Article 6(1) of the ECHR enshrines the right to a fair and public hearing before an independent and impartial tribunal established by law in the determination of civil rights and obligations. Article 6(2) protects the presumption of innocence in the criminal sphere. Article 6(3)(a)–(e) provides a number of specific guarantees which are expressed to apply only to criminal proceedings. However, since Article 6(3)(a)–(e) emphasizes the minimum constituent elements or specific aspects of the protection in Article 6(1),[2] it has also been considered to embody the requirements of fairness in civil proceedings outside the criminal sphere.[3] In addition to these express rights, the European Court has, applying a teleological approach to construction, read in a number of implied rights into Article 6. The status of the right—whether express or implied—assumes importance on the question of whether implied limitations are permissible.[4]

5.8   In the fields to which it applies, the Article ensures a minimum threshold of fairness and justice. The object and purpose of Article 6 is 'to enshrine the fundamental principle of the rule of law' (*Salabiaku* v *France* (1988) 13 EHRR 379, para. 28).[5] The European Court has held that since the right to the fair administration of justice holds such a prominent place in a democratic society, the Article is to be given a broad and purposive construction (*Delcourt* v *Belgium* (1970) 1 EHRR 355, para. 25).

5.9   Domestically, procedural rights in immigration matters are primarily protected by the procedure rules regulating appeals and, where such rules are proven deficient, by the common law.

5.10   We have seen in chapter 1 that in the UK there is a system of appeals for challenging immigration decisions. Thus, irrespective of whether the determination of immigration issues and the exercise of immigration rights of appeal involve 'civil rights', some element of remedial protection is provided. The common law and procedural rules impart fairness to the procedure in a manner

---

[2]   See e.g. *Kamasinski* v *Austria* (1989) 13 EHRR 36, para. 62; *Hadjianastassiou* v *Greece* (1992) 16 EHRR 219, para. 31.
[3]   See *R* v *Secretary of State ex parte Quaquah* [2000] INLR 196; *Albert and Le Compte* v *Belgium* (1983) 5 EHRR 533; *In re M (Child)* [2001] EWCA Civ 458, para. 25, per Thorpe LJ; para. 34 per Brooke LJ.
[4]   See per Lord Hope in *Brown* v *Stott* [2001] 2 WLR 817.
[5]   See further the Preamble to the ECHR and *Klass* v *FRG* (1978) 2 EHRR 214, para. 55.

that meets most if not all of the requirements of Article 6 and Article 13. Some immigration rights of appeal require the demonstration of preconditional facts: e.g. that a visitor in the UK holds entry clearance. Where those facts cannot be shown, judicial review is available. If the subject matter involves human rights, the High Court will apply intense scrutiny to the decision challenged, commensurate with the gravity of the issues raised.

Article 6(1): scope

5.11   In the context of immigration the question of the scope of application of Article 6 is the key question. The European Court in *Maaouia v France* (2001) 33 EHRR 42 answered this in the negative: the Article does not apply to immigration. The Tribunal in a starred decision has reached a similar result in *MNM* v *Secretary of State* [2000] INLR 576.

Article 6(1): access to court

5.12   While there is no express right of access to court in Article 6(1), in *Golder* v *UK* (1979–80) 1 EHRR 524 the European Court decided that such a right was implicit in the protection afforded by Article 6(1). The ECHR as a whole is designed to ensure protection which is practical and effective rather than theoretical and illusory, and so the right is a right of effective access to the court. This requires, in appropriate cases, the provision of legal aid to indigent persons (*Airey* v *Ireland* (1979) 2 EHRR 305).[6] The right of effective access also requires an element of due process: the individual must be given reasonable notice of the decision which interferes with his civil rights, so that a proper opportunity is afforded to challenge it in court (*de la Pradelle* v *France* (1992) A 253-B, para. 34).

5.13   The right of access is not absolute, and states are afforded a margin of appreciation by the European Court since the obvious need for regulation will vary according to local conditions (*Golder* v *UK* (1979–80) 1 EHRR 524, para. 38). But restrictions must not impair the very essence of the right, must proportionately pursue a legitimate aim (*Ashingdane* v *UK* (1985) 7 EHRR 528, para. 57), and should be legally certain (*Société Levage Prestations* v *France* (1996) 24 EHRR 351, paras. 40–50). Reasonable time limits are permissible restrictions on the right of access to a court (*Stubbings* v *UK* (1996) 23 EHRR 213, paras. 54, 55).

5.14   There is an overlap between the right of access to a court and the right to an effective national remedy under Article 13 (e.g. *Aksoy* v *Turkey* (1996) 23 EHRR 553) where the ECHR right qualifies as a civil right under Article 6.

---

[6] See also the cases cited in *R (Jarrett) v Legal Services Commission* [2001] EWHC Admin 389.

5.15 Article 6(1) does not guarantee the right of appeal from a decision of a *court*, but where a right of appeal is provided, Article 6 applies to appellate proceedings (*Tolstoy Miloslavsky* v *UK* (1995) 20 EHRR 442, para. 59).[7] Moreover, where the initial decision is taken by the executive, or an Article 6 non-compliant administrative body, the right of access to a court requires that the state provide a right to challenge the decision before a judicial body possessing full jurisdiction complying with Article 6(1). The European Court in *Albert and Le Compte* v *Belgium* (1983) 18 EHRR 533 stated (at para. 29):

> The Convention calls for one of the two following systems: either the jurisdictional organs themselves comply with the requirements of Article 6(1), or they do not so comply but are subject to control by a judicial body which has *full* jurisdiction and does provide the guarantees of Article 6(1). (emphasis supplied)

5.16 Whether an appeal on a point of law, with a restricted factual jurisdiction, complies with the requirement that the appellate body is to have 'full jurisdiction' is context-dependent. Where questions of policy are decided by an inferior expert tribunal, which reviews factual questions in a quasi-judicial manner, and the non-compliance with Article 6 arises through a technicality, an appeal on a point of law is likely to comply with Article 6.[8] Where the breach of Article 6 is more substantive, even where policy questions are involved, or where the inferior body is non-specialist and no questions of policy are engaged, a limited factual jurisdiction may not suffice.[9] The enquiry entailed is thus holistic and the demands of Article 6 flexible, the relevant factors being the subject matter of the dispute, the nature of the inferior decision-making process, and the desired grounds of appeal (*Zumbotel* v *Austria* (1983) 17 EHRR 116, paras. 31, 32).

Access to court at common law

5.17 The common law regards the right of access to the appellate authorities as a fundamental or basic constitutional right, akin to the common law right of access to the courts. This proposition forms part of the binding *ratio* of the important decision of the Court of Appeal in *R* v *SSHD ex parte Saleem* [2001] 1 WLR 443 and means that the right of access can only be abrogated by express enactment or

---

[7] This was applied by Hale LJ in *R v Secretary of State for the Home Department, ex parte Saleem* [2001] 1 WLR 443.

[8] See *Bryan* v *UK* (1995) 21 EHRR 342, paras. 44–7 where the decision of an independent planning inspector was binding, but the lack of objective independence stemmed solely from a rarely exercised power of revocation.

[9] See *Albert and Le Compte* v *Belgium* (1983) 18 EHRR 533; *Alconbury and others* v *Secretary of State for the Environment, Transport and the Regions* (2001) TLR 21 April reversed on 'leapfrog' appeal by the House of Lords [2001] 2 WLR 1389: policy questions, or matters of 'expediency' militate against a violation of Article 6 where there is an appeal on a point of law.

necessary implication.[10] A 'necessary implication' is one which necessarily follows from the express provision as a matter of express language and logic, not interpretation (see *R (Morgan Grenfell)* v *Special Commissioner of Income Tax* [2002] HRLR 42, para 45.

Saleem

5.18   The case of *Saleem*, which we consider at some length, concerned a challenge by an asylum claimant to the vires of a procedure rule, rule 42(1)(a) of the 1996 Asylum Appeals (Procedure) Rules which deemed her to have received notice of a determination of a special adjudicator dismissing her asylum appeal two days after it was sent, excluding week-ends and bank holidays, 'regardless of when or whether it was received'. The stringency of the provision crystallized in another procedure rule which stipulated a non-extendible, five working days' time limit for lodging applications for leave to appeal to the IAT (rule 13(2)). The effect was that persons such as the applicant who had not received notice of a determination through no fault of their own until the time limit for appealing had expired were entirely deprived of the right of appeal to the IAT. Dismissing the appeal of the Secretary of State for the Home Department from the decision of Hooper J, the Court of Appeal declared the deemed receipt rule ultra vires in so far as it sought to determine conclusively the moment at which the asylum seeker received notice of the special adjudicator's determination for the purpose of triggering the five-day time limit for appealing to the IAT. The position under the 2000 Procedure Rules is far more relaxed, with the deeming receipt provision subject to contrary proof, and the power in the IAT (for the first time) to extend time for submitting an application for leave to appeal (rules 18(3), 48(2)). Nevertheless, the decision of the Court of Appeal and the methodology used remains highly instructive.

5.19   Before the Court of Appeal the Secretary of State for the Home Department contended that the rule was not outside the broad rule-making power in s. 22 of the IA 1971 (see now IAA 1999, Sch. 4, paras. 3, 4). The Secretary of State's first argument was that the right of appeal to the appellate authority was not akin to the fundamental common law right of access to the courts because before 1993, asylum seekers had had no right of access to appellate authorities at all. The Secretary of State also argued that there was no right to asylum in the same way in which rights are determined in the ordinary courts, nor was the right to asylum recognized as a civil right for the purposes of Article 6. Hale LJ was 'quite unable to accept that argument' ([2001] 1 WLR 443 at p. 457). In an important passage she said (at p. 457):

---

[10]   See *Raymond* v *Honey* [1983] AC 1; *R* v *SSHD ex parte Leech* [1994] QB 198; *R* v *Lord Chancellor ex parte Witham* [1998] QB 575; see also *R* v *Lightfoot* [2000] QB 597. In *Witham* Laws LJ held at p. 585 that 'the common law provides no lesser protection of the right of access to the Queen's courts than might be vindicated in Strasbourg'. See most recently the novel approach to Community law in *Thoburn* v *Sunderland City Council* [2002] EWHC Admin 934.

There are now a large number of tribunals operating in a large number of specialist fields. Their subject matter is often just as important to the citizen as that determined in the ordinary courts. Their determinations are no less binding than those of the ordinary courts: the only difference is that tribunals have no direct powers of enforcement and, in the rare cases where this is needed, their decisions are enforced in the ordinary courts. In certain types of dispute between private persons, tribunals are established because of their perceived advantages in procedure and personnel. In disputes between citizen and state they are established because of the perceived need for independent adjudication of the merits and to reduce resort to judicial review. This was undoubtedly the motivation for grafting asylum cases onto the immigration appeals system in 1993. In this day and age a right of access to a tribunal or other adjudicative mechanism established by the state is just as important and fundamental as a right of access to the ordinary courts.

Roch LJ similarly held that 'the right created by section 20 of the Act (the right of appeal to the IAT) is a basic or fundamental right, akin to the right of access to courts of law' (at p. 449). Mummery LJ agreed with both Roch and Hale LJJ (at p. 452).

5.20 The Secretary of State's next argument was that the interference with the right was not as drastic as that claimed: the chain of events in the case were extraordinary and could scarcely recur without fault on the part of an appellant or his or her advisers. The small risk of injustice to a small number of people had to be set against the overriding objective of securing the 'just, timely and effective' disposal of asylum appeals[11] and the scale of the problems facing the system. This was in effect a proportionality argument. Hale LJ (at p. 458) was again unable to accept it, since it did not simply interfere with the opportunity of an appeal which Parliament has decided that an asylum seeker should have, but completely deprived the asylum seeker of it, irrespective of fault. In coming to this conclusion, Hale LJ drew support from principles established under Article 6:

There is an analogy here with the principles established under Article 6 of the European Convention on Human Rights. Immigration and asylum cases have not been held by the European Court of Human Rights to be 'the determination of his civil rights and obligations' for the purpose of Article 6. Furthermore, Article 6 does not guarantee a right of appeal. *But if the State establishes such a right it must ensure that people within its jurisdiction enjoy the fundamental guarantees in Article 6.* It is for national authorities to regulate the procedures governing the exercise of such rights, but these requirements must not be such that 'the very essence of the right is impaired'. They must pursue a legitimate aim and the means employed must be proportionate to that aim: see, for example, *Tolstoy* v *United Kingdom* (1995) 20 EHRR 475, para. 59. The effect of rule 42(1)(a) is in certain circumstances to destroy 'the very essence of the right'. (emphasis supplied)

---

[11] As prescribed in rule 23(2) of the 1996 Asylum Appeals (Procedure) Rules.

5.21 The analogical force of Article 6, explicitly acknowledged by Hale LJ, also underlies Roch LJ's judgment (at p. 450):

> the rule will be ultra vires the rule-making power if the rule as framed is unreasonable: if it is wider than is necessary; if it infringes the fundamental right to a greater extent than is required.

While this is couched in terms of reasonableness, it is clear that ECHR concepts of proportionality, and the enquiry as to whether a less intrusive option was available, determinatively inform what is reasonable.

5.22 A further aspect of the Secretary of State for the Home Department's proportionality argument was that the effect of the rule was not as drastic as claimed and the interference with the right of access not as severe owing to the alternative remedies available to an asylum seeker. These were the possibility of a fresh claim for asylum, a section 21 request,[12] or judicial review. Hale LJ again rejected the argument [2001] 1 WLR 443 at p. 459):

> The intention of the legislature in granting asylum seekers rights of appeal to the immigration appellate authorities was that there should be a binding adjudication of the merits of their case by an independent adjudicator who was able to hear the oral evidence of the appellant. Credibility is a vital issue in many asylum appeals (see *R v Immigration Appeal Tribunal, ex parte S* [1998] Imm AR 252, at 261), yet those making decisions on behalf of the Secretary of State are not those who interview the asylum seekers. The Secretary of State will only consider a fresh application if it raises new material not available before. A reference under section 21 leaves the decision to him. Judicial review can challenge only the legality and not the merits.

Funding and access to court at common law

5.23 A basic condition to gaining access to the courts is the ability to sustain life. The issue arose in the context of proposals to withdraw income support from asylum seekers who were not permitted to work whilst appeals were pending. The secondary legislation producing such a result was held ultra vires by the Court of Appeal in *R v Secretary of State for Social Security ex parte Joint Council for the Welfare of Immigrants* [1997] 1 WLR 275. Simon Brown LJ for the majority held that:

> After all, the [Asylum and Immigration Appeals Act 1993] confers on asylum seekers fuller rights than they had ever previously enjoyed, the right of appeal in particular. And yet these regulations for some genuine asylum seekers at least must now be regarded as rendering these rights nugatory. Either that, or the regulations necessarily

---

12 Section 21 of the IA 1971 was repealed by the IAA 1999.

contemplate for some a life so destitute that to my mind no civilised nation can tolerate it . . . Primary legislation alone could in my judgment achieve that sorry state of affairs.

5.24 The position moved on: primary legislation was indeed introduced (Asylum and Immigration Act 1996), but the Court of Appeal held that s. 21 of the National Assistance Act 1948 conferred a duty upon local authorities to give care and assistance to destitute asylum seekers (*R* v *Westminster City Council, ex parte M* [1997] 1 CCLR 85). Section 116 of the IAA 1999 abolished s. 21 of the IA 1971 for those asylum appellants whose need arises solely out of destitution: if another reason for their need, e.g. infirmity, can be identified s. 21 is still available. As Simon Brown LJ put it in *O* v *Wandsworth Borough Council* [2000] 1 WLR 2539 'if there are to be immigrant beggars on our streets, let them at least not be old and infirm'. What of those who are 'simply' destitute? They are afforded a sub-income level of support in the form of vouchers and mandatory dispersal by the National Asylum Support Service established under the IAA 1999. But those who have exhausted appeal rights are not eligible. So, an asylum seeker (or immigrant) conducting judicial review litigation against a decision of the IAT refusing leave to appeal, has no support whatsoever, and cannot lawfully take employment.[13] Similar considerations then arise to those which prompted the Court of Appeal's decision in the *JCWI* case (see above at 5.23): there is a 'hard cases fund' administered by the National Asylum Support Service under s. 4 of the IAA 1999, and it is likely that in cases where there is an interference with the right of access to the judicial review court by reason of a failure to give support under s. 4 of the IAA 1999, such as interference will be held to be unlawful.

5.25 Public funding is now available for representation in immigration appeals under the scheme of Controlled Legal Representation. Rule 35 of the 2000 Procedure Rules guarantees the right to legal representation. Prior to this, public funding was available for preparation under the Green Form scheme. Funding under the Legal Aid scheme and now the Public Funding scheme has always been available for immigration cases in the higher courts. Plans in 1992 by the Conservative government to abolish legal aid for immigration attracted widespread criticism.

Fees and access to court
5.26 The principle in *Witham* [1998] QB 575 that the right of access to the court was a fundamental constitutional right, extended to apply to tribunals by the

---

[13] See s. 8 of the Asylum and Immigration Act 1996; *R* v *Secretary of State ex parte Jammeh* [1999] Imm AR 1.

Court of Appeal decision in *Saleem* (above at 5.18), may have implications for the legality of prescribing a context-insensitive payment of fees as a precondition for the right of appeal in family visitor cases, with no discretion to lower or waive the fee in individual cases. Similarly, inflexibly applied fee requirements for entertaining entry clearance applications may violate the principle of access to court for e.g. a destitute relative stranded abroad.[14]

Due process and access to court

5.27   Due process is also applied to appellate proceedings so that the right of access to court is meaningful. In *R v IAT ex parte Omar Mohamed Ali* [1995] Imm AR 45 Sedley J held that since the interpolation of appellate machinery in 1993 (Asylum and Immigration Appeals Act 1993, s. 8) between the decisions of the Secretary of State on asylum matters and the review jurisdiction of the court, the eye of the court shifts to ensure that the *Bugdaycay v Secretary of State for the Home Department* [1987] AC 514 standards of most anxious scrutiny have been upheld in the appellate process and the appellate decisions are in no way flawed. Where the Secretary of State's reasons for refusing an application are modified before the appellate authority, procedural fairness demands that the appellant be given a fair opportunity to deal with the amended basis of refusal (*R v Secretary of State, ex parte Hubbard* [1985] Imm AR 110). Where an Adjudicator takes against an appellant a point not raised by the Secretary of State and prejudice results, fairness will normally require that notice to deal with the point is given.[15]

5.28   Where there is no meaningful right of appeal, due process has been held to require that the Secretary of State give an individual notice of the matters that are presently militating against him, so that the right to make representations can be meaningful. This applies both in the asylum (*R v Secretary of State, ex parte Thirukumar* [1989] Imm AR 270)[16] and non-asylum (*R (Cakmak and Uluyol) v Immigration Officer* [2001] INLR 194) spheres.

Access to court and unappealable decisions of the Secretary of State

5.29   It is perhaps in the situation where a raw judicial review challenge is

---

[14] Note however that the Diplomatic Service Procedure (DSP), August 2000, guidelines chapter 7.4 and 7.5, contemplate waiver of the fee for inter alia destitute applicants and dependants of refugees under s. 1(1) of the Consular Fees Act 1980, and the Consular Fees Regulations 1981, the Consular Fees Order 1994, and the Consular Fees (Amendment) Order 1994. There may be a duty to consider the payment of fees in instalments.

[15] See *R (Maheshwaran) v Secretary of State* [2001] EWHC Admin 562, an appeal: [2002] EWCA Civ 173; *R v IAT ex parte Gunn* (22 January 1998); *R v IAT ex parte Keles* (18 November 1998); cf. *R v IAT ex parte Davila-Puga* (31 August 2000); *R v IAT and Special Adjudicator ex parte Kumakech* (17 May 2000); *R v Special Adjudicator ex parte John* [1999] Imm AR 432.

[16] This was decided at a time when there was no right of appeal against asylum refusals at port.

brought to a discretionary decision of the Secretary of State that the applicability of Article 6 to immigration may have some significant impact. Where a right of appeal was available, but was not exercised or was ineffectively exercised,[17] Article 6 is unlikely to demand any difference of approach at judicial review on the basis that it is quite proper for states to regulate the principle of access to court by imposition of time limits. The position under the rules has always allowed for flexibility for late notices of appeal at first instance (now see Procedure Rules 2000, rule 7), and there is for the first time in the current regime a discretion in the IAT to extend time for accepting late applications for leave to appeal (rule 18(3)).

5.30 But where no right of appeal exists at all, and no such right was lost by delay or incompetence, Article 6 may require a more muscular approach to questions of fact on a raw challenge from some decisions of the Secretary of State. Thus for example in a third country appeal where the in-country human rights appeal is excluded by a manifestly unfounded certificate issue by the Secretary of State, Article 6 would probably make a difference (see *R (Razgor)* v *Secretary of State for the Home Department* [2002] EWHC Admin 2554, para. 14). Here, the court on judicial review would probably be required to apply an approach fulfilling the requirement for judicial control by a body possessing 'full jurisdiction'. In this context where issues of risk are concerned, and since the court is hardly less well placed than the Secretary of State to evaluate such issues and may even be advantaged by the lack of any conscious or unconscious desire to remain committed to an original decision taken,[18] the court would be able and required to conduct a far more searching evaluation of the factual material. Where the underlying decision concerned matters of policy rather than risk, the ordinary approach of the court on judicial review is likely to fulfil the requirement of judicial supervision by a body of full jurisdiction (*R (Alconbury)* v *Secretary of State for the Environment, Transport and the Regions* [2001] 2 WLR 1389).

Access to court and abandoned immigration appeals
5.31 The decision in *Gremesty* v *Secretary of State* [2001] INLR 132, where the IAT preserved the right of appeal to itself following a finding of abandonment made by an Adjudicator under the Procedure Rules 2000, rule 32, was informed essentially by the importance afforded to the right of access.

---

[17] See *JED* v *UK* (2 February 1999) (complaint that no appeal against renewed application for asylum following dismissal of first claim. Court did not deal with the question since it regarded judicial review as an adequate remedy.)

[18] See *R* v *Secretary of State ex parte Turgut* [2000] 1 All ER 719; see also *Rehman* v *Secretary of State* [2001] 3 WLR 877; M. J. Beloff QC in [2001] 6(3) JR 154–160 para. 24.

Article 6(1): fair hearing

5.32 The principle of 'equality of arms' as an aspect of fairness demands that a fair balance is struck between the parties and requires that a party has a reasonable opportunity of presenting his case to the court under conditions which do not place him at a substantial disadvantage vis-à-vis his opponent.[19] The principle applies to proceedings between an individual and the state (*Ruis Mateos* v *Spain* (1993) 16 EHRR 505), and may require the ability to cross-examine witnesses. It also finds expression in the more general requirement that judicial proceedings should be adversarial in nature, with the ability to comment effectively on material used by the court in the resolution of the dispute.[20] Where a state without good cause prevents an applicant from gaining access to, or falsely denies the existence of documents in its possession which are of assistance to the applicant's case, the right to a fair hearing will be violated (*McGinley and Egan* v *UK* (1999) 27 EHRR 1, para. 86).

5.33 A fair hearing also imposes a duty on the Court to give reasons for its judgment,[21] although what is adequate by way of reasons will depend on the context and nature of the decision (e.g. *Georgiadis* v *Greece* (1997) 24 EHRR 606).

Fair hearing at common law

5.34 The common law has long considered that in the asylum context, given the gravity of the decision, only the highest standards of fairness will suffice.[22] The courts have held that there is a legitimate expectation that asylum seekers will be interviewed and given reasons for rejection of their claim (*R* v *Secretary of State, ex parte Ramarajah* [1994] Imm AR 472). A failure to listen to representations will lead to a decision being overturned (*Aftab Ahmed* v *Secretary of State* (IAT, 1 March 2000).

Equality of arms and the common law

5.35 The principle of equality of arms is now firmly enshrined in the Civil Procedure Rules (CPR) and obliges the parties to assist the court in ensuring that they are on an 'equal footing' (CPR Rule 1.1(2)). Moreover, although not equi-

---

[19] See e.g. *Neumeister* v *Austria* (1968) 1 EHRR 91, para. 22; *Delcourt* v *Belgium* (1970) 1 EHRR 355, para. 28; *Dombo Debeer* v *Netherlands* (1993) 18 EHRR 213.

[20] See *McMichael* v *UK* (1995) 20 EHRR 205, paras. 80, 83 (non-disclosure of vital documents in family proceedings).

[21] See the cases discussed in *Stefan* v *GMC* [1999] 1 WLR 1293, 1299, Lord Clyde for the Privy Council.

[22] See *R* v *Secretary of State, ex parte Thirukumar* [1989] Imm AR 270; *R* v *Secretary of State, ex parte Gaima* [1989] Imm AR 205.

valent in all respects to civil proceedings in court,[23] proceedings before the appellate authority are essentially adversarial.[24] Thus, Home Office Presenting Officers are not permitted to give evidence (*Aitsaid* v *Secretary of State* (IAT, 11 March 1991)) in hearings on grounds of apparent unfairness, and Adjudicators are not permitted to 'enter the fray' and adopt the role of the Home Office Presenting Officers in testing the account of the appellant, albeit they may make interventions (*R* v *IAT and Secretary of State, ex parte Kumar* (Commission 5073/98, 17 April 2000); but if they overstep the line, their findings of credibility will be overturned on grounds of unfairness.[25]

The decision in Abdi and Gawe

5.36　The House of Lords held by majority in *R* v *Secretary of State, ex parte Abdi and Gawe* [1996] 1 WLR 298 that the Home Office was, in the light of time-constraints involved in third country appeals and the provisions of the Procedure Rules then in force, under no duty to disclose information held by it which was adverse to its case that a particular third country was safe. This is perhaps the most notable example of the common law failing to remedy a shortfall in procedural protection granted by the Procedure Rules. It has consequences for human rights appeals under s. 65 of the IAA 1999 in third country cases, where the Secretary of State is proposing to remove an asylum seeker to a safe third country without substantive consideration of the claim.

5.37　The case was considered to be one of fundamental importance ([1996] 1 WLR 298 at p. 302). The leading speech was given by Lord Lloyd, who gave five reasons for holding that imposing a duty of disclosure would frustrate the intention of Parliament:

(a)　the omission in the asylum procedure rules[26] of a requirement to serve an explanatory statement of facts, as then required by the immigration procedure rules[27] was irreconcilable with the duty contended for by the appellants, since 'an explanatory statement would be as quick a method for serving that purpose as any other';

(b)　further, the obligation only to disclose specific documents in asylum

---

[23]　See e.g. *Kesse* v *Secretary of State* (8 February 2000) C/2000/2955, where the Court of Appeal held that the IAT had power under the Procedure Rules to call a witness of its own motion whom neither side wished to call.

[24]　See *R* v *IAT ex parte Demeter* [2000] Imm AR 424; *MNM* v *Secretary of State* [2000] INLR 576; *Carbacuk* v *Secretary of State for the Home Department* (IAT, 18 May 2000); *R (Ganidagli* v *Secretary of State for the Home Department* [2001] INLR 479..

[25]　See *R* v *IAT ex parte Demeter* [2000] Imm AR 424; *Muwinyi* v *Secretary of State* (00052) IAT; *MNM* v *Secretary of State* [2000] INLR 576, endorsing the Surendran guidelines.

[26]　The relevant rules were then the 1993 Procedure Rules.

[27]　The relevant rules were the 1984 Procedure Rules.

appeals (1993 Procedure Rules, rule 5(6)) was wholly inconsistent with the appellants' submissions;

(c)   the issue did not concern 'substantive rights to asylum' but rather the forum in which the claim would be determined, where speed was of the essence;

(d)   the power in the Special Adjudicator to extend time limits for giving notice of appeal and for determination meant that justice was not sacrificed in the interests of speed;

(e)   there was provision for the UN High Commissioner for Refugees to intervene and the Special Adjudicator could always ask for information.

Revisiting Abdi and Gawe

5.38   *Abdi and Gawe* was a case concerning return to a safe third country where there was an in-country right of appeal. Since 1999, challenges by way of judicial review, let alone appeal,[28] are precluded in almost all cases by a statutory presumption that member states of the EU and designated states are safe in Refugee Convention terms (IAA 1999, s. 11). The continuing relevance of the approach endorsed in *Abdi and Gawe* arises in the context of third country removals where a breach of ECHR rights is asserted. Unless the Secretary of State issues a manifestly unfounded certificate under s. 72, s. 65 will guarantee an in-country human rights appeal where, for example, breaches under Article 3 could ventilated.[29] In other words, the IAA 1999 contemplates at least 'third country' human rights appeals. Moreover, the general principle involved of full disclosure by the Home Office of material both pointing in favour of and against its case is of obvious general importance in substantive asylum and indeed immigration appeals. In this context, we consider that the approach upheld in *Abdi and Gawe* ought to be revisited for the following reasons.

5.39   First, we respectfully suggest that the reasoning of the majority of the House of Lords needs to be considered in the light of developments in the common law itself. Fairness requires disclosure of data relevant to the decision in hand, in the absence of statutory wording conclusively prohibiting such disclosure. In *Simms and O'Brienn* [2000] 2 AC 115 the House of Lords held that even in the absence of ambiguity, neutral words had to be interpreted so as to ensure compliance with fundamental rights. This is the 'principle of legality'. Unless a rights-incompatible conclusion was mandated by express words of Parliament or by necessary implication, it should not be upheld.

---

[28] The in-country right of appeal was abolished by ss. 1 and 2 of the Asylum and Immigration Act 1996.

[29] The fact that removal is proposed from one ECHR state to another is not determinative: *TI* v *UK* [2000] INLR 211.

(a) This approach would in effect place an onus on the Secretary of State to show that Parliament, by omitting in the Procedure Rules the requirement on the Home Office to produce an explanatory statement, *necessarily* meant that material adverse to the Home Office argument need not be placed before the independent Adjudicator. This contrasts with the position in *Abdi and Gawe*, where the appellants sought to show that the common law should supplement the procedural protection conferred by Parliament (*Wiseman* v *Bourneman* [1971] AC 297). Instead, it would be for the Secretary of State to show that no other reading of the Procedure Rules could be arrived at other than the interpretation that he was not required to disclose material adverse to his case. See *R (Morgan Grenfell)* v *Special Commissioner for Income Tax* [2002] UKHL 21, [2002] HRLR 42, para. 45.

(b) In *R* v *Bentley* [1999] Crim LR 330 Lord Bingham CJ held that the right to a fair trial was the birthright of every British citizen. Such a birthright would no doubt extend to those within the jurisdiction (*Khawaja* v *Secretary of State* [1984] AC 74, 111 per Lord Scarman). The importance of the principle of equality of arms is underscored by the CPR which ensures that the parties are on an equal footing (rule 1.1(2)).

(c) Against such a background, and the emphasis in *Simms and O'Brienn* [2000] 2 AC 115 on a strong common law principle for the divination of a human rights compatible legislative intent, there appears to be determinative force in Lord Slynn's observation (at [1996] 1 WLR 298 at p. 305) that the obligation to disclose the material was necessary 'if the proceedings were to be conducted fairly':

An appellant is required frankly to disclose relevant information to the immigration officer; on these appeals what is sauce for the goose is sauce for the gander and prima facie there is no reason why the appellant and the Special Adjudicator should not see the material on which the Secretary of State took his decision.

(d) It is difficult to see how, other than using a wholly human rights-neutral approach to Parliamentary intent, the conclusion of the majority in *Abdi and Gawe* could be reached that an omission to produce an explanatory statement permitted an unequal procedure.

(e) The point is re-enforced by the observation that, since at common law on judicial review a party is required to make full and frank disclosure once permission to apply for judicial review is granted (*R* v *Lancashire CC, ex parte Huddleston* [1986] 2 All ER 941), it is unlikely that the approach successfully contended for by the Secretary of State in *Abdi and Gawe* in the context of proceedings before the appellate authority would pass muster before the High Court.

5.40 Secondly, it was the practice even at the time if *Abdi and Gawe* that an explanatory statement of the facts produced under the 1984 Procedure Rules, rule 4 merely set out the Home Office case, annexing material generated in the application process. It was for the appellant to produce material supportive of his/her case. The omission of a requirement to produce an explanatory statement accordingly seems not to deserve the weight given to it: Parliament in approving the 1993 Rules laid by the Lord Chancellor could be taken to know of such practice. In any event now there is no requirement to produce an explanatory statement in either an asylum case or an immigration case. This appears consistent with the view that there was no 'magic' in the explanatory statement procedure, the omission of which in asylum appeals permitted the Home Office not to disclose material adverse to its case in the asylum context. For similar reasons the point that only specific documents are obliged to be produced seems an unstable basis upon which to reason that disclosure, which would at least promote fairness (leaving aside for the moment whether such disclosure was *necessary* for fairness), need not be made.

5.41 This leads on to the third consideration: all the 'third country' judicial review applications have recognized the fact that in the third country process, fundamental rights are very much at stake (*R v Secretary of State, ex parte Adan and Aitsegur* [2001] 2 WLR 143. *Bugdaycay v Secretary of State for the Home Department* [1987] AC 514 itself was a third country case. While the substantive claim is not being determined, the ancillary question of the safety of the forum in which such determination is to take place is equally if not more important.[30] Lord Lloyd's reasoning is with respect circular: it assumes that which is at issue, namely the safety of the third country, in order to downplay the importance of the proceedings and the standards of fairness attracted.

5.42 Fourthly, as to the time limits, as Lord Slynn observed, the strict time limits applicable to third country appeals were not conclusive, given the power in the Adjudicator to extend time for the just disposal of the case, and the power in the Secretary of State to dispense with providing an explanatory statement in ordinary immigration appeals. In other words Parliament had contemplated the interests of justice requiring a slower procedure in appropriate asylum cases, and a faster procedure in immigration cases. The human rights appeal is not however governed by such a fast procedure.

5.43 Fifthly, the idea that the UN High Commissioner for Refugees could intervene and the Special Adjudicator could always ask for information appears of limited force. The UN High Commissioner for Refugees rarely intervenes at

---

[30] For an indication, see Lord Woolf in *R v Secretary of State ex parte Canbolat* [1997] 1 WLR 1569 on the standard of proof.

appellate level, and does not do so to make submissions as to the facts.[31] And if the Special Adjudicators do not ask for information, 'there is a risk that . . . something of importance will not be seen' ([1996] 1 WLR 298 at p. 305 per Lord Slynn) and this procedure would tend to lengthen proceedings.

5.44 Sixthly, the imposition of a duty of disclosure does not appear impracticable, since the Secretary of State's practice was in any event to produce bundles before the Adjudicator, containing information that was exclusively favourable to him:

> If it is possible to give information which supports the Secretary of State's decision I wholly fail to see why to disclose material supporting or tending to support the Appellant's contention frustrates the aim of Parliament. ([1996] 1 WLR 298 at p. 307)

5.45 Accordingly Lord Slynn concluded ([1996] 1 WLR 298 at p. 307), concurring with Steyn LJ in the Court of Appeal, that 'the current procedure is not such as to enable the Special Adjudicators fully to perform their task and is calculated to produce unfairness'.

5.46 An indication of the direction in which the common law is moving is the decision in *R* v *Secretary of State ex parte Vuckovic* [2000] All ER D 234 where Newman J held a failure by the Home Office Presenting Officer to present to the Adjudicator an updated country bulletin in the absence of the appellant at the hearing to be unfair.

5.47 Thus both the common law and considerations from Article 6 raise the question as to whether *Abdi and Gawe* has been overtaken by incremental developments in standards of fairness: where a state without good cause prevents an applicant from gaining access to materials helpful to the Applicant, a right to a fair hearing will be violated (*McGinley and Egan* v *UK* (1999) 27 EHRR 1, para. 86). Moreover, the recent Turkish cases (e.g. *Jabari* v *Turkey* [2001] INLR 136) highlight the importance of the state not obstructing the right to an effective remedy. The disclosure cases in the criminal sphere,[32] having regard to the gravity of the consequences of an adverse decision in the asylum field, further support the proposition that it would not be legitimate for the Secretary of State not to disclose information in the course of the appellate process that was adverse to his case, and peculiarly within his possession.

---

[31] *Gashi* v *Secretary of State* [1997] INLR 96 is a notable exception.

[32] See, e.g., *R* v *Keane* (1994) 99 Cr App R 1; *R* v *Hallett* [1986] Crim LR 462; *R* v *Agar* (1990) 90 Cr App R 318 at 324; *R* v *A* [2001] 2 WLR 1546, per Lord Hutton at para. 161; Attorney-General's Guidelines on Disclosure, November 2000.

The duty to give reasons at common law

5.48 There is a statutory duty obliging the Secretary of State in relation to appealable decisions[33] to give reasons for his decision. In the asylum field the courts have held that there is a legitimate expectation arising out of practice that an asylum seeker will be interviewed and reasons given (*R* v *Secretary of State, ex parte Ramarajah* [1994] Imm AR 472). Since one purpose of the giving of reasons both domestically and at the European Court is to enable proper access to court[34] and given the gravity of the issue arising in asylum decisions, the Secretary of State's practice of giving reasons for his decision is, we consider, a mandatory requirement of fairness under the common law.[35]

5.49 Until 2 October 2000, there was a statutory obligation on the appellate authority to give reasons for its decision.[36] The omission of such a duty in the 2000 Procedure Rules which apply to both immigration and asylum appeals is unlikely to affect the position given likely developments at common law. While there is no general duty in public law to give reasons, the position may well change owing to the influence of Article 6 jurisprudence. In *Stefan* v *GMC* [1999] 1 WLR 1293 at pp. 1300, 1301[37] Lord Clyde for the Privy Council stated that:

> The trend of the law has been towards an increased recognition of the duty upon decision-makers of many kinds to give reasons. This trend is consistent with current developments towards an increased openness in matters of government and administration . . . the law does not at present recognise a general duty to give reasons for administrative decisions. But it is well established that there are exceptions where the giving of reasons will be required as a matter of fairness and openness. These may occur through the particular circumstances of a particular case. Or . . . there may be classes of cases where the duty to give reasons may exist in all cases of that class. Those classes may be defined by factors relating to the particular character or quality of the decisions, as where they appear aberrant, or to factors relating to the particular character or particular jurisdiction of a decision-making body, as where it is concerned with matters of special importance, such as personal liberty. There is certainly a strong argument for the view that what were once seen as exceptions to the rule may now be becoming examples of the norm, and the cases where reasons are not required may be taking on the appearance of exceptions. (Their Lordships) are conscious of the poss-

---

[33] See the Immigration and Asylum Appeals (Notice) Regulations 2000 (SI 2000 No. 2246), rule 5.

[34] See the cases cited in *Stefan* v *GMC* [1999] 1 WLR 1293.

[35] The issue may assume greater significance following reconsideration after non-compliance refusals.

[36] See the Immigration Appeals (Procedure) Rules 1984, rule 39 (non-asylum); Asylum Appeals (Procedure) Rules 1996, rule 2(3)(b).

[37] See also M. Fordham, 'Reasons: The Third Dimension' [2000] Judicial Review 158; and the written answer of 12 January 1998, Hansard, HL, WA 122, given by the Solicitor-General as to the requirement to give reasons for decisions directly affecting the citizen's rights and interests, noted at [1998] Judicial Review 92.

ible reappraisal of the whole position which the passing of the Human Rights Act 1998 may bring about. The provisions of Article 6(1) . . . will require closer attention to be paid to the duty to give reasons, at least in relation to those cases where a person's civil rights and obligations are being determined. But it is in the context of the application of that Act that any wide-ranging review of the position at common law should take place.

5.50 The common law adopts a context driven approach to fairness depending upon the individual circumstances of the case, rather than erecting a rigid dichotomy between civil and non-civil rights to determine the applicability of Article 6. It would thus be inconsistent with principle not to apply an Article 6 inspired approach to the duty to give reasons to immigration decisions.[38] Furthermore, the existing approach of the common law which requires reasons in the immigration field and insists on adequate reasons where the context demands it[39] as a fundamental requirement of fairness is, we suggest, not affected by an omission of a complementary statutory duty to provide reasons.

Article 6(1): public hearing

5.51 The protection of the right to a public hearing is a fundamental guarantee designed to protect litigants from 'the administration of justice in secret with no public scrutiny' (*Pretto* v *Italy* (1983) 6 EHRR 182, para. 21) and to maintain public confidence in the courts and the administration of justice (*Diennet* v *France* (1995) 21 EHRR 554, para. 33). The right is subject to the express limitations set out in Article 6(1) (interests of morals, public order, national security, protection of the private life of the parties, interests of justice). The limitation must be 'strictly required by the circumstances' (para. 34) and must not be disproportionate (*Campbell and Fell* v *UK* (1984) 7 EHRR 165, para. 37).

5.52 The right implies an oral hearing unless there are exceptional circumstances justifying dispensing with such a hearing (*Werner* v *Austria* (1997) 26 EHRR 310, para. 50). The right to be present at the hearing is mediated in the civil context in that it extends only in cases where there is an issue as to the conduct of the party (*Muyldermans* v *Belgium* (1991) 15 EHRR 204, para. 64).

Public hearing at common law

5.53 Proceedings before the appellate authority and immigration judicial reviews are public proceedings. There is a strong common law presumption in

---

[38] See analogously the Article 6 inspired change to the common law on bias in *Director-General of Fair Trading* v *Proprietary Association of Great Britain* [2001] 1 WLR 700.

[39] See e.g. *R* v *IAT ex parte Amin* [1992] Imm AR 267; *R* v *IAT ex parte Iqbal* [1993] Imm AR 270.

favour of public justice.[40] This is reflected in rule 40 of the Asylum and Immigration (Appeals) Procedure Rules 2000 which stipulates that subject to the exceptions set out in the rule 'any hearing before the appellate authority shall take place in public'. The exceptions are those listed in Article 6(1) itself (rule 40(3)) and additionally the circumstance where the appellate authority considers an allegation that a document is forged and disclosure of the method of detection of the forgery would be contrary to the public interest. In this circumstance the appellant and their representative must be excluded from the hearing (IAA 1999, Sch. 4, para. 6(1), (2)). This situation falls within the permissible public order or interests of justice limitation to the right to a public hearing, and given that the scheme envisages exclusion for only that part of the hearing where the allegation is being tested, we consider that it would be compatible with Article 6 were that article to apply to immigration.

Article 6(1): hearing within a reasonable time

5.54 The right to a hearing within a reasonable time is designed to protect against excessive procedural delay. Time generally runs from the institution of court proceedings until the case is finally determined (including appellate or judicial review proceedings[41]). What is 'reasonable' depends on all the circumstances, including in particular the complexity of the issues raised, the conduct of the parties, and what is at stake for the applicant (*Zimmerman* v *Switzerland* (1983) 6 EHRR 17, para. 24). States are obliged to organize their legal systems so as to permit compliance with Article 6(1): a long-term backlog of work where insufficient remedial measures have been taken will not prevent a breach (paras. 27–32). Where the backlog is temporary or exceptional and necessary action has been taken by the state no breach will be found (*Buckholz* v *FRG* (1981) 3 EHRR 597, para. 51).

Hearing within a reasonable time at common law

5.55 The right to a hearing within a reasonable time has been construed domestically as a right which crystallizes without the need to show prejudice (*McLean* v *HM Advocate* [2000] UKHRR 73; *R* v *HM Advocate* (PC, 28 November 2002). At common law, delay may amount to an abuse of power (*R* v *Secretary of State, ex parte Phansopkar* [1976] QB 606), and considerations of staleness of evidence are likely to be dealt with in the proceedings themselves, rather than requiring a more drastic result such as the abandonment of those proceedings.

5.56 With considerable delays with first instance decisions and the appellate

---

[40] See e.g. *R* v *Legal Aid Board ex parte Kaim Todner* [1999] QB 966, Lord Woolf MR.
[41] See *Eckle* v *FRG* (1982) 5 EHRR 1, para. 78; *Konig* v *FRG* (1978) 2 EHRR 170, para. 98.

system a frequent aspect of immigration practice, the IAT in *MNM* v *Secretary of State* [2000] INLR 576 considered this to be the only area where the applicability of Article 6 might make a difference. Even then, since there will be no violation where efforts are made to remedy a temporary influx of cases, the establishment of a violation would not be straightforward. Even if a violation was found, there would be an issue as to the appropriate remedy which should follow. See the diverging views in the criminal context in *R* v *HM Advocate* (PC, 28 November 2002) of Lords Hope, Rodger and Clyde on the one hand, and Lords Steyn and Walker on the other. It is unlikely that the grant of the sought after immigration status would be required, more that an award of damages may be made.[42]

Article 6(1): independent and impartial tribunal established by law

5.57 For a body to have the features of a 'tribunal' it must perform a judicial function, have jurisdiction to examine all questions of fact and law, and its decisions must be legally binding rather than merely advisory (*Van de Hurk* v *Netherlands* (1994) 18 EHRR 481, para. 52).

5.58 Independence requires independence from the executive, the parties and the legislature. Regard will be had to the manner of appointment of the members of the tribunal, their term of office, the existence of guarantees against outside pressures and to the objective appearance of independence (*Bryan* v *UK* (1995) 21 EHRR 342). Relatively short terms of office (three years for prison visitors) have been accepted (*Campbell and Fell* v *UK* (1984) 7 EHRR 165, para. 80).

5.59 Impartiality requires an absence of bias, both from a subjective and objective perspective. The subjective test requires an enquiry into the personal convictions of the judge, while the objective test demands that there were sufficient guarantees to exclude legitimate doubt.[43] The approach of the European Court is evolutive having regard to the increased sensitivity of the public to the fair administration of justice.[44]

Independence and impartiality at common law

5.60 In *Director-General of Fair Trading* v *Proprietary Association of Great Britain* [2001] 1 WLR 700 at p. 711 Lord Phillips MR stated that 'The requirement that the Tribunal should be independent and impartial is one that has long

---

[42] There is a marked tendency against the award of exemplary damages for breaches of 'constitutional rights', so any award for compensatory damages would not be particularly substantial.
[43] See e.g. *Piersack* v *Belgium* (1983) 5 EHRR 169; see also cases cited and the test arrived at in *Director-General of Fair Trading* v *Proprietary Association of Great Britain* [2001] 1 WLR 700.
[44] See *Bulut* v *Austria* (1997) 24 EHRR 84; *Borgers* v *Belgium* (1991) 15 EHRR 92.

been recognised by English common law.' The decision of the Privy Council in *Millar* v *Dickson* 2002 SC (PC)30 endorsing *Starrs* v *Ruxton* 2000 JC 208 indicates that this requirement cannot be impliedly waived.

The modification of the *Gough* test

5.61 The common law has reacted to the incorporation of ECHR rights by adapting the decision in *R* v *Gough* [1993] AC 646 where Lord Goff had held that appearances had to be judged from the perspective of the court rather than the objective and well-informed onlooker. The House of Lords preferred the test of 'real danger' of bias to that of 'real apprehension' of bias. This decision was the subject of criticism by the Australian High Court in *Webb* v *The Queen* (1994) 181 CLR 41, which considered the juridical basis of protection against bias, namely the maintenance of public confidence in the law, to be irreconcilable with an approach which regarded as determinate the court's view of events, rather than the court's view of the public's perception of events. In the leading judgment Mason CJ and McHugh J stated (at pp. 50–2):

> In *Gough*, the House of Lords rejected the need to take account of the public perception of an incident which raises an issue of bias except in the case of a pecuniary interest. Behind this reasoning is the assumption that public confidence in the administration of justice will be maintained because the public will accept the conclusions of the judge. But the premise on which the decisions in this court are based is that public confidence in the administration of justice is more likely to be maintained if the court adopts a test that reflects the reaction of the ordinary reasonable member of the public to the irregularity in question. . . . They indicate that it is the court's view of the public's view, not the court's own view, which is determinative. If public confidence in the administration of justice is to be maintained, the approach that is taken by fair-minded and informed members of the public cannot be ignored . . . in considering whether an allegation of bias on the part of a judge has been made out, the public perception of the judiciary is not advanced by attributing to a fair-minded member of the public a knowledge of the law and the judicial process which ordinary experience suggests is not the case.

5.62 Even before incorporation a Court of Appeal constituted of the heads of division in *Locobail* v *Bayfield Properties* [2000] QB 451[45] proposed a relaxation to the *Gough* test by opening up a space between the Court and the onlooker, stipulating that the objective onlooker was not to be imputed with detailed knowledge of procedure (at p. 477):

---

[45] Convened in the wake of *R* v *Bow Street Metropolitan Stipendiary Magistrate ex parte Pinochet Ugarte No. 2* [2000] 1 AC 119 HL.

Provided that the court, personifying the reasonable man, takes an approach which is based on broad common sense, without inappropriate reliance on special knowledge, the minutiae of court procedure or other matters outside the ken of the ordinary, reasonably well-informed member of the public, there should be no risk that the courts will not ensure both that justice is done and that it is perceived by the public to be done.

5.63 In *Director-General of Fair Trading* v *Proprietary Association of Great Britain* [2001] 1 WLR 700 at p. 721 Lord Phillips MR considered this technique to be difficult to reconcile with *Gough* and, following a review of European Court jurisprudence,[46] held (at p. 727) that a 'modest adjustment' of the *Gough* test was required:

> The court must first ascertain all the circumstances which have a bearing on the suggestion that the judge was biased. It must then ask whether those circumstances would lead a *fair-minded and informed observer* to conclude that there was a real possibility, or a real danger, the two being the same, that the Tribunal was biased. (emphasis supplied)

5.64 The import of this is of course that an Article 6 inspired change in the domestic law has the result of affording greater domestic procedural protection to the sphere of immigration. Lord Phillips's test was endorsed by Lord Hope in *Porter* v *Magill* [2002] 2 WLR 37 who emphasized that a tribunal's denial of apparent bias was to be disregarded.

Independence and impartiality in the appellate authority

5.65 The requirement of independence and impartiality in immigration appeals is promoted by the appointment of Adjudicators by the Lord Chancellor, for a period to ensure sufficient security of tenure,[47] rather than the Secretary of State as was previously the position,[48] and by the fact that the Procedure Rules were initially laid under s. 22 of the IA 1971 by the Secretary of State, but following an amendment, they are also now made by the Lord Chancellor.

5.66 So, to prevent appearances of bias arising through a judge holding office

---

[46] The Court of Appeal at p. 726 noted in particular that the decision of the European Court in *Borgers* v *Belgium* (1991) 15 EHRR 92 effectively reversed the decision in *Delcourt* v *Belgium* (1970) 1 EHRR 355. The European Court observed (at p. 108) that the rights of the defence and the principle of equality of arms had 'undergone a considerable evolution in the court's case law, notably in respect of the importance attached to appearances and to the increased sensitivity of the public to the fair administration of justice.

[47] *Starrs* v *Ruxton* 2000 JC 208: 'In the case of temporary Sheriffs, where the appointment is frequently a career move, the combination of a one-year appointment with liability to either recall or suspension or limited use is in my opinion wholly inconsistent with the requirement of independence.'

[48] Contrast the position with regard to the appointment of members of the Employment Tribunal: *Scanfuture UK Ltd* v *Secretary of State for Trade and Industry*, *The Times*, 26 April 2001.

for a short term renewable at discretion and thus vulnerable to pleasing the paymaster, Adjudicators have been given greater security of tenure.[49]

5.67 Also to prevent appearances of bias, Adjudicators are not permitted to 'enter the fray' and adopt the role of the Home Office Presenting Officers, and if they do so findings of credibility will be overturned on grounds of unfairness.[50] Where flawed credibility findings are made by an Adjudicator, the Tribunal's practice is to remit afresh to a new Adjudicator where all issues are open. Collins J regarded the power of the Tribunal in the Procedure Rules (see now rule 23) to remit an appeal to be determined by the same Adjudicator from whom the appeal is brought, as 'remarkable', and commented 'It is, to say the least, surprising that Parliament should have intended that to happen' *(Secretary of State* v *Zengin* [2001] INLR 88 at p. 93; see also *R (Secretary of State)* v *IAT* [2001] QB 1224 and *R (Sarkisian)* v *IAT* [2002] INLR 80). While the second Adjudicator may have regard to the notes of hearing before the first Adjudicator, regard may not be had to the determination *(R* v *IAT, ex parte Nalokweza* [1996] Imm AR 230). It is desirable for the second determination to be removed from the file *(R* v *Secretary of State, ex parte Aissaoui* [1997] Imm AR 184). Where the Tribunal's refusal of leave is quashed on judicial review, the practice is again to have the substantive appeal listed before a fresh chairperson.[51]

Article 6(3)(e): right to free interpretation

5.68 We have noted above that while the specific guarantees in Article 6(3) are expressed to apply to criminal proceedings, since they encapsulate minimum aspects of the right to a fair trial as a whole in Article 6(1), they have been considered to apply *mutatis mutandis* to the civil sphere.[52] The right to an interpreter under Article 6(3)(e) in order to comprehend proceedings is part of a wider aspect of the right to participate effectively in the proceedings. It is an absolute right, albeit that there is no hard requirement for verbatim interpretation, provided the gist of the proceedings is interpreted and no matters of substance remain uninterpreted. The right also covers the translation of documents, but again it is not necessary to translate all documents, provided fairness as a whole is guaranteed.

---

[49] See *Starrs* v *Ruxton* 2000 JC 208 (temporary sheriffs not independent owing to insufficient security of tenure arising out of year's renewals of appointment).

[50] See *Muwinyi* v *Secretary of State* (00052) IAT; *MNM* v *Secretary of State* [2000] INLR 576, endorsing the Surendran guidelines.

[51] But note the comments of Laws LJ granting permission on a different point in *Mwakulua* v *Secretary of State for the Home Department* 4 March 1999; SLJ 98/7806/4 and see *Sengupta* v *Holmes* [2002] EWCA Civ 1104.

[52] See *R* v *Secretary of State ex parte Quaquah* [2000] INLR 196; *Albert and Le Compte* v *Belgium* (1983) 18 EHRR 533.

Interpretation domestically

5.69 The practice in the appellate authority is to provide for free interpretation. It is obvious that there cannot be any fair hearing if the appellant cannot participate effectively in the hearing.

Extra-territorial application

5.70 The European Court has contemplated a limited, extra-territorial application of Article 6. Expulsion is prohibited where it would lead to a flagrant breach of Article 6:[53]

> The right to a fair trial in criminal proceedings, as embodied in Article 6, holds a prominent place in democratic society. The Court does not exclude that an issue might exceptionally be raised under Article 6 by an extradition decision in circumstances where the fugitive has suffered or risks suffering a flagrant denial of a fair trial in the requesting country.

5.71 In *MAR* v *UK* (1997) 23 EHRR CD 120 the former European Commission declared admissible a complaint that removal by the UK of an immigrant to risks of detention and trial in breach of Articles 5 and 6 would be attributable to the UK. The case was settled before an opinion on the merits was adopted by the former European Commission. See also the recent decision in *Bankovic* v *Belgium and other NATO states* (12 December 2001) discussed above at 1.20 et seq. But see, however, *Ullah* v *Special Adjudicator* [2002] EWCA Civ 1856 where leave has been granted to appeal to the House of Lords.

Are Article 6 rights absolute?

5.72 The question as to which Article 6 rights are absolute was considered by the Judicial Committee of the Privy Council in *Brown* v *Stott* [2001] 2 WLR 817 in the criminal sphere in the specific context of the privilege against self-incrimination. The Judicial Committee held that the privilege was not an absolute right, and that the interference proportionately pursued the public interest in addressing in an effective manner the high incidence of death and injury on the roads caused by road crime.[54] Lord Hope held (at [2001] 2 WLR 817 at p. 851) that:

---

[53] *Soering* v *UK* [1989] 11 EHRR 439 para. 113; *Drozd and Janouesek* v *France* (1992) 14 EHRR 725 para. 110.
[54] The dual requirement that a limitation with an Article 6 right must pursue a legitimate aim and be proportionate to that aim is sometimes referred to as the *Ashingdane* principles (*Ashingdane* v *UK* (1985) 7 EHRR 528, para. 57).

A similar approach to the function of the rule of law can be seen in the fact that the court has consistently recognised that, while the right to a fair trial is absolute in its terms and the public interest can never be invoked to deny that right to anybody under any circumstances, the rights which it has read into Article 6 are neither absolute nor inflexible.

Lord Bingham went further and stated (at p. 825):

> There is nothing to suggest that the fairness of the trial itself may be qualified, comprom- ised or restricted in any way, whatever the circumstances and whatever the public inter- est in convicting the offender. If the trial as a whole is judged to be unfair, a conviction cannot stand.

And Lord Bingham also said (at p. 836):

> The jurisprudence of the European Court very clearly establishes that while the over- all fairness of a criminal trial cannot be compromised, the constituent rights comprised, whether expressly or implicitly, within Article 6 are not themselves absolute. Limited qualification of these rights is acceptable if reasonably directed by national authorities towards a clear and proper public objective and if representing no greater qualification than the situation calls for.

5.73 There appears to be a tension in the judgments of Lord Bingham and Lord Hope: Lord Hope's view that it is only the rights implied into Article 6 which may be qualified may be preferable to the view expressed by Lord Bingham that while the general right to a fair trial under Article 6(1) is absolute, the other express minimum rights, relating on their face specifically to criminal proceedings, are not. In practice, however, the difference between the approaches of Lord Hope and Lord Bingham is likely to be one without distinction, because the balancing act which, in Lord Bingham's view, can be undertaken to defeat an express right can be conducted to ascertain the mean- ing or content of the right, i.e. whether or not the right has been breached in the first instance. The approach gaining prominence appears to be that of Lord Bingham: see the decisions of the House of Lords in *R* v *Forbes* [2001] 2 WLR 1; *R* v *A* [2001] 2 WLR 1546.

ARTICLE 13

5.74 Article 13 provides that:

> Everyone whose rights and freedoms as set forth in this Convention are violated shall have an effective remedy before a national authority notwithstanding that the violation has been committed by persons acting in an official capacity.

Relevance to domestic law and practice

5.75 Article 13 is not incorporated in Sch. 1 to the HRA 1998. The justification advanced by the government was that the HRA 1998 itself was intended to give the effective remedy guaranteed by Article 13 to a determination on an ECHR rights question.[55] The European Court has stated that 'Article 13, giving direct expression to the States' obligation to protect human rights first and foremost within their own legal system, establishes an additional guarantee for an individual in order to ensure that he or she effectively enjoys those rights.' (*Kudla* v *Poland* (26 October 2000, para. 152)).

5.76 Another reason for the failure to incorporate Article 13 was that judges might fashion unpredictable new remedies.[56] However, the fact that Article 13 is not incorporated does not render it irrelevant to domestic law and practice. In essence, and first, the UK continues to be bound as a matter of international law to the developing European Court jurisprudence. A decision from the European Court that judicial review procedure in the UK failed to afford an effective remedy will require, as a matter of international law, remedial measures to be taken. Secondly, s. 2 of the HRA 1998, as we have seen above at 1.61 et seq, obliges the domestic courts to take into account the jurisprudence of the ECHR organs.

5.77 Sedley LJ said in *R* v *Camden and Islington Health Authority ex parte K* [2001] EWCA Civ 240:

> While Article 13 of the Convention is not among those scheduled to the Human Rights Act 1998, its requirement that there must be an effective remedy for violations of Convention rights reflects the long-standing principle of our law that where there is a right there should be a remedy. Parliament's intention was, of course, that the Human Rights Act itself should constitute the United Kingdom's compliance with Article 13; but this makes it if anything more important that the courts, as part of the State, should satisfy themselves so far as possible that the common law affords adequate control, in conformity with Article 13, of the legality of official measures which interfere with personal autonomy.[57]

The requirements of Article 13

5.78 The essential features of Article 13 are as follows:

(a)   although the Article states that 'Everyone whose rights and freedoms as set forth in this Convention *are violated* shall have an effective remedy',

---

55 See *Hansard*, 583 HL Official Reports (5th Series) col. 475 (18 November 1997).
56 See Lord Irvine LC, 18 November 1997, Hansard, HL, Vol. 583, col. 475.
57 Note, however, the comments of the same judge in *Keenan* v *UK* (2001) 33 EHRR 38.

the European Court has made it clear that to bring a claim under Article 13 it is not necessary to establish a violation of another ECHR right (*Klass* v *FRG* (1979–80) 2 EHRR 214, para. 64). Claims under Article 13 may be successful even though the European Court finds no violation of another ECHR right.[58] The Article is thus triggered where there is an arguable case that an ECHR right has been breached;[59]

(b)　the remedial authority must be sufficiently independent of the body which is challenged (*Silver* v *UK* (1983) 5 EHRR 347);

(c)　the scope of the obligation under Article 13 varies according to the nature of the complaint;[60]

(d)　the degree of effective redress required in a particular case depends on the importance of the right at stake (*Hasan and Chaush* v *Bulgaria* (App. No. 30985/96), para. 98). The body need not satisfy Article 6 requirements (*Golder* v *UK* (1979–80) 1 EHRR 524, para. 33). However, purely discretionary remedies will not suffice: there must be an element of compulsion (*Silver* v *UK* (1983) 5 EHRR 347, paras. 115–17). But a practice of compliance with the outcome of the judicial process has been held to be sufficient in the contexts of e.g. national security (*Leander* v *Sweden* (1987) 9 EHRR 433, and extradition (*Soering* v *UK* (1989) 11 EHRR 439);

(e)　the remedy must be practical and effective and not theoretical: thus out of country appeals in the asylum context would fall foul of this rule;[61]

(f)　the availability of the remedy must not be hindered by the acts or omissions of the state;[62]

(g)　success before the national body is not a necessary condition for the remedy to be effective for the purposes of Article 13. The requirement is that there is a remedy which *could* be granted, even if it was not granted in the particular case.[63] The critical enquiry is whether the remedy is *capable* of scrutinizing the substance of the complaint.[64]

---

[58] See *Leander* v *Sweden* (1987) 9 EHRR 433; *Kaya* v *Turkey* (1999) 28 EHRR 1, para. 107; *Iatridis* v *Greece* (2000) 30 EHRR 97.

[59] See e.g. *Bensaid* v *UK* [2001] INLR 325, para. 54, *Boyle and Rice* v *UK* (1988) 10 EHRR 425, paras. 52–5, *Kaya* v *Turkey* (1999) 28 EHRR 1, para. 113.

[60] See *Hilal* v *UK* [2001] INLR 595, para. 75; *Bensaid* v *UK* [2001] INLR 325, para. 53.

[61] See *Vilvarajah* v *UK* (1991) 14 EHRR 248; *Canbolat* [1997] Imm AR, QBD (per Bingham LCJ) contrasted with *Canbolat* [1997] 1 WLR 1569, CA (per Woolf MR).

[62] See *Aydin* v *Turkey* (1998) 25 EHRR 251, para. 103; *Iatridis* v *Greece* (2000) 30 EHRR 97, para. 66.

[63] See *Soering* v *UK* (1989) 11 EHRR 439.

[64] See *Vilvarajah* v *UK* (1991) 14 EHRR 248, para. 122; *Bensaid* v *UK* [2001] INLR 325, para. 56.

5.79 Historically there has been a live issue as to whether or not the scrutiny capable of being afforded on judicial review was compatible with Article 13 requirements.[65] The case law appears to indicate that judicial review is compliant with the requirements of Article 13 where fundamental rights are engaged, provided that rigorous scrutiny is applied by the court, the material closely examined, and the functions demanded to be performed by the ECHR are indeed performed by the domestic court. This was the view of the Court of Appeal in *Turgut v Secretary of State* [2001] 1 All ER 719, a 'raw' challenge to the exercise of the Secretary of State's discretion to refuse exceptional leave to a Turkish Kurd asylum seeker who was wholly lacking in credibility, on the basis that no violation of Article 3 could be demonstrated on return to Turkey. In a case heard before the coming into force of the HRA 1998, the Court of Appeal held that it was not necessary for the judicial review court to adopt the role of the primary fact finder in order to remain faithful to the requirements of Article 13. Leave was granted to appeal to the House of Lords, but proceedings compromised on the offer of a human rights appeal under s. 65 of the IAA 1999. The Court of Appeal's view in *Turgut*, reached after a comprehensive review of European Court authority, therefore remains binding authority for the position at common law.

5.80 *Turgut* decides that where the court applies a more than usually intensive review, Article 13 requirements will be met. This indeed appears to be the state of the common law where fundamental rights are concerned.[66] It follows that any reversion to the standard approach to judicial review absent increased scrutiny commensurate to the nature of the decision sought to be impugned will fail to comply with Article 13 requirements. Equally where the remedy of judicial review is incapable of performing functions required by the substantive ECHR right (e.g. assessing the proportionality of the impugned measure) Article 13 will be violated.[67] We return in more detail to the impact of Article 13 on the degree of scrutiny to be afforded on judicial review following the coming into force of the main provisions of the HRA 1998 below at 5.126 et seq.

Article 13—an effective remedy

5.81 The original and essentially fact-finding jurisdiction of the Adjudicator,[68]

---

[65] See also the related issue in EC law: opinion of A-G in *R v Secretary of State, ex parte Radiom and Shingara* ECJ [1997] ECR I-3341; the European Court cases are *Vilvarajah v UK* (1991) 14 EHRR 248; *Cruz Varas v Sweden* (1991) 14 EHRR 1; *Chahal v UK* (1997) 23 EHRR 413; *D v UK* (1997) 24 EHRR 423; *Lustig Prean v UK* (1999) 29 EHRR 548; *Bensaid v UK* [2001] INLR 325.

[66] See *R v Ministry of Defence ex parte Smith* [1996] QB 517; *R v Lord Saville ex parte A* [2000] 1 WLR 1855; *Bugdaycay v Secretary of State* [1987[AC 514.

[67] See *Lustig-Prean v UK* (1999) 29 EHRR 548; *Khan v UK* 8 BHRC 310; *Hatton v UK* (2002) 34 EHRR 1.

[68] See e.g. Hale LJ in *R v Secretary of State, ex parte Saleem* [2001] 1 WLR 443; *Husbadak* [1982] Imm AR 8; *R v IAT ex parte DS Abdi* [1996] Imm AR 148.

having seen and heard witnesses at an oral hearing where there is a right to legal representation, is consonant with the substance of the guarantees afforded by Article 13.

5.82 The suspensive effect of asylum and human rights appeals is also consistent with the requirement of effectiveness. The principle was recognized at common law in the case of *R v Secretary of State ex parte Canbolat* [1997] 1 WLR 1569; affirming [1997] Imm AR 281, one of the first 'third country' cases under the Asylum and Immigration Act 1996 regime which abolished in-country rights of appeal against third country certificates, leaving judicial review as the only in-country (and suspensive) remedy. The Secretary of State argued that since Parliament had legislated for a right of appeal (albeit one that could not be initiated or pursued in-country), the court should refuse relief in its discretion on the basis that the applicant had failed to exhaust an alternative statutory remedy. Lord Bingham CJ at first instance rejected the argument in the case itself, but nevertheless considered that the question of a discretionary withholding of relief should be considered on a case-by-case basis. On appeal in the Court of Appeal, however, Lord Woolf MR took a more robust view and held that the alternative remedy was non-suspensive, ineffective and could not afford a ground for withholding relief in third country judicial reviews.

5.83 The cases where the IAT has been anxious to preserve a role enabling it to examine the substance of the issue on its merits are wholly consistent with Article 13: thus the IAT has held that a non-compliance refusal still requires a merits consideration of the overall claim, rather than being restricted to a consideration of whether there was a failure to co-operate.[69]

CONCLUSIONS ON THE COMPATIBILITY OF DOMESTIC IMMIGRATION LAW WITH ARTICLES 6 AND 13

5.84 The foregoing survey of the procedural protection afforded by the common law and the Procedure Rules to immigrants demonstrates that in large measure, the requirements of Articles 6 and 13 are complied with.

5.85 We have seen that independence and impartiality,[70] absence of bias,[71] access to court[72] and funding, and natural justice,[73] the right to reasons (*R v IAT*

---

[69] See *Ali Haddad v Secretary of State* [2000] INLR 117.
[70] The Procedure Rules were initially laid under s. 22 of the IA 1971 by the Secretary of State; but they are now made by the Lord Chancellor.
[71] *Director-General of Fair Trading v Proprietary Association of Great Britain* [2001] 1 WLR 700.
[72] Public funding has for long been available for representation in immigration appeals, as well as for preparation; *R v Secretary of State, ex parte Saleem* [2001] 1 WLR 443.
[73] See *R v Secretary of State, ex parte Gunn* (22 January 1998, CO 4630/97); *R (Maheshwaran) v Secretary of State* [2001] EWHC Admin 562 (9 July 2001), on appeal: [2002] EWCA Civ 173.

ex parte Iqbal [1993] Imm AR 270; *R* v *IAT, ex parte Amin* [1992] Imm AR 367) are reflected in the common law or statute. Moreover, where there is a shortfall in the procedural protection provided by the procedure rules, the courts have been willing to imply fairness (*R* v *Special Adjudicator ex parte S* [1998] INLR 168) and in extreme cases declare a procedural rule ultra vires the rule-making power (*R* v *Secretary of State, ex parte Saleem* [2001] 1 WLR 443).

5.86 The courts have also held that Article 6 both as a matter of *de facto* practice[74] and arguably as a matter of hard law (*R* v *Secretary of State, ex parte Saleem* [2001] 1 WLR 443) applies to the system of immigration appeals and the importance of access to a hearing has informed decisions on the exercise of the Secretary of State's discretion under s. 21 of the IA 1971 to refer cases back to the appellate authority (*R* v *Secretary of State, ex parte Yousef* [2000] INLR 432).

5.87 Where there is no right of appeal and the remedy is judicial review, the courts have consistently required the Secretary of State to apply the requirements of fairness both in the asylum (*R* v *Secretary of State, ex parte Thirukumar* [1989] Imm AR 402; *R* v *Secretary of State, ex parte Gaima* [1989] Imm AR 205) and non-asylum (*R (Cakmak and Uluyol)* v *Immigration Officer* [2001] INLR 194) context by requiring the decision-maker to give immigrants notice of the matters currently going against them, an opportunity to be heard on those matters, and proper reasons once the decision is taken. The application of fair standards in the *decision-making process* as well as to the final decision reflects the principle that it may be more difficult for a person to overturn a concluded decision than it is to influence an on-going process.[75]

5.88 Given the above, we consider that Article 6 would not confer significantly greater procedural protection in the immigration sphere. Rather, the importance lies in providing a juridical basis to protect against incursions into the standards presently applied by the common law, and ensuring that present standards are maintained.

5.89 Thus Collins J stated in *MNM* v *Secretary of State* [2000] INLR 576 at para. 16 that:

> whether Article 6(1) applies or not will make little if any difference. The fact is that the IAA provides an independent and impartial tribunal established by law. The hearing is

---

[74] As long ago as 1979, in *Mustafa* v *Secretary of State* [1979–80] Imm AR 32 at pp. 37–8 the IAT held that the UK had accepted the principles set out in Article 6 long before it signed the ECHR. Tucker J said in *R* v *Secretary of State ex parte Jamil* [2000] IAR 55: 'I am bound to say that in my view the portions of (Article 6) which apply to the present case do no more than reflect what has been part of the common law in England for many years' and that Article 6 adds 'nothing to our already established practices.' See also Collins J in *MNM* v *Secretary of State* [2000] INLR 576.

[75] See *R* v *Home Secretary ex parte Hickey No. 2* [1995] 1 WLR 734 per Simon Brown LJ in another context; *R* v *SSHD ex parte Oladehinde* [1991] 1 AC 254.

in public and the procedures are designed to ensure that it is fair. If there is any unfairness, the Tribunal or the Court of Appeal[76] will correct it. Thus any complaints that the Special Adjudicator conducted an unfair hearing fall to be considered by us *and we apply the same tests as would be applicable if Article 6(1) applied.* The only advantage which Article 6(1) might confer is the requirement that the hearing be held within a reasonable time. That does not arise in this case and should not, unless some disaster occurs, arise in any case having regard to the timetables and procedures laid down by the Adjudicator and the Tribunal. (emphasis supplied)

5.90 As we have noted, the two areas where we consider there is a lacuna where Article 6 may make some difference are:

(a) the intensity of judicial review to questions of fact against decisions of the Secretary of State where appeal rights were excluded, in categories of immigration decisions such as businessmen or students which do not raise human rights, and where no or limited policy questions were engaged;

(b) the right to a hearing within a reasonable time (see above at 5.54 et seq).

5.91 The next issue is: what is the scope, in light of the judgment in *Maaouia* v *France* (2001) 33 EHRR 42 and the decision of the IAT in *MNM* v *Secretary of State*, for the argument that Article 6 should be held to apply domestically to the field of immigration. It is to this that we now turn.

ARTICLE 6(1): SCOPE REVISITED—THE DECISION IN *MAAOUIA* V *FRANCE* AND THE DOMESTIC POSITION

The road to *Maaouia* v *France*

5.92 In *Maaouia* v *France* (2001) 33 EHRR 42 the Court was for the first time seised with the question of whether a decision by a state in the immigration field attracted Article 6 safeguards. The European Commission had consistently applied to itself a self-denying ordinance on the imposition of Article 6 standards to administrative tribunals dealing with immigration matters across the Council of Europe states. In some early cases the European Commission appeared to indicate that Article 6 might apply if the right to respect for family life under Article 8 was at issue,[77] or if expulsion violated the right to education (*X* v *UK* (App. No. 7841/77)), but in later cases it held that the expulsion decision did not determine

---

[76] See, however, the judgment of Sedley LJ in *Macharia* v *Secretary of State* [2000] INLR 156 at para. 32 on the propriety of the Court of Appeal entertaining natural justice complaints: the better recourse is to judicial review where the court can receive evidence as to 'what happened'.

[77] See *X, Y, Z, V and W* v *UK* (1967) 25 CD 117; *Alam Khan and Singh* v *UK* (App. Nos. 2991 and 2992/66); see also *Singh Uppal and others* v *UK* (1980) 17 DR at pp. 149, 157.

the right to respect for family life (*X* v *UK* (App. No. 8971)). The European Commission also held that Article 6 did not apply to the right to apply for a passport (*Peltonnen* v *Finland* 84-A DR 129), the right to challenge a refusal of nationality status (*S* v *Switzerland* 59 DR 256) or political asylum,[78] the right to enter for employment (*X* v *UK* (1977) 9 DR 224 at p. 226) and confirmed that Article 6 did not apply to the right of an alien to challenge an expulsion decision,[79] even where a deportation leads to the loss of employment as a 'secondary and indirect result' (*Saleem* v *UK* (App. No. 38294/97, 4 March 1998)).

5.93 The European Commission also held that even where the immigration 'right' was founded in directly applicable provisions of EC law relating to rights of free movement,[80] the public nature of the right meant that Article 6 was excluded: *Adams and Benn* v *UK* (App. Nos. 28979/95 and 30343/96, 13 January 1997), noting the lack of personal, economic or individual aspects which are characteristic of the private law sphere. The decision is curious given the economic basis underlying the Treaty and the case law of the ECJ using Article 6 as a standard of fairness in EC law. Perhaps more plausibly, the European Commission held that the removal of an illegal entrant is not a disguised criminal penalty engaging criminal fair trial rights, since a determination of a breach of immigration law is not necessarily a criminal offence (*Zamir* v *UK* (1983) 5 EHRR 242).

5.94 In *JED* v *UK* (2 February 1999) the European Court considered a complaint that a failure to provide an appeal against a refusal of a renewed application for asylum following dismissal of a first claim violated Article 6. Instead of dismissing the application on the usual grounds that Article 6 simply did not apply, the European Court dismissed the case on the basis that judicial review was a sufficient remedy. This apparent change of emphasis was consistent with predictions that the European Court may adopt a more expansive approach to 'civil' rights which embraced immigration decisions.[81] These predictions were not to bear fruit.

The decision in *Maaouia* v *France*

5.95 Maaouia was a Tunisian national resident in France who failed to comply with a deportation order made against him. He was prosecuted and sentenced to one year's imprisonment and a 10-year exclusion order. Having successfully

---

[78] See *Slepecik Dezider* v *Netherlands* 86-A DR 176; *P* v *UK* 54 DR 211.

[79] See *Urrutikoetxea* v *France* App. No. 31113/96; 87 DR 151; *Agee* v *UK* App. No. 7729/64; 7 DR 164; *Omkaranda and Divine Light Zentrum* v *Switzerland* App. No. 8118/77; 25 DR 105; *Uppal* v *UK* (1979) 3 EHRR 391; see also *X, Y, Z, V and W* v *UK* (1967) 25 CD 117 at pp. 122–3.

[80] See Article 8A(1) EC Treaty, now EC Treaty (as amended by Treaty of Amsterdam) Article 18.

[81] P. Van Dijk, G. J. H. Van Hoof, *Theory and Practice of The European Convention on Human Rights* (Kluwer Law, 1998) p. 402.

challenged the underlying deportation order on the basis of marriage to a French national, the applicant applied for rescission of the exclusion order. The application for rescission was granted. The applicant brought proceedings in the European Court contending that the length of the proceedings had been unreasonable and in breach of Article 6(1).

5.96 The European Court noted that the concepts of 'civil rights and obligations' and 'criminal charge' had autonomous ECHR meanings.[82] However, in concluding that neither applied to the field of immigration, the European Court reasoned as follows:

(a)   It noted that the ECHR had to be construed holistically in the light of the entire ECHR system, including the Protocols: 'In that connection, the Court notes that Article 1 of Protocol No. 7, an instrument . . . which France has ratified, contains procedural guarantees applicable to the expulsion of aliens' and its preamble referred to the need to take 'further steps to ensure the collective enforcement of certain rights and freedoms by means of the Convention . . . .'. Taken together, those provisions showed that the states were aware that Article 6(1) did not apply to procedures for the expulsion of aliens and wished to take special measures in that sphere.

(b)   'The fact that the exclusion order incidentally had major repercussions on the applicant's private and family life or on his prospects of employment cannot suffice to bring those proceedings within the scope of civil rights protected by Article 6(1) of the Convention'.[83]

(c)   The European Court further considered that an exclusion order did not concern the determination of a criminal charge: 'the Court notes that, in general, exclusion orders are not characterised as criminal within the member States of the Council of Europe. Such orders, which in most States may also be made by the administrative authorities, constitute a special preventive measure for the purposes of immigration control and do not concern the determination of a criminal charge against the applicant for the purposes of Article 6(1). The fact that they are imposed in the context of criminal proceedings cannot alter their essentially preventive nature. It follows that proceedings for rescission of such measures cannot be regarded as being in the criminal sphere either'.[84]

---

[82] See *Konig* v *FRG* (1978) 2 EHRR 170.

[83] Cf, *mutatis mutandis*, the judgment in *Neigel* v *France* (17 March 1997), *Reports of Judgments and Decisions* 1997-II, pp. 410, 411, §§ 43, 44 and the judgment in *Maillard* v *France* (9 June 1998) *Reports* 1998-III, pp. 1303, 1304, §§ 39–41.

[84] Cf, *mutatis mutandis*, no. 32809/96, the former European Commission's decision of 26 February 1997.

(d)   However, in a concurring judgment, Judge Bratza held that the 'situation would be different if the order for deportation were made by a court following a conviction for a criminal offence and formed an integral part of the proceedings resulting in the conviction. In such a case, the procedural guarantees of Article 6 would clearly apply to the criminal proceedings as a whole, whether or not the deportation order which resulted was to be regarded as a penalty or having an exclusively preventative function. The same is true of the making of an exclusion order following the Applicant's conviction for refusing to comply with the deportation order made against him: the proceedings leading to imposition of the order were required to comply with Article 6 of the Convention, whether the order is to be regarded as a penalty or as essentially a preventative measure.'

5.97   The reasoning of the European Court in *Maaouia* v *France* (2001) 33 EHRR 42 is disappointing. However, as we have seen in the sections above, there is no reason to believe that Article 6 standards will not continue to inspire the development of the common law, where the UK has an established system of immigration appeals and a requirement of substantive and procedural fairness in their determination.

Analysis of *Maaouia* v *France*

5.98   On the first occasion that the European Court was called upon to consider whether Article 6 applied to the immigration sphere, the only reason given for the European Court's negative answer was the existence of Article 1 Protocol 7, demonstrative of state practice as to the applicability of Article 6. We would suggest that this is an unsatisfactory solution to the issue of procedural justice in immigration tribunals across Council of Europe states. As the dissenting judges, Judge Louciades and Judge Traja stated, the reference by the European Court to the former European Commission's jurisprudence 'without any analysis of the reasoning of such jurisprudence and the grounds for its adoption by the Court itself on a question on which the Court was expected to indicate its own legal approach is not by itself convincing'.

5.99   While state practice in the operation of a Treaty is a legitimate means of interpreting its terms,[85] it hardly seems appropriate to base a landmark decision exclusively on that footing, especially where the provisions of a Protocol were being used to support incursions on the protection afforded by Article 6.

5.100   Article 1 Protocol 7, which the UK has not ratified, provides as follows:

---

[85]   Vienna Convention 1969, Article 32; *Fothergill* v *Monarch Airlines* [1981] AC 251.

1. An alien lawfully resident in the territory of a State shall not be expelled therefrom except in pursuit of a decision reached in accordance with law and shall be allowed:

(a)   to submit reasons against his expulsion;
(b)   to have his case reviewed;
(c)   to be represented for these purposes before a competent authority or a person or persons designated by that authority;

2. An alien may be expelled before the exercise of his rights under paragraph 1(a), (b) and (c) of this Article, when such expulsion is necessary in the interests of public order or is grounded in reasons of national security.

5.101   The European Court's use of the Protocol to come to its decision in *Maaouia* is open to debate. First, the original aim of the Protocol was to 'insert as many as possible of the substantive provisions of the (ICCPR)'.[86] There is no reason why Protocol 7 could not be read as providing a minimum floor of rights in the determination of immigration public law cases without prejudice to the requirements of fairness in Article 6 being capable of application. Secondly, the Protocol only confers protection on 'lawfully resident' aliens. In contradiction to the ECHR scheme which requires terms such as 'law' to be given autonomous meaning, the domestic classification of 'lawfully' is determinative. Port applicants for asylum would be excluded. Thirdly, the 'minimum guarantees'[87] afforded are indeed minimal: while expulsion may only take place in 'accordance with law', domestic law is again exhaustive of 'law'. Fourthly, domestic law can govern the circumstances in which the rights in Article 1 are to be enjoyed. There is no requirement for review by a judicial organ: the competent authority may be the same as the original decision-taker. There is no right to an oral hearing, or to be present at any hearing, or to legal representation. The decision of the competent body need not be binding; a recommendation suffices. As to the exception in Article 1, paragraph 2, where the state grounds the exception on reasons of national security, 'this in itself should be accepted as sufficient justification',[88] a provision inconsistent with the supervisory system of the ECHR.

5.102   Thus the dissenting judges commented on the Protocol that:

(a)   Special provisions in a Protocol providing certain minimum procedural rights regarding persons who become the object of expulsion cannot reasonably be interpreted as limiting or derogating from any human rights and fundamental freedoms of those persons if such rights are already safeguarded by the Convention. Protocols add to the rights of the individual. They do not restrict or abolish them. Article 53 of the Convention provides that: '*Nothing in this*

---

[86] See the Explanatory Report on Protocol 7, Council of Europe, Strasbourg 1985, p. 5.
[87] See the Explanatory Report on Protocol 7, Council of Europe, Strasbourg 1985.
[88] ibid., p. 9.

Convention shall be construed as limiting or derogating from any of the human rights and fundamental freedoms which may be ensured under the laws of any High Contracting Party or under any other agreement to which it is a party'. In the light of that provision it would be strange to find that later additions to the Convention in the form of Protocols, which are part and parcel of the Convention, were intended to qualify or abolish rights which . . . were provided in the main body of the Convention.[89]

(b) The statement in the preamble to Protocol No. 7 regarding the decision to take 'further steps to ensure the collective enforcement of certain rights and freedoms by means of the Convention' cannot possibly mean that the procedural administrative guarantees in question were provided because the persons intended to benefit from them were not entitled to judicial guarantees in the assertion or determination of their rights and obligations. Both guarantees can coexist because they serve different purposes.

5.103 We have seen the decisive role played by state practice as divined by the existence of Article 1 Protocol 7 in the *Maaouia* decision. In addition to state practice, the drafting history of a Treaty is a permissible 'supplementary means of interpretation' where the ordinary meaning of the Treaty provision is not clear.[90] References to the *trauvaux préparatoires* are, in keeping with most decisions of the European Court on scope, conspicuously lacking in the majority decision in *Maaoiua*. Van Dijk and Van Hoof suggest, building on a seminal article by Newman[91] that the drafting history supports a broad meaning to be given to Article 6 and is inconsistent with the reduction of 'civil' to 'private',[92] which appears to be the driving force of the ECHR case law on the applicability of Article 6 in the civil sphere. While the term 'civil rights and obligations' is to be given an autonomous meaning, and domestic classification is not determinative, the European Court looks for objective indications of whether or not the right is a civil right. In doing so the practice of the European Court is effectively to

---

[89] Indeed the same reasoning technique relied upon by the UK government to argue that Article 8 did not apply in the field of immigration was rejected by the European Court in *Abdulaziz, Cabales and Balkandali v UK* (1985) 7 EHRR 471.

[90] Vienna Convention on the Law of Treaties 1969, Articles 31(1), 32.

[91] Newman, 'Natural Justice, Due Process and the New International Covenants on Human Rights: Prospectus' [1967] PL 274.

[92] Van Dijk, Van Hoof (above at footnote 81) pp. 392–3, 404. There is a strong indication 'that it was not the intention to restrict the scope of the right of access to court, apart from determinations of a criminal-law character, to determinations of rights and obligations of a private law character. On the contrary, one is struck by the fact that proposals which might imply the risk of such a restriction, were criticised for that reason and rejected or amended.' See also in particular Pieter Van Dijk, 'The interpretation of "civil rights and obligations" by the European Court of Human Rights—one more step to take' in Matscher and Petzold (eds) *Protecting Human Rights: The European Dimension, Studies in honour of Gerard J. Wiarda* (Kohn, Carl Heymanns Verlag KG, 1990), pp. 131 et seq. For a contrary view however, see Sir Vincent Evans, in his dissenting judgment in *Le Compte, Van Leuven and De Meyere v Belgium* (1981) 4 EHRR 1, 36, and the dissenting judgment in *König v Federal Republic of Germany* (1978) 2 EHRR 170 of Judge Matscher.

assimilate civil to 'private',[93] albeit that the European Court has stopped short of synonymizing the two adjectives.[94]

5.104   A perhaps more fundamental objection to the decision in *Maaioua* is its failure to promote the rule of law in the context of relations between a politically vulnerable class of individuals[95] in their dealings with a powerful state. The concept of the rule of law has a pervasive influence in the ECHR scheme: in *Klass* v *FRG* (1979–80) 2 EHRR 214 the European Court held that:

> The rule of law implies, *inter alia*, that an interference by the executive authorities with an individual's rights should be subject to an effective control which should normally be assured by the judiciary, at least in the last resort, judicial control offering the best guarantee of independence, impartiality and a proper procedure.

As the dissenting judges noted in *Maaoiua* (at p. 1052):

> It would be absurd to accept that the judicial safeguards were intended only for certain rights, particularly those between individuals, and not to any legal rights and obligations including those vis à vis the administration where an independent judicial control is especially required for the protection of the individuals against the powerful authorities of the State. In other words, it is inconceivable in a Convention which, according to its preamble, was intended to safeguard 'those fundamental freedoms which are the foundation of justice... in the world' and implement the principle of 'the rule of law'[96] to provide for a fair administration of justice only in respect of certain legal rights and obligations, but not in respect of rights concerning relations between the individual and Government.

---

[93] See *Ringgeisen* v *Austria (No 1)* (1971) 1 EHRR 455 at para. 94; *Schouten and Meldrum* v *Netherlands* (1994) 19 EHRR 432; *Ettl and others, Erkner and Hofauer and Poiss* v *Austria* (1988) 10 EHRR 255; the IAT in *MNM* adopted precisely such an assimilation of private to civil: [2000] INLR 576 paras. 14 and 15.

[94] See e.g. *Feldbrugge* v *Netherlands* (1986) 8 EHRR 425 at para. 27: 'Court does not consider that it has to give on this occasion an abstract definition'; *Konig* v *FRG* (1978) 2 EHRR 170 at para. 195: not necessary 'in the present case to decide whether the concept . . . extends beyond those rights which have a private nature . . .': *Le Compte, Van Leuven and De Meyere* v *Belgium* (1981) 4 EHRR 1 at para. 48.

[95] The approach of the US Supreme Court has been to guard certain rights jealously such as free speech and the rights of 'discrete and insular minorities': Stone J in *US* v *Carolene Products Co.* 304 US 144 (1938) at pp. 152, 153, n. 4. See further Rabinder Singh, 'The Place of the Human Rights Act in a Democratic Society' in J. Jowell and J. Cooper (eds.) *Understanding Human Rights Principles* (Hart Publishing, 2001), noting that sometimes there is a systemic failure in democracies in promoting or protecting the rights of certain groups, and observing that the primary group of litigants against the UK before the European Court have been immigrants or potential immigrants.

[96] *Golder* v *UK* (1979–80) 1 EHRR 524; *Klass* v *Federal Republic of Germany* (1979–80) 2 EHRR 214.

5.105 The failure to promote the rule of law in this context is perhaps even more surprising given the view that the meaning of the words 'determination of his civil rights and obligations' was considered vague from inception, allowing for creative interpretation and 'judicial policy',[97] and the subsequent case-law has been considered 'vague and unclear'.[98]

5.106 The European Court has liberally interpreted the rights found in Article 6 so as to read into its provisions ancillary rights such as the right of access to the courts (*Golder* v *UK* (1979–80) 1 EHRR 524) and had held that there was no warrant for a restrictive interpretation given the central importance of the Article in the ECHR scheme (*Delcourt* v *Belgium* (1970) 1 EHRR 355). However, by excluding immigration from the concept of civil rights it has in fact restrictively construed the term. This was even more surprising given that the trend of the European Court had been to include more and more situations within the term 'civil rights and obligations', even though such situations could not easily be explained by reference to the criterion of private law. The dissenting judges in *Maaouia* considered that the reasoning and distinctions reached in those cases appeared 'artificial'.

5.107 The minority also considered that the term 'civil' when examined in the context in which it appears, did no more than denote 'non-criminal': 'once the term "criminal charge" had been used, inevitably for technical reasons, another term intended to cover the rest of the adjudicative procedures distinguishing them from the criminal procedures, would have also to be used'.[99]

5.108 The *Maaoiua* judgment is contrary to the prediction of Van Dijk and Van Hoof that 'In view of the Court's very extensive interpretation of "civil rights and obligations" in disputes of an administrative character, it would seem to be doubtful that it will follow the Commission in its restrictive approach'.[100] They consider that 'the most satisfactory way to end legal uncertainty and maximise effective legal protection is to recognise that [Article 6(1)] is applicable to all cases in which a determination by a public authority of the legal position of a private party is at stake, regardless of whether the rights and obligations involved are of a private character.'[101]

---

[97] Van Dijk and Van Hoof (above at footnote 81) p. 392, citing the submission of Fawcett in *Konig* v *FRG* (1978) 2 EHRR 170: 'There is no obvious demonstration of what the purpose and scope of Article 6 really is. I submit that there are choices here of judicial policy on the part of the Court in the interpretation of Article 6'.

[98] Pieter Van Dijk 'The interpretation of "civil rights and obligations" by the European Court of Human Rights—one more step to take' (above at footnote 92) p. 133.

[99] Van Dijk and Van Hoof (above at footnote 81) p. 392.

[100] ibid. at p. 402.

[101] ibid. at p. 406.

The potential for the applicability of Article 6 to immigration in domestic law

5.109 Whether or not the decision in *Maaouia* proves durable at the international level, we suggest there is no reason why it should require a domestic court to exclude immigration from the scope of Article 6.

5.110 First, the European Court as an international court may be reluctant to impose unattainably high standards on differing administrative law systems amongst Council of Europe states. This as we have seen is hardly the position in the UK. The threadbare provisions of Article 1 Protocol 7 bear little resemblance to the established level of procedural protection given to immigrants by the common law. We suggest that the logic of the inapplicability of the margin of appreciation to a purely internal situation promotes a result that Article 6 should apply to immigration. This is surely an example of the situation contemplated by the Lord Chancellor in stating:

> The Courts will often be faced with cases that involve factors perhaps specific to the United Kingdom which distinguish them from cases considered by the [European Court].[102]

5.111 Secondly, there already is the Court of Appeal authority of *R* v *Secretary of State, ex parte Saleem* [2001] 1 WLR 443 which indicates that Article 6 in substance applies to immigration *appeals*: '. . . if the State establishes such a right (of appeal) it must ensure that people within its jurisdiction enjoy the fundamental guarantees in Article 6' (at p. 458). In the starred Tribunal case of *MNM* v *Secretary of State* [2000] INLR 576 Collins J considered that this was the de facto position (other than with respect to the right to a hearing within a reasonable time), but was not prepared to hold that Article 6 formally applied to immigration appeals. The basis of this decision was that immigration rights were not private law rights, and the distinction drawn between public and private law rights was fundamental to the issue. We have seen above at 5.103 that there is a certain artificiality of approach in the erection of such a distinction, and its use appears not to be supported by the *trauvaux préparatoires*. Further the Tribunal was not, it appears, referred to the important dicta of Hale LJ in *Saleem*.

5.112 Thirdly, the distinction between a civil right as distinct from an administrative law right is unfamiliar to the common law. Commentators have traditionally regarded the distinction between ordinary private law and public law as

---

[102] Lord Irvine LC, 19 January 1998, Hansard, HL, vol. 484, cols. 1270, 1271; Francesca Klug, 'The Human Rights Act 1998, *Pepper* v *Hart* and All That' [1999] PL 246, 251–2.

incompatible with the basic assumptions of the common law.[103] It does not map across to the public/private divide known to the domestic courts (*O'Reilly* v *Mackman* [1983] 2 AC 287). Richards J writing extra-judicially[104] has said that:

> The precise basis for the distinction between public law and private law (for Article 6 purposes) is not wholly clear and it is difficult to know where precisely the dividing line is to be drawn and whether the line is still moving . . . The domestic courts will have to decide how to apply and *to develop* the existing Convention case law on this subject. The lack of symmetry between the Convention concepts and existing domestic law concepts of private law and public law may occasion some difficulty.[105]

5.113 Moreover distributing procedural protection according to a fact-insensitive criterion, namely whether it is a civil right, rather than on the basis of the individual factors present in the situation is anathema to the common law.[106] It harks back to distinctions between administrative and judicial acts which are now considered outmoded given the recognition that administrative tribunals will often determine issues of great moment to the individual and that a commensurately demanding level of fairness will be required of them (*R* v *Secretary of State, ex parte Saleem* [2001] 1 WLR 443).

5.114 Thus it is potentially unreal and illusory to say that Article 6 does not apply to immigration whilst simultaneously acknowledging that under the common law, asylum and family life immigration decisions attract the most anxious scrutiny and the highest standards of fairness.[107] The other side of the same argument is that under the European Court's case law Article 6 applies to improve the procedural safeguards available in, for example, the planning context (*Alconbury and others* v *Secretary of State for the Environment, Transport and the Regions* [2001] 2 WLR 1389) but does not apply where issues of at least comparable gravity are concerned in the immigration context.

5.115 Fourthly, there is the anomaly that while Article 6 safeguards would be available to an immigrant for the determination by an appeals tribunal or by a

---

[103] Dicey, A. V., *Introduction to the Study of the Law of the Constitution* (8th edn, 1915) (Liberty Classics Reprint, 1987) p. 256; Allison, J., *A Continental Distinction in the Common Law: A Historical and Comparative Perspective on English Public Law* (1996). See the comprehensive and insightful contribution by Herberg, J., Le Seur, A. and Mulcahy, J., 'Determining Civil Rights and Obligations' in J. Jowell and J. Cooper (eds.) *Understanding Human Rights Principles* (Hart Publishing, 2001).

[104] 'The Impact of Article 6 of the ECHR on Judicial Review' [1999] JR 106, 107 (emphasis supplied).

[105] See further Harris, D. J., Warbrick, C. and O'Boyle, M., *Law of the European Convention on Human Rights* (Butterworths, 1994) pp. 174–86.

[106] See e.g. Janis, Kay and Bradley, *European Human Rights Law* (Oxford, 2000) 418.

[107] *Bugdaycay* v *Secretary of State* [1987] AC 514; *R* v *IAT ex parte Omar Ali* [1995] Imm AR 45; *Thirukumar* [1989] Imm AR 402; *R* v *Secretary of State ex parte Gaima* [1989] Imm AR 205.

Social Security Commissioner of social security entitlement,[108] or to determinations by the Asylum Support Adjudicators under Part VI of the IAA 1999,[109] the dominant issue of immigration status would not attract such safeguards.

5.116   Fifthly, the mode of patriation of the ECHR may give rise to the conclusion that Article 6 applies in the immigration context. An immigration decision in the UK after 1 October 2000 gives rise not only to pecuniary consequences parasitically on the immigration decision, but directly. This is because s. 6 of the HRA 1998 may be seen as constituting a private right, namely a statutory tort, breach of which sounds in damages under s. 8 of the HRA 1998 (see s. 9).

5.117   The European Court's case law on the issue of social security and welfare benefits and contributions is illuminating. In *Feldbrugge* v *Netherlands* (1996) 8 EHRR 425, a case concerning the statutory sick pay allowance, the European Court noted that in Dutch law the right was classified as 'public', but having conducted a balancing exercise held that the private law features were dominant: the personal and economic nature of the right, the close connection with the employment contract and the analogies with insurance. The European Court found determinative the fact that 'the Applicant was claiming an individual economic right flowing from specific rules laid down in statute'. The welfare and social insurance cases[110] decided subsequently are significant: the European Court considered Article 6 applied even though the pecuniary entitlements were non-contributory and non-employment related, depending wholly upon a statutory basis. A pecuniary element to the claim is a pointer to the civil character of the right.[111]

5.118   Thus Article 6 will apply if the effect of the decision is directly to affect civil rights and obligations. In *Le Compte, Van Leuven and De Meyere* v *Belgium* (1981) 4 EHRR 1 the court observed (at para. 46):

---

[108] *Salesi* v *Italy* (1996) 16 EHRR 187; *Feldbrugge* v *Netherlands* (1986) 8 EHRR 425.

[109] This is perhaps more arguable given the non-means tested nature of the benefit, but see *R (Husain)* v *Asylum Support Adjudicator and Secretary of State* (5 October 2001), *The Times*, 15 November 2001.

[110] See e.g. *Salesi* v *Italy* (1993) 26 EHRR 187; *Schuler-Zgraggen* v *Switzerland* (1993) 26 EHRR 405.

[111] See *Ortenburg* v *Austria* (1994) 19 EHRR 524 para. 28; *Tinnelly and McElduff* v *UK* (1998) 27 EHRR 249 (claim under anti-discrimination law is civil right since decision might result in financial benefit to the applicant). *Werner* v *Austria* (1997) 26 EHRR 310, para. 347: 'For a right to be a 'civil' one it is *sufficient* that the subject-matter of the action should be pecuniary and that the action should be founded on an alleged infringement of rights which are likewise pecuniary rights'. Note however the dicta of the European Court that a pecuniary element may not be sufficient: *Schouten and Meldrum* (1994) 19 EHRR 432, para. 57; *Pierre-Bloch* para. 51; *Pellegrin* v *France* para. 60.

it must be shown that the 'contestation' (dispute) related to 'civil rights and obligations', in other words that the 'result of the proceedings' was 'decisive' for such a right.

But it must have a direct effect of deciding rights or obligations. The court continued (at para. 47):

> As regards the question whether the dispute related to the above-mentioned right, the court considers that a tenuous connection or remote consequences do not suffice for Article 6 (1) in either of its official versions ('contestation sur'; 'determination of'): civil rights and obligations must be the object—or one of the objects—of the 'contestation' (dispute): the result of the proceedings must be directly decisive for such a right.[112]

5.119   Winfield's classic definition of the law of tort is as follows:

> Tortious liability arises from the breach of a duty primarily fixed by the law; such duty is towards persons generally and its breach is redressible by an action for unliquidated damages.[113]

While a tort is classically considered to be a wrong at common law,[114] the qualification arising from EC law which contemplates actions for damages for breach in certain circumstances (e.g. *Garden Cottage Foods* v *Milk Marketing Board* [1984] AC 130), apply equally in our view to the provisions of the HRA 1998: damages for breach are available consequent on the breach of the right.

5.120   Given the modern approach to questions of procedural exclusivity exemplified in *Boddington* v *BT Police* [1992] 2 AC 143—a public law challenge may be ventilated in private law proceedings—there is a cogent argument that wherever damages are sought, Article 6 should apply. This principle is not required in the appellate authority, where damages cannot be sought and resort would have to be had to the county court, given the dicta of Hale LJ in *R* v *Secretary of State, ex parte Saleem* [2001] 1 WLR 443. A judicial review application for a breach of an ECHR right contemplates an action for damages, and proceedings for damages in administrative proceedings have attracted the application of Article 6 in the European Court.[115] The enforcement by a victim of the statutory duty in s. 6 of the HRA 1998 not to infringe an ECHR obligation is a civil right.

---

[112] Followed in *Sporrong and Lönnroth* v *Sweden* (1982) 5 EHRR 35 para. 80.

[113] Winfield, *Province of the Law of Tort* (1931), p. 32.

[114] See e.g. *Banque Bruxelles Lambert SA* v *Eagle Star Insurance Co. Ltd* [1997] AC 191 where Lord Hoffman defined a tort as a breach of a non-contractual duty which gave a private law right to the party injured to recover damages at common law from the party causing the injury.

[115] See *Baraona* (1987) A122; *Neves e Silva* (1989) A153; *H* v *France* (1992) A162A; *Editions Periscope* (1992) A234-B; *Scopelliti* (1993) A 278; *Zimmerman and Steiner* (1983) A 66 p. 10.

5.121 Further support for this proposition is given by the decision of Turner J in *R* v *Secretary of State, ex parte Quaquah* [2000] INLR 196 where the Secretary of State's decision to remove an immigrant was quashed owing to his failure to consider properly the claimant's rights to a fair trial under Article 6 in relation to his pending civil litigation against the Home Office and its private detention contractor, Group 4. There the nexus between the purported act of expulsion and the tort was far less direct than the situation we contend for here: given the absence of a general tort of maladministration in English law, there was no question in *Quaquah* that the impropriety of the purported immigration decision would or could *itself* sound in damages. While of course *Quaquah* did not decide that the immigration procedures themselves were subject to Article 6 guarantees, Article 6 applied to the consequences of the immigration decision and therefore had to be properly considered by the Secretary of State. The effect of the HRA 1998 we suggest is to effectively 'concertina' the position: where the consequences of the immigration decision can *without more* result in a pecuniary award on the basis of a breach of s. 6 of the HRA 1998, and where that action for damages can be pleaded *simultaneously* with the challenge to the immigration decision, Article 6 safeguards should be held to apply.

5.122 Sixthly, quite apart from the *direct* pecuniary consequences of a breach of a human right in the immigration realm, rights to liberty and family life will typically be engaged. In Sir Robert Walker's view Article 6 would make little difference to the *R* v *Secretary of State for Social Security, ex parte Joint Council for the Welfare of Immigrants* [1997] 1 WLR 275 kind of case (concerning access to court) since immigration decisions are one of the 'likely no-go areas'. It is interesting to note that this view (a) was couched in tentative terms, with the qualification that this would be the case 'at any rate where there is no strong family element founding an argument on Article 8 of the Convention'[116] and (b) was impliedly predicated on the strength of the common law.

5.123 Seventhly, immigration decisions clearly constitute the determination of a 'right'.[117] Whilst in some systems, the field of immigration is entirely within the discretion of the relevant Ministry, in the UK there are criteria governing the entitlement to leave set out in the Immigration Rules, and in published instructions and policies in extra-rule cases which govern the Secretary of State's residual discretion under s. 4 of the IA 1971.[118] The Immigration Rules have the force

---

[116] 'Opinion: The Impact of European Standards on the Right to a Fair Trial in Civil Proceedings in UK Domestic Law' [1999] EHRLR 4, 7.

[117] See *Masson and Van Zon* v *Netherlands* (1996) 22 EHRR 491; *Georgiadis* v *Greece* (1997) 24 EHRR 606.

[118] The issue of whether extra-rule applications fall under the prerogative or under statutory powers conferred by the IA 1971 is yet to be authoritatively resolved, but see the submission of David Pannick QC for the Secretary of State in *Adan* v *Secretary of State* [1999] 1 AC 293 at 301.

of law given the appellate jurisdiction to allow an appeal where the decision is not in accordance with the law (IAA 1999, Sch. 4, para. 21), and policies will give rise to legitimate expectations and in appropriate cases confer substantive benefits.[119] Perhaps the one area where the status of an immigration entitlement may not unequivocally qualify as a right is the situation concerning naturalization as a British citizen: here the criteria spelt out in the British Nationality Act 1981 are necessary[120] but not sufficient conditions, with the ultimate decision resting with the Secretary of State in exercise of his residual discretion. Judicial review is ousted. But even here, the Court of Appeal held in *R* v *Secretary of State ex parte Fayed* [1997] 1 All ER 228 that the requirements of natural justice apply and that the Secretary of State must give notice to the applicant of the factors militating against him before the decision is made, notwithstanding the purported ouster clause in s. 44(2) of the British Nationality Act 1981. The overriding point, amply demonstrated by the *Fayed* decision, however, is the often stated view that in English law there is probably no such thing as an unfettered discretion,[121] and the distinction between rights and privileges in English law has not been valid[122] since *Ridge* v *Baldwin* [1964] AC 40 and *Re HK* [1967] 2 QB 617.

5.124 We have seen in chapter 3 that Article 6 safeguards apply to immigration detention, and it is clear that they apply to proceedings where a recommendation for deportation is made by a criminal court following a determination of guilt.[123] Moreover in the national security context, the Special Immigration Appeals Act 1997 was enacted following the judgment of the European Court that the 'advisory' panel procedure violated Article 5(4) which, as we have seen, attracts the protection afforded by Article 6—and there is a growing acceptance that the right to liberty is a civil right: *Aerts* v *Belgium* (2000) 29 EHRR 50. In *Secretary of State for the Home Department* v *A* [2002] EWCA Civ 1502 it was decided that a challenge to immigration detention involved the determination of a civil right.

5.125 We have also seen that the application of Article 6 to the immigration sphere is unlikely to have significant repercussions for domestic law. We suggest that given the developed system of protection afforded domestically, which contrasts with the position across Europe, there is no reason why Article 6 should

---

[119] See *R* v *North and East Devon Health Authority ex parte Coughlan* [2000] WLR 622, 645; *Montana* v *Secretary of State* [2001] 1 WLR 552. See the IAT decisions on the long residence policies, e.g. *Odozi* v *Secretary of State* (9582); *Umujakprone* v *Secretary of State* (12448).

[120] i.e. necessary in the absolute sense: there is no discretion in the Secretary of State to waive them.

[121] Wade and Forsyth, *Administrative Law* (Oxford) approved in *R* v *Tower Hamlets LBC ex parte Chetnik Developments Ltd* [1988] AC 858, 872; the key consideration is whether the relevant discretion is governed by 'recognised administrative and legal principles': *Allan Jacobsen* v *Sweden* (1989) 12 EHRR 56 at para. 69.

[122] See de Smith, Woolf and Jowell, *Judicial Review of Administrative Action* (Sweet & Maxwell, 1995) para. 7-029.

[123] See the concurring opinion of Bratza J in *Maaoiua* v *France* (2001) 33 EHRR 42.

not be held to apply to immigration. The policy concerns of imposing an over-demanding and rigid regime of procedural protection carry little weight in the sphere of immigration: the domestic protection afforded already approximates to Article 6 standards, the appellate machinery attracts Article 6, and the requirements of Article 6 are themselves flexible according to the subject matter of the dispute, the nature of the inferior decision-making process, and the desired grounds of appeal.

JUDICIAL REVIEW AND ARTICLE 13

5.126 We have seen above at 5.74 et seq that the question of the compatibility of judicial review with Article 13 has been a live issue at the European Court. The position, as decided by the Court of Appeal in *R* v *Secretary of State, ex parte Turgut* [2000] 1 All ER 719 in a pre-HRA 1998 case, is that an enhanced *Wednesbury* approach to decisions engaging human rights will comply with Article 13. The court need not adopt the role of the primary fact finder in order to adhere to Article 13 requirements. Whether this will be the position on judicial review in Article 3 cases brought under the HRA 1998 remains to be seen.[124] There may be scope at least in domestic law for the proposition that $3 + 13 = 6$. We now consider the impact of Article 13 in more detail.

5.127 The starting point in the case law of the European Court is *Soering* v *UK* (1989) 11 EHRR 439, a case concerning a West German national who had unsuccessfully challenged the Home Secretary's decision to extradite him to the USA to face trial in Virginia for capital murder, a trial which could expose him to the so-called 'death row phenomenon'. The complaint to the European Court succeeded under Article 3 but failed under Article 13. At paragraph 121 of its judgment, the European Court said:

> According to the United Kingdom Government, a court would have jurisdiction to quash a challenged decision to send a fugitive to a country *where it was established that there was a serious risk of inhuman or degrading treatment*, on the ground that in all the circumstances of the case the decision was one that no reasonable Secretary of State could take. Although the Convention is not considered to be part of United Kingdom law, the Court is satisfied that the English courts can review the 'reasonableness' of an extradition decision in the light of the kind of factors relied on by Mr Soering before the Convention institutions in the context of Article 3. (emphasis supplied)

---

[124] See *Rehman* v *Secretary of State* [2001] 3 WLR 877; see Introduction to this book; and see M. J. Beloff QC [2001] 6(3) JR 154–60.

5.128 *Soering* was followed and applied in *Vilvarajah* v *UK* (1991) 14 EHRR 248. This case concerned five Tamils who were refused asylum in the UK and returned to Sri Lanka but who, following return, continued to suffer ill-treatment. Their complaints to the European Court were rejected under both Articles 3 and 13.

5.129 The European Court described its adjudicative role in the context of Article 3 as follows (at para. 108):

> The court's examination of the existence of a risk of ill-treatment in breach of Article 3 at the relevant time must necessarily be a rigorous one in view of the absolute character of this provision and the fact that it enshrines one of the fundamental values of a democratic society making up the Council of Europe

5.130 As to Article 13 the European Court concluded:

> 125. It is not in dispute that the English courts are able in asylum cases to review the Secretary of State's refusal to grant asylum with reference to the same principles of judicial review as considered in the *Soering* case and to quash a decision in similar circumstances and that they have done so in decided cases. Indeed the courts have stressed their special responsibility to subject administrative decisions in this area to the most anxious scrutiny where an applicant's life or liberty may be at risk. Moreover, the practice is that an asylum seeker will not be removed from the UK until proceedings are complete once he has obtained leave to apply for judicial review.

> 126. While it is true that there are limitations on the powers of the courts in judicial review proceedings the Court is of the opinion that these powers, exercisable as they are by the highest tribunals in the land, do provide an effective degree of control over the decisions of the administrative authorities in asylum cases and are sufficient to satisfy the requirements of Article 13.

5.131 *Chahal* v *UK* (1997) 23 EHRR 413 concerned a Sikh separatist leader who was refused asylum and whom the Secretary of State proposed to deport to India as a threat to national security in the UK. Following the failure of his judicial review challenge, *Chahal* succeeded at the European Court under both Articles 3 and 13. The European Court described its own evaluative role in Article 3 cases as follows (at para. 96):

> Indeed, in cases such as the present the *Court's examination of the existence of a real risk of ill-treatment must necessarily be a rigorous one,* in view of the absolute character of Article 3 and the fact that it enshrines one of the fundamental values of the democratic societies making up the Council of Europe. (emphasis supplied)

5.132 With regard to Article 13 the European Court said this:

> 150. It is true, as the Government have pointed out, that in the cases of *Klass and Others* v *Germany* and *Leander* v *Sweden*, the Court held that Article 13 only required

a remedy that was 'as effective as can be' in circumstances where national security considerations did not permit the divulging of certain sensitive information. However, it must be borne in mind that these cases concerned complaints under Articles 8 and 10 of the Convention and that their examination required the Court to have regard to the national security claims which had been advanced by the Government. The requirements of a remedy which is 'as effective as can be' is not appropriate in respect of a complaint that a person's deportation will expose him or her to a real risk of treatment in breach of Article 3, where the issues concerning national security are immaterial.

151. In such cases, given the irreversible nature of the harm that might occur if the risk of ill-treatment materialised and the importance the Court attaches to Article 3, *the notion of an effective remedy under Article 13 requires independent scrutiny of the claim that there exist substantial grounds for fearing a real risk of treatment contrary to Article 3.* This scrutiny must be carried out without regard to what the person may have done to warrant expulsion or to any perceived threat to the national security of the expelling State.

152. Such scrutiny need not be provided by a judicial authority but, if it is not, the powers and guarantees which it affords are relevant in determining whether the remedy before it is effective.

153. In the present case, neither the advisory panel nor the courts could review the decision of the Home Secretary to deport Mr Chahal to India with reference solely to the question of risk, leaving aside national security considerations. On the contrary, the courts' approach was one of satisfying themselves that the Home Secretary had balanced the risk to Mr Chahal against the danger to national security. It follows from the above considerations that these cannot be considered effective remedies in respect of Mr Chahal's Article 3 complaint for the purposes of Article 13 of the Convention. (emphasis supplied)

5.133   The next case to examine the issue was *D* v *UK* (1997) 24 EHRR 423, the case of an AIDS sufferer whom the Secretary of State proposed to return to St Kitts as a refused applicant for leave to enter the UK. D's complaint (like Soering's) succeeded under Article 3 but not under Article 13. As to Article 13 the European Court noted that:

70. In its *Vilvarajah and Others* judgment and its *Soering* judgment the Court considered judicial review proceedings to be an effective remedy in relation to the complaints raised under Article 3 in the contexts of deportation and extradition. It was satisfied that English courts could effectively control the legality of executive discretion on substantive and procedural grounds and quash decisions as appropriate. It was also accepted that a court in the exercise of its powers of judicial review would have power to quash a decision to expel or deport an individual to a country *where it was established that there was a serious risk of inhuman or degrading treatment, on the ground that in all the circumstances of the case the decision was one that no reasonable Secretary of State could take.*

. . .

72. The applicant maintained that the effectiveness of the remedy invoked first before the High Court and subsequently before the Court of Appeal was *undermined on account of their failure to conduct an independent scrutiny of the facts in order to determine whether they disclosed a real risk that he would be exposed to inhuman and degrading treatment.* He relied on the reasoning in the Chahal v United Kingdom *judgment.* However the Court notes that in that case the domestic courts were precluded from reviewing the factual basis underlying the national security considerations invoked by the Home Secretary to justify the expulsion of Mr Chahal. No such considerations arise in the case at issue. (emphasis supplied)

5.134 Here the European Court was stating that judicial review is an effective remedy if it has the capacity to ask the correct questions. It is irrelevant that the particular court failed to ask it. But equally, it is hardly encouraging for the domestic court that the European Court in *D* v *UK* found a violation of this fundamental human right, where the Court of Appeal could not even see an arguable case fit for the grant of leave to appeal.

5.135 The European Court revisited the issue in the different non-immigration context of *Smith, Grady, Beckett and Lustig-Prean* v *UK* [1999] IRLR 734 the well-known case concerning the expulsion of homosexuals from the army. The complaint succeeded under Article 8, and under Article 13. At paragraph 138 of the judgment the Court of Human Rights said:

> In such circumstances, the Court considers it clear that, even assuming that the essential complaints of the applicants before this Court were before and considered by the domestic courts, *the threshold at which the High Court and the Court of Appeal could find the Ministry of Defence policy irrational was placed so high that it effectively excluded any consideration by the domestic courts of the question of whether the interference with the applicants' rights answered a pressing social need or was proportionate to the national security and public order aims pursued, principles which lie at the heart of the Court's analysis of complaints under Article 8 of the Convention.*
>
> The present applications can be contrasted with the cases of *Soering* and *Vilvarajah* cited above. In those cases, the Court found that the test applied by the domestic courts in applications for judicial review of decisions by the Secretary of State in extradition and expulsion *matters coincided with the Court's own approach under Article 3 of the Convention.* (emphasis supplied)[125]

---

[125] The basis for the distinction (as subsequently elucidated—see *Hilal* and *Bensaid,* and the Court of Appeal's decision in *Turgut,* below at 5.137 et seq) namely that *Soering* and *Vilvarajah* were Article 3 cases, while *Smith, Grady* etc concerned Article 8 has been criticized by M. Hunt, 'The European Convention on Human Rights', [1999–2000] YEL 531 as hardly amounting to a persuasive reason. The author continues that 'In effect the Court has finally found that judicial review is not, after all, an effective remedy for the purposes of Article 13, because the approach which courts take to assessing the justification for an interference with a Convention right is too deferential, and prevents them from properly considering the questions of proportionality which a proper Convention analysis requires.'

5.136   At paragraph 38 of its judgment the Court of Human Rights commented on the approach taken in the Court of Appeal by Sir Thomas Bingham MR as follows:

> He observed that to dismiss a person from his or her employment on the grounds of a private sexual preference, and to interrogate him or her about private sexual behaviour, would not appear to show respect for that person's private and family life *and that there might be room for argument as to whether the policy answered a 'pressing social need' and, in particular, was proportionate to the legitimate aim pursued. However, he held that these were not questions to which answers could be properly or usefully proffered by the Court of Appeal but rather were questions for the European Court of Human Rights, to which court the applicants might have to pursue their claim.* (emphasis supplied)

5.137   The Court of Appeal in *R* v *Secretary of State, ex parte Turgut* [2000] 1 All ER 719 considered these cases. It interpreted the first limb of para. 138 in *Smith, Grady* etc as follows:

> In effect the ECHR were saying in the first part of paragraph 138: it is all very well to say that 'the more substantial the interference with human rights, the more the court will require by way of justification before it is satisfied that the decision is reasonable'; *if, however, the domestic court is prepared to regard a policy as justifiable whether or not it answers a pressing social need or is proportionate to the aims pursued, then this approach (the Smith approach) accords insufficient weight to interference with human rights.* It is plain that by October 2000, the threshold of irrationality will have to be lowered in cases of that sort.

5.138   The Court of Appeal then considered the second limb of para. 138 of *Smith, Grady* etc. The appellant's argument in *Turgut* was that 'The Court's own approach under Article 3 of the Convention' (see the concluding words of para. 138) was that set out in para. 108 of its judgment in *Vilvarajah* v *UK* (1991) and in paras. 95 to 97 of its judgment in *Chahal* v *UK* (1997): *the ECHR will rigorously examine all the material before it and make its own assessment of risk as at the date of the hearing.* That, therefore, must be the approach required of the domestic court too: only thus will it have 'coincided with' the ECHR's approach (as para. 138 states that it does) and so explain why the European Court regards judicial review as an 'effective remedy' in Article 3 cases (save, of course, in *Chahal* v *UK* (1997) where the national security aspect of the case precluded the domestic courts from forming their own view upon it), but not in a case like *Smith, Grady et al* itself.

5.139   The Court of Appeal concluded as follows ([2001] 1 All ER 719 at 727–8):

Plausible though this argument appears, in my judgment it reads too much into paragraph 138. As the cited passages from the court's judgments show, the ECHR knows full well the nature of the judicial review process and cannot be thought to suppose that the reviewing court ever adopts the role of primary fact finder. It is one thing to say that an administrative decision to deport will be rigorously examined and subjected to the most anxious scrutiny: quite another to say that the court will form its own independent view of the facts which will then necessarily prevail over whatever view has been formed by the Secretary of State.

Where, therefore, the Court in *Soering, Vilvarajah* and *D* speaks of the domestic court in judicial review having the power to quash a decision 'where it was established that there was a serious risk of inhuman or degrading treatment', that can only mean 'where it was established that on any reasonable view of the facts there was a serious risk of inhuman or degrading treatment,' i.e. where it was established that no rational Secretary of State could have reached a different conclusion upon the material in the case.

. . .

I therefore conclude that the domestic court's obligation on an irrationality challenge in an Article 3 case is to subject the Secretary of State's decision to rigorous examination, and this it does by considering the underlying factual material for itself to see whether or not it compels a different conclusion to that arrived at by the Secretary of State. Only if it does will the challenge succeed.

5.140 The Court of Appeal's interpretation of the European Court's case law on Article 13 focuses on the functional capability of the judicial review court to perform the tasks required by the ECHR, rather than insisting on the adoption of an original factual jurisdiction to determine whether (in an Article 3 case) substantial grounds for the prohibited treatment have been established. It is because the judicial review court in *Chahal* v *UK* (1997) was unable to review the factual basis of the national security complaint that Article 13 was breached; and it was because the judicial review court in *Smith, Grady et al* could not examine questions of proportionality and legitimate aim that a violation was found. This accords with the principle that the focus under Article 13 is on the *capability* of the remedy to examine the substance of the complaint and afford redress, rather than deliver redress in the particular instance. It is thus not a precondition of an effective remedy that the challenge succeed domestically, even if at the European Court the substance of the complaint is allowed (*Vilvarajah* v *UK* (1991) 14 EHRR 248, para. 122). This paradox perhaps explains why the European Court desists from requiring the judicial review court to adopt an original fact finding jurisdiction, even though the European Court itself considers that its role is to examine the factual material for itself, and if necessary, substitute its assessment of risk (in an Article 3 case) for that of the respondent government. But the cases in which a breach of a substantive Article have been found by the European Court without reliance on fresh material, by necessary implication involve some criticism of the domestic judicial protection afforded in those cases, either because the domestic court failed to remedy the Secretary of State's assessment of risk (e.g. *Chahal* v *UK*, *Hilal* v *UK*), or because it misunderstood the nature of the protection afforded by the Convention (*Chahal* v *UK*, *D* v *UK*, *Soering* v *UK*). As we discuss above, whatever the approach adopted by the judicial review court to factual evaluation, it would be antithetical to the incorporation of the ECHR for *adjudicators* to depart from their intrinsically fact-finding role.

5.141 In any event, the *ex parte Turgut* analysis yields the following propositions:

(a)   in order to comply with Article 13, the judicial review court in the context of a case involving human rights must not place the threshold of irrationality too high (*Smith, Grady et al* para. 138);

(b)   it must perform the particular schematic functions required by the ECHR (e.g. whether the decision proportionately pursues a legitimate aim) rather than applying a broadbrush *Wednesbury* approach (*Smith, Grady et al* para. 138, *ex parte Turgut*);

(c)   it must examine the underlying factual material upon which the complaint is based for itself in a necessarily rigorous fashion (*Vilvarajah* v *UK* para. 108, *Chahal* v *UK* paras. 95 to 97, *Smith, Grady et al* para. 138; *ex parte Turgut*);

(d)   it is not necessary on judicial review for compliance with Article 13 for the Court to adopt an original factual jurisdiction: its rigorous examination should be with a view to determining whether another conclusion than that reached by the Secretary of State was compelled.

5.142 The position under the common law therefore was that the English courts on judicial review had a weapon that could potentially prevent violations of Article 3 through heightened scrutiny of the rationality of the expulsion decision, but on a number of significant occasions failed to exercise the jurisdiction they possessed to prevent such breaches. In reality the difference between the common law and the ECHR has been what primary facts render the Secretary of State's decision unreasonable.

5.143 *Bensaid* v *UK* (2001) 33 EHRR 10 concerned an Algerian schizophrenic suffering from a psychotic illness, who argued that he would not be able to access treatment in Algeria and would therefore be exposed to treatment contrary to Article 3 if returned there. The case under Article 3 failed on evidential grounds, the European Court concluding that while the treatment complained of, if eventuated, was of sufficient severity to breach Article 3, the risk was merely speculative. Dismissing the complaint under Article 13, the European Court said (at paras. 55–7):

In its *Vilvarajah and Others* v *the United Kingdom* judgment and its *Soering* v *the United Kingdom* judgment of 7 July 1989, the Court considered judicial review proceedings to be an effective remedy in relation to the complaints raised under Article 3 in the contexts of deportation and extradition. It was satisfied that English courts could effectively control the legality of executive discretion on substantive and procedural grounds and quash decisions as appropriate. It was also accepted that a court in the exercise of its powers of judicial review would have power to quash a decision to expel or deport an individual to a country where it was established that there was a serious risk of inhuman or degrading treatment, on the ground that in all the circumstances of the case the decision was one that no reasonable Secretary of State could take. This view was followed in the more recent judgment of *D* v *the United Kingdom.*

56. While the applicant argued that the courts in judicial review applications will not reach findings of fact for themselves on disputed issues, the Court is satisfied that the domestic courts give careful and detailed scrutiny to claims that an expulsion would expose an applicant to the risk of inhuman and degrading treatment. The judgment delivered by the Court of Appeal did so in the applicant's case. The Court is not convinced therefore that the fact that this scrutiny takes place against the background of the criteria applied in judicial review of administrative decisions, namely, rationality and perverseness, deprives the procedure of its effectiveness. The substance of the applicant's complaint was examined by the Court of Appeal, and it had the power to afford him the relief he sought. The fact that it did not do so is not a material consideration since the effectiveness of a remedy for the purposes of Article 13 does not depend on the certainty of a favourable outcome for an applicant (see the *Vilvarajah and Others* v *the United Kingdom* judgment).

57. The case of *Smith and Grady* v *the United Kingdom*, relied on by the applicant, in which there was a breach of Article 13 due to the ineffectiveness of judicial review, does not alter the Court's conclusion. In that case, the domestic courts were concerned with the general policy applied by the Ministry of Defence in excluding homosexuals from the army, in which security context there was a wide area of discretion afforded to the authorities.

5.144 In *Hilal* v *UK* [2001] INLR 595, a Tanzanian national challenged the Secretary of State's refusal to grant him asylum. The European Court found a violation of Article 3, accepting that the Special Adjudicator's assessment of credibility was flawed in the light of subsequent material presented to the Secretary of State in support of a s. 21 of the Immigration Act 1971 request. However, adopting the reasoning of the European Court in *Bensaid* v *UK* [2001] INLR 325 at paras. 55–7 (quoted above at 5.143), it dismissed the complaint under Article 13.

JUDICIAL REVIEW AND STATUTORY APPEALS TO THE COURT OF APPEAL: THE APPROACH UNDER THE HUMAN RIGHTS ACT 1998

The position before the Human Rights Act 1998

5.145 This section reviews the position under judicial review[126] prior to the coming into force of the main sections of the HRA 1998. We consider first the standard *Wednesbury* test noting its considerably deferential standards for judicial review. We then consider the impact of human rights on the operation of *Wednesbury* and conclude that *Wednesbury* is not a monolithic 'bludgeon'[127] and has provided a flexible and more intrusive standard of review where human rights are involved. Next we consider the harder-edged approach to judicial review in the human rights context, where the boundaries of source power are deemed to be constrained as a matter of legislative intent. Lastly, we consider the place of proportionality in the domestic legal framework prior to the HRA 1998.

Orthodox *Wednesbury*

5.146 A classic formulation of the grounds on which the High Court may intervene on an application for judicial review is the (non-exhaustive) three-fold test set out in the GCHQ case (*Council for Civil Service Unions v Minister for the Civil Service* [1985] AC 374) of illegality, irrationality and procedural impropriety (at p. 410). Lord Diplock held that 'illegality' requires the decision-taker to 'understand correctly the law that regulates his decision-making power and must give effect to it'; 'irrationality' is 'what can now be succinctly referred to as "*Wednesbury* unreasonableness" . . . It applies to a decision which is so outrageous in its defiance of logic or of accepted moral standards that no sensible person who had applied his mind to the question to be decided could have arrived at it.'; and 'procedural impropriety extends to breaches of natural justice, a failure to act with procedural fairness or a failure to observe procedural rules' (at pp. 410, 411).

---

126 The authoritative works on judicial review are Wade and Forsyth, *Administrative Law*, 8th edn. (OUP, 2000); de Smith, Woolf and Jowell, *Judicial Review of Administrative Action*, 5th edn. (Sweet & Maxwell, 1998); Craig, *Administrative Law*, 4th Edn. (Sweet & Maxwell). For a novel approach, winning increasing acclaim by the courts, see also the modestly titled and encyclopaedic M. Fordham, *Judicial Review Handbook* (Hart Publishing, 2001). What follows owes much to M. Fordham and T. de la Mare, 'Identifying the Principles of Proportionality' in J. Jowell and J. Cooper (eds.), *Understanding Human Rights Principles* (Hart Publishing, 2001).

127 Laws J in *Child B* [1995] 1 FLR 1055, 1058; overturned in the result (if not the reasoning) by the Court of Appeal at [1995] 1 WLR 898.

5.147 The speech of Lord Diplock in the GCHQ case is one example of how the approach of the High Court on judicial review to discretionary exercises of power by a public authority has been dominated by *Wednesbury* (*Associated Provincial Houses Ltd* v *Wednesbury Corporation* [1948] 1 KB 223) even though Lord Greene MR in that case was summarizing principles that were well understood (at p. 228).

5.148 Primarily the *Wednesbury* approach focuses on the reasoning process, requiring the decision-taker to ask the right questions and take into account relevant considerations, leaving out of consideration irrelevant factors (at p. 229). The weight to be attributed to the answers to those questions or to the relevant factors is classically a matter for the authority, subject only to the long-stop criterion of substantive *Wednesbury* unreasonableness:

> it is entirely for the decision maker to attribute to the relevant considerations such weight as he thinks fit, and the courts will not interfere unless he has acted unreasonably in the *Wednesbury* sense (*Tesco Stores Ltd* v *Secretary of State for the Environment* [1995] 1 WLR 759 at 764).

5.149 The formulation of substantive unreasonableness in the *Wednesbury* case is excessively deferential: 'something so absurd that no sensible person could ever dream that it lay within the powers of the authority' and, classically, 'a decision . . . so unreasonable that no reasonable authority could ever have come to it.' This latter formulation and the similarly deferential variants[128] have featured significantly in the approach to substantive intervention by the High Court on judicial review. Sedley LJ has attempted to emphasize standards of logicality rather than moral outrage or temporary insanity as a touchstone of *Wednesbury* unreasonableness: something that is in logic untenable is in law irrational.[129]

---

[128] See *Council for Civil Service Unions* v *Minister for the Civil Service* [1985] AC 374 at 410 per Lord Diplock 'a decision which is so outrageous in its defiance of logic or of accepted moral standards that no sensible person who had applied his mind to the question to be decided could have arrived at it.'; *R* v *Secretary of State ex parte Nottinghamshire County Council* [1986] AC 240 at 247 per Lord Scarman: 'the consequences of his guidance were so absurd that he must have taken leave of his senses' (note however that this was an example of a 'super-*Wednesbury*' situation where unusually great deference was required; see Fordham (above at footnote 126) para. 41.3.10); *R* v *Devon County Council ex parte G* [1988] 3 WLR 49 at 51 per Lord Donaldson: a decision 'which elicits the explanation—"my goodness, that is certainly wrong"' adopting May LJ's formulation in *Neale* v *Hereford and Worcester County Council* [1986] ICR 471, 483.

[129] See *R* v *Secretary of State ex parte Abdi and Gawe* [1994] Imm AR 402, 414 (quotation from Sedley J at first instance); see further *R* v *Parliamentary Commissioner for Administration ex parte Balchin* [1998] 1 PLR 1, 13: *Wednesbury* unreasonable is apt to mean 'an error of reasoning which robs the decision of logic', and see *R* v *North and East Devon Health Authority ex parte Coughlan* [2000] 2 WLR 262, per Lord Woolf MR para. 65.

5.150 Only recently has the formulation been explicitly criticized: de Smith, Woolf and Jowell considered that 'Its tautological definition . . . fails to guide us with any degree of certitude',[130] and Lord Cooke in *R v Chief Constable of Sussex ex parte International Trader's Ferry Ltd* [1998] 3 WLR 1260 said (at p. 1289):[131]

> It seems to me unfortunate that *Wednesbury* and some *Wednesbury* phrases have become established incantations in the courts of the United Kingdom and beyond. *Associated Provincial Picture Houses Ltd v Wednesbury Corporation* [1948] 1 KB 223, an apparently briefly-considered case, might well not be decided the same way today; and the judgment of Lord Greene MR twice uses (at 230 and 234) the tautologous formula 'so unreasonable that no reasonable authority could ever have come to it.' Yet judges are entirely accustomed to respecting the proper scope of administrative discretions. In my respectful opinion they do not need to be warned off the course by admonitory circumlocutions. When, in *Secretary of State for Education and Science v Tameside Metropolitan Borough Council* [1977] AC 1014, the precise meaning of 'unreasonably' in an administrative context was crucial to the decision, the five speeches in the House of Lords, the three judgments in the Court of Appeal and the two judgments in the Divisional Court all succeeded in avoiding needless complexity. The simple test used throughout was *whether the decision in question was one which a reasonable authority could reach.* The converse was described by Lord Diplock (at 1064) as 'conduct which no sensible authority acting with due appreciation of its responsibilities would have decided to adopt.' These unexaggerated criteria give the administrator ample and rightful rein, consistently with the constitutional separation of powers. (emphasis supplied)

Convention modification of *Wednesbury* where human rights engaged

5.151 It would however be wrong to consider *Wednesbury* as a monolithic inflexible standard.[132] The human rights context has been recognized to require a modified approach. Certain fundamental rights have been recognized by the common law to have a special status. Those rights are those 'largely articulated in the principal provisions of the European Convention on Human Rights'.[133] In a third country asylum judicial review, *Bugdaycay v Secretary of State* [1987] AC 514 at 531, the House of Lords recognized that the common law requires that a

---

[130] De Smith, Woolf and Jowell, *Judicial Review of Administrative Action*, 5th edn. (Sweet & Maxwell, 1998) para. 13-002; *R v IRC ex parte Taylor (No 2)* [1989] 3 All ER 353, 357: 'we still adhere to (the *Wednesbury* definition of unreasonableness) out of usage if not affection'.

[131] See also Lord Cooke's valedictory comments in *Daly* [2001] 2 AC 532 at 539 discussed above in the Introduction.

[132] For a full review see M. Fordham and T. de la Mare, 'Anxious Scrutiny, the Principle of Legality and the Human Rights Act' [2000] JR 40, and Jeffrey Jowell QC, 'In the Shadow of *Wednesbury*' [1997] JR 75 where the author surveys 'more defined principles and approaches which, practically, may not contain the *Wednesbury* hurdle but nevertheless address themselves to the unreasonable exercise of power.'.

[133] *R v Lord Chancellor ex parte Lightfoot* [1999] 2 WLR 1126 at 113 per Laws J at first instance; see also Sedley J in *R v Secretary of State ex parte McQuillan* [1995] 4 All ER 400 at 422.

claimed violation of such a fundamental right is to be subject to the most anxious scrutiny.

5.152 While *R* v *Secretary of State, ex parte Brind* [1991] AC 696 is frequently cited as authority for the position that broad statutory discretions are not required to be exercised consistently with ratified but incorporated human rights standards, since this would amount to back-door incorporation and usurpation of Parliament, the House of Lords also took a considerable step towards the present protection afforded by the courts on judicial review to human rights. Lord Bridge stated (at pp. 748, 749) that the courts were 'perfectly entitled to start from the premise that any restriction of the right to freedom of expression requires to be justified and that nothing less than an important competing public interest will be sufficient to justify it.'

5.153 This approach culminated in *R* v *Ministry of Defence ex parte Smith* [1996] QB 517 where Lord Bingham CJ accepted the following formulation of David Pannick QC:

> The court may not interfere with the exercise of an administrative discretion on substantive grounds save if the court is satisfied that it is beyond the range of responses open to a reasonable decision maker. But in judging whether the decision maker had exceeded this margin of appreciation the human rights context is important. The more substantial the interference with human rights, the more the court will require by way of justification before it is satisfied that the decision is reasonable in the sense applying above.

5.154 The *standard* of justification to be provided by the decision-taker is required to be commensurate with the significance of the right at issue (*R* v *Secretary of State, ex parte McQuillan* [1995] 4 All ER 400 at 422). Moreover, and in contrast to the position under 'classic' or unmodified *Wednesbury* (see above at 5.148: *Tesco* v *Secretary of State*), Laws LJ recognized that the dictum in *Smith* meant that in the human rights context it was appropriate and indeed necessary for the court to review the *weight* to be given to competing interests. In a case concerning compulsory purchase orders and involving property rights, Laws LJ said this (*Chesterfield Properties Ltd* v *Secretary of State for the Environment* [1998] JPL 568 at 579, 580):

> *Wednesbury*, however, is not, at least not any longer, a monolithic standard of review. Where an administrative decision abrogates or diminishes a constitutional or fundamental right, *Wednesbury* requires that the decision-maker provide a substantial justification in the public interest for doing so . . . The identification of any right as 'constitutional', however, means nothing in the absence of a written constitution unless it is defined by reference to some particular protection which the law affords it. The common law affords such protection by adopting, within *Wednesbury*, a variable standard of review. There is no question of the court exceeding the principle of reasonableness. *It means only that*

reasonableness itself requires in such cases that in ordering the priorities which will drive his decision, the decision-maker must give a high place to the right in question. He cannot treat it merely as something to be taken into account, akin to any other relevant consideration; he must recognise it as a value to be kept, unless in his judgment there is a greater value that justifies its loss. In many arenas of public discretion, the force to be given to all and any factors which the decision-maker must confront is neutral in the eye of the law; he may make of each what he will, and the law will not interfere because the weight he attributes to any of them is for him and not the court. But where a constitutional right is involved, the law presumes it to carry substantial force. Only another interest, a public interest, of greater force may override it. The decision-maker is, of course, the first judge of the question whether in the particular case there exists such an interest which should prevail. (emphasis supplied)

5.155　The *Smith* test was approved in *R* v *Lord Saville ex parte A* [2001] 1 WLR 1855 a challenge to the refusal of the 'Bloody Sunday' Tribunal to afford anonymity to testifying soldiers, who claimed that publicity would put them in peril. The Court of Appeal said:

34. . . . when a fundamental right such as the right to life is engaged, the options available to the reasonable decision maker are curtailed. They are curtailed because it is unreasonable to reach a decision which contravenes or could contravene human rights unless there are sufficiently compelling significant countervailing conditions. In other words it is not open to the decision maker to risk interfering with fundamental rights in the absence of compelling justification. Even the broadest discretion is constrained by the need for there to be countervailing circumstances justifying the interference with human rights. The courts will anxiously scrutinise the strength of the countervailing circumstances and the degree of interference with the human right involved and then apply the test accepted by the Lord Chief Justice in *Smith* which is not in issue.

5.156　The Court of Appeal then subjected the reasoning processes of the Tribunal to close examination, and identified six factors which it considered had not been afforded 'sufficient significance'—an approach going to the *weight* to be given to relevant factors—before concluding that the grant of anonymity was the only possible conclusion.

Human rights and legality

5.157　A more powerful approach, based on a strong principle of interpretation, has been developed by the courts in the human rights context. It enjoins reading general wide words, even in the absence of ambiguity, in a human rights-compatible manner. This has become known as the 'principle of legality'. Rather than reviewing the discretionary decision of the public authority in order to consider its rationality and justification by focusing on the *result* or *outcome* according to common law standards of abuse of power, the principle of legality[134] mandates construing the *source power*, which confers the discretion, in a human rights-compliant manner, and holding the decision to be ultra vires as a matter of legality if human rights are intruded upon. The exercise of administrative discretion has thus to be seen against a prior restriction placed on the scope of the source power in a human rights-compliant manner. The limiting condition is where Parliament expressly or by necessary implication approves the intrusion.

5.158 This approach was applied in essence by Simon Brown LJ in *R v Secretary of State for Social Security ex parte Joint Council for the Welfare of Immigrants* [1997] 1 WLR 275,[135] where the Joint Council sought to challenge regulations[136] which had the effect of depriving certain categories of asylum seekers of entitlement to state welfare benefit. Simon Brown LJ held that the policy change embodied in the regulations sought to deprive asylum seekers of pre-existing statutory rights of appeal, and was so significant that it could only be accomplished by unambiguous provisions of primary legislation.[137]

5.159 The leading case[138] is *R v Secretary of State for the Home Department ex parte Simms* [1999] 3 WLR 328 where the House of Lords held to be unlawful the Home Secretary's policy and prison governors' decisions refusing to allow prisoners to have oral interviews with journalists for the purposes of investigating possible miscarriages of justice, unless the journalists signed written undertakings not to publish any part of the interviews. Those decisions were taken pursuant to a policy which the Secretary of State claimed to be entitled to adopt under provisions in the Prison Rules[139] governing visits by journalists or writers. Those rules were in turn made by the Secretary of State pursuant to broad discretion conferred by s. 47 of the Prison Act 1952 to make rules for the regulation and management of prisons and for the discipline and control of prisoners. Lord Steyn construed the wide and unambiguous power in the Prison Act 1952 and the Prison Rules to be limited by the principle of legality in the following manner (at p. 340):

---

[134] i.e. at least in its most powerful form, see discussion of its application to discretionary decisions below at 5.161.

[135] See further Poole, 'Proportionality: A New Strain' [2000] JR 33, para. 3; Harvey 'Asylum seekers, ultra vires, and the Social Security Regulations' [1997] PL 394; Stevens 'The Asylum and Immigration Act 1996: Erosion of the Right to Seek Asylum' (1998) 61 MLR 207.

[136] Social Security (Persons from Abroad) (Miscellaneous Amendments) Regulations 1996 (SI 1996 No. 30).

[137] The other basis for the decision was that the new regime was so intrusive that it had to be considered immoral and unlawful: 'the Regulations necessarily contemplate for some a life so destitute that to my mind no civilised nation can tolerate it.'

[138] See also *R v Secretary of State ex parte Leech (No. 2)* [1994] QB 198; *R v Lord Chancellor ex parte Witham* [1998] QB 575, refined in *R v Lord Chancellor ex parte Lightfoot* [2000] 2 WLR 318; *R v Secretary of State ex parte Pierson* [1998] AC 539 at 575 per Lord Browne-Wilkinson; and see *R (Morgan Grenfell) v Special Commissioner of Income Tax* [2002] UKHL 21, [2002] HRLR 42.

[139] Prison Rules 1964, rule 33; Prison Service Standing Order 5A, paras. 37 and 37A.

Literally construed there is force in the extensive construction put forward. But one cannot lose sight that there is at stake a fundamental or basic right, namely the right of a prisoner to seek through oral interviews to persuade a journalist to investigate the safety of the prisoner's conviction and to publicise his findings in an effort to gain access to justice for the prisoner. In these circumstances *even in the absence of an ambiguity*[140] there comes into play a presumption of general application operating as a constitutional principle as Sir Rupert Cross explained in successive editions of his classic work: *Statutory Interpretation*, 3rd ed. (1995) 165–166. This is called 'the principle of legality': *Halsbury's Laws of England*, 4th ed. reissue, vol. 8(2), (1996), p. 13, para. 6. Ample illustrations of the application of this principle are given in the speech of Lord Browne-Wilkinson, and in my speech, in *R v Secretary of State for the Home Department, ex parte Pierson* [1998] AC 539, at 573G–575D and 587C–590A. Applying this principle I would hold that (the standing orders) leave untouched the fundamental and basic rights asserted by the prisoners in the present case.

On this basis the policy of a blanket ban, and the individual decisions reached by the governors under it, were unlawful, because the Home Office had failed to establish a case of pressing social need, a classic European Court test. However neither the Prison Rules nor the Standing Orders were unlawful: they merely had to be construed so as not to be in conflict with the prisoners' basic rights.

5.160   Lord Hoffman explained the basis for the principle of legality as a strong principle of discerning a human rights-compliant legislative intent as follows (at p. 341):

> the principle of legality means that Parliament must squarely confront what it is doing and accept the political cost. Fundamental rights cannot be overridden by general or ambiguous words. This is because there is too great a risk that the full implications of their unqualified meaning may have passed unnoticed in the democratic process. In the absence of express language or necessary implication to the contrary, the courts therefore presume that even the most general words were intended to be subject to the basic rights of the individual. In this way the courts of the United Kingdom, though acknowledging the sovereignty of Parliament, apply principles of constitutionality little different from those which exist in countries where the power of the legislature is expressly limited by a constitutional document.

5.161   The decision in *Simms* requires a particular reasoning process to be conducted in human rights contexts and allows for an intrusive review of the substantive results reached by the public authority. This case is highly significant in two further respects:

---

[140] Emphasis supplied; note the departure (in spirit if not in letter) from *Brind*, where the House of Lords had held that unincorporated Treaties such as the ECHR were relevant to construction only in cases of ambiguity, and that wide general words such as 'may' were not ambiguous. The decision in *Simms* is arguably consistent with *Brind* in so far as the rights identified, free speech and access to the courts, were rights considered to be protected by the common law as well as the ECHR.

(a)   The approach of the House of Lords was to exercise a *primary judgment* as to whether a pressing social need had been demonstrated by the prison authorities (at p. 339). We return to the importance of the methodology adopted by the House of Lords below, when considering the issue of whether it is for the judicial review court to exercise a primary or a secondary judgment on proportionality.

(b)   *Simms* establishes that the principle of legality applies to discretionary fact-specific decisions and discretionary policies, rather than merely to the construction of legislative provisions. In *R v Secretary of State, ex parte Leech (No. 2)* [1994] QB 198 Steyn LJ held that a *prison rule,* made by statutory instrument pursuant to s. 47 of the Prison Act 1947, authorizing interference with correspondence between a prisoner and his solicitor was outwith the rule-making power conferred by primary legislation and ultra vires. This led to attempts to narrow the ambit of *ex parte Leech.* Prior to *Simms,* the Court of Appeal confined (*R v Secretary of State, ex parte O'Dhuibhir* [1997] COD 315) the *Leech* approach to questions of construction of legislative provisions, and applied an irrationality test to administrative instructions issued pursuant to such provisions.[140a] But in *Simms* Lord Steyn used the principle of legality in *Leech as an alternative to the rationality test* set out in *R v Ministry of Defence, ex parte Smith* to defeat a submission made by the Secretary of State based on US case law requiring a 'measure of judicial deference' to be given to decisions of the prison authorities. Moreover, the decisions quashed in *Simms* were themselves discretionary decisions of the Secretary of State and the prison governors. It is difficult to see, in the light of *Simms,* how a distinction between primary and secondary legislation and discretionary decisions taken thereunder can continue to be made for the purposes of determining whether the principle of legality applies. Indeed it is difficult to see how if the source legislative power (in *Simms,* the rule-making power in the Prison Act 1952; in the immigration context, ss. 3 and 4 of the IA 1971) prohibits the making of ultra vires secondary legislation (the Prison Rules; the Immigration Rules[141]), it can permit the taking of a discretion decision (Home Office policy, or an individual decision) which may be ultra vires the source power, notwithstanding that the relevant secondary legislation (the Rules) is *intra*

[140a] See *R v Secretary of State ex parte Simms* [1999] QB 349 at 360, 361, CA; see also *R v Broadmoor Special Hospital Authority ex parte S* [1998] COD 199 (policy of searching mental patients); *Broadmoor Special Hospital Authority v Robinson* [1999] QB 957 (implied power to seize manuscript of book).

[141] See e.g. *R v Secretary of State ex parte Manshoora Begum* [1986] Imm AR 385, Simon Brown J.

vires.[142] This entails the unattractive consequence that lesser protection is afforded when a fundamental right is infringed not by the express terms of subordinate legislation but instead by a non-statutory policy or internal instruction.

Proportionality in domestic law before the Human Rights Act 1998[143]

Common law and proportionality

5.162 The House of Lords in *Brind* considered proportionality not to be a discrete ground of review (see at [1991] AC 766, 767, per Lord Lowry), but also appeared to endorse the proposition that proportionality 'feeds' *Wednesbury*.[144] The requirement to justify interferences with human rights has led some judges to consider that domestic law contemplated at least some form of proportionality as a principle of domestic review of administrative action. Thus in *R v Secretary of State ex parte McQuillan* [1995] 4 All ER 400 Sedley J said (at p. 422):

> the standard of justification of infringements of rights and freedoms by executive decision must vary in proportion to the significance of the right which is at issue. Such an approach is indeed already enjoined by *ex parte Bugdaycay* . . . in relation to a predominant value of the common law—the right to life—which, as it happens, the European Convention reflects. Whether this is in itself a doctrine of proportionality I do now pause to ask; if it is, the House of Lords has long since contemplated its arrival with equanimity.[145]

5.163 Professor Jowell argued in 1996[146] that it would be worthwhile to recognize proportionality as a ground of judicial review in domestic law, and that proportionality fitted within the sliding *Wednesbury* scale of review. Explicit acknowledgement of proportionality would improve the intelligibility and coher-

---

[142] See T. Owen, 'Prisoners and Fundamental Rights' [1997] JR 81, para. 19.

[143] See M. Fordham and T. de la Mare 'Identifying the Principle of Proportionality' in J. Jowell and J. Cooper (eds) *Understanding Human Rights Principles* (Hart Publishing, 2001).

[144] Lord Lowry also said that 'Clearly' *Wednesbury* unreasonableness applies to a decision 'which suffers from a total lack of proportionality'.

[145] See de Burca, G., 'Proportionality and *Wednesbury* Unreasonableness: the Influence of European Legal Concepts in UK Law' (1997) EPL 561, where the author considers that there are three classes of cases where proportionality has been raised: those where the courts have declared that proportionality is not a distinct ground of review in English law (e.g. *Brind*), those where proportionality has by contrast been explicitly acknowledged as a discrete ground of review or impliedly used as a permissible ground under colour of *Wednesbury* (e.g. the penalty cases: *R v Barnsley Metropolitan Borough Council ex parte Hook* [1976] 1 WLR 1052 at 1057, 1058 per Lord Denning MR; *R v Newham LBC ex parte X* [1995] ELR 303, 307, and cases which have used the EC law concept of proportionality (as to which see below at 5.154 et seq). See further Lord Lester of Herne Hill QC, 'The Impact of Human Rights Law' [1996] JR 21, para. 12; Craig, P. in E. Ellis (ed) *The Principle of Proportionality in the Laws of Europe* (Hart, 2000).

[146] Jeffrey Jowell QC, 'Is Proportionality an Alien Concept?' (1996) 10 EPL 401.

ence of English law, as well as the quality of the decision-making process. In *R (Alconbury)* v *Secretary of State for the Environment, Transport and the Regions* [2001] 2 WLR 1389, 1407, para. 51 Lord Slynn considered that the time had come to recognize the principle of proportionality as part of domestic public law.

EC law and proportionality[147]

5.164 Proportionality has entered domestic law most visibly through the gateway of EC law, which recognizes proportionality as a key 'general principle of law'.[148] Essentially a four-fold test is applied:

(a) an examination of the legitimacy of the end pursued;
(b) the suitability of the measure to promote that end;
(c) its necessity; and
(d) the overall question of balance: does the end justify the means?

Thus in *R* v *Minister of Agriculture, Fisheries and Food, ex parte FEDESA* (Case C-331/88) [1990] ECR 1-4023, 4063 the ECJ stated as follows (at para. 13):

By virtue of [the proportionality principle], the lawfulness of the prohibition of an economic activity is subject to the condition that the prohibitory measures are appropriate [test (b)] and necessary in order to achieve [test (c)] the objectives legitimately pursued [test (a)] by the legislation in question; where there is a choice between several appropriate measures recourse must be had to the least onerous [test (c)] and the disadvantages caused must not be disproportionate to the aims pursued [test (d)].[149]

5.165 The ECJ applies the principle of proportionality in two different contexts.[150] The first context is where the ECJ reviews the measure of an EC Institution under Article 230, EC Treaty (formerly Article 173). Here, typically, issues of economic policy are involved and while the four-fold schematic approach is applied, the ECJ is essentially deferential to the administration, applying a 'manifestly inappropriate' or 'manifest error' test. Proportionality is here seen as an instrument promoting economic integration. Thus in *ex parte FEDESA* the ECJ held ([1990] ECR 1-4023 at para. 14):[151]

However, with regard to judicial review of compliance with those conditions it must be stated that in matters concerning the common agricultural policy the Community

---

[147] See also de Burca, (above at footnote 145).
[148] See the landmark case of *Internationale Handelsgesellschaft* (Case 11/70) [1970] ECR 1125.
[149] For an analogous approach under an Article 234 reference, see *Kraus* [1993] ECR I-1663, para. 32.
[150] See generally Ellis, E. (ed) *The Principle of Proportionality in the Laws of Europe* (Hart, 2000).
[151] See further Van Verven AG in *SPUC* v *Grogan* (Case C-159/90) [1991] ECR I-4685 at 4719, 4720.

legislature has a discretionary power which corresponds to the political responsibilities given to it by Articles 40 and 43 of the Treaty. Consequently, the legality of a measure adopted in that sphere can be affected only if the measure is manifestly appropriate having regard to the objective which the competent institution is seeking to pursue.

5.166   The second situation is where, following a reference for a preliminary ruling under Article 234 (formerly Article 177),[152] the ECJ adopts an essentially advisory role and rules on a principle of EC law to be applied by the national court which is itself reviewing a decision of a public authority. Here the ECJ tends to apply a high intensity review, given that typically the reference by the national court will concern a claimed interference with a fundamental right in the Treaty scheme and the member state will be seeking to claim justification on grounds of public health, public policy or national security. Close scrutiny is typically given to test (d) in the four-fold test, whether there is available a less restrictive alternative to promote the legitimate end.[153] Here proportionality is a doctrine essentially guarding individual rights. It was described by Sedley LJ in *B* v *Secretary of State* [2000] INLR 361 as a 'fundamental principle of the common law of the EU'. However, even in this context, the ECJ will give a measure of latitude to the public authority where issues of general social policy are involved.[154]

5.167   De Burca states that 'The way the proportionality principle is applied by the Court of Justice covers a spectrum ranging from a very deferential approach, to quite a rigorous and searching examination of the justification for a measure which has to be challenged.'[155]

5.168   These principles of proportionality have been applied domestically by the courts. For example, in *R* v *CC Sussex Police ex parte ITF* [1998] 3 WLR 1260 where legitimacy (test (a)) was not in issue Lord Slynn said (at pp. 1275, 1277):

> I am satisfied, as was the Court of Appeal, that the Chief Constable has shown here that what he did in providing police assistance was proportionate to what was required. To protect the lorries, in the way he did, was a suitable [test (b)] and necessary [test (c)] way of dealing with potentially violent demonstrators. To limit the occasions when sufficient police could be made available was, in the light of the resources available to him to deal with immediate and foreseeable events at the port, and at the same time to carry out all his other police duties, necessary and in no way disproportionate to the restrictions which were involved [test (d)].

---

[152]   See *R* v *Stock Exchange ex parte Else* [1993] QB 534.

[153]   See e.g. *Bela-Mühle Josef Bergmann* v *Grows-Farm* (Case 114/76) [1977] ECR 1211; *Conegate* v *Customs and Excise Commissioners* (Case 121/85) [1986] ECR 1007; *De Peijper* (Case 104/75) [1976] ECR 613.

[154]   See e.g. *Schindler* [1994] ECR I-1039, para. 63.

[155]   'The principle of proportionality and its application in EC law' [1993] YEL 105, 111; see further C. Weir, 'Is EC Proportionality the same as *Wednesbury* unreasonableness?' [1999] JR 263.

5.169 Lord Slynn also, however, considered that there would often be little difference, at least in *result* between *Wednesbury* review and proportionality (at p. 1277):

> In *R v Secretary of State for the Home Department, ex parte Brind* [1991] 1 AC 696 the House treated *Wednesbury* reasonableness and proportionality as being different. So in some ways they are though the distinction between the two tests in practice is in any event much less than is sometimes suggested. The cautious way in which the European Court [of Justice] usually applies this test, recognising the importance of respecting the national authority's margin of appreciation, may mean that whichever test is adopted, and even allowing for a difference in onus, the result is the same.[156]

5.170 That said, it is plain that proportionality is a more rigorous and structured test capable of affording a greater intensity of review than *Wednesbury*. This is well illustrated by Laws J in *R v Minister of Agriculture, Fisheries and Food, ex parte First City Trading* [1997] 1 CMLR (at 278, 279, paras. 68, 69):[157]

> It is not the court's task to decide what it would have done had it been the decision-maker, who (certainly in the case of an elected Government) enjoys a political authority, and carries a political responsibility, with which the court is not endowed. The court's task is to decide whether the measure in fact adopted falls within the range of options legally open to the decision-maker. In the nature of things it is highly unlikely that only one of the choices available to him will pass the test of objective justification: and the court has no business to give effect to any preference for one possible measure over another when both lie within the proper legal limits. In this sense it may be said that the decision-maker indeed enjoys a margin of appreciation. The difference between *Wednesbury* and European review is that in the former case the limits lie further back. I think that there are two factors. First, the limits of domestic review are not, as the law presently stands, constrained by the doctrine of proportionality. Secondly, at least as regards a requirement such as that of objective justification in an equal treatment case, the European rule requires the decision-maker to provide a fully reasoned case. It is not enough merely to set out the problem, and assert that within his discretion the Minister chose this or that solution, constrained only by the requirement that his decision must have been one which a reasonable Minister might make. Rather the court will test the solution arrived at, and pass it only if substantial factual considerations are put forward in its justification: considerations which are relevant, reasonable and proportionate to the aim in view. But as I understand it the jurisprudence of the Court is not concerned to agree or disagree with the decision: that would be to travel beyond the boundaries of proper judicial authority, and usurp the primary decision maker's function. Thus *Wednesbury* and European review are different models—one looser, one tighter—of the same juridical concept . . .

---

[156] See also Lord Cooke at p. 1288.
[157] See also *R v Secretary of State for Health ex parte Eastside Cheese* [1999] Eu LR 968.

5.171 In the field of sex discrimination, where the issue under EC law is often whether an 'objective justification' is made out, the doctrine of proportionality is applied.[158] In *R* v *Secretary of State for Employment ex parte Equal Opportunities Commission* [1995] 1 AC 1 the House of Lords held to be unlawful a procedural rule which prevented part-time workers (predominantly women) from claiming unfair dismissal. While the measure in question had a legitimate social policy aim, namely increasing the number of jobs, it was neither suitable nor requisite to achieve that aim. While the Secretary of State submitted that a margin of appreciation should be afforded given the essentially political nature of the judgment, there was no mention of this concept in the leading speech of Lord Keith.

Constitutional review and proportionality

5.172 The experience of the Privy Council in hearing constitutional cases has meant that judges have become used to applying the principle of proportionality. For example, in *Thomas* v *Baptiste* [2000] 2 AC 1[159] the applicants appealed against an order for their execution on the grounds inter alia that the instructions governing the exercise of the right of petition to the UN Human Rights Committee were unlawful. Lord Millet, for the majority, reasoned as follows (at pp. 20, 21):

> (The instructions) were unlawful because they were disproportionate . . . the instructions were disproportionate because they curtailed the prisoners' rights further than was necessary to deal with the mischief created by the delays in the international appellate processes. It would have been sufficient to prescribe an outside period of (say) 18 months for the completion of all such processes. This could apply whether the petitioner made only one application or applied successively to more than one international body or made successive applications to the same body. It was unnecessary and inappropriate to provide separate and successive time limits for each application and for each stage of each application. This had the effect of drastically and unnecessarily curtailing the time limits within which the first such body could complete the processes.

Other human rights Conventions and common law

5.173 Prior to the coming into force of the HRA 1998 the ECHR was of course a ratified but unincorporated Treaty. The provisions which are not included in Schedule 1 remain unincorporated although all European Court jurisprudence must be taken into account, including the case law on the unincorporated articles.

---

[158] See classically *Bilka-Kaufhaus* v *Weber von Hartz* (Case 170/84) [1986] ECR 1607; Ellis, E., 'The Concept of Proportionality in EC Sex Discrimination Law' in *The Principle of Proportionality in the Laws of Europe* (Hart, 2000).

[159] See also *De Freitas* v *Permanent Secretary of Ministry of Agriculture Fisheries Lands and Housing* [1998] 3 WLR 675 (Lord Clyde); approved of in *R* v *A* [20002] 1 AC 45 and *R (Daly)* v *Secretary of State* [2001] 2 AC 532; see above at Introduction, 1.73, and below at 5.185 et seq.

Section 11 of the HRA 1998 further provides a safeguard for existing human rights: 'A person's reliance on a Convention right does not restrict (a) any other right or freedom conferred on him by or under any law having effect in any part of the UK'. This reflects Article 53 of the ECHR which provides that 'Nothing in this Convention shall be construed as limiting or derogating from any of the human rights and fundamental freedoms which may be ensured under the laws of any High Contracting Party or under any other agreement to which it is a Party.' These provisions provide the background for consideration of the impact of non-incorporated Treaty obligations in domestic law.

5.174 A non-incorporated but ratified Treaty will continue to impact on domestic public law. First, its provisions may assist in identifying a right recognized by the common law, and thus engage the *Simms/Smith* approach. Secondly, even where this is not possible, the Treaty obligation is capable of founding a legitimate expectation that its terms will be complied with. The most notable use of this technique in the immigration sphere is perhaps to be found in *R v Home Office ex parte Adimi and others* [2000] 3 WLR 434 where the Divisional Court held that the policy of prosecuting refugees travelling on false instruments was contrary to Article 31 of the Refugee Convention,[160] an unincorporated Treaty obligation conferring in effect substantive benefits. The Divisional Court used the endorsement by the Court of Appeal in *R v Secretary of State ex parte Ahmed and Patel* [1998] INLR 570 of the seminal judgment of the Australian High Court in *MIEA v Teoh* (1995) 183 CLR 273 to the effect that ratification of a Treaty founded a legitimate expectation that its provisions would be followed, absent any contrary indication from the executive.[161] *Ahmed and Patel* is also notable for the following dicta of Hobhouse LJ on the juridical nature of legitimate expectations:

> The principle of legitimate expectation in English law is a principle of fairness in the decision-making process. It differs from the doctrine of estoppel in private law. In the present context, it is a wholly objective concept and is not based upon any actual state of knowledge of individual immigrants or would be immigrants; indeed, if it had to be based upon a subjective understanding of the content of these Conventions and their legal effect in English law, there would be no basis for the application of the principle in cases such as these. However, the application of the principle must be based upon some objectively identifiable legitimate expectation as to how decisions will be made and discretions exercised.

---

[160] Convention relating to the Status of Refugees, 1951, Geneva, as amended by the 1967 Protocol thereto, New York.

[161] For a detailed consideration of the *MIEA v Teoh* (1995) 183 CLR 273 and related Canadian and New Zealand and domestic jurisprudence, see M. Taggart, M. Hunt and D. Dyzenhaus, 'The Internationalisation of Public Law'.

5.175 Thirdly, the obligation can be relied upon where the decision-maker professes to have taken the provision into account,[162] or as a relevant consideration in the exercise of a discretion.[163]

5.176 These techniques mark a considerable shift forward from the position in *R v Secretary of State, ex parte Brind* [1991] AC 696 that the Treaty obligation can only be used in cases of legislative ambiguity (defined to exclude neutral or general words) (at p. 721) or where the legislation was enacted to give effect to or promote the Treaty provisions (*R v Secretary of State for the Home department, ex parte Norney* (1995) 7 Admin LR 861).

5.177 Returning to the HRA 1998, we have noted above at 5.159 et seq that the decision in *Simms* is a significant pointer to the role to be adopted by the court on judicial review (and in statutory appeals on a point of law) and the intensity to be given to challenged decisions following the coming into force of the main provisions of the HRA 1998. It is to those issues that we now turn.

JUDICIAL REVIEW AND STATUTORY APPEALS IN THE LIGHT OF THE HUMAN RIGHTS ACT 1998

5.178 We now consider the approach to be adopted by the higher courts when considering an allegation on judicial review or on statutory appeals on a point of law that a public authority[164] acted incompatibility with a claimant's ECHR right under s. 6 of the HRA 1998. The position for the appellate authority is of course wholly different and uncontroversial: it will continue to exercise its traditional original factual jurisdiction and apply the facts found to the new legal regime.[165]

5.179 In this section we first consider the question of what is involved in the concept of proportionality, noting that proportionality requires the performance of a particular schematic exercise by the decision-maker and, on review or appeal, the court. We then consider the factors that are relevant when the court is determining the extent to which it should give due deference to a decision-maker. We next consider the approach required of the courts on judicial review under s. 6 of the HRA 1998; are the courts to exercise a primary judgment on proportionality, or merely a secondary judgment to determine whether or not the inferior decision-taker's view was within *Wednesbury* parameters? It is this question which

---

[162] *R v Secretary of State ex parte Mirza* [1996] Imm AR 413; *R v Secretary of State ex parte Launder* [1997] 1 WLR 839.

[163] See *Jordan Iye v Secretary of State* [1994] Imm AR 63, 65–6; *R v Secretary of State ex parte Ozminos* [1994] Imm AR 287, 291–3.

[164] Usually the Entry Clearance Officer, Immigration Officer, or Secretary of State.

[165] See e.g. Hale LJ in *R v Secretary of State for the Home Department, ex parte Saleem* [2001] 1 WLR 443. See also *Noruwa v Secretary of State for the Home Department* (IAT, 11 December 2001), starred, paras. 44–57.

has given rise to inconsistent decisions in the Court of Appeal, although the decisions are perhaps not as far apart as first appears given the different contexts involved.

Proportionality: the content of the test[166]

5.180 The ECHR itself does not contain a doctrine of proportionality. The doctrine has been developed, if not definitively codified, by the European Court, the point of entry being the concept of necessity which governs the express limitations in Articles 2, and 8 to 11, and which constitutes an important aspect of the autonomous ECHR concept of 'law' which permeates the entire ECHR scheme.

5.181 In the immigration context, Dyson LJ held in *Samaroo v Secretary of State* [2002] INLR 55 that proportionality does not require the examination of a less intrusive alternative to pursue the legitimate aim of deterring international drug traffickers by a policy of deportation. No suitable other measure could be capable of achieving that aim. Further it was unrealistic to expect the Secretary of State to prove that by not proceeding with deportation, the efficacy of the policy would be undermined. That was not a matter susceptible of proof. The only proportionality question for the Secretary of State was whether the deporation represented a fair balance between the interests of the community and those of the individual. Significant deference would be afforded to the Secretary of State in the evaluation of his balance: he was better placed to adjudicate upon the balance than the court.

5.182 This is an important judgment, explicable on the basis that in the immigration context, since there is no right under the ECHR as such to remain, it is inappropriate to speak of proportionality as to means (the less intrusive alternative test), and also inappropriate to ask if the essence of the right remains, because there is no such right enjoyed in the first place. The sole question is thus proportionality as to ends: are the effects on the individual in light of the particular circumstances so compelling that the countervailing considerations are outweighed? It is of note that while the Court of Appeal in *B* v *Secretary of State* [2000] Imm AR 478 considered the less intrusive alternative test, it also recognized that this had no purchase in the deportation context, and allowed the appeal because the appellant was facing not only deportation but exile having lived practically all his life in the UK. This was proportionality as to ends.

5.183 In the following paragraphs we set out the ways in which the concept of proportionality has been applied by the European Court in its case law.

---

[166] See generally Ellis, E., (ed) *The Principle of Proportionality in the Laws of Europe* (Hart, 2000).

5.184   In *Sunday Times* v *UK* (1979) 2 EHRR 245, para. 59 the phrase 'necessary in a democratic society' was held to imply a 'pressing social need', the question for the European Court being:

> whether the interference complained of corresponded to a pressing social need, whether it was proportionate to the legitimate aim pursued, and whether the reasons given by the national authorities to justify it are relevant and sufficient.

5.185   Although as we have stated, the four-fold test evident in the EC law concept of proportionality has not been definitively set out in the case law of the European Court, such a test appears also to be required by the ECHR version, save that on occasion the European Court has held that while 'necessary' does not mean desirable or reasonable, it also does not equate with 'indispensable'.[167] However, in domestic law the position appears to have been clarified. In *R* v *A* [2001] UKHL 25 Lord Steyn stated as follows:

> 38. It is well established that the guarantee of a fair trial under Article 6 is absolute: a conviction obtained in breach of it cannot stand. *R* v *Forbes* [2001] 2 WLR 1, 13, para. 24. The only balancing permitted is in respect of what the concept of a fair trial entails: here account may be taken of the familiar triangulation of interests of the accused, the victim and society. In this context proportionality has a role to play. The criteria for determining the test of proportionality have been analysed in similar terms in the case law of the European Court of Justice and the European Court of Human Rights. It is not necessary for us to re-invent the wheel. In *De Freitas* v *Permanent Secretary of Ministry of Agriculture, Fisheries, Lands and Housing* [1999] 1 AC 69 Lord Clyde adopted a precise and concrete analysis of the criteria. In determining whether a limitation is arbitrary or excessive a court should ask itself:
>
>> 'whether: (i) the legislative objective is sufficiently important to justify limiting a fundamental right; (ii) the measures designed to meet the legislative objective are rationally connected to it; and (iii) the means used to impair the right or freedom are no more than is necessary to accomplish the objective.'
>
> *The critical matter is the third criterion.* (emphasis supplied)

5.186   *De Freitas* v *Permanent Secretary of Ministry of Agriculture, Fisheries, Lands and Housing* [1999] 1 AC 69 concerned the constitutionality of provisions of Antigua and Barbuda's Civil Service Act which made inroads into the constitutional free speech rights of civil servants by prohibiting comment on controversial matters. The Privy Council held that the section had a legitimate aim, namely the preservation of neutrality in the civil service, was rationally connected to the objective since it promoted it, but was over-wide and therefore not necessary, and was excessive.

---

[167]   See e.g. *Handyside* v *UK* (1979–80) 1 EHRR 737; *Silver* v *UK* (1983) 5 EHRR 347.

5.187   The observation of the European Court that 'necessary' does not mean 'indispensable' appears to have been superseded by the endorsement of this test, from *De Freitas*, a case which concerned sensitive matters in opposition to the constitutionally enshrined right to freedom of expression. The four-stage process evident in EC law appears to be the correct approach in ECHR cases, with emphasis being placed upon the centrality of the 'least intrusive alternative' and 'fair balance' (tests (c) and (d)) aspects of the proportionality doctrine.

5.188   Further support for this view is given by the decision of the Court of Appeal in *B* v *Secretary of State* [2000] Imm AR 478 where Sedley LJ held (at para. 17) that 'in essence' proportionality amounts to this:

> a measure which interferes with a . . . human right must not only be authorised by law but must correspond to a pressing social need and go no further than is strictly necessary in a pluralistic society to achieve its permitted purpose; or, more shortly, must be appropriate and necessary to its legitimate aim.[168]

However the strictness of the review of necessity may depend upon the context of the right engaged.

5.189   Moreover, this is the test which is applied by the Home Office itself to decisions concerning detention,[169] and to assess the justification of interferences with family life, at least in the detention context.[170]

5.190   At the very least it can be said that a restriction on an ECHR right is unlikely to be proportionate if the same ends could be achieved by a less restrictive means.[171]

5.191   Thus, where intrusion into a right is permitted by the ECHR scheme, in order to pass the test of justification, the intruding measure must satisfy the following requirements.[172]

---

[168]   Sedley LJ then cited the following works: Schwarze, *European Public Law*, ch. 5; Tridimas, T., *The General Principles of EC Law* (Clarendon Press, 1999) pp. 89–93; Lester, Lord and Pannick, D., *Human Rights Law and Practice* (Butterworths, 1999) para. 3.10; Grosz, S., Beatson, J. and Duffy, P., *Human Rights: The 1998 Act and the European Convention* (Sweet & Maxwell, 1999) pp. 112–14; Starmer, K., *European Human Rights Law* (LAG, 1999) pp. 169–80; Mountfield, H. and Wadham, J., *Guide to the Human Rights Act 1998* (Blackstone Press, 2000) pp. 13–16.

[169]   Chapter 38, Operation Enforcement Manual, 21 December 2000 (see above at chapter 3).

[170]   Chapter 38, 1.1.2, ibid. (see above at chapter 4).

[171]   See Starmer, K., *Blackstone's Human Rights Digest* (Blackstone Press, 2001) lxi.

[172]   See Supperstone, M. and Coppell, J., 'Judicial Review after the Human Rights Act' EHRLR [1999] 312–315; M. Fordham and T. de la Mare, 'Identifying the Principle of Proportionality' in Jowell and Cooper (eds.) (above at footnote 143).

5.192	First, does the measure pursue a legitimate aim? The legitimate aim is provided by the express restrictions set out in the relevant ECHR Article. Thus a bland incantation of immigration control is not sufficient where Article 8(2) is concerned. The nominate aim must be identified. This is because there is no room for implied limitations on qualified rights beyond the express limitations provided for in the ECHR itself (*Golder* v *UK* (1975) 1 EHRR 524, para. 44). Where the issue is the limitation of an *implied* right, e.g. under Article 6, again the legitimate aims are those recognized in general by the ECHR (*Ashingdane* v *UK* (1985) 7 EHRR 528). Article 18 reinforces close supervision of legitimate aims by providing that permitted restrictions may only be applied for prescribed purposes.

5.193	Secondly, is the measure pursued *suitable* to the aim advanced? Thus in the 'Spycatcher case' (*Observer and Guardian* v *UK* (1991) 14 EHRR 153, para. 68), the European Court held to be unjustified injunctions obtained by the Attorney-General against newspapers preventing them from publishing extracts from the biography of a former secret service agent, Peter Wright, since the book had been published outside the UK. The UK's argument, that the restrictions on the right to freedom of expression were justified in the interests of national security, was justified only until the point of publication abroad; after that point, the restrictions were not suitable to achieve their objectives.

5.194	Thirdly, is there a less intrusive alternative to the measure pursued? In *Campbell* v *UK* (1993) 15 EHRR 137 the European Court found that a blanket rule which permitted the routine searching of prisoners' correspondence to their legal representatives was over-wide. The argument that the interference with the right to respect for correspondence under Article 8 was necessary in order to check for prohibited material failed: a less intrusive measure, namely the opening of letters in the prisoner's presence without reading them, would have met these objectives. A good domestic example of this aspect of the proportionality review, albeit as a feeding constituent of irrationality, is found in *R* v *Secretary of State, ex parte Joint Council for the Welfare of Immigrants* [1997] 1 WLR 275, where Simon Brown LJ held that the Secretary of State could have implemented measures less destructive of asylum seekers' rights than denying benefits altogether in order to achieve his stated objective of deterring unmeritorious claims.[173] Related to this aspect of the test is the enquiry as to whether the measure 'impairs the very essence of the right' (*F* v *Switzerland* (1988) 10 EHRR 411), or whether the 'substance of the right' is left intact *Campbell* v *UK* (1992) 15 EHRR 137, paras. 41, 60.

---

[173]	See also *R* v *Secretary of State, ex parte Leech (No. 2)* [1994] QB 198.

5.195 Fourthly, even if the measure promotes the aim, and there is no less intrusive alternative available, does it strike a fair balance having regard to the effects on the individual? Does it have an unacceptably severe or disproportionate effect on the individual's interests? Does the end justify the means? An example of this residual balance exercise, or proportionality in its narrowest sense, is *Nasri* v *France* (1996) 21 EHRR 458. Here, the European Court weighed the consequences of the deportation of an Algerian national from France, where he had been convicted of serious crimes, against the impact on the applicant. While the deportation pursued a legitimate aim—the prevention of crime and disorder—the consequences on the applicant were severe and excessive: the applicant was deaf and dumb, and dependent on his family for social development. A good domestic example is again *R* v *Secretary of State, ex parte Joint Council for the Welfare of Immigrants* [1997] 1 WLR 275[174] where the Court of Appeal held that the impact of the Secretary of State's policy went beyond its design: it deterred not only unmeritorious claimants (the design) but also genuine asylum seekers. Its effects were excessive.

5.196 Fifthly, and in contrast to the approach in domestic law prior to the Human Rights Act 1998 even in its most intrusive form, the burden is squarely on the decision-maker to provide by 'convincing reasons' (*Bartold* v *Germany* (1985) 7 EHRR 383) or 'relevant and sufficient reasons' (*Sunday Times* v *UK* (1979) 2 EHRR 245) that the measure passes these tests. In the absence of reasons, just as in classic domestic judicial review the court is entitled to infer that the decision has no rational basis,[175] the European Court has held that justification was not made out.[176]

5.197 It is plain that proportionality requires the application of a structured and schematic test, with an emphasis on the decision-maker providing a justification once an interference is made out. This is in contrast to *Wednesbury* which typically mandates a holistic approach, with a concomitant tendency to analyse failures of proportionality as constituent elements in, but not determinative of, legality or rationality. While the *ex parte Smith* test requires justification where there is an interference with human rights, with a variable threshold commensurate with the importance of the right interfered with, the nature of that justification is left unstructured, and there are question marks as to the intensity of review afforded by the *ex parte Smith* test, which are addressed below at 5.229 et seq. Proportionality is certainly apt to require more from a decision-maker than *Wednesbury*. The ultimate question is 'is the decision justified?' rather than 'is it reasonable?' Whether or not this *necessarily* demands a more intensive review is a topic addressed by the next section.

---

[174] See, Poole, 'Proportionality: A New Strain' [2000] JR 33.
[175] See e.g. *R* v *Secretary of State ex parte Amankwah* [1994] Imm AR 420.
[176] See *Kokkanis* v *Greece* (1993) 17 EHRR 397; *Bartold* v *Germany* (1985) 7 EHRR 383.

Due deference

5.198   We have seen above that Articles 1 (the obligation to secure to all in the jurisdiction the substance of ECHR rights), 35 (requirement to exhaust domestic remedies) and 13 (right to an effective remedy before a national remedy) cumulatively provide for a principle of subsidiarity in the ECHR scheme. It is the national courts that are expected to conduct the primary review of the decision by the public authority.

5.199   This scheme, and the European Court's resulting role as a supervisory, supra-national court as distinct from a court which determines principles for direct application in pending litigation,[177] has led it to afford states a 'margin of appreciation' in the observance and implementation of ECHR rights. It is a notion which allows the European Court to give latitude to the national authorities given their greater proximity to the relevant vital social and moral forces. But it has no application domestically.[178] In *Brown* v *Stott* [2001] 2 WLR 817, 842 Lord Steyn stated:

> Under the Convention system the primary duty is placed on domestic courts to secure and protect Convention rights. The function of the ECHR is essential but supervisory. In that capacity it accords to domestic courts a margin of appreciation, which recognises that national institutions are in principle better placed than an international court to evaluate local needs and conditions. That principle is logically not applicable to domestic courts. On the other hand, national courts may accord to the decisions of national legislatures some deference *where the context justifies it*: see *R* v *DPP ex parte Kebilene* [1993] 3 WLR 972 per Lord Hope at 993–994; see also: Singh, Hunt and Demetriou: 'Is there a role for the "Margin of Appreciation" in National Law after the Human Rights Act ?' [1999] EHRLR 15–22. (original emphasis)

5.200   In *R* v *DPP, ex parte Kebilene* [1993] 3 WLR 972, the first case in the House of Lords to examine the HRA 1998, Lord Hope of Craighead said (at pp. 993, 994), drawing on the phrase 'discretionary area of judgment' from Lester and Pannick, *Human Rights Law and Practice,* para. 3.21:

> In this area difficult choices may have to be made by the executive or the legislature between the rights of the individual and the needs of society. In some circumstances it will be appropriate for the courts to recognise that there is an area of judgment within which the judiciary will defer, on democratic grounds, to the considered opinion of the elected body or person whose act or decision is said to be incompatible with the Convention . . . It will be easier for such an area of judgment to be recognised where

---

[177] See the role of the ECJ on references under Article 234 (formerly Article 177) of the EC Treaty.
[178] See Pannick, D., 'Principles of Interpretation of Convention Rights under the Human Rights Act and the Discretionary Area of Judgment' [1998] PL 454, 458.

the Convention itself requires a balance to be struck, much less so where the right is stated in terms which are unqualified. It will be easier for it to be recognised where the issues involve questions of social or economic policy, much less so where the rights are of high constitutional importance or are of a kind where the courts are especially well placed to assess the need for protection.

5.201 It is important to note that the existence of a margin of appreciation even at European Court level does not limit the supervision of the European Court merely:

to ascertaining whether the respondent State exercised its discretion reasonably, carefully and in good faith.[179]

This affords a greater intensity of review than orthodox *Wednesbury*: a discretion that was exercised reasonably, carefully and in good faith would not be *Wednesbury* unreasonable.[180] The margin afforded does however depend on context: where the margin is broadest (property rights under Article 1 Protocol 1) the 'manifestly unreasonable' test applied by the European Court is akin to *Wednesbury*. Thus the extent of the margin afforded correlates to the intensity of review conducted by the European Court. The European Court has also been prepared to conduct searching views of the factual background to a case, holding that the state has failed to justify its assessment (*Autronic v Switzerland* (1990) 12 EHRR 485).

5.202 The passage from Lord Steyn's speech in *Brown v Stott* (2001) indicates that an analogous domestic doctrine is required 'where the context justifies it'. This is partly because the concept of margin of appreciation has a secondary element, deriving from the European Court's status as a *court*, an institution which will show restraint in reviewing the decisions of a body whose authority is underpinned by a democratic mandate.[181]

5.203 Notwithstanding the ability of the European Court to conduct a more searching review than *Wednesbury* even in the presence of a margin of appreciation, 'reading across' from a margin of appreciation into a domestic equivalent doctrine is not appropriate. This is because the factor in the European Court's approach which is essential in setting the distance between it and the decision of the domestic authority, namely the lack of proximity between the European Court and the social conditions in the state, is not present where a domestic human rights review of a decision is being conducted. A 'reading across' of a margin

---

[179] See e.g. *Sunday Times v UK* (1979) 2 EHRR 245; *Vogt v Germany* (1996) 21 EHRR 205, 235.
[180] See also R. Singh, M. Hunt and M. Demetriou: 'Is there a role for the 'Margin of Appreciation' in National Law after the Human Rights' [1999] EHRLR 15, 17.
[181] See Fordham and de la Mare, Supperstone and Coppell above at footnote 172.

from the European Court will almost by definition lead to an insufficiently intense review, and will therefore be defective in the *substantive* protection afforded to ECHR rights.

5.204   The European Court has been criticised for over-use of the notion of margin of appreciation, which obfuscates the promulgation of a clear and coherent legal analysis of the issues.[182] Singh, Hunt and Demetriou state that:[183]

> it has become commonplace to talk of 'applying' [the notion of margin of appreciation] to the facts of particular cases and of discovering its 'width' or 'ambit' in different circumstances . . . however, far from being a doctrine or principle capable of abstract definition and concrete application, the margin of appreciation is a conclusory label which only serves to obscure the true basis on which a reviewing court decides whether or not intervention in a particular case is justifiable. As such, it tends to preclude courts from articulating the justification for and limits of their role as guardians for human rights in a democracy.

5.205   This has consequences for the analogous doctrine of 'due deference'[184] or 'discretionary area of judgment'[185] or 'margin of discretion',[186] which must be applied domestically in order for the courts to remain faithful to democratic claims to power. We have seen above that a simple 'reading across' of the doctrine will not suffice in setting the *substantive* level of intensity to be afforded. The observations as to the obfuscatory and conclusory nature of the concept also indicate that reading across will not be appropriate *qualitatively* in articulating the basis of review.

5.206   As we have seen, the passage from Lord Steyn's speech in *Brown* v *Stott* indicates that an analogous domestic doctrine is required *where the context justifies it.* The question of deference is normative rather than descriptive: in the particular circumstances, *ought* the European Court to be deferential, rather than *does* the European Court defer? What, then, are the factors which determine the existence and extent of the due deference that is to be afforded?

5.207   The starting point is the *relative* margin applied by the European Court. By considering the *relative* margin, as opposed to the absolute margin applied by the European Court, the flaws in simply reading across the margin applied by the European Court are avoided. Analysis of the relative margin should abstract out

---

[182] See e.g. MacDonald, R. St J., 'The Margin of Appreciation' in Macdonald, Matscher and Petzold (eds) *The European System for the Protection of Human Rights* (Martinus Nijhoff, 1993).
[183] Is there a role for the 'Margin of Appreciation' in National Law after the Human Rights Act ?' [1999] EHRLR 15, 20–21.
[184] Ibid.
[185] Lester and Pannick (above at footnote 168).
[186] See Laws LJ in *R* v *Secretary of State, ex parte Mahmood* [2001] 1 WLR 840.

that element of deference which arises from the supra-international character of the European Court. Beyond that, we suggest the following factors:[187]

(a)   the importance of the right at stake: whether derogable or non-derogable even in time of war or public emergency (Articles 2 and 3, save that deaths arising from lawful acts of war will not violate Article 2); whether absolute (Article 3, Article 6(1)) or qualified (Articles 5, 8);

(b)   the extent and seriousness as well as the mere fact of the interference;

(c)   whether the aim of the measure is to promote other rights, including social and economic rights, and whether the measure raises a 'polycentric dispute'[188] i.e. a dispute which has a direct 'domino' effect on other policies;

(d)   the relative specialist knowledge or experience of the decision-maker as against that of the European Court;

(e)   whether the decision-maker is electorally accountable;

(f)   whether the applicants are likely to be particularly vulnerable and unpopular, for whom a minimum set of human rights guarantees are especially relevant.

5.208   Accordingly, the adoption of proportionality, applied with a domestic doctrine of due deference where the context justifies it, would not we believe lead to 'an abuse of the Court's supervisory jurisdiction' (*R* v *Secretary of State, ex parte Brind* [1991] AC 696 at 766–7 per Lord Lowry). While in some cases no deference will be due, so that the range of permissible answers will reduce to one, in others the European Court will defer to the view of the decision-maker to observe the limits of its democratic role.

Deference in the immigration context

5.209   As a starting point, there is a cogent case for the proposition that in a democracy there may be a systemic failure to promote the interests of vulnerable minority groups such as immigrants, and that cognizance of this failure should inform the level of scrutiny applied by the courts to decisions of the executive:

---

[187] See also Pannick, D., 'Principles of interpretation of Convention rights under the Human Rights Act and the discretionary area of judgment' [1998] PL 545, 549–51; *Libman* v *Attorney-General of Canada* (1998) 3 BHRC 269; Lester and Pannick (above at footnote 168); Singh, Hunt and Demetriou (above at footnote 180); Fordham and de la Mare (above at footnote 143); Supperstone and Coppell (above at footnote 172). In the field of EC law see Tridimas, T., 'Searching for the Appropriate Standard of Scrutiny' in E. Ellis (ed), *The Principle of Proportionality in the Laws of Europe* (Hart, 2000) 76–7. See also *International Transport Roth GmbH* v *Secretary of State for the Home Department* [2002] 3 WLR 344.

[188] See Fuller, 'The forms and limits of adjudication' [1978] 92 Harvard LR 353, 394–404.

It is important to note that the phrase 'in a democratic society' has substantive content and is not mere verbiage. The European Court of Human Rights has stressed that the concept of a democratic society which is reflected in the ECHR is not one in which the majority as it is from time to time simply has its way. Rather it is characterised by pluralism, tolerance and broad mindedness . . . It is worth dwelling on what a pluralist society is. It is one in which there are fluctuating groups which overlap and which may come together from time to time to form a majority. For example, a person may be wealthy or poor, unemployed or in work, male or female, a trade union member or not, of a particular religion or no religion, gay or straight, black or white. Most of the time the democratic process should allow people to decide for themselves how they want their political representatives to coalesce around these various interests. The main political parties are coalitions, sometimes uneasy ones, of all these groups and others. Most of the time, at least in theory, it should be possible for today's minorities to become tomorrow's majority by joining forces with others around a common programme. *But sometimes there is a systemic failure.* There may be no conventional political party that has much interest in representing the interests of a particular group or it may take their support for granted. They may not have the vote at all. It is in such circumstances that the ordinary give and take of the democratic process is unlikely to protect the rights of a vulnerable and unpopular minority. To make the point less abstract, look at the groups of people who have been 'clients' of the European Court of Human Rights from this country . . . The first main groups comprised immigrants or potential immigrants . . . These groups had to go to Strasbourg because they had nowhere else to go for legal remedies. English law had failed them . . .[189]

5.210 We have seen from the preceding chapters that the substantive Articles engaged in immigration cases are likely to be Articles 3, 5, and 8.

Article 3

5.211 In the context of Article 3 no balance can ever be involved. Article 3 enshrines an absolute right. No derogation is possible under Article 15. Two questions are likely to be involved in Article 3 challenges: (1) whether the treatment complained of reaches the minimum threshold of severity and (2) whether substantial grounds for a real risk are made out.

5.212 As to the first question, no deference is due. Classification of the severity of risk is a task that the courts are well used to performing. We do not consider that it would be appropriate for a court to say that the Secretary of State or appellate authority enjoyed a margin of latitude in determining whether the established risk fell within the area proscribed by Article 3. This contrasts with the position under refugee law, where the Court of Appeal has held that the question of persecution is a matter of fact (*Kagema* v *Secretary of State* [1997] Imm AR 137).

---

[189] Singh, R., 'The Place of the Human Rights Act in a Democratic Society', in Jowell and Cooper (eds), *Understanding Human Rights Principles* (Hart Publishing, 2001) 191–3.

5.213 Equally we consider that on the second essentially evidential question, where material is produced before the court, the discretionary margin afforded to the inferior decision-taker will be very narrow. Where the issue of risk is decided by the appellate authority, deference will be due to conclusions reached in light of the appellate authority's fund of knowledge about conditions abroad 'save to the extent that it could be shown to be *wrong*' (*B* v *Secretary of State* [2000] Imm AR 478, para. 26 (emphasis supplied)) (as opposed to *irrational*), by production of relevant material. This view is supported by the comments of Lord Hoffman in *Rehman* v *Secretary of State* [2001] 3 WLR 877 at paras. 54, 57 noting that no constitutional privilege can be claimed by the executive in this context.

5.214 The position is stronger when the primary adjudicator of risk is the Secretary of State. As noted above, the courts are well used to making a dispassionate assessment of risk, a function which may be more difficult to perform for a politically vulnerable executive. Further the Secretary of State and appellate authority, despite their familiarity with the material, enjoy no special advantage where the material is produced before the court, and where a situation is ongoing, the court is also free from the momentum that a previous adverse decision may generate in the executive. These points are well illustrated by the following passage of the judgment of Simon Brown LJ in *R* v *Secretary of State, ex parte Turgut* [2000] 1 All ER 719):[190]

All that said, however, this is not an area in which the Court will pay any especial deference to the Secretary of State's conclusion on the facts. In the first place, the human right involved here—the right not to be exposed to a real risk of Article 3 ill-treatment—is both absolute and fundamental: it is not a qualified right requiring a balance to be struck with some competing social need. Secondly, the Court here is hardly less well placed than the Secretary of State himself to evaluate the risk once the relevant material is placed before it. Thirdly, whilst I would reject the applicant's contention that the Secretary of State has knowingly misrepresented the evidence or shut his eyes to the true position, we must, I think, recognise at least the possibility that he has (even if unconsciously) tended to depreciate the evidence of risk and, throughout the protracted decision-making process, may have tended also to rationalise the further material adduced so as to maintain his pre-existing stance rather than reassess the position with an open mind. In circumstances such as these, what has been called the 'discretionary area of judgment'—the area of judgment within which the Court should defer to the Secretary of State as the person primarily entrusted with the decision on the applicant's removal (see Lord Hope of Craighead's speech in *R* v *DPP ex parte Kebilene* [1999] 3 WLR 972 at 993–4)—is a decidedly narrow one.

---

[190] And see also *Oladehinde* [1991] 1 AC 245 and *Hickey* [1995] 1 WLR 734.

5.215   It is noteworthy that the foregoing passage appears in the context where, by virtue of the UK appellate system, the appellate courts and tribunals cannot grant status such that the decision is always for the Secretary of State.[191] This indicates that the simple question of whether Parliament has left the question for the decision-maker is not determinative of and merely of marginal relevance to the question of whether deference should be afforded to the views of the inferior decision-taker.[192]

5.216   The question which arises is whether there is *any* room for latitude being given to the view of the Secretary of State. The decision in *Turgut* stops short of saying that the discretionary area reduces to vanishing point, although the thrust of the reasoning points towards that conclusion. All the six factors identified above at 5.207 point in favour of no margin, save for the electoral accountability of the Secretary of State—but that factor would appear to have little relevance in the present context: why should democratic accountability be relevant to an assessment of risk? It is difficult to see how the question *in this context* of 'is the decision justified?' makes any sense other than if it means 'is the decision correct?' We return to this theme below at 5.222 et seq.

5.217   The importance of protecting against Article 3 type risks is demonstrated by the decisions of the Court of Appeal in *R* v *Secretary of State for Social Security, ex parte Joint Council for the Welfare of Immigrants* [1997] 1 WLR 275 and in the subsequent case of *R* v *Westminster CC ex parte M* [1997] 1 CCLR 85 where the Court of Appeal held that s. 21 of the National Assistance Act 1948 gave rise to an obligation to provide care and assistance to destitute asylum seekers. The decision landed local authorities with a considerable increase in expenditure and had a fairly direct consequence on other policy considerations. But the polycentric nature of the issue was essentially irrelevant given the nature and severity of the situation faced by the applicants.

Article 5

5.218   In the context of challenges to detention under Article 5 the issue is quintessentially within the court's experience and competence, and it is vested with the final decision. It does not seem appropriate therefore for any deference to be afforded to the decision-taker where liberty is at stake: the courts are 'the traditional guardians of personal liberties' (*Amuur* v *France* (1996) 22 EHRR 533, para. 43). This however appears not to have been the view taken by the Court of Appeal in *R (on the application of Sezek)* v *Secretary of State* [2001] INLR 675.

---

[191]   See *Bugdaycay* v *Secretary of State* [1987] AC 514; the position is different in most other European states.

[192]   See also Lester and Pannick (above at footnote 168) para. 3.21, approved by Lord Hope in *R* v *DPP, ex parte Kebilene* [1993] 3 WLR 972 and contrast *Samaroo* (20 December 2000, Thomas J); but see Court of Appeal in *Samaroo* v *Secretary of State* [2001] EWCA Civ 1139.

5.219   The High Court has original jurisdiction in all cases to grant bail as ancillary relief on judicial review.[193] A demonstration of how the momentum built up by a decision to detain may obscure a considered perspective is contained in the following passage from *Doku v Secretary of State* (CA, 30 November 2000), which concerned a challenge to the refusal to grant bail by the first instance judge:

> (Counsel) advances three grounds which he submits might in another case be no more than arguments on the facts, but in this case, he submits, are elevated to issues of law by their starkness. He says, first, that there was simply no evidence upon which a risk of the nature spelt out in Schedule 1 of the Bail Act could be held to exist. Secondly, and it is perhaps another way of putting the same point, he says that Keene J engaged in a speculation about the risk, which in its nature was impermissible. Thirdly, he submits that, entering into the argument although it does not enter into the judgment, was the submission that if he was given bail Mr Doku might leave the United Kingdom. As to the last of these it is certainly right that counsel for the Home Secretary in an unguarded moment did so submit. Keene J however was not seduced by that argument. It is as well he was not.

Article 8

5.220   More difficult questions arise in the context of Article 8. We suggest the following approach:

(a)   Where economic well-being is concerned, or protection of the rights and interests of others, typically by exercise of frontier control (i.e. exclusion or expulsion of illegals cases), deference is due to the Secretary of State's view of the *importance* of the aim pursued, given the constitutional and democratic position, in the light of other policy objectives such as employment and race relations (that is, the rights and freedoms of others). However it may be appropriate for the court to accept a call for proof of 'legislative facts' by way of something analogous to Brandeis briefs, especially in the current climate of promoting some skilled immigration, and the indication of considerable public support even for unskilled immigration.[194] The rationale for the acceptance by the courts of third party public interest intervenors would suggest it would be appropriate in test cases for the proposition that e.g. expulsion is in the economic interests of the UK to be tested by comprehensive evidence.[195]

---

[193] See *R v Secretary of State, ex parte Kelso* [1998] INLR 603; *Doku v Secretary of State* (CA, 30 November 2000); see above at 3.94 et seq.

[194] See, *Guardian*, 21 May 2001 'Majority want to let in unskilled migrants'.

[195] This is perhaps an apposite example in the current climate of tolerance and encouragement of immigration of labour.

(b)   Where the aim is prevention of crime, typically where a legally resident non-national has committed offences, the court is well used to the issue, and we consider that it is not appropriate for great deference to be afforded to the Secretary of State's view of the *importance* to be attached to the aim pursued: tribunals have the final say in conducive to the public good deportation issues. The criminal courts decide, as part of sentence, whether they should recommend deportation. The fact that the ultimate decision is for the Secretary of State is not determinative of the issue:[196] the critical question remains whether the subject matter of the decision is something that commands deference or whether it requires the performance of a task with which the court is acquainted, and as to which it suffers from no relative lack of experience and expertise as compared to the decision-maker.

(c)   Similarly where issues under proportionality arise as to whether the measure is suitable or whether there is a less intrusive alternative to expulsion which will achieve the end, the court can decide the issues: it will typically concern a logical reasoning process.

(d)   Even where this otherwise logical process is infused by a greater requirement for evaluation, again where the interest is prevention of crime in the expulsion context, and the deterrent aspect of the sentence on the rights and freedoms of others is involved parasitically rather than directly, the question of less intrusive alternative—mere incarceration, as opposed to deportation—can equally well be decided by the court.

(e)   Where the issue is whether the measure is excessive or disproportionate in the narrow sense, the courts are able to evaluate the unique or near-unique nature of the claim and the consequent impact on the interests asserted by the Secretary of State as justification. This was precisely the approach in *R* v *Secretary of State ex parte Quaquah* [2000] INLR 196,[197] where Turner J considered it was difficult to see how the interests of immigration control could be served by removing an immigrant who wished to sue the Home Office for malicious prosecution following his acquittal of charges relating to the 'Campsfield riots', given the unique or near-unique nature of his application. In R v *Secretary of State, ex parte Mahmood* [2001] 1 WLR 840 at paras. 23, 26 in the course of his reasoning, Laws LJ held that the 'Firm immigration control requires consistency of treatment between one aspiring immigrant and another' and that a benevolent waiver of the requirement would 'in the absence of exceptional circumstances to justify the waiver, disrupt and

---

[196] Contrast the decision of Thomas J in *R* v *Secretary of State, ex parte Samaroo* (20 December 2000), [2001] EWCA Civ 1139.
[197] See also *R* v *Immigration Officer ex p Hashim* CO 2052 99, 12 June 2000.

undermine firm immigration control because it would be manifestly unfair to other would-be entrants who are content to take their place in the entry clearance queue in their country of origin.'. Even where the Home Office actually accepts that the applicant meets the rule's substantive requirements, 'it is simply unfair that he should not have to wait in the queue like everyone else. At least it is unfair unless he can demonstrate some exceptional circumstance which reasonably justifies his jumping the queue.' Thus the policy end of promoting a regulated immigration control is served by enforcing the policy. But pursuit of that end, as we have noted above, may be disproportionate where an individual case is distinguishable from the generality, and there is no longer a comparison of like with like so that the potential for undermining policy is correspondingly lowered. The court would be able to draw on its experience, perhaps if appropriate by evidence from the Secretary of State, in order to consider the 'atypicality' of the instant case. No particular deference would be due.

The approach of the courts to s. 6 of the HRA 1998 and proportionality

5.221   Our basic thesis is that the courts, when faced with a human rights challenge under s. 6 of the HRA 1998, are required to conduct a primary rather than secondary review of the decision. The ground of complaint, in the traditional nomenclature, would be illegality,[198] or perhaps more appropriately 'breach of an ECHR right'. Proportionality is a legal concept. The latitude which the courts afford to conclusions reached by decision-makers is observed by the principle of due deference or discretionary area of judgment: there is no need for the additional deferential doctrine of *Wednesbury* to be grafted onto those principles. This is indeed the effect of the important judgment of the House of Lords in *R (Daly)* v *Secretary of State* [2001] 2 AC 532. The court is the ultimate arbiter of the legality of the decision, and itself asks whether the measure is proportionate to the aim pursued. This may involve a deeper scrutiny than that required even under the heightened *Wednesbury* approach. But it does not become an appeal court. It does not substitute its own decision for that of the decision-taker. Where appropriate it will defer to the decision-maker and grant a principled distance between itself and the decision-taker commensurate with the circumstances of the case.

Article 3
5.222   The standard of review applied by the Court of Appeal in *R* v *Secretary of State, ex parte Turgut* [2000] 1 All ER 719 was informed, as we have seen, by

---

[198] *Council for Civil Service Unions* v *Minister for the Civil Service* [1985] AC 374 per Lord Scarman.

the European Court's case law on Article 13. The question was whether the Court of Appeal should adopt a primary fact finding approach on the raw data, or a review approach. The review approach was held appropriate but the nature of the exercise meant that very little deference was due to the decision-maker. An independent assessment of claim was required to see if the conclusion that substantial grounds for a real risk was compelled.

5.223   We consider that reliance on Article 13 is not an appropriate basis on which to determine the intensity of review to be afforded in an Article 3 case. First, there is an inescapable element of levelling down or margin of appreciation in the European Court even in its consideration of Article 13 standards arising from its status as an international court. Article 13 requires the ability to examine the substance of the complaint, and does not guarantee success. It does not require incorporation. Section 6 of the HRA 1998 however requires success to be guaranteed. Otherwise the court will be in breach of *its* own duty.[199] A court operating under the s. 6 duty not to breach an ECHR right, we suggest, should not afford *any* margin of deference to the primary decision-maker in an Article 3 case, where the relevant material has been placed before it. There is no external rule prohibiting a correctness standard being applied to assessment of risk, merely a self-denying ordinance: s. 6(2) would not save the court. *Turgut* of course concerned the position prior to the coming into force of s. 6, with the appellant urging the court to develop the common law in line with alleged Article 13 standards. The issue in the result did not arise since Article 13 was not out of line with the common law. But Simon Brown LJ pointed out that on the coming into force of the HRA 1998, 'the threshold of irrationality will have to be lowered'.

5.224   Secondly, a challenge which failed domestically but won at the European Court owing to an insufficiently intense review being operated at home would frustrate the objective of the Human Rights Act 1998. It is clear that the European Court conducts a searching review of the factual basis for the allegation of risk for itself without affording the views of the state any latitude.

5.225   Thirdly, the factual basis of the application in *Turgut* is worth recalling: it was a challenge to the Secretary of State's refusal of exceptional leave to an asylum seeker found to be devoid of credibility: he was no more than a failed Kurdish Alevi asylum seeker. The Court of Appeal held that the evidence was not clear as to the fate that would befall him on return. Where the evidence was clear, it seems that an adverse conclusion on risk could *now* not be upheld.

5.226   It is perhaps interesting that the Court of Appeal in *R v Secretary of State ex parte X* [2001] 1 WLR 745, where the issue was another judicial review

---

[199] See the analogous approach to horizontality in *Douglas v Hello! Ltd* [2001] 2 WLR 992.

concerning Article 3 in the context of removal powers under the IA 1971 for detainees held under Mental Health Act 1983 powers, was prepared to assume, without deciding, that Article 3 requires the court to conduct a primary review of the factual basis of the decision. Lord Hoffman in *Rehman* v *Secretary of State* [2001] 3 WLR 877 was perhaps contemplating such a role.

5.227 The final point is that the force of the decision as it stands in *Turgut* can be seen when juxtaposed against the approach adopted in *Secretary of State* v *Javed and others* (CA, 17 May 2001) at para. 9. Even though, or perhaps because, *Javed* did not raise any human rights issues, the contrast between the approach of the court in *Javed* and that in *Turgut* is illuminating. The issue in *Javed* was the validity of the Secretary of State's Order[200] which designated Pakistan as a 'white list' country on the basis that there was in general no serious risk of persecution there. The Order was subject to affirmative resolution by both Houses of Parliament. The Secretary of State submitted that the court could only review the legality of the Order if the Secretary of State had taken leave of his senses or had acted in bad faith. Lord Phillips MR, giving the judgment of the court, rejected this submission, drawing a contrast between cases concerning the distribution of the tax burden and national economic policy[201] where 'rationality could not be measured by any yardstick available to the Court' and the instant case where the validity of the Order depended on the existence of a state of affairs: 'was there in general no serious risk of persecution?' (at para. 49) (a question of fact) and then: 'should Pakistan be designated?' (at para. 56) (a question of policy). But since there were no human rights issues involved in including Pakistan in the Order,[202] there was no requirement to subject the decision to 'particularly rigorous scrutiny' nor was the 'discretionary area of judgment' (para. 54) a particularly narrow one. Lord Phillips continued (at para. 57):

> ... on analysis, the challenge by the Applicants to the inclusion of Pakistan in the Order was to its legality rather than to its rationality. However the language defining the state of affairs that had to exist before a country could be designated was imprecise. Whether there was *in general* a serious risk of persecution was a question which might give rise to a genuine difference of opinion on the part of two rational observers of the same evidence. A judicial review of the Secretary of State's conclusion needed to have regard to that considerable margin of appreciation. There was no question here of conducting a rigorous examination that required the Secretary of State to justify his conclusion. If the applicants were to succeed in showing that designation of Pakistan

---

[200] Asylum (Designated Countries of Destination and Designated Safe Third Countries) Order 1996 (SI 1996/2671).

[201] See *Notts CC* v *Secretary of State for the Environment* [1986] AC 240; *R* v *Secretary of State for the Environment ex parte Hammersmith LBC* [1991] 1 AC 521.

[202] The submission that access to the IAT was a fundamental right (*ex parte Saleem*) denied or intruded upon by inclusion in the Order appears not to have been advanced.

was illegal, they had to demonstrate that the evidence clearly established that there was a serious risk of persecution in Pakistan and that this was a state of affairs that was a general feature in that country.

Having conducted a thorough review of the evidence, and the failure by the Secretary of State to address other than in bland terms the decision of the House of Lords in *Shah and Islam* [1999] 2 AC 629 concerning the general position of women in Pakistan, the court concluded that the Secretary of State could not have reasonably concluded that Pakistan was apt for designation.

5.228   This decision gives rise to three important issues. First, the court's methodology in conducting a thorough review of the evidence in order to form a benchmark against which to adjudicate upon the reasonableness of the Secretary of State's conclusion, indicates that this is an appropriate *starting* point in judicial review or statutory appeals on a point of law in Article 3 cases. Secondly, the court afforded a margin to the Secretary of State because (a) the language required was imprecise: 'it appears to him that there was *in general* a *serious* risk of persecution'; (b) human rights issues were not engaged; (c) accordingly, there was no warrant for an approach requiring the Secretary of State to justify his conclusions. These factors will not be present in an individual case concerning an individual and fact-specific adjudication of risk: in particular there will be no imprecision in language ('substantial grounds for a real risk' contrasted with 'in general a serious risk'). Thirdly, even on this approach, the applicants were merely required to demonstrate that the evidence 'clearly established' the obverse of that which had 'appeared' to the Secretary of State in order to succeed. In an Article 3 case if the evidential threshold is clearly crossed, the decision cannot stand, whether because the Secretary of State's conclusion is unreasonable as required by *ex parte Turgut* (the parameters of reasonableness being tightly drawn) or simply wrong as suggested by Sedley LJ in *B v Secretary of State for the Home Department* [2000] Imm AR 478.

Proportionality

B v Secretary of State for the Home Department
5.229   The first case to raise the issue of the role of the higher courts in reviewing decisions involving proportionality was *B v Secretary of State for the Home Department* [2000] Imm AR 478. In this case an EU national appealed against the decision of the IAT dismissing his appeal from the Secretary of State's decision to deport him on conducive grounds as a result of his conviction for sexual assaults on his child. It was common ground that the question of proportionality was a matter of law, and as such Sedley LJ held that the 'question whether deportation constitutes a proportionate response to the appellant's offending' has to be

'answered afresh even if reaching an answer involves taking a much closer look than we are accustomed to the merits' (para. 18).

5.230 The Secretary of State submitted that while proportionality was a matter of law, 'proper regard must be shown for the IAT's view' that deportation would be proportionate. That begged the question as to what proper regard, or deference, involved in the context of the case. Sedley LJ considered that the court was hardly less well placed to evaluate the issues than the inferior bodies: the Home Secretary's decision was superseded in its entirety by the IAT, findings of primary fact were not in issue, and on appeal it was appropriate to scrutinize carefully the inferences drawn, while issues of law and the IAT's reasoning were entirely open on appeal. While the Home Secretary's view was legitimately open to him, 'our public law . . . now has to accommodate and give effect to the requirements of EU law and, through EU law, of the ECHR. It means making up our own minds of the proportionality of a public law measure—not simply deciding whether the Home Secretary's or IAT's view of it is lawful and rational.' (para. 36). Since the appellant had lived in the UK since he was a small boy, what was proposed was 'although in law deportation, . . . in substance more akin to exile' and as such 'so severe as to be disproportionate' to the appellant's previous offending and propensities.

5.231 Simon Brown LJ, also allowing the appeal, held (at para. 47) that:

It was common ground before us that proportionality involves a question of law and that, on a statutory appeal of this nature, the court is required to form its own view on whether the test is satisfied, although, of course, in doing so it will give such deference to the IAT's decision as appropriately recognises their advantage in having heard the evidence. This task is, of course, both different from and more onerous than that undertaken by the court when applying the conventional *Wednesbury* approach. It would not be proper for us to say that we disagree with the IAT's conclusion on proportionality but that, since there is clearly room for two views and their view cannot be stigmatised as irrational, we cannot interfere. Rather, if our view differs from the IAT's, then we are bound to say so and to allow the appeal, substituting our decision for theirs.

5.232 Ward LJ agreed with both judgments.

5.233 The important issue which emerged from the judgment was whether the court on judicial review or statutory appeal on a point of law was required, as part of its supervisory legal functions and its ultimate responsibility[203] to secure ECHR rights, to exercise an original or primary judgment on questions of proportionality,

---

[203] As Lord Steyn said of the intrusive effect of the road traffic requirement to name a driver of an offending vehicle in *Brown* v *Stott* [2001] 2 WLR 817: 'it . . . boils down to the question whether in adopting the procedure enshrined in s. 172 rather than a reverse burden technique, [the legislature] took more drastic action than was justified. While this is ultimately a question for the court, it is not unreasonable to regard both techniques as reasonable.'

having 'inputted' deference,[204] or whether it exercises a traditional *Wednesbury* secondary judgment, asking itself whether the decision-maker reached a decision on proportionality which was rationally open to him.

Mahmood v Secretary of State for the Home Department

5.234 A different approach was adopted by the Court of Appeal in the case of *Mahmood v Secretary of State for the Home Department* [2001] 1 WLR 840. This concerned the removal of an illegal entrant and failed asylum seeker who had married a British citizen prior to enforcement action, but the marriage had not taken place two years before enforcement action as required by the Secretary of State's policy DP 3/96 for removal to be presumptively abandoned. The Secretary of State considered that the appellant's wife and children could join him in Pakistan, or alternatively that the appellant himself could apply for an entry clearance following removal so that again family life could be enjoyed (para. 14). Accordingly there were no exceptional circumstances warranting the cancellation of removal. The appellant argued that enforcing removal for the mere purpose of an entry clearance being obtained was a disproportionate interference with the appellant's family life, especially since the consequential loss of the appellant's employment in the UK might jeopardize his ability to meet the public funds requirements of the rules from abroad (para. 20).

5.235 Two issues of general importance were raised. The first was the application of the HRA 1998 to decisions taken before 2 October 1998 which were to be executed subsequently. This issue is explored above at 1.51. The second issue was whether 'this court is effectively in as good a position as was the Secretary of State to form a judgment as to the competing interests which militate for and against the Appellant's removal' (para. 3). Laws LJ, giving the leading judgment, considered there were three approaches (at para. 16):

> The first is the conventional *Wednesbury* position . . . On this model the court makes no judgment of its own as to the relative weight to be attached to this or that factor taken into account in the decision-making process; it is concerned only to see that everything relevant and nothing irrelevant has been considered, and that a rational mind has been brought to bear by the Secretary of State in reaching the decision. The second approach recognises that a fundamental right, here family life, is engaged in the case; and in consequence the court will insist that that fact be respected by the decision-maker, who is accordingly required to demonstrate either that his proposed action does not in truth interfere with the right, or if it does, that there exist considerations which may reasonably be accepted as amounting to a substantial objective justification for the interference. The third approach directly engages the rights guaranteed by the

---

[204] Sedley LJ's reference to 'making up our minds' (see above at 5.230) obviously must be seen in the context that no deference was due to the decision of the IAT.

European Convention; it would require the court to decide whether the removal of the appellant would constitute a breach of Article 8.

5.236 Laws LJ rejected the first approach as affording an insufficient intensity of review in cases raising human rights issues. The common law indicated that in such cases (para. 19):

> the second approach . . . as to the intensity of review is generally to be followed, leaving aside incorporation of the Convention; but that approach and the basic *Wednesbury* rule are by no means hermetically sealed one from the other. There is, rather, what may be called a sliding scale of review; the graver the impact of the decision in question upon the individual affected by it, the more substantial the justification that will be required. It is in the nature of the human condition that cases where, objectively, the individual is most gravely affected will be those where what we have come to call his fundamental rights are or are said to be put in jeopardy. In the present case, whether or not the Convention is under consideration, any reasonable person will at once recognise the right to family life, exemplified in the right of the parties to a genuine marriage to cohabit without any undue interference, as being in the nature of a fundamental right (I prefer the expression fundamental *freedom*).[205]

5.237 Laws LJ held (a para. 30) that the second approach would:

> *in broad terms and in most instances suffice also at least as the beginning of a proper touchstone for review when the Convention is directly in play.* It will of course fall to be tailored and adapted as the courts confront disparate situations in which, by force of s. 2 of the Act of 1998, they are obliged to take account of the Strasbourg jurisprudence . . . There will be occasions when the court's duty is to be more muscular than has been its habit; but at every turn its decisions will form part of a continuum with what the common law has already said. (emphasis supplied)

5.238 On this approach, the decision of the Secretary of State that there were no exceptional circumstances justifying 'queue jumping' through the waiver of the need to obtain entry clearance was reasonable. Maintaining the requirement to obtain entry clearance was a matter of firm immigration control. There was no error of law. Even if the ECHR were directly applied, no breach could be found: the Secretary of State's decision by no means compelled the couple to live apart. In *Abdulaziz* v *UK* (1985) 7 EHRR 471 at para. 67, by its reference to Contracting Parties enjoying a wide margin of appreciation:

> the court expressed the view . . . that the State owes no duty generally to give effect to a couple's choice of place of residence, and it will be very much up to the State to strike the balance between the requirements of immigration control and the immigrant's freedom to choose how and where he will enjoy his Article 8 rights.

---

[205] See also Sir John Laws [1998] PL.

5.239   As to the third approach, and the issue of whether the court was in as good a position as the Secretary of State to decide whether Article 8 was breached, Laws LJ observed (at para. 33) that this engaged a question of some constitutional significance:

> much of the challenge presented by the enactment of the 1998 Act consists in the search for a principled measure of scrutiny which will be loyal to Convention rights, but loyal also to the legitimate claims of power.

Without reference to *B* v *Secretary of State for the Home Department* which was not apparently cited to him, and without having to decide the question as part of the ratio for the decision, he rejected a 'judge for yourself' approach (at para. 33):

> In this case [Counsel's] submission comes close to the proposition that the court should stand in the shoes of the Secretary of State and re-take the decision in the case on its merits. In fairness, when tested, she disavowed such a proposition. But in that case her submission is without principle: the courts are in as good a position as the Secretary of State to decide; but they must not decide as if they were his surrogate. This antithesis at the same time commends but deprecates the imposition by the courts of their own views of the merits of the case in hand. It is of no practical assistance and lacks intellectual coherence. The Human Rights Act 1998 does not authorise the judges to stand in the shoes of Parliament's delegates, who are decision-makers given their responsibilities by the democratic arm of the state. The arrogation of such a power to the judges would usurp those functions of government which are controlled and distributed by powers whose authority is derived from the ballot-box. It follows that there must be a principled distance between the court's adjudication *in a case such as this*, and the Secretary of State's decision, based on his perception of the case's merits. *For present purposes* that principled distance is to be found in the approach I have taken to the scope of judicial review in this case, built on what the common law has already done in *Smith, Launder,* and *Lord Saville. For the future, when the court is indeed applying the Convention as municipal law, we shall no doubt develop a jurisprudence in which a margin of discretion (as I would call it) is allowed to the statutory decision-maker; but in the case of those rights where the Convention permits interference with the right where that is justified by reference to strict criteria (Arts. 8–11, paragraph 2 in each case) its length will no doubt be confined by the rigour of those criteria in light of the relevant Strasbourg case-law, and the gravity of the proposed interference as it is perceived here. But that is for the future.* (emphasis supplied)

5.240   May LJ agreed. Lord Phillips MR held (at para. 38) that the approach to whether the Secretary of State had breached Article 8 was as follows. First, the jurisdiction remained supervisory. The court did not substitute its own decision for that of the executive. The issue was whether the decision was permitted by law, namely the HRA 1998. Just as states were afforded a margin of appreciation by the European Court to respond in a way that is not uniform, so there will often be an area of discretion permitted to the executive of a country before a response can be demonstrated to infringe the ECHR. Secondly, the decision would be subjected to the most anxious scrutiny. Thirdly, and here the pre-HRA 1998 position at common law required to be modified, interference with human rights could only be justified to the extent permitted by the ECHR itself.

Isiko

5.241 Judgment was given in *Mahmood* after the Court of Appeal had prepared its judgment in draft in *R v Secretary of State ex parte Isiko* [2001] 1 FLR 930. That case concerned a challenge to the deportation of two Applicants with complex family relationships in the UK. They had married each other, divorced and one applicant had married a British citizen at a time when they knew that the immigration authorities were likely to deport them. Their deportation was likely to have adverse effects on a number of family relationships. Hidden J had allowed the applications for judicial review.

5.242 Giving the judgment of the Court, Schiemann LJ held that 'Immigration policy has been delegated by Parliament to the Home Secretary, and many factors will play their part in framing that policy. Amongst those factors will be those contained in Article 8(2) of the ECHR (para. 5).' The policy DP 3/96 which erected a presumption in favour of removal even in marriage cases where the marriage took place after enforcement action, was not itself unlawful. Of course however this did not mean that every act of implementation of the policy was unlawful.

5.243 Schiemann LJ then considered the rival approaches on judicial review to consideration of such cases. Counsel for the Secretary of State submitted that *B v Secretary of State for the Home Department* was not binding since it proceeded on a concession, and that 'it may have been overlooked that the Courts may not be as well placed as the Secretary of State to consider the weight to be given on wider grounds to the prevention of disorder and crime when they are considering the deportation of those who have committed serious offences.' Citing Article 1 Protocol 1, the submission continued (at para. 19) that there had to be 'a reasonable relationship of proportionality between the means employed and the aims sought to be realised. The ECHR will examine whether the means chosen *could* be regarded as reasonable and suited to achieving the legitimate aim being pursued, regard being had to the need to strike a fair balance. It does not consider whether deprivation *is in its judgment* the best solution for dealing with the problem amongst those available.' The Court was required to form a supervisory judgment on the legality of any decision of the Secretary of State.

5.244 The applicants' submission (at para. 21) was that the court was 'in just a good as position to make a judgment as the original decision-maker' having given due deference.

5.245   The court then reviewed extensively the decision in *B* v *Secretary of State* and that in *R* v *Secretary of State ex parte Mahmood*, holding (at para. 29) that the approach in *Mahmood* 'was arguably marginally different from that adopted by consent in *B*' and that 'the approach in *Mahmood* is the correct approach in these cases. It is not entirely clear whether, read as a whole, the judgments in *B* are at variance with it, particularly since there is no indication that Sedley LJ disagreed with the approach of Lord Hope of Craighead in *Kebilene*' (para. 30).

5.246   Schiemann LJ then set out the position as follows (at para. 31):

1. Where the Court reviews a decision which is required to comply with the Convention by the Human Rights Act 1998 it does not substitute its own decision for that of the executive. It reviews the decision of the executive to see if it was permitted by law— in this instance the Human Rights Act. In performing this exercise the Court has to bear in mind that, just as individual States enjoy a margin of appreciation which permits them to respond within the law in a manner which is not uniform, so there will often be an area of discretion permitted to the executive of a country which needs to be exceeded before an action must be categorised as unlawful. In this area difficult choices may have to be made by the executive or the legislature between the rights of the individual and the needs of society. In cases involving immigration policies and the rights to family life, it will be appropriate for the courts to recognise that there is an area of judgment within which the judiciary will defer, on democratic grounds, to the considered opinion of the elected body or person whose decision is said to be incompatible— see *Mahmood* para 38.

2. Where, as here, a fundamental right is engaged the court will, applying the law as it was established prior to the coming into force of the Human Rights Act 1998, insist that this fact be respected by the decision maker, who is required to demonstrate either that his proposed action does not in truth interfere with the right, or if it does, that there exist considerations which may reasonably be accepted as amounting to a substantial objective justification for the interference. The graver the impact of the decision in question upon the individuals affected by it, the more substantial the justification that will be required—*Mahmood* para. 19.

3. This more intrusive mode of supervision will in broad terms and in most instances suffice as the beginning of a proper touchstone for review when the Convention is in play—*Mahmood* para 30.

4. Within the framework of the approach outlined above the court can give the due deference to the primary decision maker which Mr MacDonald accepts that it should give. In the framework suggested by him the concept is too vague to be of any practical use as a judicial tool.

5.247   On the facts of the case, the Secretary of State had not exceeded the discretion given to him. The Secretary of State's appeal was accordingly allowed.

Reconciliation of the authorities

5.248 We suggest that the differences in approach can be reconciled to a significant degree in the following manner.

(a) *B* v *Secretary of State* concerned the expulsion of a settled Italian national who had committed odious sexual offences but was unlikely to reoffend. We have seen above in chapter 4 how respect would be demanded by the immigration authorities for his family and private life in these circumstances.

(b) There was nothing for the court to defer on: the primary facts had been found and were not challenged. There was nothing peculiarly in the province of the Secretary of State or the IAT that was in issue. Importantly in essence it was the balance question (see *Nasri* v *France* (1996) 21 EHRR 458) in the proportionality test that was live. The court decided that the expulsion of *B* would be exile rather than deportation. In that sense it was disproportionate.

(c) Sedley LJ's comment that changes brought about by EU law and the HRA 1998 entailed 'making up our own minds about the proportionality of a public law measure' have to be read in this context: they plainly were not intended to exclude the principle of due deference, a principle which he and Simon Brown LJ expressly avowed. The Court of Appeal in *B* v *Secretary of State* plainly was not saying that it was, *in every case*, in as good a position as the IAT or Home Secretary to adjudicate on proportionality.

(d) By stark contrast *Mahmood* concerned the expulsion of a person with no status in circumstances where he could apply for a visa and rejoin his family. The issue was within the province of the Secretary of State: namely the rights and freedoms of others in the queue, and the economic interests of the nation. This was a frontier case raising these nominate interests through the medium of immigration policy. Deference was due. Even without deference, the challenge would have failed (Laws LJ).

(e) Similarly in *Isiko,* the complex family lives which had arisen were all formed at a time when the immigration position of the applicants was not only uncertain, but when it was likely that they would be deported. We have seen from the case law that this is a powerful factor militating against a breach, even when the European Court is conducting a primary review of the decision.

(f) In both *Mahmood* and *Isiko*, the position adopted in *B* was considered to amount to the position that the court was 'effectively in as good a position as was the Secretary of State to form a judgment as to the competing interests which militate for and against the applicant's removal'.[206] But in *B* the approach was more subtle: it was only in *context* that the Court of Appeal had to make up its own mind and effectively stand in the shoes of the IAT.

(g) Moreover, the judgment of at least Laws LJ in *Mahmood* again is context-driven. In the key passage of his judgment he is careful to stress that 'in a case such as this' there must be a principled distance between the court's adjudication and the Secretary of State's perception of the merits. That sufficed 'for present purposes' but the common law would no doubt be developed when the ECHR was being applied as municipal law.

(h) If the cases cannot be reconciled in this manner, on the basis that notwithstanding the lack of dispute as to primary fact in *B*, the question of *weight* as to the interest in removal was something on which the Court of Appeal was required to defer, the difference in approach is perhaps explicable by the different jurisdictional routes to the Court of Appeal in the cases. *Mahmood* and *Isiko* were judicial review appeals. By contrast *B* was a statutory appeal on a point of law: the Secretary of State's decision was superseded by that of the IAT, which by virtue of its long-standing, 'conducive to the public good' appellate jurisdiction, was in as good a position to reach an original view and indeed was mandated to do so by Parliament. See *Noruwa* v *Secretary of State for the Home Department* (IAT, 11 December 2001), a starred decision, at paras. 44–57.

(i) But this has the curious and unsatisfactory result that it may be that in the appellate context, where there is the decision of the appellate authority between the courts and the Secretary of State, the protection afforded to ECHR rights is greater than on judicial review of raw decisions of the Secretary of State.

(j) The answer may lie in the role of deference in the two approaches. In *B* the approach endorsed was that of the court reaching a primary judgment on proportionality, *having given deference* to the decision-maker: principled distance was achieved in this manner, and the court's role remained supervisory because of this distance. The *Wednesbury* modified *Smith* test was seen by both Laws LJ in *Mahmood* and Schiemann LJ in *Isiko* as 'the *beginning of a proper touchstone* for review when the Convention is in play'. In *Mahmood* Laws LJ envisaged developments in the common law where a margin of discretion would be afforded to the decision-maker, but whose length would be confined by the rigour

---

[206] See e.g. *Mahmood* paras. 3, 33: 'The Human Rights Act 1998 does not authorise the judges to stand in the shoes of Parliament's delegates'; *Isiko* para. 21: Court of Appeal is 'in just as good a position to make a judgment as the original decision-maker'.

of the criteria in the ECHR in light of the case law of the European Court, and the gravity of the interference If this was an envisaged tightening of the secondary judgment required by the *Wednesbury* modified *Smith* test (see para. 33 of *Mahmood*), deference would then, it appears, operate in setting the stringency of the *Wednesbury* parameters. *If no deference was due* and there was room for only one view, a decision with which the court simply disagreed would be unreasonable. The result would be the same as under the *B* approach. Under the *B* approach the latitude afforded to the decision-maker would be a function of the deference that was due in context; under *Mahmood* and *Isiko* the latitude would be the function of *Wednesbury* parameters also set by context-dependent considerations of due deference.

5.249 As we have already noted in the Introduction, the House of Lords, in *Daly* v *Secretary of State for the Home Department* [2001] 2 AC 532, have endorsed the approach that the question of proportionality is for the courts, paying such deference as is due, in context, to the decision-maker.

Proportionality on judicial review or statutory appeal: primary or secondary review?

5.250 We consider that the approach of the Court of Appeal in *B*, that the court is required to make a primary judgment on proportionality having given deference where that is due, is the correct approach. It is neither enough nor appropriate to ask: could a reasonable Secretary of State have concluded that the interference with respect for family life was proportionate? The approach we would suggest is: 'does the court consider that the Secretary of State has justified the interference as necessary and proportionate' or 'on the agreed, found or rational view of the primary facts, giving due deference to the Secretary of State's policy of deportation, and his assessment of the need, was the deportation no more than was necessary to effectively promote the legitimate ECHR consideration?' We suggest this for the following reasons.

5.251 First, proportionality is a legal concept, and a decision which is disproportionate will not be lawful under s. 6 of the HRA 1998. Requiring the court to form a primary view of the *legality* of a decision is no heretical departure from its supervisory function. Section 6 reinforces the view of Lord Steyn in *Brown* v *Stott* that the courts have the 'primary task of securing and enforcing Convention rights. . . . Under the Convention system the primary duty is placed on domestic courts to secure and protect Convention rights.'

5.252 Secondly, a *Wednesbury* approach to proportionality runs the risk of blurring what is necessary with what is reasonable: see Lord Slynn's comments in *R (Alconbury)* v *Secretary of State for the Environment, Transport and the Regions*

[2001] 2 WLR 1389, 1407 at para. 51. The court is required, under that approach, to ask whether 'there exist considerations which may *reasonably* be accepted as amounting to a substantial objective justification for the interference.' Such a conflation of reasonable and necessary is not appropriate in the Article 8 context. The Secretary of State's submission in *Isiko* (at para. 19) was that the European Court asks 'whether the means chosen *could* be regarded as reasonable and suited to achieving the legitimate aim being pursued, regard being had to the need to strike a fair balance. It does not consider whether deprivation *is in its judgment* the best solution for dealing with the problem amongst those available.' This appears to have been drawn from the inapposite context of property rights under Article 1 Protocol 1,[207] which provides for the weakest form of proportionality review by introducing an explicit subjective element into the equation ('*deems necessary*').

5.253 Powerful support for this view is ironically demonstrated by the case most often cited in support for the maintenance of a *Wednesbury* style secondary judgment on proportionality. When the case of *R v Ministry of Defence, ex parte Smith* [1996] QB 517 reached the European Court (*Smith, Grady, Beckett* and *Lustig-Prean v UK* [1999] IRLR 734) it was held that there had been a violation of Article 13 since the threshold of irrationality was set too high and the Court of Appeal was unable to decide matters of proportionality.

5.254 Thirdly, adherence to *Wednesbury* may allow considerations external to the ECHR to enter into adjudicative exercise, despite Laws LJ's prediction that the length of discretion would be determined by the criteria in Article 8(2) and depending on the gravity of the interference. Thus for example in *Isiko* Schiemann LJ held that 'Immigration policy has been delegated by Parliament to the Home Secretary, and many factors will play their part in framing that policy. Amongst those factors will be those contained in Article 8(2) of the ECHR.' ([2001] 1 FLR 930 at para. 5). Yet we have seen that in the case of expressly qualified rights such as Article 8, the ECHR brooks no additional implied grounds for interference (*Golder v UK* (1979-80) 1 EHRR 524). Thus any reference to immigration control must relate to Article 8(2) criteria; promotion of extra-Article 8(2) ends through immigration control would be illegitimate under the ECHR scheme.

5.255 Fourthly, the *B v Secretary of State* approach is no more nor less vague

---

[207] 'Every natural or legal person is entitled to the peaceful enjoyment of his possessions. No one shall be deprived of his possessions except in the public interest and subject to the conditions provided for by law and by the general principles of international law. The preceding provisions shall not, however, in any way impair the right of a State to enforce *such laws as it deems necessary to* control the use of property in accordance with the general interest or to secure the payment of taxes or other contributions or penalties.' (emphasis supplied)

than allowing a margin of discretion in a *Wednesbury* framework to the decision-maker. In both approaches the margin is undefined and context-dependent. Indeed, *Wednesbury* may even introduce more vagueness by permitting a residual area of discretion as to what is reasonable after deference has already been afforded.

5.256 Fifthly, many commentators have contemplated the *B* v *Secretary of State* approach. Speaking extra-judicially, the Lord Chancellor described the role of the judiciary under the 1998 Act as follows:[208]

The Court's decision [under the Human Rights Act 1998] will be based on a more overtly principled, and perhaps moral, basis. The Court will look at the positive right. It will only accept an interference with that right where a justification, allowed under the Convention, is made out. The scrutiny will not be limited to seeing if the words of an exception can be made out. The Court will need to be satisfied that the spirit of this exception is made out. It will need to be satisfied that the interference with the protected right is justified in the public interest in a free democratic society. *Moreover, the Courts will in this area have to apply the Convention principle of proportionality. This means the Court will be looking substantively at that question. It will not be limited to a secondary review of the decision making process but at the primary question of the merits of the decision itself.*

In reaching its judgment, therefore, the Court will need to expand and explain its *own view* of whether the conduct is legitimate. It will produce in short a decision on the *morality* of the conduct and not simply its compliance with the bare letter of the law.

Similarly Lord Bingham, again speaking extra-judicially, said:[209]

[W]hen they come to decide whether any restriction relied upon is 'necessary' in a democratic society, then I think that *the judges will be undertaking a task which will be, to some extent at least, novel to them. They* will have to decide whether there is a pressing social need for the restriction, and whether the restriction is proportionate to the mischief against which it is directed: both of these are problems which do not ordinarily confront judges in their familiar task of deciding applications for judicial review according to the three-fold tests of illegality, irrationality, and procedural impropriety.

Lester and Pannick state:[210]

It would be wrong for the national court or tribunal to apply the *Wednesbury* principle of domestic judicial review, and simply to ask itself whether an impugned decision is 'so unreasonable that no reasonable authority could ever have come to it'.

---

[208] Tom Sargent Memorial Lecture, 16 December 1997 (emphasis supplied).
[209] Earl Grey Memorial Lecture [1998] 1 Web JCLI (emphasis supplied).
[210] *Human Rights Law and Practice* (Butterworths, 1999) at paras. 3.24 and 3.27.

Even where the court thinks it appropriate to accord some degree of deference to the decisions of the legislature or other bodies, the court must comply with its responsibility to give a judgment consistent with the Convention, having regard to the principles set out above, *in particular whether the principle of proportionality has been satisfied.*

5.257 Perhaps the most powerful objection to the *B* v *Secretary of State* approach is that it is unfaithful to the claims of democratic power. There is, however, a cogent case that, far from being constitutionally inappropriate, it is the *B* v *Secretary of State* approach that gives proper recognition to the constitutional balance *which the HRA 1998* strikes between the judiciary, legislature and executive. We have seen that s. 6(1) of the HRA 1998 makes it unlawful for a public authority to act in a way which is incompatible with an ECHR right unless the statutory defence in s. 6(2) applies. Article 8(2), which determines the legality of an interference with Article 8(1), sets down an *objective* test (in common with Articles 9(2), 10(2) and 11(2)): 'no interference by a public authority with the exercise of this right except such as is in accordance with the law and is necessary in a democratic society . . .'. The courts are required to ask for themselves whether each of the *objective* elements under Article 8(2) has been established.

5.258 Moreover, in requiring the judiciary to be the final arbiter of whether an ECHR right is being violated, the HRA 1998 does not arrogate to the judges powers that have been democratically conferred on the executive. Rather the 1998 Act recognizes that embedded in the very notion of a democracy is a respect for fundamental human rights and that the protection of these rights creates a brake upon the exercise of legislative or executive power. It is incompatible with the very principle that there exists an area of inviolability into which public authorities cannot step, save where mandated by express legislative provisions, to leave to those same authorities the power to determine where the border lies. These considerations are all the more pertinent in the immigration context where as we have seen there may be a systemic failure to promote rights, and where the idea of a minimum irreducible core of rights tempering unbridled democratic 'tyranny of the majority' is especially apt.

5.259 Further, even before the HRA 1998, through the principle of legality, the courts have already been exercising a primary judgment whether and when the legislature (in enacting delegated legislation), or the executive acting under the purported authority of a statutory power, has improperly stepped into the inviolable territory defined by the ambit of the right. In other words, a primary judgment is already exercised in the very same areas that are within the reach of ss. 3 and 6 of the 1998 Act. Lord Hoffmann in *R* v *Secretary of State for the Home Department, ex parte Simms* [1999] 3 WLR 328, 341 drew no distinction between the approach of the court when applying the principle of legality and that which it would apply under the HRA 1998.

5.260   The decision in *Simms*, reached in the interregnum between Royal Assent being given to the HRA 1998 and the coming into force of its principal provisions, is highly significant. There it was clear that Lord Steyn conducted a *primary* review as to whether or not the prison authorities had justified their policy by their affidavit evidence. He concluded that they had not. This was in an area—freedom of expression, but essentially access to court—where the European Court afforded states a margin of appreciation. But this did not translate into a margin of discretion for the prison authorities, notwithstanding their obvious proximity to matters of prison discipline and abuse of privileges and rights. We have seen above at 5.161 that *Simms* established that the principle of legality applied both to the vires of secondary legislation *and* to discretionary decisions taken thereunder.[211] In *R (on the application of Mellor)* v *Secretary of State* [2001] EWCA Civ 472 Lord Phillips MR held that the common law approach in *Simms* was the same as that under the ECHR. It is accordingly difficult to sustain the view that a direct primary judgment on proportionality should not be taken by the courts to challenges to administrative decisions, or that such an approach would be constitutionally inappropriate.

5.261   There is also a jurisdictional point. There is an important distinction between the jurisdiction conferred by Parliament under the HRA 1998 and that which the courts have themselves developed under the common law as the foundation of the principles of administrative law. In exercising their supervisory jurisdiction, the courts have had to be acutely sensitive to their own constitutional position and particularly to Parliamentary sovereignty. But even there, the development of the principle of irrationality was justified as an expression of the will of Parliament rather than a usurpation of it: while Parliament intended the powers conferred by it to be exercised by the chosen recipient, it did not intend or authorize the recipient to exercise the power in a manner that is perverse, unreasonable or irrational. But there is no reason to adopt such a self-denying ordinance towards exercising a primary judgment in relation to the test of proportionality for the very reason that Parliamentary intent, as directly expressed in ss. 3 and 6 of the HRA 1998, is that the courts should be charged with the primary duty of securing the observance of ECHR rights. The HRA 1998 obliges the court to reach a view on the proportionality question for itself: there accordingly is no illegitimate or non-democratic expansion of the judicial role, or usurpation of the legislative or executive functions.

Conclusion

5.262   For reasons articulated above, we consider that where the ECHR right

---

[211] Contrast the Court of Appeal decision in *R* v *Secretary of State, ex parte O'Dhuibhir* [1997] COD 315, above at 5.161.

permits a justificatory intrusion, proportionality has a place in public law as an independent doctrine of administrative review. See Lord Slynn in *R (Alconbury) v Secretary of State for the Environment, Transport and the Regions* [2001] 2 WLR 1389, 1407 at para. 51 for the wider proposition that the time has come for proportionality to be recognized as a principle of domestic public law. Just as the common law recognizes that the previously monotholic *Wednesbury* standard applies differentially depending on context, so too the intensity of review on a proportionality standard will vary according to the nature of the decision challenged. In some policy-intensive contexts, the courts will allow a significant measure of deference to the decision-taker. Deference will no doubt be due to the primary facts reached by the inferior body: proportionality will not convert review into an appeal on the facts. But, the deference due to a decision-taker's view of the facts will be decidedly narrow where the court is able to reach a view on the material before it as to the critical facts that are determinative of the legality of the decision and where the decision-taker enjoys no special functional advantage, e.g. in the context of an Article 3 evaluation of risk, or where detention is concerned, and also, as we argue, where the issue is the expulsion of a settled immigrant under Article 8. We consider that it is only in entry or frontier cases that issues of policy are properly and fully engaged justifying a greater measure of deference to the decision-taker on democratic grounds. We conclude that there are no pragmatic objections to this approach—it entails nothing vaguer than the results yielded by the application of *Wednesbury* parameters to a decision-maker's view on proportionality or on risk.

Chapter Six

Discrimination

SCOPE OF ARTICLE 14

6.1 In this chapter we examine the contribution that Article 14 of the ECHR may make in immigration and asylum cases. Article 14 provides:

> The enjoyment of the rights and freedoms set forth in this Convention shall be secured without discrimination on any ground such as sex, race, colour, language, religion, political or other opinion, national or social origin, association with a national minority, property, birth or other status.

No general right to non-discrimination

6.2 It is apparent from this wording that Article 14 does not provide an independent or freestanding right not to be discriminated against. It is merely a prohibition of discrimination in the field of application of the ECHR rights (*Abdulaziz, Cabales and Balkandali* v *UK* (1985) 7 EHRR 471). The scope of Article 14 will normally be narrower than the provisions of domestic law under the Race Relations Act 1976, s. 19B as amended by the Race Relations Act 2000. This makes it unlawful for a public authority (including the Immigration Service) to do any act that constitutes discrimination, subject to the statutory defence of an authorized person acting in accordance with relevant authorization: s. 19D. Article 14 is only *normally* narrower in scope than domestic law because the 1976 Act controversially permits discrimination in asylum, immigration and nationality matters on grounds of ethnic or national origins.[1] The provisions of Article 14 are also narrower than the general principles of EC law (Article 12 (formerly Article 6) of the Amended Treaty and the law-making powers conferred under Article 13 (formerly Article 6a)).

---

[1] See Race Relations (Immigration and Asylum) Authorisation, Immigration Directorate Instructions (IDI) March/2001, Chapter 1, s. 11; Annexe EE. See also Lord Steyn's lecture in honour of Lord Cooke (18 September 2002) cited in *R (Gurung)* v *Ministry of Defence* [2002] EWHC Admin 2463, para. 18.

6.3 Conscious of the limits of Article 14 and the case law, and the central importance of a clear principle of non-discrimination in the treatment of 'foreigners' for the development of peace and justice in Europe, the Council of Europe has developed and drafted an additional Protocol 12 providing for a freestanding right against discrimination.[2] The present indications are that the United Kingdom will not ratify this Protocol nor bring it within the scope of the HRA 1998. This is a decision to be regretted. It fails to give a strong lead on a matter of serious concern throughout Europe. Indeed it can be said that discriminatory treatment by the state has been at the foundation of the most serious violations of public order and threats to peace and security within the region from Hitler's Germany to Milosevic's actions in Kosovo. Discriminatory treatment of minorities takes forms very similar to discriminatory treatment of foreigners within the territory of the contracting state; if a state can get away with discriminatory practices in one area, it may undermine rights in another. The principle of equality is now recognized as an important principle of national and international law.[3]

6.4 It is unlikely that a new international obligation would create insuperable difficulties in the field of immigration and asylum. After all, the immigration rules have long required officers not to discriminate in the exercise of their functions. The notion of discrimination itself always permits differences in treatment of people who are not in the same material position. The freedom from immigration control of own nationals is not in itself discriminatory even in the heightened context of the EU.[4] People whose immigration status and the need for authority to remain make their position materially different will not normally be the victims of discrimination. Further differences may be capable of justification by sufficient compelling evidence of a justificatory reason. At present, however, this chapter is only concerned with Article 14 of the ECHR.

6.5 We have already noted in the preceding chapters that the other ECHR rights do not grant a right of residence or remaining in the United Kingdom. States have the right to make distinctions on the grounds of nationality and control their frontiers with respect to the admission or expulsion of those who have no rights of residence there. We have also noted that discriminatory actions will not be engaged unless they raise matters within the ambit of another Convention. Usually Article 14 will apply in conjunction with rights under Articles 3, 5, and

---

[2] For the implications and effects of Protocol 12, see Parliamentary Assembly Report of 14 January 2000 (Doc. 8614) and the opinion of the European Court dated 5 January 2000 (Doc. 8608) both available on the Council of Europe website.

[3] See the observations of Lord Hoffman in *Matadeen v Pointu* [1999] 1 AC 98 and *Arthur JS Hall & Co v Simons* [2000] 3 WLR 543. See also *Gurung* above at 6.2, footnote 1.

[4] See *Roque v Lieutenant Governor of Jersey* [1998] ECR I-4607; see also *Kaba v Secretary of State* (Case C-356/98) [2000] All ER (EC) 537.

8. Thus racial prejudice may be illegal under other measures of domestic law, but will not automatically result in a violation of the ECHR.

6.6   In the case of *Aslan* v *Malta* (App. No. 29493/95, 3 February 2000) Turkish citizens were refused admission to Malta having travelled from Libya on dubious grounds. They were detained for at least 10 hours in poor conditions pending being placed on the next boat home. They alleged that one of the police officers made insulting remarks about religion and about the historic conflict between Turkey and Malta in the sixteenth century. None of this gave rise to an admissible case under Articles 3 and 8 however. Although the European Court could not condone the making of racist or other provocative utterances, the conduct did not meet the severity of degrading treatment. Further, Article 8 did not guarantee the right to honour and dignity in the absence of any prejudice to respect for private life that had not been substantiated. The European Court's conclusion on Article 8 is particularly unfortunate, and may have been reached because the treatment complained of was not more securely established by evidence. In our opinion this is precisely the kind of case that might well have benefited from being considered under Article 14, in conjunction with Article 8.

6.7   We suggest that a British judge examining this question would hold that insulting remarks made by a police officer to a detainee about his nationality and his religion were precisely within the scope of respect for dignity protected both by Article 3 and Article 8. In *Abdulaziz, Cabales and Balkandali* v *UK* (1985) 7 EHRR 471 the Article 3 claim was rejected because:

> The Court observes that the difference of treatment complained of did not denote any contempt or lack of respect for the personality of the applicants and that it was not designed to, and did not, humiliate or debase but was intended solely to achieve (legitimate) aims.

The same could hardly be said of the conduct complained of here. If there is no legitimate reason for racially provocative questioning, it is likely at the least to be discriminatory treatment in the field of respect for private life. Telling questions would be whether the police officers insulted everybody or just immigration detainees, and whether in the class of immigration detainees, there was evidence of particular animus against certain nationalities.

Connection with other rights

6.8   The adjectival nature of the right does not however mean that a violation of Article 8, for example, must be made out before Article 14 comes into play. It is sufficient to show that the treatment in question was within the sphere of the right to respect for family or private life, for example, for Article 14 to be engaged. Reflecting the European Court's well-established case law (see, e.g., the *Belgian*

Linguistics case (1968) 1 EHRR 252, para. 9), in *Thlimmenos v Greece* (2001) 31 EHRR 15, para. 40 the European Court observed:

> the application of Article 14 does not presuppose a breach of one or more . . . provisions and to this extent it is autonomous. For Article 14 to be applicable it suffices that the facts of a case fall within the ambit of another substantive provision of the Convention or its Protocols.

If this is done, a lack of respect or interference which is discriminatory may well contravene Article 14, unless it is strictly justified.

6.9   It is a moot point whether Article 14 applies to discriminatory treatment in the field of a Protocol that has not been ratified by a member state or has not been brought into the HRA 1998. In our opinion, it would. First, there is authority for the proposition that there must be no discrimination in the application of a derogating measure under Article 15 (*Ireland v UK* (1978) 2 EHRR 25 at paras. 225–32). Secondly, the European Court has held in the *Belgian Linguistics* case (1968) 1 EHRR 252, para. 9 that even where the ECHR does not require a right to be extended, where it is extended to some persons there must be no discrimination in that area. Some guidance may be obtained from the approach of the ECJ in *Department of Employment v Barr and Montrose Holdings* (Case C-355/89) (1991) ECR I-3479 at paras. 16–18 where the European Court held that the principle of non-discrimination in the scope of the EC Treaty even applied to the treatment of foreigners in the Isle of Man, which was a territory to which the free-movement provisions of the Treaty did not apply. If this is right, it would mean that although there was no obligation to establish procedural safeguards for the expulsion of aliens under Article 1 of Protocol 7, discrimination between aliens in the application of those safeguards would be contrary to Article 14 unless strictly justified. We give particular consideration to the discriminatory nature of British nationality below at para. 6.41 et seq.

Reasons for discrimination

6.10   Once another ECHR right is in issue, Article 14 is broader in scope than prohibiting discrimination merely on the grounds of sex or race etc. Reflecting Article 2 of the Universal Declaration of Human Rights, 1948, discrimination for reasons of language, religion, political or other opinion, national or social origin,[5] association with a national minority, property or birth is included. Moreover, the list is not closed and can develop as new socially significant characteristics emerge. Discrimination on grounds of *any other status* is also prohibited. A broad

---

[5] Contrast authorization given under s. 19D of the Race Relations Act 1976; see above at 6.2.

meaning is to be given to 'other status'.[6] It includes discrimination on the grounds of sexual orientation,[7] for example, an issue that has not traditionally been covered by anti-discrimination legislation.[8]

6.11 Thus in the case of *Sutherland* v *the United Kingdom* (1997) 24 EHRR 22, the applicant complained of the lower age of consent for young people who were heterosexual as opposed to male homosexuals. The former European Commission concluded that there was unjustified discriminatory treatment and it did not matter whether this was seen on the grounds of sex or sexual orientation.[9] The case did not proceed to the European Court because the government undertook to amend the legislation.

6.12 Another status covered by the ECHR is illegitimacy. The European Court has found that laws that interfere with the enjoyment of family or private life on the grounds of the illegitimate status of a child may violate Article 8.[10] Such distinctions may equally engage Article 14. In the case of *Camp and Bourimi* v *the Netherlands* (App. No. 28369/95, 3 October 2000) a child was born after the death of his father, who had a long-established family life with the mother, and had intended to get married at the time of his death. The fact that the child was born illegitimate and could not inherit did not constitute a violation of Article 8. His status did not impinge on his ability to enjoy family life with his mother. The problem was that the relatives of the deceased father wanted to exclude the child from the distribution of the assets. Their 'unequal' treatment of the child was not attributable to any action or lack of action on the part of the authorities. However, intestate succession fell within the scope of Article 14. The fact that the second applicant was unable to inherit, unlike children born in wedlock or recognized by their fathers, constituted a difference in treatment between persons in similar situations, based on birth, and a violation was found.

Discrimination

6.13 In *Abdulaziz, Cabales and Balkandali* v *UK* (1985) 7 EHRR 471, para. 72 the European Court summarized its jurisprudence:

For the purposes of Article 14, a difference of treatment is discriminatory if it 'has no

---

[6] See Simor, J. and Emmerson, B., *Human Rights Practice* (Sweet & Maxwell, 2000) para. 14.013 for a review of its scope.

[7] See *Salgueiro da Silva Mouta* v *Portugal* (2001) 31 EHRR 47 (custody of child granted to mother on exclusive basis of father's sexual orientation; while the decision pursued the legitimate aim of protecting the child's interests, no reasonable relationship of proportionality between the means used and the end pursued could be shown).

[8] See *Grant* v *South West Trains* (Case C-249/96) [1998] ECR I-621 ECJ.

[9] Contrast *Toonen* v *Australia* CCPR/C/50/D488/1992.

[10] *Marckx* v *Belgium* (1979) 2 EHHR 330; *Inze* v *Austria* (1987) 10 EHRR 394.

objective and reasonable justification', that is, if it does not pursue a 'legitimate aim' or if there is not a 'reasonable relationship of proportionality between the means employed and the aim sought to be realised[11]. . . . The Contracting States enjoy a certain margin of appreciation in assessing whether and to what extent differences in otherwise similar situations justify a different treatment in law . . . but it is for the Court to give the final ruling in this respect.

6.14   There are thus three stages. First, is there a difference in treatment between persons similarly placed with respect to issues for which the state has responsibility within the ambit of other Articles of the ECHR? Secondly, does the state seek to justify such difference in treatment with legitimate aims? Thirdly, does the European Court conclude that such difference is a proportionate response to such aims? The process looks familiar to the approach adopted in Article 8 itself, although under Article 14 the case law develops the concept from the inherent idea of discrimination rather than the express language of necessary interference found elsewhere in the ECHR. In practice, once the first stage has been reached, the margin of appreciation afforded to contracting states to justify unequal treatment is a narrow one. See also the transfer of this test into UK law in *Wandsworth LBC v Michalak* [2002] EWCA Civ 271 and *Mendoza v Ghaidan* [2002] EWCA Civ 1533; and see below at 6.39.

6.15   In *Abdulaziz etc.* v *UK* (1985) the promotion of immigration rules that precluded women settled in the United Kingdom from sponsoring an application for entry clearance by spouses living abroad was held not to contravene a right to respect for family life, as we have already noted. Although a state enjoyed a wide margin of appreciation in deciding what its immigration rules should be when considering the admission of foreigners, rules that were overtly discriminatory engaged Article 14. Since men could sponsor spouses but women could not, and since the European Court considered that the distinction was not based on sufficiently convincing reasons, a violation of Article 14 was made out.

Difference in treatment

6.16   For the inference of discrimination to arise there must be unequal treatment of people similarly placed or equal treatment of those in materially different circumstances. Gaudron J sitting in the Australian High Court in the case of *Minister for Immigration and Multicultural Affairs* v *Ibrahim* [2000] HCR 55 stated (at paras. 29–34) in the context of persecution:

There are two distinct aspects to discrimination. The first, which needs no elaboration,

---

[11]   The European Court cited the *Belgian Linguistics* judgment (above at 6.8) para. 10, the *Marckx* judgment (above at footnote 10) para. 33, and *Rasmussen v Denmark* (1985) 7 EHRR 37, para. 38.

is the different treatment of people who are not relevantly different; the second is the treatment of people who are relevantly different in a manner that is not appropriate and adapted to that difference . . . If an individual can establish that conduct to which all are subject has significantly greater consequences for the group of which he or she is a member, then he or she may well establish a well-founded fear of persecution . . . undifferentiating conduct may constitute discrimination against persons who are different or who are differently circumstanced . . .[12]

6.17　We have seen that to some extent the whole of immigration law is based on distinctions with respect to nationality. The mere denial of admission to non-nationals is not discrimination, because the fact of difference in rights of free movement means that there is no comparison between similarly situated people. See *Moustaquim* v *Belgium* (1991) 13 EHRR 802.

6.18　The government laid stress on this aspect in *Abdulaziz et al* v *UK* (1985). It sought to argue that because Protocol 4 of the ECHR covered procedures for the regulation of immigration control, it could not come within the subject matter of Article 8. The European Court rejected this frontal assault on the scope of the ECHR, and held that where immigration policies engaged family and private life, those polices would have to be subject to the requirements of the ECHR. The fact that detailed provisions were spelt out in a specific Protocol did not exclude the application of a more general ECHR right. This is a significant conclusion for the interpretation of the Convention, although it is not one that has always been consistently applied by the European Court.[13]

6.19　Elsewhere in its judgment, when it proceeded to determine whether the difference in treatment was discrimination, the European Court responded to the 'immigration right' argument in a rather contradictory fashion. First, with respect to the claim based on sex discrimination, it rejected the notion that traditional legislative support for the right of the male worker to bring over his family was simply more favourable treatment in the field of immigration that was not discriminatory. It noted:

> The notion of discrimination within the meaning of Article 14 includes in general cases where a person or group is treated, without proper justification, less favourably than another, even though the more favourable treatment is not called for by the Convention.

It accordingly found that the difference in treatment between overseas men and women settled in the UK, with respect to the capacity to sponsor the admission of their spouses, was discriminatory.

---

[12] Although Gaudron J's judgment was a dissenting one, the majority did not disagree with his analysis of discrimination.

[13] See most notably in *Maaouia* v *France* (2001) 33 EHRR 42.

6.20 Secondly, the immigration rule in question did not preclude *all* women from bringing over their spouses. Those born in the UK or to a British-born parent had the right so to do. This inevitably meant not just that the persons excluded were from the new Commonwealth and predominantly black or Asian, but also that white British women were more likely to be better off than black British women. There was thus a question of different treatment on the grounds of race and national origin. The European Court nevertheless rejected the claim on the grounds that it was legitimate for the rules to make special provision for those with close ancestral connection with the United Kingdom.

6.21 This is unconvincing. Ancestral connection may mean why a *foreigner* with a UK-born grandparent can be treated differently from a foreigner without one. The rules can state that people with such a connection are in a different material situation from people without one. However such reasoning cannot explain why a British woman with a UK-born parent could be joined by her husband whilst one without such a parent could not. The differences in ancestral connection were, we suggest, too remote to make any difference to the central question: can I be joined by my spouse in the country of my nationality and residence? In the illegitimacy case of *Mazurek* v *France* (App. No. 34406/97, 1 February 2000) the European Court concluded that there was no justification for a French rule that the child of an adulterous union should receive a lesser share of the family estate, in order for the state to show respect for marriage. Such discrimination would have the effect of penalizsing the child for events 'which were not his fault'. What matters, therefore, is the material comparison at the date of the difference in treatment. Applying that logic to *Abdulaziz et al* v *UK* (1985), the extraneous factor of the place of birth of a parent or grandparent merely penalized black British women in the enjoyment of their future family life for reasons that were not their fault. In our opinion, it is likely that the European Court would examine the underlying racial inequalities in *Abdulaziz et al* v *UK* (1985) a little more critically if the case for violation of Article 14 turned exclusively on this issue in the future.

6.22 In the case of *Gaygusuz* v *Austria* (1997) 23 EHRR 364, the Austrian government attempted to justify discriminatory denial of contributory benefit to a Turkish national lawfully resident in Austria *because* he was a Turkish citizen. The European Court summarily rejected this approach:

> 45. The Austrian Government submitted that the statutory provision in question was not discriminatory. They argued that the difference in treatment was based on the idea that the State has special responsibility for its own nationals and must take care of them and provide for their essential needs. Moreover, sections 33 and 34 of the Unemployment Insurance Act laid down certain exceptions to the nationality condition. Lastly, at the material time, Austria was not bound by any contractual obligation to grant emergency assistance to Turkish nationals.

46. The Court notes in the first place that Mr Gaygusuz was legally resident in Austria and worked there at certain times (see paragraph 10 above), paying contributions to the unemployment insurance fund in the same capacity and on the same basis as Austrian nationals.

47. It observes that the authorities' refusal to grant him emergency assistance was based exclusively on the fact that he did not have Austrian nationality as required by section 33(2)(a) of the 1977 Unemployment Insurance Act . . .

48. In addition, it has not been argued that the applicant failed to satisfy the other statutory conditions for the award of the social benefit in question. He was accordingly in a like situation to Austrian nationals as regards his entitlement thereto.

49. Admittedly, sections 33 and 34 of the 1977 Unemployment Insurance Act . . . lay down certain exceptions to the nationality condition, but the applicant did not fall into any of the relevant categories.

50. The Court therefore finds the arguments put forward by the Austrian Government unpersuasive. It considers, like the Commission, that the difference in treatment between Austrians and non-Austrians as regards entitlement to emergency assistance, of which Mr Gaygusuz was a victim, is not based on any 'objective and reasonable justification'.

51. Even though, at the material time, Austria was not bound by reciprocal agreements with Turkey, it undertook, when ratifying the Convention, to secure 'to everyone within [its] jurisdiction' the rights and freedoms defined in section I of the Convention.

52. There has accordingly been a breach of Article 14 of the Convention taken in conjunction with Article 1 of Protocol No. 1.

The European Court also held that nationality-based differences in treatment required 'very weighty reasons' as justification. This echoed the language of the European Court when considering the sex discrimination claim in *Abdulaziz et al*. Nationality is thus a 'suspect category' for differences in treatment (but see, however, *A, X, Y v Secretary of State for the Home Department* [2002] EWCA Civ 1502); and see para. 6.40 below.

6.23 Equally important in constituting discrimination is the same formal treatment granted to all people, irrespective of whether there is a legitimate difference between them. A recent example in the case law is the case of *Thlimmenos v Greece* (2001) 31 EHRR 15. A Greek national who was a Jehovah's Witness refused to bear arms during military service and was convicted of an offence against military discipline. Subsequently he sought employment as an accountant where a precondition for admission was the absence of previous convictions. He was rejected because of his conviction, and the local court concluded he was not being discriminated against for reasons of his religion. The European Court disagreed. It noted:

44. The Court has so far considered that the right under Article 14 not to be discriminated against in the enjoyment of the rights guaranteed under the Convention is violated when States treat differently persons in analogous situations without providing an objective and reasonable justification. . . . However, the Court considers that this is not the only facet of the prohibition of discrimination in Article 14. The right not to be discriminated against in the enjoyment of the rights guaranteed under the Convention is also violated when States without an objective and reasonable justification fail to treat differently persons whose situations are significantly different.

6.24   Here formal equality of treatment masked the fact that it was only because of his religious beliefs that the applicant had the conviction in the first place. Religion was therefore engaged in the accountancy application, although it appeared to have nothing to do with it:

In this context the Court notes that the applicant is a member of the Jehovah's Witnesses, a religious group committed to pacifism, and that there is nothing in the file to disprove the applicant's claim that he refused to wear the military uniform only because he considered that his religion prevented him from doing so. In essence, the applicant's argument amounts to saying that he is discriminated against in the exercise of his freedom of religion, as guaranteed by Article 9 of the Convention, in that he was treated like any other person convicted of a felony although his own conviction resulted from the very exercise of this freedom. Seen in this perspective, the Court accepts that the 'set of facts' complained of by the applicant—his being treated as a person convicted of a felony for the purposes of an appointment to a chartered accountant's post despite the fact that the offence for which he had been convicted was prompted by his religious beliefs—'falls within the ambit of a Convention provision', namely Article 9.

6.25   As we have seen above at 6.16 this principle has also been recognized in the analysis of Gaudron J in the Australian High Court case of *Ibrahim* (2000). The principle establishes that in international law, discrimination is constituted where the *same* treatment is administered in circumstances where the personal circumstances of the individual are relevantly different from others so as to require different or adapted treatment.

6.26   Applying this reasoning it would seem that a penal law of general application that makes no provision for the fact that people of certain race, religion or political beliefs will be unable to comply with it would be discriminatory, unless justified for very compelling reasons. Here again a practical and effective response is called for rather than a merely formal one. The European Court did not consider it necessary to examine this question. In the earlier case of *Tsirlis* v *Greece* (1997) 25 EHRR 198 the European Commission concluded that the detention of a Jehovah's Witness on the grounds of supposed non-exemption from military service was a violation of Article 14 combined with Article 9, although the European Court found a violation under Article 5.

6.27 It is to be hoped that the *Thlimmenos* case (above at 6.23) will make the European Court more amenable to arguments based on indirect discrimination. The Immigration Rules governing adoptions may be vulnerable to challenge on the basis of indirect discrimination on grounds of race or national origin, by effectively precluding the admission of children adopted by families from the Indian sub-continent.[14]

6.28 In *Ahmad* v *United Kingdom* (1981) 4 EHRR 126 a Muslim teacher who was refused time off work to attend Friday prayers in a mosque was held not to be discriminated against, because no members of other religions were given time off work and the rule was one of uniform application. This is disingenuous where the working week itself has been organized to enable Christians to attend church on Sundays. Formal equality in the rule may mask a severe difference in impact. Such questions are probably best seen as examples of discrimination, and attention would then focus on whether it was justified because there was no practical method of enabling time off for such purposes to be worked in lieu. The question is whether the situation is truly analogous and historic discrimination must be excluded in making the comparison.

Justification

6.29 There is inevitably a close connection between whether there is inequality in treatment, and whether such inequality is for a legitimate reason. The process is sometimes confused in the case law, but should be kept separate but see, however, *Wandsworth LBC* v *Michalak* [2002] EWCA Civ 271 at para. 20. Some differences will be easier to justify than others. In some areas of social and economic policy, greater deference will be afforded to the state's knowledge and understanding of social and ethical constraints and beliefs.

6.30 Thus, despite some 20 years of litigation on the issue, the European Court is still prepared to give a wide margin of discretion in the area of the legal status of transsexuals. See, however, the spectacular reversal of the European Court's case law in *Goodwin* v *UK* (2002) 34 EHRR 18, and the reasoning that the UK no longer had any margin of appreciation on the issue. The distinction between psychological and biological sex still enables states to maintain prohibitions on such people getting married in their appropriate gender[15] or even being acknowledged as the 'father' of a child born by AID.[16]

---

[14] See *Pawandeep Singh* v *Secretary of State* (2 December 1999, CA) SLJ 99/6917/4, currently pending an application to the European Court.

[15] See *Sheffield and Horsham* v *UK* (1998) 27 EHRR 163; *Bellinger* v *Bellinger* [2001] EWCA Civ 1140; *W* v *W* (*Nullity:Gender*) [2001] 2 WLR 674.

[16] See *XYZ* v *UK* (1997) 24 EHRR 143 where the European Court recognized that family life was engaged between the parents and the child. But see *Goodwin* v *UK* (2002) 35 EHRR 18.

6.31   Homosexuals have won the right to respect for their private life by preventing states using criminal laws to penalize consent to non-violent sexual conduct between adults in private.[17] The notion of respect for private life thus requires an absence of penalties and state intrusion. In *Salgueiro da Silva Mouta v Portugal* (above at footnote 7) the European Court held that there was no justification for the mother of a child being granted custody solely because the father was homosexual and living with another man. Beyond that, the case law has not recognized that same sex partners enjoy family life, and differences in treatment in the field of marriage, housing, social security and inheritance have accordingly been sanctioned as not violating Article 14.[18]

6.32   Article 14 has been increasingly used to examine the justification for such practices however. In the light of constitutional developments elsewhere in the world,[19] and domestic advances in this field,[20] it is increasingly unlikely that this case law can continue to apply without modification or adaptation to the particular level of social development in a state.[21]

6.33   The European Commission's decision in *Sutherland* v *UK* (1997) 24 EHRR CD 22 on the discriminatory aspect of the age of consent has been followed by the European Court in a series of subsequent decisions.[22] In its decision in the case of *Smith* v *UK* and *Grady* v *UK* (2000) EHRR 493 the European Court found a violation of Article 8 alone without needing to consider Article 14. It concluded that sexual orientation is a most intimate aspect of private life, and interference with it required particularly serious reasons by way of justification.

6.34   In the illegitimacy cases the European Court has concluded that once paternity has been established or acknowledged (*Inze* v *Austria* (1987) 10 EHRR 394 para. 41):

> Very weighty reasons need to be put forward before a difference in treatment on the ground of birth out of wedlock can be regarded as compatible with the Convention and

---

[17] See *Dudgeon* v *UK* (1982) 4 EHRR 149; *Laskey* v *UK* (1997) 24 EHRR 39; *Modinos* v *Cyprus* (1993) 16 EHRR 485 and *Z* v *Secretary of State for the Home Department* [2002] Imm AR 560.

[18] See *X* v *UK* (1983) 5 EHRR 601; *Simpson* v *UK* (1986) 47 DR 274.

[19] The case law has perhaps developed most in Canada under the influence of the Charter of Rights. See *Attorney-General Canada* v *Mossop* (1993) 100 DLR (4th) 656; *Egan* v *Canada* (1995) 124 DLR (4th) 609; *Vreind* v *Alberta* 4 BHRC 140; *A-G Ontario* v *M* 7 BHRC 489. See also *El Al* v *Danilowitz* (Supreme Court of Israel, 4 May 1994).

[20] See *Fitzpatrick* v *Sterling Housing* [1999] 3 WLR 1113. See also the Immigration Rules (Cmnd 4851) adding para. 295A to the Immigration Rules (HC 395), bringing unmarried partners of either sex into the field of entry clearance for family reunion.

[21] Simor and Emmerson (above at footnote 6) suggest at 14.035 that these earlier cases, including discrimination in the field of immigration, are no longer good law. See *Mendoza* and *Ghaidan* [2002] EWCA Civ 1533.

[22] See *Salguerio Mouta* v *Portugal* (above at footnote 7) discrimination in the context of child care; *ADT* v *UK* [2000] 2 FLR 697, discrimination for prosecution of group sex in private.

similarly weighty reasons are required to justify the fact that in this case the second applicant was unable to inherit.

6.35 Similar considerations lay behind the rejection of the government's justification for sexual discrimination in the case of *Abdulaziz, Cabales and Balkandali* v *UK* (1985) 7 EHRR 471 at para. 78. Social developments and the development of laws prohibiting sexual discrimination placed a particularly onerous burden on the state to justify the perpetuation of assumptions such as the male being the breadwinner in a family. The European Court noted that:

> The advancement of the equality of the sexes is a major goal in the member states of the Council of Europe.

6.36 The UK government argued that reducing unemployment amongst the indigenous community was a relevant factor in restricting immigration. The European Court accepted that this was a legitimate aim in maintaining immigration control, although on examination of the statistics not a sufficient justification. The argument that good race relations were promoted by denying black British women the right to sponsor their husbands was much more contentious. The European Commission noted (at para. 82 of the European Court's judgment):

> Neither was it established that race relations or immigration controls were enhanced by the rules: they might create resentment in part of the immigrant population and it had not been shown that it was more difficult to limit abuses by non-national husbands than by other immigrant groups.

6.37 In *Thlimennos* v *Greece* (2001) 31 EHRR 15, the European Court accepted that there was a legitimate aim to exclude convicted criminals from the accountancy profession, but conviction of an offence of refusal to wear a uniform involved no moral turpitude and there was no ground to exclude him as unfit. The alternative aim of adding to his punishment was excessive in the light of the sentence he had served.

6.38 The fact that the treatment is required under municipal law is not, of course, sufficient to justify the action of the authorities. If the laws are incompatible with ECHR obligations they must be changed. The European Court in *Thlimennos* v *Greece* noted at para. 48:

> It is true that the authorities had no option under the law but to refuse to appoint the applicant a chartered accountant. However, contrary to what the Government's representative appeared to argue at the hearing, this cannot absolve the respondent State from responsibility under the Convention. The Court has never excluded that legislation may be found to be in direct breach of the Convention (see, *inter alia*, *Chassagnou and Others* v *France* (1999) 29 EHRR 615. In the present case the Court considers that

it was the State having enacted the relevant legislation which violated the applicant's right not to be discriminated against in the enjoyment of his right under Article 9 of the Convention. That State did so by failing to introduce appropriate exceptions to the rule barring persons convicted of a felony from the profession of chartered accountants.

Proportionality

6.39 We have examined the notion of proportionality and the margin of appreciation earlier and the reader is referred to 1.63 et seq and 1.82 et seq and 5.162 for a fuller account. In the context of Article 14 the European Court has restated the position (*Gaygusuz v Austria* (1997) 23 EHRR 364 at para. 42):

> A difference of treatment is discriminatory, for the purposes of Article 14, if it 'has no objective and reasonable justification', that is if it does not pursue a 'legitimate aim' or if there is not a 'reasonable relationship of proportionality between the means employed and the aim sought to be realised'. Moreover the Contracting States enjoy a certain margin of appreciation in assessing whether and to what extent differences in otherwise similar situations justify a different treatment.

6.40 In practice once a difference in treatment is shown in analogous situations, on grounds expressly prohibited by the ECHR, compelling reasons for the discriminatory treatment are needed. Thus the European Court continued:

> However, very weighty reasons would have to be put forward before the Court could regard a difference of treatment based exclusively on the ground of nationality as compatible with the Convention.

6.41 The case law is divided on whether the fact that other satisfactory solutions could have been adopted prevents the solution from being proportionate. In the case of *Rasmussen v Denmark* (1985) 7 EHRR 371 a law providing for different time limits as between fathers and mothers to challenge the paternity of a child was held to be justified by the European Court, reversing the European Commission, even though there were other ways of providing for the legal certainty that was in the child's interest and years after Denmark had changed the legislation complained of. In the prisoners case of *Campbell and Fell v UK* (1985) 7 EHRR 165, however, the European Court found the fact that less intrusive techniques were available to be a significant indication of a lack of proportionate justification. At the very least, where a less intrusive solution could reasonably have been adopted at the material time, a compelling explanation for why it was not is needed.

6.42 Proportionality and the margin afforded by the European Court to the contracting state is dependent on the subject matter, the issues, and the discrimination sought to be justified. Different treatment on racial grounds alone will never be justified, whereas a greater margin may be afforded in cases where women have been given special consideration. Nationality-based discrimination (once it is established that the comparators are similarly placed) is a suspect category (see 6.22 above).

Positive discrimination

6.43 Where a group is disadvantaged in society, there may be a positive duty on the state to take measures to secure that the rights afforded by the ECHR are available without discrimination. Accordingly measures to promote a group may be justified as a proportionate response to a legitimate aim. In the *Belgian Linguistics* case (1968) 1 EHRR 252 the European Court noted that legal inequalities could be used to correct factual inequalities. In *Kennedy Lindsay* v *UK* (1986) 9 EHRR 555 the European Commission concluded that proportional representation in Northern Ireland was justified to promote the interests of a minority that would otherwise be under-represented.

Application

Nationality certificates on entitlement and right of abode
6.44 In the case of *Amin* v *ECO Bombay* [1983] AC 818, Mrs Amin appealed against the refusal of the Entry Clearance Officer, Bombay to issue a special voucher to her on the grounds that as a dependent married woman she was not the head of a household as required by the terms of the policy to promote the admission of United Kingdom passport holders without the right of abode. She had no right of appeal under the Immigration Rules because the rules made no reference to the criteria for the issue of special vouchers. She claimed that the decision was contrary to the law and discriminatory. The United Kingdom government denied that the policy was discriminatory and pointed out that a woman could be granted special vouchers as a principal in certain circumstances. Lord Fraser in the House of Lords rejected the government's contentions and found that the terms of the voucher clearly discriminated on the grounds of sex in assuming that the head of the household must be a man save in exceptional circumstances. The discrimination, however, did not make the decision unlawful because all the Lords were agreed that it occurred outside the field of application of the Sex Discrimination Act 1975.

6.45 The *Amin* case is but one reflection of the case law since 1962 of an aspect of British immigration and nationality law that has given cause for concern in courts in the UK and abroad, and has provoked much bitterness and resentment; namely the discriminatory denial of nationality and the rights fundamentally associated with it, i.e. freedom to come into and go from one's own country. We do not rehearse here the legislative history whereby citizens of the United Kingdom and colonies with no ancestral connection with the United Kingdom or certain other colonies, lost the right to enter the United Kingdom 'without let or hindrance'.[23] The question is whether the ECHR will now be of any assistance to those British nationals who do not have the right of residence in their state of nationality.

6.46 Protocol 4 to the ECHR, Article 3(2) provides that 'No one shall be deprived of the right to enter the territory of the state of which he is a national'. This seems a clear enough statement of international legal principle. The ECJ has referred to this principle of international law in several of its judgments concerned with the UK.[24] It avoided having to address whether the principle was part of EC law in its judgment in the case of *R v Secretary of State for the Home Department, ex parte Manjit Kaur* (Case C 192–99) [2001] All ER (EC) 250. The principle is not an absolute one: thus Protocol 4 Article 5 recognizes that a state may declare whether and to what extent the right applies to dependent territories for which it is responsible. The International Covenant on Civil and Political Rights[25] Article 12(4) provides that no one may be arbitrarily deprived of the right to enter his own country, suggesting that some restrictions according to law may be justified. The American Convention on Human Rights drafted in 1969 is the most comprehensive provision. It provides by Article 20 that everyone has the right to a nationality, has the right to the nationality of the state in which he was born if he does not have any other nationality, and cannot be arbitrarily deprived of it, and by Article 22(5) cannot be deprived of the right to enter the territory of the state of which he is a national.[26]

6.47 In its Advisory Opinion on the Nationality Provisions of the Constitution of Costa Rica[27] the Inter American Court of Human Rights stated:

> It is generally accepted today that nationality is an inherent right of all human beings. Not only is nationality the basic requirement for the exercise of political rights, it also has an important bearing on the individual's legal capacity. Thus despite the fact that it is traditionally accepted that the conferral and regulation of nationality are matters for each state to decide, contemporary developments indicate that international law does impose certain limits on the broad powers enjoyed by the states in that area, and that the manner in which states regulate matters bearing on nationality cannot be deemed within their sole jurisdiction; those powers of the state are also circumscribed by their obligations to ensure the full protection of human rights.

---

[23] A full account is given in Fransman, L., *British Nationality Law* (Butterworths, 1998).

[24] See *Van Duyn v Home Office* [1974] ECR 1337 at 1351; *R v Immigration Appeal Tribunal and Secretary of State, ex parte Surinder Singh* (Case C-370/90) [1992] ECR-1 4267; *Roque v Lieutenant Governor of Jersey* (Case C-171/98) [1998] ECR I-4607.

[25] As to which, see Brownlie, I. (ed), *Basic Documents on Human Rights* (Clarendon Press, 1992) p. 130.

[26] See ibid. at p. 504.

[27] See (1986) 5 HRLJ; see also Chan 'Nationality as a Human Right' (1991) HRLJ Vol. XII p. 1.

6.48 It is perfectly consistent with international law principles to deprive someone of nationality of the metropolitan territory upon the independence of a former dependent territory, provided that the Constitution of the new territory secures that all those with a substantial connection with the territory can acquire nationality of the new territory. It is also quite consistent with international principles to define nationality as confined to a particular dependent territory: Bermudans are nationals of Bermuda and the like. What is inconsistent with international principle and practice is to permit a class of British nationals to retain UK citizenship on independence of their state of residence, but subsequently deprive them of the incidents of citizenship without providing them with a new one. If the right to enter one's own territory is such a badge of nationality as almost to define it, deprivation of that right is equivalent to a loss of a nationality or a deprivation of nationality in breach of the UN Convention on the Reduction of Statelessness 1961, Articles 8(1) and 10.

6.49 There is no direct enforcement of any international law principle of the right to enter one's own country under the HRA 1998 or the ECHR as the UK has not ratified Protocol 4. This does not mean that discriminatory practices in this field will be outside the scope of the HRA 1998. We have already noted above at 6.9 that discrimination in the field of application of a Protocol may be within Article 14 even though the terms of the Protocol themselves are not binding. Such an approach is confirmed in the field of nationality by the UN Convention on the Elimination of All Forms of Racial Discrimination 1966.[28]

6.50 The problem is most acute where the British national is faced with expulsion from the country of residence as was the case with many East African Asians in the late 1960s and early 1970s. Denial of access to own nationals in such circumstances may amount to degrading treatment, where the element of racial difference in determining which UK nationals from Africa had the right of abode and which did not was an important aggravating factor of the shuttlecocking of those with nowhere to go. Such actions are almost certainly a violation of customary international law[29] and would found the basis of a claim for asylum in the United Kingdom (*R* v *Chief Immigration Officer Gatwick Airport, ex parte Singh* [1987] Imm AR 346), as denial of such a core right of residence on racial grounds would amount to persecution.

6.51 Absent the extreme factor of a racially motivated expulsion, the application of human rights norms in the field of nationality and the right of abode is probably more complex and dependent on the particular facts.

---

[28] Article 5(d)(i) and (iii) refers to the civil right of residence within the borders of the state, the right to nationality and the right to leave and return to one's own country.
[29] See *R* v *Secretary of State, ex parte Thakrar* [1974] QB 684.

6.52 First, it would seem that the past sexual discrimination of the nationality laws whereby children with a British citizen mother failed to acquire nationality by descent, will not be actionable many years after the age of majority has been passed, unless there was reliance on misleading representations that no application for registration need be made. The HRA 1998 is not retrospective and so some relevant discriminatory administrative action after 2 October 2000 is required. A failure to remedy past defects in the law will not suffice. A child of a British mother under 18 after commencement of the HRA 1998, can always seek to remedy the past sex discrimination by applying for discretionary registration as a minor. Any discrimination in the denial of that application would be unlawful under the terms of the Race Relations Act 1976 as amended, or under Protocol 4 taken with Article 14 or potentially Article 8 taken with Article 14.

6.53 Secondly, if Mrs. Amin were to apply for her special voucher today to come to the United Kingdom, discrimination on the grounds of her sex or social status would be capable of challenge under similar principles. The discrimination would be in the field of application of the Race Relations Act 1976 and the ECHR and it would fall on the government to justify such measures. An assumption that women should live in the country of residence of their husbands is surely not enough. Of course, this is all too late. A generation of British Asians denied their rights through the non-application of international principles have died, migrated elsewhere, changed their nationality or generally given up on the expectation of justice from their country of nationality. A few cases may still linger on, and the quota for distribution of special vouchers, where there are still long queues in India and none in Africa, may well require very careful consideration and justification. Their position has now been regularized under the Nationality and Immigration Act 2002.

6.54 Thirdly, there are the children of such 'stateless' British nationals (the British overseas citizens) who do not acquire British nationality from either parent if born after 1 January 1983. They can still apply under s. 27(1) of the British Nationality Act 1981 for discretionary registration as a minor. If this is granted they could in due course be eligible for a voucher as a head of household. But would a refusal of such registration be discrimination?

6.55 Some indication of the likely approach of the courts arose in the case of *R (on the application of Montana)* v *Secretary of State* [2001] 1 WLR 552. A child was born in Norway to a Norwegian mother and a British father, who had cohabited in the UK without marrying for 18 months. The child was a Norwegian national, resided with its mother and the father had regular access. If the parents had been married the child would have had dual nationality. The Court of Appeal did not consider that the denial of nationality was an interference with the right to respect for family life under Article 8(1) because it amounted to no real and present interference with the father's actual relationship with the child. The Court of Appeal noted that the mother was opposed to the application, the child had free movement rights in the United Kingdom as an EEA national and if the mother died there would be no difficulty in the child coming to the UK assuming that the appropriate court thought it was in its best interests to do so. These assumptions seem to pay little regard to the fact that unless a child and its parents have choices available to them in the early years, circumstances may prevent the maintenance and development of social relations later on. Nevertheless the Court of Appeal considered the impact of Article 14 on the assumption that Article 8 was engaged and so there was prima facie discriminatory treatment in the application of Article 8. It assumed that there was discrimination on the grounds of illegitimate status rather than merely differential 'treatment' but then concluded that the discrimination arose from the separate way that illegitimate children were treated under the statute rather than the exercise of discretion. It would seem that the Court of Appeal would deny discrimination in the exercise of a discretion if the *propositus* was put in the less favourable position as a result of the statute denying him automatic rights in the first place. This is troubling reasoning directly inconsistent with the policy of the Nationality Division on s. 3, Immigration Act 1971 discretion to overcome sexual discrimination. If children of British citizen fathers should be treated equally, irrespective of their social status as legitimate or not, then a statute that deprives them of that status is inconsistent with the principle of non-discrimination in the application of the ECHR save to the extent that it can be read down in a manner consistent with the ECHR. Suppose the facts of the case were different, father and mother continued to live in the United Kingdom, the child's future home looked to be there, and the mother consented to the application. It would be an unlawful perpetuation of the statutory discrimination for the decision-maker to refuse to exercise the discretion he had in order to overcome its unfortunate effects. The child is not to be punished twice in one statute for the lamentable failure of the UK to promote rules that do not discriminate. It should be noted that the previous discrimination in the Immigration Rules in respect of illegitimate children has been relaxed. Thus 'parent' for the purpose of para. 6 of HC 395 includes the father as well as the mother of an illegitimate child where paternity is proved. It is difficult to see why similar rules should not apply to nationality.

6.56 In the particular case of *Montana*, however, it seems likely that the challenge was premature and that an application should have been made for a declaration of incompatibility after commencement in respect of the British Nationality Act 1981 for the perpetuation of different treatment on the grounds of legitimacy. This would have required consideration of whether such a difference in treatment was proportionate and necessary in a democratic society. The nationality practices of other states should be examined, as should the reasons advanced by the government for not extending non-discrimination into the field of nationality law.

6.57 In other cases, where the child did not have the benefit of EEA residence rights and an effective alternative nationality, a far more intense approach is necessary to the examination of the exercise of discretion. The point about s. 3 of the HRA 1998, is that the statute should be read down to ensure that the discretion is exercised in a manner compatible with human rights, and should not permit tendentious excuses to enable the court to prevent it from engaging with them.

The Immigration Rules

6.58 Article 8 combined with Article 14 will undoubtedly be available as a means of challenge to any immigration rules that fall foul of the principle of non-discrimination on the grounds of status. The topic has been considered above in chapter 4 which deals with family life. Clearly, since the case of *Abdulaziz et al v UK* (6.13 above), the promoters of the rules have been careful not to incorporate provisions that directly discriminate on the grounds of race or sex.

6.59 In general with the abolition of the primary purposes rule, with provision now made under the rules for admission of same sex partners in stable relationships and unmarried couples of either sex who are unable to marry, the rules on family reunion look more human rights compatible than they did a few years ago. There could still be arguments in other areas that provisions that enable those with large sums of money to come in as investors, and enable the self-sufficient to come in for business discriminate against the indigent, but here the basic comparison of like with like should provide the answer. A difference in material circumstances justifies a proportionate difference in treatment, and immigration control is as much about economic advantage to the host state as about duties of admission.

6.60 One area of controversy is worth examining with a little more care, and that is the rules relating to the admission of adoptive children to the United Kingdom.[30] The problem is a long-standing one that successive changes in the rules have done little to ameliorate. First, 'parent' within the general meaning of the rules is confined to cases 'where the child was adopted in accordance with a decision taken by the competent administrative authority or court in a country whose adoption orders are recognised by the United Kingdom'. The difficulty is that some societies do not have a formal legal system of adoption, although transfers of parental responsibility take place in just the same way as in Convention adoption countries.[31] Secondly, the rules for admitting an adoptive child of

---

[30] See *Pawandeep Singh* v *Secretary of State* (2 December 1999, CA) SLJ 99/6917/4, and see 4.115 et seq above.

[31] See the Adoptions (Designation of Overseas Adoptions) Order 1973, SI 1973/19; Adoption Act 1976, s. 38(1)(d); Hague Convention on the Protection of Children and the Co-operation in Respect of Inter-Country Adoptions, signed by the UK in January 1994; and the Adoption (Intercountry Aspects) Act 1999.

parents settled in the United Kingdom, restrict recognition to cases of 'inability of the original parent(s) or current carer(s) to care for the child'. This is a much more restrictive test than the 'best interests of the child' that is the statutory criterion for adoption in the United Kingdom and other societies that apply the principles of the paramountcy of the child's interests in their family law as required by the UN Convention on the Rights of the Child. Thirdly, there is no provision in the Immigration Rules to enable family members of a child to bring him or her to the United Kingdom for the purposes of adoption by the UK courts. There has been a concessionary scheme outside the rules run for some years, but the criteria are stringent and it may take an impracticably long time to complete where the interests of a young child are concerned. Finally, the problem may increase with the suggested involvement of the criminal law in this area to deter unethical adoptions: usually raids on the orphanages of under-developed countries by wealthy childless couples or users of internet adoption agencies.

6.61 In terms of discrimination law, the problem is that there is differential access on the grounds of nationality to the principle of adoption in the best interests of the child. Thus an Indian family resident in the United Kingdom might agree to transfer the upbringing of their child to a sister or brother who is childless, or for some other genuine family reason. As a transfer between family members this is not an unlawful or undesirable step. In due course, the transfer having been affected and the child having formed a strong bond with the adoptive parents, the UK court may formalize the arrangements with an adoption order. The case law establishes that where the best interests of the child are engaged such order is lawful, even if it has the consequences of bypassing immigration decisions and conferring British nationality on the child: see *In Re W* [1986] Fam 54.

6.62 A couple living in another country party to the Hague Convention on Adoptions[32] can equally obtain an adoption order from the local court that should be respected by the Home Office on application for entry clearance applying the principles for recognition of private international law. A couple living in a predominantly Islamic country where no formal adoption laws have been promulgated will be unable to fulfil these criteria and their entry clearance claims are likely to fail on the grounds that either there has been no official adoption or that the adoption was not on the grounds of the original parents' inability to care for the child. There may be therefore a different treatment of people who are in the same position vis-à-viz the child. There may well be a genuine transfer of responsibility, making the child's exclusion from the UK undesirable, and no mere adoption of convenience. The requirements of Article 8, taken together with Article 14, may require the Immigration Rules to be read in a more flexible and humane way in such cases.

---

[32] See above at footnote 31.

Social security and social assistance

6.63   Historically, immigration controls take place at the frontier in the United Kingdom. Those who were admitted were then not subject to internal controls save for the requirement for aliens to register with the police, and the obligation on those with limited leave to enter or remain to apply in time for extensions at the risk of deportation for breach of conditions.

6.64   Now, there is a whole range of regulatory activity after entry in which immigration officers, employers, housing officers, doctors and the benefit agencies all have an interest in ascertaining the immigration status and entitlements of persons who appear to be from abroad. The potential for racial discrimination giving rise to a cause of action under the Race Relations Acts and the provisions of EC law has substantially increased. The substantive law of social security and social assistance and its relationship to immigration control is complex, detailed and beyond the scope of this work. What we will consider here is how far Article 14 in combination with Protocol 1, the right to property, or Article 8, the right to private life, is engaged in such cases.

Protocol 1

6.65   It will be seen from *Gaygusuz* v *Austria* (1997) 23 EHRR 364 that where a lawfully resident person from abroad makes contributions as an employee to a scheme of social assistance, the protection of Article 1 of Protocol 1 and the right of 'peaceful enjoyment of possessions' is engaged. This provides that no one shall be deprived of his possessions except in the public interest and subject to the conditions provided for by law and the general principles of international law. The position may be different where there is no entitlement to or expectation of a possession but merely a deficiency of need that requires a humanitarian response.

6.66   It is unlikely that the fact that a person from abroad has a home or possessions will play a significant role in the exercise of discretion against removal or deportation. Guidance may be drawn from educational decisions under Article 2 of Protocol 1 where 'no one shall be denied the right to education'. In its decision in the case of *Holub* v *Secretary of State for the Home Department* [2000] All ER (D) 2398 the Court of Appeal decided that the right to education did not give rise to a right to remain in the United Kingdom by a Polish child established in education here whose education curriculum would be interrupted by expulsion. A comparison of educational advantage between the two systems was not necessary. The position may be different if expulsion prevented access by a child to any education at all.

6.67   Discrimination in access to rights to education or peaceful enjoyment of property is another matter. The difficulty is in determining in what circumstances own nationals and foreigners are in equivalent circumstances. The Court of Appeal has concluded that the special rules granted to EU nationals do not make inferior treatment of other persons from abroad discriminatory (see *R* v *Secretary of State, ex parte Al Sabah* [1992] Imm AR 223. However, there comes a moment when a person from abroad is integrated into the host state and discriminatory treatment thereafter becomes offensive to the principles of international law.

6.68 Integration is normally effected in the UK system when the grant of indefinite leave to remain is given. The ability to revoke, curtail or restrict such leave (if lawfully obtained) disappears. Differential treatment is permitted under British law after that point, with respect to access to certain employment in the public sphere. The right to vote in national elections and perform jury service is restricted to British citizens.

6.69 More controversially, certain family members of persons entitled in the UK may have been admitted with indefinite leave to remain on the basis of an undertaking given by their sponsor. Section 115(9) of the Immigration and Asylum Act 1999 defines 'a person subject to immigration control' for the purpose of exclusion from benefits as a person who is not a national of an EEA state and who:

(a) requires leave to enter and remain in the UK but does not have it;
(b) has such leave that is subject to a condition not to have recourse to public funds;
(c) has such leave given as a result of a maintenance undertaking;
(d) has leave to enter or remain only as a result of a pending appeal.

Persons excluded from benefit by this section have to be restored to benefit by enabling regulations promoted by the Department for Social Security. As subordinate instruments these measures could be struck down if they were incompatible with Article 14 of the ECHR. At present, the regulations require that the sponsored migrant be settled for five years or the sponsor to have died before they may access benefits. This provision is probably race neutral and in any event relates to non-contributory benefits that may not amount to possession within the meaning of Protocol 1 Article 1.

6.70 Where there is differential treatment on the basis of nationality or status, there will have to be an examination of whether the discrimination is in the scope of application to the ECHR, and whether it is justified for some pressing social need. Usually the problem will be solved by more pro-active non-discrimination clauses, such as the preclusion of discrimination on the grounds of social advantage in EC Regulation 1612/68, Article 7, the non-discrimination provisions of EU Association Agreements with various other states, or the principle of non-discrimination in the field of social assistance provided for in the European Social

Charter 1961 (Revised 1996), Articles 12 and 13, and the European Convention on Social and Medical Assistance 1953, Articles 1 and 2 for nationals of states that have ratified those instruments.

Refugees and asylum seekers

6.71   Article 3 of the 1951 Refugee Convention precludes discrimination in the application of the Convention on the grounds of race, religion or country of origin. Asylum seekers are unusually dependent on the host state for their means of support and social and medical assistance, and discrimination in this sphere would be likely to engage Article 14 when combined with the concept of physical and bodily integrity under Article 8.

6.72   Although a person is a refugee from the moment he or she fulfils the qualifying criteria, and for the purposes of non-refoulement a claimant must be treated as a refugee until it is finally decided that he or she fails to qualify, it is likely that in matters relating to social assistance, the crucial moment is the recognition of a refugee by a state. Thus the Court of Appeal in *R v Secretary of State for Social Security, ex parte B and Joint Council for the Welfare of Immigrants* [1997] 1 WLR 275 was unpersuaded that there was a right to equal treatment with own nationals for asylum claimants. If so, special measures of asylum support for asylum seekers would not by themselves infringe the discrimination provisions of the ECHR.

6.73   Discriminatory policies with respect to detention of asylum seekers, however, will clearly engage Article 14 when combined with Article 5. Since personal liberty is a strong value in the ECHR, differential treatment would have to be closely reasoned and explained to avoid the conclusion of unlawful discrimination. Any suggestion that certain races, nationalities, or ethnic groups within a nationality should be detained raises a presumption of discrimination. The controversial authorization[33] permitting discrimination on the basis of nationality or national or ethnic origin in the fields of examination of a claim, detention and conditions of temporary admission, may have to be scrutinized closely to see whether a proper justification has been advanced. In *R (Tamil Information Centre) v Secretary of State for the Home Department* [2002] EWHC Admin 2155, the first such authorization was declared unlawful because it delegated judgment to an immigration officer contrary to parliamentary assurances, but no discrimination was found in *European Roma Rights Centre v Immigration Officer Prague* [2002] EWHC Admin 1989. Discrimination is permitted where there is statistical evidence or intelligence showing a trend of past or likely future

---

[33]   Race Relations (Immigration and Asylum) Authorisation 2001, IDI March/2001, cCh 1, section 1, Annex EE; Race Relations Act 1976, s. 19D, inserted by Race Relations (Amendment) Act 2000, s. 1.

breaches of the immigration laws by persons of that nationality. Tamils, Kurds, Pontic Greeks, Roma, Somalis, Albanians, Afghans, and ethnic Chinese presenting Malaysian or Japanese travel documents are currently targeted.[34] However, since discrimination is an inherently comparative concept, we suggest that this inequality of treatment would only be objectively justified if there was evidence or intelligence showing *proportionately* greater historic or likely future breaches by nationals of these countries than by others. It would not be enough to point to absolute figures. Equally, measures that routinely suggest male claimants should be detained while women and children are to be released would appear to be discriminatory on the ground of sex. Very closely reasoned evidence would be called for before a safe conclusion could be drawn that there were other objective criteria at work here, e.g. tendency to abscond, compassionate circumstances and the like.

6.74 Where susceptibility to detention is linked to a fast track procedure, again reserved to certain nationalities, there would have to be an objective basis for believing the claim to be unlikely to be well founded before treating apparently like claims differently. The London Conclusions of the EU Council of Ministers[35] stress the need for 'objective and verifiable' means for concluding that such countries do not normally generate refugees. Where the issue of discriminatory treatment is in issue, a high intensity of scrutiny of underlying facts is called for in judicial review, and we suggest that the burden of justification or explanation rests with the respondent *R (on the application of Javed, Ali, and Ali) v Secretary of State* [2001] EWCA Civ 789.

---

[34] Written answer 1 May 2001, Hansard HC, col. 636W.
[35] 30 November and 1 December 1992 reprinted in Plender, R., *Basic Documents on International Migration Law* 2nd revised edition (Martinus Nijhoff Publications, 1999) at 472.

Chapter Seven

Postscript: The Implications of the Anti-Terrorism, Crime and Security Act 2001 for Immigration and Asylum

INTRODUCTION

7.1 The events of 11 September 2001 were profoundly traumatic to all who witnessed them. The consequences in the response of the executive at home and the international community abroad have yet to be fully evaluated and the implications for the international legal order are continuing. At one level, it was deeply depressing that the first anniversary of the coming into force of the Human Rights Act 1998 was celebrated by the Secretary of State's announcement of legislation that would require a derogation from Article 5 of the ECHR, one of the provisions guaranteeing the core freedom from arbitrary detention. On the other hand, it is perhaps a tribute to the status of the ECHR in the legal and political reasoning of the United Kingdom and the European Union, that the debate focused from the first on the legality of such a derogation under international norms. The Human Rights Act 1998 has survived its first test.

7.2 The Anti-Terrorism, Crime and Security Act (ATCSA) 2001, which received a thorough examination in the impossibly short space of time afforded for legislative scrutiny and principled objection within Parliament, from both the Joint Human Rights Committee and the House of Lords, secured important modifications and changes. The legislation is time restricted and the Special Immigration Appeals Commission (SIAC) has the authority to determine the legal basis for the Secretary of State's certification in individual cases and the compatibility with the ECHR of the controversial derogation in certain cases of certified detention. The judicial function, albeit exercised in an exceptional procedure, remains intact. Moreover, the executive has acknowledged that Articles 2, 3 and Protocol 6 of the ECHR remain absolute values to be respected in the times of the gravest emergency. There can be no licence to torture, arbitrarily kill or judicially execute even those who have shown the highest disregard for human life and dignity in their acts. Most importantly for aliens these absolute obligations prevent expulsion of those suspected of terrorist activity to countries where these values are not respected. In the present context this notably includes the United States of America. See the judgment of the Bosnian Human Rights Chamber in *Boudella* v *Bosnia and Herzegovina* (11 October 2002), finding a violation of Protocol 6 (paras. 268–274). See also *R (Abassi)* v *Secretary of State for the Home Department* [2002] EWCA Civ 1502 where the regime of British detainees held in a US camp in Cuba was held to be a 'legal black hole'.

7.3   Indeed the contrast between the response of the United Kingdom and that of the USA with the different constitutional traditions in the USA remains remarkable. Aliens in the USA have only such rights as the executive or lawmaker gives them; constitutional protection is reserved for citizens and not aliens. There is no entrenched body of human rights law available to alien and citizen alike and no international court to whom the alien can turn for assistance at times of jeopardy. Although the Inter American Commission on Human Rights has authority to examine the compatibility of acts of the executive with the American Declaration of Human Rights, the opinions of this hard-worked body are frequently ignored. The death penalty is regularly pronounced in the criminal courts of most states and in federal courts, and is frequently carried into effect. The recent execution of Timothy McVeigh for terrorist murders saw the formal end to the moratorium on federal executions. The prospects for clemency in the present political climate are bleak. The USA having declared war on terrorism, special military tribunals have been promulgated by emergency legislation bypassing usual congressional procedures, enabling military courts to convict aliens abducted without due process from foreign jurisdictions, with special rules of evidence and procedure, and then sentence them to death. It seems that such trials will be held offshore in a military base occupied by the US in Cuba of all places, where it is contended that the writ of law does not run. See *R (Abassi)* above at 7.2. Whatever problems there may be for human rights lawyers in the United Kingdom following these events, it is essential to keep a sense of perspective.

7.4   Nevertheless there is little doubt that the activities of Osama Bin Laden's Al Qaeda network of dedicated anti-western terrorists, the brutal hijacking and destruction of civilian aircraft, the attack on the World Trade Centre and the Pentagon and the response to these atrocities of western governments represent a significant departure in the world order. The prospects of unilateral or bilateral action against states and aliens has increased, with the risk that the UN, the International Criminal Court and other trans-national bodies designed to secure peace and protect individual rights will be marginalized. In the United Kingdom the events provided the opportunity for a marked shift of power back in favour of the executive in the treatment of aliens liable to expulsion. Of course, in the light of the House of Lords judgment in the case of *Secretary of State* v *Rehman* [2001] 3 WLR 877, before these events became known about, it must be acknowledged that the power of SIAC to disagree with the policy of the executive when it comes to action genuinely engaging the interest of national security, was already limited.

7.5 Historically the common law had done little to protect even friendly aliens subject to immigration control from liability to expulsion on political grounds without sight of the evidence, a right to any adequate reasons for the decision or a fair hearing before an impartial tribunal as to the justification for the expulsion (*Hosenball* v *Secretary of State* [1977] 1 WLR 766). The appeal rights under the Immigration Act 1971 were excluded in the cases where the Secretary of State personally deemed exclusion or deportation to be in the public good in the interests of national security foreign relations or other matters of a political nature. It was theoretically possible to judicially review such decisions but the grounds for review were in practice excluded if the material on which such decisions were based was not placed before the court for scrutiny (*NSH* v *Secretary of State* [1988] Imm AR 389). In the absence of a human rights claim there was little possibility of mounting an argument that a person who was susceptible to the power of deportation should not be deported. At first blush the Refugee Convention might have operated as such a restraint. It would seem offensive to common justice and a long historical tradition of asylum, if persons who had a well-founded fear of persecution could be returned to the frontiers of a territory where such persecution might take place. The Refugee Convention was not absolute in terms of the protection it provided however (*Chahal* v *Secretary of State* [1995] 1 WLR 526). For persons who were seeking entry as a refugee, the exclusion clause of Article 1F operated to deny the benefit of the Refugee Convention to those in respect of whom there were serious grounds for believing that they were guilty of a crime against humanity or the principles and purposes of the UN or any other serious, non-political crime (*T* v *Secretary of State* [1996] AC 742). Those who were already in the UK and had been found guilty of a serious offence here or were considered to be a danger to the security of the UK could also be denied the benefit of the non-refoulement provision (Refugee Convention, Article 33(2)). The UK case law established merely that where a lawful resident was being deported and Article 33(2) of the Refugee Convention was being relied on, the Secretary of State had at least to balance the particular interest of national security with the individual circumstances of the claimant and the degree of risk faced abroad (*Chahal* v *Secretary of State* [1995] 1 WLR 526). Where there was no right of appeal, and deportation of an asylum claimant could be justified on public good grounds, the issue was whether the Secretary of State could lawfully claim that national security was engaged, but what national security required in a particular case was not justiciable and thus not a matter for the courts.

ANTI-TERRORISM, CRIME AND SECURITY ACT

7.6   The Anti-Terrorism, Crime and Security Act 2001 reverses these modest restraints on executive discretion and declares that henceforth Articles 1F and 33(2) of the Refugee Convention (the exclusion clauses) are not to be taken to require consideration of the gravity of the harm the person faced if he or she had not been excluded from protection (ATCSA 2001, s. 34). This excision of the international obligation enables the Secretary of State to certify that the Refugee Convention does not apply where removal is conducive to the public good and the exclusion clauses apply (s. 33). Although such a certificate can be reviewed on appeal to SIAC, SIAC has first to consider whether it agrees with the statements in the certificate applying s. 34. It if does then it must dismiss such part of the appeal as relates to a claim for asylum. The only protection claim available to such a person would then be the Article 3 claim

7.7   So, in asylum cases, the central question for SIAC is whether the evidence relied on establishes whether there are serious reasons for considering that the person has committed a crime against peace, a war crime, or a crime against humanity or a serious non-political offence or acts contrary to the purposes of the UN (Article1F) or whether there are reasonable grounds for regarding the person as a danger to the security of the country in which they are (Article 33(2)). It is to be noted that these are not the same questions as were considered by the House of Lords in *Secretary of State* v *Rehman* (above at 7.4). Article 1F cases clearly refer to past crimes committed by the applicant so a more cogent assessment of conduct is called for than intimated by the House of Lords. Also, while Article 33(2) is looking to future risk and is thus more predictive in its nature, there is a difference between an assessment that a person is a danger to the United Kingdom, and the assessment that deportation is conducive to the public good as in the interests of national security. *Rehman* (above at 7.4), it should be remembered, was neither an asylum case nor even a detention case, and so no countervailing consideration of human rights fell to be weighed. Whilst ATCSA 2001, s. 35 demonstrates that when exclusion is engaged, no balance is required, the closest attention must be given by SIAC to what past conduct is established or what future conduct justifiably feared. In respect of the former, SIAC will still be applying the test in *T* v *Secretary of State* (above at 7.5).

7.8   The other new certificate that ATCSA 2001 brings into being is a s. 21 certificate that the Secretary of State reasonably (a) believes that person's presence is a risk to national security and (b) suspects that the person is a terrorist. Given the consequences of such a certificate in terms of detention, it is highly regrettable that the term 'national security' has no precise definition. It remains to be seen how far Lord Hoffman's approach to national security in *Secretary of*

State v *Rehman* will be applied by SIAC in a s. 21 case. Again we would make the point that *Rehman* was based on the term 'interests of national security' and the draftsman has opted for the possibly narrower term 'risk to national security'.

7.9 'Terrorist' here includes a person who is a member of an international terrorist group, is or has been concerned in the commission, preparation or instigation of acts of international terrorism, or has links with an international terrorist group (ATCSA 2001, s. 21(2)). Terrorism has the same meaning as under the Terrorism Act 2000, s. 1 which is exceptionally broad and goes way beyond international instruments designed to give it an effective meaning. 'Terrorism' means the use or threat of action to advance a political, religious or ideological cause and either involves the use of firearms and explosives or is designed to influence government or to intimidate the public or a section of the public. 'Action' means serious violence against a person or endangering someone's life, serious damage to property, serious risk to the health and safety of the public or a section of the public, or designed to seriously interfere with or seriously disrupt an electronic system. A terrorist group is 'international' if it is subject to the control or influence of persons outside the United Kingdom and the Secretary of State suspects it is concerned in the commission, preparation or instigation of acts of terrorism (ATCSA 2001, s. 21(3)). Presumably in any proceedings the Secretary of State will rely on evidence of proscription of a terrorist organization under s. 3 of the Terrorism Act 2000, even though the first cases for de-proscription suggest that a 'respectable' organization can be proscribed if it has individual members who are concerned in the instigation etc of acts of terrorism. See *R (Kurdistan Workers Party)* v *Secretary of State for the Home Department* [2002] EWHC Admin 644; and see *O'Driscoll* v *Secretary of State for the Home Department* [2002] EWHC Admin 2477. A person has links with an international terrorist group if he supports or assists it (ATCSA 2001, s.21(4)).

7.10 The Home Office it seems is having its belated revenge on Lord Atkin's dissent in *Liversidge* v *Anderson* [1942] AC 206, and Humpty Dumpty's rules of statutory construction are being relied on when it comes to foreigners of whom the Secretary of State disapproves for the time being. Perhaps the most depressing aspect of events post 11 September is that terrorism by states directed against their populations has been conveniently ignored, in favour of castigation of those who respond to it. A political scientist might find it curious to distribute the epithet 'terrorist' to those Kashmiris who want an independent homeland without asking about the legitimacy of Indian rule in the first place or its methods of dealing with political dissent. The bizarre history of western interference in the affairs of Afghanistan suggests that the label 'freedom fighter' or 'terrorist' is applied depending on the foreign policy concerns of the government of the day. It is undoubtedly the case that many people in the United Kingdom and the EU of a variety of ethnic religious or political persuasions support independence struggles in Palestine, the Middle East, South Asia, Africa and elsewhere. If the government of the day were to prosecute domestic supporters of such organizations, its hypocrisy in preaching peace but doing nothing to suppress state violence would prove embarrassing.

7.11 Those without the right of abode can be more readily intimidated by detention, deportation or the threat of either, outside the glare of publicity and effective scrutiny. It is to be hoped that the judicial authorities at SIAC will exercise common sense and rigorous scrutiny to protect political expression and participation even in controversial political movements, in deciding whether there are reasonable grounds for suspecting that a person is a terrorist endangering the national security of the United Kingdom. The other side of the lesson of 11 September is that people resort to support for violent groups if the causes of oppression and denial of political justice are ignored.

7.12 The purpose behind certification of a person as an international terrorist posing a risk to national security is first made plain by ATCSA 2001, s. 22 which provides that immigration action may be taken against such a person even though such action cannot result in his removal from the United Kingdom by what is coyly called a point of law relating to an international agreement or a practical consideration. The first limb clearly covers expulsions precluded by the HRA 1998, but is wider and includes any international agreement prohibiting expulsion that the common law would accept as determinative. In our view, this would include Article 3 of UNCAT. The second limb contemplates such problems as presently bedevil the removal of failed Iraqi asylum seekers to the KAA or Somalis to Somalia.

7.13 Then comes ATCSA 2001, s. 23 which provides that a suspected international terrorist may be detained under Sch. 2 and 3 of the IA 1971 despite the fact that there is a temporary or permanent bar to his removal under that Act. Thus the critical link between detention and expulsion that we have discussed above in chapter 3 is broken and detention is made permissible even though there is no prospect of removal. Section 23(1) refers to a suspected international terrorist, but in context must refer to a s. 21(1) certified terrorist who is in principle vulnerable to deportation action. This must exclude both people immune from deportation powers by reason of nationality or long residence (IA 1971, s. 7), and those who are not considered to be a risk to national security. Given that international terrorism might potentially embrace those who support organizations whose members have thrown petrol bombs at oppressive overseas security forces, this may be of importance. It highlights the feature, however, that this new power of indefinite detention is restricted to foreigners who have the requisite profile, even though the press reports emerging suggest that British nationals may represent as great if not a greater risk in some cases than lawfully resident foreigners.

7.14 A person who is being detained or expelled under the certification arrangements introduced under ATCSA 2001 may appeal to the Commission established under the SIAC Act 1997 that has now acquired a larger and more controversial jurisdiction. The Commission (SIAC) may grant bail under procedures adopted from the 1997 Act (ATCSA 2001, s. 24). It can cancel a s. 21 certificate on an appeal lodged within three months of issue if it considers that that are no reasonable grounds for the required belief or suspicion or for some other reason the certificate should not have been issued. 'Other reason' could be constituted by an error as to nationality, or as to the power to remove, or some illegality in the certification process (such as an abuse of process where a critical charge in respect of the relevant conduct has been preferred). SIAC could also conclude 'for some other reason' that the certificate should not have been issued where *on the facts* it finds the individual not to be an international terrorist who is a risk to national security, even though the Secretary of State could reasonably believe or suspect him to be so. Irrespective of an appeal, s. 23(6) imposes on SIAC an obligation to review a certificate six months or three months after the first review or where there has been a change in circumstance. Presumably an abandonment by a detainee of political views and beliefs previously held might be a change of circumstance. The special advocate procedure and the appeal on a point of law from SIAC apply to certified appeals.

7.15 These measures are due to expire after 15 months (see s. 29(1)) unless the Secretary of State grants a twelve month renewal of the order. In any event he is obliged to appoint a person to review the operation of the section after 14 months (see s. 28(2)(a)) and the legislation ceases after five years (see s. 29(7)). Nevertheless, the United Kingdom has derogated from the terms of Article 5 of the ECHR and this derogation has been communicated to the Council of Europe enabling ATCSA 2001 to come into force on 21 December 2001 some three months after the emergency said to have required it.[1] Opinions have differed as to whether the events of 11 September 2001 justify the government's assessment that there is a public emergency threatening the life of the nation.[2] Whilst of the Council of Europe states, the UK is perhaps at heightened risk owing to its close relationship with the USA and its support for Israel, as of 15 October 2001 there was 'no immediate intelligence pointing to a specific threat to the UK'.[3]

---

[1] The relevant immigration sections come into force on the passing of the Act: s. 127(2)(a) of the ATCSA 2001.

[2] See opinion of David Pannick QC of 16 November 2001 for LIBERTY and compare with opinion of David Anderson QC and Jemima Stratford of 16 November 2001 for JUSTICE. Both SIAC and, on appeal, the Court of Appeal have concluded that there was material enabling the Secretary of State lawfully to derogate from Article 5 on the basis of a state of emergency: *A, X, Y* v *Secretary of State for the Home Department* [2002] EWCA Civ 1502.

[3] Home Secretary's speech to House of Commons, 15 October 2001, *Hansard* HC Deb, col. 925.

7.16 We have seen that British citizens and those immune from removal (IA 1971, s. 7) who are suspected international terrorists and pose a threat to national security cannot be indefinitely detained without trial. Given the absence of a domestic law power of preventative detention, they must be prosecuted or extradited. Detention is thus linked to removal, and ATCSA 2001 thus only catches those whom the Secretary of State wishes to and has the power to remove, but cannot do so because of practical considerations (lack of documents) or owing to the UK's international obligations (essentially Article 3 ECHR). The focus on immigrants in ATCSA 2001 has accordingly led to the suggestion that the derogation is not in reality a derogation from Article 5 at all, but rather a disguised derogation from Article 3, which is impermissible by virtue of Article 15(2).[4]

7.17 In *Lawless* v *Ireland* (1961) 1 EHRR 15, 31, para. 28[5] the European Court held that the words 'other public emergency threatening the life of the nation' refer to:

> an exceptional situation of crisis or emergency which affects the whole population and constitutes a threat to the organised life of the community of which the State is part.

The European Court requires the asserted emergency to be supported by evidence. A wide margin of appreciation is however left to the national authorities, on the familiar international principle that they are 'in principle better placed than the international judge . . . to decide on the presence of such an emergency'.[6] The decision in *Rehman* v *Secretary of State* (7.4 above) would suggest that substantial deference would be paid by a domestic court to the Secretary of State's assertion in recognition of its status as a court and the Secretary of State's status as an accountable Minister.

7.18 While the European Court resists the temptation to judge the efficacy of measures with the benefit of hindsight (*Ireland* v *UK* (1978) 2 EHRR 25, paras. 214, 220), the standard of strict necessity demands a high intensity of review of the proposed derogating measure. Thus in *Aksoy* v *Turkey* (1997) 23 EHRR 553 paras. 78, 83, 84 the European Court ruled that the public emergency in southeast Turkey could not justify a detention on suspicion of terrorist involvement lasting 14 days, and without judicial supervision or access to lawyers, doctors, relative or friends.

7.19 If there is a strict need for derogation to permit indeterminate detention without trial of a suspected international terrorist presenting a threat to national security, why do the same principles not apply to British citizens? Certainly a

---

[4] See Pannick's opinion above at footnote 2.
[5] See also *Aksoy* v *Turkey* (1997) 23 EHRR 553 para. 70.
[6] See *Ireland* v UK (1978) 2 EHRR 25, para. 207; *Brannigan and McBride* v *UK* (1993) 17 EHRR 539, para. 43; *Aksoy* v *Turkey* (1997) 23 EHRR 553 para. 68.

by-product of these measures seems intended to undermine reliance on Article 3 to require certain classes of claimants to undergo the pleasures of indefinite administrative detention as the price of such a claim. SIAC concluded it would be discriminatory to take action only against non-removable aliens and non-removable citizens ([2002] HRLR 45) but the Court of Appeal disagreed ([2002] EWCA Civ 1502).

7.20 In any event the only body able to review the derogation in the United Kingdom is SIAC and on appeal the Court of Appeal (ATCSA 2001, s. 30(2), (3)). In hearing such an appeal SIAC has all the powers of the High Court in a judicial review hearing (ATCSA 2001, s. 30(2), (3)). The critical question before SIAC is likely to be not so much the abstract question of whether there was a threat to the UK from terrorism, although the absence of actual attacks against the UK since the state of emergency is perhaps striking. Rather it is whether the particular measures of detention of up to 15 months, renewable for up to five years in tranches of twelve months, are strictly required by the exigencies of the situation.

7.21 Doubtless the security case for detention of any individual will be carefully reviewed. In our opinion if SIAC concludes that individuals are being certified with a view to detention and removal who do not represent any immediate threat to the population of the United Kingdom as a whole, a real issue arises as to the strict necessity of these measures. We would equate risk to national security with an immediate rather than a remote threat. Simply because foreign policy presently disapproves of the acts of the foreign organizations to which the detainee adheres, the exigency of the threat to the United Kingdom will not 'strictly require' these measures of detention. If a person is considered to be a supporter of a Palestinian militant organization, but is not connected with attacks in the UK or Europe and against British property or interests, and the UK is not at risk of Israeli retaliation, it is difficult to see why they should be detained, however much the UK may disapprove of the political affiliation. See *A, X, Y* v *Secretary of State for the Home Department* [2002] EWCA Civ 1502. If there is evidence of extra-territorial commission of offences they can be prosecuted. In our opinion, SIAC would have to be satisfied that detention was strictly necessary on the merits to prevent violence etc. that threatened the United Kingdom or its people. Otherwise we are essentially detaining at the behest of foreign regimes, including objectionable and oppressive ones, that do not apply ECHR standards in their dealings with their own inhabitants.

7.22 The risk is that what has been sold to the public as a necessary measure of defence against suicide bombers, or chemical warfare spreading terrorists, may be used against exiled dissidents and political activists who displease oppressive regimes abroad. Whether Lord Hoffman's judgment in *Rehman* has given wide authority for the executive to promote immigration policies, justifying refusal or entry or expulsion in such circumstances, is a very different question from whether internment is necessary, especially when the issue is under scrutiny by a judicial body designed to apply an exacting test. It is to be hoped that either executive self-restraint in the use of this power, or judicial perspicacity to prevent abuses, limit its functioning to the bare minimum in scope: namely detention of the truly dangerous. If the necessity of such detention justifies the derogation then it is important for traditions of liberty, diversity and decency that its duration is minimal and that the Secretary of State will not see fit to extend this inherently odious measure[7] beyond its sell by date.

---

[7] 'The power of the Executive to cast a man into prison without formulating any charge known to the law, and particularly to deny him the judgment of his peers, is in the highest degree odious and is the foundation of all totalitarian government whether Nazi or Communist.' Winston Churchill, cited in A. W. B. Simpson, *In the Highest Degree Odious, Detention Without Trial in Wartime Britain* (Clarendon Press, Oxford, 1992).

Appendix One

Human Rights Act 1998

CHAPTER 42

ARRANGEMENT OF SECTIONS

Derogations and reservations

Judges of the European Court of Human Rights

Parliamentary procedure

Supplemental

SCHEDULES:

HUMAN RIGHTS ACT 1998

1998 CHAPTER 42

An Act to give further effect to rights and freedoms guaranteed under the European Convention on Human Rights; to make provision with respect to holders of certain judicial offices who become judges of the European Court of Human Rights; and for connected purposes. [9th November 1998]

BE IT ENACTED by the Queen's most Excellent Majesty, by and with the advice and consent of the Lords Spiritual and Temporal, and Commons, in this present Parliament assembled, and by the authority of the same, as follows:—

Introduction

1. The Convention Rights

(1) In this Act 'the Convention rights' means the rights and fundamental freedoms set out in—

(a) Articles 2 to 12 and 14 of the Convention,

(b) Articles 1 to 3 of the First Protocol, and

(c) Articles 1 and 2 of the Sixth Protocol,

as read with Articles 16 to 18 of the Convention.

(2) Those Articles are to have effect for the purposes of this Act subject to any designated derogation or reservation (as to which see sections 14 and 15).

(3) The Articles are set out in Schedule 1.

(4) The [Lord Chancellor] may by order make such amendments to this Act as he considers appropriate to reflect the effect, in relation to the United Kingdom, of a protocol.

(5) In subsection (4) 'protocol' means a protocol to the Convention—

(a) which the United Kingdom has ratified; or

(b) which the United Kingdom has signed with a view to ratification.

(6) No amendment may be made by an order under subsection (4) so as to come into force before the protocol concerned is in force in relation to the United Kingdom.

2. Interpretation of Convention rights

(1) A court or tribunal determining a question which has arisen in connection with a Convention right must take into account any—

(a) judgment, decision, declaration or advisory opinion of the European Court of Human Rights,

(b) opinion of the Commission given in a report adopted under Article 31 of the Convention,

(c) decision of the Commission in connection with Article 26 or 27(2) of the Convention, or

(d)   decision of the Committee of Ministers taken under Article 46 of the Convention,

whenever made or given, so far as, in the opinion of the court or tribunal, it is relevant to the proceedings in which that question has arisen.

(2)   Evidence of any judgment, decision, declaration or opinion of which account may have to be taken under this section is to be given in proceedings before any court or tribunal in such manner as may be provided by rules.

(3)   In this section 'rules' means rules of court or, in the case of proceedings before a tribunal, rules made for the purposes of this section—

(a)   by the Lord Chancellor or the Secretary of State, in relation to any proceedings outside Scotland;

(b)   by the Secretary of State, in relation to proceedings in Scotland; or

(c)   by a Northern Ireland department, in relation to proceedings before a tribunal in Northern Ireland—

(i)   which deals with transferred matters; and

(ii)   for which no rules made under paragraph (a) are in force.

Legislation

3.   Interpretation of legislation

(1)   So far as it is possible to do so, primary legislation and subordinate legislation must be read and given effect in a way which is compatible with the Convention rights.

(2)   This section—

(a)   applies to primary legislation and subordinate legislation whenever enacted;

(b)   does not affect the validity, continuing operation or enforcement of any incompatible primary legislation; and

(c)   does not affect the validity, continuing operation or enforcement of any incompatible subordinate legislation if (disregarding any possibility of revocation) primary legislation prevents removal of the incompatibility.

4.   Declaration of incompatibility

(1)   Subsection (2) applies in any proceedings in which a court determines whether a provision of primary legislation is compatible with a Convention right.

(2)   If the court is satisfied that the provision is incompatible with a Convention right, it may make a declaration of that incompatibility.

(3)   Subsection (4) applies in any proceedings in which a court determines whether a provision of subordinate legislation, made in the exercise of a power conferred by primary legislation, is compatible with a Convention right.

(4)   If the court is satisfied—

(a)   that the provision is incompatible with a Convention right, and

(b)   that (disregarding any possibility of revocation) the primary legislation concerned prevents removal of the incompatibility,
it may make a declaration of that incompatibility.

(5)   In this section 'court' means—

(a)   the House of Lords;

(b)   the Judicial Committee of the Privy Council;

(c)   the Courts-Martial Appeal Court;

(d)   in Scotland, the High Court of Justiciary sitting otherwise than as a trial court or the Court of Session;

(e)   in England and Wales or Northern Ireland, the High Court or the Court of Appeal.

(6)   A declaration under this section ('a declaration of incompatibility')—

(a)   does not affect the validity, continuing operation or enforcement of the provision in respect of which it is given; and

(b)   is not binding on the parties to the proceedings in which it is made.

5.   Right of Crown to intervene

(1)   Where a court is considering whether to make a declaration of incompatibility, the Crown is entitled to notice in accordance with rules of court.

(2)   In any case to which subsection (1) applies—

(a)   a Minister of the Crown (or a person nominated by him),

(b)   a member of the Scottish Executive,

(c)   a Northern Ireland Minister,

(d)   a Northern Ireland department,
is entitled, on giving notice in accordance with rules of court, to be joined as a party to the proceedings.

(3)   Notice under subsection (2) may be given at any time during the proceedings.

(4)   A person who has been made a party to criminal proceedings (other than in Scotland) as the result of a notice under subsection (2) may, with leave, appeal to the House of Lords against any declaration of incompatibility made in the proceedings.

(5)   In subsection (4)—
'criminal proceedings' includes all proceedings before the Courts-Martial Appeal Court; and
'leave' means leave granted by the court making the declaration of incompatibility or by the House of Lords.

Public authorities

6.   Acts of public authorities

(1)   It is unlawful for a public authority to act in a way which is incompatible with a Convention right.

(2)   Subsection (1) does not apply to an act if—

(a)   as the result of one or more provisions of primary legislation, the authority could not have acted differently; or

(b)   in the case of one or more provisions of, or made under, primary legislation which cannot be read or given effect in a way which is compatible with the Convention rights, the authority was acting so as to give effect to or enforce those provisions.

(3)   In this section 'public authority' includes—

(a)   a court or tribunal, and

(b)   any person certain of whose functions are functions of a public nature, but does not include either House of Parliament or a person exercising functions in connection with proceedings in Parliament.

(4)   In subsection (3) 'Parliament' does not include the House of Lords in its judicial capacity.

(5)   In relation to a particular act, a person is not a public authority by virtue only of subsection (3)(b) if the nature of the act is private.

(6)   'An act' includes a failure to act but does not include a failure to—

(a)   introduce in, or lay before, Parliament a proposal for legislation; or

(b)   make any primary legislation or remedial order.

7. Proceedings

(1)   A person who claims that a public authority has acted (or proposes to act) in a way which is made unlawful by section 6(1) may—

(a)   bring proceedings against the authority under this Act in the appropriate court or tribunal, or

(b)   rely on the Convention right or rights concerned in any legal proceedings,

but only if he is (or would be) a victim of the unlawful act.

(2)   In subsection (1)(a) 'appropriate court or tribunal' means such court or tribunal as may be determined in accordance with rules; and proceedings against an authority include a counterclaim or similar proceeding.

(3)   If the proceedings are brought on an application for judicial review, the applicant is to be taken to have a sufficient interest in relation to the unlawful act only if he is, or would be, a victim of that act.

(4)   If the proceedings are made by way of a petition for judicial review in Scotland, the applicant shall be taken to have title and interest to sue in relation to the unlawful act only if he is, or would be, a victim of that act.

(5)   Proceedings under subsection (1)(a) must be brought before the end of—

(a)   the period of one year beginning with the date on which the act complained of took place; or

(b)   such longer period as the court or tribunal considers equitable having regard to all the circumstances, but that is subject to any rule imposing a stricter time limit in relation to the procedure in question.

(6) In subsection (1)(b) 'legal proceedings' includes—

(a) proceedings brought by or at the instigation of a public authority; and

(b) an appeal against the decision of a court or tribunal.

(7) For the purposes of this section, a person is a victim of an unlawful act only if he would be a victim for the purposes of Article 34 of the Convention if proceedings were brought in the European Court of Human Rights in respect of that act.

(8) Nothing in this Act creates a criminal offence.

(9) In this section 'rules' means—

(a) in relation to proceedings before a court or tribunal outside Scotland, rules made by the Lord Chancellor or the Secretary of State for the purposes of this section or rules of court,

(b) in relation to proceedings before a court or tribunal in Scotland, rules made by the Secretary of State for those purposes,

(c) in relation to proceedings before a tribunal in Northern Ireland—

(i) which deals with transferred matters; and

(ii) for which no rules made under paragraph (a) are in force,

rules made by a Northern Ireland department for those purposes,

and includes provision made by order under section 1 of the Courts and Legal Services Act 1990.

(10) In making rules, regard must be had to section 9.

(11) The Minister who has power to make rules in relation to a particular tribunal may, to the extent he considers it necessary to ensure that the tribunal can provide an appropriate remedy in relation to an act (or proposed act) of a public authority which is (or would be) unlawful as a result of section 6(1), by order add to—

(a) the relief or remedies which the tribunal may grant; or

(b) the grounds on which it may grant any of them.

(12) An order made under subsection (11) may contain such incidental, supplemental, consequential or transitional provision as the Minister making it considers appropriate.

(13) 'The Minister' includes the Northern Ireland department concerned.

8. Judicial remedies

(1) In relation to any act (or proposed act) of a public authority which the court finds is (or would be) unlawful, it may grant such relief or remedy, or make such order, within its powers as it considers just and appropriate.

(2) But damages may be awarded only by a court which has power to award damages, or to order the payment of compensation, in civil proceedings.

(3)　No award of damages is to be made unless, taking account of all the circumstances of the case, including—

　　(a)　any other relief or remedy granted, or order made, in relation to the act in question (by that or any other court), and

　　(b)　the consequences of any decision (of that or any other court) in respect of that act,

the court is satisfied that the award is necessary to afford just satisfaction to the person in whose favour it is made.

(4)　In determining—

　　(a)　whether to award damages, or

　　(b)　the amount of an award,

the court must take into account the principles applied by the European Court of Human Rights in relation to the award of compensation under Article 41 of the Convention.

(5)　A public authority against which damages are awarded is to be treated—

　　(a)　in Scotland, for the purposes of section 3 of the Law Reform (Miscellaneous Provisions) (Scotland) Act 1940 as if the award were made in an action of damages in which the authority has been found liable in respect of loss or damage to the person to whom the award is made;

　　(b)　for the purposes of the Civil Liability (Contribution) Act 1978 as liable in respect of damage suffered by the person to whom the award is made.

(6)　In this section—

'court' includes a tribunal;

'damages' means damages for an unlawful act of a public authority; and

'unlawful' means unlawful under section 6(1).

9.　Judicial acts

(1)　Proceedings under section 7(1)(a) in respect of a judicial act may be brought only—

　　(a)　by exercising a right of appeal;

　　(b)　on an application (in Scotland a petition) for judicial review; or

　　(c)　in such other forum as may be prescribed by rules.

(2)　That does not affect any rule of law which prevents a court from being the subject of judicial review.

(3)　In proceedings under this Act in respect of a judicial act done in good faith, damages may not be awarded otherwise than to compensate a person to the extent required by Article 5(5) of the Convention.

(4)　An award of damages permitted by subsection (3) is to be made against the Crown; but no award may be made unless the appropriate person, if not a party to the proceedings, is joined.

(5)　In this section—

'appropriate person' means the Minister responsible for the court concerned, or a person or government department nominated by him;

'court' includes a tribunal;

'judge' includes a member of a tribunal, a justice of the peace and a clerk or other officer entitled to exercise the jurisdiction of a court;

'judicial act' means a judicial act of a court and includes an act done on the instructions, or on behalf, of a judge; and

'rules' has the same meaning as in section 7(9).

Remedial action

10. Power to take remedial action

(1)   This section applies if—

(a)   a provision of legislation has been declared under section 4 to be incompatible with a Convention right and, if an appeal lies—

(i)   all persons who may appeal have stated in writing that they do not intend to do so;

(ii)   the time for bringing an appeal has expired and no appeal has been brought within that time; or

(iii)   an appeal brought within that time has been determined or abandoned; or

(b)   it appears to a Minister of the Crown or Her Majesty in Council that, having regard to a finding of the European Court of Human Rights made after the coming into force of this section in proceedings against the United Kingdom, a provision of legislation is incompatible with an obligation of the United Kingdom arising from the Convention.

(2)   If a Minister of the Crown considers that there are compelling reasons for proceeding under this section, he may by order make such amendments to the legislation as he considers necessary to remove the incompatibility.

(3)   If, in the case of subordinate legislation, a Minister of the Crown considers—

(a)   that it is necessary to amend the primary legislation under which the subordinate legislation in question was made, in order to enable the incompatibility to be removed, and

(b)   that there are compelling reasons for proceeding under this section, he may by order make such amendments to the primary legislation as he considers necessary.

(4)   This section also applies where the provision in question is in subordinate legislation and has been quashed, or declared invalid, by reason of incompatibility with a Convention right and the Minister proposes to proceed under paragraph 2(b) of Schedule 2.

(5)   If the legislation is an Order in Council, the power conferred by subsection (2) or (3) is exercisable by Her Majesty in Council.

(6)   In this section 'legislation' does not include a Measure of the Church Assembly or of the General Synod of the Church of England.

(7)   Schedule 2 makes further provision about remedial orders.

Other rights and proceedings

11. Safeguard for existing human rights

A person's reliance on a Convention right does not restrict—

(a)   any other right or freedom conferred on him by or under any law having effect in any part of the United Kingdom; or

(b)   his right to make any claim or bring any proceedings which he could make or bring apart from sections 7 to 9.

12. Freedom of expression

(1)   This section applies if a court is considering whether to grant any relief which, if granted, might affect the exercise of the Convention right to freedom of expression.

(2)   If the person against whom the application for relief is made ('the respondent') is neither present nor represented, no such relief is to be granted unless the court is satisfied—

(a)   that the applicant has taken all practicable steps to notify the respondent; or

(b)   that there are compelling reasons why the respondent should not be notified.

(3)   No such relief is to be granted so as to restrain publication before trial unless the court is satisfied that the applicant is likely to establish that publication should not be allowed.

(4)   The court must have particular regard to the importance of the Convention right to freedom of expression and, where the proceedings relate to material which the respondent claims, or which appears to the court, to be journalistic, literary or artistic material (or to conduct connected with such material), to—

(a)   the extent to which—

(i)   the material has, or is about to, become available to the public; or

(ii)   it is, or would be, in the public interest for the material to be published;

(b)   any relevant privacy code.

(5)   In this section—

'court' includes a tribunal; and

'relief' includes any remedy or order (other than in criminal proceedings).

13. Freedom of thought, conscience and religion

(1)   If a court's determination of any question arising under this Act might affect the exercise by a religious organisation (itself or its members collectively)

of the Convention right to freedom of thought, conscience and religion, it must have particular regard to the importance of that right.

(2)   In this section 'court' includes a tribunal.

Derogations and reservations

14. Derogations

(1)   In this Act 'designated derogation' means any derogation by the United Kingdom from an Article of the Convention, or of any protocol to the Convention, which is designated for the purposes of this Act in an order made by the [Lord Chancellor].

(2)   . . .

(3)   If a designated derogation is amended or replaced it ceases to be a designated derogation.

(4)   But subsection (3) does not prevent the [Lord Chancellor] from exercising his power under subsection (1) to make a fresh designation order in respect of the Article concerned.

(5)   The [Lord Chancellor] must by order make such amendments to Schedule 3 as he considers appropriate to reflect—

(a)   any designation order; or

(b)   the effect of subsection (3).

(6)   A designation order may be made in anticipation of the making by the United Kingdom of a proposed derogation.

15. Reservations

(1)   In this Act 'designated reservation' means—

(a)   the United Kingdom's reservation to Article 2 of the First Protocol to the Convention; and

(b)   any other reservation by the United Kingdom to an Article of the Convention, or of any protocol to the Convention, which is designated for the purposes of this Act in an order made by the [Lord Chancellor].

(2)   The text of the reservation referred to in subsection (1)(a) is set out in Part II of Schedule 3.

(3)   If a designated reservation is withdrawn wholly or in part it ceases to be a designated reservation.

(4)   But subsection (3) does not prevent the [Lord Chancellor] from exercising his power under subsection (1)(b) to make a fresh designation order in respect of the Article concerned.

(5)   The [Lord Chancellor] must by order make such amendments to this Act as he considers appropriate to reflect—

(a)   any designation order; or

(b)   the effect of subsection (3).

16. Period for which designated derogations have effect

(1)   If it has not already been withdrawn by the United Kingdom, a designated derogation ceases to have effect for the purposes of this Act at the end of the period of five years beginning with the date on which the order designating it was made.

(2)   At any time before the period—

    (a)   fixed by subsection (1), or

    (b)   extended by an order under this subsection,

comes to an end, the [Lord Chancellor] may by order extend it by a further period of five years.

(3)   An order under section 14(1) ceases to have effect at the end of the period for consideration, unless a resolution has been passed by each House approving the order.

(4)   Subsection (3) does not affect—

    (a)   anything done in reliance on the order; or

    (b)   the power to make a fresh order under section 14(1).

(5)   In subsection (3) 'period for consideration' means the period of forty days beginning with the day on which the order was made.

(6)   In calculating the period for consideration, no account is to be taken of any time during which—

    (a)   Parliament is dissolved or prorogued; or

    (b)   both Houses are adjourned for more than four days.

(7)   If a designated derogation is withdrawn by the United Kingdom, the [Lord Chancellor] must by order make such amendments to this Act as he considers are required to reflect that withdrawal.

17. Periodic review of designated reservations

(1)   The appropriate Minister must review the designated reservation referred to in section 15(1)(a)—

    (a)   before the end of the period of five years beginning with the date on which section 1(2) came into force; and

    (b)   if that designation is still in force, before the end of the period of five years beginning with the date on which the last report relating to it was laid under subsection (3).

(2)   The appropriate Minister must review each of the other designated reservations (if any)—

    (a)   before the end of the period of five years beginning with the date on which the order designating the reservation first came into force; and

    (b)   if the designation is still in force, before the end of the period of five years beginning with the date on which the last report relating to it was laid under subsection (3).

(3)   The Minister conducting a review under this section must prepare a report on the result of the review and lay a copy of it before each House of Parliament.

Judges of the European Court of Human Rights

18. Appointment to European Court of Human Rights

(1)   In this section 'judicial office' means the office of—

(a)   Lord Justice of Appeal, Justice of the High Court or Circuit judge, in England and Wales;

(b)   judge of the Court of Session or sheriff, in Scotland;

(c)   Lord Justice of Appeal, judge of the High Court or county court judge, in Northern Ireland.

(2)   The holder of a judicial office may become a judge of the European Court of Human Rights ('the Court') without being required to relinquish his office.

(3)   But he is not required to perform the duties of his judicial office while he is a judge of the Court.

(4)   In respect of any period during which he is a judge of the Court—

(a)   a Lord Justice of Appeal or Justice of the High Court is not to count as a judge of the relevant court for the purposes of section 2(1) or 4(1) of the Supreme Court Act 1981 (maximum number of judges) nor as a judge of the Supreme Court for the purposes of section 12(1) to (6) of that Act (salaries etc.);

(b)   a judge of the Court of Session is not to count as a judge of that court for the purposes of section 1(1) of the Court of Session Act 1988 (maximum number of judges) or of section 9(1)(c) of the Administration of Justice Act 1973 ('the 1973 Act') (salaries etc.);

(c)   a Lord Justice of Appeal or judge of the High Court in Northern Ireland is not to count as a judge of the relevant court for the purposes of section 2(1) or 3(1) of the Judicature (Northern Ireland) Act 1978 (maximum number of judges) nor as a judge of the Supreme Court of Northern Ireland for the purposes of section 9(1)(d) of the 1973 Act (salaries etc.);

(d)   a Circuit judge is not to count as such for the purposes of section 18 of the Courts Act 1971 (salaries etc.);

(e)   a sheriff is not to count as such for the purposes of section 14 of the Sheriff Courts (Scotland) Act 1907 (salaries etc.);

(f)   a county court judge of Northern Ireland is not to count as such for the purposes of section 106 of the County Courts Act (Northern Ireland) 1959 (salaries etc.).

(5)   If a sheriff principal is appointed a judge of the Court, section 11(1) of the Sheriff Courts (Scotland) Act 1971 (temporary appointment of sheriff principal) applies, while he holds that appointment, as if his office is vacant.

(6)   Schedule 4 makes provision about judicial pensions in relation to the holder of a judicial office who serves as a judge of the Court.

(7) The Lord Chancellor or the Secretary of State may by order make such transitional provision (including, in particular, provision for a temporary increase in the maximum number of judges) as he considers appropriate in relation to any holder of a judicial office who has completed his service as a judge of the Court.

Parliamentary procedure

19. Statements of compatibility

(1) A Minister of the Crown in charge of a Bill in either House of Parliament must, before Second Reading of the Bill—

(a) make a statement to the effect that in his view the provisions of the Bill are compatible with the Convention rights ('a statement of compatibility'); or

(b) make a statement to the effect that although he is unable to make a statement of compatibility the government nevertheless wishes the House to proceed with the Bill.

(2) The statement must be in writing and be published in such manner as the Minister making it considers appropriate.

Supplemental

20. Orders etc. under this Act

(1) Any power of a Minister of the Crown to make an order under this Act is exercisable by statutory instrument.

(2) The power of the Lord Chancellor or the Secretary of State to make rules (other than rules of court) under section 2(3) or 7(9) is exercisable by statutory instrument.

(3) Any statutory instrument made under section 14, 15 or 16(7) must be laid before Parliament.

(4) No order may be made by the Lord Chancellor or the Secretary of State under section 1(4), 7(11) or 16(2) unless a draft of the order has been laid before, and approved by, each House of Parliament.

(5) Any statutory instrument made under section 18(7) or Schedule 4, or to which subsection (2) applies, shall be subject to annulment in pursuance of a resolution of either House of Parliament.

(6) The power of a Northern Ireland department to make—

(a) rules under section 2(3)(c) or 7(9)(c), or

(b) an order under section 7(11),

is exercisable by statutory rule for the purposes of the Statutory Rules (Northern Ireland) Order 1979.

(7) Any rules made under section 2(3)(c) or 7(9)(c) shall be subject to negative resolution; and section 41(6) of the Interpretation Act (Northern Ireland) 1954 (meaning of 'subject to negative resolution') shall apply as if the power to make the rules were conferred by an Act of the Northern Ireland Assembly.

(8) No order may be made by a Northern Ireland department under section 7(11) unless a draft of the order has been laid before, and approved by, the Northern Ireland Assembly.

21. Interpretation etc.

(1) In this Act—

'amend' includes repeal and apply (with or without modifications);

'the appropriate Minister' means the Minister of the Crown having charge of the appropriate authorised government department (within the meaning of the Crown Proceedings Act 1947);

'the Commission' means the European Commission of Human Rights;

'the Convention' means the Convention for the Protection of Human Rights and Fundamental Freedoms, agreed by the Council of Europe at Rome on 4th November 1950 as it has effect for the time being in relation to the United Kingdom;

'declaration of incompatibility' means a declaration under section 4;

'Minister of the Crown' has the same meaning as in the Ministers of the Crown Act 1975;

'Northern Ireland Minister' includes the First Minister and the deputy First Minister in Northern Ireland;

'primary legislation' means any—

    (a) public general Act;

    (b) local and personal Act;

    (c) private Act;

    (d) Measure of the Church Assembly;

    (e) Measure of the General Synod of the Church of England;

    (f) Order in Council—

      (i) made in exercise of Her Majesty's Royal Prerogative;

      (ii) made under section 38(1)(a) of the Northern Ireland

Constitution Act 1973 or the corresponding provision of the Northern Ireland Act 1998; or

      (iii) amending an Act of a kind mentioned in paragraph (a), (b) or (c);

and includes an order or other instrument made under primary legislation (otherwise than by the National Assembly for Wales, a member of the Scottish Executive, a Northern Ireland Minister or a Northern Ireland department) to the extent to which it operates to bring one or more provisions of that legislation into force or amends any primary legislation;

'the First Protocol' means the protocol to the Convention agreed at Paris on 20th March 1952;

'the Sixth Protocol' means the protocol to the Convention agreed at Strasbourg on 28th April 1983;

'the Eleventh Protocol' means the protocol to the Convention (restructuring the control machinery established by the Convention) agreed at Strasbourg on 11th May 1994;

'remedial order' means an order under section 10;

'subordinate legislation' means any—

    (a)   Order in Council other than one—

      (i)   made in exercise of Her Majesty's Royal Prerogative;

      (ii)   made under section 38(1)(a) of the Northern Ireland Constitution Act 1973 or the corresponding provision of the Northern Ireland Act 1998; or

      (iii)   amending an Act of a kind mentioned in the definition of primary legislation;

    (b)   Act of the Scottish Parliament;

    (c)   Act of the Parliament of Northern Ireland;

    (d)   Measure of the Assembly established under section 1 of the Northern Ireland Assembly Act 1973;

    (e)   Act of the Northern Ireland Assembly;

    (f)   order, rules, regulations, scheme, warrant, byelaw or other instrument made under primary legislation (except to the extent to which it operates to bring one or more provisions of that legislation into force or amends any primary legislation);

    (g)   order, rules, regulations, scheme, warrant, byelaw or other instrument made under legislation mentioned in paragraph (b), (c), (d) or (e) or made under an Order in Council applying only to Northern Ireland;

    (h)   order, rules, regulations, scheme, warrant, byelaw or other instrument made by a member of the Scottish Executive, a Northern Ireland Minister or a Northern Ireland department in exercise of prerogative or other executive functions of Her Majesty which are exercisable by such a person on behalf of Her Majesty;

'transferred matters' has the same meaning as in the Northern Ireland Act 1998; and

'tribunal' means any tribunal in which legal proceedings may be brought.

(2)   The references in paragraphs (b) and (c) of section 2(1) to Articles are to Articles of the Convention as they had effect immediately before the coming into force of the Eleventh Protocol.

(3)   The reference in paragraph (d) of section 2(1) to Article 46 includes a reference to Articles 32 and 54 of the Convention as they had effect immediately before the coming into force of the Eleventh Protocol.

(4)   The references in section 2(1) to a report or decision of the Commission or a decision of the Committee of Ministers include references to a report or decision made as provided by paragraphs 3, 4 and 6 of Article 5 of the Eleventh Protocol (transitional provisions).

(5)   Any liability under the Army Act 1955, the Air Force Act 1955 or the Naval Discipline Act 1957 to suffer death for an offence is replaced by a liability to imprisonment for life or any less punishment authorised by those Acts; and those Acts shall accordingly have effect with the necessary modifications.

22. Short title, commencement, application and extent

(1)   This Act may be cited as the Human Rights Act 1998.

(2)   Sections 18, 20 and 21(5) and this section come into force on the passing of this Act.

(3)   The other provisions of this Act come into force on such day as the Secretary of State may by order appoint; and different days may be appointed for different purposes.

(4)   Paragraph (b) of subsection (1) of section 7 applies to proceedings brought by or at the instigation of a public authority whenever the act in question took place; but otherwise that subsection does not apply to an act taking place before the coming into force of that section.

(5)   This Act binds the Crown.

(6)   This Act extends to Northern Ireland.

(7)   Section 21(5), so far as it relates to any provision contained in the Army Act 1955, the Air Force Act 1955 or the Naval Discipline Act 1957, extends to any place to which that provision extends.

SCHEDULES

Section 1(3)

SCHEDULE 1
THE ARTICLES

PART I
THE CONVENTION

RIGHTS AND FREEDOMS

Article 2
Right to life

1.   Everyone's right to life shall be protected by law. No one shall be deprived of his life intentionally save in the execution of a sentence of a court following his conviction of a crime for which this penalty is provided by law.

2.   Deprivation of life shall not be regarded as inflicted in contravention of this Article when it results from the use of force which is no more than absolutely necessary:

(a)   in defence of any person from unlawful violence;

(b)   in order to effect a lawful arrest or to prevent the escape of a person lawfully detained;

(c)   in action lawfully taken for the purpose of quelling a riot or insurrection.

Article 3
Prohibition of torture

No one shall be subjected to torture or to inhuman or degrading treatment or punishment.

Article 4
Prohibition of slavery and forced labour

1. No one shall be held in slavery or servitude.

2. No one shall be required to perform forced or compulsory labour.

3. For the purpose of this Article the term 'forced or compulsory labour' shall not include:

   (a)   any work required to be done in the ordinary course of detention imposed according to the provisions of Article 5 of this Convention or during conditional release from such detention;

   (b)   any service of a military character or, in case of conscientious objectors in countries where they are recognised, service exacted instead of compulsory military service;

   (c)   any service exacted in case of an emergency or calamity threatening the life or well-being of the community;

   (d)   any work or service which forms part of normal civic obligations.

Article 5
Right to liberty and security

1. Everyone has the right to liberty and security of person. No one shall be deprived of his liberty save in the following cases and in accordance with a procedure prescribed by law:

   (a)   the lawful detention of a person after conviction by a competent court;

   (b)   the lawful arrest or detention of a person for non-compliance with the lawful order of a court or in order to secure the fulfilment of any obligation prescribed by law;

   (c)   the lawful arrest or detention of a person effected for the purpose of bringing him before the competent legal authority on reasonable suspicion of having committed an offence or when it is reasonably considered necessary to prevent his committing an offence or fleeing after having done so;

   (d)   the detention of a minor by lawful order for the purpose of educational supervision or his lawful detention for the purpose of bringing him before the competent legal authority;

   (e)   the lawful detention of persons for the prevention of the spreading of infectious diseases, of persons of unsound mind, alcoholics or drug addicts or vagrants;

(f) the lawful arrest or detention of a person to prevent his effecting an unauthorised entry into the country or of a person against whom action is being taken with a view to deportation or extradition.

2. Everyone who is arrested shall be informed promptly, in a language which he understands, of the reasons for his arrest and of any charge against him.

3. Everyone arrested or detained in accordance with the provisions of paragraph 1(c) of this Article shall be brought promptly before a judge or other officer authorised by law to exercise judicial power and shall be entitled to trial within a reasonable time or to release pending trial. Release may be conditioned by guarantees to appear for trial.

4. Everyone who is deprived of his liberty by arrest or detention shall be entitled to take proceedings by which the lawfulness of his detention shall be decided speedily by a court and his release ordered if the detention is not lawful.

5. Everyone who has been the victim of arrest or detention in contravention of the provisions of this Article shall have an enforceable right to compensation.

Article 6
Right to a fair trial

1. In the determination of his civil rights and obligations or of any criminal charge against him, everyone is entitled to a fair and public hearing within a reasonable time by an independent and impartial tribunal established by law. Judgment shall be pronounced publicly but the press and public may be excluded from all or part of the trial in the interest of morals, public order or national security in a democratic society, where the interests of juveniles or the protection of the private life of the parties so require, or to the extent strictly necessary in the opinion of the court in special circumstances where publicity would prejudice the interests of justice.

2. Everyone charged with a criminal offence shall be presumed innocent until proved guilty according to law.

3. Everyone charged with a criminal offence has the following minimum rights:

(a) to be informed promptly, in a language which he understands and in detail, of the nature and cause of the accusation against him;

(b) to have adequate time and facilities for the preparation of his defence;

(c) to defend himself in person or through legal assistance of his own choosing or, if he has not sufficient means to pay for legal assistance, to be given it free when the interests of justice so require;

(d) to examine or have examined witnesses against him and to obtain the attendance and examination of witnesses on his behalf under the same conditions as witnesses against him;

(e) to have the free assistance of an interpreter if he cannot understand or speak the language used in court.

Article 7
No punishment without law

1.   No one shall be held guilty of any criminal offence on account of any act or omission which did not constitute a criminal offence under national or international law at the time when it was committed. Nor shall a heavier penalty be imposed than the one that was applicable at the time the criminal offence was committed.

2.   This Article shall not prejudice the trial and punishment of any person for any act or omission which, at the time when it was committed, was criminal according to the general principles of law recognised by civilised nations.

Article 8
Right to respect for private and family life

1.   Everyone has the right to respect for his private and family life, his home and his correspondence.

2.   There shall be no interference by a public authority with the exercise of this right except such as is in accordance with the law and is necessary in a democratic society in the interests of national security, public safety or the economic well being of the country, for the prevention of disorder or crime, for the protection of health or morals, or for the protection of the rights and freedoms of others.

Article 9
Freedom of thought, conscience and religion

1.   Everyone has the right to freedom of thought, conscience and religion; this right includes freedom to change his religion or belief and freedom, either alone or in community with others and in public or private, to manifest his religion or belief, in worship, teaching, practice and observance.

2.   Freedom to manifest one's religion or beliefs shall be subject only to such limitations as are prescribed by law and are necessary in a democratic society in the interests of public safety, for the protection of public order, health or morals, or for the protection of the rights and freedoms of others.

Article 10
Freedom of expression

1.   Everyone has the right to freedom of expression. This right shall include freedom to hold opinions and to receive and impart information and ideas without interference by public authority and regardless of frontiers. This Article shall not prevent States from requiring the licensing of broadcasting, television or cinema enterprises.

2.   The exercise of these freedoms, since it carries with it duties and responsibilities, may be subject to such formalities, conditions, restrictions or penalties

as are prescribed by law and are necessary in a democratic society, ᵢ. ests of national security, territorial integrity or public safety, for the prevᵥ disorder or crime, for the protection of health or morals, for the protection ᵥ reputation or rights of others, for preventing the disclosure of informatiᵥ received in confidence, or for maintaining the authority and impartiality of the judiciary.

Article 11
Freedom of assembly and association

1.   Everyone has the right to freedom of peaceful assembly and to freedom of association with others, including the right to form and to join trade unions for the protection of his interests.

2.   No restrictions shall be placed on the exercise of these rights other than such as are prescribed by law and are necessary in a democratic society in the interests of national security or public safety, for the prevention of disorder or crime, for the protection of health or morals or for the protection of the rights and freedoms of others. This Article shall not prevent the imposition of lawful restrictions on the exercise of these rights by members of the armed forces, of the police or of the administration of the State.

Article 12
Right to marry

Men and women of marriageable age have the right to marry and to found a family, according to the national laws governing the exercise of this right.

Article 14
Prohibition of discrimination

The enjoyment of the rights and freedoms set forth in this Convention shall be secured without discrimination on any ground such as sex, race, colour, language, religion, political or other opinion, national or social origin, association with a national minority, property, birth or other status.

Article 16
Restrictions on political activity of aliens

Nothing in Articles 10, 11 and 14 shall be regarded as preventing the High Contracting Parties from imposing restrictions on the political activity of aliens.

Article 17
Prohibition of abuse of rights

Nothing in this Convention may be interpreted as implying for any State, group or person any right to engage in any activity or perform any act aimed at the destruction of any of the rights and freedoms set forth herein or at their limitation to a greater extent than is provided for in the Convention.

Article 18
Limitation on use of restrictions on rights

The restrictions permitted under this Convention to the said rights and freedoms shall not be applied for any purpose other than those for which they have been prescribed.

PART II
THE FIRST PROTOCOL

Article 1
Protection of property

Every natural or legal person is entitled to the peaceful enjoyment of his possessions. No one shall be deprived of his possessions except in the public interest and subject to the conditions provided for by law and by the general principles of international law.

The preceding provisions shall not, however, in any way impair the right of a State to enforce such laws as it deems necessary to control the use of property in accordance with the general interest or to secure the payment of taxes or other contributions or penalties.

Article 2
Right to education

No person shall be denied the right to education. In the exercise of any functions which it assumes in relation to education and to teaching, the State shall respect the right of parents to ensure such education and teaching in conformity with their own religious and philosophical convictions.

Article 3
Right to free elections

The High Contracting Parties undertake to hold free elections at reasonable intervals by secret ballot, under conditions which will ensure the free expression of the opinion of the people in the choice of the legislature.

PART III
THE SIXTH PROTOCOL

Article 1
Abolition of the death penalty

The death penalty shall be abolished. No one shall be condemned to such penalty or executed.

Article 2
Death penalty in time of war

A State may make provision in its law for the death penalty in respect of acts committed in time of war or of imminent threat of war; such penalty shall be applied only in the instances laid down in the law and in accordance with its provisions. The State shall communicate to the Secretary General of the Council of Europe the relevant provisions of that law.

SCHEDULE 2
REMEDIAL ORDERS

Orders

1.—(1) A remedial order may—

(a)   contain such incidental, supplemental, consequential or transitional provision as the person making it considers appropriate;

(b)   be made so as to have effect from a date earlier than that on which it is made;

(c)   make provision for the delegation of specific functions;

(d)   make different provision for different cases.

(2)   The power conferred by sub-paragraph (1)(a) includes—

(a)   power to amend primary legislation (including primary legislation other than that which contains the incompatible provision); and

(b)   power to amend or revoke subordinate legislation (including subordinate legislation other than that which contains the incompatible provision).

(3)   A remedial order may be made so as to have the same extent as the legislation which it affects.

(4)   No person is to be guilty of an offence solely as a result of the retrospective effect of a remedial order.

Procedure

2.   No remedial order may be made unless—

(a)   a draft of the order has been approved by a resolution of each House of Parliament made after the end of the period of 60 days beginning with the day on which the draft was laid; or

(b)   it is declared in the order that it appears to the person making it that, because of the urgency of the matter, it is necessary to make the order without a draft being so approved.

Orders laid in draft

3.—(1) No draft may be laid under paragraph 2(a) unless—

(a)   the person proposing to make the order has laid before Parliament a document which contains a draft of the proposed order and the required information; and

(b)   the period of 60 days, beginning with the day on which the document required by this sub-paragraph was laid, has ended.

(2)   If representations have been made during that period, the draft laid under paragraph 2(a) must be accompanied by a statement containing—

(a)   a summary of the representations; and

(b)   if, as a result of the representations, the proposed order has been changed, details of the changes.

Urgent cases

4.—(1)   If a remedial order ('the original order') is made without being approved in draft, the person making it must lay it before Parliament, accompanied by the required information, after it is made.

(2)   If representations have been made during the period of 60 days beginning with the day on which the original order was made, the person making it must (after the end of that period) lay before Parliament a statement containing—

(a)   a summary of the representations; and

(b)   if, as a result of the representations, he considers it appropriate to make changes to the original order, details of the changes.

(3)   If sub-paragraph (2)(b) applies, the person making the statement must—

(a)   make a further remedial order replacing the original order; and

(b)   lay the replacement order before Parliament.

(4)   If, at the end of the period of 120 days beginning with the day on which the original order was made, a resolution has not been passed by each House approving the original or replacement order, the order ceases to have effect (but without that affecting anything previously done under either order or the power to make a fresh remedial order).

Definitions

5.   In this Schedule—

'representations' means representations about a remedial order (or proposed remedial order) made to the person making (or proposing to make) it and includes any relevant Parliamentary report or resolution; and

'required information' means—

(a)   an explanation of the incompatibility which the order (or proposed order) seeks to remove, including particulars of the relevant declaration, finding or order; and

(b)   a statement of the reasons for proceeding under section 10 and for making an order in those terms.

Calculating periods

6.   In calculating any period for the purposes of this Schedule, no account is to be taken of any time during which—

(a)   Parliament is dissolved or prorogued; or

(b)   both Houses are adjourned for more than four days.

[7.—(1) This paragraph applies in relation to—

(a)   any remedial order made, and any draft of such an order proposed to be made,—

(i)   by the Scottish Ministers; or

(ii) within devolved competence (within the meaning of the Scotland Act 1998) by Her Majesty in Council; and

(b)   any document or statement to be laid in connection with such an order (or proposed order).

(2)   This Schedule has effect in relation to any such order (or proposed order), document or statement subject to the following modifications.

(3)   Any reference to Parliament, each House of Parliament or both Houses of Parliament shall be construed as a reference to the Scottish Parliament.

(4)   Paragraph 6 does not apply and instead, in calculating any period for the purposes of this Schedule, no account is to be taken of any time during which the Scottish Parliament is dissolved or is in recess for more than four days.]

SCHEDULE 3

[DEROGATION AND RESERVATION]

[PART I

DEROGATION

United Kingdom's derogation from Article 5(1)

The United Kingdom Permanent Representative to the Council of Europe presents his compliments to the Secretary General of the Council, and has the honour to convey the following information in order to ensure compliance with the obligations of Her Majesty's Government in the United Kingdom under Article 15(3) of the Convention for the Protection of Human Rights and Fundamental Freedoms signed at Rome on 4 November 1950.

Public emergency in the United Kingdom

The terrorist attacks in New York, Washington, D.C. and Pennsylvania on 11th September 2001 resulted in several thousand deaths, including many British victims and others from 70 different countries. In its resolutions 1368 (2001) and 1373 (2001), the United Nations Security Council recognised the attacks as a threat to international peace and security.

The threat from international terrorism is a continuing one. In its resolution 1373 (2001), the Security Council, acting under Chapter VII of the United Nations Charter, required all States to take measures to prevent the commission of terrorist attacks, including by denying safe haven to those who finance, plan, support or commit terrorist attacks.

There exists a terrorist threat to the United Kingdom from persons suspected of involvement in international terrorism. In particular, there are foreign nationals present in the United Kingdom who are suspected of being concerned in the commission, preparation or instigation of acts of international terrorism, of being members of organisations or groups which are so concerned or of having links with members of such organisations or groups, and who are a threat to the national security of the United Kingdom.

As a result, a public emergency, within the meaning of Article 15(1) of the Convention, exists in the United Kingdom.

The Anti-terrorism, Crime and Security Act 2001

As a result of the public emergency, provision is made in the Anti-terrorism, Crime and Security Act 2001, inter alia, for an extended power to arrest and detain a foreign national which will apply where it is intended to remove or deport the person from the United Kingdom but where removal or deportation is not for the time being possible, with the consequence that the detention would be unlawful under existing domestic law powers. The extended power to arrest and detain will apply where the Secretary of State issues a certificate indicating his belief that the person's presence in the United Kingdom is a risk to national security and that he suspects the person of being an international terrorist. That certificate will be subject to an appeal to the Special Immigration Appeals Commission ('SIAC'), established under the Special Immigration Appeals Commission Act 1997, which will have power to cancel it if it considers that the certificate should not have been issued. There will be an appeal on a point of law from a ruling by SIAC. In addition, the certificate will be reviewed by SIAC at regular intervals. SIAC will also be able to grant bail, where appropriate, subject to conditions. It will be open to a detainee to end his detention at any time by agreeing to leave the United Kingdom.

The extended power of arrest and detention in the Anti-terrorism, Crime and Security Act 2001 is a measure which is strictly required by the exigencies of the situation. It is a temporary provision which comes into force for an initial period of 15 months and then expires unless renewed by Parliament. Thereafter, it is subject to annual renewal by Parliament. If, at any time, in the Government's assessment, the public emergency no longer exists or the extended power is no longer strictly required by the exigencies of the situation, then the Secretary of State will, by Order, repeal the provision.

Domestic law powers of detention (other than under the Anti-terrorism, Crime and Security Act 2001)

The Government has powers under the Immigration Act 1971 ('the 1971 Act') to remove or deport persons on the ground that their presence in the United Kingdom is not conducive to the public good on national security grounds.

Persons can also be arrested and detained under Schedules 2 and 3 to the 1971 Act pending their removal or deportation. The courts in the United Kingdom have ruled that this power of detention can only be exercised during the period necessary, in all the circumstances of the particular case, to effect removal and that, if it becomes clear that removal is not going to be possible within a reasonable time, detention will be unlawful (*R* v *Governor of Durham Prison, ex parte Singh* [1984] 1 All ER 983).

Article 5(1)(f) of the Convention

It is well established that Article 5(1)(f) permits the detention of a person with a view to deportation only in circumstance where 'action is being taken with a view to deportation' (*Chahal* v *United Kingdom* (1996) 23 EHRR 413 at paragraph 112). In that case the European Court of Human Rights indicated that detention will cease to be permissible under Article 5(1)(f) if deportation proceedings are not prosecuted with due diligence and that it was necessary in such cases to determine whether the duration of the deportation proceedings was excessive (paragraph 113).

In some cases, where the intention remains to remove or deport a person on national security grounds, continued detention may not be consistent with Article 5(1)(f) as interpreted by the Court in the *Chahal* case. This may be the case, for example, if the person has established that removal to their own country might result in treatment contrary to Article 3 of the Convention. In such circumstances, irrespective of the gravity of the threat to national security posed by the person concerned, it is well established that Article 3 prevents removal or deportation to a place where there is a real risk that the person will suffer treatment contrary to that article. If no alternative destination is immediately available then removal or deportation may not, for the time being, be possible even though the ultimate intention remains to remove or deport the person once satisfactory arrangements can be made. In addition, it may not be possible to prosecute the person for a criminal offence given the strict rules on the admissibility of evidence in the criminal justice system of the United Kingdom and the high standard of proof required.

Derogation under Article 15 of the Convention

The Government has considered whether the exercise of the extended power to detain contained in the Anti-terrorism, Crime and Security Act 2001 may be inconsistent with the obligations under Article 5(1) of the Convention. As indicated above, there may be cases where, notwithstanding a continuing intention to remove or deport a person who is being detained, it is not possible to say that 'action is being taken with a view to deportation' within the meaning of Article 5(1)(f) as interpreted by the Court in the *Chahal* case. To the extent, therefore, that the exercise of the extended power may be inconsistent with the United

Kingdom's obligations under Article 5(1), the Government has decided to avail itself of the right of derogation conferred by Article 15(1) of the Convention and will continue to do so until further notice.

Strasbourg, 18 December 2001]

[PART II
RESERVATION]

At the time of signing the present (First) Protocol, I declare that, in view of certain provisions of the Education Acts in the United Kingdom, the principle affirmed in the second sentence of Article 2 is accepted by the United Kingdom only so far as it is compatible with the provision of efficient instruction and training, and the avoidance of unreasonable public expenditure.

Dated 20 March 1952. Made by the United Kingdom Permanent Representative to the Council of Europe.

SCHEDULE 4
JUDICIAL PENSIONS

Duty to make orders about pensions

1.—(1) The appropriate Minister must by order make provision with respect to pensions payable to or in respect of any holder of a judicial office who serves as an ECHR judge.

(2) A pensions order must include such provision as the Minister making it considers is necessary to secure that—

(a) an ECHR judge who was, immediately before his appointment as an ECHR judge, a member of a judicial pension scheme is entitled to remain as a member of that scheme;

(b) the terms on which he remains a member of the scheme are those which would have been applicable had he not been appointed as an ECHR judge; and

(c) entitlement to benefits payable in accordance with the scheme continues to be determined as if, while serving as an ECHR judge, his salary was that which would (but for section 18(4)) have been payable to him in respect of his continuing service as the holder of his judicial office.

Contributions

2. A pensions order may, in particular, make provision—

(a) for any contributions which are payable by a person who remains a member of a scheme as a result of the order, and which would otherwise be payable by deduction from his salary, to be made otherwise than by deduction from his salary as an ECHR judge; and

(b) for such contributions to be collected in such manner as may be determined by the administrators of the scheme.

Amendments of other enactments

3. A pensions order may amend any provision of, or made under, a pensions Act in such manner and to such extent as the Minister making the order considers necessary or expedient to ensure the proper administration of any scheme to which it relates.

Definitions

4. In this Schedule—

'appropriate Minister' means—

(a)   in relation to any judicial office whose jurisdiction is exercisable exclusively in relation to Scotland, the Secretary of State; and

(b)   otherwise, the Lord Chancellor;

'ECHR judge' means the holder of a judicial office who is serving as a judge of the Court;

'judicial pension scheme' means a scheme established by and in accordance with a pensions Act;

'pensions Act means—

(a)   the County Courts Act (Northern Ireland) 1959;

(b)   the Sheriffs' Pensions (Scotland) Act 1961;

(c)   the Judicial Pensions Act 1981; or

(d)   the Judicial Pensions and Retirement Act 1993; and

'pensions order' means an order made under paragraph 1.

Appendix Two

European Convention on Human Rights

CONVENTION FOR THE PROTECTION OF HUMAN RIGHTS AND
FUNDAMENTAL FREEDOMS AS AMENDED BY PROTOCOL NO. 11
(Date of entry into force 1 November 1998)

The governments signatory hereto, being members of the Council of Europe,
   Considering the Universal Declaration of Human Rights proclaimed by the General Assembly of the United Nations on 10th December 1948;
   Considering that this Declaration aims at securing the universal and effective recognition and observance of the Rights therein declared;
   Considering that the aim of the Council of Europe is the achievement of greater unity between its members and that one of the methods by which that aim is to be pursued is the maintenance and further realisation of human rights and fundamental freedoms;
   Reaffirming their profound belief in those fundamental freedoms which are the foundation of justice and peace in the world and are best maintained on the one hand by an effective political democracy and on the other by a common understanding and observance of the human rights upon which they depend;
   Being resolved, as the governments of European countries which are like-minded and have a common heritage of political traditions, ideals, freedom and the rule of law, to take the first steps for the collective enforcement of certain of the rights stated in the Universal Declaration,
   Have agreed as follows:

Article 1
Obligation to respect human rights

The High Contracting Parties shall secure to everyone within their jurisdiction the rights and freedoms defined in Section I of this Convention.

Section I—Rights and freedoms

Article 2
Right to life

1. Everyone's right to life shall be protected by law. No one shall be deprived of his life intentionally save in the execution of a sentence of a court following his conviction of a crime for which this penalty is provided by law.

2. Deprivation of life shall not be regarded as inflicted in contravention of this article when it results from the use of force which is no more than absolutely necessary:

(a)   in defence of any person from unlawful violence;

(b)   in order to effect a lawful arrest or to prevent the escape of a person lawfully detained;

(c)   in action lawfully taken for the purpose of quelling a riot or insurrection.

Article 3
Prohibition of torture

No one shall be subjected to torture or to inhuman or degrading treatment or punishment.

Article 4
Prohibition of slavery and forced labour

1. No one shall be held in slavery or servitude.

2. No one shall be required to perform forced or compulsory labour.

3. For the purpose of this article the term 'forced or compulsory labour' shall not include:

(a)   any work required to be done in the ordinary course of detention imposed according to the provisions of Article 5 of this Convention or during conditional release from such detention;

(b)   any service of a military character or, in case of conscientious objectors in countries where they are recognised, service exacted instead of compulsory military service;

(c)   any service exacted in case of an emergency or calamity threatening the life or well-being of the community;

(d)   any work or service which forms part of normal civic obligations.

Article 5
Right to liberty and security

1. Everyone has the right to liberty and security of person. No one shall be deprived of his liberty save in the following cases and in accordance with a procedure prescribed by law:

(a)   the lawful detention of a person after conviction by a competent court;

(b)   the lawful arrest or detention of a person for non-compliance with the lawful order of a court or in order to secure the fulfilment of any obligation prescribed by law;

(c)   the lawful arrest or detention of a person effected for the purpose of bringing him before the competent legal authority on reasonable suspicion of having committed an offence or when it is reasonably considered necessary to prevent his committing an offence or fleeing after having done so;

(d)   the detention of a minor by lawful order for the purpose of educational supervision or his lawful detention for the purpose of bringing him before the competent legal authority;

(e)   the lawful detention of persons for the prevention of the spreading of infectious diseases, of persons of unsound mind, alcoholics or drug addicts or vagrants;

(f)   the lawful arrest or detention of a person to prevent his effecting an unauthorised entry into the country or of a person against whom action is being taken with a view to deportation or extradition.

2.   Everyone who is arrested shall be informed promptly, in a language which he understands, of the reasons for his arrest and of any charge against him.

3.   Everyone arrested or detained in accordance with the provisions of paragraph 1.c of this article shall be brought promptly before a judge or other officer authorised by law to exercise judicial power and shall be entitled to trial within a reasonable time or to release pending trial. Release may be conditioned by guarantees to appear for trial.

4.   Everyone who is deprived of his liberty by arrest or detention shall be entitled to take proceedings by which the lawfulness of his detention shall be decided speedily by a court and his release ordered if the detention is not lawful.

5.   Everyone who has been the victim of arrest or detention in contravention of the provisions of this article shall have an enforceable right to compensation.

Article 6
Right to a fair trial

1. In the determination of his civil rights and obligations or of any criminal charge against him, everyone is entitled to a fair and public hearing within a reasonable time by an independent and impartial tribunal established by law. Judgment shall be pronounced publicly but the press and public may be excluded from all or part of the trial in the interests of morals, public order or national security in a democratic society, where the interests of juveniles or the protection of the private life of the parties so require, or to the extent strictly necessary in the opinion of the court in special circumstances where publicity would prejudice the interests of justice.

2.   Everyone charged with a criminal offence shall be presumed innocent until proved guilty according to law.

3.   Everyone charged with a criminal offence has the following minimum rights:

(a)   to be informed promptly, in a language which he understands and in detail, of the nature and cause of the accusation against him;

(b)   to have adequate time and facilities for the preparation of his defence;

(c)   to defend himself in person or through legal assistance of his own choosing or, if he has not sufficient means to pay for legal assistance, to be given it free when the interests of justice so require;

(d)   to examine or have examined witnesses against him and to obtain the attendance and examination of witnesses on his behalf under the same conditions as witnesses against him;

(e)   to have the free assistance of an interpreter if he cannot understand or speak the language used in court.

Article 7
No punishment without law

1.   No one shall be held guilty of any criminal offence on account of any act or omission which did not constitute a criminal offence under national or international law at the time when it was committed. Nor shall a heavier penalty be imposed than the one that was applicable at the time the criminal offence was committed.

2.   This article shall not prejudice the trial and punishment of any person for any act or omission which, at the time when it was committed, was criminal according to the general principles of law recognised by civilised nations.

Article 8
Right to respect for private and family life

1.   Everyone has the right to respect for his private and family life, his home and his correspondence.

2.   There shall be no interference by a public authority with the exercise of this right except such as is in accordance with the law and is necessary in a democratic society in the interests of national security, public safety or the economic well-being of the country, for the prevention of disorder or crime, for the protection of health or morals, or for the protection of the rights and freedoms of others.

Article 9
Freedom of thought, conscience and religion

1. Everyone has the right to freedom of thought, conscience and religion; this right includes freedom to change his religion or belief and freedom, either alone

or in community with others and in public or private, to manifest his religion or belief, in worship, teaching, practice and observance.

2. Freedom to manifest one's religion or beliefs shall be subject only to such limitations as are prescribed by law and are necessary in a democratic society in the interests of public safety, for the protection of public order, health or morals, or for the protection of the rights and freedoms of others.

Article 10
Freedom of expression

1. Everyone has the right to freedom of expression. This right shall include freedom to hold opinions and to receive and impart information and ideas without interference by public authority and regardless of frontiers. This article shall not prevent States from requiring the licensing of broadcasting, television or cinema enterprises.

2. The exercise of these freedoms, since it carries with it duties and responsibilities, may be subject to such formalities, conditions, restrictions or penalties as are prescribed by law and are necessary in a democratic society, in the interests of national security, territorial integrity or public safety, for the prevention of disorder or crime, for the protection of health or morals, for the protection of the reputation or rights of others, for preventing the disclosure of information received in confidence, or for maintaining the authority and impartiality of the judiciary.

Article 11
Freedom of assembly and association

1. Everyone has the right to freedom of peaceful assembly and to freedom of association with others, including the right to form and to join trade unions for the protection of his interests.

2. No restrictions shall be placed on the exercise of these rights other than such as are prescribed by law and are necessary in a democratic society in the interests of national security or public safety, for the prevention of disorder or crime, for the protection of health or morals or for the protection of the rights and freedoms of others. This article shall not prevent the imposition of lawful restrictions on the exercise of these rights by members of the armed forces, of the police or of the administration of the State.

Article 12
Right to marry

Men and women of marriageable age have the right to marry and to found a family, according to the national laws governing the exercise of this right.

Article 13
Right to an effective remedy

Everyone whose rights and freedoms as set forth in this Convention are violated shall have an effective remedy before a national authority notwithstanding that the violation has been committed by persons acting in an official capacity.

Article 14
Prohibition of discrimination

The enjoyment of the rights and freedoms set forth in this Convention shall be secured without discrimination on any ground such as sex, race, colour, language, religion, political or other opinion, national or social origin, association with a national minority, property, birth or other status.

Article 15
Derogation in time of emergency

1.   In time of war or other public emergency threatening the life of the nation any High Contracting Party may take measures derogating from its obligations under this Convention to the extent strictly required by the exigencies of the situation, provided that such measures are not inconsistent with its other obligations under international law.

2.   No derogation from Article 2, except in respect of deaths resulting from lawful acts of war, or from Articles 3, 4 (paragraph 1) and 7 shall be made under this provision.

3.   Any High Contracting Party availing itself of this right of derogation shall keep the Secretary General of the Council of Europe fully informed of the measures which it has taken and the reasons therefor. It shall also inform the Secretary General of the Council of Europe when such measures have ceased to operate and the provisions of the Convention are again being fully executed.

Article 16
Restrictions on political activity of aliens

Nothing in Articles 10, 11 and 14 shall be regarded as preventing the High Contracting Parties from imposing restrictions on the political activity of aliens.

Article 17
Prohibition of abuse of rights

Nothing in this Convention may be interpreted as implying for any State, group or person any right to engage in any activity or perform any act aimed at the destruction of any of the rights and freedoms set forth herein or at their limitation to a greater extent than is provided for in the Convention.

Article 18
Limitation on use of restrictions on rights

The restrictions permitted under this Convention to the said rights and freedoms shall not be applied for any purpose other than those for which they have been prescribed.

Section II—European Court of Human Rights

Article 19
Establishment of the Court

To ensure the observance of the engagements undertaken by the High Contracting Parties in the Convention and the Protocols thereto, there shall be set up a European Court of Human Rights, hereinafter referred to as 'the Court'. It shall function on a permanent basis.

Article 20
Number of judges

The Court shall consist of a number of judges equal to that of the High Contracting Parties.

Article 21
Criteria for office

1. The judges shall be of high moral character and must either possess the qualifications required for appointment to high judicial office or be jurisconsults of recognised competence.

2. The judges shall sit on the Court in their individual capacity.

3. During their term of office the judges shall not engage in any activity which is incompatible with their independence, impartiality or with the demands of a full-time office; all questions arising from the application of this paragraph shall be decided by the Court.

Article 22
Election of judges

1. The judges shall be elected by the Parliamentary Assembly with respect to each High Contracting Party by a majority of votes cast from a list of three candidates nominated by the High Contracting Party.

2. The same procedure shall be followed to complete the Court in the event of the accession of new High Contracting Parties and in filling casual vacancies.

Article 23
Terms of office

1. The judges shall be elected for a period of six years. They may be re-elected. However, the terms of office of one-half of the judges elected at the first election shall expire at the end of three years.

2. The judges whose terms of office are to expire at the end of the initial period of three years shall be chosen by lot by the Secretary General of the Council of Europe immediately after their election.

3. In order to ensure that, as far as possible, the terms of office of one-half of the judges are renewed every three years, the Parliamentary Assembly may decide, before proceeding to any subsequent election, that the term or terms of office of one or more judges to be elected shall be for a period other than six years but not more than nine and not less than three years.

4. In cases where more than one term of office is involved and where the Parliamentary Assembly applies the preceding paragraph, the allocation of the terms of office shall be effected by a drawing of lots by the Secretary General of the Council of Europe immediately after the election.

5. A judge elected to replace a judge whose term of office has not expired shall hold office for the remainder of his predecessor's term.

6. The terms of office of judges shall expire when they reach the age of 70.

7. The judges shall hold office until replaced. They shall, however, continue to deal with such cases as they already have under consideration.

Article 24
Dismissal

No judge may be dismissed from his office unless the other judges decide by a majority of two-thirds that he has ceased to fulfil the required conditions.

Article 25
Registry and legal secretaries

The Court shall have a registry, the functions and organisation of which shall be laid down in the rules of the Court. The Court shall be assisted by legal secretaries.

Article 26
Plenary Court

The plenary Court shall

(a)   elect its President and one or two Vice-Presidents for a period of three years; they may be re-elected;

(b)   set up Chambers, constituted for a fixed period of time;

(c)   elect the Presidents of the Chambers of the Court; they may be re-elected;

(d)   adopt the rules of the Court, and

(e)   elect the Registrar and one or more Deputy Registrars.

Article 27
Committees, Chambers and Grand Chamber

1. To consider cases brought before it, the Court shall sit in committees of three judges, in Chambers of seven judges and in a Grand Chamber of seventeen judges. The Court's Chambers shall set up committees for a fixed period of time.

2. There shall sit as an *ex officio* member of the Chamber and the Grand Chamber the judge elected in respect of the State Party concerned or, if there is none or if he is unable to sit, a person of its choice who shall sit in the capacity of judge.

3. The Grand Chamber shall also include the President of the Court, the Vice-Presidents, the Presidents of the Chambers and other judges chosen in accordance with the rules of the Court. When a case is referred to the Grand Chamber under Article 43, no judge from the Chamber which rendered the judgment shall sit in the Grand Chamber, with the exception of the President of the Chamber and the judge who sat in respect of the State Party concerned.

Article 28
Declarations of inadmissibility by committees

A committee may, by a unanimous vote, declare inadmissible or strike out of its list of cases an application submitted under Article 34 where such a decision can be taken without further examination. The decision shall be final.

Article 29
Decisions by Chambers on admissibility and merits

1. If no decision is taken under Article 28, a Chamber shall decide on the admissibility and merits of individual applications submitted under Article 34.

2. A Chamber shall decide on the admissibility and merits of inter-State applications submitted under Article 33.

3. The decision on admissibility shall be taken separately unless the Court, in exceptional cases, decides otherwise.

Article 30
Relinquishment of jurisdiction to the Grand Chamber

Where a case pending before a Chamber raises a serious question affecting the interpretation of the Convention or the protocols thereto, or where the resolution of a question before the Chamber might have a result inconsistent with a judgment previously delivered by the Court, the Chamber may, at any time before it has rendered its judgment, relinquish jurisdiction in favour of the Grand Chamber, unless one of the parties to the case objects.

Article 31
Powers of the Grand Chamber

The Grand Chamber shall

(a) determine applications submitted either under Article 33 or Article 34 when a Chamber has relinquished jurisdiction under Article 30 or when the case has been referred to it under Article 43; and

(b) consider requests for advisory opinions submitted under Article 47.

Article 32
Jurisdiction of the Court

1. The jurisdiction of the Court shall extend to all matters concerning the interpretation and application of the Convention and the protocols thereto which are referred to it as provided in Articles 33, 34 and 47.

2. In the event of dispute as to whether the Court has jurisdiction, the Court shall decide.

Article 33
Inter-State cases

Any High Contracting Party may refer to the Court any alleged breach of the provisions of the Convention and the protocols thereto by another High Contracting Party

Article 34
Individual applications

The Court may receive applications from any person, non-governmental organisation or group of individuals claiming to be the victim of a violation by one of the High Contracting Parties of the rights set forth in the Convention or the protocols thereto. The High Contracting Parties undertake not to hinder in any way the effective exercise of this right.

Article 35
Admissibility criteria

1. The Court may only deal with the matter after all domestic remedies have been exhausted, according to the generally recognised rules of international law, and within a period of six months from the date on which the final decision was taken.

2. The Court shall not deal with any application submitted under Article 34 that

(a) is anonymous; or

(b) is substantially the same as a matter that has already been examined by the Court or has already been submitted to another procedure of international investigation or settlement and contains no relevant new information.

3. The Court shall declare inadmissible any individual application submitted under Article 34 which it considers incompatible with the provisions of the Convention or the protocols thereto, manifestly ill-founded, or an abuse of the right of application.

4. The Court shall reject any application which it considers inadmissible under this Article. It may do so at any stage of the proceedings.

Article 36
Third party intervention

1. In all cases before a Chamber of the Grand Chamber, a High Contracting Party one of whose nationals is an applicant shall have the right to submit written comments and to take part in hearings.

2. The President of the Court may, in the interest of the proper administration of justice, invite any High Contracting Party which is not a party to the proceedings or any person concerned who is not the applicant to submit written comments or take part in hearings.

Article 37
Striking out applications

1. The Court may at any stage of the proceedings decide to strike an application out of its list of cases where the circumstances lead to the conclusion that

   (a)   the applicant does not intend to pursue his application; or

   (b)   the matter has been resolved; or

   (c)   for any other reason established by the Court, it is no longer justified to continue the examination of the application.

However, the Court shall continue the examination of the application if respect for human rights as defined in the Convention and the protocols thereto so requires.

2. The Court may decide to restore an application to its list of cases if it considers that the circumstances justify such a course.

Article 38
Examination of the case and friendly settlement proceedings

1. If the Court declares the application admissible, it shall

   (a)   pursue the examination of the case, together with the representatives of the parties, and if need be, undertake an investigation, for the effective conduct of which the States concerned shall furnish all necessary facilities;

   (b)   place itself at the disposal of the parties concerned with a view to securing a friendly settlement of the matter on the basis of respect for human rights as defined in the Convention and the protocols thereto.

2. Proceedings conducted under paragraph 1.b shall be confidential.

Article 39
Finding of a friendly settlement

If a friendly settlement is effected, the Court shall strike the case out of its list by means of a decision which shall be confined to a brief statement of the facts and of the solution reached.

Article 40
Public hearings and access to documents

1.   Hearings shall be in public unless the Court in exceptional circumstances decides otherwise.

2.   Documents deposited with the Registrar shall be accessible to the public unless the President of the Court decides otherwise.

Article 41
Just satisfaction

If the Court finds that there has been a violation of the Convention or the protocols thereto, and if the internal law of the High Contracting Party concerned allows only partial reparation to be made, the Court shall, if necessary afford just satisfaction to the injured party.

Article 42
Judgments of Chambers

Judgments of Chambers shall become final in accordance with the provisions of Article 44, paragraph 2.

Article 43
Referral to the Grand Chamber

1.   Within a period of three months from the date of the judgment of the Chamber, any party to the case may, in exceptional cases, request that the case be referred to the Grand Chamber.

2.   A panel of five judges of the Grand Chamber shall accept the request if the case raises a serious question affecting the interpretation or application of the Convention or the protocols thereto, or a serious issue of general importance.

3.   If the panel accepts the request, the Grand Chamber shall decide the case by means of a judgment.

Article 44
Final judgments

1.   The judgment of the Grand Chamber shall be final.

2.   The judgment of a Chamber shall become final
   (a)   when the parties declare that they will not request that the case be referred to the Grand Chamber; or
   (b)   three months after the date of the judgment, if reference of the case to the Grand Chamber has not been requested; or
   (c)   when the panel of the Grand Chamber rejects the request to refer under Article 43.

3.   The final judgment shall be published.

Article 45
Reasons for judgments and decisions

1. Reasons shall be given for judgments as well as for decisions declaring applications admissible or inadmissible.
2. If a judgment does not represent, in whole or in part, the unanimous opinion of the judges, any judge shall be entitled to deliver a separate opinion.

Article 46
Binding force and execution of judgments

1. The High Contracting Parties undertake to abide by the final judgment of the Court in any case to which they are parties.
2. The final judgment of the Court shall be transmitted to the Committee of Ministers, which shall supervise its execution.

Article 47
Advisory opinions

1. The Court may, at the request of the Committee of Ministers, give advisory opinions on legal questions concerning the interpretation of the Convention and the protocols thereto.
2. Such opinions shall not deal with any question relating to the content or scope of the rights or freedoms defined in Section I of the Convention and the protocols thereto, or with any other question which the Court or the Committee of Ministers might have to consider in consequence of any such proceedings as could be instituted in accordance with the Convention.
3. Decisions of the Committee of Ministers to request an advisory opinion of the Court shall require a majority vote of the representatives entitled to sit on the Committee.

Article 48
Advisory jurisdiction of the Court

The Court shall decide whether a request for an advisory opinion submitted by the Committee of Ministers is within its competence as defined in Article 47.

Article 49
Reasons for advisory opinions

1. Reasons shall be given for advisory opinions of the Court.
2. If the advisory opinion does not represent, in whole or in part, the unanimous opinion of the judges, any judge shall be entitled to deliver a separate opinion.
3. Advisory opinions of the Court shall be communicated to the Committee of Ministers.

Article 50
Expenditure on the Court

The expenditure on the Court shall be borne by the Council of Europe.

Article 51
Privileges and immunities of judges

The judges shall be entitled, during the exercise of their functions, to the privileges and immunities provided for in Article 40 of the Statute of the Council of Europe and in the agreements made thereunder.

Section III—Miscellaneous provisions

Article 52
Inquiries by the Secretary General

On receipt of a request from the Secretary General of the Council of Europe any High Contracting Party shall furnish an explanation of the manner in which its internal law ensures the effective implementation of any of the provisions of the Convention.

Article 53
Safeguard for existing human rights

Nothing in this Convention shall be construed as limiting or derogating from any of the human rights and fundamental freedoms which may be ensured under the laws of any High Contracting Party or under any other agreement to which it is a Party.

Article 54
Powers of the Committee of Ministers

Nothing in this Convention shall prejudice the powers conferred on the Committee of Ministers by the Statute of the Council of Europe.

Article 55
Exclusion of other means of dispute settlement

The High Contracting Parties agree that, except by special agreement, they will not avail themselves of treaties, conventions or declarations in force between them for the purpose of submitting, by way of petition, a dispute arising out of the interpretation or application of this Convention to a means of settlement other than those provided for in this Convention.

Article 56
Territorial application

1.   Any State may at the time of its ratification or at any time thereafter declare by notification addressed to the Secretary General of the Council of

Europe that the present Convention shall, subject to paragraph 4 of this Article, extend to all or any of the territories for whose international relations it is responsible.

2. The Convention shall extend to the territory or territories named in the notification as from the thirtieth day after the receipt of this notification by the Secretary General of the Council of Europe.

3. The provisions of this Convention shall be applied in such territories with due regard, however, to local requirements.

4. Any State which has made a declaration in accordance with paragraph 1 of this article may at any time thereafter declare on behalf of one or more of the territories to which the declaration relates that it accepts the competence of the Court to receive applications from individuals, non-governmental organisations or groups of individuals as provided by Article 34 of the Convention.

Article 57
Reservations

1. Any State may, when signing this Convention or when depositing its instrument of ratification, make a reservation in respect of any particular provision of the Convention to the extent that any law then in force in its territory is not in conformity with the provision. Reservations of a general character shall not be permitted under this article.

2. Any reservation made under this article shall contain a brief statement of the law concerned.

Article 58
Denunciation

1. A High Contracting Party may denounce the present Convention only after the expiry of five years from the date on which it became a party to it and after six months' notice contained in a notification addressed to the Secretary General of the Council of Europe, who shall inform the other High Contracting Parties.

2. Such a denunciation shall not have the effect of releasing the High Contracting Party concerned from its obligations under this Convention in respect of any act which, being capable of constituting a violation of such obligations, may have been performed by it before the date at which the denunciation became effective.

3. Any High Contracting Party which shall cease to be a member of the Council of Europe shall cease to be a Party to this Convention under the same conditions.

4. The Convention may be denounced in accordance with the provisions of the preceding paragraphs in respect of any territory to which it has been declared to extend under the terms of Article 56.

Article 59
Signature and ratification

1. This Convention shall be open to the signature of the members of the Council of Europe. It shall be ratified. Ratifications shall be deposited with the Secretary General of the Council of Europe.

2. The present Convention shall come into force after the deposit of ten instruments of ratification.

3. As regards any signatory ratifying subsequently, the Convention shall come into force at the date of the deposit of its instrument of ratification.

4. The Secretary General of the Council of Europe shall notify all the members of the Council of Europe of the entry into force of the Convention, the names of the High Contracting Parties who have ratified it, and the deposit of all instruments of ratification which may be effected subsequently.

Done at Rome this 4th day of November 1950, in English and French, both texts being equally authentic, in a single copy which shall remain deposited in the archives of the Council of Europe.

The Secretary General shall transmit certified copies to each of the signatories.

PROTOCOL [NO. 1] TO THE CONVENTION FOR THE PROTECTION OF HUMAN RIGHTS AND FUNDAMENTAL FREEDOMS, AS AMENDED BY PROTOCOL NO. 11

The governments signatory hereto, being members of the Council of Europe,

Being resolved to take steps to ensure the collective enforcement of certain rights and freedoms other than those already included in Section I of the Convention for the Protection of Human Rights and Fundamental Freedoms signed at Rome on 4 November 1950 (hereinafter referred to as 'the Convention'),

Have agreed as follows:

Article 1
Protection of property

Every natural or legal person is entitled to the peaceful enjoyment of his possessions. No one shall be deprived of his possessions except in the public interest and subject to the conditions provided for by law and by the general principles of international law.

The preceding provisions shall not, however, in any way impair the right of a State to enforce such laws as it deems necessary to control the use of property in accordance with the general interest or to secure the payment of taxes or other contributions or penalties.

Article 2
Right to education

No person shall be denied the right to education. In the exercise of any functions which it assumes in relation to education and to teaching, the State shall respect the right of parents to ensure such education and teaching in conformity with their own religious and philosophical convictions.

Article 3
Right to free elections

The High Contracting Parties undertake to hold free elections at reasonable intervals by secret ballot, under conditions which will ensure the free expression of the opinion of the people in the choice of the legislature.

Article 4
Territorial application

Any High Contracting Party may at the time of signature or ratification or at any time thereafter communicate to the Secretary General of the Council of Europe a declaration stating the extent to which it undertakes that the provisions of the present Protocol shall apply to such of the territories for the international relations of which it is responsible as are named therein.

Any High Contracting Party which has communicated a declaration in virtue of the preceding paragraph may from time to time communicate a further declaration modifying the terms of any former declaration or terminating the application of the provisions of this Protocol in respect of any territory.

A declaration made in accordance with this article shall be deemed to have been made in accordance with paragraph 1 of Article 56 of the Convention.

Article 5
Relationship to the Convention

As between the High Contracting Parties the provisions of Articles 1, 2, 3 and 4 of this Protocol shall be regarded as additional articles to the Convention and all the provisions of the Convention shall apply accordingly.

Article 6
Signature and ratification

This Protocol shall be open for signature by the members of the Council of Europe, who are the signatories of the Convention; it shall be ratified at the same time as or after the ratification of the Convention. It shall enter into force after the deposit of ten instruments of ratification. As regards any signatory ratifying subsequently, the Protocol shall enter into force at the date of the deposit of its instrument of ratification.

The instruments of ratification shall be deposited with the Secretary General of the Council of Europe, who will notify all members of the names of those who have ratified.

Done at Paris on the 20th day of March 1952, in English and French, both texts being equally authentic, in a single copy which shall remain deposited in the archives of the Council of Europe. The Secretary General shall transmit certified copies to each of the signatory governments.

PROTOCOL NO. 4 TO THE CONVENTION FOR THE PROTECTION OF HUMAN RIGHTS AND FUNDAMENTAL FREEDOMS, SECURING CERTAIN RIGHTS AND FREEDOMS OTHER THAN THOSE ALREADY INCLUDED IN THE CONVENTION AND IN THE FIRST PROTOCOL THERETO, AS AMENDED BY PROTOCOL NO. 11

The governments signatory hereto, being members of the Council of Europe,

Being resolved to take steps to ensure the collective enforcement of certain rights and freedoms other than those already included in Section 1 of the Convention for the Protection of Human Rights and Fundamental Freedoms signed at Rome on 4th November 1950 (hereinafter referred to as the 'Convention') and in Articles 1 to 3 of the First Protocol to the Convention, signed at Paris on 20th March 1952,

Have agreed as follows:

Article 1
Prohibition of imprisonment for debt

No one shall be deprived of his liberty merely on the ground of inability to fulfil a contractual obligation.

Article 2
Freedom of movement

1. Everyone lawfully within the territory of a State shall, within that territory, have the right to liberty of movement and freedom to choose his residence.

2. Everyone shall be free to leave any country, including his own.

3. No restrictions shall be placed on the exercise of these rights other than such as are in accordance with law and are necessary in a democratic society in the interests of national security or public safety, for the maintenance of *ordre public*, for the prevention of crime, for the protection of health or morals, or for the protection of the rights and freedoms of others.

4. The rights set forth in paragraph 1 may also be subject, in particular areas, to restrictions imposed in accordance with law and justified by the public interest in a democratic society.

Article 3
Prohibition of expulsion of nationals

1.   No one shall be expelled, by means either of an individual or of a collective measure, from the territory of the State of which he is a national.

2.   No one shall be deprived of the right to enter the territory of the state of which he is a national.

Article 4
Prohibition of collective expulsion of aliens

Collective expulsion of aliens is prohibited.

Article 5
Territorial application

1.   Any High Contracting Party may, at the time of signature or ratification of this Protocol, or at any time thereafter, communicate to the Secretary General of the Council of Europe a declaration stating the extent to which it undertakes that the provisions of this Protocol shall apply to such of the territories for the international relations of which it is responsible as are named therein.

2.   Any High Contracting Party which has communicated a declaration in virtue of the preceding paragraph may, from time to time, communicate a further declaration modifying the terms of any former declaration or terminating the application of the provisions of this Protocol in respect of any territory.

3.   A declaration made in accordance with this article shall be deemed to have been made in accordance with paragraph 1 of Article 56 of the Convention.

4.   The territory of any State to which this Protocol applies by virtue of ratification or acceptance by that State, and each territory to which this Protocol is applied by virtue of a declaration by that State under this article, shall be treated as separate territories for the purpose of the references in Articles 2 and 3 to the territory of a State.

5.   Any State which has made a declaration in accordance with paragraph 1 or 2 of this Article may at any time thereafter declare on behalf of one or more of the territories to which the declaration relates that it accepts the competence of the Court to receive applications from individuals, non-governmental organisations or groups of individuals as provided in Article 34 of the Convention in respect of all or any of Articles 1 to 4 of this Protocol.

Article 6
Relationship to the Convention

As between the High Contracting Parties the provisions of Articles 1 to 5 of this Protocol shall be regarded as additional Articles to the Convention, and all the provisions of the Convention shall apply accordingly.

Article 7
Signature and ratification

1. This Protocol shall be open for signature by the members of the Council of Europe who are the signatories of the Convention; it shall be ratified at the same time as or after the ratification of the Convention. It shall enter into force after the deposit of five instruments of ratification. As regards any signatory ratifying subsequently, the Protocol shall enter into force at the date of the deposit of its instrument of ratification.

2. The instruments of ratification shall be deposited with the Secretary General of the Council of Europe, who will notify all members of the names of those who have ratified.

In witness whereof the undersigned, being duly authorised thereto, have signed this Protocol.

Done at Strasbourg, this 16th day of September 1963, in English and in French, both texts being equally authoritative, in a single copy which shall remain deposited in the archives of the Council of Europe. The Secretary General shall transmit certified copies to each of the signatory states.

PROTOCOL NO. 6 TO THE CONVENTION FOR THE PROTECTION OF HUMAN RIGHTS AND FUNDAMENTAL FREEDOMS CONCERNING THE ABOLITION OF THE DEATH PENALTY, AS AMENDED BY PROTOCOL NO. 11

The member States of the Council of Europe, signatory to this Protocol to the Convention for the Protection of Human Rights and Fundamental Freedoms, signed at Rome on 4 November 1950 (hereinafter referred to as 'the Convention'),

Considering that the evolution that has occurred in several member States of the Council of Europe expresses a general tendency in favour of abolition of the death penalty;

Have agreed as follows:

Article 1
Abolition of the death penalty

The death penalty shall be abolished. No-one shall be condemned to such penalty or executed.

Article 2
Death penalty in time of war

A State may make provision in its law for the death penalty in respect of acts committed in time of war or of imminent threat of war; such penalty shall be applied only in the instances laid down in the law and in accordance with its provisions. The State shall communicate to the Secretary General of the Council of Europe the relevant provisions of that law.

Article 3
Prohibition of derogations

No derogation from the provisions of this Protocol shall be made under Article 15 of the Convention.

Article 4
Prohibition of reservations

No reservation may be made under Article 57 of the Convention in respect of the provisions of this Protocol.

Article 5
Territorial application

1. Any State may at the time of signature or when depositing its instrument of ratification, acceptance or approval, specify the territory or territories to which this Protocol shall apply.

2. Any State may at any later date, by a declaration addressed to the Secretary General of the Council of Europe, extend the application of this Protocol to any other territory specified in the declaration. In respect of such territory the Protocol shall enter into force on the first day of the month following the date of receipt of such declaration by the Secretary General.

3. Any declaration made under the two preceding paragraphs may, in respect of any territory specified in such declaration, be withdrawn by a notification addressed to the Secretary General. The withdrawal shall become effective on the first day of the month following the date of receipt of such notification by the Secretary General.

Article 6
Relationship to the Convention

As between the States Parties the provisions of Articles 1 to 5 of this Protocol shall be regarded as additional articles to the Convention and all the provisions of the Convention shall apply accordingly.

Article 7
Signature and ratification

The Protocol shall be open for signature by the member States of the Council of Europe, signatories to the Convention. It shall be subject to ratification, acceptance or approval. A member State of the Council of Europe may not ratify, accept or approve this Protocol unless it has, simultaneously or previously, ratified the Convention. Instruments of ratification, acceptance or approval shall be deposited with the Secretary General of the Council of Europe.

Article 8
Entry into force

1. This Protocol shall enter into force on the first day of the month following the date on which five member States of the Council of Europe have expressed their consent to be bound by the Protocol in accordance with the provisions of Article 7.

2. In respect of any member State which subsequently expresses its consent to be bound by it, the Protocol shall enter into force on the first day of the month following the date of the deposit of the instrument of ratification, acceptance or approval.

Article 9
Depositary functions

The Secretary General of the Council of Europe shall notify the member States of the Council of:

(a) any signature;

(b) the deposit of any instrument of ratification, acceptance or approval;

(c) any date of entry into force of this Protocol in accordance with Articles 5 and 8;

(d) any other act, notification or communication relating to this Protocol.

In witness whereof the undersigned, being duly authorised thereto, have signed this Protocol.

Done at Strasbourg, this 28th day of April 1983, in English and in French, both texts being equally authentic, in a single copy which shall be deposited in the archives of the Council of Europe. The Secretary General of the Council of Europe shall transmit certified copies to each member State of the Council of Europe.

PROTOCOL NO. 7 TO THE CONVENTION FOR THE PROTECTION OF HUMAN RIGHTS AND FUNDAMENTAL FREEDOMS, AS AMENDED BY PROTOCOL NO. 11

The member States of the Council of Europe signatory hereto,

Being resolved to take further steps to ensure the collective enforcement of certain rights and freedoms by means of the Convention for the Protection of Human Rights and Fundamental Freedoms signed at Rome on 4 November 1950 (hereinafter referred to as 'the Convention'),

Have agreed as follows

Article 1
Procedural safeguards relating to expulsion of aliens

1.   An alien lawfully resident in the territory of a State shall not be expelled therefrom except in pursuance of a decision reached in accordance with law and shall be allowed:

    (a)   to submit reasons against his expulsion,

    (b)   to have his case reviewed, and

    (c)   to be represented for these purposes before the competent authority or a person or persons designated by that authority.

2.   An alien may be expelled before the exercise of his rights under paragraph 1.a, b and c of this Article, when such expulsion is necessary in the interests of public order or is grounded on reasons of national security.

Article 2
Right of appeal in criminal matters

1.   Everyone convicted of a criminal offence by a tribunal shall have the right to have his conviction or sentence reviewed by a higher tribunal. The exercise of this right, including the grounds on which it may be exercised, shall be governed by law.

2.   This right may be subject to exceptions in regard to offences of a minor character, as prescribed by law, or in cases in which the person concerned was tried in the first instance by the highest tribunal or was convicted following an appeal against acquittal.

Article 3
Compensation for wrongful conviction

When a person has by a final decision been convicted of a criminal offence and when subsequently his conviction has been reversed, or he has been pardoned, on the ground that a new or newly discovered fact shows conclusively that there has been a miscarriage of justice, the person who has suffered punishment as a result of such conviction shall be compensated according to the law or the practice of the State concerned, unless it is proved that the non-disclosure of the unknown fact in time is wholly or partly attributable to him.

Article 4
Right not to be tried or punished twice

1.   No one shall be liable to be tried or punished again in criminal proceedings under the jurisdiction of the same State for an offence for which he has already been finally acquitted or convicted in accordance with the law and penal procedure of that State.

2. The provisions of the preceding paragraph shall not prevent the reopening of the case in accordance with the law and penal procedure of the State concerned, if there is evidence of new or newly discovered facts, or if there has been a fundamental defect in the previous proceedings, which could affect the outcome of the case.

3. No derogation from this Article shall be made under Article 15 of the Convention.

Article 5
Equality between spouses

Spouses shall enjoy equality of rights and responsibilities of a private law character between them, and in their relations with their children, as to marriage, during marriage and in the event of its dissolution. This Article shall not prevent States from taking such measures as are necessary in the interests of the children.

Article 6
Territorial application

1. Any State may at the time of signature or when depositing its instrument of ratification, acceptance or approval, specify the territory or territories to which the Protocol shall apply and state the extent to which it undertakes that the provisions of this Protocol shall apply to such territory or territories.

2. Any State may at any later date, by a declaration addressed to the Secretary General of the Council of Europe, extend the application of this Protocol to any other territory specified in the declaration. In respect of such territory the Protocol shall enter into force on the first day of the month following the expiration of a period of two months after the date of receipt by the Secretary General of such declaration.

3. Any declaration made under the two preceding paragraphs may, in respect of any territory specified in such declaration, be withdrawn or modified by a notification addressed to the Secretary General. The withdrawal or modification shall become effective on the first day of the month following the expiration of a period of two months after the date of receipt of such notification by the Secretary General.

4. A declaration made in accordance with this Article shall be deemed to have been made in accordance with paragraph 1 of Article 56 of the Convention.

5. The territory of any State to which this Protocol applies by virtue of ratification, acceptance or approval by that State, and each territory to which this Protocol is applied by virtue of a declaration by that State under this Article, may be treated as separate territories for the purpose of the reference in Article 1 to the territory of a State.

6. Any State which has made a declaration in accordance with paragraph 1 or 2 of this Article may at any time thereafter declare on behalf of one or more of

the territories to which the declaration relates that it accepts the competence of the Court to receive applications from individuals, non-governmental organisations or groups of individuals as provided in Article 34 of the Convention in respect of Articles 1 to 5 of this Protocol.

Article 7
Relationship to the Convention

As between the States Parties, the provisions of Article 1 to 6 of this Protocol shall be regarded as additional Articles to the Convention, and all the provisions of the Convention shall apply accordingly.

Article 8
Signature and ratification

This Protocol shall be open for signature by member States of the Council of Europe which have signed the Convention. It is subject to ratification, acceptance or approval. A member State of the Council of Europe may not ratify, accept or approve this Protocol without previously or simultaneously ratifying the Convention. Instruments of ratification, acceptance or approval shall be deposited with the Secretary General of the Council of Europe.

Article 9
Entry into force

1.   This Protocol shall enter into force on the first day of the month following the expiration of a period of two months after the date on which seven member States of the Council of Europe have expressed their consent to be bound by the Protocol in accordance with the provisions of Article 8.

2.   In respect of any member State which subsequently expresses its consent to be bound by it, the Protocol shall enter into force on the first day of the month following the expiration of a period of two months after the date of the deposit of the instrument of ratification, acceptance or approval.

Article 10
Depositary functions

The Secretary General of the Council of Europe shall notify all the member States of the Council of Europe of:

(a)   any signature;

(b)   the deposit of any instrument of ratification, acceptance or approval;

(c)   any date of entry into force of this Protocol in accordance with Articles 6 and 9;

(d)   any other act, notification or declaration relating to this Protocol.

In witness whereof the undersigned, being duly authorised thereto, have signed this Protocol.

Done at Strasbourg, this 22nd day of November 1984, in English and French, both texts being equally authentic, in a single copy which shall be deposited in the archives of the Council of Europe. The Secretary General of the Council of Europe shall transmit certified copies to each member State of the Council of Europe.

PROTOCOL NO. 12 TO THE CONVENTION FOR THE PROTECTION OF HUMAN RIGHTS AND FUNDAMENTAL FREEDOMS

The member states of the Council of Europe signatory hereto,

Having regard to the fundamental principle according to which all persons are equal before the law and are entitled to the equal protection of the law;

Being resolved to take further steps to promote the equality of all persons through the collective enforcement of a general prohibition of discrimination by means of the Convention for the Protection of Human Rights and Fundamental Freedoms signed at Rome on 4 November 1950 (hereinafter referred to as 'the Convention');

Reaffirming that the principle of non-discrimination does not prevent States Parties from taking measures in order to promote full and effective equality, provided that there is an objective and reasonable justification for those measures,

Have agreed as follows:

Article 1
General prohibition of discrimination

1. The enjoyment of any right set forth by law shall be secured without discrimination on any ground such as sex, race, colour, language, religion, political or other opinion, national or social origin, association with a national minority, property, birth or other status.

2. No one shall be discriminated against by any public authority on any ground such as those mentioned in paragraph 1.

Article 2
Territorial application

1. Any state may, at the time of signature or when depositing its instrument of ratification, acceptance or approval, specify the territory or territories to which this Protocol shall apply.

2. Any state may at any later date, by a declaration addressed to the Secretary General of the Council of Europe, extend the application of this Protocol to any other territory specified in the declaration, in respect of such

territory the Protocol shall enter into force on the first day of the month following the expiration of a period of three months after the date of receipt by the Secretary General of such declaration.

3.   Any declaration made under the two preceding paragraphs may, in respect of any territory specified in such declaration, be withdrawn or modified by a notification addressed to the Secretary General. The withdrawal or modification shall become effective on the first day of the month following the expiration of a period of three months after the date of receipt of such notification by the Secretary General.

4.   A declaration made in accordance with this article shall be deemed to have been made in accordance with paragraph 1 of Article 56 of the Convention.

5.   Any state which has made a declaration in accordance with paragraph 1 or 2 of this article may at any time thereafter declare on behalf of one or more of the territories to which the declaration relates that it accepts the competence of the Court to receive applications from individuals, non-governmental organisations or groups of individuals as provided by Article 34 of the Convention in respect of Article 1 of this Protocol.

Article 3
Relationship to the Convention

As between the States Parties, the provisions of Articles 1 and 2 of this Protocol shall be regarded as additional articles to the Convention, and all the provisions of the Convention shall apply accordingly.

Article 4
Signature and ratification

This Protocol shall be open for signature by member states of the Council of Europe which have signed the Convention. It is subject to ratification, acceptance or approval. A member state of the Council of Europe may not ratify, accept or approve this Protocol without previously or simultaneously ratifying the Convention. Instruments of ratification, acceptance or approval shall be deposited with the Secretary General of the Council of Europe.

Article 5
Entry into force

1.   This Protocol shall enter into force on the first day of the month following the expiration of a period of three months after the date on which ten member states of the Council of Europe have expressed their consent to be bound by the Protocol in accordance with the provisions of Article 4.

2.   In respect of any member state which subsequently expresses its consent to be bound by it, the Protocol shall enter into force on the first day of the month

following the expiration of a period of three months after the date of the deposit of the instrument of ratification, acceptance or approval.

Article 6
Depositary functions

The Secretary General of the Council of Europe shall notify all the member states of the Council of Europe of:

(a)　any signature;

(b)　the deposit of any instrument of ratification, acceptance or approval;

(c)　any date of entry into force of this Protocol in accordance with Articles 2 and 5;

(d)　any other act, notification or communication relating to this Protocol.

In witness whereof the undersigned, being duly authorised thereto, have signed this Protocol.

Done at ...., this .... day of .... 2000, in English and French, both texts being equally authentic, in a single copy which shall be deposited in the archives of the Council of Europe. The Secretary General of the Council of Europe shall transmit certified copies to each member state of the Council of Europe.

Index